Finance and Business Law

Third Edition

Certified Professional Secretary® Examination Review Series

Betty L. Schroeder, *Series Editor*

CERTIFIED PROFESSIONAL SECRETARY®
EXAMINATION REVIEW SERIES

FINANCE AND BUSINESS LAW
Third Edition

Betty L. Schroeder, Ph.D., Editor
Northern Illinois University

John Lewis, Ph.D.
Northern Illinois University

Sally A. Webber, M.S., CPA
University of Texas at Arlington

Lawrence S. Clark, J.D., L.L.M.
Sonoma State University

Philip DiMarzio, J.D., L.L.M.
Sycamore, Illinois

A joint publication of
PSI® Professional Secretaries International and

PRENTICE HALL CAREER & TECHNOLOGY
Englewood Cliffs, New Jersey 07632

Library of Congress Cataloging-in-Publication Data

Certified professional secretary review series for finance and
  business law / Betty L. Schroeder . . . [et al.]. — 3rd ed.
        p.   cm.
     Rev. ed. of: Certified professional secretary examination review
series. Module 2, Business law and module 4, Accounting.
c1986–c1992.
     ISBN 0–13–312133–X
     1. Secretaries—United States—Examinations, questions, etc.
2. Corporations—Accounting—Examinations, questions, etc.
3. Corporations—Finance—Examinations, questions, etc.
4. Commercial law—United States—Examinations, questions, etc.
I. Schroeder, Betty L.   II. Certified professional secretary
examination review series.
HF5547.5.C443   1995
651.3′74′076—dc20   94–14313
                                                                CIP

Acquisitions editor: Elizabeth Sugg
Editorial/production supervision and
   interior design: Tally Morgan, WordCrafters Editorial Services, Inc.
Cover design: Marianne Frasco
Manufacturing buyer: Ed O'Dougherty
Supplements editor: Judy Casillo
Editorial assistant: Maria Klimek

© 1995, 1992, 1984 by Prentice-Hall, Inc.
A Simon & Schuster Company
Englewood Cliffs, New Jersey 07632

The following are registered marks owned by Professional Secretaries International:

Trademarks and Registered Service Marks

PSI®

Professional Secretaries International®
Since 1942 known as The National Secretaries Association (International)
10502 N.W. Ambassador Drive, Kansas City, MO 64153, 816-891-6600

A.I.S.P. (French equivalent of PSI®)
L'Association Internationale des Secretaries Professionailes

CPS®
Certified Professional Secretary®
Professional Secretaries Week®
Professional Secretaries Day
The Secretary®

FSA®
Future Secretaries Association®
International Secretary of the Year®

Printed in the United States of America

10   9   8   7   6   5

ISBN 0-13-312133-X

Prentice-Hall International (UK) Limited, *London*
Prentice-Hall of Australia Pty, Limited, *Sydney*
Prentice-Hall Canada, Inc., *Toronto*
Prentice-Hall Hispanoamericana, S.A., *Mexico*
Prentice-Hall of India Private Limited, *New Delhi*
Prentice-Hall of Japan, Inc., *Tokyo*
Simon & Schuster Asia Pte. Ltd., *Singapore*
Editora Prentice-Hall do Brasil, Ltda., *Rio de Janeiro*

Contents

Section II: Accounting

6   INTRODUCTION TO ACCOUNTING, 113

7   THEORY AND CLASSIFICATION OF ACCOUNTS, 123

Section III: Business Law

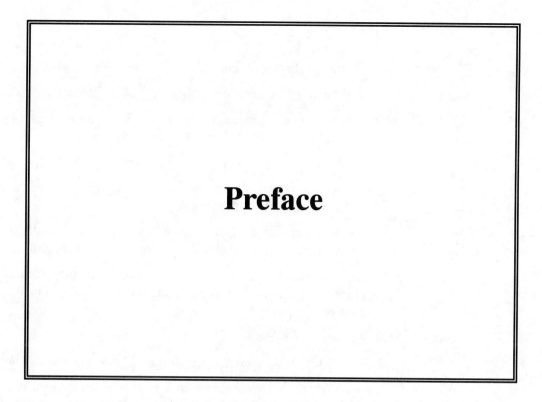

Preface

The Certified Professional Secretaries Examination® (CPS) Review Series, three review manuals and their corresponding Study Guides prepared for each of the three parts of the Certified Professional Secretary Examination, is a joint publication of Prentice Hall and Professional Secretaries International. The content of each module is based on the current *Outline and Bibliography* published by Professional Secretaries International. *Capstone,* the official publication of the Institute for Certification, provides detailed information about the examination and an application form.

CPS Examination

The rewards for achieving the Certified Professional Secretaries (CPS) rating are numerous, as attested to by the more than 45,000 CPS holders. These include: pride in accomplishment, increased self-esteem, greater respect from employers and peers, confidence to assume greater responsibilities, college credit toward a degree, pay increases, bonuses, and opportunities for advancement. In today's workplace, having the CPS credential can be assurance of employability.

The CPS Examination is a one-day, three-part examination based on the premise that a professional secretary should know how to apply the principles of good human relations and have basic knowledge of finance, business law, economics, communication, and management. It is expected that a competent secretary is thoroughly familiar with current techniques in secretarial practice and procedures and is aware of developments in office systems and technology.

CPS Review Series

The CPS Review Series provides valuable assistance to the secretary or the secretarial student preparing for the CPS Examination, whether it is used for group review sessions or for self-study. The series provides an excellent teaching tool that is focused on key topics that are necessary for passing the exam.

The format used for each of the modules of the series is identical. The CPS Examination Review Series provides as much relevant information as possible to help secretaries in preparing for the CPS Examination. However, this does not imply that all information presented in the series will be included on the examinations.

Each chapter contains:

- An overview introducing the reader to the chapter and its content

- A complete sentence/paragraph outline, with examples highlighted in italic type within the text to enhance the explanation given

- Illustrations to aid understanding of concepts difficult to understand

- Review questions at the end of each chapter, developed in formats similar to those found in the CPS Examination

- Solutions to the review questions, with some explanation of correct answers, where needed, and references to the sentence/paragraph outline within the manual

The solutions to the review questions should be particularly helpful since they include references to the portion of the outline that explains the answer more fully. For example:

> 1.   (b)   [A-2]
>
> *The outline reference pertains to: Section A, Point 2 in the chapter.*

When a solution seems unclear, it is recommended that the section of the sentence/paragraph outline be reviewed for further clarification. Review questions have been included to give candidates for the CPS Examination further review and practice with questions similar to those found on the examination.

At the end of each module is presented a complete Glossary of terms and definitions included in the module. A reference is made to the chapter where the term may be found in context.

CPS Review Series Study Guides

Each module has a corresponding Study Guide. The CPS Review Series Study Guides were developed specifically for self-study. They enhance material presented in CPS Exam Review courses for laboratory assignments or for test applicants who choose to prepare for the exam on their own.

The question arises as to why this series is formatted in this particular way. The response is simple: We want you to have a thorough, efficient, review of the content that may appear on the CPS Examination this year. In addition to your study of the CPS Examination Review Series, you are encouraged to consult other references for more detailed explanations and/or a variety of learning materials to test your knowledge and skill in the particular subject areas.

Paulette Gladis, CSJ, Ph.D.
Dean, Institute for Certification

Acknowledgments

Through the sincere and dedicated efforts of a number of individuals interested in the preparation of professional secretaries, the third edition of the *Certified Professional Secretary® Review for Finance and Business Law* was prepared to complement the current Study Outline for the Certified Professional Secretary® Examination. Like the other two reviews in the series, *Finance and Business Law* will be a successful review tool because of the reviews and contributions of the following people.

Professional Secretaries International, through the Institute for Certification, has provided not only the incentive for the development of the third edition of this review but also valuable input during the review process. We are sincerely grateful and thank PSI and the Institute for their continued support and enthusiasm for the development and revision of the series.

Specifically, we acknowledge the many contributions of Paulette Gladis, CSJ, Ph.D.; Estella H. Gillette, BBA, CPS; Colleen R. Lloyd, CPS; Dr. Arnola C. Ownby; and Kathy L. Schoneboom, CPS for their extremely helpful reviews and critiques of the manuscript.

In addition, a very special acknowledgment is directed to those Certified Professional Secretaries who served as professional reviewers for this manuscript: Candace Barr, CPS, Dresselhuis Niemi & Barr P.A., Minneapolis, Minnesota; Shirley A. Calvin, CPS, Moberly Junior College, Moberly, Missouri; and Nancy Moran, CPS, Zurich American Insurance Group, Schaumburg, Illinois. Not only have these individuals earned their professional certification, but they also teach review courses that prepare secretaries for the examination. Their input is invaluable in making this review and the others in the series appropriate for individual or group review for the CPS Examination.

Another special acknowledgment recognizes the Illinois Division of Professional Secretaries International and, in particular, those members of the Kishwaukee Chapter, DeKalb, Illinois, who are pursuing or have received their professional certification. These groups have continued to be extremely supportive and positive about this review series; their friendship is very much appreciated.

A very special "thank you" is given to Charnelle Lewis, Sycamore, Illinois, for her excellent writing and editing assistance with the economics manuscript.

Lastly, we are most appreciative of the assistance and leadership demonstrated by Liz Kendall and Elizabeth Sugg of Prentice Hall and for their continued support of this series. It is a joy to work with individuals so professional in their judgment of what professional secretaries need to prepare appropriately for the CPS Examination.

We hope that all the input provided by professionals throughout the revision process will continue to make this review (and the others in the series) the "leaders" in preparing professional secretaries everywhere for the CPS Examination in the future.

Betty L. Schroeder, Ph.D.
John L. Lewis, Ph.D.
Sally A. Weber, M.S., CPA
Lawrence S. Clark, J.D., LL. M.
Philip DiMarzio, J.D., LL.M.

Finance and Business Law
Third Edition

CHAPTER 1

Basic Concepts of Economics

OVERVIEW

Economics is one of the many social sciences that attempt to analyze our complex society. Economics deals with understanding and predicting human behavior in an effort to solve the universal economic problem of scarcity. In studying human behavior, economics analyzes decisions relative to consumption, production, distribution, and the exchange of goods and services in a society.

In this chapter we develop basic concepts used by economists to study human behavior. These concepts include types of economic systems, the demand for and supply of goods and services, markets for goods and services, and the structural environment in which firms operate. These concepts provide a basis for understanding such questions as: How will people react to an increase in the price of goods? *or* How will the farming community react to declining crop prices?

KEY TERMS

Capital	Explicit costs	Perfect competition
Command economy	Factors of production	Private goods
Complementary goods	Imperfect competition	Private property
Consumption	Implicit costs	Production possibility
Demand	Inelastic demand	curve
Economic efficiency	Inelastic supply	Profit
Economic equity	Labor	Public goods
Economic freedom	Laissez-faire	Scarcity
Economic security	Land	Shortage
Economic stability	Law of demand	Substitute goods
Elasticity	Law of supply	Supply
Entrepreneur	Market	Surplus
Entrepreneurial ability	Mixed economy	Utility
Equilibrium price	Opportunity cost	Wants

A. The Basis of Economics

The basis of economics is the existence of scarcity. Scarcity exists whenever society's desire for goods and services exceeds society's ability to produce these goods and services, or whenever wants exceed resources. The consequences of scarcity are that choices must be made. Scarcity affects individuals in much the same manner as it affects society. When individuals must choose between paying bills and taking a vacation, scarcity is the basis for the decision.

The government must also deal with scarcity and choices. The Department of Defense may want to increase expenditures at the same time that the Department of Agriculture wishes to increase support for agricultural commodities. Since the resources available are limited, the government must also make choices.

It is sometimes convenient to distinguish between individual choices and societal choices. Societal choices are limited by the availability of technology and resources which set the boundaries for the production possibilities of an economy. Within these bounds, decisions must be made concerning how much of each type of good will be produced. A typical societal choice is the decision concerning how many public goods versus private goods should be produced.

EXAMPLE: Society must decide whether to use its scarce resources for public parks or to devote these resources to the production of private goods.

1. *Scarcity*: In economics, the concept of scarcity is derived from the idea that individuals and societies have unlimited wants and limited resources. As a result of scarcity, society makes choices among alternative uses of its resources. If no conflict between wants and resources exists, choices do not have to be made and no economic problem exists.

    a. *Unlimited wants*: Economists accept the fact that society desires a vast amount of goods and services that provide utility (a measure of satisfaction) to the consumers within society. Taken together, the desires for all goods and services are so great they could be considered unlimited. It is assumed that as people satisfy more of their wants, they will continue to work and to make decisions in an attempt to satisfy additional wants. There is no limit to the wants that individuals within society wish to have satisfied.

    b. *Limited resources*: At any given point in time, the resources of society are limited. Resources, as classified by economists, include land, labor, capital, and entrepreneurial ability.

        (1) *Land*: All land, waterways, and natural resources that come from them.

        (2) *Labor*: Human resources; the ability of individuals to perform labor services in society.

        (3) *Capital*: Those human-made resources that are used in the production of other goods and services. Capital is defined somewhat uniquely by economists and in a substantially different way from the definition used by accountants.

            EXAMPLE: The machines on an assembly line that are used to produce automobiles are capital.

        (4) *Entrepreneurial ability*: The ability to organize the factors of production (land, labor, capital) to produce goods in such a way as to make a profit.

2. *Societal Choices*: As a result of scarcity, societies must make choices. With the given state of technology and limited resources, society can produce only a finite number of goods and services at a particular point in time. The maximum amount of goods and services that a society can produce at any given point in time is called its production possibilities curve.

   a. *Production possibility*: The production possibilities of an economy can be illustrated graphically by using a simplified economy in which only two types of goods are produced. The maximum quantities of each type of good that can be produced are measured on horizontal and vertical axes (see Figure 1–1).

   EXAMPLE: In Figure 1–1, if a society uses all of its resources to produce capital goods (for example, tractors), it can produce no consumer goods (for example, cars). This is illustrated by point A on the figure, where 25 tractors are produced and no cars.

   Society could use all its resources to produce cars (consumer goods) and no tractors. This is illustrated by point B, showing society producing 100 cars and no tractors.

   In addition to these possibilities, a society could choose to produce anywhere along the curve between points A and B. If a society is producing on the production possibility curve, it is using all its available resources in an efficient manner. If it is producing inside the curve, for example, point C, it is not using all of its resources efficiently and can increase its output of tractors and cars, or both, without reducing the output of the other.

   The production possibility curve also illustrates the necessity of choice. If society uses all of its resources fully (full employment), it will produce somewhere on the production possibility curve. However, once society has

Figure 1–1   Production Possibility Curve

achieved a point on the production possibility curve, such as combination D, to get more tractors, it must give up cars, and vice versa.

In this example, if society wanted to move from point D to point E, it must give up five tractors to get 30 additional cars.

b. *Opportunity costs*: Opportunity cost is the value of the opportunity foregone when a decision is made. The movement from point E to point D in Figure 1–1 illustrates the principle of opportunity cost.

EXAMPLE: In Figure 1–1, if society changed the use of its resources and produced 15 tractors and 90 cars as opposed to 20 tractors and 60 cars, the opportunity costs of the 30 additional cars would be the five tractors that could no longer be produced.

A basic principle in economics is: "There is no such thing as a free lunch." This statement attests to the fact that scarcity exists and there are insufficient resources to satisfy all of society's wants. If society wants to increase production of one good or service, it must reduce production of another good or service.

c. *Fundamental problems of economic systems*: The existence of scarcity and thus the necessity of making choices presents three fundamental, independent questions that every economic system must answer. This is true no matter what type of organization exists within the economic system. The three basic questions are: what to produce, how to produce, and for whom to produce.

(1) *What to produce*: The question of what goods and services to produce and the quantity to produce is determined by societal demand. Society must choose among consumer goods, capital goods, and present and future consumption. In effect, if all resources are fully employed, a society is choosing a unique point on the production possibility curve at which to produce.

EXAMPLE: Should more automobiles or more airplanes be produced with our limited resources? Should more resources be used to produce military goods or social services?

(2) *How to produce*: Deciding "how to produce" involves choosing among different combinations of resources to produce a particular good or service. The problem is to find the most efficient combination of resources to produce a given level of output.

EXAMPLE: A choice has to be made regarding how to produce electricity. Should we use petroleum, energy from the sun, or nuclear power to fulfill our energy needs?

(3) *For whom to produce*: The question concerning for whom to produce is basically a distribution problem. The solution to this problem will determine how the total output of society is distributed among its members. Output can be distributed equally among everyone, or large portions of output can be directed to certain subgroups while others receive very little. To a large extent, politics, ethics, and economics are all involved in deciding for whom to produce.

EXAMPLE: The concept of welfare and progressive income taxes are attempts to address the issue of "for whom to produce" by reducing the purchasing power of the top income groups and increasing the purchasing power of the low-income groups.

3.   *Individual Choices*: Just as society must make choices, individuals also live within limited resources and must make choices.

a.   *Consumption*: Consumers have limited incomes; thus each individual must choose what goods and services to purchase with that limited income. If an individual consumer purchases more of one good (good X), then less of another good (good Y) can be purchased. Therefore, the opportunity cost of increasing the consumption of good X is the value of good Y that must be foregone.

EXAMPLE: If an individual has $15 to spend on refreshments, and the choice is between buying a hot dog for $1.50 or a soft drink for 75 cents, the choices are limited to 10 hot dogs and no soft drinks, 20 soft drinks and no hot dogs, or some combination of the two. Using this example, the opportunity cost of one hot dog would be two soft drinks or the opportunity cost of two soft drinks would be one hot dog.

b.   *Employment*: Individuals in society own productive resources and must decide how to use these resources. A decision must be made about how much of these resources to sell (a choice between work and leisure) and to whom the resources should be sold (a decision about what type of work to perform and for how much money).

c.   *Saving*: Another important personal decision-making application is the use of current income versus future income. Individuals can increase consumption now at the expense of future consumption, or can save now and have additional income for future consumption. The opportunity cost of saving is the value of present consumption that is foregone.

B.   Organization of an Economic System

Different societies attempt to solve the universal problem of scarcity, and address the basic question of what to produce, how to produce, and for whom to produce in different ways. Some societies do this through custom, some through decree, and some through the price and/or market system. Historically, the United States has relied primarily on price and markets to answer the basic questions of what, how, and for whom to produce.

l.   *Types of Economic Organization*: Different types of economic systems have often been classified as "isms" (socialism, communism, capitalism, market socialism). Each of these "ism" systems can be classified as a combination of alternative forms of economic organization: authoritarian, individualistic, traditional, and mixed economy. Capitalism has traditionally been identified with the individualistic type of economic organization; socialism and communism are identified with authoritarian types of economic organizations. In reality, all economic systems are a combination of authoritarian (command) and individualistic (market) types of economic systems.

a. *Authoritarian (command)*: An authoritarian economic organization is one within which people respond without choice to the commands of the state (government).

   (1) An authoritarian type of economic organization is characterized by centralized state (government) control over the direction of economic activity. The questions of what to produce, how to produce, and for whom to produce are answered by the state. This can be done through very structured central planning, or by a dictator simply making the decisions.

   EXAMPLES: Communism, authoritarian socialism, and fascism.

   (2) Citizens of the country have little freedom to choose among various occupations, and the choice of consumer goods is limited.

b. *Individualistic (market)*: In an individualistic economic system, people respond by choice to the dictates of their own self-interests. Individualistic economic organization allows the basic economic decisions and activities to be carried out by individuals and businesses without substantial interference by the government. An individualistic (or market) system is often referred to as "laissez-faire" capitalism.

   (1) Decisions of "what to produce" (how to use society's resources) are made through the market, and its resources are used in the production of those goods and services that derive the most profit.

   (2) The question of "how to produce" is also answered by market forces. Producers organize resources in the production process to make the maximum profit.

   (3) The question "for whom to produce" is answered through the market as individuals express their choices by buying. This relates back to the question of "what to produce," since increases in consumer preferences for goods and services lead to increases in profit, thus to additional resources being devoted to the production of particular goods or services.

c. *Traditional*: People respond on the basis of past practice and custom in a traditional economic organization. This mode is based on procedures devised in the distant past and solidified by a long process of historical trial and error. In many cases the traditions are sustained by belief, custom, and, in some cases, law. Many underdeveloped countries have traditional economies.

   (1) Occupational choices of children are often determined by the family's occupation.

   (2) Decisions on "what to produce" are based upon what has been produced in the past.

   (3) The traditional type of economic organization leads to very little change or economic growth.

d. *Mixed economy*: In a mixed economy individuals within the system and the government have an impact upon basic decisions of "what to produce," "how to produce," and "for whom to produce." People respond to a mixture of both coercion and economic incentives.

   (1) Mixed types of economic systems can be almost totally authoritarian, almost completely individualistic or market economy, or anywhere between.

   (2) In the recent past, economies labeled as democratic or market socialism have developed wherein the state owns the means of production and, therefore, determines what is produced. However, the decision of "for whom" production takes place may remain in the hands of the people through the operation of the market.

2. *Institutions of Modern Capitalism*: The fundamental concepts of modern capitalism include private ownership of property, freedom of contract, freedom of choice in enterprise, a relatively competitive free market, and some limited governmental responsibilities. Government responsibility comes about because markets cannot satisfy all of a society's goals. While markets may be very effective in satisfying such goals as economic freedom and economic efficiency, markets are less able to meet goals of economic stability, equity, and economic security. In most countries it has become the responsibility of government to implement policies that will aid in meeting the latter goals. It is important to remember, however, that the goals mentioned above are often competing. Societies are continually making choices that reduce economic efficiency but increase economic security or stability or establishing policies that reduce stability to improve economic freedom.

  a. *Private property*: The concept of private property is fundamental to a capitalistic (individualistic or market) economic system. Private property is the right of individuals to own the factors of production and to do with these resources what they see fit. Private property is distinguished from public property by the form of ownership. Public property implies ownership by the government or state.

  b. *Freedom of contract*: Coupled with private property rights, freedom of contract allows owners of resources, goods, and services to obtain, control, and dispose of economic resources within rather broad legal limits. Freedom of contract is important in a capitalistic system since it ensures that individuals may dispose of personal property as they wish.

  c. *Government's responsibilities*: Government has the responsibility for providing public services, maintaining general economic stability and security, and preventing economic abuses. Historically, laissez-faire capitalism did not meet the goals of all people within society. Thus, the role of government has been extended to meet economic goals such as stability, equity, and security in addition to the goals of economic freedom, efficiency, and growth that a market-oriented system would meet.

   (1) *Economic freedom*: The right and ability to choose how to use income to buy goods and services and use owned resources in the production process.

   (2) *Economic efficiency*: The production of goods and services in the most efficient (least costly) manner.

   (3) *Economic growth*: An increase in the output of goods and services per capita over a period of time.

(4) *Economic stability*: The existence of low rates of inflation (price increases) and low rates of unemployment within the society.

(5) *Economic equity*: The distribution of resources in society and the degree of equality that is proper for the distribution of resources and income.

(6) *Economic security*: The absence of fear of losing possessions as a result of unexpected events.

d. *Goals not met by economic system*: Goals generally not met by market-oriented economic systems are stability, equity, efficiency, and security. Typically, government assumes the responsibility for meeting these goals.

3. *Structure of Modern Capitalism*: When discussing modern capitalism, it is helpful to look at the economic system in terms of a model utilizing a circular flow of income that shows input and output flows and how they interrelate within the economy. This simple model visually illustrates how markets operate and the interaction of households, businesses, and governments within a market economy. As shown in Figure 1–2, there are three major institutions within modern capitalism: households, business, and government. Modern capitalism is an example of a mixed economy.

a. *Households*: Households are units within the economic system. Under modern capitalism, households are the owners of the factors of production. Households make these resources available to business firms and to government. In return, households receive income in the form of wages (the payment to labor), rents (the payment to land), interest (the payment to capital), and profits (the payment to entrepreneurial ability). Households use the income earned from selling their resources to buy the final goods and services.

Figure 1–2   Circular Flow of an Economic System

b. *Business firms*: Business firms are organizations that buy a variety of resources from households and organize them to produce goods and services that households wish to purchase. In modern capitalism, business firms can be sole proprietors (one person owning a business), partnerships (at least two people owning a business), or corporations (ownership of the firm is in the hands of many people known as stockholders). Business firms make the ultimate decision on how goods and services are produced and buy resources from households, organizing them in such a way as to make a product that households want to buy—at a profit. Businesses also sell goods and services to the government.

c. *Government*: The role of government is one of maintaining law and order, providing social services desired by the public, and providing national defense. To make these services available, the government has to buy resources from the household sector (as business firms do) and, in return, produce services that are desired by individuals. Restrictions that government places on the markets are attempts to meet goals that markets will not meet.

C.   Markets

Markets are fundamental to the functioning of a market economy. Markets exist for goods and services as well as for resources, and firms operate under varying competitive conditions often referred to as "market conditions."

1. *Basic Components of a Market*: The basic components of any market are demand, supply, and equilibrium.

  a. *Demand*: Demand is the relationship between a series of prices and corresponding quantities that individuals are able and willing to purchase at these prices.

  b. *Supply*: Every market needs suppliers of goods and services. Supply is the relationship between a series of prices and the associated quantities that producers will be able and willing to make available at those prices.

  c. *Equilibrium*: Supply and demand yield an equilibrium in quantity when considered together. Since the demand curve is downward sloping and the supply curve is upward sloping, they will intersect at some point. This intersection will establish a price at which all goods supplied at a given price will be purchased.

   (1) *Price below equilibrium*: If the price of a good is below equilibrium, the quantity demanded will be greater than the quantity supplied. This shortage will result in an upward pressure on price to restore equilibrium.

   (2) *Price above equilibrium*: If the price is above equilibrium, the quantity supplied will be greater than the quantity demanded. There will be a pressure for prices to fall, again approaching equilibrium.

     In reality, this equilibrium is seldom obtained. Market forces constantly affect the shifting of demand and/or supply. Thus, the market is constantly moving toward an equilibrium. This is most obvious in purely competitive markets, such as the grain market, where the quotes on the board of trade change on a minute-by-minute and day-by-day basis.

2. *The Price System*: The price system is synonymous with the market system in explaining economic behavior. The equilibrium price established by the market performs basic functions for a market-oriented economic system. Not only does it ration goods and services, but it also allocates resources to the most productive use. Inherent in the price system is the demand for and supply of goods and services.

a. *The demand for goods and services*:

(1) *The law of demand*: The law of demand is a very important relationship in economics. This law states that as price decreases, individuals will buy more of a good or service; and as price increases, individuals will buy less of a good or service.

(a) *Income effects*: As price increases, the real purchasing power of individuals declines; therefore, they are able to purchase fewer goods and services.

(b) *Substitution effects*: Substitution effects relate to the consumer's desire to get the best buy. If the price of good A increases and the price of good B stays the same, then A becomes relatively more expensive than B, and some consumers are likely to shift their consumption patterns to B.

(2) *Individual demand*: Demand is the quantity of goods that an individual is willing and able to buy at a variety of prices within a given period of time. As the price of a good decreases, the consumer will purchase a greater quantity of that good. As price increases, the consumer will purchase less of that good. This inverse relationship between the price of a good and the quantity of that good demanded is referred to as the law of demand. The following example shows this demand relationship.

EXAMPLE: In Figure 1–3, if the price of shoes is $40 a pair and John Q. Donaldson is willing to pay $40 for shoes this year, he will be willing to buy only one pair of shoes this year. If the price is $20, John will be

Figure 1–3 Individual Demand Curve

willing to buy two pairs. However, if the price drops to $10, he may be willing to purchase four pairs of shoes this year.

It is important to note that the demand schedule does not indicate or reflect the market price of a good. It simply indicates the quantity of a commodity that a person is willing to buy at various prices.

(3) *Market demand*: The total market demand for goods is the summation of all individual demands for that good. To find the market demand, one must add the quantity that will be bought by all individuals at a specific price. This total becomes the total market demand for the commodity at that given price level.

> *EXAMPLE: If there were 40,000 consumers, each with a demand curve equivalent to that pictured in Figure 1–3, at a price of $40 there would be 40,000 pairs of shoes bought within a year at a price of $40. If the price of shoes were $20, there would be 80,000 pairs of shoes purchased. If the price of shoes were $10, there would be 160,000 pairs of shoes purchased. The market demand would then resemble Figure 1–4. It is unlikely that all 40,000 consumers would have the same demand curve as that pictured in Figure 1–3. Thus, to find the market demand, you would have to add the number of pairs of shoes each of the 40,000 consumers would purchase at a price of $40 to find the total market quantity that would be bought at a price of $40.*

(4) *Determinants of demand*: While the price of the good will affect the quantity that individuals will purchase, other changes in our economic system will affect the amount that people purchase at all prices. These

Figure 1–4   Market Demand Curve

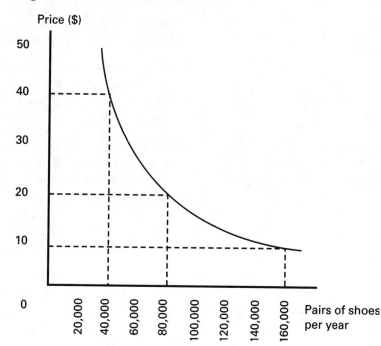

factors include consumer tastes and preferences, consumer income, prices of related goods, and expectations.

(a) *Consumer tastes and preferences*: People alter the goods and services which they desire over a period of time. As society feels that a good is something that it wants to purchase, the demand increases; and as society moves away from that good, the demand decreases. Tastes and preferences are also influenced by sections of the country and, to some extent, by the ethnic or religious background of individuals.

EXAMPLES:

Each year clothing fashions change.

The styles of automobiles change each year.

In the late 1960s hula hoops were in demand; today hula hoops are rarely seen.

(b) *Income of consumers*: Income definitely has an impact upon the demand for goods and services. As an individual's income increases, the demand for most goods and services will increase. When income and the demand for a good are positively related, economists refer to the good as a *normal* good. However, in a few cases income and demand for a good are inversely related; that is, an increase in income will result in a decrease in demand for a good. This type of good is labeled as an *inferior* good.

EXAMPLE: A good typically classified as an inferior good would be hamburger. As income increases, individuals consume less hamburger and consume more of other types of meat.

(c) *Prices of related goods*: The prices of related goods also have an impact upon the demand for goods and services. Two types of relationships are common. A good may be a substitute for another type of good, or a good may be complementary to another good.

If two goods are substitutes, that implies that both goods, to some extent, satisfy the same want of an individual. Therefore, they can substitute one for the other. If the price of a substitute increases, the demand for the original good would increase.

EXAMPLES OF SUBSTITUTES: If the price of Coca-Cola increases, the demand for other types of cola would also increase. As a result of the Coca-Cola price increase, people would start substituting other colas because of the new price of Coca-Cola relative to its substitutes. A rise in the price of beef could cause an increase in the demand for chicken since beef and chicken are both meats and can substitute for one another.

If two goods are complementary (goods that are used together), an increase in the price of one good will cause a decrease in the demand for the other.

EXAMPLES OF COMPLEMENTARY GOODS:

Gasoline and automobile tires: As the price of gasoline goes up, the demand for automobile tires goes down since they are complementary goods. As the price of gasoline goes up, people will drive fewer miles and, therefore, need (or demand) fewer automobile tires.

Tennis racquets and tennis balls.

Golf clubs and golf balls.

(d) *Buyers' expectations*: Individual expectations on the future of the market also have an impact on the demand for goods and services. An individual who expects future prices to increase is inclined to purchase now instead of paying the higher prices later. This leads to an increase in demand during the current period.

(e) *Population*: As the population increases, the total number of consumers increases. This results in an increase in demand.

(5) *Changes in demand and changes in quantity demanded*: Several factors affecting the demand for a good or service have been discussed. It is important to distinguish changes in quantity demanded from changes in demand. Changes in quantity demanded are changes in the amount of goods resulting from changes in price.

EXAMPLE: A movement from point A to point B on demand curve D1 in Figure 1–5 is an example of a change in quantity demanded. As the price goes down, the quantity demanded increases.

Figure 1–5 Shift in Demand

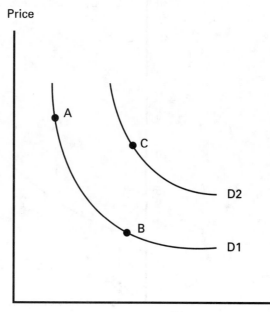

Changes in demand indicate changes in the quantity bought at all prices. A movement from one demand curve to another indicates a change in demand.

EXAMPLE: A movement from demand curve D1 to demand curve D2 in Figure 1–5 is an example of a change in demand. Changes in demand can be caused by changes in one of the determinants of demand: tastes and preferences, income, price of related goods, or expectations. A shift in demand for hamburger would result from the price of steaks increasing.

b. *The supply of goods and services*:

(1) *The law of supply*: The law of supply states that as price increases, the quantity of a good or service produced by a business in a given period of time increases.

(2) *The supply curve of a firm*: Supply is defined as the maximum quantity of a good that a firm or supplier will make available at various prices over a certain period of time. Like demand, supply is a schedule of price-quantity relationships. Figure 1–6 represents a typical supply curve. The supply curve is upward sloping, whereas a demand curve is always downward sloping. The reason for the upward slope can be explained in this way. If a producer is to increase the quantity of a good or service, the producer must receive a higher price. This is a result of increases in output requiring additional resources. If a firm is going to get additional resources in a competitive market, it is going to have to pay a higher

Figure 1–6   The Supply Curve of a Firm

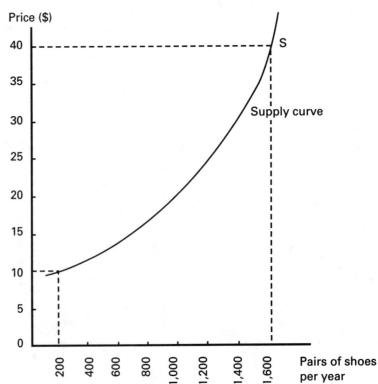

price for those resources than the ones currently being used. (This relationship is also referred to as the law of increasing costs.)

EXAMPLE: In Figure 1–6 the supplier is willing to make 200 units (pairs of shoes) available at a price of $10 and 1,600 units (pairs of shoes) available at a price of $40. The quantity made available is measured within a given time period, in this case, a year.

(3) *The market supply curve*: The total market supply curve of an industry is the horizontal summation of the supply curves of all the firms within the industry; that is, the number of units each firm is willing to make available at a given price is added to quantities other firms are willing to make available to arrive at the market supply. Figure 1–7 represents the market supply if there were 100 producers in the industry, all facing identical costs.

EXAMPLE: Referring to Figure 1–7, at a price of $10 there would be 10,000 units made available by the suppliers in any given year. If the price were $40, 110,000 units would be made available.

The process of developing the market supply curve is thus very similar to the process of developing the market demand curve.

(4) *Quantity supplied*: As price changes the quantity demanded, price also changes the quantity supplied. Changes in quantity supplied are move-

Figure 1–7   The Market Supply Curve

ments along a supply curve, as in movement from point A to point B in Figure 1–7.

(5) *Changes in supply*: As other determinants cause a change in demand (a shift in the total curve), there are determinants that result in a shift in supply (a change in the quantity made available at all possible prices). There are five determinants of supply: technology, resource prices, number of suppliers, price of related goods, and expectations. A change in one or more of the determinants will cause a shift in supply.

(a) *Technology*: Since technology affects the cost of production, it also affects supply. An improvement in technology suggests a more efficient means of production; thus producers can make more units available at lower prices. This would cause an increase in supply and shift the supply curve to the right, as shown in Figure 1–8 in the movement from supply curve S1 to supply curve S2.

(b) *Resource prices*: As the cost of resources used in production decreases, the supply of a certain number of goods can be made at a lower cost. This would result in an increase in supply as shown in the move from S1 to S2 in Figure 1–8. The opposite, of course, would be true if a firm experienced an increase in resource cost.

(c) *Number of suppliers*: The number of firms in the market also affects the market supply of goods and services. As the number of producers of a good increases, the market supply would increase, and vice versa.

(d) *Price of related goods*: As the price of related goods affects the demand curve, prices of related goods also affect the supply curve. If the price of related goods increases and the production of those goods appears more profitable, firms will reduce their supply of

Figure 1–8　Shift in Supply

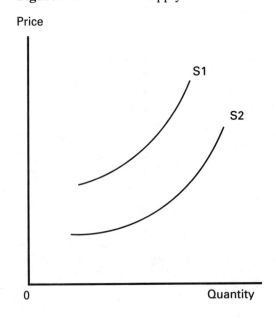

one good to increase the supply of the good whose price has increased.

EXAMPLE: This may be illustrated by the basic decision a farmer has to make each year concerning what crops to plant. If the market price of corn is high, corn is expected to be a profitable crop; the farmer would use a larger portion of land for corn and a smaller amount for beans for the following year. This would cause an increase in the supply for corn and a decrease in the supply for beans. If the market prices for corn decreased, beans would become relatively more profitable and the supply of beans would increase.

    (e) *Expectations*: Similar to the role they play in determining demand, expectations play a role in determining supply. If prices are expected to rise, suppliers will attempt to supply less now in the hope that more can be supplied when prices increase, thus increasing profits.

c. *Elasticity*: An additional function of demand and supply is elasticity. Elasticity measures the degree of responsiveness of buyers (sellers) to changes in the price of a commodity. If a small reduction in price results in a large change in the quantity bought (supplied), the demand (supply) is *elastic*. This means that the consumers (producers) are responsive to price changes.

EXAMPLE: The price of Crest toothpaste goes up. Since there are many brands of toothpaste on the market, consumers will tend to switch to a lower-priced brand.

If a large change in price results in a small change in quantity bought (supplied), the demand (supply) is *inelastic*. This means that the consumers (producers) are unresponsive to price changes.

EXAMPLE: If the price of salt increases, the amount of salt purchased would decline very little.

d. *Equilibrium*: A market is in equilibrium when all goods and services that consumers want to purchase at a given price are willingly supplied by producers. At this point both the suppliers and the demanders are satisfied. As long as the determinants of supply and demand are constant, there is a tendency for price and quantity demanded and supplied to remain at the same point. Changes in the determinants of demand and/or supply will stimulate market adjustments and bring the price toward a new equilibrium.

EXAMPLE: Figure 1–9 illustrates market equilibrium. At a price of $10, consumers are willing to purchase 8,000 units of the good and producers are willing to make available 8,000 units. This equilibrium will be maintained unless the demand or supply changes. For example, if individual incomes increase, demand for the good might increase and the demand curve would shift to D2. As the demand curve shifts to D2, the quantity that people would now buy at a price of $10 would increase to 10,000 units, but only 8,000 units would be made available by suppliers. This shortage would indicate to businesses that people were willing to pay a higher price, and the price would move toward the new equilibrium of $11 and a quantity of 9,000.

Figure 1–9   Market Equilibrium

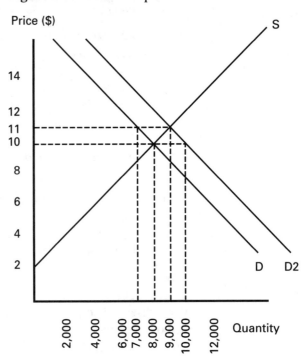

If the opposite had happened, similar results would take place. Suppose that the original equilibrium was at $11 and 9,000 and the demand declined from D2 to D. Now at a price of $11, only 7,000 units would be bought by consumers and suppliers would make available 9,000. This surplus would be eliminated by suppliers lowering the price to get rid of excess inventory, and a new equilibrium price of $10 and quantity of 8,000 would be established. Similar effects can be traced by analyzing changes in supply and their impact on equilibrium price and quantity.

One unique feature of the market is that it will automatically adjust to an equilibrium. With private property and the freedom of consumers to purchase what they want and producers to produce what they want, price will provide the proper incentive for market adjustments to take place.

e.   *Functions of prices*: Prices in an economic system have a variety of functions. One function is providing signals to consumers and producers which result in the clearing of the market. Another way of saying this is that prices allocate resources among alternative uses and ration goods and services.

(1)   *The distribution function of prices*: Because society's wants exceed its scarce resources, there must be some way to ration the available goods and services. Price serves the rationing function by distributing goods to anyone capable of and willing to pay the market price. If a good becomes scarce, its price increases until the quantity demanded and the quantity supplied are equal. Thus, a price increase eliminates the shortage. Price adjustments are automatic and need no direction from government agencies or institutions.

(2) *The allocation function of prices*: Along with distributing goods and services, price also performs the function of allocating scarce resources. If one type of good is more valuable to society than another, consumers are willing to pay more for a given quantity of the more valued good. As consumers are willing to pay more for more valued goods, the profit for producing those goods will increase. This is the signal to producers to use resources to produce more of that good relative to other goods. Therefore, producers seek to maximize profits by responding to the desires of consumers and use productive resources in a way that fulfills societal wants. If the producer fails to heed consumer demand, competitive firms will meet this need; the unresponsive firm will lose money and be forced out of business. This allocation function of prices is what Adam Smith (the father of economics) referred to as "the invisible hand."

EXAMPLE: As a resource such as petroleum becomes scarce, its price increases relative to other forms of energy. As the price of petroleum increases, some users will find it more economical to use other forms of energy. Therefore, the higher prices will provide an incentive to reallocate resource use from petroleum to other forms of energy.

3. *Types of Markets*: The discussion of markets would not be complete without a review of the types of markets within which producers operate.

   a. *Competitive markets*: If a market economic system is to be effective, there must be competition among producers. Competition results in products being manufactured at the lowest possible price and in the most efficient manner. The equilibrium market price, determined by the intersection of supply and demand, not only determines the market price that a consumer must pay for a good or service, but also has an influence upon the industry that produces the good. The industry that produces the good can be characterized as one that is competitive or which contains elements of monopoly power. For perfect competition to exist, several characteristics must be fulfilled:

      (1) *Homogeneous products*: All producers within a market (industry) offer products that are identical; quality and other aspects of the good are all the same.

         EXAMPLE: Grains produced by farmers are homogeneous products. Number 2 corn is number 2 corn, no matter what farmer happened to produce it.

         Since all products are exactly the same, one interesting aspect of homogeneous products is that producers find it unnecessary to advertise their product. Therefore, advertising plays a very minor role. The only role advertising would play would be to inform consumers of the availability of a good or of the market for the good.

         Brand-name products represent nonhomogeneous products since they are packaged differently. There can be an allegiance to the brand even though it is similar or identical to other products.

      (2) *Many buyers and sellers*: Another characteristic of perfect competition is that there are many buyers and sellers. Many people wish to buy the

product, and many producers are making the product available for sale. *Many*, in this case, is defined as a sufficient number so that no one buyer or seller could have any impact on the market price for the good.

EXAMPLE: The market for grain is an industry that characterizes many buyers and sellers. There are many farmers producing grain, and any one farmer could substantially increase the amount of acreage of corn without affecting the market price. By the same token, there are many buyers of grain, and no single buyer can substantially affect the market for grain. With many buyers and sellers, no single producer or consumer can influence the market.

(3) *Freedom of entry and exit*: For a market to be competitive, there must be freedom of entry into and exit from the industry. Firms should be able to begin producing a given product at any time they see fit, and they should also be able to leave the industry at any point in time they see fit. There are three common barriers to a firm's freedom of entry and exit into an industry:

(a) *Restricted entry*: Existing firms or groups of firms may restrict entry to an industry. Historically, this has been the case where existing firms use cutthroat competition to prevent new firms from becoming established in the industry. Also, if a firm (or a few firms) has exclusive ownership of raw materials or patent rights, this exclusive ownership allows control of the flow of firms into the industry.

(b) *Government action*: Legislation often limits entry and exit by establishing rates, prices, and conditions of operation in many industries, including utilities, transportation, and communications. In addition, governments may require some type of accreditation or licensing before a firm can enter into an industry.

EXAMPLE: The government may require licensing to practice a particular occupation. Teachers, accountants, and other professionals must acquire some license to practice their professions. Requiring licenses allows a certain control over the market.

(c) *Mobility of resources*: Entry into an industry may require large cash outlay due to heavy fixed investments to initiate production. In the case of the steel industry and the automobile industry, the amount of cash necessary to begin the industry is substantial.

(4) *Sufficient information*: There must be sufficient information available to both buyers and sellers to enable them to make good judgments. This condition provides for complete information to be available on production, technology, and investment opportunities so that one firm does not have an advantage over another firm. All buyers and sellers would know the price and quality of goods that are available in the market.

EXAMPLE: The New York Stock Exchange, which records and distributes, almost instantly, prices and quantities of stocks sold, is an example.

In most markets this information is dispensed through advertising which provides buyer and seller identity, reliability, price, terms of sale, overall quality, and so on. In perfect competition, however, there would be no persuasive advertising of the "ours is better than yours" variety. This would not be necessary because of product homogeneity.

Economists have set perfect competition as the ideal to judge the structure of industry. This is true because under perfect competition the producer of a product would have to accept the prevailing market price, and produce as efficiently as other producers, or not make a profit. As a result, products would be made available at the lowest possible costs and the price charged to the consumer would be equivalent to the cost of production for the producer. One cost of production is a normal rate of return (or normal profit) to the producer.

b. *Noncompetitive markets*: The term *noncompetitive* is used to describe those industries that do not fit the definition of the perfect competition model. Noncompetitive markets typically result because one of the conditions of perfect competition is not met, and the result is monopoly power.

Since the perfect competition model is used as the ideal by economists and most market systems, government attempts to ensure that the impact of noncompetitive markets on society is minimized. These actions include the passage of various laws to limit the amount of monopoly power that a firm can obtain. In the U.S. economy this has been done through a series of antitrust laws and through government regulation of some industries. In noncompetitive markets, one or more of the following characteristics exist:

(1) *Some type of concentration of buyers and sellers*: When noncompetitive markets exist, there is typically some concentration of buyers and sellers. This concentration is sufficient when buyers or sellers have some impact on the price of the good they are buying or producing. If this is the case, the buyer or seller will charge a higher price and provide a smaller quantity of the good for sale than if the market was competitive. In many instances, this will result in the producers earning a profit greater than the normal profit, thus making monopoly profits. In any case, the welfare of the buyer is reduced since the price will be higher and the product less available.

EXAMPLE: In a town with only one grocery store, that store would have the ability to charge prices higher than the competitive level due to lack of competition.

(2) *Product differentiation*: Product differentiation is an attempt to make consumers partial to a given product. Therefore, the producer is able to charge a slightly higher price for one product than for another product by packaging it differently or changing it slightly.

EXAMPLES: Toothpaste, soft drinks, and other such commodities.

Producers often package similar products differently or make small ingredient changes to develop brand loyalty. While the increase in selection made available to consumers may have some benefit, product differentiation also results in a slightly higher price than under conditions of perfect competition. Product differentiation also leads to promotional advertising rather than informational advertising described under perfect competition. The goal of promotional advertising is to create an image that a particular product is better than similar products.

(3) *Lack of product information*: Under perfect competition, it is assumed that buyers and sellers have adequate information concerning price and quality of products in the market. In noncompetitive markets, buyers may lack information; therefore, producers are able to exploit this lack of information to avoid normal price competition. Thus, the firm operating in the nonperfect competitive market is able to exert greater control over the market than the competitive firm.

(4) *Barriers to entry*: In noncompetitive markets barriers to entry may exist. These entry barriers can be the result of the use of a variety of techniques:

(a) *Cutthroat competition*: A firm using this technique cuts prices when a new firm enters the industry so that the new firm is unable to make a profit and is rapidly forced out of business.

(b) *High entry cost*: A second barrier is high entry cost, which may prohibit firms from entering a particular industry. These costs could include high capital costs or high promotional costs of making a product known.

(c) *Patents and other exclusive rights granted to products*: Although a patent protects a product developer against other people benefiting from the fruits of the developer's time and effort, it also gives a legal monopoly to the patent owner. A firm's exclusive rights to all materials also precludes other firms from entering into the production of a good or service.

(d) *Ownership of resources*: A firm's exclusive right to raw materials also precludes other firms from beginning production of a good or service. At one point, Alcoa owned rights to all bauxite deposits in the world. Since bauxite is necessary for the production of aluminum, Alcoa had a monopoly in the production of aluminum.

c. *Types of noncompetitive markets*: There are basically three types of noncompetitive markets: monopoly, oligopoly, and monopolistic competition.

(1) *Monopoly*: A market consisting of only one producer of a product with no competition is known as a monopoly. Since there is only one firm in the industry, the industry and the monopolist are one and the same. In the United States the only pure monopolies are those created by government, which we refer to as natural monopolies (local electric companies, local telephone companies, and other types of utilities). Where these natural monopolies exist, a regulatory commission is usually established to control the price charged.

(2) *Oligopoly*: In an oligopoly a few sellers control the majority of the market. A balanced oligopoly is characterized by several firms all with equal

market power. An unbalanced oligopoly consists of one or two firms with substantial power.

EXAMPLES IN UNITED STATES: Automobiles (balanced), breakfast cereals (unbalanced), cigarettes (balanced), and appliances (balanced).

Since there are only a few producers in the market, it is easy for these firms to charge a slightly higher price and earn a higher profit than would be charged in a competitive situation.

(3) *Monopolistic competition*: There are many producers, but each firm has a slight degree of monopoly power because its product is slightly different from other products in its group. (Product difference may be in the service that is offered.) While the perfectly competitive firm must accept the market price for a good, a monopolistically competitive firm may be able to charge slightly above the market price, because it has slightly differentiated its product.

EXAMPLES: Toothpaste, soft drinks, soaps.

Review Questions

DIRECTIONS: Select the best answer from the four alternatives. Write the letter of your answer in the blank to the left of the number.

_____ 1. The distinguishing characteristic of an economic good is

    a. that it is scarce.
    b. that it is sold in the marketplace.
    c. that it possesses utility.
    d. that the consumer derives utility from owning it.

_____ 2. The law of demand implies that people would

    a. never choose work over leisure.
    b. buy less gas if the gasoline tax were raised 6 cents.
    c. buy as much milk at 90 cents per half gallon as at 75 cents per half gallon.
    d. eat more beef if the price of beef were increased.

_____ 3. Which of the following statements is consistent with the law of demand?

    a. Farmers produce fewer bushels of wheat because the price of wheat has recently increased.
    b. A politician votes against a proposal because most constituents oppose it.
    c. More students attend lectures in an introductory economics class because attendance counts 20 percent of the grade.
    d. People drive less because of higher gas prices.

_____ 4. Goods are

    a. scarce for the poor but not for the rich.
    b. scarce neither for the poor nor for the rich.
    c. scarcer for the poor than for the rich.
    d. scarce for both poor and rich.

_____ 5. Scarcity means that

    a. human desires will never be satisfied.
    b. human desire for a good is greater than the amount that is freely available.
    c. temporarily, some good is in short supply.
    d. humans have failed to achieve a basic standard of living.

6. Which of the following is not a basic question faced by each economy?

  a. What goods are subject to the law of demand?
  b. What will be produced?
  c. To whom will the goods that are produced be allocated?
  d. How will the goods be produced?

7. Which of the following factors would not affect the supply of computers?

  a. Higher wage rates for workers in the electronics industry
  b. Higher prices for resources used to produce computers
  c. Technological improvement reducing the cost of production of computers
  d. Increase in consumer income

8. Which of the following was not a result of the higher prices of gasoline and petroleum-derived products in early 1974?

  a. The demand for small cars expanded.
  b. The incentive to use solar heating units increased.
  c. The demand for used Cadillacs and Lincoln Continentals increased.
  d. Tourism in Florida declined relative to that in 1973.

9. Criteria for rationing goods and resources must be established because of

  a. the law of comparative advantage.
  b. capitalist economic organizations.
  c. the scarcity imposed by nature.
  d. the inability of political entrepreneurs to develop efficient forms of economic organizations.

10. The law of demand refers to

  a. the phenomenon that prices decrease as more units of a product are demanded and more are produced.
  b. the increase in price that results from an increase in demand.
  c. the inverse relationship between the price of a good and the quantity of the good demanded.
  d. the increase in the quantity of a good available as the price of the good increases.

11. Profit can be defined as

  a. the difference between the revenue derived from the sale of a product and the opportunity cost of employing the resources required to produce the product.
  b. the difference between the income and disbursements of a firm.
  c. the difference between the price of a product and the cost of the raw materials used to produce it.
  d. the total compensation received by the firm's owners.

12. According to the law of supply

    a. more of a good is supplied as the price of the resources rise.
    b. there is a positive relationship between price of a good and the amount that buyers choose to purchase.
    c. there is a positive relationship between the price of a good and the amount of it offered for sale by suppliers.
    d. there is a negative relationship between the price of the good and the amount of it purchased by suppliers.

13. Technological advancements in the production of computer products will cause

    a. the supply curve for computer products to shift to the right.
    b. the supply curve for computer products to shift to the left.
    c. the quantity supplied to increase along the existing supply curve.
    d. little change, since the computer industry is controlled by a few corporations.

14. When a shortage of a good exists

    a. the amount demanded is greater than the amount supplied at all prices except the existing price.
    b. price must be controlled to avoid the need for rationing.
    c. only an increase in production will eliminate the shortage.
    d. if the price is not permitted to rise, nonprice factors such as quality deterioration will play more of a role in the allocation process.

15. Under competitive conditions, market prices

    a. are always in long-run equilibrium.
    b. can be determined only after a detailed study of supply and demand conditions has been made.
    c. are incapable of coordinating the actions of buyers and sellers.
    d. generally bring the self-interest of individual consumers and producers into harmony with the general welfare (economic efficiency).

16. Which of the following exists in a market in which producers have monopoly power?

    a. Free entry and exit
    b. Product differentiation
    c. Large numbers of buyers and sellers
    d. Complete information

_____ 17. Bill said, "If I didn't have a date tonight, I would save $20 and spend this evening playing chess." The opportunity cost of the date is

a. $20.
b. $20 plus the cost of foregoing a night playing chess.
c. dependent on how pleasant a time one has on the date.
d. the cost of foregoing a night playing chess.

_____ 18. A new hospital is being built in your home town. The opportunity cost of building the new hospital would be

a. the money cost of constructing the hospital.
b. the highest-valued bundle of other goods and services that might be foregone because of the hospital construction.
c. the necessary increase in tax revenues to finance the construction.
d. increased if the money cost of building the hospital decreases.

_____ 19. In this diagram, point A is

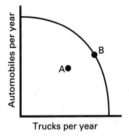

a. unattainable.
b. inefficient.
c. efficient.
d. preferred to point B.

_____ 20. Which of the following conditions would be most likely to cause the production possibility curve for corn and beans to shift from AA to BB?

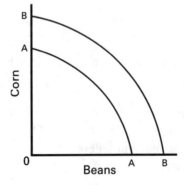

a. A reduction in the labor force
b. Choosing more corn and less beans
c. Choosing more beans and less corn
d. Increasing the capital used to produce corn and beans

_____ **21.** Based on the graph below, if the current price of beef was $4 per pound, which of the following conditions would be accurate?

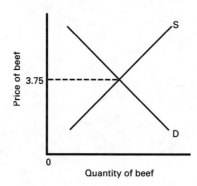

a. Producers would want to supply more beef than consumers would wish to buy.
b. Producers would be supplying less than the equilibrium quantity of beef.
c. Equilibrium could only be reached if demand increased.
d. The price of beef would have to rise to bring establish equilibrium.

Solutions

1. (a)   [A-1] The concept of scarcity is derived from the idea that individuals and societies have unlimited wants and limited resources.

2. (b)   [C-2-a] The law of demand states that as price increases, individuals will buy less of a good or service.

3. (d)   [C-2-a] As the price of gas increases, people will buy less gas and travel less if possible.

4. (d)   [A-1] Scarcity of goods affects everyone, rich or poor.

5. (b)   [A-1-a] Scarcity of goods means that there is more demand than supply.

6. (a)   [A-2-c] What to produce, for whom to produce, and how to produce are the three basic questions an economic system must answer.

7. (d)   [C-2-b] Answers (a), (b), and (c) all affect the supply, while answer (d) affects the demand.

8. (c)   [C-2-b] Answers (a), (b), and (d) all describe the proper relationship between substitute goods: As price increases, demand for substitutes will increase. The demand for cars with low mileage per gallon of gas decreased at that time.

9. (c)   [C-2-e(1)] Society's wants exceed its scarce resources. Therefore, there must be a way to ration available goods and services.

10. (c)   [C-2-a(1)] The law of demand states that as price decreases, individuals will buy more of a good or service; and as price increases, individuals will buy less of a good or service.

11. (a)   [C-2-b] Answers (b) and (c) refer only to explicit costs and do not take into consideration opportunity costs. Answer (d) refers to cost only.

12. (c)   [C-1-b] The law of supply states that as price increases, the individual or firm will be willing to sell a greater quantity of goods and services.

13. (a)   [C-2-b] Improvements in computer technology suggest more efficient production and possibly lower prices. This would cause an increase in supply and shift the supply curve to the right.

14. (d)   [C-2-e] Price also performs the function of allocating scarce resources.

15. (d)   [C-3-a] Competition results in products being manufactured at the lowest possible price and in the most efficient manner.

16. (b)   [C-3] Answers (a), (c), and (d) are requirements of perfect competition and would not be present if monopoly power were present.

17. (b)   [A-2-b] Opportunity cost is the value of the opportunity foregone when a decision is made. In this case, one would spend $20 on the date and forego a night of chess.

18. (b)   [A-2-a,b] Opportunity cost is the value of the opportunity foregone when a decision is made. The opportunity cost of building the hospital would be the value of any goods or services that will not be offered because of the new construction.

19. (b)   [A-2-a] Point A is inside the curve. Therefore, it is not using all of its resources efficiently and can increase output of one without increasing output of the other.

20. (d)   [A-2-a] Once a specific point on the production possibility curve is achieved, to get more output more capital must be invested.

21. (a)   [C-2-c] Producers are responsive to price changes. As the price increases, producers may want to produce more, but consumers might not be willing to purchase more at the increased price.

CHAPTER 2

National Income
and its Determinants

From an economist's standpoint, the study of national income and its determinants has a variety of implications. National income and its determinants allow us to take a look at the economy, analyze the growth that has taken place in past years, identify weaknesses or strengths in our economy that will lead to future growth or future recession, and identify the impact of changes in economic policy by either the federal government or monetary authorities.

In this chapter we develop measures for economic performance and discuss policy issues, such as unemployment and inflation. The solutions to these policy issues will be analyzed, and the role of fiscal and monetary policy will be discussed.

KEY TERMS

Aggregate demand (aggregate expenditures)
Aggregate supply
Average propensity to consume (APC)
Built-in stabilizers
Capital consumption allowance
Ceteris paribus
Classical school of economics
Consumer price index (CPI)
Consumption
Cost-push inflation
Cyclical unemployment
Demand-pull inflation (inflationary gap)
Disposable personal income (DPI)
Economic growth

Factors of production
Fiscal policy
Frictional unemployment
GNP implicit price deflator index
Gross national product (GNP)
Inflation
Investment
Keynesian economics
Marginal propensity to consume (MPC)
Marginal tax rate
Monetary policy
National income
Near money
Net national product (NNP)
Output per capita

Personal income (PI)   Structural unemployment
Prime interest rate   Supply-side economics
Producer price index (PPI)   Technological unemployment
Production possibilities curve (PPC)   Transfer payments
Real income (purchasing power)

A. Economic Growth

Economic growth is an increase in the per capita output of an economy. Economic growth involves both benefits and costs to a society. Although the concept has been challenged in recent years, economic growth is essential if society is to experience increased capacity to produce and consume goods and services. National income measures whether economic growth has taken place. The average rate of growth in the United States was extremely high, by most measures, until the mid to late 1970s. Since then, the rate of growth in the United States has slowed substantially.

1. *Maintaining Economic Growth*: To maintain economic growth a society must be able to increase the availability of goods and services to individuals within that society. A system of national income accounting has been devised to provide a yardstick for measuring economic growth. For a society to have continued economic growth, however, it is necessary from time to time to investigate those factors that control economic activity to stimulate economic growth.

   a. *Factors controlling economic activity*:

      (1) *Production*: Transforming resources within the society into goods and services is the process of production.

      (2) *Income*: Income is the flow of net production of goods and services over a period of time (e.g., a year).

      EXAMPLES: Basic income concepts used to measure economic well-being are:

      Gross national product (GNP)

      Net national product (NNP)

      National income (NI)

      Personal income (PI)

      Disposable personal income (DPI)

      (3) *Wealth*: The net assets on hand at any given point in time are considered the wealth of an economy. If an economy is not growing at the desired rate, policy can be implemented to affect wealth and move the economy toward its production possibility curve, rather than operating at less than full employment or with high rates of inflation.

   b. *Other factors affecting the level of economic activity*: The level of gross national product and other economic variables is affected by the level of employment and the level of inflation within our society. These variables in turn affect the level of consumption, level of investment, and level of government activity necessary for society to operate at its full-employment equilibrium. If society is not functioning efficiently, resources remain unused and/or inflation is at an undesirable rate. The level of consumption, investment, and government spending can affect the level at which the economy is operating and the level of employment and inflation.

    c. *The need for consistent economic policy*: For society to grow, there must be an economic policy consistent with the growth rate of gross national product, the rate of unemployment existing within society, and the rate of inflation within society.

        (1) *The Classical School of economic theory*: The first writings by economists (commonly referred to as the Classical School) developed a philosophy wherein any fluctuations in the economy would be self-correcting. These economists included Adam Smith, David Ricardo, and Alfred Marshall, among others. They believed that if inflation was at a higher rate than desirable, the real value of wages would decline, leading to declines in demand for goods and services. Therefore, a reduction of pressure on prices occurred. Conversely, if the rate of unemployment became higher than desirable, individuals would offer their services for less than the existing market wage. The reduction in the market wage would cause an increase in the number of people employed and reduce unemployment.

        (2) *Keynesian economic theory*: In the mid-1930s a new philosophy of economics was developed that did not rely on market self-adjusting mechanisms to achieve economic stability. John Maynard Keynes, a British economist, developed the concept of employment theory relying on government to take an active step in the economic stabilization of a country.

        (3) *Supply-side economic theory*: In the 1970s and early 1980s Keynes' assumptions were challenged. A new school of thought referred to as supply-side economics emerged. Supply-side economics gives consideration not only to affecting the aggregate *demand* for goods and services, but also to those factors affecting aggregate *supply* of goods and services. The supply-side economist argues that we should rely more on natural market mechanisms and provide sufficient incentives for these market mechanisms to solve societal problems of unemployment, inflation, and economic growth.

  2. *Measuring Economic Growth*: Economic growth may be based on changes in the standard of living, output per capita, real income, or gross national product of individuals within a society.

    a. *Standard of living as a measure of economic growth*: Standard of living historically has been measured by the per capita consumption of individuals within society, the literacy rate of society, and measures of other types of amenities available to people in the society.

    b. *Output per capita as a measure of economic growth*: In terms of pure economic growth, societies tend to look at the *output per capita* (society's output divided by its population) as a measure of the standard of living in society.

        (1) If output per capita of a country increases, economic growth is taking place.

(2)   If output per capita declines or remains constant, there is either a declining rate of growth or a zero rate of growth, respectively.

c.   *Real income as a measure of economic growth*: *Real income* is income measured in constant dollars. The primary drawback is that there is no reference to the distribution of income within the society. Thus, a society can be extremely wealthy on a per capita basis, but wealth is actually held by only a small percentage of the population while the standard of living for the general population may not be very high.

d.   *Total aggregate output or gross national product as a measure of economic growth*: The basic yardstick for measuring economic growth is gross national product (GNP). GNP is the market value of the nation's total output of new final goods and services within a period of time, usually one year. Although this measure for economic growth does not take into consideration all aspects of the economy, and therefore does not indicate the welfare of a society, GNP does give us an indication of the direction in which a society is advancing. This type of measurement does not identify how much output is available per person or the distribution of the output among individuals in society.

3.   *Economic Growth and Economic Welfare*: It is important to distinguish between economic growth and increases in economic welfare. When we use increases in output per capita or some other measure of GNP to indicate that economic growth has taken place, this says nothing about the types of goods and services that are being produced or the possible negative aspects of experiencing economic growth.

a.   *Effects of increased production output*: As economic growth takes place, society tends to use scarce resources at a more rapid rate. Thus, increased production can have a negative result.

EXAMPLES:

As production increases, pollution also increases.

Increases in production may cause increases in urbanization, which may lead to increases in crime.

b.   *Net economic welfare as an indication of economic growth*: Instead of using gross national product to indicate economic growth, some economists have proposed using a net economic welfare measure. This net measure would subtract the increased cost of pollution, crime, and so on, from the GNP to arrive at a net economic welfare.

4.   *Factors Affecting Economic Growth*: For economic growth to occur, there must be net production of goods and services over a period of time, typically a year. *Net production* refers to the fact that, in production, resources must be used up. For *growth* to take place, the value of the goods and services produced must exceed the value of the resources used up in the production process. This may be accomplished by increased efficiency or by advances in the level of technology. In measuring economic growth, it is necessary to distinguish between net production from a dollar standpoint and net production from a *real goods and services* standpoint.

EXAMPLE: If GNP is used to measure the economic growth of a country, an increase in GNP this year over last year does not necessarily indicate whether the in-

crease in GNP is attributed to (1) an increase in the quantity of goods and services produced or (2) an increase in the price level or (3) a combination of these two.

To measure the impact of increases in prices, a series of price indices has been developed so that we can subtract the impact of price increases on GNP. Real growth takes place only when real income changes over time.

a.   *Effects of factors of production on growth*: The growth of society over time is affected by the factors of production: land, labor, capital, and entrepreneurial ability. As these factors of production are used more efficiently, more output can be produced for the same quantity of resources.

   (1)   *Land*: The more productive land a country possesses and the more resources the land contains, the more rapidly that country can grow over time.

   (2)   *Labor*: The size and composition of the labor force also has a strong impact on the growth of a country over a period of time.

   (a)   Size of the labor force simply accounts for increases in the number of people who work, or are willing to work, at prevailing wages in the production process.

   (b)   Quality of the labor force is another important factor. As the average education of the labor force increases, the labor force typically becomes more productive and adds to the potential growth rates for a country.

   (c)   If the age distribution of the population moves toward a higher percentage in the prime working years, the output of that society will be greater.

   (d)   As the average hours of work per week change, the output of a society will be affected.

   (e)   The degree of specialization of the labor force will also affect the total production.

   (3)   *Capital*: The capital stock of a country includes resources such as buildings, equipment, and other assets (but not money) that are used in the production process. If the capital stock of a country is large relative to other countries, that country will possess a greater ability to grow, since it has greater productive capacity.

   (4)   *Entrepreneurial ability*: The unique talents that individuals have of combining resources to produce goods or services more efficiently than other individuals is called entrepreneurial ability. The human resource needed to manage the development of new goods and services, continue to expand output, and accept the risks of business ownership is a very important part of the production process.

b.   *Effects of other factors on growth*:

   (1)   A country's level of technology influences methods of production and the applicability of scientific principles utilized in the production

process. As technology enables production to increase, efficiency typically increases and economic growth takes place.

(2) The sociopolitical framework of the country provides the economic incentives within that country for growth to take place. If society provides incentives for businesses to invest and increase capital stock, a foundation for future economic growth is developed.

B. National Income Measurement

National income accounting provides the system for measuring production, income, and wealth of a society (refer to Section A-1-a for definitions of the terms—production, income, and wealth). As a result, it is possible to monitor fluctuations in economic activity and, if necessary, to stimulate growth. The concepts of income and wealth are interrelated since real wealth and real income both result from production. The exception to this is natural wealth, which includes land, mineral deposits, lumber, and other resources taken from the land.

1. *Measuring Economic Variables*: Income and production may be measured using a variety of yardsticks: gross national product (GNP), net national product (NNP), national income (NI), personal income (PI), and disposable personal income (DPI). Figure 2–1 provides national income accounts for the United States for the year 1992.

   a. *Gross national product (GNP)*: GNP is the broadest concept of national income accounting and represents the aggregate money value, at market prices,

Figure 2–1 Summary of National Income Accounts for 1992 (in billions of dollars)

Gross national product (GNP)	$6,046
− Capital consumption allowance	− 658
= Net national product (NNP)	$5,388
− Indirect business taxes	− 503
− Business transfer payments	− 51
+ Subsidies less current surplus of government enterprises	+ 3
= National income	$4,837
− Corporate profits	− 407
− Net interest	− 442
− Contributions to Social Security	− 536
+ Government transfer payments	+ 694
+ Personal interest income	+ 140
+ Personal dividend income	+ 837
+ Business transfer payments	+ 22
= Personal income	$5,145
− Personal taxes	− 644
= Disposable personal income	$4,501
− Personal outlays	−4,262
= Personal savings	$ 239

of all the final goods and services produced within an economy in a given year. The use of final goods and services rules out double counting of values. If a good was counted both in the intermediate stages of production and at the time it was purchased for consumption, the value of net production would be exaggerated. GNP also includes all government expenditures except transfer payments. Transfer payments are disbursements from government or private firms for which no products or services are received in exchange.

EXAMPLES OF TRANSFER PAYMENTS: Social security payments, unemployment compensation, and government welfare programs.

Although GNP is a measure of all final goods and services produced for sale within a year, certain items are omitted. GNP only includes market transactions. Nonmarket transactions, such as the value of a homemaker's services, the value of criminal activity, and the value of family production are not included in the gross national product of a country.

Note: Moreover, these figures are not counted in any of the national income accounting figures discussed below.

b. *Net national product (NNP)*: Not all of a country's output within a given period of time is a net increase in output. Part of the output is used to replace the capital goods that were used during the production of other goods and services. These are called capital consumption allowances.

net national product = gross national product – capital consumption allowances (depreciation)

Net national product gives us a measure of the value of the goods and services available for consumption during a given time period.

c. *National income (NI)*: Where GNP and NNP measure the value of the goods and services produced within an economy within a given period of time, national income (NI) measures the sum of payments to the factors of production which resulted from production that occurred. Each of the four factors of production (land, labor, capital, and entrepreneurial ability) has its own return: returns, wages, interest, and profit, respectively.

National income = net national product – indirect business taxes

EXAMPLES OF INDIRECT BUSINESS TAXES: Sales taxes, excise taxes.

d. *Personal income (PI)*: Not all income paid for the factors of production is retained by households in the form of personal income. The amount of income available to households is the national income minus earnings of factors of production that households do not receive from employers (for example, corporate profits, corporate social security contributions, corporate net interest). In addition, transfer payments and nonlabor income must be added to the national income figure to get personal income. Transfer payments are not direct payments to the factors of production but are transfers of income from the government and business to households. Transfer payments include unemployment compensation, welfare payments, and farm subsidy payments.

Nonlabor income would include interest, dividend, and business transfer payments.

e. *Disposable personal income (DPI)*: Not all national income is available to households, and not all income available to households can be used for consumption or saving. From personal income, one must deduct payment of personal income taxes, personal property taxes, and inheritance taxes to get disposable personal income. Disposable personal income is the amount that people have available to buy consumer goods, to save, and to pay interest. In the United States, approximately 93 percent of DPI is spent on consumption and interest and about 6 to 8 percent goes into personal savings.

2. *Real versus Nominal Measures*: GNP, defined as the total value of all final goods and services produced within a society within a year, can also be explained using the following equation

$$GNP = \Sigma \; P_i Q_i$$

where *P* is the price of a good and *Q* is the quantity.

This means that gross national product (GNP) equals the sum (Σ) of the value of all goods, or the price of a good times the quantity of goods, for all goods and services produced.

a. *Reasons for change in GNP*:

(1)   The quantity of goods and services increases (real increases in GNP).

(2)   The price of goods and services increases (nominal increases in GNP).

To separate the impact of increases in GNP from these real and nominal phenomena, we use a measure of changes in the value of the dollar and deflate the GNP figures by the price index. To deflate GNP, the ratio of the price index of the base year to the price index of the year in question is computed, and then the GNP (in money) is multiplied by that ratio.

EXAMPLE: If prices in 1982 were 100 and prices in 1989 were 120, multiply the 1989 GNP by 100/120 to get the real output of 1989 in terms of 1982 dollars.

b. *Basic price indices used in United States*:

(1)   *Consumer price index (CPI)*: The consumer price index compares the costs of a given market basket (a sampling) of goods and services at different points in time. The CPI is based on the food, housing, recreation, clothing, and other expenditures made by a typical suburban family. The cost of buying these items is calculated on a monthly basis, and the index is figured from these calculations. The CPI is the most common price index.

(2)   *Producers price index (PPI)*: The producers price index is the calculation of the cost of goods at the producer level versus the retail level used for the CPI. The PPI is often used as an indicator for increases in the CPI for the future.

(3) *GNP implicit price deflator index*: The GNP implicit price deflator index is computed only once a year using the prices of all goods and services produced in the United States. This index gives the most accurate measure of increases in prices and is the most comprehensive index used. This index excludes prices of imports, whereas the consumer price index (CPI) and producers price index (PPI) do not.

C. Signposts for Economic Conditions

Gross national product and other measures of the state of the economy fluctuate from month to month and from year to year. While GNP gives a measure of the output of society, other measures help analyze how the economy is operating with respect to its efficiency and ability to meet consumer needs. These other measures include unemployment and inflation.

1. *Unemployment*: Unemployment is the result of an economic system operating below its maximum level of activity. To be unemployed, one must be a member of the labor force, that is, a person who is willing and able to work in a productive activity. This excludes people who are old and infirm, children under legal working age, students, and people who work without pay, such as volunteer workers, and who are not considered part of the labor force. Unemployment can be classified into four types:

   a. *Cyclical unemployment*: Cyclical unemployment exists when people who are willing and able to work at prevailing wage rates do not have jobs and whose employment is not explained by one of the other types explained below.

   b. *Frictional unemployment*: Frictional unemployment results when people are caught between jobs or are looking for their first job. This type of unemployment is a healthy sign for society since it indicates that people are moving up. Changing jobs typically means increasing one's status within a profession. A frictional unemployment rate of about 1 percent is considered normal for society.

   c. *Technological unemployment*: Technological unemployment is typical of an industrialized society—when people are displaced temporarily as a result of technological advance. Technological unemployment ranges from 2 to 3 percent in the United States.

   d. *Structural unemployment*: Structural unemployment (often referred to as "hard-core" unemployment) is the result of changes in consumer tastes and preferences and changes in types of labor needed. This type of unemployment is the most difficult since it usually means that retraining of workers is necessary. Governmental policy to affect the level of economic activity will not often change structural unemployment. Historically, programs to retrain workers have been a basic corrective measure for structural unemployment.

   Given these four types of unemployment, economists have often assumed that a 5 percent unemployment rate is a "full employment level" of activity. The 5 percent would include an acceptable level of frictional, technological, and structural unemployment. Since the late 1960s the unemployment rate in the United States has typically averaged above the 5 percent level. This is the result of a variety of circumstances. Foremost is the increase in the number of women in the workforce. As the number of families with two working members increases, the rate of frictional, technological, and structural unemployment may increase somewhat. Many economists are arguing that a 6 or 7 percent unemployment rate is considered a full employment rate today.

2. *Inflation*: Inflation is the increase in prices of goods and services. Historically, inflation has been the greatest problem when a society is producing at, or near, full employment. Inflation can be discouraged by reducing the demand for goods and services or by increasing the amount of goods and services supplied by the business sector.

    a. *Effects of inflation on the economy*: Inflation has adverse effects on different sectors of the economy. It is believed that debtors benefit from inflation. As inflation takes place, the purchasing power of a dollar declines. Debtors would be paying off loans made now with dollars that will have lower purchasing power in the future. People on fixed incomes are often hurt by inflation. An individual with a fixed income has no way to protect against inflation. Similarly, creditors are hurt by inflation since they are being repaid in less valuable dollars.

    b. *Types of inflation*: The two types of inflation are demand-pull inflation and cost-push inflation.

        (1) *Demand-pull inflation*: The classical version of inflation is demand-pull inflation, caused by excessive aggregate demand. It is often expressed as "too much money chasing too few goods."

        (2) *Cost-push (or seller's) inflation*: Cost-push inflation is caused by increases in the cost of factors of production, resulting in reductions of aggregate supply and, therefore, increases in prices. One common cause of cost-push inflation is the increase in wages in excess of labor productivity.

        EXAMPLE: In the 1970s substantial cost-push inflation was the result of the Arab oil embargo's impact on the cost of energy to producers in the United States and its eventual effect on the price of gasoline to the consumer.

    The impact of both types of inflation on society is the same. The cures for the inflation, however, differ depending on the type of inflation. If the inflation is demand-pull, the proper cure is to decrease the demand for goods and services. This could be done by increased taxation, reduction in government spending, or other measures that would affect the demand for goods and services. If the inflation type is cost-push, the solutions have to come as a result of increasing the productive capacity of the economy.

D. Determinants of National Income

The level of national income for the economy is determined by demand for goods and services within the economic system. This aggregate demand for goods and services is dependent on the levels of consumption by households, investment by businesses, spending by government, and the level of net exports. Each of these factors has an impact on national income through aggregate demand.

For an economy to be in equilibrium, the level of aggregate demand must be equal to the level of aggregate supply. Aggregate supply is the quantity of goods and services that a society can make available within a specific period of time. Aggregate supply is determined by the productivity of labor, the amount and quality of land available, technology, and the stock of capital that a country has available for use.

1. *Aggregate Demand*: In a market-oriented economic system, the activities within a society are carried out through the interaction of households and business, with some activities by government. This interaction of households and business generates demand for goods and services that results in expenditures for resources and consumption of goods and services. Changes in the level of these aggregate expenditures by households, business, government, and foreign countries have an impact on the total demand for goods and services for society and on the expenditures for goods and services made by each unit.

   a. *Consumption*: Consumption is the expenditure incurred by households on final goods and services that yield direct satisfaction to consumers. Household consumption is the most stable of the various components of aggregate expenditures. The level of household expenditures (or consumption expenditures) is determined by several factors that influence individual decision making.

      (1) *Stock of goods owned*: The existing stock of goods owned by consumers affects future consumption. The larger the stock of goods, *ceteris paribus* (all other things remaining equal), the smaller is the amount of consumption that will take place in the near future.

      (2) *Rate of interest*: The rate of interest may have an impact on the rate of consumption. If the interest rate is high, people who are saving for a desired goal in the future will have to save fewer dollars to reach that goal. With high interest rates, the rate of return on investments will be greater, and people can reach their goals by saving less money. With this reduction in the rate of savings, there is an increase in the amount of money available for consumption. It is also true that with a higher interest rate, saving becomes more attractive. Therefore, an increase in the incentive to save exists. It is unclear which of these influences is stronger. Thus, it is difficult to predict the impact that the interest rate has upon consumption. In our society it appears that consumption increases as interest rates remain high.

      (3) *Level of taxes*: Individuals can dispose of their income in basically three ways:

         (a) Consume goods and services

         (b) Save (postponed consumption)

         (c) Pay taxes

         As the level of taxes individuals are required to pay increases, the money available for saving and consumption decreases. There is an inverse relationship between tax rates and consumption. The rate of taxation is a variable that can be controlled by the government, and changing the level of taxation to affect the level of consumption is one type of fiscal policy.

(4) *Level of personal income*: The major determinant of consumption expenditures is the level of personal income. As personal income increases, individuals will increase their purchases of goods and services, and increases in the level of consumption expenditures will occur. Most individuals, however, will not increase their level of consumption by the total amount of their increase in income.

EXAMPLE: If an individual's income increases by $1,000 per year, this will not necessarily lead to a $1,000 increase in consumption expenditures. Part of the $1,000 increase will be saved for future consumption.

The ratio of increases in consumption expenditures to increases in disposable income is referred to as the marginal propensity to consume (MPC). The marginal propensity to consume is the change in consumption resulting from a given change in disposable income.

EXAMPLE: If an individual's personal income (PI) increases by $1,000 and, as a result, taxes (T) increase by $300, the disposable personal income (DPI) would be $700. If an individual increases consumption expenditures by $560, the marginal propensity to consume (MPC) would be 0.8 ($560 divided by $700). The marginal propensity to save, the change in savings from a given change in disposable income, is equal to 1 minus the marginal propensity to consume (1 - MPC); in this example the marginal propensity to save is 0.2.

A corresponding relationship to the marginal propensity to consume is the level of consumption divided by the level of income. This is distinguished from marginal propensity, which refers to changes in consumption as a result of changes of income. This relationship is referred to as the average propensity to consume (APC).

b. *Investment*: Another variable that affects the level of income in society is the level of investment by business firms. Investment is defined as expenditures for capital goods. Net investment does not include replacement of existing capital stock or depreciation, but includes only those expenditures that are intended to lead to new productive capacity (for example, investments in new equipment, new buildings, new production capacity). While investment affects the level of national income, there are several variables that determine the level of investment at a given point in time. Investment is the *most volatile* GNP component.

(1) *Interest rate*: The interest rate is the price firms must pay for the privilege of using someone else's money. It is important to remember that the interest rate affects business decisions to invest even when the business is financing the investment project from undistributed corporate profits or some other form of internal financing. The interest rate, then, represents the income given up by not taking the undistributed corporate profits and investing them elsewhere at a given rate of return. When a firm is making an investment decision, the interest rate is important, either in

terms of the actual cost of borrowing money or of the opportunity cost of using its money for the investment versus some other type of project. In general, the lower the interest rate the larger the amount of investment that business firms are willing to undertake. For business to invest, the interest rate must be less than the expected return on the investment project. Thus, as the interest rate lowers, more projects become profitable.

(2) *Expectations*: A second factor that has a major influence on the level of investment is expectations. As business firms expect the future outlook of the economic situation to be positive, they will increase their investments to be able to meet the expected increase in demand. Things that change the expectations of business include changes in population growth or changes in the behavior of consumers or government, leading to a change in demand for specific products.

(3) *Corporate taxation*: The level of corporate taxation also has a major impact on investment decisions. Corporate taxation takes many forms, including corporate income tax and various types of investment taxes and/or tax credits. These taxes provide an incentive or deterrent for businesses to undertake investment projects. If the corporate income tax is high, there is less income after taxes for paying dividends. During the 1980s the U.S. government passed a series of investment tax credit laws which allows for increased depreciation of capital equipment. This, in essence, reduced the level of taxation for corporations. It was intended that through investment tax credits, the demand for investment by firms would be stimulated.

c.   *Government expenditures*: The level of government expenditures within an economic system is, to some extent, determined by budgets developed by the president and approved by Congress. Government expenditures include those expenditures incurred by federal, state, and local governments.

EXAMPLES OF GOVERNMENT EXPENDITURES:

National defense expenditures

Cost of administration of the government

Education, training for employment, and social services

Health care for senior citizens and the poor

Agriculture support programs

It is important to note, however, that certain transfer payments do not count as government expenditures because they do not represent current production. These transfer payments simply transfer expenditures from one time period to another.

EXAMPLES OF TRANSFER PAYMENTS (payment not for GNP):

Interest on the national debt

Social security benefits

Pensions

Historically, the level of government expenditures in the United States has increased both absolutely and relatively in regard to consumption and investment. There has been a trend in recent years to reduce that rate of growth. An additional factor considered very important is that government expenditures are, to some extent, tied to taxation. However, these expenditures are not limited to the level of taxation imposed on the people. In any given year the level of government expenditures may be greater than or less than the level of taxes. Depending on the particular situation, the government may have either a surplus or a deficit at the end of the year. The level of government expenditures includes federal, state, and local expenditures.

EXAMPLE: In the 1980s the level of state government expenditures increased at a more rapid rate than the level of federal government expenditures, primarily because of increases in the cost of providing public education and a reduction in federal government support for such programs.

    d. *Net exports*: The portion of national income designated as net exports is the difference between the value of goods and services produced in the United States and exported overseas and the value of goods and services produced overseas and imported into the United States. The level of net foreign trade, relatively small in the past, has had little impact on the level of national income until the early 1980s. Since then, negative net exports have been increasing. (Additional information on the determinants is presented in Chapter 5.)

  2. *Aggregate Supply*: Just as consumption, investment, government expenditures, and net export affect the total demand for goods and services, other factors affect the supply of goods and services made available within the society. These factors include productivity of labor, level of taxation, technology, and natural resources available to a country.

    a. *Productivity of labor*: Productivity is defined as the output per worker during a given period of time. As the output per worker increases, the quantity of goods and services made available also increases, depending on the supply of labor resources. Productivity is influenced dramatically by the worker's level of education in society. A large portion of the growth in aggregate supply of goods and services within the United States has been attributed to increased productivity of labor.

    b. *Level of taxation*: The level of taxation has an impact on aggregate supply from a dual standpoint. Taxes impact the incentive of individuals to work as well as on businesses to invest in capital goods that increase productive capacities in the future.

      (1) *Impact on individual incentives*: As the marginal tax rate on income increases, the net take-home pay for working additional hours declines. This influences the incentive of the individual to work and to engage in nonmarket transactions (transactions that are not taxable). For example, fixing a friend's car in exchange for help in painting the house is a nonmarket transaction. If individuals engage in nontaxable activities, those individuals are withholding a portion of their labor from the market, thereby not increasing the supply of goods and services counted in the GNP. Thus, aggregate supply does not expand at an acceptable rate.

    (2) *Impact on business incentives*: By the same token, corporate taxation has an impact on decisions to invest in capital goods which will increase future productive capacity. As tax rates on profits increase, the amount of money available for investment is reduced and capital stock will not grow as rapidly.

  c. *Level of technology*: As technology increases, firms will be able to produce more goods and services with a given set of resources, thus increasing society's output, or producing a given quantity of goods and services at a lower cost. Increasing the output and lowering production costs enables the aggregate supply of goods and services available to society to increase.

  d. *Availability of natural resources*: The quantity and quality of natural resources available for a country's use also have an impact on the aggregate supply of goods and services. Resources include land, labor, capital, and entrepreneurial ability.

    (1) *Land*: Countries with an ample stock of land, including natural resources and capital, will have a larger aggregate supply than will countries with fewer of the factors of production.

    (2) *Labor*: As the quality of labor increases, so does the productivity of labor and thus the aggregate supply.

    (3) *Capital*: In combination with other resources, availability of capital affects a country's aggregate supply of goods and services.

    (4) *Entrepreneurial ability*: A country must have appropriate incentives for entrepreneurs to take risks and ultimately to expand output and develop new goods and services. If these incentives exist, there will be a long-term impact on the productivity of the country and the aggregate supply of goods and services. If these incentives do not exist, the ability of a country to produce goods and services at a constant or increasing rate is greatly reduced.

E.   Fluctuations in National Income

An economy is not always operating at its full employment level. There are times when it is operating below its full employment level and where the economic activity is declining. These time periods are referred to as periods of recession. When a country is producing at full employment and growing, the time period is referred to as prosperity.

EXAMPLES: The worst economic recession or depression was the period from 1929 to 1938. This was the longest prolonged period of depression that the U.S. economy has known, resulting in unemployment rates as high as 25 to 30 percent in some groups and even higher among certain other groups of people. The period of the 1950s through the 1970s was a period of intermittent prosperity with slight recessions.

For a country to be operating at full employment, the amount paid to produce goods and services must be received back when those same goods and services are sold. Another way of saying this is: The value of consumption (C) plus savings (S) plus government taxes (T) must equal the value of consumption (C) plus investment (I) plus government spending (G):

$$C + S + T = C + I + G$$

There are both self-correcting and government policy measures that can minimize the fluctuations of economic activities. These self-correcting aspects are "built-in" stabilizers that occur in the economy. They include unemployment compensation, welfare payments, and other government payments that fluctuate inversely to the level of economic activity. Other government policies that can be instituted are those affecting consumption, investment, and the level of government spending to stimulate or retard the economy.

The overall purpose of government policies to affect fluctuations in national income is to create a stable economy, an economy with a low level of unemployment and inflation. If the national income is not at a sufficient level, unemployment will be relatively high. If the economy is at full employment and still trying to grow, we will experience high rates of inflation.

1. *Natural Forces to Moderate Fluctuations*: In our economy today "built-in" stabilizers help offset downturns in business activity and moderate recovery. These stabilizers moderate the fluctuations in business cycles and the level of inflation and unemployment which society experiences. Stabilizers that reverse an economic downturn are unemployment compensation or welfare benefits, among others, which require increased government expenditures during periods of decline in economic activity.

   EXAMPLES:

   As economic activity declines, the unemployment rate rises and unemployment insurance payments increase.

   As the economy declines, various welfare programs increase.

   As the economic conditions decline, some people will experience decreased work hours versus layoffs. As a result of moving into a lower marginal tax bracket, these people will not experience a decline in salaries equivalent to the decline in the value of the hours they are working.

   If the economy becomes very competitive during an economic downturn and firms try to counteract decreased sales or increased inventories by reducing prices, these changes will result in a relatively rapid change in the cycle.

   If labor is willing to accept lower wage rates, the impact of the downturn will be minimized and will result in a faster recovery.

2. *Policies to Moderate Economic Fluctuations*: Policies that alleviate pressure on inflation or moderate downturns in the business cycle can be classified as *fiscal* policy or *monetary* policy. These policies can be used to correct either inflation or unemployment.

   a. *Fiscal policy measures to counteract business cycles*: While some factors automatically operate within an economy to counteract business cycles, on occasion the government intervenes to stimulate activity or to reduce pressure on inflation. The impact of government occurs because of policies implemented to affect consumption, investment, or level of government spending.

      (1) *Effect on consumption*: The level of consumption is changed by a number of different variables. One variable is the level of taxation. As the level of taxation increases, the level of disposable personal income declines, and vice versa. During periods of economic recession, the intent

E. Fluctuations in National Income

of government policy is to stimulate the demand for goods and services, leading to increased employment and a recovery from the recession. By reducing tax rates, government can increase the level of individual consumption, thus having an impact on the long-term equilibrium level of the economy.

(2) *Effect on investment*: In much the same way, government can affect the level of investment.

   (a) *Tax incentives*: During periods of recession, government can provide incentives for business, through investment tax credits and reductions in the corporate income tax rate, to expand and continue appropriate levels of employment. Similarly, during a period of prosperity, the government may eliminate the tax credits and increase the rate of corporate income tax.

   (b) *Financing the government deficit*: In periods of prosperity, with high rates of interest and inflation, the government can finance the government deficit by competing with private firms for money available for investments. During periods of recession, however, the government may want a deficit so that the borrowed money would provide more money to the economy and thus stimulate economic recovery.

b. *Monetary policy*: While the level of government spending can have an impact on business cycles, so can the amount of money that is in our economic system. The amount of money is controlled by the Federal Reserve System and can be increased or decreased depending on the actions of that institution. The Federal Reserve System is independent of the federal government and can follow policies complementary or contradictory to the federal government administration.

(1) *Control of money supply during economic recession*: During periods of economic recession, one way to stimulate the economy is simply to make more money available to people. If people have more money, they will have a tendency to spend more and reverse the decline in business activity.

(2) *Control of money supply during periods of prosperity and inflation*: By taking money out of circulation during periods of prosperity and inflation, the pressure on inflation can be reduced.

(3) *Monetary controls*: Monetary authorities have a variety of controls that help to affect the money supply.

   (a) *Reserve ratio for banks*: This ratio represents the percentage of a bank's assets that must be held in reserve with the Federal Reserve System. If the reserve ratio is reduced, the money that banks can lend increases, thus increasing the money supply.

   (b) *Discount rate*: The cost to banks for borrowing from the Federal Reserve System is known as the *discount rate*. Higher discount rates discourage borrowing and limit the money supply.

   (c) *Open-market operations*: These controls refer to buying or selling domestic government securities by the Federal Reserve System. If the FED sells securities, they receive money in exchange for the securities. This reduces the money supply.

3. *Supply-Side Economics*: Supply-side economics involves those factors that influence the supply of goods and services available in society. If the United States is experiencing an economic recession, one possible remedy is to increase the demand for goods and services. When there is a period of high unemployment with high inflation, traditional demand management policy may not work. To reverse the recession, there must be increases in the supply of goods and services as well as increases in the demand. Supply-side economists use basically the same tools that demand management economists use; however, the outcome is somewhat different.

    a. *Marginal tax rates*: The supply-side economists argue that if a society has *high* marginal tax rates, the incentives for individuals to work are reduced. As incentives are reduced, the hours people are willing to work and the total quantity of resources available for society are also reduced. With the lowering of the marginal tax rates, incentives to work are increased, the output of the labor force is increased, and as a result of the increased number of working hours, the revenues collected through taxation may actually increase, too.

        EXAMPLE: This philosophy was used to sell the 1963 tax cuts under the Kennedy administration and did have the desired impact of increasing output and tax revenues at the same time.

    b. *Encouragement of investment and savings*: An additional component of supply-side economics is equivalent to that of the demand side. Under supply-side economics, the emphasis would be on encouraging investment and savings, resulting in increasing the capacity and productive potential of the economy. Measures used to encourage investment and saving include investment tax credits, corporate income tax reductions, tax credit incentives on individual savings accounts, and other stimuli for the investment sector.

F. Sources of Economic Information

For current economic information, a variety of reference material is available through public and business libraries. Here is a brief list of some of the major sources:

1. *Challenge*: A bimonthly periodical covering stories about our economy written for the lay person.

2. *Economic Indicators*: Prepared by Council of Economic Advisors, published by the Joint Economic Committee.

3. *Economic Report of the President*: Published annually by the U.S. Government Printing Office.

4. *Federal Reserve Bulletin*: Published monthly by the Board of Governors of the Federal Reserve System.

5. *Survey of Current Business*: Published monthly by the Bureau of Economic Analysis, U.S. Department of Commerce.

6. *Wall Street Journal*: A daily newspaper covering economic events and activities in the business world.

Review Questions

DIRECTIONS: Select the best answer from the four alternatives. Write the letter of your answer in the blank to the left of the number.

_____ 1. In contrast to nominal GNP, real GNP refers to

    a. nominal GNP minus exports.
    b. nominal GNP minus personal income taxes.
    c. nominal GNP corrected for price changes.
    d. nominal GNP corrected for depreciation.

_____ 2. The consumer price index is a tool designed to measure the extent to which

    a. the cost of a typical bundle ("market basket") of consumer goods has changed over time.
    b. consumers have increased their spending over time.
    c. GNP is allocated to consumers, not business or government, over time.
    d. prices paid by employers to resource owners have changed over time.

_____ 3. Which of the following is _not_ included in the calculation of net national product?

    a. Depreciation
    b. Net exports
    c. Government purchases
    d. Net investment

_____ 4. Disposable income is equal to

    a. national income − personal income − federal taxes.
    b. personal income − personal taxes.
    c. net national product per capita − personal taxes.
    d. national income − social security − taxes + dividends.

_____ 5. The real output of goods and services and the real income of resource suppliers

    a. must increase at the same rate for prices to be stable.
    b. will be constant during periods of price stability.
    c. will never increase at the same rate.
    d. are generally determined by the rate of inflation.

_____ **6.** Structural unemployment is a result of

       a. an inadequate matching of qualified workers and available jobs.
       b. inaccurate and costly information about job opportunities.
       c. insufficient employment in the building trades.
       d. not enough employees.

_____ **7.** Inflation

       a. occurs whenever any price in the economy rises.
       b. has been more severe in the United States than for other Western nations.
       c. is measured by changes in the cost of a typical "market basket" of goods at different times.
       d. causes the purchasing power of a dollar to rise.

_____ **8.** The portion of disposable income a consumer does not spend on current consumption is called

       a. investment.
       b. saving.
       c. supply.
       d. temporary income.

_____ **9.** Aggregate demand is equal to

       a. consumption + saving − government spending.
       b. consumption + saving − taxes.
       c. consumption + saving + investment.
       d. consumption + investment + government spending.

_____ **10.** The marginal propensity to consume (MPC) is

       a. consumption expenditures divided by saving.
       b. consumption expenditures divided by disposable income.
       c. consumption expenditures divided by personal income.
       d. additional current consumption expenditures divided by additional current disposable income.

_____ **11.** Consumption is equal to

       a. disposable income − taxes.
       b. disposable income − saving.
       c. investment + saving.
       d. saving − disposable income.

12. Which of the following would be considered an investment by an economist?

   a. A corporation buying a car for its sales staff
   b. A new television set bought by a household
   c. A corporate bond purchased by a financial investor
   d. Purchase of a corporate stock

13. A planned deficit

   a. would stimulate aggregate demand more than the same level of expenditures
      with a balanced budget.
   b. is rejected by most Keynesians as acceptable fiscal policy.
   c. became widely accepted as a policy tool just before the Great Depression.
   d. means that tax revenues exceed the level of government spending.

14. Which of the following is not a built-in stabilizer?

   a. Unemployment compensation
   b. The investment multiplier
   c. Corporate profit tax
   d. Progressive income tax

15. According to the supply-side view

   a. aggregate demand is the major determinant of real output and aggregate em-
      ployment.
   b. tax rates are a major determinant of real output and aggregate employment.
   c. an increase in government expenditures and taxes will cause real income to
      rise.
   d. expansionary monetary policy will cause real output to expand without causing
      the rate of inflation to accelerate.

16. Which of the following would a supply-side fiscalist be most likely to propose as a
    policy for effectively promoting economic growth and halting inflation during the
    1990s?

   a. An increase in government expenditures coupled with a tax increase.
   b. An across-the-board reduction in tax rates coupled with a reduction in govern-
      ment expenditures.
   c. An increase in taxes to attain a budget surplus.
   d. A large budget deficit coupled with an acceleration in the growth of the money
      supply.

_____

17. The balanced-budget rule would require Congress to establish tax rates such that

a. the saving on the part of households and the investment of business decision makers were in balance.
b. the consumption expenditures and savings of households were in balance.
c. government expenditures and tax revenues were balanced annually.
d. the Federal Reserve expanded the money supply at a noninflationary rate.

_____

18. You have been asked to study the production of the economy over the past five years. Why would you use the real GNP series rather than the nominal series?

a. The real series is less complicated than the nominal series because the exports are not included.
b. The real series is more precise because it accounts for imports, whereas the nominal series does not.
c. The nominal series fails to account for transfer payments; the real series does not.
d. The nominal series reflects changes in both output and prices; the real series reflects changes in output.

_____

19. Suppose that U.S. policymakers decide that to stimulate the growth rate of the GNP, investment must be increased. What is needed, they conclude, is a reallocation of resources *away* from the production of consumer goods and *toward* the production of capital goods. Which of the following policy alternatives would be most likely to accomplish that objective?

a. A reduction in personal income taxes
b. A reduction in state sales taxes
c. A higher tax credit allowance for business investment in capital equipment
d. A restrictive monetary policy

_____

20. An economy is currently experiencing a high rate of unemployment as the result of deficient aggregate demand. Which of the following policy alternatives would be most likely to push the economy toward full employment?

a. A tax cut coupled with an equal reduction in government expenditures
b. An increase in government expenditures, coupled with an increase in taxes
c. A decrease in tax rates, leaving government expenditures unchanged
d. A level of taxes and government spending that keeps the budget in balance

Solutions

Answer	Refer to:

1. (c)   [B-2] Real GNP refers to nominal GNP corrected for price changes.

2. (a)   [B-2-b] The consumer price index consists of the costs of a given sampling of goods and services at different points in time.

3. (a)   [B-1-b] Net national product is gross national product minus depreciation. Although the other responses are all components of GNP, only depreciation is subtracted from GNP to obtain NNP.

4. (b)   [B-1-e] The definition of disposable income is personal income minus personal taxes.

5. (a)   [D-1 and D-2] For an economy to be in equilibrium, the level of aggregate demand must be equal to the level of aggregate supply.

6. (a)   [C-1-d] This is the definition of structural unemployment.

7. (c)   [C-2] Inflation is the increase in prices of goods and services during a given period of time.

8. (b)   [D-1-a] Disposable income minus consumption is the definition of saving.

9. (d)   [D-1] The definition of aggregate demand is consumption plus investment plus government spending.

10. (d)   [D-1-a] The definition of marginal propensity to consume is change in consumption divided by the change in disposable income.

11. (b)   [D-1-a] Consumption is defined as disposable income minus saving.

12. (a)   [D-1-b] Investment is defined as an expenditure for capital goods. An economist would view the purchase of corporate cars for business use as an investment.

13. (a)   [E-2-a] The government can affect the level of investment through planned deficits.

14. (b)   [E-1] The investment multiplier is not an automatic stabilizer since it helps perpetuate economic cycles.

15. (d)   [E-3] Under supply-side economics, investment and savings are encouraged, resulting in increased capacity and productive potential of the economy.

16. (b)   [E-3] Lowering of marginal tax rates will provide more opportunity for incentives to work to increase, and thus the output of the labor force is increased as well as revenues from taxation.

17. (c)   [E-2] This is the correct definition of a balanced budget.

18. (d)   [B-2-a] Real increases or decreases in GNP reflect changes in the quantity of goods and services produced.

19. (c)   [E-2-a] Government can provide incentives for business, through investment tax credits, to produce more capital goods.

20. (c)   [E-2] Reductions in the corporate income tax rate are incentives to business to expand and continue appropriate levels of employment.

CHAPTER 3

Money and Banking

OVERVIEW

Money and its availability are prime determinants of the level of economic activity within our country. Money serves as a standard of value, a medium of exchange, a store of value, and a standard of deferred payment.

Financial markets in the United States are complex and represent very fluid markets. The financial markets, always extremely competitive, have become even more so as a result of changes in banking laws over the past several years.

The basis for the financial system is the Federal Reserve System, the country's central bank. The Federal Reserve System (the "FED") controls the supply of money and develops regulations under which banks and other financial institutions (savings and loan associations, credit unions, and thrift institutions) must operate. The Federal Reserve System is independent of the U.S. government and acts independently of the executive and legislative branches of the government.

Modern fractional reserve banking stems from the experiences of early goldsmiths who found that 100 percent reserves were not needed to carry on daily business and to hold money for individuals. With the reserve requirement of less than 100 percent, financial institutions can expand the money supply at a multiple of the reserve requirement. The FED has control over this reserve requirement and thus the financial institution's ability to create money.

KEY TERMS

Currency
Discount rate
Excess reserves
Federal Deposit Insurance Corporation (FDIC)
Federal Housing Administration (FHA)
Federal Reserve note

Federal Reserve System (FED)
Gresham's law
Margin requirements
Monetary policy
Money
Moral suasion
NOW account

57

Open-market operations   Small Business Administration (SBA)
Primary deposit   Supply of money
Required reserves   Transaction account
Reserve ratio   Usury laws
Secondary deposit

A. The Nature and Value of Money

Money and its availability are prime determinants of the level of economic activity within our country. Money serves as a standard of value, a medium of exchange, a store of value, and a standard of deferred payment. For money to serve its functions adequately, the *commodity value* of money (the value of the materials from which money is made) must be less than the exchange value of money. This is certainly the case with paper money and coins that are in existence in the United States today. If, on occasion, the value of coins in exchange is less than the value of the commodities that make up the coins, the coins are withdrawn from the market and replaced with ones of less commodity value.

1. *Money*: Money refers to the coins, currency, and checking account balances that people have available for use. This definition stems from the use of money as a medium of exchange. In the United States, coins, currency, and instruments drawn upon transaction accounts are commonly accepted as "money."

2. *Components of the Money Supply*:

    a. *Coins and currency*: Currency represents about 27 percent of the money supply.

    b. *Transaction deposits*: Transaction deposits (about 73 percent of the money supply) include deposits in checking accounts at commercial banks, deposits in NOW accounts in savings and loan associations and savings banks, and deposits in share draft accounts in credit unions.

    c. *"Near monies"*: "Near monies" include credit cards, balances in savings accounts, and other instruments that can be converted easily into money. However, in their present form they do not serve as money since near monies are not acceptable as payment for most transactions.

       In addition, short-term government securities are often classified as near monies because they have to be converted into money before they can be used in exchange. These securities are highly liquid and can be converted to money in a relatively short period of time.

       EXAMPLE: Groceries cannot be bought with a U.S. government bond or with a savings account, but both of these instruments are easily convertible into money; thus, they are classified as near monies.

    d. *Credit cards*: A credit card is, in essence, a line of credit issued by a credit card company to an individual. When a credit card is used to purchase goods or services, a debt is incurred or a loan made. The credit card itself is not money but is access to credit.

3. *Functions of Money*: Money performs four important functions in any economic system:

a. *Standard of value*: Money serves as a common denominator in expressing the value of other goods or services. If money did not exist, we would have to express the value of items in terms of other commodities.

EXAMPLE: The value of wheat, clothes, or household goods is expressed in terms of money rather than relative to other goods and services. The value of a coat might be four pairs of shoes, or the value of a steak could be one-half of a shoe if the standard of value were shoes.

By using money as the standard of value, we eliminate the problem of comparing one commodity to another by expressing the value of goods in a manner easily understood by all.

b. *Medium of exchange*: Money is accepted in all transactions of goods bought and sold and for the discharging of debts. When a unit of money is no longer accepted as a medium of exchange, it no longer performs its primary function and is usually replaced by another medium of exchange.

c. *Store of value*: Money provides a mechanism by which a given dollar amount may be reserved for the future.

EXAMPLE: If you put $100 into a savings account today, ten years from now you will still have $100 plus interest. However, if the price level changes, the purchasing power of that $100 in the future would be less than the purchasing power today. This does not mean that you do not have $100; it simply means that the purchasing power of that $100 has changed.

d. *Standard of deferred payment*: Money also allows agreements to be made for future payments. Thus, it becomes a standard of deferred payment. Without money, deferred payment would have to be made in terms of commodities rather than money. Again, money increases the efficiency with which exchange takes place and allows for agreements between individuals in regard to both current and future transactions.

4. *The Value of Money*: The value of money is determined by the quantity of goods and services that a given amount of money will purchase. To say that the value of money has declined means that the purchasing power of money has declined. The dollar is still worth a dollar, but the amount of goods and services that the dollar will purchase has decreased.

a. *Changes in the value of money*: The value of money has changed in the United States as well as in most of the world. Since World War II, the purchasing power of a dollar in the United States has continually declined due to inflation. There are three explanations for the fluctuation in the value of money:

(1) *The commodity theory of money*: The value of money depends on the value and quantity of materials (examples: gold, silver) contained in the unit of money. The commodity theory of money has lost prominence in the United States especially since the use of fiat money (paper money and demand deposits are not backed by any commodity at the present time).

(2) *The quantity theory*: A second explanation for changes in the value of money, the quantity theory, emphasizes the principle that the larger the

quantity of money the less valuable each unit will be. This theory hypothesizes that the stock of money is equal to some constant times the price level. If the stock of money increases, prices will go up automatically. The quantity theory, however, better explains periods of full employment. If the economy is operating at less than full employment, the relationship between quantity of money and the price level is not as consistent.

(3) *The income theory*: Another theory attempting to explain the fluctuation in the value of money is referred to as the income theory. The income theory emphasizes that the value of money depends on the growth of money income and real income or the value of total spending in the economy. This theory reasons that an increase in the quantity of money will not necessarily cause an increase in prices, production, and employment but will cause an increase in production and employment if the increase in the money stimulates total spending. The increase in total spending will have an impact on prices, production, and employment.

b. *Decline in purchasing power of a dollar*: Decline in purchasing power tends to benefit debtors since the purchasing power of money used for paying debts is less than the purchasing power of money that was borrowed. Similarly, when prices rise, industrial profits tend to be high, which stimulates output and employment.

EXAMPLES:

In times of rising prices, creditors are hurt because they are being paid back in dollars with less purchasing power than that of the dollars which were loaned.

Individuals on fixed incomes are hurt because they must pay higher prices for goods and services but their income does not change.

The average worker has usually not been hurt by rising prices (inflation) because wages usually increase at a rate equal to or higher than the rate of price increases. The real purchasing power of the worker's salary has increased over time.

B. The Supply of Money

The supply of money consists of coins, currency, and transaction accounts in financial institutions owned by the nonbanking public. One important aspect of money is that the commodity value of money must be less than the exchange value of money. If the commodity value becomes greater than the exchange value, people will keep their money for its real value and not for its exchange value. Referred to as Gresham's law, this may be stated another way: "Bad money drives good money out of circulation."

EXAMPLE OF GRESHAM'S LAW: In the late 1960s, the value of silver in a quarter became greater than the exchange value of a quarter. People began keeping the quarter for its silver value, so the U.S. government began to replace the old quarter with a "sandwich" quarter which included more copper, a metal of less value than the silver in the old quarter.

1. *Forms of Money*:

   a. *Currency*: Currency consists of coins and paper money issued by the federal government. Today, paper money is in the form of federal reserve notes because the money is issued through the Federal Reserve System. Paper currency has been backed by 40 percent gold and later by 25 percent gold. However, today, federal reserve notes are not backed by any commodity. Historically, there have been other kinds of paper money used in the United States besides federal reserve notes. These were called treasury currency and included treasury notes of the 1890s, U.S. notes referred to as "greenbacks," and silver certificates and gold certificates. The silver and gold certificates could be redeemed at the U.S. Treasury for an amount of gold or silver equal to the value of the paper money. Since 1968, no silver or gold certificates have been issued by the U.S. government. Today, all paper money can be redeemed at the U.S. Treasury or the Federal Reserve banks for an equivalent amount of currency or other federal reserve notes.

   b. *Transaction accounts in financial institutions*: Prior to the Bank Regulation Act of 1980, commercial banks had a virtual monopoly on transaction accounts (checking accounts). With a checking account, an individual would have a bank balance against which checks could be written. With the Bank Regulation Act of 1980, savings and loan associations, savings banks, and credit unions could establish similar accounts. These are referred to as NOW accounts in savings and loan associations and savings banks and share-draft accounts in credit unions. These accounts originate in these two ways:

   (1) *Primary deposits*: The initial deposit into an account is called the primary deposit.

   (2) *Secondary deposits*: Accounts can also be established with secondary deposits, created by a financial institution granting a loan and depositing the balance into an individual's account.

   Financial institutions do not have to keep all of their depositors' assets in the form of cash. The probability that all depositors would want to convert their accounts into cash at a given point in time is very small. The financial institution only needs to keep cash on hand equivalent to that portion of the deposits that is expected to be withdrawn at a given point in time. Reserve ratios are established by the Federal Reserve System. While ratios provide protection for depositors, their primary purpose is to give the Federal Reserve System the ability to regulate the money supply.

2. *Types of Financial Institutions*:

   a. *Federal Reserve System*: The Federal Reserve System (FED) was organized in 1913 with the passage of the Federal Reserve Act. This act divided the United States into 12 districts, with each district having its own Federal Reserve bank. The act gave the FED the power to control the activities of commercial banks. With the Bank Regulation Act of 1980, the controlling authority of the Federal Reserve System expanded to other financial institutions. The FED is a nonprofit organization, independent of the federal government. The FED's main purpose is to control and service financial institutions.

Federal Reserve activities are coordinated by a seven-member Board of Governors chosen by the President of the United States. Their 14-year terms are staggered so that no president has substantial impact on the board, thus keeping the operation of the system independent of the executive and judicial branches of the federal government.

b.   *Other financial institutions*: Commercial banks, savings and loans associations, credit unions, thrift institutions, and insurance companies provide financial services to citizens in society. Each of these types of institutions has a unique function, with their activity limited to that function by law. With the Bank Regulation Act of 1980, the activities in which each of these institutions can engage became similar. Each type of institution is governed by a specific set of regulations enforced by this country's central bank, the Federal Reserve System.

EXAMPLES OF BANKING SERVICES:

Transaction accounts[1]

Personal loans

Savings accounts

Consumer loans

Credit cards in the name of the institution

Financial planning services

Estate planning services

Commercial loans

(1)   *Commercial banks*: Historically, commercial banks have been the major financial institutions within society: making loans, accepting both transaction account balances and time deposit accounts, and providing the full services of a financial institution. Before the Bank Regulation Act of 1980, commercial banks were the only financial institutions that had transaction accounts and were the only institutions able to expand the money supply through fractional reserves. Deposits up to $100,000 in banks are insured by the Federal Deposit Insurance Corporation (FDIC).

(2)   *Savings and loan associations*: These institutions were originally established to make home loans. Loans could be made to the limit of the company's assets. People deposited savings that the association would, in turn, be used to make home and home construction loans. Since the Bank Regulation Act of 1980, savings and loan associations have been permitted to issue checking privileges against savings accounts and offer other services previously available only through commercial banks.

Since deregulation, many savings and loan companies have experienced financial difficulties. In many cases the difficulties resulted from expan-

---

[1]A financial institution's issuance of transaction accounts has a very direct impact on the economy.

sion into areas of business in which the company had little experience. Even with failure of some savings and loan associations, deposits were protected by the Federal Savings and Loan Insurance Corporation (FSLIC), which has recently been merged with the FDIC. This organization guarantees deposits up to $100,000 per depositor if the company has financial difficulties.

(3)   *Credit unions*: Credit unions are organizations that receive money deposited into savings accounts and make loans. In the past, credit unions have made consumer loans at an interest rate equivalent to or slightly lower than bank interest rates and have paid dividends on savings accounts slightly higher than banks. Credit unions are owned by their depositors (members). Since the Bank Regulation Act of 1980, credit unions have expanded their sphere of operation to include issuance of drafts against savings accounts deposited with the credit union.

(4)   *Insurance companies*: Insurance companies are a unique form of financial institution. Historically, they have provided substantial amounts of money for large investment. The premiums collected on policies are loaned out for investment purposes; thus the insurance company can earn a rate of return on the money until it is paid out on life insurance policies. In addition, with standard life insurance, there is usually a clause that allows individuals to borrow against the cash value of the insurance policy. The Bank Regulation Act of 1980 did not have a substantial impact on insurance companies.

3.   *Creation of Money*: A bank, like any business, attempts to make a profit by providing a service for which it receives payment. Banks have certain assets, and these assets must equal liabilities plus net worth. The assets of a bank are the value of anything the bank owns. The liabilities are the bank's debts to others, and the net worth is the difference between the bank's assets and the liabilities. For most banks, the majority of its liabilities are its transaction account deposits, which are payable upon demand. Since the proportion of these liabilities that will be paid out at any point in time is predictable, only a fraction of the liabilities must be kept on hand at any point in time. This allows the bank to create money.

EXAMPLE: If a bank has $1,000,000 in liabilities in the form of transaction accounts and does not expect more than 20 percent of those balances to be demanded at any point in time, the bank has $800,000 that it can use for other purposes. The bank may use this $800,000 to make loans to its customers and thus put the deposits of other customers to work. When the bank makes loans in this manner, it is creating money.

Banks are required by law to keep a portion of their assets on reserve with the Federal Reserve Bank. This reserve and the cash kept in the bank's vault are termed the bank's *required reserves*. Monies available in excess of required reserves are *excess reserves*. The availability of excess reserves is what allows the bank to create money.

EXAMPLE: Assume that the legal reserves against transaction deposits is 20 percent: that is, for every dollar in a transaction account, a bank must have 20 cents in reserves either with the Federal Reserve System or in vault cash. If Bank A has

$10,000,000 deposited in transaction accounts, it would be required to have $2,000,000 in reserves.

(The actual reserve requirement for banks, historically, has ranged from 15 to 20 percent.)

EXAMPLE: Figure 3–1 demonstrates the ability of banks to create money. Assume that a bank must have 20 percent reserves on its demand deposits. These five transactions increased the money supply to $29,520. Of that amount, $19,520 was the result of the initial increase of $10,000. If this example were expanded to include additional loans based on excess reserves, the final level of money supply would be $50,000. Of this, $10,000 would be due to the initial transaction, and $40,000 would result from the loans the bank made as a result of having excess reserves.

As the example above illustrates, the banking system can expand the money supply by a multiple of its excess reserves. This multiple is equal to 1 divided by the reserve ratio. In the foregoing example, the multiple was 1 divided by 0.2, or 5. Thus, an initial $8,000 in excess reserves could result in a $40,000 increase in the money supply after banks had made loans based on excess reserves. As the reserve ratio of banks increases, the ability of banks to expand money through loaning excess reserves declines, and vice versa, as the reserve ratio declines, the ability of the banking system to create money expands.

4. *The Banking System and Monetary Policy*: The actions of the Federal Reserve System determine the monetary policy of the country. Monetary policy is activity that would have an impact on the availability of money in society. Monetary pol-

Figure 3–1   Ability of Banks to Create Money

Transaction	Banking System T-Account			
	Assets		Liabilities	
1. Bank A receives a new deposit for $10,000 in the form of a check issued by the Federal Reserve Board for bonds purchased. This is a $10,000 increase in the money supply.	1. Cash	$10,000	1. DD	$10,000
2. Bank A sends required reserves (RR) to Fed; the remainder of the cash assets are excess reserves (ER).	2. RR ER	2,000 8,000	2. DD	10,000
3. Bank A loans its excess reserves. (The result is: DD, 18,000; RR, 3,600; and ER, 6,400.) Money Supply (MS) is now increased by $8,000.	3. RR ER Loans	3,600 6,400 8,000	3. DD	18,000
4. Bank A now loans its current ER (6,400), increasing DD to 24,400 and changing RR to 4,880. MS is increased by $6,400.	4. RR ER Loans	4,880 5,120 14,400	4. DD	24,400
5. Bank A now loans its ER of 5,120. This increases DD to 29,520; RR becomes 5,904; ER equals 4,096; and total loans equal 19,520. MS has again increased by the amount of ER of the bank.	5. RR ER Loans	5,904 4,096 19,520	5. DD	29,520

DD, demand deposit; RR, required reserves; ER, excess reserves; MS, money supply.

icy could have an impact on economic fluctuations since increases in the money supply tend to stimulate the economy, and declines in the money supply tend to retard the economy. During periods of inflation, the appropriate monetary policy would be to restrict the growth of the money supply, whereas in times of high unemployment the appropriate monetary policy would be to expand the money supply. The Federal Reserve System has a variety of weapons that can be used to assist in stabilizing the economy: open-market operations, discount rate, changes in the reserve requirement, moral suasion, selective controls over margin requirements for loans made to purchase stocks and bonds, selective controls over installment contracts and other forms of consumer credit, and selective controls over the terms of home mortgage contracts.

a. *Open-market operations*: The most important set of policies used by the FED to control the money supply is open-market operations. These involve the buying and selling of government securities by the open-market committee of the Federal Reserve Board. Open-market operations occur daily in New York City with the objective of tightening or loosening member banks' reserve positions. In periods of inflation, the committee sells securities, and in periods of recession it buys securities.

EXAMPLE: If the FED sells $1,000 worth of bonds to the public and the public pays for the bonds in cash, the FED has exchanged $1,000 worth of government securities for $1,000 worth of cash and the money supply has been reduced by $1,000. (Cash held by the FED is not part of the money supply.) If the payment for the securities issued by the FED is in the form of a check (assuming a reserve requirement of 0.2), a 5:1 reduction in the money supply of member banks will take place as the excess reserve positions of the banks are altered. Thus, in the case of selling $1,000 worth of bonds, the total money supply could be reduced by $5,000 (the initial $1,000 plus $4,000 as a result of changes in excess reserves).

b. *Discount rate*: The rate that the Federal Reserve Bank charges if member banks wish to borrow from the FED is known as the discount rate. To increase reserves, a bank can discount its assets (loans, securities, etc.) to the FED. The Federal Reserve Bank will pay the borrowing bank a fraction of the face value of the assets. This discount, usually in the range of 6 to 10 percent, would affect the willingness of banks to borrow money from the FED. If the discount rate is extremely high, banks will not want to borrow money and will maintain a reserve position that will guarantee they won't have to borrow. This, in turn, has the impact of reducing the banking system's willingness to create money. Similarly, if the discount rate is extremely low, banks will be encouraged to discount some of their assets and thus to expand the money supply.

c. *Changing the reserve requirement*: A powerful tool that the Federal Reserve System has available is the changing of the reserve requirement. Although this tool is used infrequently, its impact is both dramatic and immediate. Changes in the reserve requirement, in essence, change the banking system's ability to create money.

EXAMPLE: If the reserve requirement was 20 percent, the banking system would have the potential to expand the money supply by a 5:1 ratio. If the re-

serve requirement were 25 percent, however, the expansion could only be on a 4:1 ratio. Thus, by changing the reserve requirement from 20 percent to 25 percent, a dramatic 25 percent increase of reserves would be necessary to back the deposits of banks. To comply with this, the banks would have to reduce their loans or excess reserves would become required reserves. Each of these would have the effect of reducing the supply of money in the economy. Similarly, if the reserve requirement changed from 25 percent to 20 percent, the banks would have a 20 percent increase in excess reserves and thus could expand the money supply.

d. *Moral suasion ("jawboning")*: Historically, the Federal Reserve System has used moral suasion to promote certain socially beneficial policies. Moral suasion does not involve actual policy action but simply tries to encourage member banks to follow a policy that the FED prefers member banks to follow. Although use of a moral-suasion approach lacks the clout of open-market operations, the discount rate, and reserve requirements, it has occasionally provided some success over short periods of time.

e. *Margin requirements on loans for purchases of securities*: Margin requirements necessary on loans for securities (stocks and bonds) are controlled by the Federal Reserve System. Margin requirements refer to the percentage of the stock purchase price an individual must deposit with a broker or bank before the difference can be made up by a loan. Margin requirements have ranged from 25 to 100 percent since 1964. At the present time, margin requirements are in the 50 to 60 percent range. As margin requirements increase, the money supply is reduced since people need more cash to buy securities. A reduction in the margin requirements allows people to purchase more stocks and bonds with a limited amount of cash, which increases the money supply.

f. *Other selective controls*: The Federal Reserve System's remaining selective controls are designed to affect two specific markets: installment contract buying and home mortgage rates. The FED has imposed restrictions on these markets at different points in time, especially during war. At present, the FED places limited restrictions on installment contracts and home mortgages since they are controlled by state usury laws or other types of legislation.

The Federal Reserve System can implement a variety of controls to change the level of the money supply. These tools are used to help stabilize the economy and minimize the rate of inflation and unemployment.

C. The Involvement of Government in Availability of Credit

The federal government intervenes in the credit market by providing a series of regulations that affect individuals wanting credit. These regulations are administered through a variety of government agencies, including the Federal Housing Authority (FHA), the Federal Deposit Insurance Corporation (FDIC), and the Small Business Administration (SBA).

1. *Federal Housing Authority (FHA)*: The Federal Housing Authority (FHA) is a government agency that helps finance housing projects for low-income families and makes loans available to families at lower than market interest rates. On occasion, the FHA will simply guarantee the home loans as opposed to providing the

loan. The FHA obtains revenue by selling bonds to the public. The revenue from the bonds is used to finance housing projects. The bonds are retired by borrowers paying off their debt to the agency.

2. *Federal Deposit Insurance Corporation (FDIC)*: The FDIC was developed after bank failures in the early 1930s. The FDIC insures an individual's deposits, up to $100,000, against bank failure. An association similar to the FDIC, the Federal Savings and Loan Insurance Corporation (FSLIC), was formed to guarantee deposits in savings and loan associations to a maximum of $100,000. In the late 1980s and early 1990s, much attention was given to the cost of the savings and loan bailout. During that time many savings and loan associations failed. Since deposits were insured by the FSLIC, the government had to augment the FSLIC assets to meet obligations. Recently, the FSLIC was merged into the FDIC.

3. *Small Business Administration (SBA)*: The SBA provides small business services similar to the FHA. In essence, the SBA provides loans at a low market interest rate to small businesses to help maintain small business as a viable unit within society. The SBA, like the FHA, sells bonds to the public and uses the revenue from the bonds to operate the agency and make loans to businesses. These bonds are then retired by repayment of the loans.

Review Questions

DIRECTIONS: Select the best answer from the four alternatives. Write the letter of your answer in the blank to the left of the number.

_____ 1. Which of the following is not a function of money?

    a. Measure of output
    b. Medium of exchange
    c. Standard of value
    d. Store of value

_____ 2. The most frequently used monetary tool of the Federal Reserve System is

    a. changes in the discount rate.
    b. changes in reserve requirements.
    c. moral suasion.
    d. open-market operations.

_____ 3. The value (purchasing power) of each unit of money

    a. is largely independent of the money supply.
    b. tends to increase as the money supply expands.
    c. increases as the level of prices rises.
    d. tends to decline as the money supply expands relative to the availability of goods and services.

_____ 4. Which of the following is not a function of money?

    a. A store of value
    b. A medium of exchange
    c. It earns income for its holders
    d. A standard of value

_____ 5. The major income-earning asset of financial institutions is

    a. demand deposits.
    b. time deposits.
    c. reserve deposits with the Federal Reserve System.
    d. loans outstanding.

_____   **6.** Which of the following comprise the required reserves of financial institutions?

    a. Demand deposits and time deposits
    b. Vault cash and deposits of the bank with the Federal Reserve
    c. U.S. securities and stock equity
    d. Cash and U.S. securities

_____   **7.** Uncertainty in general business conditions will cause financial institutions to hold excess reserves. Other things constant, this will

    a. have no effect on the money supply.
    b. tend to reduce the money supply.
    c. tend to increase the money supply.
    d. tend to reduce the money supply during a period of inflation while increasing it under recessionary conditions.

_____   **8.** Excess reserves of financial institutions are

    a. actual reserves minus required reserves.
    b. federal reserves held by banks minus their liabilities.
    c. assets minus the liabilities of banks.
    d. actual reserves minus demand deposits.

_____   **9.** A reserve requirement of 20 percent

    a. implies a potential money deposit multiplier of 20.
    b. implies a potential money deposit multiplier of 5.
    c. implies a potential money deposit multiplier of 4.
    d. is mandatory at all times, according to Federal Reserve policy.

_____   **10.** The establishment of a stable monetary environment is

    a. the responsibility of the U.S. Treasury.
    b. the responsibility of the Federal Reserve System.
    c. the joint responsibility of the Treasury and the Federal Reserve System.
    d. the result of an automatic mechanism built into the independent decision making of our commercial banking system.

_____   **11.** Which of the following is not a function of the Federal Reserve System?

    a. Limiting the national debt
    b. Setting the reserve required for deposit holdings of member banks
    c. Buying and selling government bonds to control the size of the money supply
    d. Establishing a money supply consistent with the business stability of the entire economy

12. The major purpose of the Federal Reserve System is

    a. to keep the discount rate flexible.
    b. to be a lender of last resort.
    c. to regulate the money supply and thereby provide a monetary climate in the best interest of the economy.
    d. to regulate the levels of excess reserves held by member banks.

13. Monetary policy

    a. is determined by commercial banks.
    b. is determined by the U.S. Treasury.
    c. is the major concern of the Federal Reserve System.
    d. is a responsibility shared equally by the Treasury and the Federal Reserve System.

14. Open-market operations are

    a. the tool most often used by the Federal Reserve System to alter the money supply.
    b. the least effective tool the Federal Reserve System has to alter the money supply.
    c. the tool used by the Treasury to raise tax revenues.
    d. the tool used by the Federal Reserve System to regulate stock market activities.

15. In recent years the primary tool used by the Federal Reserve System to control the money supply has been

    a. jawboning.
    b. open-market operations.
    c. changes in the discount rate.
    d. changes in reserve requirements.

16. An expansion in the money supply is desired as part of an antirecession policy. The Federal Reserve Board might

    a. increase reserve requirements.
    b. buy U.S. securities.
    c. increase the discount rate.
    d. urge the Treasury to sell more U.S. securities.

17. Suppose that a member bank of the Federal Reserve System has $8,000 in demand deposits, is able to loan out $5,000 of this amount, and still keep $1,000 in excess reserves in the bank. What is the legal reserve requirement?

    a. 62.5 percent
    b. 75 percent
    c. 37.5 percent
    d. 25 percent

_____   **18.** The Federal Reserve System wants to reduce the supply of money as part of an
anti-inflation policy. The Federal Reserve System might

a. reduce reserve requirements.
b. sell U.S. securities.
c. reduce the discount rate.
d. urge the Treasury to sell more U.S. securities.

Solutions

Answer	Refer to:

1. (a) [A-3] The four functions of money are standard of value, medium of exchange, store of value, and standard of deferred payment. Answer (a) is the only option not a function of money.

2. (d) [B-4-a] Open-market operations are engaged in daily by the FED, while reserve requirements are seldom changed and discount rates rarely change more than once every two months.

3. (d) [A-4] The money supply is a prime determinant of the value of money. The impact of changes in money supply or value of money is dependent on corresponding changes in output of goods and services.

4. (c) [A-3] Answers (a), (b), and (d) are all functions of money.

5. (d) [B-2-b] Financial institutions lend money to individuals and businesses as income-earning ventures.

6. (b) [B-3] This is the definition of required reserves.

7. (b) [B-4] If a financial institution holds excess reserves, it is not expanding the money supply to its potential. This will result in a reduced money supply.

8. (a) [B-3] This is the definition of excess reserves.

9. (b) [B-3] The multiplier is found by using the formula: 1 divided by the reserve requirement. If the reserve requirement is 0.2, the multiplier is 1/0.2 or 5.

10. (b) [B-2] All monetary policy is the responsibility of the Federal Reserve System.

11. (a) [B-2-a] Answers (b), (c), and (d) all refer to monetary policy, which is controlled by the FED. The national debt is controlled by Congress.

12. (c) [B-2-a] Answers (a), (b), and (d) refer to measures the FED can use to control the money supply, not the purpose of the FED.

13. (c) [B-2] The Federal Reserve System has sole responsibility for monetary policy.

14. (a)   [B-4-a] Open-market operations are most often used by the FED to alter the money supply.

15. (b)   [B-4-a] Open-market operations are the primary tool for controlling the money supply.

16. (b)   [B-4-a] Buying U.S. securities would expand the money supply. Selling securities cannot be done by the Treasury.

17. (d)   [B-3] If $5,000 is loaned and $1,000 is excess reserves, $2,000 is left for required reserves. $2,000/8,000 = 25 percent, which is the reserve ratio.

18. (b)   [B-4-e] This is the only means identified here that would *reduce* the money supply.

CHAPTER 4

Business Involvement in Current Social and Economic Programs

OVERVIEW

The degree to which business has a responsibility to assist in solving current social problems is an issue that is often discussed. Trying to define exactly what responsibility business has in finding solutions to social problems and what responsibility individuals and government have in solving these social problems is difficult.

One solution is a laissez-faire type of capitalism in which business has no responsibility in solving social problems. In a laissez-faire society, solving social problems would be the responsibility of private individuals or groups, not business or government. For example, unemployment insurance or social security would be organized by private groups.

Another solution is that business must share the responsibility in solving social problems. It is hard to imagine solving such problems as pollution and conservation of natural resources solely through the efforts of private individuals and groups. Individuals who believe that the government has a responsibility to impose regulations on the private sector that would result in solutions of social problems support this argument.

In this chapter, four social problems, their significance, and related economic issues are reviewed. These problems are conservation of natural resources, consumerism, pollution control, and equal employment opportunity.

KEY TERMS

Age Discrimination in Employment Act
  of 1967
Americans with Disabilities Act (ADA)
Antitrust laws
Civil Rights Act of 1964
Consumerism
Cost–benefit analysis

Discrimination
Economics of pollution
Environmental Protection Agency (EPA)
Equal Employment Opportunity Act
  of 1972
Equal Employment Opportunity
  Commission (EEOC)

Federal Aviation Administration (FAA)   Laissez-faire
Federal Food and Drug Administration   Pollution
  (FDA)   Price ceiling
Federal Power Commission (FPC)   Productivity
Federal Trade Commission (FTC)   Vocational Rehabilitation Act of 1973

A. Conservation of Natural Resources

Conservation of natural resources can best be examined as a problem of current versus future consumption. If a society engages in large amounts of current consumption, resources are depleted, which reduces the amount of resources available for future production, thus future consumption. A variety of methods can be utilized to encourage the conservation of natural resources.

1. *Using Minimum Quantity of Resources for Production*: For businesses to produce goods and services efficiently, markets must be able to operate without restrictions. Restrictions promote inefficiency.

    EXAMPLE: If the government imposes import quotas or import tariffs on foreign steel, this action encourages the use of domestic steel in production. In turn, the use of domestic steel encourages the extraction of more iron ore within the United States. This process increases the price of iron ore and depletes the supply of domestic ore. The increased use of domestic resources might be reversed if the import duties were eliminated, but other social problems, such as higher unemployment in the domestic steel industry, might be the result.

2. *Deterring Use of Natural Resources*: If resources are to be conserved in the short run, policies must be enacted to deter their use. One such policy might be excise taxes placed on some resources to discourage their use. As the price of the resource increases, business would attempt to find a different resource to make their products in an efficient manner. This would result in the conservation of a given natural resource.

    EXAMPLE: If the United States placed an excise tax on domestic crude oil, the price of domestic crude oil would increase relative to foreign crude oil as well as the price of crude oil relative to other forms of energy. Business firms would then have two choices: (1) Use foreign crude oil to produce petroleum products; or (2) find an alternative form of energy to continue their production processes.

    The long-term impact would be to reduce the demand for domestic petroleum and conserve domestic petroleum reserves. This would increase the price for goods and services since cost of energy would increase.

3. *Voluntary Conservation by Business*: Another argument often heard is that business has a responsibility to conserve natural resources and should introduce conservation programs voluntarily. The basic problem is one of cooperation.

    EXAMPLE: If one firm within an industry attempts to conserve a natural resource, the production costs for that firm will increase. The firm will be placed in a position where the cost of using their production methods and resources is greater than that of competing firms. Therefore, either the business profits will decline or their product prices will be higher.

    Consumers must be willing to pay a higher price for goods produced using resource conservation methods. Firms cannot be expected to use expensive conservation methods "out of the goodness of their hearts." If some business firms cooperated to ensure conservation of natural resources, other problems might develop. For example, the cooperative firms might run the risk of violating antitrust laws as a result of the cooperative effort.

When considering future conservation of natural resources in the United States, consumers must consider the way in which the markets function and either accept the results of such market operations or impose restrictions to change the results. If we accept the market results, we allow prices of resources to increase and/or decrease as demand dictates. The elimination of such government policies as price ceilings on natural gas, gasoline, and other resources would allow the prices of those resources to increase to a point where consumers and producers would actively search for alternative resources to conserve natural resources.

B. Consumerism

Consumerism is a movement shared by a large number of people who believe that society is not always getting "a fair shake" in the economic system. The primary economic reason for consumerism is the enhancement of consumer welfare.

1. *Business Practices Adverse to Consumer Interests*: Some of these business practices include:

    a. Unsafe, impure, and low-quality products

    b. Deceptive advertising of goods and services

    c. Techniques that obscure or hide real prices

    d. Poor or inadequate servicing of products

    Each of these practices provides, at minimum, inconvenience to the consumer, at maximum increased expenditures for goods and services that may or may not be needed. In addition, the availability of unsafe, impure, and low-quality products can result in personal injury or even death.

2. *The Consumer's Bill of Rights*: At the core of consumerism is the Consumer's Bill of Rights, first declared by President John F. Kennedy. The original draft of consumers' rights included:

    a. The right to safety

    b. The right to be informed

    c. The right to choose

    d. The right to be heard

    Since Kennedy's original declaration, two others have been added:

    e. The right to recourse and redress

    f. The right to a physical environment that will enhance the quality of life

3. *The Economics of Consumerism*: The primary economic reason for consumerism is the enhancement of consumer welfare. When looking at the overall activities of the country relative to consumerism, one must look at the benefits as well as the costs to the consumer of having that protection available.

a. *Economic benefits of consumerism*: There are three possible avenues through which consumerism may help improve consumer welfare:

(1) *Improvements in product and service information*: To obtain the greatest satisfaction from a limited income, the consumer must have information on the prices and quality of a variety of goods and services to make rational decisions.

EXAMPLE: We expect that weights and measures will be represented correctly by sellers. This information is essential in making appropriate buying decisions.

It is helpful to know the ingredients comprising a product, the product's uses, how it operates, and how long it is expected to last, assuming average usage. This type of information is essential for the consumer to make informed purchasing decisions.

EXAMPLE: If someone wanted to purchase a skill saw for home use, the price might range from $30 to $70. By having accurate information about the different intensity of use, one might find that the lesser-priced saw was fine for home use.

(2) *Reduction in deceptive advertising*: Everyone at some time or another has been taken in by a deceptive sales promotion. While a reduction in deceptive sales activities increases consumer welfare, the cost of enforcing these reductions cannot be ignored. Deceptive sales tactics are the opposite of informational advertising and generate "fog" or confusion to the consumer. One problem with deceptive sales practices is that it is difficult to draw the line between what is a deceptive practice and what is not. A sales promotion considered useless and deceptive by one consumer may not be considered so by another consumer.

(3) *Increased consumer protection*: The largest part of consumerism activities is directed toward the protection of the consumer rather than the education of the consumer. These activities are directed toward protecting consumers from unsafe, impure, and low-quality products and from unfair practices. Results of consumerism activities in this area include the following:

(a) Laws preventing smoking in elevators

(b) Regulations requiring seat belts and shoulder harnesses in automobiles

(c) Laws requiring the wearing of helmets by motorcycle riders

(d) Government inspection of meat

(e) Licensing of professionals, such as medical doctors, before they can provide services

Other consumerism measures are intended to protect consumers from unscrupulous sellers. Price controls on gasoline and maximum rents for housing units fall into this category. Consumers who can get as much at the controlled price as they would be able to purchase at an uncontrolled price clearly gain. However, other consumers who might like to purchase some of the good may be unable to do so because of the lower quantity supplied.

b. *The economic costs*: In economic terms, all goods and services have a cost. Consumerism activities and legislative measures are not a free service to consumers. Two sets of costs can readily be identified:

(1) *The cost to consumers for providing protection to other consumers*: Direct costs to consumers for consumerism activities consist of the reduction in well-being felt by some consumers as the presumed benefits of these activities are extended to others.

EXAMPLE: As a result of the consumerism movement, seat belts are now required in all automobiles. People purchasing a new car must pay the seat belt costs whether they wish to use the seat belt or not. Therefore, the values of those involved in the consumerism movement—in this case, seat belts are beneficial—are imposed on all society by forcing all persons who own cars to bear the costs.

(2) *Costs of resources used in consumerism activities*: The costs of resources used in affecting any given consumerism activity must be taken into consideration. The resources used by the Federal Trade Commission, the Federal Aviation Agency, the Federal Food and Drug Administration, and other consumer protection agencies could be used elsewhere if they were not being used to protect the consumer. In 1988 the cost of operating federal agencies whose sole responsibility was providing consumer protection exceeded $3 billion.

4. *Consumerism Activities and Measures*: Specific types of activities, stemming from the Consumer's Bill of Rights, are employed to bolster the consumer's position with respect to producers and sellers. These activities include consumer information and educational services, performed by such organizations as Consumers Union; the investigation of practices thought to be adverse to consumer interests; the publication of reports by a number of consumer-oriented groups; and the extension of regular activities by government agencies for the purpose of protecting the consumer.

a. *Providing informational services*: Most individuals agree that the provision of information as a form of consumerism has positive benefits at a minimum cost. There is virtually no economic argument against consumerism measures that require truth in advertising or a listing of ingredients on labels. The benefits of these activities are obvious, and the costs are no more than the cost of providing false or misleading advertising.

b. *Minimizing risk to the consumer*: Consumerism measures that attempt to minimize the impact on individuals from actions of others are relatively easy to justify on a cost–benefit basis.

EXAMPLE: In the absence of regulation, people would drive automobiles with defective brakes or without headlights, imposing substantial risk on other people who happened to be driving on the highway. Legislation that regulates automobile safety increases the benefit to society as a whole, and the cost of this regulation is somewhat minimal.

    c. *Protection from business manipulation*: Protection of the individual from business manipulation is probably the most questionable set of consumerism activities. Manipulation of individual consumers means that a business firm can do with the consumer whatever it desires. To protect a consumer from business manipulation, one has to assume that the consumer can be manipulated by businesses. Business can be prevented from manipulating consumers if societal measures are available which provide information to individual consumers or which enable individual consumers to be protected from such activities by other consumers.

5. *Government Support for Consumerism*: Much of the consumer's power and thrust comes from government support through legislation. Several governmental agencies on the federal level are actively engaged in consumer affairs: Federal Trade Commission, Food and Drug Administration, Interstate Commerce Commission, Federal Aviation Agency, Department of Agriculture Consumer and Marketing Services, Federal Power Commission, Occupational Safety and Health Administration, and Securities and Exchange Commission, to name a few. The function of these agencies (as well as state and local consumer affairs agencies) is to protect the consumer from unfair business practices.

C. Pollution Control

Economic analysis of pollution provides a perspective on its causes and effects. The absence of property rights to our shared resources of air, land, and water provides the major incentive to pollute. The elimination of pollution can be accomplished through three primary avenues: direct controls which eliminate pollution, indirect controls which would tax polluters for the right to pollute, and the establishment of property rights to whatever is being polluted, typically air, land, and water. Each of these has advantages and disadvantages and must be evaluated carefully before effective and efficient pollution controls can be implemented.

1. *Pollution*: Pollution is present in all industrial societies—capitalist, socialist, and communist countries alike. In general, pollution is a result of increased economic growth. Pollution is defined as the use of the environment by producers and consumers as a dumping ground for waste. The environment is able to recycle some degree of pollution, but pollution becomes a problem when the quantity of pollutants is greater than what the environment can recycle. There are three common forms of pollution: air pollution, water pollution, and land pollution.

    a. *Air pollution*: Air pollution is the emission of waste, such as carbon monoxide, sulfa oxides, nitrogen oxides, hydrocarbons, and particulates into the air. These waste materials typically come from the production and consumption processes in our economic system.

    b. *Water pollution*: Water pollution is ordinarily measured in terms of the capacity of water to support aquatic life. This capacity depends on the level of dissolved oxygen in the water and the presence of matters or materials injurious to plant and animal life existing in the water. The capacity of the water to support aquatic life is reduced when various kinds of materials and matters are dumped into it. Among these are toxins which do not settle out of the water and are not easily broken down by biological means.

    EXAMPLES OF TOXINS: Mercury, dioxins, herbicides, pesticides.

In recent years there have also been questions as to whether the oceans should be used for the dumping of nuclear wastes or for undersea nuclear explosions.

c. *Land pollution*: Land pollution results from the dumping of a wide variety of wastes onto the terrain and from tearing up the earth's surface through such activities as strip mining. Garbage dumps and landfills grow as cities dispose of waste. The strip mining of the land for coal has, in the past, left unsightly blemishes on the countryside and has taken productive land out of use in some cases.

2. *The Economics of Pollution*: In general, pollution occurs in areas where no well-defined property rights exist. Air, water, and land pollution occurs when the rights to the air, water, or land are not well defined.

EXAMPLE: Air is unlike other resources—no one owns air. Since air is not owned, it can be used without being paid for. As a result, business can minimize the cost of production by eliminating waste into the air rather than using expensive recycling technology.

a. *Reducing pollution costs*: From a business standpoint, production costs can be reduced by using air, water, and land which have no property owners. By disposing of pollutants into the air or water, business does not have to pay the cost of recycling or cleanup technology. Thus, the costs of production are reduced, and goods are made available to consumers at a lower cost. From a societal point of view, if industries put too much pollution into the environment, the quality of air is reduced and all society members must then bear the cleanup costs.

EXAMPLES:

In a residential area close to a steel plant, the particulates from the steel blast furnace cause the paint on homes and automobiles to deteriorate faster.

If a firm pollutes a stream, the quality of the water as well as the surrounding area is reduced. The quality and quantity of fish in the stream may also be reduced, thereby reducing the satisfaction people receive who use the stream.

b. *The cost of eliminating pollution*: The consumer's initial reaction to pollution is that it should be eliminated totally. However, substantial costs are involved in pollution elimination.

EXAMPLES:

If steel companies were required not to pollute, they would have to invest large amounts of capital to collect the particulates from the blast furnaces before these pollutants were emitted into the air.

Similarly, if producers were required not to emit pollutants into streams, they would have to install some type of waste treatment system for the water before it would be allowed to enter a stream.

If producers were required to eliminate all pollution, the result would be an increase in the cost of production and an increase in the cost of any products made by the producer or, as in the case of steel, products made from the original product produced.

    c. *Factors for analyzing effects of pollution*: In analyzing the economics of pollution, three factors are important:

        (1) The environment can recycle some pollution: we do not need to reduce the level of pollution to zero.

        (2) Eliminating pollution benefits society.

        (3) Eliminating pollution costs society. These costs will be in the form of higher prices for goods and services due to increased production costs.

3. *Control of Pollution*: Pollution can be reduced through the use of direct controls, indirect controls, and through the establishment of property rights.

    a. *Direct controls*: Direct controls involve government banning of activities that result in pollution. These controls are most useful for types of pollution that nature cannot recycle. Such items as plastic bags or tires will not disintegrate on their own. To control the disposal of these items, direct controls may be necessary.

    EXAMPLE: Government's banning the use of pesticides such as DDT.

    Such policies are enforced by the Environmental Protection Agency (EPA) at the federal level and by various state and local agencies established for this purpose. Problems may arise from the use of such direct controls, for example:

        (1) Using direct controls does not always consider that the use of certain polluting products, for example pesticides, might be necessary to obtain a salable crop.

        (2) The benefits from using the pollutants are not the same for all producers. If outright prohibition of pollutants takes place, this prohibition imposes higher costs on some producers than on others.

            EXAMPLE: Abolishing the use of DDT may have substantial effects on the cost to farmers of growing grain but have a minimal effect on the cost to groundskeepers for maintaining golf courses.

        (3) A third problem with direct controls is the enforcement that becomes necessary. Since direct controls fail to provide incentive to polluters not to pollute, it is necessary for some type of enforcement to ensure that the controls are not violated.

    b. *Indirect controls*: A second method used to control pollution is through indirect controls. Typically, indirect controls include taxing for pollution activities. Producers or individuals would pay a tax for the right to pollute. This method is especially useful in cases where the amount of pollution can be measured. However, substantial problems occur if the pollution cannot be measured directly.

    EXAMPLES OF INDIRECT CONTROLS: Taxes or deposits on bottles and cans are imposed to encourage recycling. The high tax or deposit placed on these: (1) provides an incentive to recycle, and (2) makes it profitable for some individuals to clean up discarded containers.

This process could also be used for firms that emit pollutants into the air or water simply by taxing them for the emission of pollutants and then using the tax dollars to clean up the water or to install devices that would minimize the impact of pollution on the environment.

c. *Use of property rights*: A third solution to pollution elimination is to assign property rights to the air and water. By assigning property rights, individuals who own the property (air and water) could charge for the use of the air and water. Therefore, the water and air would become a private good and susceptible to supply and demand conditions for resources that exist in other parts of the market.

D. Employment Opportunities

Substantial attention has been given to discrimination in the labor market. Laws have been passed in an attempt to alleviate this discrimination and to provide equal employment opportunity for all. The major employment law passed in recent years is the Equal Employment Opportunity Act of 1972. Previous legislation included the Civil Rights Act of 1964 and the Age Discrimination Act of 1967. The Vocational Rehabilitation Act of 1973 also affected the employment of handicapped persons as part of the workforce. Each of these laws attempted in some way to alleviate discrimination in the labor market.

1. *Discrimination*: The term *discrimination* means that equals are treated unequally or that unequals are treated equally. More specifically, discrimination exists in the labor market when persons with equal productivity are paid different wages or persons with differences in productivity are paid equal wages. Some types of discrimination found in labor markets are:

   a. *Wage discrimination*: In 1985 the average income of males between the ages of 35 and 44 was $25,886; and those between 45 and 54 earned an average of $26,702 annually. At the same time the average annual income of females between the ages of 35 and 44 was $16,114. The Women's Bureau of the U.S. Department of Labor reports that the average annual salary for women is currently $18,000, compared with $27,000 for men. Since 1985, the average annual income for males has been increasing each year after hitting a plateau for a few years. Female workers have much lower income than males, but their incomes have been steadily rising over the past several years.

   On the surface, this would indicate that females have been discriminated against in terms of salaries, even though the average income for females has been increasing steadily. However, before a case for discrimination can be justified, jobs held by men and those held by women must be examined to discover if production is at equal levels in the same types of jobs. It is very difficult to talk about wage discrimination on an aggregate scale instead of talking about wage discrimination on the basis of equal pay for equal work.

   b. *Employment discrimination*: Employment discrimination means that some people are not hired because of noneconomic characteristics such as race or gender. Employment discrimination, like wage discrimination, is difficult to identify. Differences among employment rates comparing Caucasians and minority groups or males and females may suggest discrimination, but may not prove that it exists.

EXAMPLE: When productivity is examined, it may be discovered that unemployment rates are much higher among some particular ethnic groups. Or when educational level is examined and individuals are compared who have identical educational levels, unemployment rates may be much higher among some ethnic groups compared with other ethnic groups.

Such evidence for employment discrimination becomes more conclusive.

    c. *Occupational discrimination*: Another type of discrimination in the labor market is occupational discrimination. Certain occupations may be more available to people of one sex or race. Several studies have been completed recently which show that more high-paying occupations are held by men, and women are often relegated to lower-paying occupations. This would indicate that occupational discrimination exists.

2. *The Costs of Discrimination*: Discrimination represents a substantial loss not only to individuals, but also to society. To individuals, the loss may be less income and the inaccessibility of occupations in which they would like to be employed. The social loss is in terms of a lower output and lower productivity than if discrimination did not exist. This lower output is a result of high unemployment of certain groups which results in a smaller production possibility curve for society than would otherwise be possible.

3. *Legislation Regulating Discrimination Practices*: Five basic laws have been passed to minimize discrimination within the labor market in the United States.

    a. *The Civil Rights Act of 1964*: Instrumental in eliminating many forms of discrimination, this act was the first legislation of its kind. Title VII was concerned with equal employment opportunities and specified that employees or labor organizations with 25 or more employees must treat all persons equally regardless of sex, race, national origin, or religion. It also provided for the creation of the Equal Employment Opportunity Commission to help with enforcement of the act.

    b. *The Age Discrimination in Employment Act of 1967*: This legislation applies to private employers of 20 or more persons and all federal, state, and local governments regardless of the number of people employed. This act prohibits discrimination based on the age of the applicant. Specifically, it prohibits discrimination against individuals between the ages of 40 and 65 in the hiring, compensation, working conditions, and privileges of employment. This act also made it illegal for an employer to specify an applicant's age on an employment application form or in the advertising of employment opportunities.

    c. *The Equal Employment Opportunity Act of 1972*: This act involves a series of amendments to the Civil Rights Act of 1964. Perhaps the most significant amendment provided an independent agency for the first time at the federal level—the Equal Employment Opportunity Commission (EEOC). The EEOC was empowered to enforce laws prohibiting discrimination based on sex, color, national origin, or religion. In addition, the EEOC received the power to institute civil action as a means of eliminating discrimination in employment. As a result of this act, coverage was also extended to state and local government employees and employees of labor organizations with 15 or more members.

d. *The Vocational Rehabilitation Act of 1973*: Job-related discrimination was specifically eliminated against handicapped individuals in the Vocational Rehabilitation Act of 1973.

e. *The Americans with Disabilities Act*: The Civil Rights Act of 1964 was extended in 1992 to cover the physically and mentally disabled, including AIDS patients, cancer patients, and treated, recovering substance abusers. Individuals with emotional disorders, however, were excluded. Businesses are required to make reasonable accommodations to workers and job applicants with disabilities unless the required changes present an undue hardship for the business. The act is considered the most comprehensive civil rights legislation in 30 years.

Each of these federal laws relates to economic discrimination in the labor market and attempts to minimize the amount of discrimination that might take place. The EEOC is the major enforcer of the various laws and is empowered to initiate civil proceedings against firms, labor unions, and government agencies that have violated one of these acts.

Review Questions

DIRECTIONS: Select the best answer from the four alternatives. Write the letter of your answer in the blank to the left of the number.

_____ 1. Which of the following statements describes a choice that involves conservation?

    a. Produce wheat or corn
    b. Use resources for current or future consumption
    c. Have private industry or government pay for education
    d. Produce automobiles

_____ 2. Of the following statements, which business practices are generally thought to be adverse to consumer interests?

    a. Advertising goods or services in local papers
    b. Many firms making similar products
    c. Production of low-quality products
    d. Production of high-cost products

_____ 3. Which of the following is generally not assumed to be a consumer right?

    a. Right to safety
    b. Right to choose
    c. Right to low-priced products
    d. Right to be heard

_____ 4. With respect to consumerism,

    a. there are neither costs nor benefits to the consumer.
    b. there are both costs and benefits to the consumer.
    c. there are only benefits to the consumer.
    d. there are only costs to the consumer.

_____ 5. Increased information about the quality of a product will

    a. leave no impact on the economic costs of the item.
    b. result in a lower price for the product to the consumer.
    c. help consumers make decisions that result in increasing their welfare.
    d. confuse consumers and thus result in irrational decisions being made.

6. Which of the following is not generally considered a regulation aimed at protecting the consumer?

a. Inspection of meat
b. Prohibition of smoking in elevators
c. Seat belts in cars
d. Licensing of accountants

7. The economic costs of regulation include

a. costs of government agencies that enforce regulations.
b. value of resources used to meet regulations that could be available for another use.
c. loss of freedom to engage in those activities prohibited by regulation.
d. all of the above.

8. Which of the following activities is not considered an activity to help consumers?

a. Providing information
b. Regulations minimizing risk to consumers of products
c. Providing national defense by government
d. Protection from business manipulation

9. Which of the following government agencies is most actively engaged in consumer affairs?

a. Bureau of the Budget
b. Department of Commerce
c. Food and Drug Administration
d. Congress

10. The major reason for pollution is

a. lack of social conscience of business.
b. lack of property rights.
c. greediness of consumers.
d. absence of government regulations.

11. Three general ways to control pollution are the uses of

a. direct controls, extension of property rights, and government regulation.
b. indirect controls, extension of property rights, and tax placed on polluters.
c. elimination of property rights, indirect controls, and government regulation.
d. direct controls, indirect controls, and extension of property rights.

12. Which of the following best describes discrimination?

    a. Equals are treated equally.
    b. Persons with the same productivity are paid the same.
    c. Unequals are treated unequally.
    d. Equals are treated unequally.

13. A specific example of discrimination in the labor market is

    a. a man is employed in an occupation for which he does not meet the basic qualifications.
    b. an employee receives a wage commensurate with education and experience.
    c. a worker is displaced by technology.
    d. a woman is denied a promotion to manager even though she has the basic qualifications for the position.

14. Costs of discrimination are borne by

    a. individuals only.
    b. individuals and society together.
    c. society alone.
    d. producers alone.

15. Which of the following pieces of legislation has attempted to reduce discrimination?

    a. Age Discrimination Act of 1967
    b. Civil Rights Act of 1964
    c. Vocational Rehabilitation Act of 1973
    d. All of the above

16. In a market-oriented economic system

    a. it is possible to eliminate discrimination, but the costs are high.
    b. discrimination would never exist.
    c. discrimination should be eliminated since the costs are very low.
    d. discrimination can never be eliminated.

17. In an office building a number of signs can be found posted in various corridors. Which one is the result of consumer action designed to protect the consumer?

    a. "Directions for tornado watches/warnings"
    b. "Building hours 7 a.m. to 10 p.m."
    c. "No smoking in elevator"
    d. "Caution—wet floors!"

18. ABC Autos, Inc. is a retail automobile dealership. A series of sales promotions is being developed and considered for use in promoting the sale of new automobiles. Which of the following statements most likely represents deceptive advertising?

    a. "The new Rally is the best car you'll ever own!"
    b. "The moment you sit behind the wheel, you will want to drive it away!"
    c. "More miles to the gallon!"
    d. "No money down! You can drive it away for $199 a month plus a moderate finance charge!"

Solutions

Answer	Refer to:

1. (b)   [A-1] Answers (a), (c), and (d) all involve choices on current resource use, not conservation of resources for the future.

2. (c)   [B-1] The production and marketing of low-quality products are thought of as practices adverse to the consumer's interest. Firms that are making similar products are typically competitive and therefore beneficial to consumers. Advertising goods and services keeps consumers informed about products coming onto the market.

3. (c)   [B-2] Answers (a), (b), and (d) state some of the rights of consumers. Answer (c) is something consumers might like to have but has not been declared a right.

4. (b)   [B-3] For any decision involving the use of scarce resources, there are costs and benefits to both the consumer and the producer.

5. (c)   [B-3-a(1)] The consumer must have information about the prices and quality of a variety of goods and services to make rational decisions.

6. (d)   [B-3-a(3)] Answers (a), (b), and (c) all relate to areas that affect the consumer directly. Answer (d) affects the consumer only indirectly.

7. (d)   [B-3-b] All answers list economic costs of regulations.

8. (c)   [B-3] The provision of national defense by the government is usually considered necessary since it is impossible to have it provided by business but is not considered an activity that helps consumers.

9. (c)   [B-5] Answer (c) is correct since it is the only alternative that lists a government agency engaged in consumer affairs.

10. (b)   [C-1] Although some pollution may be caused by answers (a), (c), and (d), the major reason for pollution is lack of property rights.

11. (d)   [C-3] Answer (d) lists the three general methods of controlling pollution. Answers (a), (b), and (c) all have a specific policy listed with the general method.

12. (d)   [D-1] If equals were treated unequally, some individuals would be discriminated against for one reason or another.

13. (d)   [D-1-c] This is the only situation that appears to be discriminatory. A woman who has the basic qualifications for a managerial position who is denied the promotion may have just cause to feel that discrimination has taken place.

14. (b)   [D-2] If discrimination exists, the individual loses; but society also loses the potential output of the person being discriminated against.

15. (d)   [D-3] Each of the acts mentioned in (a), (b), and (c) attempts to eliminate a form of discrimination.

16. (d)   [D-3] A market requires choices to be made, and choices will always result in some form of discrimination. The role of society is to define what criteria can be used to discriminate.

17. (c)   [B-3-a(3)] A large part of consumerism activities is directed toward the protection of the consumer.

18. (d)   [B-3-a(2)] The statement is vague, not stating a definite finance charge or any other "hidden" costs in purchasing the automobile.

CHAPTER 5

International Trade

OVERVIEW

The United States is involved in substantial amounts of international trade. In 1992 over $640 billion worth of goods and services were exported from the United States, that is, sold to other countries around the world. In addition, U.S. citizens bought slightly over $670 billion in foreign goods and services in 1989. This resulted in a negative balance of trade of close to $30 billion.

All countries in the world engage in some form of international trade. In relation to the total level of production in society, the United States engages in a relatively small amount of trade. However, in absolute dollars, the total amount of trade is substantial for the country. The reasons countries engage in trade are numerous, but one principle is always present: The country is better off *after* trade than it was *before* trade.

In this chapter we review the fundamentals of international trade, the economic basis of international trade (especially geographic specialization, absolute advantage, and comparative advantage), and special problems of international trade. The balance of payments in international finance and international exchange is also discussed. The effects of tariffs and quotas as policies established by individual countries are emphasized as an important part of international trade.

KEY TERMS

Absolute advantage
Ad valorem
Balance of payments
Common Market
  (European Economic
  Community)
Comparative advantage

Compound tariff
Embargo
Excise tax
Foreign exchange rate
Geographic specialization
Import quota
Import tariff

International finance
Nationalism
Protective tariff
Revenue tariff
Specific tariff
Tariff
Tariff quota

A. Fundamentals of International Trade

In addition to economic concepts, international trade encompasses the political economy and the sociocultural climate of different nations. These determine the movement of goods, services, people, and capital across national political boundaries and thus set the stage for international trade. The fundamentals of international trade involve its economic theory and importance in our society.

1. *Theory of international trade*: To explain the basic theory of international trade, we must look at each of the following questions:

   Why does international trade take place?

   What determines the composition, pattern, and direction of international trade?

   On what kinds of terms does international trade take place?

   What are the economic results of international trade?

   a. *The need for international trade*: International trade exists because of differences in the productive capacities of various countries. These differences lead to differences in production costs for goods. Thus, it becomes mutually advantageous for countries to trade with one another. For trade among countries to become beneficial, geographic specialization must take place based on the comparative advantages of producing a different commodity.

   b. *Composition, pattern, and direction of international trade*: Three primary factors determine the composition, pattern, and direction of international trade:

      (1) *The relative endowments of factors of production*: The term *relative endowments* refers to the amount of land, capital, available labor, and skills possessed by the labor force in any particular country. Countries have unequal endowments of these factors; thus they will differ in their abilities to produce certain types of goods.

      (2) *Economics of large-scale production*: The economics of large-scale production deal with the relationship of the average cost of production to the amount produced. For some goods, as the output increases, the average cost of production declines. If countries have small internal or domestic markets, they would be unable to produce in an efficient manner. Through international trade and marketing products overseas, the output of goods can increase and the average cost of production can be reduced, which will result in more efficient production.

      (3) *Minimization of transportation costs*: In a free market, industries tend to locate where the costs of transportation are minimized. In some cases it is advantageous for a country to specialize in a particular commodity because the transportation costs for getting the resources to the place of production or the finished products from production to the final markets will be minimized.

   c. *Terms of trade*: The terms of trade at which exchange takes place are often referred to as the foreign exchange rate for currency. Foreign exchange refers to the monetary means for making payments in currencies other than a country's own currency. The rate of exchange is the price of foreign currency in terms of domestic currency.

EXAMPLE: In the United States, the exchange rate indicates the number of American dollars per unit of foreign currency. If the British pound sterling is quoted as $2.50, this means that one pound sterling is worth $2.50 in American money.

The demand for foreign exchange stems from countries buying foreign goods.

EXAMPLE: If Americans buy more Japanese products, Americans have a demand for Japanese yen to pay for these products. This also increases the supply of American dollars in Japan.

    d. *Economic results of international trade*: Through international trade, each country gains as the gap between prices of goods and services and the prices of factors of production are narrowed among countries. International trade reduces the opportunity cost of obtaining certain commodities in which a country has a comparative cost disadvantage.

2. *The Importance of International Trade*: Commodity and service trade comes to 10 to 15 percent of world income. However, for some countries trade is much more important.

EXAMPLE: As a percentage of gross national product, exports are around 30 to 35 percent for the Netherlands, about 15 percent for Germany, Great Britain, and Italy, and about 10 percent for France.

For a few countries, such as the United States, international trade is less important. U.S. exports are usually around 6 to 10 percent of gross national product. Yet, trade contributes much to our standard of living.

    a. *U.S. involvement in international trade*: While international trade represents a relatively small portion of the gross national product, the United States is the world's largest exporter and importer and the largest provider of international capital and grants.

        (1) *Volume of imports*: The volume of U.S. imports is of vital significance to other countries. These sales provide the dollar earnings that other countries need to pay for the importation of American goods. The volume of U.S. imports is closely related to the level of national income. The higher the level of national income in the United States, the greater the quantity of imports we consume. This fact results in close ties between the U.S. economy and economies of foreign countries.

            EXAMPLE: If the U.S. economy enters a period of recession, the demand for imports is decreased and the quantity of dollars that foreign countries have to purchase goods from the United States is reduced. Along with the decreased demand for foreign goods is reduced income (in U.S. dollars) to buy American goods and services that foreign countries do not produce domestically.

        (2) *Volume of exports*: The U.S. exports are lower than the world average (usually around 6 to 10 percent of the gross national product). However, international trade is important to the United States because of its contribution to our standard of living. International trade is the product of a world in which countries are dependent on each other to maintain their respective standards of living.

B. Economic Basis of International Trade

The economic basis of international trade involves an analysis of geographic specialization, absolute advantage, and comparative advantage. These three concepts are explained in this section, along with specific problems relating to international trade, domestic policies leading to restrictions in trade, the idea of nationalism, and artificial barriers that interfere with international trade.

1. *Geographic Specialization*: Geographic specialization is based on the premise that differences in production capabilities lead to differences in comparative costs for production. Geographic specialization is also the basis for mutually beneficial international or interregional trade. Two conditions are the foundation for specialization and trade: the relative prices of the factors of production, and differences in the level of technology in various countries. Both of these factors lead to differences in relative costs of production. Countries gain from trade by specializing in the production of goods they can produce at a low cost and importing commodities that are expensive to produce domestically. Production specialization in which the country or area has a cost advantage is referred to as geographic specialization.

   The basis for trade among regions within a country or among different countries is the same. Each region within a country has comparative advantages for producing particular goods and services because of the presence of soil, climate, topography, natural resources, labor supply, and capital supply best suited to produce those goods or services.

   EXAMPLES:

   In the United States, Florida and California have a comparative advantage in producing citrus fruits; the Plains states, in grain and pork; the north-central and northeastern states, in heavy manufacturing; and the east coast, in fresh fish.

   Historically, in international trade, the United States has had an advantage in agriculture and technology; Canada, in wheat and wood pulp; Japan, in textiles; Australia, in wool; and France, in wine and perfumes.

   Through geographic specialization, world production efficiency is increased and standards of living improved.

2. *Absolute Advantage and Comparative Advantage*: The principles of absolute advantage and comparative advantage are the basis for international trade and interregional economics. The principles by which geographic specialization takes place stem from the concepts of absolute advantage and comparative advantage:

   a. *Principle of absolute advantage*: The principle of absolute advantage, in relation to the concept of comparative advantage, illustrates the benefits of interregional and international trade.

      EXAMPLE: Figure 5–1 provides information about two manufacturers of electronic products, each with an identical quantity of land, equipment, and quality of labor available. The U.S. manufacturer can produce 200 television sets or 400 stereo systems with the same resources that the manufacturer in Japan needs to produce only 20 television sets or 200 stereo systems.

      The U.S. producer can manufacture more of each product—television and stereo systems—with a given amount of resources because the quality of labor in the United States is better suited to produce electronic equipment

Figure 5–1 Televisions/Stereos—U.S./Japan

	Television Sets	Stereo Systems
U.S. producer	200	400
Japanese producer	20	200
Opportunity cost		
Television sets (U.S.)	1	2
Television sets (Japan)	1	10

than are those same resources in Japan. We say that the United States has an absolute advantage in producing both television sets and stereo systems. Initially, it might seem that the U.S. manufacturer should produce both products and the Japanese manufacturer should find something else to produce. However, this would not result in efficient production of television sets and stereo systems.

b. *Principle of comparative advantage*: The principle of comparative advantage refers to the ability of a particular country to produce a good at a lower opportunity cost, compared to the opportunity costs of other goods, than can other countries with whom it trades. This principle emphasizes that each country tends to specialize in production and exportation of commodities in which it has a comparative advantage and to import those commodities in which it has a comparative disadvantage.

EXAMPLE: Use the example illustrated in Figure 5–1 to analyze the opportunity costs for a U.S. manufacturer and a Japanese producer. When analyzing the opportunity costs for the U.S. manufacturer, the opportunity cost of producing television sets must first be considered. If the U.S. producer can manufacture 200 television sets with the same resources, some of both products can be produced by diverting resources from televisions to stereos. In the extreme case, 200 televisions and no stereos or 400 stereos and no televisions could be produced with the same resources. If the U.S. producer started producing only televisions and then changed to producing only stereos, 200 televisions would be foregone to produce 400 stereos. The U.S. producer would be giving up one-half of a television set for every stereo produced. The opportunity cost of producing a stereo system would be one-half that of a television set. This opportunity cost represents the real cost of producing stereo systems.

A similar analysis can be used for the Japanese producer. If only television sets are produced, production would be 20 television sets. If the manufacturer then moves from producing only televisions to producing only stereos, 20 televisions must be given up to produce 200 stereos. The Japanese producer is giving up one-tenth of a television set for every stereo system produced. The opportunity cost to the manufacturer for producing television sets is one-tenth that of a stereo. Therefore, the cost of producing stereos by the Japanese producer is less than the cost of producing stereos by the U.S. producer (the cost to the Japanese producer is one-tenth of a television set compared to the cost to the U.S. producer, one-half of a television set).

Result: Since the cost of producing stereos is less, the Japanese producer would want to specialize in stereo production.

A similar analysis could be completed for the production of television sets. The cost of producing television sets to the U.S. producer is one television set for two stereos. For the Japanese producer, one television set is equal to 10 stereos. The U.S. producer has a comparative advantage in television production since what must be foregone in terms of stereos is less.

Result: The U.S. producer has an absolute advantage in the production of both televisions and stereos. However, the real cost of producing televisions and stereos is different for the two companies. As a result, the U.S. producer should specialize in producing televisions, and the Japanese manufacturer should specialize in stereo production.

3. *The Establishment of Trade*: Once specialization takes place, the profitability for the two countries (United States and Japan) to establish trade would be determined by the terms of trade.

EXAMPLE: Continuing the U.S./Japan example, for the U.S. manufacturer to produce televisions, 10 stereos must be foregone for every television set produced. If televisions can be purchased from the United States for an amount equivalent to less than 10 stereos, the U.S. producer would gain from the trade. On the other hand, for every television the U.S. producer foregoes, only two stereos can be produced. The U.S. producer would gain if the value of two stereos was traded for the value of one television set. Using that knowledge as the basis for trade, the U.S. producer will give up televisions for stereos if the value of the televisions exceeds that of two stereos. Similarly, the Japanese producer will give up stereos for televisions if a television set can be obtained by giving up less than 10 stereos. Thus, each producer can benefit from specialization and trade.

The principles in this example can be used to understand the establishment of international trade as well as interregional trade. Trade between two countries takes place in a manner similar to that of trade between regions within a country.

EXAMPLE: Figure 5–2 shows that the United States produces 100 bushels of wheat or 50 gallons of wine with a given set of resources. With those same resources, France can produce 50 bushels of wheat or 40 gallons of wine. Assuming that the quality of wheat and the quality of wine are the same, the United States has an absolute advantage in the production of both wheat and wine. However, according to the principle of comparative advantage, the United States must give up only one-half gallon of wine to produce a bushel of wheat, whereas France must give up four-fifths of a gallon of wine to produce a bushel of wheat. The United States has a comparative advantage in wheat production, and trade will take place as long as the United States has to give up less than two bushels of wheat for every gallon of wine. In return, France would receive more than four-fifths of a bushel of wheat for every gallon of wine. If the terms of trade were within this range, both countries could gain; and efficiency in the production of both wheat and wine would be attained.

4. *The Value of Establishing Trade*: The establishment of trade between two countries provides the opportunity for the following cooperative efforts to occur:

Figure 5-2   Wheat/Wine—U.S./France

	Wheat (bushels)	Wine (barrels)
United States	100	50
France	50	40

a. *Reallocation of resources*: Resources will be reallocated as each country expands employment of those resources needed for the production of goods for which that country holds a comparative advantage.

b. *Equalization of cost and commodity price differentials*: Relative price and cost differentials are a primary reason for trade, but trade will result only if these differences tend to be eliminated in the international market. It is the equalization of commodity prices and factor cost that must be gained from international trade. As long as price and cost disparities exist among nations, there will be the opportunity cost for gain by engaging in international trade.

C. Special Problems of International Trade

While the international trade theory presented above explains how countries gain from trade, particular circumstances often lead countries into minimizing the amount of international trade involvement. These circumstances can be classified as domestic policy and nationalism.

1. *Domestic Policy*: Traditionally, independent countries have monetary and fiscal controls that cause some exchange rate problems. If a country is attempting to reduce its rate of unemployment by expanding its economy through increased money supply, this has an adverse effect on that country's international trade position. Domestic inflation would increase the demand for imports and reduce the demand for exports. A country may want to follow an official policy of restricting imports during that period of time, so it can achieve domestic stability even though it does not gain as much from trade as possible. Barriers that a country imposes to achieve domestic goals include tariffs (taxes placed on imported commodities), quotas, and embargoes.

2. *Nationalism*: Nationalism is a belief that one's country should be self-sufficient and should not depend on other countries for goods and services. Nationalism often interferes with and restricts international trade.

   EXAMPLE: The common market in Europe is an example of the spirit of nationalism among countries in a region of the world. Among the common market countries, there is relatively free trade. However, there are restrictions to trade among members of the common market and the rest of the world. This is an attempt by the members of the common market to expand the ability of common market countries to be self-sufficient at the expense of international trade.

D. Elements of International Finance

International finance is the movement of monies from one country to another. Basic balance sheet accounting is used to analyze the flow of monies among countries. This balance sheet is referred to as the balance of payments.

1. *The Balance of Payments*: The balance of payments is an international summary statement of all economic and financial transactions between one country and the rest of the world for one year. The balance of payments distinguishes between debit payments and credits and receipts. Because of the double-entry nature of the accounting system, the debits must be equal to the credits in any balance of payments statement.

   a. *Debit*: A debit is any transaction that gives rise to a claim for payment against a resident of a country.

      EXAMPLE: John Q. American receives wine from France as a purchase or a gift. The fact that the wine from France enters the United States gives rise to a claim for payment from the United States to France. Thus, the value of the wine coming into the country is a debit item to the U.S. balance of payments.

      Any commodity or service coming into a country is a debit whether payment is made or not. Similarly, a cash outflow would be a capital outflow and a debit on the U.S. balance of payments.

      EXAMPLES:

      The purchase of a foreign corporation's stocks and bonds by an American citizen would be a debit on the U.S. balance of payments.

      Payments to U.S. military overseas represent debits to the U.S. balance of payments account.

   b. *Credit*: A credit to the balance of payments account would be a claim of the United States against a foreign country.

      EXAMPLES:

      The export of any good or service

      The purchase of American stocks and bonds by a citizen of a foreign country

      Any foreign investment in U.S. companies

   c. *Categories of debits and credits*: The debits and credits are divided into five categories within the balance of payments account:

      (1) *Current account*: Commodities and services, imports and exports.

      (2) *Net remittances and pensions*: Unilateral transfer or private gifts or grants between countries.

      (3) *Net government transactions*: Loans and grants made between countries.

      (4) *Net capital movements*: U.S. investment in foreign countries minus foreign countries' investments in the United States.

      (5) *Financing transactions*: Involvement of international reserves to make the balance of payments balance.

      A nation's balance of payments is considered in disequilibrium when the nation's autonomous payments are not sufficient to meet its autonomous receipts, thereby necessitating corresponding balancing, financing, or accommodating transactions, including foreign money sales and increases in nonresident liquid liabilities.

2. *International Exchange*: International exchange can be summarized in terms of payment for imports, export of goods and services, import surplus/unfavorable balance of trade, and long-term international capital movements.

   a. *Payment for imports*: To pay for its imports, a country must have foreign monies (foreign exchange) which will be demanded by the exporters. The possible sources for this exchange are

      (1)   The export of goods and services from one country to another

      (2)   The borrowing of money from abroad

      (3)   The receipt of gifts from abroad

      (4)   The liquidation of home-owned foreign assets

   b. *Export of goods and services*: The export of goods and services is the only way that will result in the acquisition of foreign dollars by a country over a long-term basis. Other forms of obtaining foreign capital can be used only temporarily or over short periods of time.

      EXAMPLE: When John Q. American borrows from abroad, this loan must be repaid at some point in time. Similarly, gifts from abroad cannot continue indefinitely.

      The export of goods and services is necessary for a country to have the long-term ability to trade.

   c. *Import surplus or unfavorable balance of trade*: Over short periods of time, a country may have an import surplus, also called an unfavorable balance of trade. The normal method of financing a persistent import surplus over several years is through long-term borrowing or long-term capital movement into the country.

   d. *Long-term international capital movements*: Long-term international capital movements are the means by which most developed countries obtain capital without reducing consumption. These capital movements rank second in importance to international imports and exports.

   International finance is simply a financial accounting of international transactions. The two important aspects of international finance are the balance of trade (the difference between the value of exports and the value of imports) and the balance of movement of capital. For a country to participate continually in the international market, it must have a balance, or surplus balance, trade account to finance other types of transactions.

E.   Commercial Policies

Countries may occasionally wish to engage in activities that may restrict international trade. These commercial policies are usually import tariffs, export tariffs, transit tariffs, and quotas. Tariffs and quotas are discussed in this section along with the economic effect and some arguments for these types of protection.

1. *Tariffs*: Tariffs are taxes levied on commodities as they move through a custom boundary.

   a. *Purposes of tariffs*: There are two general purposes of tariffs: protection and revenue.

      (1) *Protective tariffs*: Protective tariffs are typically import tariffs levied to protect domestic industry against foreign competition. The use of protective tariffs increases the cost of imported products, making it easier for domestic producers to compete. Most tariffs in the United States today are protective tariffs.

      (2) *Revenue tariffs*: Revenue tariffs are levied to benefit the country levying the tariff. Early tariffs levied in the continental United States, and some developing countries' tariffs levied in recent years, were based on revenue considerations. The impact of revenue tariffs on trade gains is less than that of the protective tariff. If revenue tariffs restricted trade, they would defeat their primary purpose, to gain revenue, since revenue could not be received if trade for the commodities ceased.

   b. *Types of tariffs*: There are three different types of tariffs: *ad valorem* tariffs, specific tariffs, and compound tariffs.

      (1) *Ad valorem tariffs*: *Ad valorem* tariffs are based on the value of the commodity.

         EXAMPLE: A tariff of 10 percent of the price of the goods, or some percentage of the price of the goods.

      (2) *Specific tariffs*: Specific tariffs are charges per physical unit of the good.

         EXAMPLE: A tariff of 10 cents per pound on imported beef.

      (3) *Compound tariffs*: Compound tariffs are based on *ad valorem* and physical units.

         EXAMPLE: A tariff of $100 per ton of steel plus 50 percent of its value.

      Each of these tariffs increases the price of the foreign good in the country imposing the tariff.

2. *Quotas*: Another form of commercial policy to restrict the amount of international trade is the *quota*. Two types of quotas are used: import quota and tariff quota.

   a. *Import quota*: Import quotas put a limit on the amount or value that can be imported into a country.

      EXAMPLE: An import quota could be initiated allowing only 500,000 tons of beef into the country in any given year. Once that quota is reached, no more beef may come in until the next quota period.

   b. *Tariff quota*: A tariff quota puts a low tariff or no tariff on goods imported into the country up to a certain amount. After that quota is reached, a higher tariff goes into effect. Tariffs provide revenues, while quotas benefit only those with import licenses.

EXAMPLE: There may be no tariff on imported beef for the first 100,000 pounds and a tariff of 50 cents per pound after that quota has been reached.

Quotas are generally considered to be more harmful than tariffs since quotas completely sever the price–cost relationship. Tariffs merely distort this relationship.

    c. *Embargo*: A unique form of quota is an embargo. During an embargo, no units of a particular commodity can be imported or, in some cases, exported.

        EXAMPLE: The United States placed an export embargo on all exports to Iraq in 1990.

3. *General Restrictive Devices*: A country can choose to place general restrictions on goods imported into or exported from the country.

EXAMPLES:

Sanitary regulations

Administrative protection

Milling regulations

Marks of origin

These practices would, in essence, restrict the amount of trade with a given country. U.S. commercial history shows wide swings between extremely high protective tariffs, such as those used in the 1930s, to low tariffs in the 1960s and 1970s. In general, vested self-interest groups have lobbied for tariffs which, though harmful to the country, benefit some workers in the protected industries.

4. *Economic Effects of Tariffs and Quotas*: The immediate impact of a tariff is to change the price–cost conditions of the importing and exporting countries. The price of the commodity in competitive equilibrium must be higher by exactly the amount of the tariff in the levying country compared to the exporting country. Free trade tends to equalize prices.

    a. *Economic effects of tariffs*: A tariff creates a price differential which, in competitive equilibrium, is exactly equal to the tariff. The differential can be achieved in three ways:

      (1) The price of the good can stay the same in the exporting country but rise in the importing country by the full amount of the tariff.

          EXAMPLE: Suppose that an English bicycle costs $100, and an import tariff of $25 is levied by the United States. In this instance, the price of the bicycle in England and in the international market would be $100, while in the United States the price would be $125.

      (2) The price in the exporting country would fall by the full amount of the tariff and stay the same in the importing country.

          EXAMPLE: In the example above, the price of the bicycle might fall to $75 in England and remain at $100 in the United States.

(3)   The price would fall some in the exporting country and rise some in the importing country.

EXAMPLE: The price of the bicycle in the United States would be between $100 and $125 or, in England, between $75 and $100, with the differential being $25.

Which country would bear the brunt of the tariff depends on the elasticity of the demand for the item and the supply of the item. A country with the judicious use of tariffs can improve its terms of trade and make foreigners pay part, or the major portion, of the tariff.

b.   *Economic effects of quotas*: The imposition of a quota tends to lower the supply, quantity demanded, and hence the price for the importing country, thereby improving its terms of trade.

(1)   A quota has no limits to its price effect; in contrast, a tariff has price-effect limits.

(2)   With a tariff, government gets the price differential; with a quota, the importer gets the price differential. When a quota is imposed, the availability of the goods demanded is reduced, which results in a higher price being paid by the consumer. The difference between the competitive price and the higher price is received by the importer.

c.   *Arguments against tariffs*: The economic argument against tariffs is that they prevent full realization of potential benefits from specialization in trade. The basis for a mutual gain in trade is the relative cost differences between countries. These differences narrow and eventually disappear with free trade as the world achieves more efficient allocation of its scarce resources. If protective tariffs or quotas are imposed, the movement toward the production cost differences is eliminated and, therefore, the need for countries to trade.

d.   *Arguments for protective tariffs*: There are five basic arguments for protective tariffs: protecting terms of trade, protecting infant industry, preventing unemployment, increasing military or political security, and protecting domestic wage levels.

(1)   *Protecting terms of trade*: It is possible for a country to have lower prices as a result of imposing import tariffs. This is true if the country is a large importer of goods or services and the country exporting the good depends on that as a substantial market. Thus, the exporting country would have to reduce its prices to an extent where the tariff had no negative effect on sales in the importing country. This is much like the monopolist who raises prices above the competitive level and gains monopoly profits. Of course, any gain realized with the country imposing the tariff is at the direct expense of the exporting country. The possibility of a country improving its terms of trade with a tariff depends heavily on that country being a world power in the importing of goods and services. That country must also be strong enough to prevent any retaliation on these types of tariffs from other countries.

(2)   *Protecting infant industry*: It is argued that tariffs can encourage economic growth and industrialization. Newly emerging industry finds it

difficult to develop in the face of competition from already established foreign firms in the same industries. Granting protection to infant industries allows them to become established.

EXAMPLE: The infant industry thesis was developed in the United States by Alexander Hamilton, the first Secretary of the Treasury. This thesis argued that new countries with newly developed industries could not compete with the same industries in established countries without protection during their "growing-up" or infancy period. Once the infancy period was completed, the protective tariffs would be eliminated.

While the infant industry argument has validity, it is difficult to determine which particular industries fit into the "infant" category. What happens in actual practice is that protection continues indefinitely and the protected industry continues to argue for protection indefinitely.

(3) *Preventing unemployment*: One way to reduce unemployment is to raise import tariffs and decrease imports. This decrease in imports would cause an increase in the demand for domestic goods and services and increase employment. The use of tariffs for prevention of unemployment simply transfers the unemployment in the country imposing the tariffs to other countries around the world. The imposition of tariffs for preservation of employment can also be answered by retaliation from foreign countries by imposing similar tariffs that would reduce the ability to export.

(4) *Increasing military or political security*: The military and political security argument has been the most popular argument for tariffs in recent years. This argument states that a country should continue to produce items essential for military security regardless of its inefficiency in that area.

EXAMPLE: During the 1973 Arab oil embargo, many people argued that the United States should become energy self-sufficient from a military protection standpoint. If the United States were not energy self-sufficient, we would be at the mercy of foreign countries to provide us with sources of energy during periods of war; and our ability to wage war would be reduced substantially.

One problem with limiting imports of foreign products to ensure domestic production is that the desired results may not be achieved. If restrictions were placed on importation of foreign crude oil, domestic reserves would have to be used. This would deplete a nonrenewable domestic resource faster than if foreign oil was imported.

EXAMPLE: If the United States becomes energy self-sufficient, we will be using domestic resource deposits of oil, uranium, and other energy forms more rapidly than we would if we also imported some of these energies from the rest of the world.

(5) *Protecting domestic wage levels*: Proponents of this theory argue that high-priced home labor will have to compete with low-priced foreign labor. As a result, home labor may be unemployed and/or have to accept

lower wages if industries in which these home laborers work are not protected. Individuals who are pro-tariff often cite the low wage levels that allow goods to be produced inexpensively in Hong Kong as an example of low-priced foreign labor.

This argument often confuses wage rates with wage costs. Wage rates are the wages per unit of labor, while wage costs are the wages per unit of output. The only meaningful comparison for international trade purposes is the wage cost. If labor productivity in the United States is five times higher than that in a foreign country, the wages in the United States could be as much as five times greater without any difference in wage costs.

Although each argument has some validity in terms of restriction of international trade, each will also prevent the efficient operation of a world economy. Another consequence would be higher costs and less output than free trade would produce. When considering policies that restrict trade, the real cost to a society and whether those costs are offset by domestic gains must be taken into account.

Review Questions

DIRECTIONS: Select the best answer from the four alternatives. Write the letter of your answer in the blank to the left of the number.

_____ 1. An increase in the tariff on foreign-produced automobiles would be least likely to benefit

    a. producers of automobiles.
    b. domestic consumers of automobiles.
    c. workers in the automobile industry.
    d. steel producers, if steel were used to produce domestic automobiles.

_____ 2. Each trading nation can gain by specializing in the production of those items for which they are low-opportunity-cost producers while trading for those things for which they are high-opportunity-cost producers. This statement best describes the implications of

    a. the export–import link.
    b. the industrial diversity argument.
    c. the law of comparative advantage.
    d. the equation of exchange.

_____ 3. A trade policy that reduces government-imposed restrictions preventing foreign goods from freely entering the U.S. market (for example, a reduction in tariffs) will

    a. reduce the demand for U.S. export goods.
    b. benefit producers at the expense of consumers.
    c. reduce the nation's income by failing to protect domestic jobs from foreign competition.
    d. enhance economic efficiency by allocating more resources to the areas of their greatest comparative advantage.

_____ 4. Which of the following is not an argument for protecting certain domestic industries from foreign competitors?

    a. The law of comparative advantage
    b. The national defense for protection argument
    c. The present unemployment argument
    d. The infant-industry argument

5. The share of GNP in the United States that results from exports is approximately

    a. 25 percent.
    b. 10 percent.
    c. 15 percent.
    d. 20 percent.

6. Specialization and trade, according to comparative advantage, tend to reduce cost while directing each output toward its highest valued use. Thus, total benefits increase while total output

    a. is reduced as a cost of specialization.
    b. is reduced in physical terms not in value.
    c. increases in the region gaining most and is reduced to the region gaining least.
    d. increases in the trading regions.

7. The law of comparative advantage explains why a nation will benefit from trade when

    a. it exports more than it imports.
    b. its trading partners are experiencing offsetting losses.
    c. it exports goods for which it is a high-opportunity-cost producer while importing those for which it is a low-opportunity-cost producer.
    d. it exports goods for which it is a low-opportunity-cost producer while importing those for which it is a high-opportunity-cost producer.

8. Which of the following is a credit to a government's balance of payments?

    a. U.S. citizen's purchase of stock in an English company
    b. Purchase of U.S. stock by an English citizen
    c. Payment to U.S. military personnel in Asia
    d. Value of a gift given by a U.S. citizen to a Canadian citizen

9. For which of the following reasons do producers export goods to other nations?

    a. They export goods because they believe in the law of comparative advantage.
    b. They export goods because they seek to increase the standard of living of persons in other countries.
    c. They export goods because they plan to use the compensation received as payment for resources to produce more goods and services and to purchase imports.
    d. They export goods so that they can obtain the currency of other nations, which they will attempt to hold indefinitely.

10. Which of the following does not restrict the volume of international trade?

    a. Quotas
    b. Tariffs
    c. High transportation cost
    d. A stable international monetary framework

11. A tariff differs from a quota in that

    a. a tariff is levied on imports, whereas a quota is imposed on exports.
    b. a tariff is levied on exports, whereas a quota is imposed on imports.
    c. a tariff is a tax levied by a foreign country, whereas a quota is a limit on the total trade allowed.
    d. a tariff is a tax imposed on imports, whereas a quota is an absolute limit to the number of units of a good that can be imported.

12. The infant-industry argument about tariffs states that

    a. it is unfair to levy tariffs on items intended for use by infants.
    b. tariffs should be levied on foreign products that compete with new domestic industries.
    c. tariffs should be levied on items intended for infants in order to protect domestic infant industries.
    d. permanent tariffs should be levied on foreign products that compete with those produced by domestic industries.

13. Suppose that the United States imposed a tariff on television sets, preventing foreign-produced television sets from freely entering the U.S. market. Which of the following would be most likely to occur?

    a. The price of television sets to U.S. consumers would increase, and the demand for U.S. export products would rise.
    b. The price of television sets to U.S. consumers would fall, and the demand for U.S. export products would fall.
    c. The price of television sets to U.S. consumers would increase, and the demand for U.S. export products would fall.
    d. The price of television sets to U.S. consumers would fall, and the demand for U.S. export products would rise.

14. Suppose that the Swiss government subsidized the watchmaking industry, enabling Swiss producers to undersell foreign watch producers. A watch-importing nation would take best advantage of the Swiss subsidization policy by

    a. setting a tariff high enough to discourage foreign competition against its domestic watchmaking industry.
    b. setting a declining quota on the import of Swiss watches such that its domestic watchmaking industry would continue to grow at the same rate as the rest of the economy.
    c. setting a tariff such that the prices of Swiss and domestic watches to the consumer are equal.
    d. gladly accepting the subsidy of the Swiss government, displacing the appropriate adjustment for the resources temporarily from the domestic watchmaking industry.

15. A no-trade situation exists in which the U.S. exports wheat to a foreign country. The U.S. domestic price

    a. and output of wheat would decline.
    b. and output of wheat would rise.
    c. of wheat would rise, but the domestic output would fall.
    d. of wheat would decline, but the domestic output would rise.

16. A situation exists where labor-intensive textile products can be produced more cheaply in low-wage countries than in the United States. The United States would gain if it

    a. levied a tariff on the goods produced by the cheap foreign labor.
    b. subsidized the domestic textile industry so that it could compete in international markets.
    c. used its resources to produce other items, while importing textiles from foreigners.
    d. levied a tax on the domestic textile products to penalize the industry for inefficiency.

Solutions

1. (b)   [E-1] Domestic consumers of foreign-produced automobiles would most likely experience the higher prices placed on the imported automobiles.

2. (c)   [B-2] The law of comparative advantage is based on specialization according to opportunity cost.

3. (d)   [E-1] A reduction in trade restrictions will increase imports and make more dollars available for foreigners to buy U.S. exports, thus increasing the demand for exports. In turn, this trade policy will make it possible for the United States as well as other countries to allocate resources to goods that can be produced to the greatest comparative advantage.

4. (a)   [E-4] Answers (b), (c), and (d) are all arguments for restricting trade, while (a) is the basis for trade.

5. (b)   [A-2] The figure for U.S. exports as a percent of GNP averages between 6 and 10 percent.

6. (d)   [B-2] Physical output is increased with specialization and trade.

7. (d)   [B-2] The principle of comparative advantage explains why one country would specialize in producing certain goods and importing others rather than producing all goods domestically.

8. (b)   [D-1] A purchase of U.S. stock by an English citizen would result in money moving into the United States from England and thus would be a credit to that government's balance of payments.

9. (c)   [A-1, B-2-b] The law of comparative advantage provides a rationale for specialization and trade, but belief in it alone does not justify exports. Producers export goods in order to market their products, thus receiving payment that can be invested in future production.

10. (d)   [E-1, E-2] A stable international monetary framework would encourage the increase in international trade. Quotas place restriction on imports. Tariffs increase price, thus reducing quantity demand and the level of imports.

11. (d)   [E-1, E-2] This statement identifies a primary difference between tariffs and quotas.

12. (b)   [E-4-d(2)] The infant industry agreement applies to the short run only. Tariffs are imposed only on foreign products that, in the long run, will compete with new domestic industries.

13. (c)   [E-1] Restrictions on imports would increase the cost of imports, leading to increased demand for domestic television sets that would result in price increases. In addition, since sales of foreign television sets would decrease, the supply of U.S. dollars in foreign countries would fall and reduce the demand for U.S. exports.

14. (d)   [E-4] Accepting the subsidy of the Swiss government would enable trade to continue between the countries, and the watchmaking industry would certainly benefit over time within both countries.

15. (b)   [A-1] A no-trade situation would result in a rise in domestic prices, and producers would want to increase output. The export of wheat will reduce the domestic supply and cause prices to increase.

16. (c)   [E-4] Those products that could be produced more inexpensively in low-wage countries should be imported by the United States so that resources could be used more wisely for the production of other goods.

CHAPTER 6

Introduction to Accounting

OVERVIEW

This chapter is designed to introduce the candidate to the study of accounting. Understanding the basic concepts, principles, and functions of accounting should aid the candidate in preparing for the CPS examination.

KEY TERMS

Accounting
Accounting entity
Assets
Audit (independent external)
Bookkeeping
Conservatism
Consistency
Corporation
Estimation
External financial reports
External users
Full disclosure

Generally accepted accounting
  principles (GAAP)
Going concern
Historical cost
Internal financial reports
Internal users
Materiality
Money measurement
Objectivity
Partnership
Periodicity

A. Accounting Process

Accounting is the process of recording, measuring, summarizing, analyzing, and interpreting financial information and communicating this information to various users for decision-making purposes.

1. *Accounting Entity*: Accounting information is recorded separately for each accounting entity. An accounting entity is any business, individual, or not-for-profit organization whose financial affairs can be viewed as being distinct from those of any other entity or unit.

EXAMPLE: John Jones owns and operates a small grocery store. John Jones is one accounting entity, and his grocery store is an entirely separate business entity. Separate accounting records should be kept for John and his store. If John Jones mixes the recording of his personal and business expenses, he will be unable to make valid decisions about the profitability of his business.

2. *Types of Business Entities*: Accountants are concerned primarily with three basic types of business entities: the sole proprietorship, the partnership, and the corporation.

   a. *Sole proprietorship*: A business owned by one individual. A sole proprietorship is not a separate legal entity from its owner; however, it is a separate accounting entity.

   b. *Partnership*: A business with two or more owners who have agreed to operate as co-owners and who share the profits and losses of the business in an agreed-upon proportion. For most purposes a partnership is not a separate legal entity from its owners; however, it is a separate accounting entity.

   c. *Corporation*: A separate legal entity created by state or federal law. Corporations usually have the same legal rights and obligations as individuals. To form a corporation, a corporate charter must be obtained from the state where the business is formed. A corporation issues shares of capital stock in exchange for money, assets, or services. Owners of the capital stock are called *stockholders* or *shareholders* of the company; stockholders are the owners of the corporation.

      Corporations are both separate legal entities and separate accounting entities. Characteristics of corporations as well as the advantages and disadvantages of the three types of business entities are discussed further in Chapter 16.

3. *Recording Financial Information*: Financial information is normally recorded when an economic transaction takes place.

   a. *Money measurement*: There must be a common unit of measure for recording economic events. In accounting, money is that unit of measure. This is known as the *money measurement principle*.

      EXAMPLE: A business has $500 in the bank and owns a building. If the business wishes to determine the total value of its assets, a monetary value must first be assigned to the building.

   b. *Historical cost*: If accountants are to record the building in the previous example as a monetary value, it is necessary to make an assumption in determining that value. There are a number of possible alternatives for valuation. For example, cost of replacing the building, potential selling price of the building, the owner's estimation of the fair market value, or original purchase cost might be used to value the building. In accounting, it has been decided that the original purchase (historical) cost should be used to value assets.

      (1) Historical cost was chosen because it can be determined with objectivity. The term *objective* in accounting refers to valuations that can be factually substantiated and can be verified by an independent party. Historical cost is determined in a market transaction, and it is easily verifiable. At the time an asset is acquired, the cost represents the fair market value of

the asset. The other valuation methods suggested result in subjective estimates of value that are changing constantly.

    (2)   As time passes, historical cost may not represent the current fair market value of the asset. Because operational assets are not intended for resale, however, current market value may not be relevant to accounting purposes.

    c. *Stable dollar*: Another assumption of accounting is the *stable dollar concept*. The stable dollar concept assumes that a dollar today is worth the same amount as a dollar used to buy an asset in the past.

4. *Classifying Financial Information*: After financial information is recorded, it must be classified according to the areas that are affected. This is done by recording information in different accounts.

5. *Summarizing Financial Information*: Due to the large number of economic transactions that are recorded, the information must be summarized into reports in order for decision makers to be able to use it effectively.

EXAMPLE: Ajax Company recorded 5,000 transactions in June. These transactions related to purchases of materials; sales of goods to customers; payments for utilities, rent, and services; salaries paid to employees; and various other business activities. Accountants summarize the financial data into reports before providing the information to decision makers.

6. *Using Accounting Information*: A number of different groups use accounting information. Such users may be *internal* or *external* users of accounting information.

    a. *Internal users*: The managers of a business represent one important group of users of accounting information. Managers are generally referred to as internal users of accounting data.

    b. *External users*: There are a number of users of accounting data external to the company's management. A business would be unable to issue one set of financial statements that meets the specific needs of all groups of external users. General purpose financial statements are prepared and issued for use by external users of accounting data.

    EXAMPLES OF EXTERNAL USERS: Bankers, creditors, investors, stockholders, employees, customers, and governmental agencies.

B.   Reporting Accounting Information

1. *External Financial Statements*: The standard general-purpose reports (financial statements) that are issued are the balance sheet (the statement of financial position), the income statement, the statement of retained earnings, and the statement of cash flows.

    a. *Generally accepted accounting principles*: The format of these statements and the methods of recording the data summarized within them are governed by a set of rules called *generally accepted accounting principles*. These rules are considered necessary because external users do not normally have access to financial information other than that provided by management of the company. Generally accepted accounting principles (GAAP) consist of pronouncements issued by the accounting profession, industry-wide practices, and other methods developed over the history of accounting which have authoritative support. GAAP are currently set by a private-sector organization called the Financial Accounting Standards Board (FASB). The rules comprising generally accepted accounting principles will be discussed throughout the rest of this module.

b. *Audits*: In order that external users may have more confidence in external financial reports, they may be audited by an independent Certified Public Accountant (CPA). An audit consists of an independent auditor (CPA) reviewing the financial statements to determine their conformity with generally accepted accounting principles. The auditor then issues an opinion regarding the fairness of the financial statements. A CPA might also perform a number of accounting services for a business such as management advising or tax return preparation. The major function of a CPA is to perform an audit of the financial statements.

2. *Internal Financial Reports*: Internal reports generated for use by managers within the particular accounting entity do not need to follow generally accepted accounting principles. Internal users have access to the entity's accounting information system and are able to request reports in any form they desire. Internal financial reports are generally more detailed than external reports. There are certain accounting reports and techniques frequently used by managerial accountants. These are discussed in more detail in Chapter 19. Managers of the business also use the financial statements generated for external users in making decisions about the operations of the company.

C. Basic Concepts and Principles

Some of the basic concepts, principles, and methods used in accounting are introduced here. Many of them are elaborated on in later chapters.

1. *Going Concern*: In accounting, the going-concern assumption states that the accountant assumes that the entity is going to exist for an indefinite period of time. The going-concern assumption is often used to justify the historical cost concept. Since we assume that the business entity will continue in existence for an indefinite period of time, the fixed assets of the entity will be needed to continue its operations. The fixed assets cannot be sold without disrupting the operations of the business. Thus, historical cost is a relevant measure of the value of the fixed assets being used by the business.

2. *Relevance*: Accounting information must be relevant or pertain to the specific decisions that are to be made from the information.

3. *Periodicity*: The life of an entity is divided into time intervals for reporting purposes. The only time an *exact* accounting of the financial affairs of an entity can be made is at the end of the life of the entity. If an entity is a going concern, decision makers need accounting information about the entity prior to its termination in order to make decisions. The accountant must make periodic reports about the economic affairs of the entity. The traditional time period for financial reporting is one year. An accounting period that consists of 12 consecutive months is called a *fiscal year*. When a fiscal year ends on December 31, it is called a *calendar year-*

end. A fiscal period may also follow the natural business year and end when inventories are at their lowest point and business activities are at their lowest level.

4. *Estimation*: The student of accounting needs to realize that much of what is included in financial reports is an estimate. Since accountants divide the life of an entity into arbitrary periodic time intervals, it is necessary to estimate many of the amounts included in the periodic financial reports.

5. *Consistency*: Consistency is the accounting principle which requires that once an accounting or reporting method is selected, it should be used from one period to another. This ensures that financial reports of an entity will be comparable from period to period. If a change in accounting method is made, the consistency principle requires that the change be disclosed in the financial statements.

6. *Conservatism*: The principle of conservatism requires that when doubt exists about the valuation of an asset or the recording of an accounting transaction, the accounting method that is the least likely to overstate income and financial position should be chosen.

7. *Full Disclosure*: The full disclosure principle requires that all information that may be relevant to decision makers be communicated to them through the financial statements.

8. *Materiality*: Materiality refers to the relative importance of an item or event to the decisions that users will be making. If an item is very insignificant when compared to other items, it is not necessary to follow accounting theory precisely. In determining materiality, the important consideration is whether knowledge of the item would influence the decisions of users. Materiality is a relative concept.

EXAMPLE: For a company with sales of $100,000, $10,000 would be material; whereas $10,000 would be immaterial for a company with $10,000,000 in sales.

Review Questions

DIRECTIONS: Select the best answer from the four alternatives. Write the letter of your answer in the blank to the left of the number.

_d_

1. The process that involves identifying, recording, measuring, and communicating *summarizing, analyzing* financial information is

   a. bookkeeping.
   b. relevance.
   c. generally accepted accounting principles.
   d. accounting. *for decision making purposes.*

_c_

2. The principle which requires that the accounting method used be the one least likely to overstate income and financial position is called

   a. the consistency principle.
   b. the objectivity principle.
   c. the conservatism principle.
   d. the periodicity concept.

_b_

3. The accounting concept which states that accounting information should pertain to the problem at hand and provide useful information about the problem is

   a. objectivity.
   b. relevancy.
   c. full disclosure.
   d. materiality.

_a_

4. The accounting principle which requires that once an accounting or reporting method is selected it should be used from one period to another is

   a. consistency.
   b. periodicity.
   c. estimation.
   d. comparability.

_d_

5. Accounting reports issued solely for use by the management of a company are called

   a. external reports.
   b. periodic reports.

c. balance sheets.

d. internal reports.

a

6. The going-concern assumption

a. states that the accountant assumes that the entity will exist for an indefinite period of time.

b. requires that assets be written up to market value when market value is higher than the cost of the asset.

c. requires that the accounting method least likely to overstate income and financial position be chosen.

d. states that the life of an entity is limited.

a

7. Generally accepted accounting principles

a. are currently set by the Financial Accounting Standards Board.

b. must be followed when reporting to internal financial statement users.

c. consist only of pronouncements issued by the accounting profession.

d. state that assets should be reported at replacement cost.

d

8. A corporation

a. is a separate legal entity.

b. normally has the same rights and obligations as an individual.

c. requires obtaining a corporate charter.

d. all of the above.

c

9. The principal function of an independent CPA is to

a. prepare tax returns.

b. conduct an audit the purpose of which is to guarantee that the financial statements are free of fraud.

c. conduct an audit to determine whether the company's financial statements are presented fairly in accordance with GAAP.

d. provide advisory services to management.

b

10. Lew Co. purchased a plot of land for $100,000 five years ago. The appraised value of the land at that time was $105,000. Land in this area is generally worth about 50 percent more today than it was five years ago. The value of the land on Lew Co.'s current records should be

a. $105,000.

b. $100,000.

c. $150,000.

d. $152,000.

Solutions

Answer	Refer to:		Answer	Refer to:
1. (d)	[A]		**6.** (a)	[C-1]
2. (c)	[C-6]		**7.** (a)	[B-1-a]
3. (b)	[C-2]		**8.** (d)	[A-2-c]
4. (a)	[C-5]		**9.** (c)	[B-1-b]
5. (d)	[B-2]		**10.** (b)	[A-3-b]

Answer *Refer to:*

CHAPTER 7

Theory and Classification of Accounts

OVERVIEW

The theory and classification of accounts is the most fundamental area in accounting. The candidate must thoroughly understand the recording of debits and credits in asset, liability, owners' equity, revenue, and expense accounts in order to understand the discipline of accounting.

The candidate should understand the definitions of asset, liability, owners' equity, revenue, and expense accounts; how to record transactions in the accounts; and the accounting equation and its relationship to debits and credits in the accounts.

KEY TERMS

Account
Account balance
Accounting equation
Accounts payable
Accounts receivable
Accrual
Assets
Capital stock
Credit
Debit
Dividend
Double-entry accounting
Expenses
Inventory
Journal

Ledger
Liability
Matching
Net income
Owners' equity
Permanent accounts
Posting
Retained earnings
Revenue
Revenue realization
Source document
Stockholders' equity
T-account
Temporary accounts

A. Accounts

Accounts are used for the collection and summarization of data resulting from economic transactions. An account is a device used to collect and summarize information. Accounts are sometimes called ledger accounts.

1. *Recording Information in Accounts*: The data comprising an account may be recorded in a number of forms.

   a. *Computerized systems*: Many companies keep their accounting records on a computer; their accounts are recorded in the form of magnetic tape or disks.

   b. *Manual systems*: A company using a manual accounting system might use a three-column account format (see Figure 7–1).

2. *Using T-Accounts*: The easiest way to represent an account for instructional or problem-solving purposes is to use a T-account. A T-account resembles a capital T. T-accounts are *teaching tools* and are not used in the actual recording of data by businesses.

EXAMPLE:

Name of the Account

| debit side (abbreviated *dr*) | credit side (abbreviated *cr*) |

3. *Recording Debits and Credits*: A debit is an entry recorded on the left-hand side of a T-account. A credit is an entry recorded on the right-hand side of a T-account. It is important that the candidate understand that debit and credit simply mean left- and right-hand sides of an account, respectively. Debits and credits also connote adding to or deducting from an account.

4. *Recording Entries*: Entries for individual transactions are recorded in the various accounts. Each account serves as a summary of a particular type of transaction during a period of time.

5. *Calculating the Account Balances*: The difference between the total debits and total credits recorded in an account is called the *account balance*. (Note that the T-account in Figure 7–2 is a record of the same information as Figure 7–1.)

Figure 7–1   Three-Column Account—Cash Account

Date	Explanation	Ref	Receipts (dr)	Payments (cr)	Balance
1/1	Beginning balance	√			100.00
1/5	Purchased materials	CD #1		50.00	
1/10	Sold materials	CR #2	25.00		75.00

Figure 7–2   Cash Account

Cash

	dr	cr	
Balance 1/1	100.00		
1/10 Sold merchandise	25.00	50.00	1/5 Purchased merchandise
Balance 1/10	75.00		

6.   *The Ledger:* A record of all the accounts of a business is called the ledger.

B.   Classification of Permanent Accounts

1.   Assets: Assets are economic resources from which an owner can expect to receive benefits now or in the future. Here is another way of defining the term assets: things of value that are owned by the entity.

a.   Asset accounts: Some asset accounts are cash, accounts receivable, notes receivable, inventory, prepaid expenses, land, buildings, equipment, supplies, investments, patents, copyrights, and goodwill. The term receivable refers to an asset that is an amount the business has the right to collect in the future from another party.

b.   *Debits and credits*: Increases in assets are recorded as *debits*. Decreases in assets are recorded as *credits*. Asset accounts normally have debit balances. The normal balance of any account falls on the increase side of the account.

EXAMPLE:

Asset Account

dr	cr
Normal balance	
Increases are recorded as debits	Decreases are recorded as credits

c.   *Recording of assets*: As discussed earlier, assets are recorded at cost following the money measurement, stable dollar, and historical cost conventions of accounting. This is done because costs can be objectively determined and verified.

2.   *Liabilities*: Liabilities are obligations or debts of an entity that are owed to other parties. Liabilities come about from purchasing goods or services on credit; borrowing cash to finance the operations of the business; receipt of payment in advance of providing a product or service; and the adjustment process discussed in Chapter 9, Section F. Accounts payable constitute one of the liabilities of a business. Accounts payable arise when a company purchases merchandise on credit for use in its business.

a. *Liability accounts*: Some liability accounts are accounts payable, notes payable, mortgages payable, bonds payable, wages payable, and unearned income. The term *payable* refers to an obligation the entity owes another party.

b. *Debits and credits*: Increases in liabilities are recorded as *credits*. Decreases in liabilities are recorded as *debits*. Liability accounts normally have credit balances.

EXAMPLE:

Liability Account

dr	*cr*
	Normal balance
Decreases are recorded as debits	Increases are recorded as credits

3. *Owners' Equity (Stockholders' Equity)*: Owners' equity represents the resources invested in the business by owners. Owners' equity is a residual claim. This means that legally, the claims of creditors (liabilities) come first and owners are entitled to whatever remains after creditors are paid.

owners' equity = total assets − total liabilities

EXAMPLE: The ABC Company has total assets equaling $5,000. The firm owes suppliers $1,000 for goods purchased on credit (accounts payable) and has a $2,000 note owed to the bank. Therefore, total liabilities at this time are $3,000. Owners' equity is the residual amount of $2,000 ($5,000 total assets minus $3,000 total liabilities).

a. *Sole proprietorship*: In a sole proprietorship, owner's equity is recorded in the owner's capital account.

EXAMPLE: John Jones owns a sole proprietorship. His owner's equity account is called John Jones, Capital.

b. *Partnership*: In a partnership, each owner has a separate capital account.

c. *Corporation*: In a corporation, owners' equity is divided into two categories. Investment by owners of the corporation is classified as contributed capital, and earnings of the company that have been retained in the business are classified as retained earnings.

d. *Increases in owners' equity*: Owners' equity may be increased in two ways:

(1) From investment by owners

(2) From retention of earnings generated by the business

e. *Decreases in owners' equity*: Owners' equity may be decreased in two ways:

(1) Through distribution of cash or other assets of the business to its owners

(2) Through losses incurred in the operation of the business

f. *Debits and credits to owners' equity*: Increases in owners' equity are recorded as *credits*. Decreases in owners' equity are recorded as *debits*. The normal balance of owners' equity is a credit.

EXAMPLE:

Owners' Equity Account

dr	*cr*
	Normal balance
Decreases are recorded as debits	Increases are recorded as credits

4. *Balance Sheet Accounts:* Asset, liability, and owners' equity accounts are included on the *balance sheet* of an entity. They are called balance sheet, permanent, or real accounts. These accounts remain on the books of the business permanently. The balance sheet is also known as the *statement of financial position.* (The balance sheet is discussed in Chapter 8.)

C. The Accounting Equation

The accounting equation is a representation of the relationship: "Assets are equal to liabilities plus owners' equity":

$$\text{assets} = \text{liabilities} + \text{owners' equity}$$

1. *Equality Represented*: This equality must always hold true in accounting since assets must always be equal to the rights or claims associated with the assets.

2. *Sources of Assets*: Another way of looking at the liabilities and owners' equity side of the equation is to view liabilities and owners' equity as sources of the assets. All of the resources used to obtain assets are provided either through creditors' holdings (liabilities) or through owners' investments (owners' equity).

EXAMPLE: Sara Stone has started a business that sells bicycles. She has named the business Stone's Bicycles. She purchased 20 bicycles for $2,000 on June 1, 19XA. She used $1,000 of her own money to buy the bicycles and borrowed $1,000 from the bank. She gave the bank a six-month note payable in exchange for the $1,000. Stone's Bicycles has $2,000 worth of assets represented by the bicycles. Sara has ownership rights or owners' equity in the amount of $1,000 which she contributed toward the purchase of the bicycles. Since Sara used $1,000 of borrowed money to purchase the bicycles, she does not have owners' equity equal to the total amount of the cost of the bicycles. The bank owns some of the equity in the bicycles in the form of a claim against the assets (a liability). The bank's claim is the right to be repaid $1,000 six months from now. The accounting equation for Stone's Bicycles would appear as follows:

$$\text{assets} = \text{liabilities} + \text{owners' equity}$$
$$\$2,000 = \$1,000 \quad + \quad \$1,000$$

3. *Continual Changes in Composition*: The composition of the assets, liabilities, and owners' equity of a business changes continually. However, the equality of the basic equation must always be maintained.

4. *Residual Aspect of Owners' Equity*: The accounting equation may be written as assets − liabilities = owners' equity. When written in this way, it emphasizes the residual aspect of owners' equity.

5. *Double-Entry Accounting*: Whenever an accounting transaction is recorded, the total dollar amount of the debits recorded must equal the total dollar amount of the credits recorded. If a larger amount of debits were recorded than credits, or vice versa, the accounting equation would be out of balance. This recording of an equal amount of debits and credits is called *double-entry accounting*. It is also sometimes referred to as the duality concept. By recording data in this fashion, a periodic check of the equality of the total debit and credit balances in the accounts can be made and used to help in discovering errors made in recording transactions.

D. Recording Accounting Transactions

1. *Journalization*: Accounting transactions are first recorded in *journals* or books of original entry. This is called journalization. Transactions are recorded in a journal in chronological order.

   a. *Source document*: When accounting transactions occur, some sort of document is usually prepared. This document is called a *source document*. Source documents serve as the source of information for recording transactions in the journal. Examples of source documents include checks, sales invoices, purchase orders, and receipts. Source documents are often called business papers.

   b. *General journal*: This is the most common type of journal. When a business keeps only a general journal, all types of transactions are recorded in the general journal. (Some businesses may keep special journals as well as a general journal. Special journals are discussed in Chapter 10.)

      (1) The general journal serves as a complete record of each accounting transaction since both sides of the transaction are recorded in one place.

      (2) The general journal entry contains the following elements:

          (a) Date of the transaction

          (b) Ledger account to be debited and the amount

          (c) Ledger account to be credited and the amount

          (d) An explanation of the transaction including an identification of the source document

Figure 7–3   General Journal

Page 10

Date	Explanation	Ref	Debit	Credit
Aug. 8	Machinery Cash Purchased stamping machine, check number 112		2,000	2,000

EXAMPLE: ABC Company purchased a machine for $2,000 cash on August 8. This transaction would be recorded in the general journal as shown in Figure 7–3. The account (or accounts) to be debited is listed first, and the amount is recorded in the debit column. The account (or accounts) to be credited is listed next, and the amount is recorded in the credit column. Note that the account to be credited is indented. This indentation is used to indicate that the account is credited. Following the debit and credit entries is an explanation of the transaction. The reference column is provided so that the journal entry may be cross-indexed to the ledger account.

To conserve space, the journal entries throughout the rest of the book will be presented in the following format:

	dr	cr
Aug. 8 Machinery	2,000	
Cash		2,000
Purchased stamping machine		
Check number 112		

Note that the position of the accounts indicates which account is to be debited and which is to be credited. The explanation may be omitted from journal entries when the transaction is routine and the entry is clear without the explanation.

2. *Posting to the Ledger*: Information that is recorded in the journal is transferred periodically to the ledger accounts. The transfer of information from the journal to the ledger is called *posting*.

Figure 7–4 shows the posting of the transaction journalized in Figure 7–3 to the ledger. The debit side of the journal entry is posted first. The machinery ledger account is located, the debit amount from the journal entry is recorded in the debit column, the date of the transaction is recorded, and the journal page number from which the entry was taken is recorded in the reference column. The ledger account number is then recorded in the reference column of the journal. This is done to cross-reference the entry and to record that the transaction has been posted. The referencing procedure may be somewhat different depending on the business involved. Some sort of referencing is necessary to provide an audit trail. The *audit*

Figure 7–4   Cash/Machinery Accounts

Acct. #01 Cash

Date	Explanation	Ref	Debit	Credit	Balance
					10,000
Aug. 8		10		2,000	8,000

Acct. #10 Machinery

Date	Explanation	Ref	Debit	Credit	Balance
					100,000
Aug. 8		10	2,000		102,000

trail is the information that makes it possible for the accountant to trace each transaction back to its source document to determine that it was recorded properly. The same procedure would be followed for transferring the credit entry to the cash account.

3. *Typical Accounting Transactions*: In the following examples, journal entries are shown, and the amounts are posted to T-accounts. The T-accounts represent the general ledger. The explanations will be omitted from the journal entries, although in reality they would be included.

a. Henry Smith starts a small business repairing television sets. On August 1, he invests $1,000 of his own money in the business. This transaction results in an increase in the asset Cash of $1,000 and an increase in Owner's Equity of $1,000. The journal entry would be:

		dr	cr
Aug. 1	Cash	1,000	
	Owner's equity		
	(Henry Smith capital)		1,000

This is posted as transaction A in the T-accounts in Figure 7–5.

Figure 7–5   Cash/Equipment Accounts

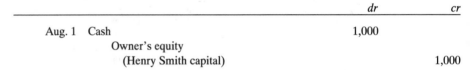

dr Cash			cr
A. Aug. 1	1,000		
B. Aug. 3	2,000	C. Aug. 8	1,500
		D. Aug. 10	500
		E. Aug. 20	250
Bal. Aug. 20	750		

Equipment and Tools

C. Aug. 8	1,500		
Bal. Aug. 20	1,500		

Notes Payable

		B. Aug. 3	2,000
		Bal. Aug. 20	2,000

Inventory of Parts

D. Aug. 10	750		
Bal. Aug. 20	750		

Accounts Payable

E. Aug. 20	250	D. Aug. 10	250
		Bal. Aug. 20	-0-

Owners' Equity

		A. Aug.1	1,000
		Bal. Aug. 20	1,000

b. Henry borrowed $2,000 from the bank on August 3. He gave the bank a note payable. As a result of this transaction, the asset *cash* is increased by $2,000 and the liability *notes payable* is increased by $2,000. The journal entry would be:

	dr	cr
Aug. 3 Cash	2,000	
Notes payable		2,000

See transaction B in the T-accounts in Figure 7–5.

c. Henry purchased $1,500 of testing equipment and tools for use in his business on August 8. He paid for the equipment in cash. This transaction resulted in an increase in the asset *equipment and tools* of $1,500 and a decrease in the asset *cash* of $1,500. The journal entry would be:

	dr	cr
Aug. 8 Equipment and tools	1,500	
Cash		1,500

See transaction C in the T-accounts in Figure 7–5.

d. Henry purchased $750 worth of parts to use in repairing television sets on August 10. He paid for the parts by using $500 cash and charging the other $250 on open account. This transaction resulted in an increase of $750 in the asset *inventory of parts,* a decrease of $500 in the asset *cash*, and an increase of $250 in the liability *accounts payable.* The journal entry would be:

	dr	cr
Aug. 10 Inventory of parts	750	
Cash		500
Accounts payable		250

This journal entry is called a *compound journal entry* because more than two accounts are affected by the transaction. This transaction is posted as transaction D in Figure 7–5.

e. Henry paid the $250 account payable on August 20 using cash. As a result of this transaction, the asset *cash* decreased by $250 and the liability *accounts payable* decreased by $250. The journal entry would be:

	dr	cr
Aug. 20 Accounts payable	250	
Cash		250

See transaction E in the T-accounts in Figure 7–5.

f. After recording transactions A through E, the T-accounts have been totaled to determine the account balances. When the increases and decreases recorded in an account are separately added and the sum of the decreases is subtracted from the sum of the increases, the procedure is called *determining the account balance.* Note that the asset accounts *cash, inventory of parts,* and *equipment and tools* all have debit balances. The liability *accounts payable* has a zero balance, and the liability *notes payable* has a credit balance. The *owner's equity* account also has a credit balance.

Total Assets		Total Liabilities and Owner's Equity	
Cash	750	Notes payable	2,000
Inventory of parts	750	Owner's equity	1,000
Equipment and tools	1,500		
Total	3,000	Total	3,000

Total Assets = Total Liabilities and Owner's Equity
Total Debits = Total Credits

E. Classification of Temporary Accounts

1. *Revenues*: Revenues are earnings resulting from the receipt of cash or other assets (or the reduction of a liability) in exchange for goods sold by an entity or services performed by an entity.

    a. *Revenue realization principle*: Revenue is usually recognized only after exchange has taken place or a service has been rendered.

    EXAMPLES:

    Henry Smith repaired his neighbor's television set and received $85 for his services. The $85 represents revenue earned by Henry in exchange for his services. The account used to record revenue from services is called service fees or service revenue.

    Stone's Bicycles sold two bicycles for a total of $250. The person who purchased the bicycles promised to pay for them within 30 days. The $250 represents revenue earned from the sale of goods. The fact that the $250 has not yet been received in cash does not affect the recording of revenue since an exchange has taken place. The account used to record revenue from the sale of goods is called sales.

    b. *Increases and decreases in revenues*: Increases in revenues are recorded as credits. Decreases in revenues are recorded as debits. Revenue accounts normally have a credit balance.

    EXAMPLE:

    Revenue Account

dr	*cr*
	Normal balance
Decreases are recorded as debits	Increases are recorded as credits

2. *Expenses*: Expenses are the costs of goods and services consumed (used up) by the entity as a result of earning revenue.

    a. *Incurring expenses*: To earn revenue, it is necessary to incur expenses.

    EXAMPLES:

    The cost of the parts that Henry Smith used in repairing his neighbor's television set represents an expense or cost used up in earning revenue.

The rent for the building where Sara Stone stores her bicycles represents an expense. It is a cost incurred to produce revenue.

b. *Increases and decreases in expenses*: Increases in expenses are recorded as debits. Decreases in expenses are recorded as credits. Expense accounts normally have a debit balance.

EXAMPLE:

Expense Account

dr	*cr*
Normal balance	
Increases are recorded as debits (+)	Decreases are recorded as credits (−)

3. *Net Income*:

$$revenues - expenses = net\ income$$

The excess of total revenues over total expenses of an entity represents the *net income* of the entity. Net income is measured over a specific period of time. If total expenses exceed total revenues, a *net loss* is incurred.

a. *Reporting net income*: Net income is reported periodically on the income statement.

b. *Accrual concept*: Revenues should be reported when earned rather than when the cash is received, and expenses should be reported when incurred rather than when paid.

EXAMPLE: The previous example, where Stone's Bicycles sold two bicycles in exchange for an account receivable, illustrates the accrual concept. The revenue was reported when earned (at the time of the sale) rather than when the cash was received.

c. *Matching principle*: The matching principle states that expenses incurred in earning revenues should be matched with those revenues to determine net income. Expenses should be reported in the same period as the revenues to which they correspond.

EXAMPLE: Arnold is a salesman for the ABC Company. During July, he sold merchandise totaling $100,000. His sales commission will be included as part of his August paycheck. The sales commission should be reported as an expense on ABC's records in July. In this way the sales revenue and sales commission expense are matched.

d. *Increases in owners' equity*: Net income represents an increase in owners' equity. A net loss represents a decrease in owners' equity.

e. *Income summary account*: At the end of an accounting period, revenues and expenses are closed to an income summary account, which is then closed to owners' equity. Revenue, expenses, income summary, and drawing accounts are called temporary accounts since they are closed periodically to owners' equity. The closing process is discussed in Chapter 9.

4. *Investments by Owners*:

    a. *Increases in assets and owners' equity*: Additional investments by owners of a business are not revenue. They are recorded as increases in assets and increases in owners' equity.

    b. *Sale of stock*: If a corporation sells shares of stock, the resulting cash obtained is not revenue but an additional investment by owners. The sale of stock is recorded as an increase in the asset *cash* and an increase in the owners' equity account *capital stock.*

5. *Withdrawals and Dividends*:

    a. *Withdrawal of assets*: Withdrawals of assets from a business by the owners are not expenses. They are a decrease in the owners' equity in the business. A withdrawal is recorded as a decrease in cash and a decrease in owners' equity.

    b. *Dividends*: Dividends represent distributions of assets by a corporation to its owners (stockholders).

        (1) Dividends are paid to stockholders when declared by the corporation's board of directors.

        (2) Payment of a dividend is not an expense. It is a distribution of assets similar to a withdrawal of assets by owners in a sole proprietorship.

6. *Typical Transactions Including Revenues and Expenses*: In the following examples, journal entries are shown, as well as postings to T-accounts. The T-accounts are shown in Figure 7–6. Waldorf Corporation sells widgets. The following are some of the transactions for Waldorf Corporation for the month of January.

    a. Waldorf Corporation sold 10,000 widgets during January. Two thousand widgets were sold for cash, and 8,000 widgets were sold on account. Widgets sell for $10 each. As a result of this transaction, sales revenue was increased by $100,000 (10,000 units sold × $10 per unit); cash was increased by $20,000 (2,000 units sold for cash × $10 per unit) and accounts receivable was increased by $80,000 (8,000 units sold on open account × $10 per unit). The journal entry to record this transaction would be:

	dr	cr
Cash	20,000	
Accounts receivable	80,000	
Sales revenue		100,000

This transaction was recorded as transaction A in the T-account in Figure 7–6.

    b. The cost of the widgets sold during January was $50,000. This cost represents an expense in the period the widgets were sold. When the widgets were purchased, the asset account *inventory* was debited. *Expensing* of the cost of the widgets in the same period they are sold results in proper matching of rev-

Figure 7–6   T-Accounts for Waldorf Corporation

dr Cash		cr
Bal. Jan. 1/9- $30,000	D.	$20,000
A. 20,000	F.	7,000
C. 50,000	H.	40,000
	I.	5,000

Accounts Receivable

Bal. Jan. 1/9- $50,000		
A. 80,000	C.	$50,000

Inventory of Widgets

Bal. Jan. 1/9- $50,000		
G. 90,000	B.	$50,000

Accounts Payable

	45,000 Bal.	Jan. 1/9-
H. $40,000	G.	$90,000

Sales Commissions Payable

	7,000 Bal.	Jan. 1/9-
F. $7,000	E.	$8,000

Sales Revenue

	A.	$100,000

Salaries Expense

D. $20,000	

Sales Commission Expense

E. $8,000	

Cost of Goods Sold

B. $50,000	

Rent Expense

I. $5,000	

enues and expenses. As a result of this transaction, the asset *inventory of widgets* decreased by $50,000 and the expense *cost of goods sold* increased by $50,000. The journal entry for this transaction would be:

	dr	cr
Cost of goods sold	50,000	
Inventory		50,000

Note: This is the entry that would be prepared using the perpetual inventory method. Another method of recording inventory transactions is called the periodic method. Both the perpetual and periodic methods are discussed in Chapter 12. This transaction was recorded as transaction B in Figure 7–6.

c. Waldorf Corporation collected $50,000 for widgets sold on account in December. The revenue from the sales of these widgets was recorded in December when the sale took place (revenue realization). At that time, an account receivable was set up for the $50,000. Now Waldorf Corporation will record the collection of that account receivable. As a result of this transaction, cash was increased by $50,000 and accounts receivable was decreased by $50,000. The journal entry to record this transaction would be:

	dr	cr
Cash	50,000	
Accounts receivable		50,000

See transaction C in the T-account in Figure 7–6.

d. Waldorf Corporation paid the sales representatives $20,000 in salaries for the month of January. This payment represents an expense incurred in generating the revenue from sales of widgets. As a result of this transaction, salaries expense was increased by $20,000 and cash was decreased by $20,000. The journal entry to record this transaction would be:

	dr	cr
Salaries expense	20,000	
Cash		20,000

This transaction was recorded as transaction D in the T-accounts in Figure 7–6.

e. The sales representatives earned $8,000 in selling commissions related to the January sales. These selling commissions will be paid in February. The selling commissions relate to January revenue and should be expensed in January according to the matching principle. To record the expense in January, a liability account *sales commissions payable* must be set up. As a result of this transaction, sales commissions expense was increased by $8,000 and sales commissions payable was increased by $8,000. The journal entry to record this transaction would be:

	dr	cr
Sales commissions expense	8,000	
Sales commissions payable		8,000

This transaction was recorded as transaction E in Figure 7–6.

f. Sales commissions incurred in December were $7,000. These commissions were paid to the sales representatives in January. The sales commissions expense related to this transaction was recorded in December according to the matching principle. When the expense was recorded in December, sales commissions payable was increased by $7,000. This transaction represents payment of that $7,000 liability. As a result of this transaction, sales commissions payable was decreased by $7,000 and cash was decreased by $7,000. The journal entry to record this transaction would be:

	dr	cr
Sales commissions payable	7,000	
Cash		7,000

This transaction was recorded as transaction F in the T-accounts in Figure 7–6.

g. During the month of January, Waldorf Corporation purchased $90,000 worth of widgets from its suppliers on account. As a result of this transaction, the asset *inventory of widgets* was increased by $90,000 and the liability *accounts payable* was increased by $90,000. The journal entry to record this transaction would be:

	dr	cr
Inventory of widgets	90,000	
Accounts payable		90,000

This transaction was recorded as transaction G in the T-accounts in Figure 7–6.

h. During January, Waldorf Corporation paid for $40,000 worth of widgets that had been purchased on open account previously. As a result of this transaction, the liability *accounts payable* decreased by $40,000 and the asset *cash* decreased by $40,000. The journal entry for this transaction would be:

	dr	cr
Accounts payable	40,000	
Cash		40,000

This transaction was recorded as transaction H in the T-accounts in Figure 7–6.

i. During January, Waldorf Corporation paid $5,000 rent on the building used for operations. The rent on the building represents an expense of doing business. It is necessary to have a building to operate from in order to earn revenue. The rental expense cannot be matched with any specific revenues. Therefore, the rent expense is matched with the revenues earned in the same accounting period that the expense is incurred. As a result of this transaction, the rent expense account increased by $5,000 and the cash account decreased by $5,000. The journal entry to record this transaction would be:

	dr	cr
Rent expense	5,000	
Cash		5,000

This transaction was recorded as transaction I in the T-accounts in Figure 7–6.

Review Questions

DIRECTIONS: Select the best answer from the four alternatives. Write the letter of your answer in the blank to the left of the number.

1. An account is

   a. always kept in computerized form.
   b. used to ensure that debits equal credits.
   c. used to collect and summarize information.
   d. a record where business transactions are recorded in chronological order.

2. In accounting the term *credit* means

   a. an entry made on the right-hand side of an account.
   b. increases in accounts.
   c. decreases in accounts.
   d. an increase in an asset.

3. The left-hand side of an account is called

   a. the journal.
   b. the balance.
   c. the increase side.
   d. the debit side.

4. The difference between total debits and total credits recorded in an account is called

   a. the accounting equation.
   b. the balance.
   c. the inventory.
   d. owners' equity.

5. The normal balance of an account may be described as follows:

   a. The normal balance is indicated by the increase side.
   b. The normal balance is indicated by the decrease side.
   c. The normal balance is indicated by the debit side.
   d. The normal balance is indicated by the credit side.

_____   **6.** An obligation or debt of an entity owed to one of its creditors is called

     a. an asset.
     b. an expense.
     c. a liability.
     d. owners' equity.

_____   **7.** Which of the following accounts would be classified as a temporary account?

     a. Cash
     b. Buildings
     c. Accounts payable
     d. Service fees

_____   **8.** Economic resources from which future benefits can be received are called

     a. debits.
     b. assets.
     c. capital.
     d. dividends.

_____   **9.** Which of the following is a correct form of the accounting equation?

     a. Assets = liabilities + owners' equity
     b. Assets + liabilities = owners' equity
     c. Assets + owners' equity = liabilities
     d. Assets = liabilities + contributed capital

_____   **10.** A net loss results in

     a. no change in owners' equity.
     b. a decrease in owners' equity.
     c. an increase in owners' equity.
     d. a credit to the capital account.

_____   **11.** Accounting transactions are first recorded in

     a. the general ledger.
     b. the journal.
     c. a T-account.
     d. alphabetical order.

_____   **12.** The stock of goods that an entity holds for future sale is called

       a. accounts receivable.
       b. cost of goods sold.
       c. inventory.
       d. accounts payable.

_____   **13.** The periodic transfer of information from the journal to the ledger is called

       a. journalizing.
       b. matching.
       c. crediting.
       d. posting.

_____   **14.** Liabilities

       a. can arise from purchasing goods on credit.
       b. can arise from borrowing cash in order to finance the operations of the business.
       c. are decreased by recording a debit.
       d. All of the above statements pertain to liabilities.

_____   **15.** Owners' equity

       a. is a residual claim that is equal to: total assets – total liabilities.
       b. represents the resources invested in the business by creditors.
       c. is increased by debiting an owners' equity account.
       d. is usually called capital in a corporation.

_____   **16.** Owners' equity can be decreased through

       a. investment by owners.
       b. payment of a note payable.
       c. retention of earnings generated by the business.
       d. withdrawals made by owners.

_____   **17.** In double-entry bookkeeping

       a. total increases in the accounts must always equal total decreases in the accounts.
       b. total debits must always equal total credits.
       c. the accounting equation may be out of balance temporarily after certain types of transactions occur.
       d. whenever an asset account is debited, a liability account or owners' equity account must be credited.

_____ **18.** Expenses

a. should always be reported in the period during which they are paid.
b. normally have a credit balance.
c. are recorded according to the realization principle.
d. should be matched with the revenues to which they correspond.

_____ **19.** Which of the following statements about revenues is false?

a. Revenue should be realized when cash is received.
b. Revenues are increased by recording a credit and decreased by recording a debit.
c. Revenue is usually recognized only after an exchange has taken place or a service has been performed.
d. Revenues are the earnings of a business normally resulting from the sale of goods or the performance of services.

_____ **20.** Net income

a. is reported periodically on the statement of cash flows.
b. is equal to: revenues – liabilities.
c. is reported periodically on the income statement.
d. represents a decrease in owners' equity.

_____ **21.** Investments made in the entity by owners

a. represent revenue to the entity.
b. are recorded in the capital account in a sole proprietorship.
c. are recorded in the retained earnings account of a corporation.
d. all of the above.

_____ **22.** Dividends

a. should be reported on the income statement.
b. are paid on the request of stockholders.
c. are an expense incurred by a corporation.
d. result in a reduction of stockholders' equity.

_____ **23.** A journal entry contains

a. the date of the transaction.
b. an explanation of the transaction.
c. the ledger accounts and amounts to be debited or credited.
d. all of the above.

24. When an account receivable is collected,

    a. total assets increase.
    b. total assets decrease.
    c. total assets remain unchanged.
    d. total owners' equity increases.

25. Which of the following items could not result from the correct recording of a transaction?

    a. An increase in assets and an increase in owners' equity
    b. A decrease in an asset and a decrease in a liability
    c. A decrease in an asset and a decrease in owners' equity
    d. An increase in an asset and a decrease in a liability

26. The journal entry to record the purchase of office supplies on account would be

    a. debit office supplies; credit cash.
    b. debit accounts payable; credit supplies expense.
    c. debit office supplies; credit accounts payable.
    d. debit supplies expense; credit office supplies.

27. A typewriter having a list price of $1,200 was purchased by Jones Co. for $1,100 cash. Which of the following entries represents the correct recording of the transaction?

    a. Office equipment   1,100
          Jones capital   1,100
    b. Cash   1,100
          Office equipment   1,100
    c. Office equipment   1,100
          Cash   1,100
    d. Office equipment   1,200
          Cash   1,200

28. Arnold Co. purchased a building in exchange for $20,000 cash and an $80,000 note payable that will come due in four years. Which of the following journal entries records the transaction correctly?

    a. Building   80,000
          Note payable   80,000
    b. Building   80,000
       Cash   20,000
          Note payable   100,000

c. Building	100,000	
Cash		20,000
Note payable		80,000
d. Building	20,000	
Cash		20,000

Solutions

Answer	Refer to:	Answer	Refer to:
1. (c)	[A]	**15.** (a)	[B-3]
2. (a)	[A-3]	**16.** (d)	[B-3-e]
3. (d)	[A-3]	**17.** (b)	[C-5]
4. (b)	[A-5]	**18.** (d)	[E-2, E-3-c]
5. (a)	[B-1-b, B-2-b]	**19.** (a)	[E-1]
6. (c)	[B-2]	**20.** (c)	[E-3-a]
7. (d)	[E-3-e]	**21.** (b)	[B-3-a, E-4-a]
8. (b)	[B-1]	**22.** (d)	[E-5]
9. (a)	[C]	**23.** (d)	[D-1-b(2)]
10. (b)	[B-3-e]	**24.** (c)	[E-6-c]
11. (b)	[D-1]	**25.** (d)	[C]
12. (c)	[B-1]	**26.** (c)	[D-3-d]
13. (d)	[D-2]	**27.** (c)	[D-3-c, A-3]
14. (d)	[B-2]	**28.** (c)	[D-3-d]

CHAPTER 8

Basic Financial Statements

OVERVIEW

This section is designed to introduce the candidate to the basic financial statements of accounting. These statements are the final product of financial accounting.

    The candidate should know the format and classification of the balance sheet and what is included in the various asset, liability, and owners' equity accounts. The candidate should know the classified forms of the income statement and the nature of revenue, expense, gain, and loss accounts. The candidate should also know how the statement of retained earnings shows the changes in the retained earnings account from one period to the next.

KEY TERMS

Allowance for uncollectible accounts	Investments
Balance sheet	Liquidity
Bonds payable	Long-term liabilities
Book value or carrying value	Losses
Common stock	Mortgage
Contra-asset account	Notes payable
Cost of goods sold	Notes receivable
Current assets	Operating cycle
Current liabilities	Other assets
Depreciation	Other liabilities
Earnings per share	Preferred stock
Fixed assets	Prepaid expenses
Gains	Statement of cash flows
Gross margin (or gross profit)	Statement of changes in capital
Income statement	Statement of retained earnings
Intangible assets	Temporary investments

A. Balance Sheet   The balance sheet is a financial statement that shows the financial position of an entity as of a specific time. The balance sheet lists all the assets, liabilities, and owners' equity of an entity. The balance sheet is formally called the statement of financial position.

1. *Accounting Equation*: The balance sheet is a formal statement that shows the accounting equation (assets = liabilities + owners' equity) at a specific time.

2. *Heading*: Every balance sheet should have a proper heading. The heading includes the following information:

   a. The name of the company

   b. The title of the statement

   c. The date of the statement (the balance sheet is dated as of a specific day)

   EXAMPLE:

   Stone's Bicycles
   Statement of Financial Position
   December 31, 19XA

3. *Classification of Assets on the Balance Sheet*: Assets are typically classified as current assets, investments, fixed assets, intangible assets, and other assets.

   a. *Current assets*: The first category of assets shown on the balance sheet is current assets. Current assets are those assets expected to be used in the operations of an entity within its operating cycle or one year, whichever is longer. The operating cycle is defined as the period of time it takes a firm to buy merchandise (or produce it), sell the merchandise, collect the customers' accounts receivable resulting from sale of the merchandise, and pay the accounts payable of the firm. This cycle will vary depending on the nature of the business. Most businesses have an operating cycle shorter than one year, and they use a period of one year for the purpose of classifying current assets.

   Within the category of current assets, the individual asset accounts are listed according to their degree of liquidity. *Liquidity* is a measure of the speed with which an asset can be converted into cash. The more easily an asset can be converted into cash, the more liquid it is considered to be. The normal order in which current assets are listed is:

   (1) *Cash*: Cash includes coins, paper money, checks, money orders, and money on deposit in banks.

   (2) *Temporary investments*: Temporary investments consist of government bonds, corporate securities, or other securities that can be converted into cash very quickly. These may also be called short-term marketable securities. Temporary investments are expected to be held for less than one year or one operating cycle.

   (3) *Notes receivable*: Notes receivable are promissory notes given to a business by its customers. These notes normally indicate the amount of the future payment, the interest rate, and the time at which payment is to be made by the customers. Notes receivable are signed documents that are transferable.

(4) *Accounts receivable*: Accounts receivable are amounts owed to a business by customers for sales made on open account.

    (a) *Uncollectible accounts receivable*: It is usually not realistic to assume that the total amount of the accounts receivable will be collected. Some portion of the accounts receivable will normally prove to be uncollectible.

    (b) *Allowance for uncollectible accounts*: The amount of the accounts receivable that is estimated to be uncollectible is recorded in the allowance for uncollectible (or doubtful) accounts.

    (c) *Contra-assets*: The allowance for uncollectible accounts is a contra-asset account. Contra-asset accounts have credit balances and are shown as deductions from their related asset accounts on the balance sheet. The allowance account is shown as a deduction from the total account receivable balance on the balance sheet, showing the *net* amount that is expected to be collected. (See disclosure in Figure 8–2.)

    EXAMPLE: ABC Company has accounts receivable totaling $100,000. Of this amount it is estimated that $10,000 will be uncollectible. The balance in the allowance for uncollectible accounts before recording the $10,000 uncollectible estimate is zero. The entry to record the estimate of the uncollectible accounts would be made as follows:

	dr	cr
Bad debt expense	10,000	
Allowance for		
uncollectible accounts		10,000

(5) *Inventory*: Inventory is an asset that consists of goods on hand held by a business for future sale.

    (a) Merchandising firms normally have one inventory control account.

    (b) Manufacturing firms normally have three types of inventory control accounts:

        • *Raw materials*: Raw materials inventory is made up of the store of raw materials a company holds for use in producing goods.

        • *Work in process*: Work-in-process inventory consists of goods on hand that are still in the process of being completed.

        • *Finished goods*: Finished goods inventory consists of products completed and on hand awaiting sale to customers.

(6) *Prepaid expenses*: Prepaid expenses consist of the cost of goods or services bought for use in the business which are not used up by the end of the accounting period. Prepaid expenses are assets for as long as future benefits may be obtained from them. Examples of prepaid expense accounts are supplies, prepaid rent, and prepaid insurance.

EXAMPLE: A company pays rent one year in advance on a building used in operating the business. The payment of the rent in advance results in an asset called prepaid rent expense. The prepaid rent is an asset because the company has the right to use the building for 12 months without paying rent.

The amounts in the prepaid expense accounts are written off to expense as their potential for future benefit is consumed.

b. *Investments*: The second category of assets listed on the balance sheet is investments. Investments are assets held by the company for investment purposes, not for use in the operations of the business. The investments category is used for assets that are expected to be held for longer than one year.

EXAMPLES OF INVESTMENTS: Stocks of other corporations, cash surrender value of life insurance, savings accounts kept for a specific purpose (debt retirement, construction of a new building), and bonds of other corporations.

c. *Fixed assets*: The third category of assets listed on the balance sheet is fixed assets. Fixed assets are often called plant and equipment. Fixed assets are long-lived assets used in the operations of the business and not held for sale to customers.

(1) *Tangible nature of fixed assets*: Fixed assets are *tangible property* such as land, machinery, equipment, buildings, furniture, and fixtures.

(2) *Depreciation*: Depreciation is the systematic and rational allocation of the original cost of an asset over its expected useful life. Depreciation takes place even though an asset is not in use—such as during a strike. Depreciation is the process of allocating the cost of an asset to the periods in which it is used. Fixed assets normally wear out or deteriorate with time and use. Land is an example of a fixed asset that does not deteriorate. However, machinery, equipment, buildings, furniture, and fixtures do deteriorate. These types of assets are subject to depreciation. The depreciation of an asset is recorded in an account called *accumulated depreciation*.

EXAMPLE: ABC Company purchased a machine for $12,000. The machine is expected to last for six years. The decision has been made to depreciate the asset an equal amount during each year of its life. After the first year of use, the following entry is made to record depreciation:

	dr	cr
Depreciation expense	2,000	
Accumulated depreciation		2,000
To record depreciation on machine		
($12,000/6 years = $2,000 per year).		

There are a number of different methods of computing depreciation expense. These methods are discussed in Chapter 13, Section B-1.

(3) *Accumulated depreciation account*: The accumulated depreciation account is a contra-asset account. Accumulated depreciation is shown as a deduction from the related fixed asset account on the balance sheet. The

fixed asset account contains the original cost of the asset. (See Figure 8–2 for disclosure.)

(4) *Book value*: The original cost of an operational asset less the accumulated depreciation related to that asset is equal to the book value or carrying value of the asset.

d. *Intangible assets*: The fourth category of assets listed on the balance sheet is intangible assets. Intangible assets are long-lived assets that do not have any tangible existence. Intangible assets represent rights that the company owns.

EXAMPLES: Patents, copyrights, trademarks, franchises, leaseholds, and goodwill.

e. *Other assets*: The last category of assets listed on the balance sheet is "other assets." Other assets include long-lived assets that do not fit the criteria for classification in another area.

4. *Classification of Liabilities on the Balance Sheet*: Liabilities are typically classified as current liabilities, long-term liabilities, and other liabilities.

a. *Current liabilities*: Current liabilities are obligations of a business that are due to be paid within the next operating cycle or one year, whichever is longer.

EXAMPLES OF CURRENT LIABILITIES: accounts payable, short-term notes payable, wages payable, taxes payable, unearned revenue, interest payable, and *current interest due on long-term debt.*

b. *Long-term liabilities*: Long-term liabilities are obligations of a business that will not come due during the next operating cycle.

EXAMPLES OF LONG-TERM LIABILITIES: mortgages payable, bonds payable, and long-term notes payable.

(1) *Mortgage*: A mortgage is a long-term obligation that is usually secured by real estate and is usually repaid in installments made up partially of interest and partially of a repayment of the principal of the loan.

(2) *Bond*: A bond is a security issued by an entity wishing to borrow a large sum of money. Bonds are issued in stated denominations, and they pay a stated rate of interest.

(3) *Long-term notes payable*: A note payable is an obligation of an entity consisting of a signed document that promises to pay a specific amount of money plus interest at a specific time in the future. Ordinarily, a long-term note payable does not come due within the next operating cycle.

The current portion of long-term liabilities should be classified as a current liability.

EXAMPLE: ABC Company has a $200,000 note on one of their buildings. They make yearly payments of $20,000 on this note. They would have to reclassify $20,000 of this long-term liability as a current liability on the balance sheet since the $20,000 comes due within the next year.

  c. *Other liabilities*: "Other liabilities" is the category used in some balance sheets to classify long-term liabilities that do not fit the criteria for classification in another area.

 5. *Classification of Owners' Equity on the Balance Sheet*: Owners' equity is classified in the accounts differently depending on the form of the ownership of the business.

  a. *Sole proprietorship*: In a sole proprietorship, there is one owner's equity account called *Capital*. This account reflects all increases and decreases in the owner's equity.

  b. *Partnership*: In a partnership, there is a separate owner's equity (capital) account for each partner. This account shows an individual partner's contributions of capital to the business, any distribution of assets to the partner from the business, and the partner's share of any profits or losses incurred by the business. The sum of all of the individual partners' equity accounts would equal the total owners' equity of the partnership.

  c. *Corporation*: The stockholders' equity in a corporation is disclosed in two amounts: the amount invested by stockholders of the corporation and the amount generated by retention of earnings from the business.

   (1) *Capital stock*: Investments in the business by stockholders are shown in the contributed capital section. When stockholders invest in a corporation, they receive capital stock. There may be two classes of capital stock: common stock and preferred stock.

    (a) *Common stock*: All corporations *must* issue common stock. Common stock is sold to owners who receive no assurance of income from ownership of their stock. They have the rights to all residual assets left after creditors' and preferred stockholders' claims have been met. Common stockholders have the right to vote.

    (b) *Preferred stock*: Preferred stock is issued mostly by large corporations. Preferred stock has a preference over common stock. Preferred stockholders often have the right to receive a specified but limited amount of dividends before any distribution of dividends may be made to common shareholders. Preferred stockholders usually do not have the right to vote. (Preferred and common stock are discussed further in Chapter 16.)

   (2) *Retained earnings*: The amount generated by retention of earnings is called retained earnings. Retained earnings consist of the cumulative income and losses of a corporation less any dividends paid out to shareholders.

 Figure 8–1 shows the balance sheet presentation of owners' equity for a sole proprietorship, a partnership, and a corporation.

 6. *Basic Forms of the Balance Sheet*: The balance sheet may appear in account form or report form. The account form is usually used for internal managerial purposes whereas the report form is usually used in presenting information such as an annual report to stockholders.

Figure 8–1   Balance Sheet Presentations of Owners' Equity

Sole proprietor:	Owner's equity		
	John Jones, capital		20,000
Partnership:	Partners' equity		
	Alice Smith, capital	10,000	
	Robert Adams, capital	8,000	
	Total partners' equity		18,000
Corporation:	Stockholders' equity		
	Capital stock	1,000,000	
	Retained earnings	523,000	
	Total stockholders' equity		1,523,000

a. *Account form:* The form of the balance sheet that shows assets on the left side and liabilities and owners' equity on the right side is called the *account form.* Figure 8–2 shows a balance sheet for a corporation in account form.

b. *Report form*: The form of the balance sheet that shows assets on the top and liabilities and owners' equity below assets is called the *report form.*

B.   Income Statement

The income statement is a financial report that summarizes the operations of the business resulting in revenues, expenses, gains, and losses. The income statement shows the increase or decrease in owners' equity resulting from the operation of the business over a period of time (the accounting period).

1. *Net Income Related to Revenues and Expenses*: This equation defines net income from normal operations of a business as revenues minus expenses:

$$\text{net income} = \text{revenues} - \text{expenses}$$

2. *Gains and Losses*: A business may earn revenues that are not part of the normal operations of the business (gains) or incur expenses that do not result from normal operations of the business (losses). Gains and losses result in increases and decreases in owners' equity and are a part of the net income of a company. Since gains and losses do not result from the normal operations of a business, they are usually reported separately on the income statement.

a. *Gain*: One example of a gain might be the sale of a fixed asset for more than its book value. Assume that the DEF Corporation owns land which cost $20,000 and is currently being used as a parking lot. DEF Corporation is in the business of selling lawn mowers. DEF sells this land for $30,000. The land did not constitute goods held for sale in the normal course of the business; therefore, the sale results in a gain.

Gains and losses are measured on a net basis. Rather than report revenue of $30,000 from the sale of the land and an expense of $20,000 for the cost of the land, accountants report only a gain of $10,000 (the net amount).

Figure 8–2 Statement of Financial Position/Account Form

ABC Company
Statement of Financial Position
December 31, 19XB

Assets			Liabilities and Owners' Equity			
Current assets			**Current liabilities**			
Cash		25,000	Notes payable			5,000
Temporary investments		20,000	Accounts payable			70,000
Notes receivable		10,000	Salaries payable			10,000
Accounts receivable	100,000		Taxes payable			2,000
Less: Allowance			Current portion			
for uncollectible			of mortgage			36,000
accounts	10,000	90,000	Total current			
Inventory		100,000	liabilities			123,000
Prepaid insurance		2,000				
Total current		247,000	**Long-term liabilities**			
assets			Mortgage payable		200,000	
			Less: Current			
Investments			portion		36,000	164,000
Investment in			Notes payable			50,000
securities		80,000	Bonds payable			
Cash surrender			10% due 2000			150,000
value of life			Total long-term			
insurance		20,000	liabilities			364,000
Total						
investments		100,000	**Other liabilities**			
			Estimated warranty			
Fixed assets			liability			56,000
Land		60,000	Deferred income			
Buildings	900,000		taxes			23,000
Less: Accumulated			Total other			
depreciation	200,000	700,000	liabilities			79,000
Machinery and			Total liabilities			566,000
equipment	1,000,000					
Less: Accumulated			**Owners' equity**			
depreciation	450,000	550,000	Contributed capital			
Total fixed			Preferred stock,			
assets		1,310,000	7%, $100 per 500			
			shares outstanding			50,000
Intangible assets			Common stock,			
Patents		25,000	100,000 shares			
			outstanding			616,000
			Total contributed			
			capital			666,000
			Retained earnings			450,000
			Total stockholders'			
			equity			1,116,000
			Total liabilities and			
			stockholders'			
Total assets		1,682,000	equity			1,682,000

Revenue from sale of land	$30,000
– Cost of land	– 20,000
Net gain on sale of land	$10,000

b. *Loss*: Assume that DEF Corporation sold the parking lot land for $18,000 instead of $30,000. In this case a net loss of $2,000 would be incurred.

Revenue from sale of land	$18,000
– Cost of land	– 20,000
Net loss on sale of land	$–2,000

Gains and losses may also occur as a result of uncontrollable events such as fires, floods, or tornadoes. If the damages received from an insurance company exceed the book value of the property destroyed, a gain would result. If the damages received were less than the book value of the property lost, a loss would result.

3. *Net Income Related to Gains and Losses*: This equation describes the net income from normal operations of a business as well as revenues or expenses which are not a part of the business's normal operations:

$$\text{net income} = \text{revenues} - \text{expenses} + \text{gains} - \text{losses}$$

4. *Heading*: Every income statement should have a proper heading. The heading includes the following information:

a. The name of the company

b. The title of the statement

c. The period of time the statement covers

(*Note:* The income statement is dated over a period of time while the balance sheet is as of a *specific* date.)

EXAMPLE:

Stone's Bicycles
Income Statement
For the Year Ending December 31, 19XA

5. *Basic Forms of the Income Statement*: An income statement may be reported in a classified form or an unclassified form. Figure 8–3 shows a classified income statement, and Figure 8–4 shows an unclassified income statement.

a. *Format of a classified income statement*:

(1) *Operating income*: Operating income consists of the revenues and expenses that result from the normal operations of the business. The expenses incurred in the normal operations of the business are subtracted from the revenues generated in the normal operations of the business to arrive at operating income. Operating income is the first section of a classified income statement.

(a) *Revenue*: Revenue from sales of goods or services is reported first in the operating income section.

Figure 8–3 Income Statement for a Corporation

ABC Company
Income Statement
For the Year Ending December 31, 19XB

Sales		5,000,000	
Less: Cost of			
goods sold		2,450,000	
Gross margin			2,550,000
Selling expenses			
Sales salaries	300,000		
Sales commissions	210,000		
Advertising	175,000		
Travel	25,000		
Total selling expense		710,000	
General and administrative expenses			
Salaries	458,000		
State and local taxes	47,600		
Telephone	8,400		
Legal and professional fees	9,200		
Insurance	12,450		
Depreciation	198,550		
Bad debt expense	10,000		
Total general and administrative expenses		744,200	
Total operating expenses			1,454,200
Operating income			1,095,800
Other income and expenses			
Investment revenue	98,000		
Gain on sale of land	12,000	110,000	
Interest expense	(85,000)		
Loss on equipment due to fire	(8,500)	(93,500)	
Total other income			16,500
Net income before income taxes			1,112,300
Less: Applicable income taxes			444,920
Net income after income taxes			667,380
Earnings per share			
(on 100,000 shares)			6.67

(b) *Cost of goods sold*: Next, the cost of goods sold is reported in the classified income statement of a merchandising firm. Cost of goods sold is the cost of merchandise sold to customers. Sales of goods minus cost of goods sold is called margin (or gross profit) on sales. In a firm that only provides services rather than selling a product, there is no cost of goods sold.

(c) *Operating expenses*: Operating expenses are divided into at least two categories: selling expenses and general and administrative expenses. Selling expenses are expenses that are directly related to

Figure 8–4   Income Statement for a Partnership

XYZ Company
Income Statement
For the Year Ending December 31, 19XB

Revenues and gains		
Service fees		225,000
Gain on sale of equipment		7,500
Total revenues and gains		232,500
Less expenses and losses		
Salaries	120,000	
Rent for office building	30,000	
Supplies	2,500	
Depreciation	2,000	
Bad debts	1,800	
Interest	1,600	
Maintenance	500	
Total expenses and losses		158,400
Net income		74,100

Note: XYZ is a partnership. Therefore, there is no income tax expense shown on the income statement. On an unclassified income statement of a corporation, income taxes would be included under expenses and losses.

the selling of a product. General and administrative expenses are expenses related to the office and administrative costs.

gross profit – total operating expenses = operating income

(2) *Other income and expenses*: Other income and expenses are reported after operating income. Other income and expenses consist of revenues and expenses that are not connected with the primary operations of the business. This category would include gains and losses, investment income (dividends received or interest earned on investments), interest expense, and incidental rental revenue. Interest expense is considered to be a financing expense rather than an operating expense and as such is included in the *other income and expense* category.

(3) *Net income before income taxes*: Operating income plus other income or minus other expenses results in "net income before income taxes" (corporate use only).

(4) *Net income after income taxes*: Income tax expense is deducted from "net income before income taxes" to arrive at "net income after income taxes."

(a) *Corporations*: As separate legal entities, corporations pay taxes on their net income. The steps for reporting income taxes on the income statement refer only to corporations.

(b) *Sole proprietorships*: Because sole proprietorships are not separate legal entities, the business is not responsible for the payment of income taxes. The *owner* must include the income of the business on his or her personal tax return and pay the taxes individually. Hence income tax expense is not reported on the income statement of a sole proprietorship. Operating income plus other income or minus other expenses would result in the net income of the business, and the income statement would be complete.

(c) *Partnerships*: The individual partners are responsible for paying the taxes on their share of the income of the partnership. They report this income on their personal tax returns. The partnership pays no income taxes; thus, no income taxes are reported on the income statement of a partnership. As with a sole proprietorship, operating income plus/minus other income/expenses would result in the net income of the business, and the income statement would be complete.

(5) *Earnings per share*: A corporation also reports earnings per share on the income statement. Earnings per share is determined by dividing net income after taxes by the average number of shares of common stock held by owners during the period. "Earnings per share" is abbreviated EPS. The detailed calculation of earnings per share will not be discussed in this module. (See the presentation of simple EPS in Figure 8–3.)

Note: Partnerships and sole proprietorships do not issue common stock and, therefore, do not report earnings per share.

b. *Format of an unclassified income statement*:

(1) *Revenues and gains*: In an unclassified or single-step income statement all revenues and gains are grouped together first.

(2) *Expenses and losses*: Next, all expenses and losses are deducted from total revenues and gains to arrive at net income.

C. Statement of Retained Earnings

A corporation may present a statement of retained earnings. The statement of retained earnings shows the changes in retained earnings from one period to another. Figure 8–5 shows an example of a statement of retained earnings.

Figure 8–5   Statement of Retained Earnings

ABC Company
Statement of Retained Earnings
For the Year Ending December 31, 19XB

Retained earnings, December 31, 19XA	282,620
Add: Net income	667,380
Total	950,000
Less: Dividends	500,000
Retained earnings, December 31, 19XB	450,000

    1. *Increases in Retained Earnings*: Net income results in an increase in retained earnings.

    2. *Decreases in Retained Earnings*: Net loss results in a decrease in retained earnings. Dividends decrease retained earnings.

D. Statement of Changes in Capital

If the business is a sole proprietorship or a partnership, the company may present a statement of changes in capital. This statement shows the changes in the capital account from one period to another.

    1. *Increases in Capital*: Increases in capital result from total net income and additional contributions.

    2. *Decreases in Capital*: Decreases in capital result from total net losses and withdrawals.

E. Statement of Cash Flows

The final basic financial statement is the statement of cash flows. This statement shows the cash flows provided or used by the operating, investing, and financing activities of the business. This statement is discussed further in Chapter 18.

Review Questions

DIRECTIONS: Select the best answer from the four alternatives. Write the letter of your answer in the blank to the left of the number.

_____ 1. Which of the following headings would be correct for the income statement of Morrison Company?

    a. Morrison Company
       Income Statement
       December 31, 19XA
    b. Morrison Company
       Income Statement
    c. Income Statement
       For the year ending December 31, 19XA
    d. Morrison Company
       Income Statement
       For the year ending December 31, 19XA

_____ 2. Current assets are listed on the balance sheet according to

    a. size of dollar amount.
    b. importance to the owner.
    c. liquidity.
    d. order of acquisition.

_____ 3. The financial statement that shows cash provided and used by operating, financing, and investing activities is called the

    a. statement of financial position.
    b. statement of changes in financial position.
    c. retained earnings statement.
    d. statement of cash flows.

_____ 4. In a classified (multiple-step) income statement, interest revenue would be reported

    a. as an other income or expense item.
    b. along with sales.
    c. as part of operating expenses.
    d. after income tax expense.

_____   **5.** Obligations of a business that will not come due within one year or the current operating cycle are called

a. other equities.
b. current liabilities.
c. long-term liabilities.
d. prepaid expenses.

_____   **6.** Revenues that are generated from operations not a part of the normal operations of the business are called

a. gains.
b. operating revenues.
c. losses.
d. intangible revenue.

_____   **7.** Which of the following transactions would result in the recording of a prepaid expense account?

a. Payment of a two-year insurance policy on January 1, 19XA. The policy expires on December 31, 19XB.
b. Payment of an account payable that resulted from the purchase of office supplies.
c. Payment of rent for June on June 30.
d. Purchase of stock in another corporation.

_____   **8.** Income tax expense would be shown on the income statement for

a. corporations, sole proprietorships, and partnerships.
b. corporations and partnerships.
c. partnerships.
d. corporations.

_____   **9.** Current liabilities

a. will normally require the use of current assets for repayment.
b. include trademarks, franchises, and good will.
c. should include the current portion of long-term liabilities.
d. Both (a) and (c) are correct answers.

_____   **10.** Which of the following statements is true of owners' equity?

a. In a partnership, there is a separate capital account for each partner.
b. The owner's equity of a sole proprietorship is divided into two categories for balance sheet disclosure purposes: the amount invested by the owner and the retained earnings.

    c. Retained earnings consists of the cumulative income and losses of a corporation.

    d. Total stockholders' equity in a corporation includes only the contributed capital accounts.

_____ **11.** Within the statement of retained earnings

    a. decreases in retained earnings result from dividends and net losses.

    b. net income is shown as an increase in retained earnings.

    c. the change in the retained earnings balance during the period is explained.

    d. All of the above statements are true.

_____ **12.** In a classified (multiple-step) income statement

    a. operating expenses typically include selling and general and administrative expenses.

    b. other income and expense items are included with operating expenses.

    c. earnings per share are shown on all classified income statements.

    d. All of the above statements are true.

_____ **13.** Contra-asset accounts

    a. are related to asset accounts.

    b. have debit balances.

    c. are shown as a deduction from their related accounts on the income statement.

    d. include the allowance for uncollectible accounts and the depreciation expense accounts.

_____ **14.** Rohas Corporation purchased a machine for $50,000. The post-closing balance in the accumulated depreciation account that relates to the machine was $20,000 on December 31, 19XA. The machine could be sold currently for $24,000. Depreciation expense for 19XA was $5,000. What is the book value of the machine?

    a. $30,000

    b. $25,000

    c. $24,000

    d. $50,000

_____ **15.** During 19XC, Steve's Grocery, a sole proprietorship, had revenues of $500,000 and expenses of $300,000. Owner's equity was $150,000 on January 1, 19XC. Steve withdrew $50,000 cash from the business during 19XC. What was the balance in Steve's capital account on December 31, 19XC?

    a. $350,000

    b. $300,000

c. $100,000
d. $200,000

Use the following information in answering Questions 16 and 17.

Miller Corporation had sales of $1,000,000 during 19XB. Cost of goods sold was $500,000; selling expenses were $100,000; general and administrative expenses were $50,000; other expenses were $10,000; and income taxes were $20,000.

_____ **16.** What was Miller Corporation's gross profit for 19XB?

a. $400,000
b. $350,000
c. $340,000
d. $500,000

_____ **17.** What was Miller Corporation's net income before tax for 19XB?

a. $340,000
b. $320,000
c. $400,000
d. $500,000

Solutions

Answer	Refer to:		
1. (d)	[B-4]		
2. (c)	[A-3-a]		
3. (d)	[E]		
4. (a)	[B-5-a(2)]		
5. (c)	[A-4-b]		
6. (a)	[B-2]		
7. (a)	[A-3-a(6)]		
8. (d)	[B-5-a(4)]		
9. (d)	[A-4-a, A-4-b(3)]		
10. (a)	[A-5]		
11. (d)	[C]		
12. (a)	[B-5-a]		
13. (a)	[A-3-a(4) (c), A-3-c(3)]		
14. (a)	[A-3-c(4)]		
	Cost	$50,000	
	−Accumulated depreciation	− 20,000	
	Book value	$30,000	
15. (b)	[D]		
	Capital 1/1/XC	$150,000	
	+Net income		
	(revenues − expenses)	+ 200,000	
	−Withdrawals	− 50,000	
	Capital 12/31/XC	$300,000	
16. (d)	[B-5-a(1) (b)]		
	Sales	$1,000,000	
	−Cost of goods sold	− 500,000	
	Gross profit	$ 500,000	

17. (a)

[B-5-a]

Sales		$1,000,000
−Cost of goods sold		− 500,000
Gross profit		$ 500,000
−Operating expenses:		
Selling expenses	$100,000	
General/adm. exp.	50,000	− 150,000
Net operating income		$ 350,000
−Other expenses		10,000
Net income before income tax		$ 340,000

CHAPTER 9

The Accounting Cycle

OVERVIEW

In this chapter we introduce the candidate to the steps involved in the accounting cycle. An understanding of the accounting cycle is necessary in understanding how transactions are recorded in the accounts and how financial statements are prepared.

The candidate should know the basic steps involved in the accounting cycle and how to complete each of the steps. Journalizing and posting of transactions were discussed in Chapter 7, and financial statement format was discussed in Chapter 8.

KEY TERMS

Accounting cycle   Trial balance
Adjusting entries   Worksheet
Closing entry

The accounting cycle consists of all the accounting procedures performed during each accounting period. The accounting period for most businesses is one year. The following are the steps in the accounting cycle.

A. Analyzing Transactions and Recording

Accounting transactions occur, and source documents are prepared. The transactions are recorded in the journal(s) as they occur.

EXAMPLE: Stone's Bicycles sold a bicycle for $90 cash. A sales invoice (source document) was prepared when the transaction occurred. From the sales invoice, the transaction was recorded in a journal.

B. Posting

The debits and credits recorded in the journal entries are posted to the appropriate ledger accounts.

C. Trial Balance
A trial balance is a listing of all the ledger account balances. Taking a trial balance is a process of summarizing all the ledger accounts.

1. *Equality of Debits and Credits*: The trial balance proves the equality of total debits and total credits in the accounts.

    a. If total debits do not equal total credits in the trial balance, an error has been made in recording and/or posting the transactions.

    b. If total debits do equal total credits in the trial balance, this does *not* ensure that no errors have been made in recording and posting transactions. An entry could have been posted twice, posted to an incorrect account or for an incorrect amount; yet the trial balance could still balance.

2. *Preparation of Trial Balance*: A trial balance can be prepared at any time. Many companies prepare trial balances on a regular basis to provide a check on the equality of total debits and total credits in the accounts.

    a. The first step in the end-of-period accounting processes is to prepare an unadjusted trial balance from the ledger accounts.

    b. This unadjusted trial balance can be included as a portion of the worksheet and might not be prepared as a separate step in the accounting cycle.

The accounts of PALS Partnership are presented below:

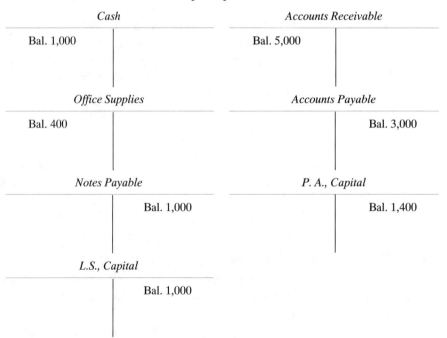

The trial balance of PALS Partnership is shown in Figure 9–1.

D. Worksheet
The worksheet is an accounting tool that makes the end-of-period processes of adjusting the accounts, closing the accounts, and preparing the financial statements easier (see Figure 9–4).

1. *Columns on the Worksheet*: A worksheet has columns for the unadjusted trial balance, the adjusting entries, the adjusted trial balance, the income statement, and the balance sheet.

Figure 9–1   Trial Balance of PALS Partnership

PALS Partnership
Trial Balance
December 31, 19XB

	Debits	Credits
Cash	$1,000	
Accounts receivable	5,000	
Office supplies	400	
Accounts payable		$3,000
Notes payable		1,000
P.A., capital		1,400
L.S., capital		1,000
Totals	$6,400	$6,400

2. *End-of-Period Adjustments*: The worksheet provides a place for recording all the end-of-period adjustments where errors may be detected and corrected easily.

3. *Journalizing and Posting*: After the worksheet has been completed, financial statements are prepared and the adjusting and closing entries are journalized and posted.

It is possible to complete the end-of-period processes without the use of a worksheet. Using a worksheet helps to minimize the errors made in adjusting and closing the accounts and preparing the financial statements.

E. Preparing Financial Statements

The basic financial statements are prepared using the worksheet information. The financial statements are prepared following the formats discussed in Chapter 8.

F. Adjusting Entries

Adjusting entry information is taken from the worksheet, recorded in the journal, and posted to the ledger. Adjusting entries are necessary to bring accounts up to date which have incorrect balances as of the end of the accounting period. In preparing financial statements, it is necessary to follow the accounting principles of revenue realization, accrual accounting, and matching. Since we prepare financial statements at periodic intervals, there are some accounts that have incorrect balances at year end. This occurs because an event that should be reported in accounting has occurred, but no formal transaction has occurred that resulted in preparation of a source document and recording of the transaction in the accounts. The following are basic types of adjusting entries:

1. *Estimates*:

   a. *Depreciation expense*: Depreciation expense recorded for a machine is an example of one of these types of adjustments. The cost of the machine is capitalized, and this cost is apportioned systematically to each period of the asset's useful life. There is no source document to initiate the recording of depreciation expense. Therefore, an adjusting entry must be made to reflect properly the asset valuation and the depreciation expense at the end of each accounting period. See Chapter 13 for an example of the recording of depreciation expense.

b. *Allowance for uncollectible accounts*: The recording of the correct amount in the allowance for uncollectible accounts is also done through an adjusting entry at the end of the period. See Chapter 14 for an example of the recording of bad debt expense and the allowance for uncollectible accounts.

2. *Prepaid/Unearned Accounts*:

a. *Expenses*:

(1) *Expenses recorded initially as an asset*: Goods or services purchased for future use and paid for in advance may be recorded initially as assets. The adjustment process for expenses paid for in advance and recorded as assets is illustrated by some typical examples in (a) and (b), which follow.

(a) *Insurance expense*: Suppose that Company A purchased a fire insurance policy on March 1, 19XB, for $2,000. The policy had a two-year life. When the policy was purchased, Company A made the following journal entry:

	dr	cr
Prepaid insurance	2,000	
Cash		2,000

The end of Company A's fiscal year is August 31. On August 31, 19XB, the asset account *prepaid insurance* still has a $2,000 balance. An adjusting entry must be made to reflect the expiration of six months of insurance coverage benefits. Company A would make the following adjusting journal entry on August 31:

	dr	cr
Insurance expense	500	
Prepaid insurance		500

To record insurance expense for the period March 1 through August 31 ($2,000 × 6/24 months).

If this adjusting entry was not made, the asset *prepaid insurance* would be overstated and the amount of *insurance expense* would be understated in the financial statements.

(b) *Supplies expense*: Another type of adjusting entry is the entry to record use of supplies when the original purchases of supplies were recorded in an asset account. Assume that GEF Company purchased $500 of office supplies on April 12. The following journal entry was made on that date:

	dr	cr
Office supplies inventory	500	
Cash		500

GEF Company wishes to prepare financial statements on June 30. No entries were made between April 12 and June 30 to record the usage of office supplies. A physical count on June 30 reveals that there are $232 worth of office supplies left on hand. From this count, GEF Company can determine that $268 ($500 − $232) of office supplies were used. An adjusting entry must be made to record the expense and reduce the asset account *office supplies*. GEF Company would make the following adjusting entry on June 30:

	dr	cr
Office supplies expense	268	
Office supplies inventory		268

(2)   *Recorded initially as an expense*: Goods or services purchased for future use and paid for in advance might be recorded initially in an expense account rather than an asset account as discussed in Section F-2-a(1).

(a)   *Supplies expense*: If GEF Company had originally recorded the purchase of the office supplies on April 12 as an expense, it would be necessary to record an adjusting entry to reflect that some of the office supplies are still on hand. Assume that GEF Company made the following journal entry on April 12.

	dr	cr
Office supplies expense	500	
Cash		500

Assume that the physical count still indicated that $232 of office supplies were on hand on June 30. If no adjusting entry were made, office supplies expense would be overstated and assets would be understated. GEF Company would make the following adjusting entry on June 30:

	dr	cr
Office supplies inventory	232	
Office supplies expense		232
To record office supplies on hand on June 30.		

Figures 9–2 and 9–3 show two different methods of recording the same transaction. Whether a company originally records the purchase of office supplies as an asset or as an expense is up to the managers of the company. Regardless of whether office supplies are originally recorded as an asset or as an expense, the final end-of-period amounts recorded in the office supplies inventory and office supplies expense accounts should be the same.

(b)   *Insurance expense*: When the purchase of an insurance policy is originally recorded as insurance expense and the life of the policy covers two or more accounting periods, an adjusting entry must be made to reduce the amount of expense recorded and to set up the asset *prepaid* (or *unexpired*) *insurance*. Assume that Company A made the following entry when they purchased the fire insurance policy for $2,000 on March 1.

Figure 9–2 Office Supplies Inventory/Expense Accounts

Figure 9–3 Office Supplies Expense/Inventory Accounts

Office Supplies Inventory

April 12	500		
		June 30	268
June 30	Bal. 232		

Office Supplies Expense

June 30	268		
June 30	Bal. 268		

Office Supplies Expense

April 12	500		
		June 30	232
June 30	Bal. 268		

Office Supplies Inventory

June 30	232		
June 30	Bal. 232		

	dr	cr
Insurance expense	2,000	
Cash		2,000

When their fiscal year ends on August 31, it would be necessary to record the following adjusting entry:

	dr	cr
Prepaid insurance	1,500	
Insurance expense		1,500

To record the portion of the fire insurance policy that is unexpired as of August 31, 19XB ($2,000 × 18/24 months).

b. *Revenues*:

(1) *Revenue recorded initially as a liability*: Revenue received in advance may be recorded initially in an unearned revenue (liability) account. The adjustment process for revenue received in advance and recorded as liabilities is illustrated in the following example.

(a) *Rental revenue*: Z Company received payment in advance for rental of a building for 12 months. The payment of $1,200 was received on June 1, 19XB, and the end of the company's accounting year is December 31, 19XB. Assume that Z Company made the following journal entry on June 1:

	dr	cr
Cash	1,200	
Unearned rental revenue		1,200

(b) *Adjusting entry*: As of December 31, the amount of seven months of the total rental revenue has been earned. If no adjusting entry were made, rental revenue would be understated and unearned rental revenue would be overstated. Z Company would make the following adjusting entry on December 31:

	dr	cr
Unearned rental revenue	700	
Rental revenue		700

To record the portion of rent received in advance which has been earned
through December 31.

Examples b(1) (a) and b(2) (a) show two different ways of recording the
same transactions. The end-of-period balances in the accounts are the
same regardless of the method used.

(2) *Revenue recorded initially as a revenue*: Revenue received in advance
     might be initially recorded in a revenue account.

   (a) *Rental revenue*: Z Company received payment in advance for rental
        of a building for 12 months. The payment of $1,200 was made on
        June 1 and the end of the company's accounting year is December
        31, 19XB. Assume that Z Company made the following entry to
        record the transaction on June 1:

	dr	cr
Cash	1,200	
Rental revenue		1,200

   (b) *Adjusting entry*: As of December 31, all of the rental revenue was
        not earned. If no adjusting entry were made on December 31, rental
        revenue would be overstated and the liability unearned rental rev-
        enue would be understated. Z Company would make the following
        adjusting entry on December 31:

	dr	cr
Rental revenue	500	
Unearned rental revenue		500

To record the portion of rent received that has not yet been earned
($1,200 × 5/12 months).

3. *Accruals*:

   a. *Accrued expenses*: Accrued expenses should be recorded when expenses have
       been incurred but have not yet been recorded as of the end of the accounting
       period. When an adjusting entry of this type is made, it results in the record-
       ing of an accrued liability.

   (1) *Accrued salaries*: Salaries have been earned by employees but have not
        yet been paid. Assume that Y Company's year end is November 30,
        19XB, which is a Thursday. The employees of Y Company are paid
        weekly on Friday. As of November 30, the employees have earned
        salaries for four days' work which have not been paid or recorded.
        Assume that the amount earned by the employees from Monday through
        Thursday was $9,820. If no adjusting entry were made, *salaries expense*
        would be understated for the period and the liability *salaries payable*
        would be understated. Y Company would make the following adjusting
        entry on November 30:

	dr	cr
Salaries expense	9,820	
Accrued salaries payable		9,820

To record salaries earned for the period ending November 30 which have
not yet been paid.

(2) *Accrued interest expense*: Interest expense on borrowed money accumulates on a day-to-day basis, but it is not normally recorded until it is paid. At the end of an accounting period, it is necessary to make an adjusting entry to record any interest expense incurred since the last payment date and to record the liability for payment of that interest at a future time. Assume that Z Company borrowed $5,000 from the bank on September 1, 19XB. Z Company signed a promissory note which stated that the note would be repaid on February 28, 19XC, with 15 percent interest. Z Company's year end is December 31. On September 1, Z Company made the following entry:

	dr	cr
Cash	5,000	
Note payable to bank		5,000

To record six-month 15% loan obtained from bank.

It is necessary for Z Company to make the following adjusting entry on December 31 to record the interest expense accrued from September 1 through December 31:

	dr	cr
Interest expense	250	
Accrued interest payable		250

To record interest expense from September 1 through December 31
($5,000 \times 0.15 \times 4/12$ months).

Note: Interest rates are always quoted on an annual basis. In this example, interest had accrued for four months so it was necessary to multiply by 4/12 to determine the interest expense for the fraction of the year that had passed.

b. *Accrued revenues*: Accrued revenues should be recorded when revenues have been earned but have not yet been recorded as of the end of the accounting period. When an adjusting entry of this type is made, an accrued asset (receivable) and revenue are recorded.

(1) *Interest revenue*: Interest revenue is earned with the passage of time on notes receivable held by a company, but interest revenue is not normally recorded until it is received. At the end of an accounting period, it is necessary to make an adjusting entry to record any interest revenue earned that has not been received. Assume that Z Company accepted a four-month, 16 percent note receivable for $3,000 from a customer on November 1, 19XB. Z Company's year-end is December 31. As of December 31, Z Company has earned two months of interest revenue which has not been recorded. It would be necessary for Z Company to make the following adjusting entry on December 31:

	dr	cr
Accrued interest receivable	80	
Interest revenue		80

To record interest earned on note receivable from November 1 through
December 31 ($3,000 × 0.16 × 2/12 months).

4.   *Use of the Worksheet*: Figure 9–4 shows a typical worksheet that includes columns for the unadjusted trial balance, the adjustments, the adjusted trial balance, the income statement, and the balance sheet.

Columns 1 and 2 show the unadjusted trial balance of Handy Corporation. This trial balance was taken from Handy Corporation's general ledger.

Columns 3 and 4 show the adjustments necessary to bring the accounts in the unadjusted trial balance to the proper year-end amounts.

Adjustment a records the bad debt expense for the period and adjusts the allowance for uncollectible accounts balance. On December 31, 19XB, Handy Corporation estimated that $800 of the $10,000 accounts receivable balance would prove to be uncollectible. Since the allowance account had a credit balance of $40, it was necessary to make an adjusting entry crediting the allowance for uncollectible accounts for $760. The following adjusting entry was made on the worksheet:

	dr	cr
a. Bad debt expense	760	
Allowance for uncollectible		760
accounts		

Adjustment b records the amount of supplies used during the period. Handy Corporation records purchases of office supplies in the asset account *office supplies*. On December 31, 19XB, a physical count of the office supplies on hand was taken and $150 of supplies were on hand. The following adjusting entry was made to record the use of $400 ($550 – $150) of the supplies recorded in the office supplies account.

	dr	cr
b. Supplies expense	400	
Office supplies		400

Adjustment c records the portion of the asset *prepaid insurance* that has expired during the current period. Handy Corporation purchased a 20-month insurance policy on May 1 and made full payment for the policy at that time. The payment on May 1 of $200 was recorded as follows:

	dr	cr
Prepaid insurance	200	
Cash		200

As of December 31, eight months of the life of the policy have expired. Handy Corporation made the adjusting entry to record the insurance expense and the reduction in the value of the insurance policy:

Figure 9–4 Worksheet

Handy Corporation
Worksheet
Year Ending 12/31/XB

	Unadjusted Trial Balance		Adjustments		Adjusted Trial Balance		Income Statement		Balance Sheet	
	dr (1)	cr (2)	dr (3)	cr (4)	dr (5)	cr (6)	dr (7)	cr (8)	dr (9)	cr (10)
Cash	2,230				2,230				2,230	
Accounts receivable	10,000				10,000				10,000	
Allowance for uncollectible accounts		40		a. 760		800				800
Office supplies	550			b. 400	150				150	
Prepaid insurance	200			c. 80	120				120	
Furniture and fixtures	12,000				12,000				12,000	
Accumulated depreciation		2,200		d. 1,000		3,200				3,200
Accounts payable		5,400				5,400				5,400
Notes payable		2,000				2,000				2,000
Capital stock		5,000				5,000				5,000
Retained earnings 12/31/XB		5,920				5,920				5,920
Service revenue		65,700				65,700		65,700		
Loss of sales of equipment	2,420				2,420		2,420			
Salaries expense	57,860		e. 540		58,400		58,400			
Dividends	1,000				1,000				1,000	
Totals	86,260	86,260								
Bad debt expense			a. 760		760		760			
Supplies expense			b. 400		400		400			
Insurance expense			c. 80		80		80			
Depreciation expense			d. 1,000		1,000		1,000			
Salaries payable				e. 540		540				540
Interest expense			f. 50		50		50			
Interest payable				f. 50		50				50
Totals			2,830	2,830	88,610	88,610	63,110	65,700	25,500	2,590
Net income							2,590			2,590
							65,700	65,700	25,500	25,500

	dr	*cr*
c. Insurance expense	80	
Prepaid insurance		80
($200 × 8/20 months)		

Adjustment d records depreciation expense for the period. Handy Corporation esti-mated that the $12,000 of furniture and fixtures had a useful life of 12 years when purchased. The straight-line depreciation method is used. Depreciation expense for the year would be $1,000, calculated as follows:

$$\$12,000/12 \text{ years} = \$1,000 \text{ per year}$$

The following adjusting entry was made to record depreciation expense:

	dr	*cr*
d. Depreciation expense	1,000	
Accumulated depreciation		1,000

Adjustment e records the salaries earned by employees in the final week of December, 19XB, which have not yet been paid or recorded. Handy Corporation employees earned $540 which had not been paid. The following adjusting entry was made to reflect the year-end liability for salaries earned and not paid.

	dr	*cr*
e. Salaries expense	540	
Salaries payable		540

Adjustment f records the interest that has accrued on the note payable through December 31. Handy Corporation borrowed $2,000 from the bank on November 1, 19XB. They agreed to pay the balance of the note plus 15% interest in 12 months. As of December 31, interest expense for two months has been incurred. The calculation of the interest expense was made as follows:

$$\$2,000 \times 0.15 \times 2/12 \text{ months} = \$50$$

Handy Corporation made the following adjusting entry to record the accrued inter-est expense:

	dr	*cr*
f. Interest expense	50	
Interest payable		50

Columns 5 and 6 show the adjusted trial balance with the account balances after adjustment. Column 5 or 6 is the sum of the account balance shown in column 1 or 2 plus or minus any adjustments made in column 3 or 4. Note that debits = credits in columns 1 and 2, 3 and 4, and 5 and 6.

Columns 7 and 8 show the accounts taken from the adjusted trial balance (columns 5 and 6) which make up the income statement. The amount needed to make debits equal credits in the income statement column is the amount of net in-come or loss. Note that in Figure 9–4 the net income is $2,590. This amount of net income is carried over to the balance sheet credit column (column 10) because it is a portion of the ending retained earnings balance.

Columns 9 and 10 show the accounts taken from the adjusted trial balance (columns 5 and 6) that make up the balance sheet. The new retained earnings balance as of December 31, 19XB, consists of the sum of the December 31, 19XA, retained earnings balance ($5,920 credit), the dividends balance ($1,000 debit), and the net income balance ($2,590 debit) carried over from the income statement.

G. Closing Entries

It is necessary to prepare entries to close the temporary accounts at the end of the accounting period. Revenue, expense, gain, and loss accounts are summarized in the income statement and net income is added to the owners' equity or retained earnings account. Thus, the revenue, expense, gain, and loss accounts are actually subdivisions of the owners' equity account which are used to accumulate information during the accounting period. At the end of the accounting period, they have served their purpose and should be closed or "zeroed out." The income summary account is used in the closing procedures to summarize the amounts of revenues and expenses. The following are the procedures used in closing the temporary accounts:

1. *Closing Revenue and Gain Accounts*: Revenue and gain accounts are closed by debiting the individual revenue/gain accounts and crediting the income summary account.

2. *Closing Expense and Loss Accounts*: Expense and loss accounts are closed by debiting the income summary account and crediting the individual expense/loss accounts.

3. *Closing the Income Summary Account*: The income summary account is closed to owners' equity in a partnership or sole proprietorship or to retained earnings in a corporation. If a profit was earned during the period, the income summary account is closed by debiting the income summary and crediting owner's capital or retained earnings. If a loss was incurred during the period, the income summary account is closed by debiting owner's capital or retained earnings and crediting the income summary account.

4. *Closing Withdrawal and Dividend Accounts*: Withdrawal (or drawing) accounts and dividends declared accounts are also closed at the end of the period. They are temporary accounts. However, they are not income statement accounts. The withdrawal account is closed by debiting owner's capital and crediting withdrawals (drawings). The dividends declared account is closed by debiting retained earnings and crediting dividends declared.

5. *Journalizing and Posting*: The closing entries are first journalized and then posted to the ledger. See Figure 9–5 for an illustration of the closing journal entries and the T-account posting of the closing entries.

H. Postclosing Trial Balance

The final step of the accounting cycle is to take a postclosing trial balance. This ensures that debits still equal credits in the accounts after the adjusting and closing entries have been journalized and posted. The postclosing trial balance of Handy Corporation is shown in Figure 9–6. The postclosing trial balance includes only permanent accounts.

I. The Next Accounting Cycle

The accounting cycle begins again on the first day of the next accounting period.

Note: The Certified Professional Secretary Examination Study Outline combines steps G and H into one step. Because of this, the CPS Study Outline includes seven, rather than eight, steps in the accounting cycle.

Figure 9–5   Closing Journal Entries and T-Account Posting of Closing Entries for Handy Corporation

1. Service revenue	65,700	
Income summary		65,700
2. Income summary	63,110	
Salaries expense		58,400
Bad debt expense		760
Supplies expense		400
Insurance expense		80
Depreciation expense		1,000
Interest expense		50
Loss on sale of equipment		2,420
3. Income summary	2,590	
Retained earnings		2,590
4. Retained earnings	1,000	
Dividends declared		1,000

Service Revenue

	65,700 Bal.
65,700	
	-0- Bal.

Salaries Expense

Bal. 58,400	
	(2) 58,400
Bal. -0-	

Bad Debt Expense

Bal. 760	
	(2) 760
Bal. -0-	

Supplies Expense

Bal. 400	
	(2) 400
Bal. -0-	

Insurance Expense

Bal. 80	
	(2) 80
Bal. -0-	

Depreciation Expense

Bal. 1,000	
	(2) 1,000
Bal. -0-	

Interest Expense

Bal. 50	
	(2) 50
Bal. -0-	

Loss on Sale of Equipment

Bal. 2,420	
	(2) 2,420
Bal. -0-	

Income Summary

	(1) 65,700
(2) 63,110	
(3) 2,590	
Bal. -0-	

Retained Earnings

	5,920 Bal.
	(3) 2,590
(4) 1,000	
	7,510 Bal.

Dividends Declared

Bal. 1,000	
	(4) 1,000
Bal. -0-	

Figure 9–6 Postclosing Trial Balance

Handy Corporation
Postclosing Trial Balance
December 31, 19XB

	Debits	Credits
Cash	2,230	
Accounts receivable	10,000	
Allowance for uncollectible accounts		800
Office supplies	150	
Prepaid insurance	120	
Furniture and fixtures	12,000	
Accumulated depreciation		3,200
Accounts payable		5,400
Salaries payable		540
Interest payable		50
Notes payable		2,000
Capital stock		5,000
Retained earnings		7,510
Totals	24,500	24,500

Review Questions

DIRECTIONS: Select the best answer from the four alternatives. Write the letter of your answer in the blank to the left of the number.

_____ 1. A trial balance that is prepared after all adjusting and closing entries have been posted is called the

  a. unadjusted trial balance.
  b. postclosing trial balance.
  c. adjusted trial balance.
  d. balance sheet.

_____ 2. The withdrawals account would normally be closed to

  a. the income summary account.
  b. the retained earnings account.
  c. the owner's capital account.
  d. the common stock account.

_____ 3. The financial statements are normally prepared

  a. after the worksheet is completed.
  b. before beginning the worksheet.
  c. using the postclosing trial balance.
  d. from information taken from the unadjusted trial balance.

_____ 4. Taking a trial balance means

  a. making a listing of the account balances in the general journal.
  b. adjusting the books of the company.
  c. transferring the debits and credits from the journal to the ledger.
  d. making a listing of the general ledger accounts and their balances.

_____ 5. Which of the following accounts would not be included on a postclosing trial balance?

  a. Accounts receivable
  b. Unearned revenue
  c. Buildings
  d. Interest revenue

6. Accounts that are closed at the end of each accounting period are called

a. permanent accounts.
b. temporary accounts.
c. closing accounts.
d. real accounts.

7. Which of the following is the first step in the accounting cycle?

a. Posting transactions
b. Adjusting the accounts
c. Taking a trial balance
d. Analyzing and recording transactions in the journal

8. On a worksheet, the net income amount is recorded

a. only in the income statement credit column.
b. only in the income statement debit column.
c. in both the income statement debit column and the balance sheet credit column.
d. in both the income statement credit column and the balance sheet debit column.

9. Failing to make an adjusting entry to record accrued wages payable would result in

a. an overstatement of assets and an understatement of net income.
b. an understatement of liabilities and an understatement of net income.
c. an understatement of liabilities and an overstatement of net income.
d. an understatement of liabilities but would have no effect on net income.

10. Little Company purchased an insurance policy that covers 18 months. At the time the policy was purchased, the payment was recorded as a debit in the prepaid insurance account. The adjusting entry at the end of the accounting period would require

a. a debit to insurance expense and a credit to the prepaid insurance account.
b. a debit to prepaid insurance and a credit to the cash account.
c. a debit to prepaid insurance and a credit to the insurance expense account.
d. no adjusting entry at the end of the period.

11. Green Company originally recorded the purchase of office supplies in an expense account. At year end, Green Company counted the office supplies and found that $100 of supplies were still on hand. As a result of this

a. no adjusting entry would be needed.
b. an adjusting entry debiting office supplies expense and crediting the asset office supplies should be made for $100.

c. an adjusting entry debiting the asset office supplies and crediting office supplies expense should be made for $100.

d. an adjusting entry debiting cash and crediting the asset office supplies should be made for $100.

_____ **12.** Miller Company failed to record accrued rent receivable as of the end of the accounting period. As a result

a. total assets would be understated and total net income would be understated.
b. total assets would be understated and total net income would be overstated.
c. total assets would be understated and total liabilities would be understated.
d. total assets would be understated and net income would be unaffected.

_____ **13.** Which of the following statements regarding trial balances is true?

a. A trial balance may be taken any time.
b. The last step of the accounting cycle is to prepare an adjusted trial balance.
c. If total debits are equal to total credits in the trial balance, no errors have been made in the recording and posting of transactions.
d. All of the above statements are true.

_____ **14.** The worksheet

a. is a tool that makes the end-of-period accounting processes easier.
b. makes it unnecessary to record the adjusting entries in the journal and the ledger.
c. ensures that no errors were made in the adjusting process if all column sets balance when it is completed.
d. is required to complete the end-of-period accounting process.

_____ **15.** Adjusting entries are needed to

a. correct errors in the accounts.
b. bring accounts that have incorrect balances as of the end of the accounting period up to date.
c. bring the trial balance into balance.
d. All of the above statements pertain to adjusting entries.

_____ **16.** Which of the following entries would be considered to be an adjusting entry?

a. The recording of accrued interest payable on a note payable held by Company Z
b. The recording by Company Z of the portion of unearned revenue that has been earned

c. The recording by Company Z of the expiration of a portion of the asset *prepaid rent*

d. All of the above would be considered adjusting entries.

Use this information in answering Questions 17 to 20.

Alex Company rented a building from Bates Co. for 18 months on June 1, 19XA. The amount of the rent was $3,600. Alex Company's year end is October 31. Alex Company recorded the payment of $3,600 as rent expense on June 1.

_____ 17. What is the amount of the rent expense related to this lease that should be reported on Alex Company's income statement for October 31, 19XA?

   a. $3,600
   b. $2,600
   c. $1,000
   d. $1,400

_____ 18. What is the amount of prepaid rent that should be shown on Alex Company's October 31, 19XA balance sheet?

   a. $3,600
   b. $2,600
   c. $1,000
   d. $2,200

_____ 19. On October 31, 19XA, the correct adjusting entry to record this transaction would be

   a. debit rent expense and credit prepaid rent for $1,000.
   b. debit prepaid rent and credit rent expense for $2,600.
   c. debit prepaid rent and credit rent expense for $1,000.
   d. debit rent expense and credit prepaid rent for $1,400.

_____ 20. Using the same information in Questions 17 to 19, assume that Alex Company originally recorded the $3,600 payment as a debit to prepaid rent and a credit to cash. The necessary adjusting entry would be

   a. debit rent expense and credit prepaid rent for $1,000.
   b. debit prepaid rent and credit rent expense for $1,000.
   c. debit rent expense and credit prepaid rent for $2,600.
   d. debit prepaid rent and credit rent expense for $2,600.

Use this information in answering Questions 21 to 24.

The following accounts and balances appear on the adjusted trial balance of Alice's Hair Salon. The accounts are not listed in chart of account order.

Accumulated depreciation expense	$ 300
Cash	1,764
Wages expense	1,700
Advertising expense	126
Revenue from services	3,917
Equipment	3,974
Rent expense	750
Alice Stowe, capital	4,820
Alice Stowe, drawing	1,200
Accounts receivable	721
Accounts payable	1,424
Supplies	116
Depreciation expense	110

21. Total debits in the trial balance are

    a. $9,261.
    b. $10,461.
    c. $10,761.
    d. $10,161.

22. Net income for Alice's Hair Salon is

    a. $1,231.
    b. $931.
    c. $31.
    d. $1,041.

23. Total assets as shown on the balance sheet are

    a. $6,575.
    b. $7,775.
    c. $7,475.
    d. $6,275.

24. After closing entries are posted, the balance in the Alice Stowe, capital account will be

    a. $6,051.
    b. $4,551.
    c. $4,851.
    d. $4,661.

Solutions

Answer	Refer to:
1. (b)	[H]
2. (c)	[G-4]
3. (a)	[E]
4. (d)	[C]
5. (d)	[H]
6. (b)	[G]
7. (d)	[A]
8. (c)	[Figure 9–4]
9. (c)	[F-3-a]
10. (a)	[F-2-a(1) (a)]
11. (c)	[F-2-a(2) (a)]
12. (a)	[F-3-b]
13. (a)	[C]
14. (a)	[D]
15. (b)	[F]
16. (d)	[F]
17. (c)	[F-2-a(2)] $3,600/18 months = $200/month $200/month × 5 months = $1,000 rent expense
18. (b)	[F-2-a(2)]
19. (b)	[F-2-a(2)]
20. (a)	[F-2-a(1)]

21. (b)   [C]

	dr	cr
Accumulated depreciation	$	$ 300
Cash	1,764	
Wages expense	1,700	
Advertising expense	126	
Revenue from services		3,917
Equipment	3,974	
Rent expense	750	
Alice Stowe, capital		4,820
Alice Stowe, drawing	1,200	
Accounts receivable	721	
Accounts payable		1,424
Supplies	116	
Depreciation expense	110	
Totals	$10,461	$10,461

22. (a)   [Chapter 8, B-1]

Revenue from services		$3,917
Less expenses:		
Wages expense	$1,700	
Advertising expense	126	
Rent expense	750	
Depreciation expense	110	2,686
Net income		$1,231

23. (d)   [Chapter 7, B-1]

Cash		$1,764
Accounts receivable		721
Supplies		116
Equipment	$3,974	
Less accumulated		
depreciation	(300)	3,674
		$6,275

24. (c)   [Chapter 8, D]

Alice Stowe, capital beginning	$4,820
Add: Net income	1,231
Less: Alice Stowe, drawing	(1,200)
Alice Stowe, capital ending	$4,851

CHAPTER 10

Accounting for Cash

OVERVIEW

Cash is an area of accounting with which candidates should be familiar. The procedures for performing a bank reconciliation for a business account are the same as those used to reconcile an individual's checking account. Other aspects of accounting for cash, such as internal control and the recording of transactions, may be less familiar to the candidates.

The candidate should understand the recording of cash receipts and cash disbursements, the procedures needed for proper internal control over cash, the treatment of trade and cash discounts, the handling of a petty cash fund, the use of a voucher system, and the procedures for reconciling a bank account, and be familiar with the types of checks and the check register.

KEY TERMS

Bank reconciliation
Cash
Cash disbursements journal
Cash discount
Cash receipts journal
Certified check
Check register
Control account
Deposits in transit
Internal controls

NSF check
Outstanding checks
Petty cash fund
Purchases journal
Sales journal
Special journal
Subsidiary account
Trade discount
Voucher
Voucher system

A. Cash Receipts

1. *Cash*: Coins, paper money, checks, money orders, and money on deposit in bank accounts are all classified as cash. If an item is accepted as a deposit by a bank, it should be considered to be a part of the cash of the company.

2. *Major Types of Cash Receipts*: Cash may be received for the immediate sale of merchandise, performance of services, or for payment of a sale on credit.

3. *Internal Controls*: The procedures and rules used by a company to ensure that its assets are being used for legitimate business purposes are known as *internal controls*. Internal controls aid in the efficient operation of a business.

   a. *Procedures and rules*: The establishment of procedures and rules by a company usually fall into the following five categories:

      (1) *Adequate separation of duties among employees*: Custody of an asset and recordkeeping for it should be separated. This helps prevent an individual from stealing assets and changing the accounting records to cover up the theft.

      (2) *Proper authorization*

      (3) *Maintenance of adequate documents and records*

      (4) *Limiting access to assets and to accounting records*

      (5) *Performing independent checks on the performance of individuals*

   b. *Internal controls for cash receipts*: Cash is very easily misappropriated, so it is essential that a business maintain good internal controls over cash receipts and disbursements. The following items are examples of good internal control procedures for cash receipts:

      (1) *Recording cash sales*: Cash sales should be recorded on a cash register.

      (2) *Depositing cash receipts*: Cash receipts should be deposited intact daily.

      (3) *Daily reconciliation of cash sales*: At the end of the day, an individual not involved in the collection of cash receipts should reconcile the total cash on hand with the record of cash sales for the day.

      (4) *Endorsement of checks received*: Any checks received should be restrictively endorsed immediately.

      (5) *Recording cash receipts*: Recording of cash receipts should be separated from custody of cash.

      (6) *Opening mail cash receipts*: Responsibility should be assigned for opening mail receipts. Payments on outstanding account receivable balances are typically received in the mail.

         (a) The person who is assigned responsibility for opening mail receipts should restrictively endorse all checks and prepare a list of checks received.

         (b) The individual opening the mail may prepare the bank deposit slip and make the deposit, or the checks may be forwarded to a cashier who deposits the receipts intact daily.

         (c) A copy of the list of checks received [see Section (6) (a)] should be sent to the accounting department.

(d)   The accounting department should receive a duplicate deposit slip that can be compared with the list of mail receipts. Any differences must be reconciled.

(e)   The accounting department enters the amounts received in the accounting records.

(7)   *Preparation of bank reconciliation*: An independent bank reconciliation should be prepared monthly. The individual preparing the bank reconciliation should not be involved in the cash depositing or recording functions.

B.   Subsidiary Ledgers and Special Journals

1.   *Control Account*: A control account has a balance that is the total of all the balances of a related subsidiary ledger. For example, the general ledger accounts receivable account is a control account because its balance shows the total amount owed to the company by its customers. The individual accounts for each customer are kept in the *subsidiary accounts receivable ledger*. The general ledger accounts payable account is also a control account.

2.   *Subsidiary Account*: The detailed accounts of individual balances are kept in a subsidiary ledger.

   a.   *The subsidiary accounts receivable ledger*: The subsidiary accounts receivable ledger contains an account for each credit customer of the company. The total of all the individual accounts contained within the subsidiary accounts receivable ledger should be equal to the balance in the general ledger. The balance in a single account of the subsidiary accounts receivable ledger (if it is up-to-date) represents the amount owed to the business by that particular customer.

   b.   *The subsidiary accounts payable ledger*: The subsidiary accounts payable ledger contains a separate account for each supplier from whom the company has purchased on account. The total of all the balances of the individual accounts contained within the subsidiary accounts payable ledger should be equal to the balance in the general ledger accounts payable control account. Each individual subsidiary accounts payable account shows all credit purchases made by the company from a particular supplier, all payments made to the supplier, and any adjustments made to the account. The balance in an individual subsidiary accounts payable account represents the amount owed by the company to that supplier.

3.   *Special Journals*: Special journals may be used in the recording of transactions that occur very frequently. In earlier chapters, all transactions were assumed to be recorded in a general journal. In reality, it is more efficient to use special journals for recording routine transactions that occur often. Many businesses have special journals to record cash receipts, cash disbursements, sales of goods on account, and purchases of inventory on account. It is possible that a company might have more special journals than these. However, these are the four most common special journals.

   a.   *Cash receipts journal*: All receipts of cash are recorded in the cash receipts journal.

b. *Cash disbursements journal*: All payments of cash are recorded in the cash disbursements journal, sometimes called a cash payments journal.

c. *Sales journal*: Credit sales are recorded in the sales journal. Cash sales are recorded in the cash receipts journal.

d. *Purchases journal*: The purchases journal is used to record inventory purchases on account.

e. *General journal*: When special journals are used, the general journal is used to record any transaction that does not fit in a special journal. Adjusting entries, closing entries, sales returns, and purchases returns are examples of items that would be recorded in the general journal.

Note: Refer to an accounting principles textbook for examples of how to record transactions in special journals.

C. Cash Disbursements

1. *Cash Disbursement Records*: To ensure that proper control is maintained over cash disbursements, almost all cash disbursements should be made by check. Cash disbursements are usually recorded in a cash disbursements journal (see Section B-3-b).

2. *Trade and Cash Discounts*:

a. *Trade discounts*: Trade discounts are reductions from the retail list price of items in a catalog that are given by manufacturers or wholesalers to their dealers. Each dealer might have a specific discount (for example, 25, 30, or 40 percent) on items the dealer buys from the catalog. Trade discounts are not recorded on the accounting records of the buyer or of the seller. Both companies record the sale at the reduced amount. The trade discount is simply a method of determining the sales price.

EXAMPLE: Jones Distributing Company is a dealer of Ajax Wholesaling Company. Jones Distributing Company is given a 30 percent trade discount on all purchases from Ajax Wholesaling Company's catalog. Jones purchased goods with a total catalog list price of $10,000 from Ajax. The amount of the sale would be computed as follows:

List price	$10,000	
− Trade discount	− 3,000	($10,000 × 0.30)
Selling/		
purchase price	$ 7,000	

b. *Cash discounts*: Cash discounts encourage customers to pay their accounts promptly. Cash discounts are stated on the invoice and tell the customer how much of a discount may be taken if the bill is paid within a certain period.

An invoice might have the terms 2/10, n/30. This means that the customer will get a 2 percent discount if the bill is paid within 10 days of the invoice date and the net amount (the total amount) is due in 30 days.

The terms 3/15, n/30 mean that the customer will get a 3 percent discount if the bill is paid within 15 days and the net amount is due in 30 days.

The terms 3/15 EOM, n/60 mean that the customer may deduct a 3 percent discount if the invoice is paid within the first 15 days of the month following the month of the sale, and the net amount is due within 60 days from the date of the sales invoice.

EXAMPLE: Jones Company receives an invoice from Papper Company dated January 2, 19XA. The terms of the invoice are 2/10, n/30. The amount of the invoice is $100. If the invoice were paid on January 10, the amount due would be $98.

Total invoice amount	$100
− Cash discount (2% × $100)	− 2
Amount to be paid	$ 98

Using the gross method of recording cash discounts, Jones Company's journal entry to record payment of this invoice would be:

	dr	cr
Accounts payable	100	
Cash		98
Purchase discounts		2

Papper Company's entry to record receipt of the payment would be:

	dr	cr
Cash	98	
Sales discounts	2	
Accounts receivable		100

If the invoice were paid on January 15, the 10-day discount period would have passed and the total invoice amount of $100 would be due. Using the gross method of recording cash discounts, Jones Company's entry to record payment on January 15 would be:

	dr	cr
Accounts payable	100	
Cash		100

Papper Company's entry to record the receipt would be:

	dr	cr
Cash	100	
Accounts receivable		100

EXAMPLE: If an invoice is subject to both a trade and a cash discount, the cash discount is computed on the selling price after consideration of the trade discount. Jones Company received an invoice from Ajax Company. The list price of the goods purchased was $2,000. The trade discount is 30 percent and the terms of the cash discount are 3/10, n/30. Jones Company paid the invoice within the 10-day discount period. The amount paid was $1,358, which was computed as follows:

List price	$2,000	
− Trade discount	− 600	($2,000 × 0.30)
	$1,400	
− Cash discount	− 42	($1,400 × 0.03)
Amount paid	$1,358	

3. *Imprest Petty Cash*: It is not practical for a company to write checks for small expenditures. Some items, such as postage stamps, taxi fares, office supplies, and parking meter payments, can be made more easily from a special fund called a *petty cash fund*. An imprest petty cash fund has one custodian, often a secretary, who is responsible for handling cash payments from the fund. The word *imprest* means an advance of money for some specified business use.

a. *Establishing the petty cash fund*: The petty cash fund is established at some reasonable amount. Assume that a petty cash fund of $100 is to be established. A check for $100 would be written and cashed, and the money would be kept in a petty cash drawer or box. The journal entry to record the establishment of the fund is:

	dr	cr
Petty cash	100	
Cash		100

The only times an entry is made to the petty cash fund are when the fund is established or when the total amount of money in the fund is increased or decreased.

b. *Making disbursements from the petty cash fund*: When disbursements are made from the fund, the custodian prepares a petty cash voucher. A petty cash voucher is a record of the expenditure which includes the date, the amount paid, the reason for the expenditure, and the signature of the person who received the money. The petty cash drawer should always contain cash and vouchers equal to the total amount of the fund. No journal entries are prepared when the disbursements are made. The entries to record the disbursements are made when the fund is replenished.

c. *Replenishing the petty cash fund*: When the fund becomes depleted, the petty cash custodian makes a list of the petty cash vouchers and requests reimbursement. Assume that the petty cash vouchers indicate that $83.78 was disbursed from the fund. A check would be made out to the petty cash fund for $83.78. This check would be cashed and the money placed in the petty cash drawer. A journal entry would be made to record the expenditures as indicated by the petty cash vouchers. A typical journal entry to record replenishment might be:

	dr	cr
Postage expense	42.00	
Freight in	21.00	
Transportation expense	12.53	
Miscellaneous expense	8.25	
Cash		83.78

Note that the expense accounts are debited each time the fund is replenished.

d. *Reconciling petty cash*: At any time, the sum of the money and the petty cash vouchers in the petty cash drawer should equal the total amount of the fund. A periodic reconciliation should be made to ensure that this is the case. Occasional surprise audits (counts) of the fund should be made by a supervisor. This ensures that the petty cash custodian is using the fund for authorized expenditures and that vouchers are being properly completed.

4. *Checks and Check Registers*:

   a. *Check*: A check is a written document that orders a bank to pay a specific amount from the depositor's account to the payee of the check. Checks come in many different forms. Many checks have a check stub attached to the check. This stub is filled out prior to writing the check and is kept by the company writing the check. The stub may serve as a source document for recording the transaction.

   b. *Certified check*: A certified check is a check for which the bank guarantees that the depositor has enough funds in the bank account to cover the check when it is presented for payment. The depositor must take the check to the bank and have it certified prior to giving the check to the payee. The bank stamps *certified* on the check and removes the money from the depositor's account. A fee is usually charged for certifying a check. Certified checks might be issued when a large sum of money is involved.

   c. *Check register*: Check register is another term for cash disbursements journal. The check register lists all the checks issued. When a voucher system is used, a simplified version of the cash disbursements journal may be used, and this journal is usually called a check register. (See Section C-5 for further discussion of the check register.)

5. *The Voucher System and Recording of Accounts Payable*: A voucher system is used to obtain the maximum amount of internal control over cash disbursements, purchasing, and receiving. A voucher system requires that a voucher be prepared and verified prior to making any payments.

   a. *The voucher system*: A voucher is a document that is used to authorize payment of a liability. A voucher typically contains spaces for the voucher date, information from the supplier's invoice, the ledger accounts to be debited and credited, space for the approval signatures for each step of the verification process, and space for the signature for the approval of the liability. Vouchers are numbered consecutively, and a separate voucher is attached to each incoming invoice.

   b. *Recording transactions in a voucher system*:

      (1) An invoice is received and a voucher is prepared by transferring all the pertinent information from the invoice to the voucher.

      (2) The voucher with the invoice attached is sent to the appropriate individuals for verification.

      (3) After the verification process has been completed, an employee from the accounting department indicates the accounts to be debited and credited.

      (4) The voucher is approved by an official who notes that the verification procedures have been completed and the liability is valid.

      (5) After approval, the voucher is entered in the voucher register. A voucher register is similar to a purchases journal, but it has more columns for the different types of asset and expense accounts to be debited. A purchases journal records only purchases of inventory and supplies on account. A voucher register is used to record all types of expenditures. (A voucher

register replaces the purchases journal in companies using the voucher system.) All credits in the voucher register consist of a credit to the vouchers payable account.

(6) When payment is made, the date of the payment and the check number are recorded in the voucher register and the check is recorded in the check register. When a voucher system is used, all entries in the check register consist of a debit to vouchers payable and a credit to cash. The check register contains columns for debits to vouchers payable, credits to cash and credits to purchase discounts (for use when payment is made within the cash discount period).

(7) The column totals from the voucher register and the check register are posted to the general ledger periodically.

(8) Paid vouchers are filed numerically in a special file.

6. *Internal Control of Cash Disbursements*: To maintain adequate internal control over cash disbursements, the following steps should be followed:

a. *Payments*: All cash disbursements should be made by check except for minor expenditures paid through a petty cash fund.

b. *Use of prenumbered checks*: Checks should be prenumbered, and any checks that are written incorrectly should be marked *void* and filed in numerical sequence with the other canceled checks. In this way, all check numbers will be accounted for.

c. *Authorized signatures*: The individual who is authorized to sign checks should not have the authority to approve invoices or vouchers for payment or to make entries in the accounting records.

d. *Access to cash*: The individual who records cash disbursements in the accounting records should not have access to cash.

e. *Approval of voucher or invoice*: Checks submitted for signature should be accompanied by an approved voucher or invoice. The approved voucher or invoice should be stamped *paid* at the time the check is signed. This eliminates the possibility of paying the same invoice twice.

7. *Cash Over and Short*: Small errors may occur in making change during over-the-counter sales to customers. When this happens, the total of the daily cash register tapes will not be equal to the total cash collected. If there is more cash available than that reported on the total cash register tape (overage), the cash over and short account is credited. If there is less cash available than that reported on the total cash register tape (shortage), the cash over and short account is debited.

EXAMPLE: Jones Company collected $1,010.25 in cash for over-the-counter sales on March 1. The total cash sales per the cash register tapes on March 1 were $1,011.38. The entry to record the day's sales would be as follows:

	dr	cr
Cash	1,010.25	
Cash over and short	1.13	
Sales		1,011.38

D. Bank Statements and Cash Balance

Every month the bank provides each depositor with a bank statement for the bank account. This bank statement includes any checks paid by the bank and charged to the depositor's account and any deposit slips showing amounts that have been credited to the depositor's account. The bank statement is the bank's record of their account payable to the depositor. See Figure 10–1 for an example of a bank statement.

1. *Reconciliation*: When the bank statement is received, the depositor should prepare a reconciliation that explains any differences between the bank statement and the cash account in the ledger. In most circumstances, the balance per the bank statement will not agree with the cash balance per the general ledger. Preparation of a bank reconciliation by a party independent of recording cash, handling cash, or preparing checks is an important internal control tool.

   a. *Transactions not recorded by bank*: Transactions could have been recorded by the depositor which have not yet been recorded by the bank. Examples of these types of transactions are:

Figure 10–1 Bank Statement

THE FIRST NATIONAL BANK

MONTHLY
STATEMENT
OF ACCOUNT

PAGE
1

Jones Company
6491 Alameda Drive
Chicago, Illinois 60101

ACCOUNT NUMBER
31-484-6
STATEMENT DATE
11/29/19XA
LAST STATEMENT DATE
10/31/19XA

YOUR LAST CHECKING STATEMENT BALANCE WAS	From Which is Subtracted CHECKS/DEBITS/ PAYMENTS	And Added DEPOSITS/CREDITS/ ADVANCES	YOUR SERVICE CHARGE IS	RESULTING IN A CHECKING BALANCE OF
$10,423.82	$15,633.28	$16,752.41	$5.00	$11,537.95

DATE	CHECKS/DEBITS/PAYMENTS	DEPOSITS/CREDITS/ ADVANCES	BALANCE
11/1	101.23		
11/2	1,320.24		2,423.82
11/3	916.13	4,422.21	
11/5	212.10	33.24	
11/7	98.80		
11/8	100.00	893.26	4,513.17
11/10	87.50		
11/12	3,212.10	105.40	
11/13	108.20		3,123.22
11/14	56.43	157.22	
11/16	82.18		
11/18	99.50	3,310.12	2,100.10
11/19	71.33		
11/21		1,822.16	
11/26	63.25 DM	182.84	2,769.94
11/29	5.00 SC		

DM = Debit Memo, NSF Check.
SC = Service Charge

(1) *Deposits in transit*: Deposits recorded on the books of the depositor and sent to the bank which have not yet been recorded by the bank.

(2) *Outstanding checks*: Checks written and recorded on the books of the depositor which have not yet been paid by the bank and recorded on the books of the bank.

b. *Transactions not recorded by depositor*: Transactions could have been recorded by the bank which have not yet been recorded in the general ledger of the depositor. Examples of these types of transactions are:

(1) *Service charges*: The bank may charge a service charge for handling the depositor's account. Prior to receiving the bank statement, the depositor has no record of the amount of the service charge and it will not have been recorded on the depositor's books.

(2) *Notes collected by the bank*: The bank might have collected a note receivable for the depositor. If this is done, the bank usually charges a collection fee.

(3) *NSF checks*: NSF checks are nonsufficient funds checks. An NSF check is a check that has been received by the depositor company and deposited in its account. This check was returned to the bank because the account on which the check was written did not contain sufficient funds to cover the amount of the check. The bank returns the check to the depositor along with a debit memo indicating that the depositor's account was reduced by the amount of the check the bank was unable to collect.

(4) *Miscellaneous debit or credit memos*: There may be other miscellaneous types of debit or credit memos not recorded by the depositor, such as check printing costs or stop payment order charges.

2. *Detection and Correction of Errors*: The bank reconciliation may be complete after consideration of the reconciling items discussed in Section D-1. It is possible that the bank or the depositor may have made an error in recording the transactions for the month. If an error was made, it would be necessary to correct the error to reconcile the bank statement balance and the general ledger balance. Common types of errors are:

a. A check or a deposit is recorded with an incorrect amount.

b. The depositor has more than one bank account and records a check or a deposit in the wrong account.

c. The bank has made an error. The bank should be notified immediately so that the error can be corrected. There is no need to make an entry on the depositor's books since they are correct.

If the depositor made an error in recording a transaction, a correcting journal entry must be made to bring the account balance to the proper amount.

3. *Preparation of a Bank Reconciliation*: A bank reconciliation is a report that explains the difference between the bank's balance shown on the bank statement issued by the bank and the balance shown in the general ledger cash account. Figure 10–2 shows a typical form used in preparing a bank reconciliation.

EXAMPLE OF BANK RECONCILIATION: Jones Company received the bank statement shown in Figure 10–1 on December 5, 19XA. They found that the bank had not yet recorded a deposit of $1,322.93 which was mailed on November 28 and that five checks totaling $2,020.89 had not yet been presented to the bank for payment.

The outstanding checks were:

Check Number	Date	Amount
1933	11/20	$ 33.25
1938	11/25	282.65
1941	11/29	1,050.87
1942	11/29	200.00
1943	11/29	454.12
		$2,020.89

The $63.25 debit memo was for an NSF check issued by G-Var Company to Jones Company. The bookkeeper of Jones Company had recorded check number 1930 to the gas company as $65.43 in the records. The correct amount of the check was $56.43. This type of error is called a transposition error (when two figures of a number are transposed). The difference resulting from a transposition error is always divisible by 9, and this fact can be used to help in locating errors. The bank reconciliation for Jones Company is shown in Figure 10–2.

4. *Journal Entries to Record Reconciling Items*: The additions and deductions necessary to go from the balance per bank to the adjusted balance per bank and from the balance per books to the adjusted balance per books are called reconciling items. It is necessary to record journal entries for all reconciling items under the balance per books. No journal entries are necessary for the reconciling items that relate to the balance per bank, since they refer to the bank's records rather than the company's records. The journal entries to record the reconciling items on the Jones Company bank reconciliation are as follows:

   a. *Transposition errors*: The transposition error resulted in an overstatement of utilities expense of $9.00 and an understatement of cash of $9.00. The entry to correct the transposition error would be:

Figure 10–2 Bank Reconciliation for Jones Company

Balance per bank statement		11,537.95	Balance per books		10,899.24
Add: Deposit in transit		1,322.93	Add: Transposition		
		12,860.88	error		9.00
Less:			Less: Service charge	5.00	
Outstanding checks			NSF check	63.25	
No. 1933	$ 33.25				
No. 1938	282.65		Total		68.25
No. 1941	1,050.87				
No. 1942	200.00				
No. 1943	454.12	$2,020.89			
Adjusted bank balance		$10,839.99	Adjusted book balance		$10,839.99

	dr	cr
Cash	9.00	
Utilities expense		9.00

b. *Service charges*: The service charge was not yet recorded on the books of Jones Company. The entry to record the service charge would be:

	dr	cr
Bank service charge expense	5.00	
Cash		5.00

c. *NSF check*: The NSF check was originally recorded as a cash receipt. Since there were not sufficient funds to cover the check, it is not really a cash receipt but an account receivable from the customer. Jones Company would make the following entry to record the receipt of the NSF check.

	dr	cr
Accounts receivable—G-Var	63.25	
Cash		63.25

Review Questions

DIRECTIONS: Select the best answer from the four alternatives. Write the letter of your answer in the blank to the left of the number.

_____ 1. The total amount owed by Jones Company to Company X is represented by

   a. the balance in Jones Company's subsidiary accounts payable account for Company X.
   b. the balance in Jones Company's subsidiary accounts receivable account for Company X.
   c. the amount in the general ledger accounts payable control account.
   d. the amount in the general ledger accounts receivable control account.

_____ 2. Trade discounts are

   a. reductions from the list price of goods which are used in determining selling price.
   b. allowed only if the invoice is paid within a specified time period.
   c. recorded at the time of payment for the goods.
   d. all of the above.

_____ 3. Which of the following items should be classified as cash?

   a. Postage stamps
   b. Certificates of deposit
   c. Money orders
   d. IOUs

_____ 4. When the petty cash fund is reimbursed

   a. petty cash is debited.
   b. petty cash is credited.
   c. cash is debited.
   d. expenses are debited.

_____ 5. Which of the following procedures would not be considered a good internal control procedure for cash?

   a. All cash receipts should be deposited intact daily.
   b. All disbursements should be made by check (except for minor items paid from petty cash).

c. The person assigned to open cash receipts should restrictively endorse all checks immediately.

d. The bank reconciliation should be prepared by the same person who records cash receipts and disbursements since this person is familiar with the records.

_____ 6. The terms 3/15, n/60 on an invoice mean that

a. a discount of 15 percent may be taken if the invoice is paid in 60 days.

b. a discount of 3 percent may be taken if the invoice is paid within 15 days of the invoice date and the net amount of the invoice is due within 60 days.

c. if the invoice is paid within 60 days, 3/15 of the invoice may be deducted.

d. a discount of 3 percent may be taken if the invoice is paid by the fifteenth day of the month following the month of purchase.

_____ 7. Which of the following procedures should be followed to ensure good internal control over cash disbursements?

a. Disbursements made from the petty cash fund should be recorded on petty cash vouchers that are signed by the recipient of the cash.

b. The same individual who signs checks should approve vouchers for payment.

c. The individual who signs the checks should also record them in the check register.

d. Vouchers should be stamped *paid* when the canceled check is returned with the bank statement.

_____ 8. Nonsufficient funds checks are

a. checks that have been canceled by the bank to show that they have been paid.

b. checks that are guaranteed by the depositor's bank.

c. checks written by a customer and returned by the bank as uncollectible because there were insufficient funds in the customer's account.

d. checks issued by a company which have not yet been presented to the bank for payment.

_____ 9. A business paper used in summarizing a transaction and approving it for recording and payment is called a/an

a. invoice.

b. special journal.

c. control account.

d. voucher.

_____ 10. The cash over and short account might be used to record

a. a transposition error made in recording a check in the cash disbursements journal.

b. a bank service charge.

c. small errors made in making change in the petty cash fund.
d. all of the above.

11. When a voucher system is used

a. an obligation should not be recorded as a liability until a check is written for payment.
b. vouchers are prepared only for large invoices.
c. Petty cash is debited and vouchers payable is credited when the petty cash fund is reimbursed.
d. all credits in the voucher register are made to the vouchers payable account.

12. Which of the following procedures would not be considered a good internal control procedure for cash?

a. Use of a voucher system.
b. Use of a cash register.
c. Verification of the amount on an invoice before payment.
d. Checks should be numbered only after they have been written to avoid having a number assigned to a check written incorrectly.

13. After completing a bank reconciliation, it is necessary to make journal entries to record

a. errors made by the bank.
b. all reconciling items.
c. the reconciling items that explain the difference between the balance per bank and the adjusted balance per bank.
d. the reconciling items that explain the difference between the balance per books and the adjusted balance per books.

14. The correct journal entry to record a check returned as NSF by the bank would be

a. debit accounts receivable, credit cash.
b. debit bad debt expense, credit cash.
c. debit cash, credit accounts receivable.
d. debit NSF expense, credit cash.

15. A withdrawal of cash by the owner of a sole proprietorship should be recorded in the

a. cash receipts journal.
b. general journal.
c. cash disbursements journal.
d. purchases journal.

Use the following information in answering Questions 16 to 18.

Merry Co. purchased items with a list price of $10,000 on May 1, 19XA. Merry Co. was given trade discounts of 20 and 10 percent. The terms of the invoice were 2/10, n/30.

_____ **16.** Assuming that Merry Co. paid the invoice on May 9, the amount of the payment would be

    a. $6,860.
    b. $9,800.
    c. $7,056.
    d. $7,200.

_____ **17.** Assuming that Merry Co. paid the invoice on June 10, 19XA, the amount of payment would be

    a. $10,000.
    b. $6,860.
    c. $7,056.
    d. $7,200.

_____ **18.** Assuming that Merry Co. paid the invoice on May 9, the journal entry to record payment would include

    a. a debit to accounts payable, a debit to purchase discounts, and a credit to cash.
    b. a debit to accounts payable, a credit to purchase discounts, and a credit to cash.
    c. a debit to cash, a credit to accounts payable, and a credit to purchase discounts.
    d. a debit to accounts payable and a credit to cash.

Use this information in answering Questions 19 to 21.

Good Company wrote a check for $639.25 to Jones Company in payment for office equipment. The bookkeeper erroneously recorded the check in the cash disbursements journal for $369.25. The accounts used were correct; only the amount recorded was in error. The error was discovered when the monthly bank reconciliation was prepared.

_____ **19.** The item should be shown on the bank reconciliation as

    a. an addition to the balance per books.
    b. a deduction from the balance per books.
    c. an addition to the balance per bank.
    d. a deduction from the balance per bank.

_____

20. The journal entry to correct the error would be

    a. a debit to office equipment and a credit to cash for $270.
    b. a debit to cash and a credit to office equipment for $270.
    c. a debit to error correction and a credit to cash for $270.
    d. a debit to cash and a credit to error correction for $270.

_____

21. This type of error is called

    a. a slide error.
    b. a posting error.
    c. a balancing error.
    d. a transposition error.

Solutions

Answer   *Refer to:*

1. (a)   [B-2-b]

2. (a)   [C-2-a]

3. (c)   [A-1]

4. (d)   [C-3-c]

5. (d)   [A-3-b(7)]

6. (b)   [C-2-b]

7. (a)   [C-3-b]

8. (c)   [D-1-b(3)]

9. (d)   [C-5-a]

10. (c)   [C-7]

11. (d)   [C-5-b(5)]

12. (d)   [A-3, C-6-b]

13. (d)   [D-4]

14. (a)   [D-4-c]

15. (c)   [B-3-b]

16. (c)   [C-2-a, C-2-b] The correct solution is calculated as follows:

$10,000
− 2,000   ($10,000 × 0.20)   trade discount
$ 8,000
− 800   ($8,000 × 0.10)   trade discount
$ 7,200
− 144   ($7,200 × 0.02)   cash discount
$ 7,056

17. (d)   [C-2-a, C-2-b]

18. (b)   [C-2-b]

19. (b)   [D-3]

20. (a)   [D-4-a]

21. (d)   [D-4-a]

CHAPTER 11

Accounting for Investments

OVERVIEW

This chapter is intended to introduce the candidate to the basics of accounting for investments. Topics such as bond premium, discount amortization, and the equity method of accounting for investments in common stock are explained in the chapter. It is not important that the candidate fully understand these topics; however, knowledge that the various methods exist and when they are used will be useful.

   The candidate should understand the three major categories of investments and the appropriate accounting procedures for each. Accounting for stocks and bonds at cost should be emphasized over the other methods discussed.

KEY TERMS

Bond	Consolidated statements	Parent company
Bond discount	Equity method	Stock dividend
Bond premium	Investment	Subsidiary company

A. Introduction to Investments

Investments are assets held by a company which are not used in the operations of the business. These assets are held for investment purposes in the hope of earning a return or profit on the amount invested. The treatment of accounting for investments differs depending on whether the investments are of a short-term or long-term nature.

1. *Short-Term Investments*: Short-term investments, which the company intends to hold for less than one operating cycle, are classified as *temporary* investments (or marketable securities). Marketable securities are classified as current assets on the balance sheet.

2. *Long-Term Investments*: Long-term investments are investments intended to be held for longer than one operating cycle. Long-term investments are classified as *investments* on the balance sheet. There are three basic types of investments: real

estate, bonds, and stocks. Bond sinking funds and cash surrender value of life insurance are also classified as long-term investments.

B. Real Estate

Investments in real estate are usually long term in nature. The accounting treatment for
investments in real estate is the same whether the investments are of a short-term or
long-term nature. An example of a real estate investment would be land held for future
development of the business. The land is not currently used in the business but is being
held for future expansion. The land would be carried at cost on the records of the business. A gain or loss would be recorded when the land is sold if it is sold for an amount
different from its cost.

*EXAMPLE: Selzig Corp. holds 10 acres of land for investment purposes. The cost of
the land was $100,000. The land is sold for $150,000. The entry to record the sale
would be:*

	dr	cr
Cash	150,000	
Investment: Land		100,000
Gain on sale of land		50,000
To record sale of 10 acres of land held for investment purposes.		

**C. Bonds and
Interest Income**

Bonds are debt securities issued by the government or a corporation in order to raise
large sums of money. Most individual bond certificates have a stated face value of
$1,000. Bonds pay interest at a fixed rate based on the stated face value. Bond interest
is normally paid every six months. The fixed interest rate paid by a bond is called the
contract rate.

1. *Issuance of Bonds*: When bonds are issued, they may be sold for an amount
    greater or less than their face value. If a bond sells for less than its stated face
    value, it is selling at a discount. If it sells for more than its stated face value, it is
    selling at a premium. Bonds will sell for face value when the contract rate and the
    market rate are equal.

    a. *Discount*: If the market rate of interest (for bonds of the same quality) at the
        time the bonds are sold is higher than the contract rate paid by the bonds, the
        bonds will sell at a discount.

    b. *Premium*: If the market rate of interest at the time the bonds are sold is lower
        than the coupon (contract) rate paid by the bonds, the bonds will sell at a pre-
        mium.

2. *Accounting for Bonds and Interest Income*:

    a. *Short-term investments*: Short-term investments in bonds are carried at cost.

    b. *Purchase of bonds between interest dates*: The price paid for a bond includes
        a portion for purchased interest if the bond is purchased between interest
        dates. Commissions paid in acquiring a bond are considered to be a part of the
        cost.

(1) If a bond is purchased exactly on an interest payment date, the full purchase price is considered to be the cost of the bond (i.e., no "interest receivable" is purchased).

(2) If a bond is purchased between interest dates, the buyer must pay the seller for any interest that has accrued on the bond. The buyer then receives the full amount of the interest payment on the next interest payment date.

EXAMPLE: Assume that Petit Company purchased the Selzig Corp. bonds on February 1. Petit Company paid $9,658 for the bonds. Of this amount, $166.67 represented accrued interest. The interest portion was calculated as follows:

	$10,000	Face value
×	.10	Coupon rate
	1,000	Interest per year
×	2/12	Portion of year
	$166.67	Interest for 2 months

The entry to record the purchase of the bonds would be:

		dr	cr
Feb. 1	Investment in bonds	9,491.33	
	Interest receivable	166.67	
	Cash		9,658.00

When the semiannual interest payment is received, Petit Company would make the following entry:

		dr	cr
June 1	Cash	500.00	
	Interest receivable		166.67
	Interest income		333.33

To record semiannual interest receipt
($10,000 × 0.10 × 6/12 months).

c. *Interest income*: The interest income earned on bonds accrues from day to day. Bond interest is paid every six months. Therefore, it might be necessary to record an adjusting entry to recognize accrued interest receivable at the end of the accounting period.

EXAMPLE: Assume that Petit Company's year end is October 31. The Selzig Corp. bonds pay interest on June 1 and December 1. Petit Company purchased the bonds on December 1. The journal entry to record the June 1 receipt of interest would be:

	dr	cr
Cash	500.00	
Interest income		500.00

To record semiannual receipt of bond interest
($10,000 × 0.10 × 6/12 months).

It would be necessary for Petit Company to record an adjusting entry to recognize the interest that has been earned from June 1 through October 31. The adjusting journal entry to record the interest accrual would be:

	dr	cr
Accrued interest receivable	416.67	
Interest income		416.67

To record interest accrued on Selzig bond from June 1 through October 31 ($10,000 × 0.10 × 5/12 months).

3. *Amortization of Premium or Discount on Long-Term Bonds*: A premium or discount is ignored in the measurement of interest revenue for short-term bonds since the bonds are not intended to be held to maturity. The effect of any premium or discount on interest revenue should be recognized when the bonds are to be held for a long period of time. A bond premium or discount results when the market rate of interest is different from the contract rate of interest. The premium or discount paid for the bond effectively adjusts the rate of interest received on the bond to the market rate. Amortization of bond premium or discount is used to adjust the interest received to approximate the effective amount of interest earned on the investment. Amortization of bond premium decreases interest income and amortization of bond discount increases interest income.

   a. *Amortizing bond premium or discount*: When long-term bonds are acquired at a premium or discount, they are recorded at cost. As interest is received over the life of the bond, any premium or discount is amortized. This brings the carrying value (book value) of the bond closer to its face value. By the maturity date of the bond, it will be valued at face value.

   b. *Methods of bond premium or discount amortization*: There are two methods of bond premium or discount amortization: the straight-line method and the effective interest method. The effective interest method is more exact and should be used whenever the difference that results from using the straight-line method instead of the effective interest method is material.

4. *Accounting for Sale of Bond Investment*:

   a. *Sale of bonds at maturity*: If bonds are held to maturity, the holder receives the face value of the bonds from the company that issued the bonds.

   b. *Sale of bonds prior to maturity*: If a bond investment is sold prior to its maturity date, a gain or loss will probably occur. If the bonds are sold between interest dates, the purchaser must pay the seller for any interest that has accrued. If the bonds are classified as long term, any premium or discount on the bonds should be amortized up to the date of sale. There is no premium or discount amortization recorded for short-term bond investments. Any selling commission should be deducted from the selling price of the bonds.

   EXAMPLE: ABC Co. held $10,000 (face value) of XYZ Corp. bonds. The bonds were purchased at face value. The coupon rate of interest is 15 percent, and the bonds pay interest on April 1 and October 1. ABC Co. sold the bonds on May 1 for $10,750. A sales commission of $50 was paid. The entry to record the sale would be:

	dr	cr
May 1 Cash	10,700	
Investment in bonds		10,000
Interest revenue		125
Gain on sale of bonds		575

To record sale of 10 XYZ Corp. bonds for $10,750 less a broker's commission of $50. Accrued interest was $125.

D.   Stocks and Dividend Income

1. *Recording Investment in Stock*: Investments in stock are usually recorded at cost. Commissions paid in acquiring stocks are considered to be part of the cost of the stock.

   a. *Short-term investment*: Short-term investments in stock of other companies are called marketable equity securities. Marketable equity securities are recorded in the balance sheet at the lower of cost or market. Short-term investments in stock are valued at cost in the balance sheet unless the aggregate market value of all short-term equity securities is less than their cost. If the aggregate market value is less than cost, the securities are valued at market.

      EXAMPLE: Jones Corporation has the following portfolio of marketable equity securities:

	Cost	Market
Equity security 1	$100,000	$ 90,000
Equity security 2	150,000	170,000
Equity security 3	50,000	30,000
Equity security 4	60,000	60,000
Totals	$360,000	$350,000

      Since the total market value of the portfolio is less than the total cost, the marketable equity securities would be reported in the balance sheet at the cost of $360,000 less an allowance for decline in market value of $10,000 to yield a carrying amount of $350,000. Note that the carrying amount is based on the comparison of total cost and total market value of the portfolio, rather than the lower of cost or market for each individual equity security.

   b. *Long-term investment*: Long-term investments in stock are accounted for differently depending on the amount of stock the investor owns and the resulting amount of control that the investor can exercise over the operations of the investee. This amount of control is measured by the percentage of the investee's voting common stock that is owned by the investor. The three classifications used in accounting are:

      (1) *Ownership of more than 50 percent of common stock*: In this case, the investor is said to own a controlling interest in the investee, and the financial statements of the two companies are combined into a *consolidated* set of financial statements by the parent company. When financial statements are consolidated, the two accounting entities are treated as if they were one accounting entity for financial statement purposes. The investor company that owns more than 50 percent of the voting stock in the investee company is called the *parent company*. The investee company that is controlled by the parent company is called the *subsidiary*

company. The procedures for consolidating financial statements are beyond the scope of this chapter.

(2) *Ownership of 20 to 50 percent of common stock*: In this case the investor is *assumed* to have significant influence over the operations of the investee corporation. Due to the assumption of significant influence, the investor should account for the investment using the equity method. Under the equity method, the investment is originally recorded at cost. When the investee corporation reports earnings, the investor recognizes its share of the investee's reported earnings by debiting the investment account and crediting earnings. The amount recorded is based on the percentage of the stock held by the investor. Dividends and the investor's proportionate share of net losses are recorded as a reduction in the investment account. The earnings or loss account recorded by the investor for its proportionate share of the investee's income is shown on the income statement as investment income or loss.

EXAMPLE: In January, 19XA, James Co. purchased 2,000 shares (25 percent) of PRO, Inc. common stock for a total cost of $80,320. The entry to record the purchase on James Co.'s books is:

		dr	cr
Jan. 1	Investment in PRO, Inc.	80,320	
	Cash		80,320
	Purchased 2,000 shares of stock.		

On December 31, 19XA, PRO, Inc. reported net income of $100,000. The entry to record James Co.'s share of PRO, Inc.'s net income is:

		dr	cr
Dec. 31	Investment in PRO, Inc.	25,000	
	Earnings from investment in PRO, Inc.		25,000
	To record 25% equity in PRO, Inc.'s net income of $100,000.		

On January 20, 19XB, PRO, Inc. paid James Co. $5,000 in dividends. (The total dividend declaration was $20,000.) The entry to record the receipt of the dividend is:

		dr	cr
Jan. 20	Cash	5,000	
	Investment in PRO, Inc.		5,000
	To record receipt of dividends paid by PRO, Inc.		

On December 31, 19XB, PRO, Inc. reported a net loss of $28,000. The entry to record James Co.'s share of PRO, Inc.'s net loss is:

		dr	cr
Dec. 31	Loss from investment in PRO, Inc.	7,000	
	Investment in PRO, Inc.		7,000
To record 25% equity in PRO, Inc.'s net loss of $28,000.			

(3) *Ownership of less than 20 percent of common stock*: When less than 20 percent of the common stock is owned, the investor is assumed to have little influence over the operations of the investee. In this case the investment is accounted for at cost using the lower of cost or market. If the ag-

gregate market value of the long-term investment portfolio declines below the aggregate cost of the portfolio, long-term investments should be valued in the balance sheet at market. Lower of cost or market is used to satisfy the conservatism principle.

(4) *Ownership of preferred stock*: Investments in preferred stock are accounted for at cost using lower of cost or market.

2. *Recording Dividend Income*:

a. *Recording receipt of dividends*: Dividend income does not accrue as interest income does. Dividends are income when received by the investor and are usually not recorded until they are received. The entry to record the receipt of dividends when stock ownership is less than 20 percent is:

	dr	cr
Cash	XXX	
Dividend income		XXX

b. *Recording receipt of stock dividends*: Stock dividends are distributions in the form of additional shares of stock instead of cash. Stock dividends do not represent income to the recipient. The investor apportions the original cost of the shares over the new total amount of shares owned.

EXAMPLE: If XYZ Corp. owned 1,000 shares of Ajax Corp. common stock and a 5 percent stock dividend was paid by Ajax Corp., XYZ Corp. would receive an additional 50 shares of Ajax Corp. stock.

Assume that XYZ Corp. paid $10,000 for the 1,000 shares that it originally owned. After the stock dividend is received, that $10,000 is apportioned over the new number of shares owned ($10,000/1,050 shares = $9.524). The new cost per share of stock would be approximately $9.524 per share. If any of the shares of stock are sold after the stock dividend is received, the gain or loss on the sale must be computed using the new cost of $9.524 per share.

3. *Sale of Investments in Stock*: When an investment in stock is sold, the book value of the investment (which in most cases is cost) is compared to the selling price to determine any gain or loss on the sale. Any selling commissions are treated as a deduction from the total selling price.

EXAMPLE: Jones Corporation sold 10 shares of Baines Corp. common stock for $1,000. The carrying value of the stock was $800, which was its cost. Selling commissions on the sale amounted to $25. The journal entry to record the sale would be:

	dr	cr
Cash	975	
Investment in Baines Corp. stock		800
Gain on sale of stock		175

To record sale of 10 shares of Baines Corp. stock for $100/share less $25 broker's commission.

Review Questions

DIRECTIONS: Select the best answer from the four alternatives. Write the letter of your answer in the blank to the left of the number. (For simplicity, when calculating interest in this set of questions, assume 360 days per year and 30 days per month.)

1. A long-term debt security that normally has a face value of $1,000 and pays semi-annual interest at a stated rate is called a/an

   a. note.
   b. account receivable.
   c. bond.
   d. preferred stock.

2. If bonds are sold between interest dates

   a. the seller must pay the buyer the accrued interest to the date of sale.
   b. the buyer must pay the seller the accrued interest to the date of sale.
   c. the bonds will sell at a premium.
   d. the seller is allowed to deduct the interest that accrued prior to the date of purchase from the next semiannual interest payment.

3. When a bond sells for more than its face value, the difference between the face value of the bond and the selling price is called

   a. a bond discount.
   b. a bond premium.
   c. additional paid in debt.
   d. amortization.

4. When bonds receivable that were purchased at a discount are classified as long-term investments

   a. the bond investment account should be debited for the face value of the bonds purchased.
   b. the carrying value of the bonds (the book value in the investment account) will remain unchanged over the life of the bond.
   c. any discount on the purchase of the bond should be amortized over the life of the bond.
   d. accrual of bond interest at year end is not necessary.

_____   **5.** Land held by a business for future sale should be valued in the balance sheet at

    a. cost.
    b. lower of cost or market.
    c. market value.
    d. replacement cost.

_____   **6.** Puscas Co. purchased 10 shares of Schmaus Co. common stock for $100 per share. Puscas Co. paid a $50 brokerage commission on this transaction. The investment account should be debited for

    a. $150.
    b. $950.
    c. $1,000.
    d. $1,050.

_____   **7.** Short-term marketable equity securities should be reported in the balance sheet at

    a. cost.
    b. market value.
    c. lower of cost or market.
    d. replacement cost.

_____   **8.** A real estate investment that had a book value of $20,000 was sold for $22,000. The journal entry to record the sale would include

    a. a credit to cash for $22,000.
    b. a credit to a gain account for $2,000.
    c. a debit to the investment account for $20,000.
    d. a debit to cash for $20,000.

_____   **9.** When the equity method is used to account for an investment in another company

    a. the investor is assumed to have significant influence over the operations of the investee.
    b. dividends are recorded as income.
    c. the basis of the investment on the company's books remains at cost.
    d. dividends are recorded by the investor company as an increase in the investment account.

_____   **10.** A company that owns more than 50 percent of the voting stock of another corporation is called the

    a. primary company.
    b. subsidiary company.

c. parent company.

d. controlling company.

_____

11. Bart Co. sold 10 shares of Ajax Corporation preferred stock for $826 in cash. The carrying value of the stock on Bart Co.'s books was $900. Selling commissions on the transaction were $30. The journal entry to record the sale would be:

		dr	cr
a.	Loss on sale of stock	44	
	Commissions expense	30	
	Cash	826	
	Investment in Ajax Corp.		900
b.	Investment in Ajax Corp.	900	
	Cash		826
	Gain on sale of stock		74
c.	Cash	826	
	Loss on sale of stock	74	
	Investment in Ajax Corp.		900
d.	Cash	796	
	Loss on sale of stock	104	
	Investment in Ajax Corp.		900

_____

12. Financial statements that combine the results of a parent company with its subsidiaries for financial reporting purposes are called

a. parent statements.

b. consolidated statements.

c. combined statements.

d. subsidiary statements.

_____

13. Which of the following items would not be classified as a long-term investment?

a. Bond sinking fund

b. An investment in bonds that is expected to be held for more than one year

c. A building used in the business

d. Land held for future expansion of the business

_____

14. Which of the following statements about dividend income is true?

a. Dividends are recorded as income regardless of the percentage of voting stock of the investee held by the investor.

b. Dividends should be accrued at year end based on historical dividend rates.

c. Dividends are considered to be income when they are received by the investor company if the investor owns less than 20 percent of the voting shares of the investee.

d. Stock dividends increase the basis per share of stock owned by the investor.

15. Axel Co. owned 400 shares of common stock that were purchased for $4,400. Axel Co. received a common stock dividend of 40 shares of this stock. What was the carrying value per share of stock after the stock dividend was received?

   a. $11
   b. $110
   c. $9
   d. $10

Use this information in answering Questions 16 to 18. For simplicity, when calculating interest in this set of questions, assume 360 days per year and 30 days per month.

Assume Kan Co. purchased $300,000 of Lily Corp. 12 percent bonds for face value on April 1, 19XA. The bonds pay interest on January 1 and July 1. Kan Co.'s year end is August 31.

16. The total amount of cash which Kan Co. paid for the bonds on April 1 was

   a. $300,000.
   b. $318,000.
   c. $291,000.
   d. $309,000.

17. The amount of the interest payment Kan Co. will receive on July 1 is

   a. $18,000.
   b. $9,000.
   c. $36,000.
   d. $18,540.

18. The adjusting entry that Kan Co. should make on August 31 is:

   a. Debit bond interest receivable and credit bond interest revenue for $6,000.
   b. Debit bond interest revenue and credit bond interest receivable for $6,000.
   c. Debit bond interest receivable and credit bond interest revenue for $9,000.
   d. No adjusting entry should be made.

Use this information in answering Questions 19 to 21.

On January 1, 19XA, Box Co. purchased 5,000 shares (40 percent) of Bag Co.'s common (voting) stock for a total cost of $100,000. On December 31, 19XA, Bag Co. reported net income of $100,000. On January 5, 19XB, Bag Co. declared a $10,000 dividend on its common stock.

19. The entry to record the purchase of Bag Co. stock by Box Co. would be:

a. Debit cash and credit investment in Bag Co. for $100,000.
b. Debit investment in Bag Co. and credit cash for $100,000.
c. Debit investment in Bag Co. and credit cash for $40,000.
d. None of the above.

20. The entry to record the receipt of the dividend by Box Co. would be:

a. Debit cash and credit dividend income for $10,000.
b. Debit cash and credit dividend income for $4,000.
c. Debit cash and credit investment in Bag Co. for $4,000.
d. Debit cash and credit investment in Bag Co. for $10,000.

21. The entry by Box Co. to record the earnings of Bag Co. would be:

a. Debit investment in Bag Co. and credit earnings from investment in Bag Co. for $40,000.
b. Debit investment in Bag Co. and credit earnings from investment in Bag Co. for $100,000.
c. Debit cash and credit earnings from investment in Bag Co. for $40,000.
d. No journal entry would be made to recognize Bag Co.'s income.

22. Jayne Co. has the following portfolio of marketable equity securities:

	Cost	Market
Equity security 1	$ 5,000	$ 6,000
Equity security 2	10,000	5,000
Equity security 3	6,000	6,000

The marketable equity securities should be reported on the balance sheet at

a. $21,000.
b. $16,000.
c. $19,000.
d. $17,000.

Solutions

Answer	Refer to:
1. (c)	[C]
2. (b)	[C-2-b(2)]
3. (b)	[C-1]
4. (c)	[C-3-a]
5. (a)	[B]

6. (d) [D-1] Commissions paid in acquiring stock are included as part of the cost of the stock.

Cash paid for the stock	$1,000	($10 × 100)
+ Commission paid	50	
Amount to be debited	$1,050	

7. (c) [D-1-a]

8. (b) [B]

Selling price	$22,000
− Book value	20,000
Gain on sale	$ 2,000

The entry to record the transaction would be:

	dr	cr
Cash	22,000	
Gain on sale of investment		2,000
Investment		20,000

9. (a) [D-1-b(2)]

10. (c) [D-1-b(1)]

11. (d) [D-3]

Selling price	$826
− Selling commission	− 30
Amount for computing gain or loss	$796

Book value	$900
− Proceeds	− 796
Loss on sale	$104

12. (b) [D-1-b(1)]

13. (c) [A]

14. (c) [D-2-a, D-1-b(2)]

15. (d)   [D-2-b]

$$\frac{\text{total original cost}}{\substack{\text{total number of shares}\\ \text{owned after stock dividend}}} = \text{cost per share}$$

$$\frac{\$4,400}{440} = \$10$$

16. (d)   [C-2-b(2)] Since the bonds were purchased between interest dates, Kan Co. had to pay for the accrued interest as well as the face value of the bonds.

$300,000   Face value

   9,000   Accrued interest   ($300,000 × 0.12 × 3/12)

$309,000

17. (a)   [C-2-b(2)] The amount of the semiannual interest payment is $18,000 ($300,000 × 0.12 × 6/12).

18. (a)   [C-2-c] Kan Co. must make an adjusting entry to accrue the interest earned for the months of July and August. The computation of accrued interest is $300,000 × 0.12 × 2/12 = $6,000. This entry would debit bond interest receivable and credit bond interest revenue.

19. (b)   [D-1-b(2)]

20. (c)   [D-1-b(2)] Dividends reduce the investment account under the equity method. Box Company's share of the dividend was $4,000 ($10,000 × 0.40). The entry would include a debit to cash and a credit to investment in Bag Co.

21. (a)   [D-1-b(2)] Under the equity method, the investor records its proportionate share of the investee's net income as an increase in the investment account. Box Company's share of Bag Company's net income is $40,000 ($100,000 × 0.40).

22. (d)   [D-1-a]

	Cost	Market
Equity security 1	$ 5,000	$ 6,000
Equity security 2	10,000	5,000
Equity security 3	6,000	6,000
Totals	$21,000	$17,000

Since the aggregate market value of the portfolio as a whole is less than the aggregate cost, marketable equity securities should be reported on the balance sheet at market value of $17,000.

CHAPTER 12

Accounting for Inventories

OVERVIEW

This chapter is intended to introduce the candidate to the accounting procedures used in valuing and recording inventories. Inventories are often one of the most important and largest current assets held by a company. Therefore, an understanding of the topic is important.

The candidate should understand the four methods of pricing inventories, how to apply the lower of cost or market theory, how to determine cost of goods sold, and the effects that inventory valuation and inventory errors have on net income. The candidate should review the periodic inventory system thoroughly.

KEY TERMS

FIFO	Periodic inventory system
Gross profit method	Perpetual inventory system
LIFO	Weighted-average method
Lower of cost or market	

A. Types of Inventory Systems

1. *Perpetual Inventory Systems*: When a perpetual inventory system is used, a continuous record is maintained of all inventory transactions.

   a. *Merchandise inventory account*: A merchandise inventory account is kept. Inventory purchases are recorded as increases in the inventory account, and sales of inventory are recorded as decreases in the inventory account. The cost of goods sold is recorded as units are sold.

   b. *Use of perpetual inventory system*: A perpetual inventory system is often used by businesses that sell merchandise with a high per-unit value. Manufacturing firms often use a perpetual inventory system since they need accurate and timely information about costs. As computers make the processing of data easier, more companies are using perpetual inventory systems.

EXAMPLE: Assume that Nelson Co., which sells minicomputers, has 10 units of inventory on hand on January 1, 19XA. These 10 units originally cost $10,000. The 10 units would be included in the merchandise inventory account.

Merchandise Inventory

1/1/XA	10, 000		
2/2	7,700	6,000	2/10
Bal.	11,700		

Cost of Goods Sold

2/10	6,000	

On February 2, 19XA, the company purchased seven more units at $1,100 each. The journal entry to record the purchase would be:

	dr	cr
Feb 2. Merchandise inventory	7,700	
Accounts payable		7,700
Purchased 7 units of inventory P.O. #2182		

On February 10, 19XA, the company sold six of the original 10 units for $2,500 each. The entries to record this transaction would be:

	dr	cr
Feb. 10 Accounts receivable	15,000	
Sales		15,000
To record sale of six units.		
Feb. 10 Cost of goods sold	6,000	
Merchandise inventory		6,000
To record cost of goods sold for 6 units sold on February 10.		

   c. *End-of-period inventory procedure*: At the end of the period, the balance in the inventory account should represent the cost of the inventory that is on hand. The cost of goods sold account should contain the cost of all units sold during the period. A periodic physical count of inventory is taken to verify the balance of the inventory account. This count will reveal any "shrinkage."

  2. *Periodic Inventory Systems*: When a periodic inventory system is used, purchases of inventory are recorded in a purchases account. Ending inventory is determined by taking a physical count of the goods on hand at the end of the period. A value is then determined for the ending inventory that is on hand. The cost of goods sold is computed by subtracting the ending inventory from the goods available for sale. Goods available for sale is determined by adding total purchases for the period to the beginning inventory.

   a. *Use of a periodic inventory system*: Many businesses that sell a variety of low-cost items use a periodic inventory system. A perpetual inventory system is more difficult and costly to maintain than a periodic inventory system.

EXAMPLE: Use the same facts as in the previous example, with the Nelson Co. using a periodic inventory system. The beginning inventory consists of 10 units which cost $10,000.

Merchandise Inventory

Bal. 1/1	10, 000	

Purchases

2/2	7,700	

The entry to record the purchase on February 2 would be as follows:

	dr	cr
Feb. 2 Purchases	7,700	
Accounts payable		7,700

To record purchase of seven units of inventory P.O. #2182

The entry to record the sale on February 10 would be as follows:

	dr	cr
Feb. 10 Accounts receivable	15,000	
Sales		15,000

To record sale of six units.

b. *Merchandise inventory account*: When a periodic system is used, the merchandise inventory account remains unchanged for the period. Purchases of inventory are recorded in the purchases account, and no entry is made that affects inventory when a sale is made.

EXAMPLE: Assume that Nelson Co. made no other purchases or sales during the month of February. Financial statements will be prepared as of February 28. To do so, a physical count of the inventory must be taken to determine the quantity on hand. The physical count indicated that 11 units were on hand. Nelson Co. assumed that these 11 units were made up of the seven units purchased on February 2 and four units from beginning inventory (FIFO). The value of the ending inventory ($11,700) was calculated as follows:

$$7 \text{ units @ } \$1,100 = \$\ 7,700$$
$$\underline{4 \text{ units @ } \$1,000 = \quad 4,000}$$
$$11 \text{ units} \qquad = \$11,700$$

To determine cost of goods sold, Nelson Co. made the following calculation:

Beginning inventory	$10,000
+ Purchases	7,700
= Goods available for sale	$17,700
− Ending inventory	− 11,700
= Cost of goods sold	$ 6,000

B.   Inventory Pricing

To value ending inventory, the company must make an assumption about the cost flow of the goods out of the inventory account. Four basic inventory cost flow assumptions are used in accounting: FIFO, LIFO, weighted average, and specific identification.

(The implementation of various cost-flow assumptions with a perpetual inventory system will not be discussed in this chapter.)

1. *FIFO (First-In, First-Out)*: When a FIFO inventory pricing assumption is used, the units purchased first are assumed to be the first units sold. The units left in ending inventory are made up of the units purchased last.

    EXAMPLE: Petit Co. uses a periodic inventory system and uses the FIFO method of inventory pricing. The periodic inventory count indicated that 60 units were on hand on January 31. The January 31 inventory valuation and cost of goods sold for January is calculated as follows:

    Units available for sale:

    50 units from beginning inventory @ $2.00/unit
    20 units from January 3 purchase @ $2.20/unit
    30 units from January 5 purchase @ $2.30/unit
    50 units from January 30 purchase @ $2.50/unit

    If there are 60 units in ending inventory, 90 units must have been sold. Using a FIFO pricing assumption, the cost of goods sold would be calculated in this way:

50 units in beginning inventory @ $2.00/unit	$100.00
20 units from January 3 purchase @ $2.20/unit	44.00
20 units from January 5 purchase @ $2.30/unit	46.00
	$190.00

    Ending inventory:

10 units from January 5 purchase @ $2.30/unit	$ 23.00
50 units from January 30 purchase @ $2.50/unit	125.00
	$148.00

2. *LIFO (Last-In, First-Out)*: When a LIFO inventory pricing assumption is used, the units purchased last are assumed to be the first units sold. The units remaining in ending inventory consist of the units that were acquired earliest.

    EXAMPLE: Using the facts in the previous example, assume that Petit Co. now uses a LIFO inventory pricing assumption. The cost of goods sold for January would be calculated in this way:

50 units from January 30 purchase @ $2.50/unit	$125.00
30 units from January 5 purchase @ $2.30/unit	69.00
10 units from January 3 purchase @ $2.20/unit	22.00
	$216.00

    Ending inventory:

50 units from beginning inventory @ $2.00/unit	$100.00
10 units from January 3 purchase @ $2.20/unit	22.00
	$122.00

Note: The IRS requires that if LIFO is used for income tax purposes, it must be used for financial reporting purposes. In Canada, LIFO is not acceptable for income tax purposes.

3. *Weighted Average*: When a weighted-average inventory pricing assumption is used, a weighted-average unit cost is determined by dividing the cost of goods available for sale by the total units available for sale (units in beginning inventory + total units purchased). The cost of ending inventory is determined by multiplying the total number of units in the ending inventory by the weighted-average unit cost. The cost of the units sold is determined by multiplying the number of units sold by the weighted-average unit cost.

EXAMPLE: Using the facts in the previous example, assume that the Petit Co. uses the weighted-average inventory pricing assumption. The January 31 inventory valuation and the cost of goods sold for January would be determined as follows:

	Units Available for Sale		Cost of Goods Available for Sale
Beginning inventory	50 units × $2.00	=	$100.00
January 3 purchase	20 units × $2.20	=	44.00
January 5 purchase	30 units × $2.30	=	69.00
January 30 purchase	50 units × $2.50	=	125.00
	150 units		$338.00

The weighted-average unit cost is computed as follows:

$$\frac{\text{cost of goods available for sale}}{\text{units available for sale}} = \frac{\$338.00}{150.00} = \$2.253/\text{unit}$$

The cost of goods sold would be calculated as follows:

Units available for sale	150
− Units in ending inventory	− 60
Units sold	90

Cost of goods sold = units sold × weighted average per unit cost
$202.80 = 90 units × $2.2533/unit

Ending inventory = 60 units × $2.2533/unit = $135.20

4. *Specific Identification*: When a company is able to identify each item in inventory with a specific purchase, specific invoice prices may be used to assign costs to the units in ending inventory.

EXAMPLE: Using the facts in the previous example, assume that Petit Co. now uses specific invoice prices to cost ending inventory. Of the 60 units in ending inventory, they have determined that 30 units are from the January 30 purchase, 20 units are from the January 5 purchase, and 10 units are from the January 3 purchase.

Ending inventory would be valued as follows:

30 units @ $2.50/unit = $ 75.00
20 units @ 2.30/unit = 46.00
10 units @ 2.20/unit = 22.00
Total ending inventory = $143.00

Cost of goods sold:

$$50 \text{ units @ } \$2.00/\text{unit} = \$100.00$$
$$10 \text{ units @ } \ \ 2.20/\text{unit} = \ \ 22.00$$
$$10 \text{ units @ } \ \ 2.30/\text{unit} = \ \ 23.00$$
$$20 \text{ units @ } \ \ 2.50/\text{unit} = \ \ \underline{50.00}$$
$$\text{Cost of goods sold} = \overline{\$195.00}$$

C. Applying Lower of Cost or Market

Inventory is normally reported in the balance sheet at cost. If a permanent decline in the value of the inventory occurs, the conservatism principle requires that the inventory be reported at a lower value than cost. A permanent decline in the value of inventory may occur when the goods become obsolete, damaged, or shopworn or if there is a general price decline for goods of that type. When the market value of inventory is lower than its cost, the inventory should be reported at its market value.

D. Determining Cost of Goods Sold

1. *Periodic Inventory System*: When a periodic inventory system is used, the cost of goods sold is determined as follows:

Cost of goods sold:

Beginning inventory
+ Net purchases
 ──────────────
Goods available for sale
− Ending inventory
 ──────────────
Cost of goods sold

Net purchases:

Purchases
+ Transportation (freight) in
− Purchases discounts
− Purchase returns and allowances
 ──────────────
Net purchases

EXAMPLE: Sullivan Co. had beginning inventory for 19XA of $105,000. The balance in the purchases account as of the year end was $1,120,000. The ending inventory valued at LIFO was $110,000. Cost of goods sold for 19XA is:

Beginning inventory	$ 105,000
+ Purchases	1,120,000
Goods available for sale	$1,225,000
− Ending inventory	110,000
Cost of goods sold	$1,115,000

2. *Perpetual Inventory System*: When a perpetual inventory system is used, the balance in the cost of goods sold account should represent the cost of goods sold for the period, unless a physical count detects "shrinkage."

3. *Estimate as Percentage of Sales*: Cost of goods sold is sometimes estimated as a percentage of sales. This method may be used when monthly financial statements are prepared and taking a physical count is too costly. Inventory estimation may also be necessary if inventory has been stolen or destroyed by fire.

4. *Gross Profit Method*: The income statement format is:

$$
\begin{array}{l}
\text{Sales} \\
\underline{- \text{ Cost of goods sold}} \\
\text{Gross profit} \\
\underline{- \text{ Operating expenses}} \\
\text{Net operating income}
\end{array}
$$

The gross profit divided by sales revenue is called the *gross profit ratio*. If a company's gross profit ratio is consistent from period to period, that ratio can be used to estimate the cost of goods sold. Once the cost of goods sold is estimated, ending inventory can also be computed.

EXAMPLE: Crass Co.'s gross profit ratio is 40 percent and is relatively consistent from period to period. Crass Co. wishes to estimate ending inventory and cost of goods sold for the month of June. Sales for June are estimated at $100,000. Beginning inventory was $30,000 and purchases were $72,000. Figure 12–1 shows the calculation of estimated inventory and cost of goods sold.

If the gross profit percentage (ratio) is 40 percent, the average percentage for cost of goods sold is 60 percent. If sales are $100,000, cost of goods sold is estimated to be $60,000 and gross profit is estimated to be $40,000. Once cost of goods sold is estimated to be $60,000, an estimate of ending inventory can be made as follows:

Goods available for sale	$102,000
− Estimated cost of goods sold	− 60,000
Estimated ending inventory	$ 42,000

5. *Retail Inventory Method*: The retail inventory method is often used by retail businesses to compute inventory valuations. Records are kept of merchandise acquired at both cost and retail selling price. The ratio of cost to selling price is used to convert inventory from retail value to approximate cost. This method is complex, and the details of the method will not be discussed in this chapter.

E. Evaluating Effect of Inventory on Net Income

1. *Inventory Valuation*: It is important that inventory be valued accurately. An error in the ending inventory valuation will affect both the balance sheet (through inventory) and the income statement (through cost of goods sold). Since the ending inventory of one period is the beginning inventory of the next period, the income

Figure 12–1   Calculation/Gross Profit

Goods available for sale	$102,000	
− Estimated cost of goods sold	60,000	
Estimated ending inventory	$42,000	
Sales	$100,000	100%
Less: Cost of goods sold		
Beginning inventory	$30,000	
+ Purchases	72,000	
Goods available for sale	$102,000	
− Estimated ending inventory	42,000	
− Estimated cost of goods sold	60,000	60%
Gross profit	$40,000	40%

statement of the next year will also be incorrect. However, the error will cancel itself over two accounting periods.

 a. *Overstatement of ending inventory*: If ending inventory is overstated, cost of goods sold will be understated and net income for the period will be over-stated.

 b. *Understatement of ending inventory*: If ending inventory is understated, cost of goods sold will be overstated and net income will be understated.

 c. *Overstatement of beginning inventory*: If beginning inventory is overstated, cost of goods available for sale is overstated, cost of goods sold is overstated and net income is understated.

 d. *Understatement of beginning inventory*: If beginning inventory is understated, cost of goods available for sale will be understated, cost of goods sold will be understated, and net income will be overstated.

 EXAMPLE: Sullivan Corp. made an error in the ending inventory in 19XA. Ending inventory was overstated by $20,000. Due to this error, cost of goods sold for 19XA was understated by $20,000 and net income was overstated by $20,000. Figure 12–2 shows the effects of the error on the income statement for 19XA.

 If it were not corrected, the error would carry through to the income statement of 19XB since beginning inventory would be overstated. Beginning inventory would be overstated by $20,000, cost of goods available for sale would be overstated by $20,000, cost of goods sold would be overstated by $20,000, and net income would be understated by $20,000. Figure 12–3 shows the effects of the error on the income statement for 19XB.

2. *Method of Inventory Valuation Used*: The method of inventory valuation used has an effect on the amount recorded in the inventory account and also an effect on cost of goods sold, which influences the amount of net income reported by the company.

Figure 12–2 Sullivan Corporation Income Statement for 19XA

		Including Error		Without Error
Sales		1,000,000		1,000,000
Less: Cost of goods sold				
Beginning inventory	100,000		100,000	
+ Purchases	700,000		700,000	
Goods available for sale	800,000		800,000	
− Ending inventory	100,000		80,000	
Cost of goods sold		700,000		720,000
Gross profit		300,000		280,000
Less: Operating expenses		200,000		200,000
Net operating income		100,000		80,000

Figure 12–3   Sullivan Corporation Income Statement for 19XB

	Including Error		Without Error	
Sales		1,100,000		1,100,000
Less: Cost of goods sold				
Beginning inventory	100,000		80,000	
+ Purchases	800,000		800,000	
Good available				
for sale	900,000		880,000	
− Ending inventory	110,000		110,000	
Cost of goods sold		790,000		770,000
Gross profit		310,000		330,000
Less: Operating expenses		210,000		210,000
Net operating income		100,000		120,000

a. *Rising prices*: During a period of rising prices, the use of FIFO normally results in a higher reported net income and a higher ending inventory valuation than LIFO.

b. *Falling prices*: During a period of falling prices, the use of LIFO normally results in a higher reported net income and higher ending inventory valuation than FIFO.

c. *Use of weighted-average method*: The weighted-average method will always produce an amount of net income and an inventory valuation that is between the amounts determined using the FIFO and LIFO methods.

Review Questions

DIRECTIONS: Select the best answer from the four alternatives. Write the letter of your answer in the blank to the left of the number.

_____ 1. A perpetual inventory system is

   a. a method where cost of goods sold is recorded after each sale and the inventory account is updated for each purchase and sale transaction.
   b. a method of estimating inventory value using the historical gross profit percentage.
   c. a method that updates the inventory account only one time each period after a physical count of the inventory is taken.
   d. a method which requires that records be kept of merchandise acquired both at cost and at retail selling price.

_____ 2. A periodic inventory system

   a. is most often used by companies selling numerous small inexpensive items.
   b. uses a purchases account for recording inventory acquisitions.
   c. requires that a physical inventory count be taken to determine the ending inventory valuation.
   d. all of the above.

_____ 3. The method of inventory estimation that is based on the company's historical gross profit percentage is called the

   a. retail method.
   b. perpetual method.
   c. periodic method.
   d. gross profit method.

_____ 4. Inventory should not be valued at

   a. an amount higher than the original cost.
   b. the cost of the most recent purchases.
   c. market value when market value exceeds cost.
   d. cost when market value exceeds cost.

5. Jana Co. had beginning inventory of $200,000. Ending inventory is $100,000 and cost of goods sold for the year is $1,000,000. Net purchases made during the year were

   a. $1,000,000.
   b. $900,000.
   c. $1,100,000.
   d. The answer cannot be determined from the information given.

6. Sales are $100,000; goods available for sale are $90,000; and the gross profit ratio is 30 percent. The estimate of ending inventory using the gross profit method is

   a. $20,000.
   b. $30,000.
   c. $60,000.
   d. $27,000.

7. Merz Company had beginning inventory for 19XA of $95,000. The balance in the purchases account as of year end is $900,000. The ending inventory valued at FIFO is $90,000. The purchase discounts account has a balance of $5,000; the purchase returns account has a balance of $2,000; and the freight-in account has a balance of $10,000. Cost of goods sold is

   a. $888,000.
   b. $908,000.
   c. $813,000.
   d. $898,000.

8. Obsolete or damaged inventory

   a. should be excluded from inventory.
   b. should be included in inventory at historical cost.
   c. should be included in inventory at market value if market value is lower than cost.
   d. should be included in inventory at its expected selling price.

9. Which of the following statements is false?

   a. A major objective in accounting for inventories is to match revenues and expenses properly.
   b. The use of lower of cost or market to value inventory is an example of an application of the conservatism principle.

c. When a periodic inventory system is used, an error that understates the ending inventory of 19XA will result in an understatement of net income in 19XB.

d. When LIFO is used for tax purposes, the IRS requires that it also be used for financial reporting purposes (in the United States).

Use this information in answering Questions 10 to 12.

Hanes Company began a year ago and purchased merchandise as follows:

Jan. 1	Beginning inventory	20 units @ $10.00
Feb. 15	Purchased	90 units @ $11.00
May 26	Purchased	50 units @ $11.50
Aug. 10	Purchased	80 units @ $12.00
Nov. 30	Purchased	60 units @ $12.50

Hanes uses a periodic inventory system, and there are 65 units in ending inventory.

10. Assuming that Hanes Company uses FIFO to value inventory, the amount of cost of goods sold for the year would be

a. $2,665.
b. $810.
c. $695.
d. $2,780.

11. Assuming that Hanes Company uses LIFO to value inventory, ending inventory for the year would be valued at

a. $2,780.
b. $695.
c. $2,665.
d. $810.

12. Assuming that Hanes Company uses the weighted-average method to value inventory, ending inventory for the year would be valued at (rounded to the nearest dollar)

a. $760.
b. $741.
c. $2,725.
d. $753.

Solutions

Answer	Refer to:
1. (a)	[A-1-a]
2. (d)	[A-2]
3. (d)	[D-4]
4. (c)	[C]

5. (b)   [D-1] The following computations show how net purchases is derived:

Beginning inventory	$ 200,000 (given)
+ Net purchases	$ 900,000a
Goods available for sale	$1,100,000b
− Ending inventory	$ 100,000 (given)
Cost of goods sold	$1,000,000 (given)

6. (a)   [D-4] The estimate of ending inventory is computed as shown here:

Goods available for sale	$ 90,000
− Estimated cost of goods sold-	− 70,000c
Estimated ending inventory	$ 20,000

The estimated cost of goods sold percentage is 70%. Sales % − gross profit % = 100% − 30% = 70%.

7. (b)   [D-1] The following computations show how the cost of goods sold is derived:

Beginning inventory		$ 95,000
+ Net purchases		
Purchases	$900,000	
Add: Freight in	10,000	
Deduct: Purchase discounts	− 5,000	
Deduct: Purchase returns	− 2,000	903,000
Goods available for sale		$998,000
− Ending inventory		− 90,000
Cost of goods sold		$908,000

8. (c)	[C]
9. (c)	[E-1-d]

a$1,100,000 − $200,000.
b$1,100,000 + $100,000.
c$100,000 × 0.7 = $70,000.

10. (a) [B-1] Goods available for sale were:

			Units	$ Value
Jan.	1	Beg. inventory	20 units @ $10	$ 200
Feb.	15	Purchased	90 units @ $11	990
May	26	Purchased	50 units @ $11.50	575
Aug.	10	Purchased	80 units @ $12	960
Nov.	30	Purchased	60 units @ $12.50	750
		Goods available for sale	300 units	$ 3,475

Under FIFO ending inventory would be:

60 units @ $12.50 = $750
5 units @ $12.00 = 60
Ending inventory = $810

cost of goods sold = goods available for sale − ending inventory
$2,665 = $3,475 − $810

11. (b) [B-2] Ending inventory under LIFO would be:

20 units @ $10.00 = $200
45 units @ $11.00 = 495
Ending inventory = $695

12. (d) [B-3] The weighted-average cost per unit is

$$\frac{\$3,475}{300} = \$11.5833$$

Ending inventory using the weighted-average method would be:

$11.5833/unit × 65 units = $752.91 or $753

CHAPTER 13

Property, Plant, and Equipment Records

OVERVIEW

Property, plant, and equipment records are the records that relate to the fixed assets of the company. This chapter is intended to introduce the candidate to the recording of transactions involving property, plant, and equipment.

The candidate should understand what is considered to be part of the cost of a fixed asset and know the procedures for calculating depreciation and depletion, accounting for repairs of fixed assets, and recording the sale or exchange of a fixed asset.

KEY TERMS

Accelerated depreciation method
Depletion
Double-declining-balance depreciation (DDB)

Extraordinary repairs
Modified accelerated cost recovery system (MACRS)
Salvage value

Straight-line depreciation
Sum-of-the-years' digits depreciation (SYD)
Units-of-production method

A. Acquisition Cost

The first thing that must be determined when a fixed asset is acquired is the cost of the asset.

1. *Cost of Fixed Assets*: Cost of a fixed asset includes all expenses necessary to acquire the asset and to prepare the asset for its use in the operations of the business. The cost of a fixed asset should include only amounts that are reasonable and necessary. Examples of items that would be included in the cost of a fixed asset are the cash paid to acquire the asset, freight-in, insurance on the asset while in transit, installation costs, and any trial runs necessary to determine the asset's readiness for use. *Freight-in* is the term used to refer to the transportation cost of an asset when it is paid by the buyer. If a fixed asset is purchased with a note that has an interest provision, any interest paid should be recorded as interest expense rather than as a part of the cost of the asset.

2. *Cost of Acquiring Land*: If land is purchased, the cost of the land must be sepa-
    rated from the cost of any depreciable buildings or improvements that are situated
    on the land since land is not depreciable. If land is purchased for use in the busi-
    ness and there is an existing structure on the land that must be removed, the cost
    of removing the structure should be included as part of the cost of the land. Any
    surveying or grading costs should also be included in the cost of the land if these
    costs are necessary to make the land suitable for its intended use. If a building is
    to be constructed on the land, any excavation costs associated with the construc-
    tion of the building should not be included in the cost of the land. These costs are
    considered part of the cost of the building. Any commissions paid to brokers, legal
    fees, and title fees would be included as a part of the cost of the land. Land im-
    provements which may have a limited life, such as driveways, fences, and parking
    lots, should be recorded in a separate land improvements account. Land improve-
    ments have a limited life and, as such, are subject to depreciation.

**B. Allocation
of Costs:
Depreciation
and Depletion**

1. *Depreciation*: Depreciation is the systematic and rational allocation of the cost of
    an asset over its useful life. To determine the amount of depreciation to charge to
    specific periods, it is necessary to perform the following steps:

    a. *Cost of the asset*: The cost of the asset to be depreciated must first be deter-
        mined.

    b. *Useful life of the asset*: The length of the useful life of the asset is estimated,
        that is, 5 years, 10 years.

    c. *Salvage value*: Salvage value is the residual value an asset is expected to have
        when its estimated useful life is over. The amount of salvage value anticipated
        needs to be estimated. Often, no residual value is assigned because it is inde-
        terminable.

        *EXAMPLE: Jones Co. purchases a truck for $20,000. The useful life of the
        truck is estimated to be eight years. At the end of eight years, Jones Co. ex-
        pects to be able to sell the truck for $2,000. $2,000 is the salvage value of the
        truck.*

    d. *Selection of depreciation method to be used*: Depreciation expense is an ap-
        proximation that is based on a number of estimates. There are many methods
        of computing depreciation. As long as a depreciation method is systematic
        and rational, it is normally an acceptable method. There are four basic depre-
        ciation methods that you should be familiar with.

        (1) *Straight-line depreciation method*: The straight-line depreciation method
            assumes that an equal amount of depreciation should be taken for each
            year of the asset's useful life. The formula for computing straight-line
            depreciation is

            $$\text{depreciation rate} \times (\text{cost} - \text{salvage value})$$

            The depreciation rate that is used with straight-line depreciation is

            $$\frac{100\% \ (\text{or } 1.00)}{\text{number of periods of useful life}}$$

Therefore, straight-line depreciation would be computed in this way:

$$(\text{cost} - \text{salvage value}) \times \frac{100\% \ (\text{or } 1.00)}{\text{number of periods of useful life}}$$

EXAMPLE: Lox Company purchases a machine for $10,000. Freight-in on the machine was $100 and installation charges were $100. The salvage value of the machine is estimated to be $1,200. The useful life is estimated to be five years. The asset was purchased on January 1, 19XA. The calculation of depreciation for each year of useful life is shown below.

Depreciation Schedule
Straight-Line Depreciation Method

Year	Computation	Depreciation Expense	Accumulated Depreciation	Book Value
				10,200
1	$(9{,}000^a \times 0.20^b)$	1,800	1,800	8,400
2	$(9{,}000 \times 0.20)$	1,800	3,600	6,600
3	$(9{,}000 \times 0.20)$	1,800	5,400	4,800
4	$(9{,}000 \times 0.20)$	1,800	7,200	3,000
5	$(9{,}000 \times 0.20)$	1,800	9,000	1,200
		9,000		

[a] Cost   salvage value
 $10,200   –   1,200   = $9,000.

[b] 1/5 = 20% (or 0.20).

The journal entry to record the depreciation expense for each year would be:

		dr	cr
Dec. 31	Depreciation expense	1,800	
	Accumulated depreciation		1,800

(2) *Double-declining-balance method*: Some assets produce more benefits in the early years of their useful life than in the later years. For example, some machines might require substantial repair as they become older. These types of assets might be depreciated using an accelerated depreciation method. Accelerated depreciation methods assign a larger amount of depreciation expense to the earlier years of an asset's useful life than to its later years. The double-declining-balance (DDB) method is an example of an accelerated depreciation method. The DDB depreciation method uses a constant depreciation rate applied to a declining asset base.

(a) The depreciation rate used in DDB depreciation is twice or 200 percent of the straight-line rate. In the previous Lox Company example, the straight-line rate was 1/5 or 20 percent, so the DDB rate would be 40 percent.

(b) To obtain depreciation expense for a period, the DDB depreciation rate is multiplied by the book value of the asset at the beginning of the period for which depreciation is to be calculated.

(c)   Note that salvage value is not considered when computing depreci-
      ation using the DDB method. When the DDB method is used, how-
      ever, an asset should not be depreciated below its salvage value.

*EXAMPLE: Assume the same facts as were used in the Lox
Company example except that Lox Company wishes to use the
double-declining-balance depreciation method.*

Depreciation Schedule
Double-Declining-Balance Depreciation Method

Year	Computation	Depreciation Expense	Accumulated Depreciation	Book Value
				10,200
1	$(10{,}200 \times 0.40)$a	4,080	4,080	6,120
2	$(6{,}120 \times 0.40)$	2,448	6,528	3,672
3	$(3{,}672 \times 0.40)$	1,469	7,997	2,203
4	$(2{,}203 \times 0.40)$	881	8,878	1,322
5		122b	9,000	1,200
		9,000b		

a$0.40 = 2 \times$ straight-line rate of 20% (0.20).
bUnder DDB depreciation, we do not depreciate below the estimated salvage value amount.
Note that the amount of the depreciation expense recorded each year declines from that reported in the previous year.

(3)   *Sum-of-the-years' digits method*: The sum-of-the-years' digits (SYD)
      method is also an accelerated depreciation method. When the sum-of-
      the-years' digits method is used, a decreasing rate is applied to a con-
      stant asset base.

      (a)   The asset base to be depreciated in the SYD method is the cost of
            the asset minus the salvage value of the asset (as with straight-line
            depreciation).

      (b)   The decreasing rate is achieved by using a fraction, with the nu-
            merator representing the number of years remaining to be written
            off and the denominator representing the sum of the years' digits.

            In the Lox Company example, the sum of the years' digits would
            be 15 years (5 years + 4 years + 3 years + 2 years + 1 year).
            An easy formula for calculating the sum-of-the-years' digits is
            $[N(N + 1)]/2$, where N is the number of years of useful life. (This
            number is the denominator.)

            In the Lox Company example, the depreciation rate in the first year
            would be 5/15; in the second year, 4/15; in the third year, 3/15; in
            the fourth year, 2/15; and in the fifth year, 1/15. By the end of the
            fifth year, the entire asset base will have been written off: 5/15 +
            4/15 + 3/15 + 2/15 + 1/15 = 15/15.

            *EXAMPLE: Assume the same facts as were used in the Lox
            Company straight-line depreciation example, except that Lox
            Company now uses the SYD method of computing depreciation ex-
            pense.*

Depreciation Schedule
Sum-of-the-Years' Digits Method

Year	Computation	Depreciation Expense	Accumulated Depreciation	Book Value
				10,200
1	$(5/15 \times 9,000)$a	3,000	3,000	7,200
2	$4/15 \times 9,000$	2,400	5,400	4,800
3	$3/15 \times 9,000$	1,800	7,200	3,000
4	$2/15 \times 9,000$	1,200	8,400	1,800
5	$1/15 \times 9,000$	600	9,000	1,200
		9,000		

a   Cost   salvage value
    $10,200 –   1,200   = $9,000.

Note that the amount of the depreciation expense which is recorded declines in each successive year.

(4)   *Units-of-production method*: The units-of-production method of calculating depreciation may be used when the total units of service that an asset will provide can be estimated accurately.

The formula used to calculate units-of-production depreciation is

$$\frac{\text{total units produced during the period}}{\text{total estimated units of production}} \times (\text{cost} - \text{salvage value})$$

EXAMPLE: XYZ Company bought a new truck. It is expected that the truck will have a useful life of 100,000 miles. The cost of the truck was $20,000 and salvage value is expected to be $2,000. During the first year the truck was driven 25,000 miles. The depreciation expense for the first year would be calculated as follows:

$$\frac{25,000}{100,000} \times (\$20,000 - \$2,000) = \$4,500$$

2.   *Depletion*: Assets which are natural resources, such as timber, iron ore, gold, or oil reserves, are subject to depletion since the total quantity available will eventually be used up.

a.   *Estimating quantity of natural resources*: First, the company must estimate the amount of the natural resource that will be available for use. This estimate is likely to change as time progresses and the company is more aware of the actual amount of the resource left.

b.   *Calculating depletion*: The calculation of depletion is similar to the calculation of the units-of-production method.

c.   *Formula for computing depletion*: The formula for computing depletion is

$$\frac{\text{quantity of resource used in current year}}{\text{estimated quantity of the resource available}} \times (\text{cost} - \text{salvage value of natural resource})$$

d.   *Expensing depletion cost*: Depletion is an inventoriable cost. Depletion cost should be added to the cost of extracting the resource. These costs should be expensed as the product is sold.

EXAMPLE: The Sylvan Silver Co. owns a silver mine in Alaska. It is estimated that 30,000 tons of silver ore will be able to be extracted from the mine. During the past year, 5,000 tons of silver ore were mined. The cost of the silver mine was $20,000 and the salvage value of the mine is estimated to be $5,000. The calculation of depletion for the period would be

$$\frac{5,000}{30,000} \times (\$20,000 - \$5,000) = \$2,500$$

C. Repairs

Ordinary repairs are amounts spent to maintain an asset in its normal operating condition. Ordinary repairs include regular maintenance, painting, cleaning, and repair of minor parts. Ordinary repairs performed on fixed assets are considered to be expenses for the period in which they are incurred. Extraordinary repairs should be capitalized and depreciated over the remainder of the asset's life. Repairs are extraordinary when they change the quality of service provided by an asset or extend its useful life beyond the original estimate.

1. *Extraordinary Repairs*: An extraordinary repair that increases the service life of an asset is recorded by debiting accumulated depreciation and crediting cash. An extraordinary repair that materially increases the productivity of the asset is debited directly to the asset account.

2. *Effect on Depreciation*: When extraordinary repairs occur, the current year's depreciation and all future periods' depreciation are affected. (No changes are made to the depreciation expense which was recorded in the past.)

EXAMPLE: Geni Co. purchased a truck for $18,000. The truck had a six-year estimated useful life. After five years Geni Co. decided to install a new engine in the truck that would extend its useful life to a total of 10 years. The new engine cost $10,000, including installation. Prior to the extraordinary repairs, the accounts appeared as follows (straight-line depreciation was used):

Truck 4		Accumulated Depreciation	
18,000			15,000

Geni Co. recorded the extraordinary repairs as follows:

	dr	cr
(a) Accumulated depreciation/truck 4	10,000	
Cash		10,000
To record installation of new engine		
in truck 4.		

Then, the accounts appeared as follows:

Truck 4		Accumulated Depreciation	
18,000			15,000
		(a) 10,000	
			5,000

The new book value of the truck is $13,000. This amount should be depreciated over the new remaining useful life of the asset, which is five years. The depreciation expense on the truck for each of the next five years (assuming that straight-line depreciation is used) would be $13,000/5 = $2,600 per year (no salvage value is assumed).

D. Disposition of Property Items

Assets may be disposed of in one of the following three ways: sale, exchange, or abandonment. If an asset is disposed of at any time other than the end of an accounting period, depreciation should be calculated for the portion of the year for which the asset was held.

EXAMPLE: Floit Company sold a machine on June 30, 1991. The company purchased the machine on January 1, 1984, for $20,000 and estimated depreciation on the machine using the straight-line method over a 10-year period. Floit Company's year end is December 31. The entry to record the partial-year depreciation to date of sale would be:

	dr	cr
June 30 Depreciation expense	1,000	
Accumulated depreciation		1,000

To record 6 months' depreciation prior to disposal
   of machine (6/12 months × $2,000).

1. *Sale of a Property Item*: When a property item is sold, the book value of the asset is compared to the proceeds generated by the sale of the asset.

   a. *Gain*: If an asset is sold for more than its book value, a gain is recorded.

   b. *Loss*: If an asset is sold for less than its book value, a loss is recorded.

   EXAMPLE: Assume that Floit Company sold the machine in the previous example for $10,000 cash. The book value of the asset is computed as follows:

$20,000.00	Cost
− 12,916.67	Less accumulated depreciation
$ 7,083.33	Book value

   The gain on the sale is computed as follows:

$10,000.00	Proceeds
− 7,083.33	Book value
$ 2,916.67	Gain

   The journal entry to record the sale is:

	dr	cr
June 15 Cash	10,000.00	
Accumulated depreciation	12,916.67	
Machine		20,000.00
Gain on sale of machine		2,916.67

   Sold machine on June 15 for $10,000.

2. *Exchange of Property Items*: Often, a business trades in an old asset when a new one is purchased. These transactions are treated as exchanges of assets. Exchanges

of assets are treated either as an exchange of unlike assets or an exchange of like assets.

a. *Exchange of unlike assets*: An example of an exchange of unlike assets would be the exchange of a machine for a new truck. The two assets are to be used for different purposes within the business. Gains or losses on exchanges of unlike assets are calculated, based on the *fair value* of the asset given up. The fair value of the asset given up is the market value of that asset on the day it is exchanged. If no fair value can be determined, book value is assumed to be fair value. Trade-in value is often used as a measure of the fair value of the asset.

EXAMPLE: Villa Corporation traded in a stamping machine on a new truck. The stamping machine has a cost of $10,000, accumulated depreciation of $6,000, and a fair value of $4,500. The stamping machine is exchanged for a new truck with a list price of $15,000. A trade-in value of $4,500 is allowed on the exchange. The company must pay the balance of $10,500 in cash. The entry to record this transaction is:

	dr	cr
Truck	15,000	
Accumulated depreciation/stamping machine	6,000	
Stamping machine		10,000
Cash		10,500
Gain on exchange of stamping machine		500
Exchanged stamping machine for truck.		

b. *Exchange of like assets*: An example of an exchange of like assets would be the exchange of an old truck for a new truck or the exchange of an old calculator for a new calculator. No gain is reported when like assets are exchanged. Since no gain is recorded, the company must adjust the cost of the new asset. Losses are recorded on exchanges of like assets in order to satisfy the conservatism principle.

EXAMPLE 1:   No Gain on Exchange of Like Assets

Villa Corporation exchanged an old calculator with a cost of $500 and accumulated depreciation of $300 for a new calculator with a list price of $800. The seller allowed a $300 trade-in allowance for the old calculator (the trade-in value was equal to the fair value). The entry to record this transaction would be:

	dr	cr
Office equipment (new calculator)	700	
Accumulated depreciation/office		
equipment (old calculator)	300	
Office equipment (old calculator)		500
Cash		500
Exchanged old calculator for new calculator.		

EXAMPLE 2: Loss on Exchange of Like Assets

Assume that Villa Corporation exchanged the old calculator for a new one and all of the facts are the same except that the trade-in allowance was $100 instead of $300. The entry to record this transaction would be:

	dr	cr
Office equipment (new calculator)	800	
Accumulated depreciation/office equipment (old calculator)	300	
Loss on exchange of calculator	100	
Office equipment (old calculator)		500
Cash		700

Exchanged old calculator for new calculator.

Note: For federal income tax purposes, losses on exchanges of like assets are not deductible.

3. *Abandonment of Property Items*: If fully depreciated assets are abandoned, a journal entry must be made debiting accumulated depreciation and crediting the asset account, which results in the writing off of the asset. If an asset that is not yet fully depreciated is abandoned, a loss due to the abandonment must be recorded.

   If fully depreciated assets are still being used in the business, no further depreciation should be taken on the asset but the full amount of the asset and the accumulated depreciation related to it should be left on the records of the company.

E. Depreciation for Income Tax Purposes

In 1981, the tax provisions included a new system of depreciation known as the Accelerated Cost Recovery System (ACRS). In 1986, Congress modified the ACRS system. Under the Modified ACRS system (MACRS), an asset is assigned to a class of property that has a defined life for income tax depreciation purposes. The asset is depreciated over that statutory life at an assigned rate per year. Tables of class lives and depreciation rates for each year are published by the Internal Revenue Service. Although MACRS should be used for income tax purposes, it is not in accord with generally accepted accounting principles and should not normally be used for financial accounting purposes. Some small businesses may use MACRS depreciation for both financial reporting and tax purposes when the differences between MACRS and conventional methods are not material.

Review Questions

DIRECTIONS: Select the best answer from the four alternatives. Write the letter of your answer in the blank to the left of the number.

_____ 1. Any depreciation method that assigns more depreciation expense in the early years of an asset's life and less in later years is called

   a. double-declining-balance depreciation.
   b. an accelerated depreciation method.
   c. sum-of-the-years' digits depreciation.
   d. modified accelerated cost recovery system.

_____ 2. Jones Company bought a plot of land with an old building located on it. The old building was demolished to pave the land for a parking lot. The cost of demolishing the building should be

   a. capitalized as a part of the building account.
   b. charged to demolition expense.
   c. capitalized as part of the parking lot improvement account.
   d. capitalized as a part of the cost of the land.

_____ 3. Which of the following items should not be included as part of the cost of a new machine?

   a. Sales tax paid on the purchase of the machine.
   b. Installation cost of the machine.
   c. Cost of repairing damage to the machine caused when it was dropped from a forklift while carrying it into the building.
   d. Freight-in on the delivery of the machine.

_____ 4. Which of the following items may correctly be included as part of the land account?

   a. Fences
   b. Title fees
   c. Excavation costs incurred during construction of a building
   d. Concrete parking lot

_____ **5.** The amount a natural resource is reduced as a result of usage is called

     a. depreciation.
     b. amortization.
     c. depletion.
     d. accumulation.

_____ **6.** A repair that is treated as an expense in the period in which it is incurred is a/an

     a. extraordinary repair.
     b. capital item.
     c. betterment.
     d. ordinary repair.

_____ **7.** The residual value an asset is expected to have when its useful life is over is called

     a. book value.
     b. depreciated value.
     c. salvage value.
     d. current value.

_____ **8.** When like assets are exchanged

     a. gains or losses on the exchange should not be recognized.
     b. gains on the exchange should be recognized for financial reporting purposes, but losses should not be recognized.
     c. losses on the exchange should be recognized for financial reporting purposes, but gains should not be recognized.
     d. both gains and losses on the exchange should be recognized.

_____ **9.** Rohas Co. purchased a new machine for $50,000 which they estimated would be able to produce 100,000 units of product C. During the current year, they produced 10,000 units of product C. The machine is expected to last eight years and have a salvage value of $2,000. Assuming that Rohas Co. uses the units-of-production method, depreciation expense for the current period is

     a. $6,000.
     b. $5,000.
     c. $5,102.
     d. $4,800.

_____ **10.** If a fixed asset is sold for less than its book value

     a. a loss is recorded.
     b. a gain is recorded.

c. no gain or loss is recorded.

d. cash is credited.

11. Extraordinary repairs

a. should be recorded as an increase in accumulated depreciation.

b. result in a decrease in the value of the fixed asset repaired.

c. result in a prior period adjustment of depreciation taken in earlier years.

d. often extend the useful life of the asset.

12. Using U.S. tax law, which of the following statements is true?

a. Gains are not recognized on exchanges of unlike assets.

b. Depletion should be treated as an expense when the natural resource is extracted.

c. No journal entry is necessary when fully depreciated assets are abandoned.

d. Losses on exchanges of like assets are not deductible for federal income tax purposes.

13. An accelerated method of depreciation prescribed in U.S. law for assets placed in service after 1986 is the

a. accumulated cost recovery system.

b. double-declining-balance method.

c. modified accelerated cost recovery system.

d. sum-of-the-years' digits method.

14. Nelson Company sold a truck for $14,000 on August 1, 19XD. The cost of the truck was $30,000 and the balance in the accumulated depreciation/truck account on January 1, 19XD, was $9,000. The truck had an estimated useful life of 10 years with no salvage value. The sale resulted in

a. a gain of $14,000.

b. a loss of $5,250.

c. a loss of $7,000.

d. a gain of $7,000.

Use this information in answering Questions 16 to 19.

On January 1, 19XA, Hawk Co. purchased equipment for $60,000. The equipment was expected to last eight years and have a salvage value of $4,000. Hawk Co.'s year end is December 31.

15. Assuming that Hawk Co. uses straight-line depreciation, the balance in the accumulated depreciation account on January 1, 19XC, would be

    a. $7,000.
    b. $14,000.
    c. $7,500.
    d. $15,000.

16. Assuming that Hawk Co. uses the double-declining-balance method, depreciation expense for 19XB would be

    a. $10,500.
    b. $15,000.
    c. $30,000.
    d. $11,250.

17. Assuming that Hawk Co. uses the sum-of-the-years' digits method, depreciation expense for 19XC would be (rounded to the nearest dollar)

    a. $12,444.
    b. $9,333.
    c. $12,000.
    d. $10,000.

18. Assuming that Hawk Co. uses the sum-of-the-years' digits method, the book value of the equipment on December 31, 19XB (after closing) would be (rounded to the nearest dollar)

    a. $32,667.
    b. $10,889.
    c. $36,667.
    d. $25,000.

Use this information in answering Questions 19 and 20.

On January 1, 19XA, Rose Co. purchased new equipment that had a list price of $50,000. Rose Co. traded in some *like* equipment. The cost of the equipment traded in was $40,000, and the accumulated depreciation on this equipment as of January 1, 19XA, was $15,000.

19. Assuming that Rose Co. received a trade-in allowance of $30,000 (which is equal to fair value), the journal entry to record this transaction should include

    a. a debit to the equipment account for $50,000.
    b. a credit to the accumulated depreciation account for $15,000.

c. a debit to the equipment account for $45,000.
d. a credit to a gain account for $5,000.

_____

20. Assuming that Rose Co. received a trade-in allowance of $20,000 (which is equal to fair value), the journal entry to record this transaction should include

a. a debit to a loss account for $5,000.
b. a debit to the new equipment account for $55,000.
c. a credit to a gain account for $5,000.
d. a credit to the old equipment account for $25,000.

Solutions

Answer	Refer to:
1. (b)	[B-1-d(2)]
2. (d)	[A-2]
3. (c)	[A-1]
4. (b)	[A-2]
5. (c)	[B-2]
6. (d)	[C]
7. (c)	[B-1-c]
8. (c)	[D-2-b]

9. (d)   [B-1-d(4)] The calculation of depreciation using the units-of-production method is:

$$\frac{10,000}{100,000} \times (\$50,000 - 2,000)$$

10. (a)	[D-1-b]
11. (d)	[C]
12. (d)	[D-2-b]
13. (c)	[E]

14. (b)   [D-1-b] The book value of the truck was:

$30,000	Cost
− 10,750	Accumulated depreciation[a]
$19,250	Book value

The selling price of the asset is less than the book value, so there was a loss on the sale of $5,250 ($19,250 − $14,000).

---

[a]Accumulated depreciation as of January 1, 19XD + depreciation for the current year through August 1, 19XD ($3,000/year × 7/12).

15. (b)   [B-1-d(1)] Straight-line depreciation expense is $7,000 per year. $[(\$60,000 - 4,000) \times 0.125]$ or $[(\$60,000 - 4,000)/8]$

Accumulated depreciation as of January 1, 19XC would have a balance of $14,000 ($7,000 for 19XA and $7,000 for 19XB).

16. (d)   [B-1-d(2)] Double-declining-balance depreciation would be computed as follows:

Year	Beg. of Period Carrying Value	Rate[b]	Depreciation Expense	End of Period Carrying Value
19XA	$60,000	0.25	$15,000	$45,000
19XB	$45,000	0.25	$11,250	$33,750

17. (b)   [B-1-d(3)] Sum-of-the-years' digits depreciation would be computed as follows:

Year	Fraction × Cost − Salvage Value	=	Depreciation Expense
19XA	8/36[c]	$60,000 − $4,000	=	$12,444
19XB	7/36	$60,000 − $4,000	=	$10,889
19XC	6/36	$60,000 − $4,000	=	$ 9,333

18. (c)   [B-1-d(3)] Book value as of December 31, 19XB, is:

cost	− accumulated depreciation	= book value
$60,000	− $23,333[d]	= $36,667

19. (c)   [D-2-b] Book value of the old equipment is $25,000 ($40,000 − 15,000). Since the trade-in allowance of $30,000 is greater than the book value of $25,000, there is a $5,000 gain on the transaction. Gains on the exchange of like assets are not recognized for financial reporting purposes. The entry to record the transaction would be:

	dr	cr
Equipment (new)	45,000[e]	
Accumulated depreciation/equipment	15,000	
Equipment (old)		40,000
Cash		20,000[f]

20. (a)   [D-2-b] Since the trade-in allowance of $20,000 is less than the book value of $25,000, there is a $5,000 loss on the exchange. For financial

---

[b]Straight-line rate = 1/8 = 0.125. Double-declining-balance rate = 0.125 × 2 = 0.25

[c]The denominator is the sum-of-the-years' digits, which can be computed using the formula $n(n + 1)/2$.
The computation is 8(9)/2 = 36.

[d]$12,444 + $10,889 (see solution to Question 17).

[e]$50,000 cost minus $5,000 gain not recognized.

[f]$50,000 cost minus $30,000 trade-in allowance.

reporting purposes, losses are recognized on the exchange of like assets. The entry to record this transaction would be:

	dr	cr
Equipment (new)	50,000	
Accumulated depreciation/ equipment	15,000	
Loss on exchange of equipment	5,000	
Equipment (old)		40,000
Cash		30,000[g]

[g]$50,000 cost − $20,000 trade-in allowance.

CHAPTER 14

Other Assets

OVERVIEW

This chapter covers the accounting for the rest of the asset categories. Some of the topics, such as the calculation of interest and treatment of prepaid expenses, have been discussed in Chapter 9. The candidate should review Chapter 4 if necessary.

The candidate should be familiar with the recording of notes receivable and interest revenue for both interest-bearing and noninterest-bearing notes, the process of discounting a note receivable with a bank, accounting for accounts receivable and bad debts, types of insurance, co-insurance, and the recording of adjusting entries for prepaid insurance, accounting for office supplies, and accounting for intangible assets, including amortization of intangible assets.

KEY TERMS

Aging of accounts receivable	Fidelity bond
Amortization	Interest-bearing note receivable
Casualty insurance	Life and health insurance
Co-insurance	Maturity date of a note
Contingent liability	Noninterest-bearing note receivable
Direct write-off method	Property insurance
Discounting of a note receivable	Surety bond

A. Notes Receivable

A note receivable is a legal document signed by the borrower which promises to pay the lender the principal amount of the note. Notes receivable normally specify that a certain interest rate will be paid on the principal.

1. *Interest-Bearing Note Receivable*: A note receivable that requires payment of both the principal and a stated rate of interest is called an interest-bearing note receivable.

EXAMPLE: Moomey Company accepted a $5,000 60-day 10 percent note receivable from Joe Pone in exchange for merchandise on June 1. The journal entry to record the receipt of the note would be:

	dr	cr
June 1 Note receivable	5,000	
Sales revenue		5,000
Received 60-day 10% note from Joe Pone in exchange for merchandise.		

The journal entry to record the collection of the note receivable would be:

	dr	cr
July 31 Cash	5,083	
Note receivable		5,000
Interest revenue		83
Collected Joe Pone note; interest =		
$5,000 \times 0.10 \times 60/360 = \$83$.		

2. *Noninterest-Bearing Note Receivable*: A note receivable that has no provision for the payment of interest on the principal of the note is called a noninterest-bearing note receivable. Since money has a time value, the principal amount received on the due date includes an amount for implied interest. Generally accepted accounting principles require that interest be imputed on long-term noninterest-bearing notes. Imputing interest refers to the process of recognizing the implied interest through an approximation process. Short-term noninterest-bearing notes are recorded at face value since the implied interest on the note is immaterial. To determine the amount of imputed interest associated with a noninterest-bearing note, the following steps are used:

    a. *Rate of imputed interest*: Determine the rate of interest that is usually charged on transactions of the same nature as the one involving the noninterest-bearing note.

    b. *Present value of note*: Find the present value of the note using the following formula:

    $$\frac{\text{face value of the note}}{(1 + r)^n} = \text{present value of the note}$$

    In this formula, r is the interest rate and n is the number of interest periods.

    c. *Discount*: Find the amount of the discount to be recorded on the note using the following formula:

    $$\text{face value} - \text{present value} = \text{discount on note receivable}$$

    The discount amount represents the interest that is implied in the note. This amount is recorded in a discount on notes receivable account. The discount account is a contra-asset account and is deducted from the face value of the note on the balance sheet. The balance in the discount account is written off to interest income over the life of the note. The amount of interest to be recorded in any given period is based on the beginning of the period carrying value of the note (notes receivable − discount on notes receivable), times the interest rate, times the period of time for which interest is to be accrued.

    EXAMPLE: Moomey Company accepted a $10,000 two-year noninterest-bearing note receivable from Zebo Company on January 1, 19XA. The note *was taken in exchange for merchandise. The interest rate normally charged in this type of transaction is 10 percent. The computation of interest to be imputed is*

$$\frac{\$10,000}{(1 + 0.1)^2} = \frac{\$10,000}{1.21} = \$8,264$$

The discount on the note would be $1,736 ($10,000 – 8,264).

The journal entry to record the receipt of the note would be:

	dr	cr
Jan. 1 Notes receivable	10,000	
Discount on notes receivable		1,736
Sales		8,264

Received a two-year noninterest-bearing note from Zebo Co. Interest was imputed at 10%.

The journal entry to record the first year's interest on the note would be:

	dr	cr
Dec. 31 Discount on notes receivable	826	
Interest income (revenue)		826

To record interest accrued on the Zebo Co. note receivable.
(Carrying value × interest rate × time) ($8,264 × 0.10 × 1 year)

The journal entry to record the collection of the note on December 31, 19XB, would be:

	dr	cr
Dec. 31 Cash	10,000	
Discount on notes receivable	910	
Interest income (revenue)		910
Notes receivable		10,000

To record collection of the Zebo Co. note and to write off the balance in the discount account to interest income.

d. *Imputing interest on notes*: Interest should be imputed whenever a long-term (more than one year) note is noninterest-bearing or has an interest rate that is unreasonably low under the circumstances.

3. *Recording Accrued Interest Receivable*: If financial statements are prepared before a note receivable is collected, the amount of accrued interest receivable must be recorded.

a. *Interest-bearing notes receivable*: For interest-bearing notes receivable, interest is accrued in the same fashion as for bonds receivable (see Chapter 11).

b. *Noninterest-bearing notes receivable*: For noninterest-bearing notes receivable, an adjusting entry records the interest revenue that was accrued and writes off the portion of the discount that has been earned. (See the December 31 entries in the example in Section A-2-c.)

4. *Discounting of Notes Receivable*: A company may discount (sell) its notes receivable to a bank if the company needs cash immediately and does not want to hold the notes to maturity. The bank buys the note and holds it until maturity. At the

time the note matures, the bank collects the principal and interest earned on the note from the maker.

The seller of the note is liable to the bank for payment of the maturity value if the maker does not pay the note. This liability to pay the bank if the maker fails to do so is called a contingent liability. A contingent liability might become a liability at a future date but is not a liability at the present time. Contingent liabilities are potential liabilities, but they are not currently legal obligations. Contingent liabilities are usually reported in footnotes on financial statements.

The amount that a company will receive from the bank when a note is discounted may be calculated as follows:

a. *Maturity value of note*: The maturity value of the note (the principal plus the interest) is determined.

b. *Discount on note*: The amount of interest the bank will charge for the note is calculated. This is called the *discount* on the note. The formula for calculating the discount is

$$\text{maturity value} \times \text{bank discount rate} \times \text{portion of a year for which the bank will hold the note} = \text{discount}$$

c. *Proceeds*: The maturity value less the discount is equal to the proceeds that the bank will pay to the seller.

$$\text{maturity value} - \text{discount} = \text{proceeds}$$

d. *Interest expense*: If the proceeds received from the bank are less than the face value of the note, the seller will record the difference as *interest expense*.

e. *Interest revenue*: If the proceeds received from the bank are more than the face value of the note, the seller will record the difference as *interest revenue*.

EXAMPLE: Lackey Co. discounted a $10,000 8 percent 90-day note receivable with the bank. The note was issued on June 1, and Lackey Co. discounted the note with the bank on July 1. The bank charges a 10 percent discount rate. The calculation of the proceeds to be received by Lackey Co. follows:

Principal	$10,000
+ Interest ($10,000 × 0.08 × 90/360)	200
Maturity value	$10,200
Less: discount ($10,200 × 0.10 × 60/360)	− 170
Proceeds to Lackey Co.	$10,030

Lackey Co. would record the receipt of the proceeds as follows:

	dr	cr
July 1 Cash	10,030	
Notes receivable		10,000
Interest revenue		30
Discounted note receivable with the bank.		

f. *Default in payment of note*: If the maker of a note defaults, the bank requests payment from the seller. The journal entry to record payment on a defaulted note would be a debit to accounts receivable and a credit to cash. The seller would then be responsible for collection of the note from the maker.

EXAMPLE: Assume that the maker of the note Lackey Co. discounted with the bank defaulted and that the bank charged a $25 protest fee. Lackey Co. would make the following entry to record the payment to the bank of the maturity value:

	dr	cr
Accounts receivable	10,225	
Cash		10,225
To record payment of defaulted notes receivable and bank protest fee.		

B.   Accounts Receivable and Bad Debts

Accounts receivable are amounts owed to a business for sales of merchandise or services that are sold on credit. Many businesses have a credit department that analyzes prospective customers before credit is issued to them. Even if a business has a credit department that screens credit customers, some of the accounts receivable of the business will prove to be uncollectible. An allowance for uncollectible accounts (or allowance for doubtful accounts) is set up to report accounts receivable on the balance sheet at the amount that is expected to be collected.

> Total accounts receivable balance
> Less: Allowance for uncollectible accounts
> Net realizable value of accounts receivable

Using an allowance for uncollectible accounts results in a better matching of the expense related to uncollectible accounts with the sales revenue recorded when the initial sales took place. It also reports accounts receivable at a more conservative amount (net realizable value). There are a number of different methods for estimating the amount of bad debt expense to be recorded and the amount to be included in the allowance for uncollectible accounts.

1. *Aging of Accounts Receivable*: When an aging of accounts receivable is prepared, individual customers' account balances are categorized according to the length of time they have been outstanding. Based on past experience, the company estimates the probability of accounts not being collected for each category. The estimated losses in each category are totaled to determine the total amount of estimated uncollectible accounts. The aging-of-accounts-receivable method provides the best estimate of uncollectible accounts. Figure 14–1 shows an example of an aging-of-accounts-receivable schedule.

EXAMPLE: Assume that Nelson Company's accounts receivable control account had a $100,000 debit balance and the company's allowance for uncollectible accounts account had a $200 credit balance prior to adjustment.

Figure 14–1   Aging of Accounts Receivable

Nelson Company
Aging of Accounts Receivable
December 31, 19XA

Account Name	Account Balance	Not Yet Due	1–30 Days Past Due	30–60 Days Past Due	Over 60 Days Past Due
Aronson	2,500	2,500			
Bellows Co.	10,122	8,000	2,122		
Bird	8,310	8,310			
Cafen Co.	503				503
Crane	12,200	10,000		2,200	
Dulow Corp., etc.	5,110		5,110		
Total	100,000	65,000	20,000	10,000	5,000
Percentage estimated to be uncollectible from past experience		1%	3%	8%	15%
Amount estimated to be uncollectible	2,800	650	600	800	750

Accounts Receivable (Control)

Bal. 12/31   100,000

Allowance for Uncollectible Accounts

	200	Bal. 12/31
	2,600	12/31
	(adjusting entry)	
	2,800	

The entry to record bad debt expense based on the aging schedule in Figure 14–1 would be:

	dr	cr
Dec. 31 Bad debt expense	2,600	
Allowance for uncollectible accounts		2,600
To record bad debt expense.		

2. *Percentage of Accounts Receivable*: The percentage-of-accounts-receivable method estimates the balance of the allowance for uncollectible accounts based on a percentage of the ending accounts receivable balance.

EXAMPLE: Assume that based on past experience Nelson Company estimates that uncollectible accounts are about 2.5 percent of total ending accounts receiv-

able. Nelson Company would estimate that their allowance for uncollectible accounts balance should be $2,500 ($100,000 × 0.025). Since the allowance account already has a balance of $200, the entry to record bad debt expense, assuming that the percentage-of-accounts-receivable method is used, would be:

	dr	cr
Dec. 31 Bad debt expense	2,300	
Allowance for uncollectible accounts		2,300

To record bad debt expense.

3. *Percentage of Credit Sales*: The percentage-of-credit-sales method assumes that a certain percentage (based on past experience) of credit sales for the year will prove to be uncollectible. When the percentage-of-sales method is used, the company estimates the amount of bad debt expense rather than the amount of the allowance for uncollectible accounts as in the other two methods. The amount already recorded in the allowance for uncollectible accounts does not affect the adjusting entry when the percentage-of-credit-sales method is used. Bad debt expense might also be estimated using a percentage of net sales rather than credit sales.

EXAMPLE: Assume that Nelson Company had credit sales of $900,000 during 19XA. Nelson Company estimates that 0.3 percent of its credit sales will be uncollectible. The entry to record bad debt expense, assuming that the percentage-of-credit-sales method is used, would be:

	dr	cr
Dec. 3 Bad debt expense	2,700	
Allowance for uncollectible accounts		2,700

To record bad debt expense ($900,000 × 0.003).

Note that the balance in the allowance account did not affect the entry that was made, since the percentage of sales method was used.

4. *Writing Off an Uncollectible Account*: When it is determined that an individual account has become uncollectible, that account must be written off. To write off an account, the allowance for uncollectible accounts is debited and the accounts receivable account is credited. The procedure for writing off an uncollectible account is the same regardless of the method used to estimate bad debt expense and the allowance for uncollectible accounts. The writing off of a bad debt does not affect the net realizable value of accounts receivable since both accounts receivable and the allowance for uncollectible accounts are reduced by an equal amount.

EXAMPLE: Assume that Nelson Company determines, on May 1, 19XA, that Cafen Co.'s account is uncollectible. The entry to write off the account would be:

	dr	cr
May 1 Allowance for uncollectible accounts	503	
Accounts receivable		503

To write off Cafen Co.'s uncollectible account.

5. *Collection of Uncollectible Account*: It is possible that an account which has previously been written off will be collected. When this happens, it is necessary to re-

store the account as a part of the accounts receivable balance before recording the collection of the account.

EXAMPLE: Assume that on May 5, 19XB, Nelson Company collects a $300 account from J.D. Corporation that was written off in 19XA. On May 5, 19XB, the entries necessary to record the transaction would be:

	dr	cr
May 5 Accounts receivable	300	
Allowance for uncollectible accounts		300
To restore J.D. Corporation account, which was previously written off.		
May 5 Cash	300	
Accounts receivable		300
To record collection of J.D. Corporation account receivable.		

If a collection agency were used to help collect the account, its commission would need to be shown as a part of the cash received.

6. *Direct Write-off*: When the direct write-off method is used, a company does not record an allowance for doubtful accounts or attempt to match bad debt expense with the related revenues. When an account is determined to be uncollectible, an entry is made directly to bad debt expense and accounts receivable. No adjusting entry is made at the end of the period. From an accounting standpoint, the direct write-off method is deficient because no attempt is made to match revenues and expenses, and the accounts receivable balance in the balance sheet is overstated, except where the company ordinarily would not have any bad accounts.

EXAMPLE: Sullivan Co. uses the direct write-off method of recording bad debts. On October 1, 19XA, the $500 account of J.B. Harding was determined uncollectible. The entry to write off the account would be:

	dr	cr
Oct. 1 Bad debt expense	500	
Accounts receivable		500
To write off the J.B. Harding account as uncollectible.		

C. Prepaid Expenses

Prepaid expenses consist of the cost of supplies or services bought for use in the business which are not used up at the end of the accounting period.

1. *Insurance*: Insurance policies usually cover a set period of time, and frequently they are paid for in advance. When the period of time covered by an insurance policy extends beyond one accounting period, prepaid insurance should be recorded. When payment is made on an insurance policy that covers more than one accounting period, the payment may be recorded in two alternative ways:

a. *Recording original payment*: The original payment for insurance may be recorded in either of the following ways:

(1) The original payment may be recorded as a debit to the insurance expense account. When this is done, an adjusting entry must be made at the end of the period to record any remaining prepaid insurance benefits. [See Chapter 9, Section F-2-a(2) (b), for an example of the recording of the adjusting entry that must be made.]

(2)   The original payment may be recorded as a debit to the prepaid insurance account. When this is done, an adjusting entry must be made at the end of the period to record the portion of the benefits that have expired (that is, have become an expense of the period). [See Chapter 9, Section F-2-a(1) (a), for an example of the recording of the necessary adjusting entry.]

b.   *Numerous insurance policies*: A company might have a number of insurance policies which cover one or more accounting periods. When this is the case, the prepaid insurance account includes the total of all the prepaid insurance benefits for all the policies.

c.   *Types of insurance*: The major types of insurance available for businesses today include property insurance, casualty insurance, life and health insurance, fidelity bond insurance, surety bonding, and co-insurance.

(1)   *Property insurance*: Insurance protection of the property (assets) of the company from damage or destruction by fire, smoke, vandalism, and so forth, is provided through property insurance policies.

(2)   *Casualty insurance*: Casualty insurance is insurance coverage that is primarily for the liability of a party that results from negligent acts or omissions resulting in bodily injury and/or property damage to another party.

(3)   *Life and health insurance*: Business life and health insurance coverage provides funds for the normal maintenance of a business in the event of the loss of a key person. This is often called *key man insurance*.

(4)   *Fidelity bond insurance*: This type of insurance guarantees that the insurance company will pay for losses of money or property that result from the dishonest acts of bonded employees. The employees are named specifically or by position. The bond covers dishonest acts whether employees act alone or in collusion. Many companies feel that bonding is beneficial; as well as paying for losses, bonding provides a deterrent to fraud. The bonding company can uncover dishonesty in the work history of a new employee, and many employees feel that the bonding company is certain to prosecute if they are caught performing dishonest acts.

(5)   *Surety bond*: This is a contract under which the surety agrees to make good the debt or default of the principal.

(6)   *Co-insurance*: A provision is included in some insurance contracts which requires the insured party to insure property for at least a specified minimum percentage of its fair market value or to share the loss proportionately with the insurance company.

2.   *Supplies*: Office supplies are often purchased in large quantities and kept on hand for use in the business when needed. Any supplies on hand at the end of an accounting period represent a prepaid expense of the company. The original purchase of office supplies may be recorded in two alternative ways:

a.   *Debit to asset account*: When the supplies are purchased, the asset account *supplies inventory* may be debited. When this is done, an adjusting entry must be made at the end of the period to record supplies expense for the supplies that were used. [See Chapter 9, Section F-2-a(1) (b), for an example of the recording of an adjusting entry of this type.]

b. *Debit to expense account*: When the supplies are purchased, an expense account may be debited. When this is done, an adjusting entry must be made at the end of the period to record any supplies on hand as an asset. [See Chapter 9, Section F-2-a(2) (a), for an example of the recording of an adjusting entry of this type.]

D. Intangible Assets and Amortization

Intangible assets are long-lived assets that have no tangible existence. Examples of intangible assets are patents, copyrights, trademarks, franchises, leaseholds, and goodwill.

1. *Value of Intangible Assets*: Intangible assets are valued at cost. A company could have intangible assets that were acquired at no cost to the company. These assets, which have no cost, should not be recorded on the balance sheet.

2. *Capitalization of Intangible Assets*: An intangible asset should be capitalized and shown on the balance sheet *only* if a future benefit can be expected to be derived from that intangible asset.

3. *Amortization of Intangible Assets*: Intangible assets should be amortized over their useful lives. Amortization expense is recorded by debiting amortization expense and crediting the intangible asset account. Amortization is always recorded on a straight-line basis.

a. *Limited legal life*: Some intangible assets, such as patents or copyrights, have a limited legal life. Patents and copyrights should be amortized over their legal life, or their useful life if it is shorter than their legal life. Patents have legal life of 17 years, and copyrights have legal life of 50 years beyond the creator's lifetime.

b. *Indefinite useful life*: Some intangible assets, such as trademarks, organization costs, or goodwill, have indefinite useful lives. If an intangible asset has an indefinite useful life, it should be amortized over a period that does not exceed 40 years.

EXAMPLE: ABC Co. has a patent that cost $10,000. The legal life of the patent is 17 years, but the expected useful life is 10 years. The journal entry to record amortization of the patent for each of its 10 years of useful life would be:

	dr	cr
Amortization expense	1,000	
Patent		1,000

To amortize the cost of the patent over its useful life ($10,000/10 years).

Review Questions

DIRECTIONS: Select the best answer from the four alternatives. Write the letter of your answer in the blank to the left of the number. Assume 360 days per year in all interest calculations.

_____ 1. A note receivable that requires payment of principal only with no provision for interest is called

    a. an interest-bearing note receivable.
    b. a noninterest-bearing note receivable.
    c. an imputed note receivable.
    d. a discounted note receivable.

_____ 2. What is the interest on a $40,000 interest-bearing note at 9 percent for 120 days?

    a. $3,600
    b. $1,800
    c. $1,200
    d. $5,333

_____ 3. Arnold Company accepted a $10,000 three-year noninterest-bearing note from Mary Mealy. The interest rate that Arnold Company charged for similar transactions was 10 percent. The amount of the discount on notes receivable that Arnold Company should have recorded is (rounded to the nearest dollar)

    a. $7,513.
    b. $9,090.
    c. $3,030.
    d. $2,487.

_____ 4. In the United States, interest should be imputed on a note receivable

    a. when the note is noninterest bearing regardless of the due date of the note.
    b. when the interest rate on the note is unreasonably low and the note has a due date more than one year in the future.
    c. Both (a) and (b) are true.
    d. Neither (a) nor (b) is true.

_____ **5.** Selling a note receivable to a bank

  a. is called discounting the note.
  b. results in the seller assuming a contingent liability to pay the bank if the maker of the note defaults.
  c. results in a credit to interest income when the proceeds of the sale exceed the face value of the note.
  d. All of the above are correct responses.

_____ **6.** The maturity value of an interest-bearing note receivable is

  a. equal to the face value.
  b. equal to the face value plus the interest due on the maturity date of the note.
  c. the amount a bank will pay for a note if it is discounted with the bank.
  d. the principal amount of the note.

_____ **7.** The writing off of a worthless account receivable when the allowance method of recording bad debt expense is used

  a. results in a decrease in the total assets of the company.
  b. should include a debit to bad debt expense.
  c. decreases the net realizable value of accounts receivable for the firm.
  d. should include a debit to the allowance for uncollectible accounts.

_____ **8.** Which of the following items would not be included as an intangible asset?

  a. Patent
  b. Copyright
  c. Prepaid rent
  d. Goodwill

_____ **9.** ABC Co. owns a patent that has a legal life of 17 years and an expected useful life of 10 years. The patent should be amortized over

  a. 17 years.
  b. 5 years.
  c. 12 years.
  d. 10 years.

_____ **10.** Ajax Co. purchased a two-year insurance policy on June 1, 19XA, for $600. On June 1, Ajax Co. debited prepaid insurance and credited cash for $600. On December 31, 19XA (Ajax Co.'s year end), Ajax Co. should

  a. include the $600 on the balance sheet as a prepaid expense.
  b. make an adjusting entry debiting prepaid insurance and crediting insurance expense for $175.

c. make an adjusting entry debiting insurance expense and crediting prepaid insurance for $175.
d. make an adjusting entry debiting insurance expense and crediting prepaid insurance for $425.

_____

11. On the balance sheet, the allowance for uncollectible accounts

a. should be included as a current liability.
b. should be shown as an addition to the accounts receivable balance.
c. should be shown as a deduction from the balance in the accounts receivable account.
d. should not be shown on the balance sheet since it is an income statement account.

_____

12. If the interest income account has a $400 credit balance before the year-end adjustments are made, and there are adjustments for $50 of accrued interest on notes receivable, the income statement should show interest earned of

a. $350.
b. $450.
c. $400.
d. $50.

_____

13. Sun Co. uses the allowance method of recording bad debt expense. In 19XA, Sun Co. wrote off the account of Susan Wendel as uncollectible. During 19XB, Susan Wendel paid Sun Co. the amount that had been owed. Sun Co. should

a. not record the collection since the account was previously written off.
b. credit bad debt expense for the amount received.
c. first reinstate the account of Susan Wendel by debiting accounts receivable and crediting allowance for uncollectible accounts; then record the collection.
d. record the amount received as miscellaneous revenue in 19XB.

_____

14. After aging the accounts receivable at the end of the year, Ring Co. estimated that $100,000 of the accounts receivable would be uncollectible. The balance in allowance for uncollectible accounts prior to adjustment was a $2,000 debit. The correct adjusting entry would include a debit to bad debt expense of

a. $98,000.
b. $102,000.
c. $100,000.
d. $2,000.

15. Which of the following statements about intangible assets is true?

    a. Intangible assets should be amortized over their useful lives.
    b. Intangible assets with indefinite lives should be amortized over a period not exceeding 50 years.
    c. Intangible assets that are acquired at no cost should be recorded on the balance sheet at estimated market value.
    d. All of the above are true.

Use this information in answering Questions 16 to 18. Assume 360 days per year in all interest calculations.

    Millikin Co. had credit sales of $2,000,000 in 19XA. The year-end accounts receivable balance was $588,000. The allowance for uncollectible accounts had a credit balance of $1,000 prior to adjustment.

16. Assuming that Millikin Co. uses the percentage-of-credit-sales method of estimating bad debt expense and that past experience indicates 1 percent of credit sales will be uncollectible, the year-end adjusting entry should include

    a. a debit to bad debt expense for $21,000.
    b. a debit to bad debt expense for $19,000.
    c. a debit to bad debt expense for $20,000.
    d. none of the above.

17. Assuming that Millikin Co. uses the percentage-of-accounts-receivable method of estimating uncollectible accounts and that past experience indicates that 3.5 percent of the total accounts receivable prove to be uncollectible, the year-end adjusting entry should include

    a. a debit to bad debt expense for $19,580.
    b. a credit to allowance for uncollectible accounts of $20,580.
    c. a debit to bad debt expense for $21,580.
    d. none of the above.

18. Assuming that Millikin Co. uses the direct write-off method of recording bad debts, the year-end adjusting entry should include

    a. a debit to bad debt expense and a credit to accounts receivable.
    b. a debit to accounts receivable and a credit to bad debt expense.
    c. a debit to bad debt expense and a credit to allowance for uncollectible accounts.
    d. no adjusting entry would be made under the direct write-off method.

Use this information in answering Questions 19 to 22. Assume 360 days per year in all interest.

Frank Co. accepted a $10,000 10 percent 90-day note receivable from Alex Co. on June 1, 19XA. On July 1, 19XA, Frank Co. discounted the note with ABC Bank. The bank discount rate is 12 percent.

19. The maturity value of the note is

  a. $11,000.
  b. $10,300.
  c. $10,250.
  d. $11,200.

20. The proceeds received by Frank Co. from ABC Bank were (rounded to the nearest dollar)

  a. $10,079.
  b. $9,500.
  c. $10,000.
  d. $10,045.

21. Assuming that the proceeds received in Question 20 were $9,500, the entry to record the receipt of the proceeds would include

  a. a debit to cash, a credit to notes receivable, and a credit to interest income.
  b. a debit to cash, a debit to interest expense, and a credit to notes receivable.
  c. a debit to notes receivable, a credit to cash, and a credit to interest income.
  d. a debit to cash and a credit to notes receivable.

22. On September 5, 19XA, Frank Co. received a notice from ABC Bank that Alex Co. had dishonored the note. The bank charged a $50 protest fee. The entry to record Frank Co.'s payment to the bank would include

  a. a debit to notes receivable for $10,000 and a credit to cash for $10,000.
  b. a debit to accounts receivable for $10,050 and a credit to cash for $10,050.
  c. a debit to accounts receivable for $10,300 and a credit to cash for $10,300.
  d. a debit to notes receivable for $10,250 and a credit to cash for $10,250.

Solutions

Answer   *Refer to:*

1. (b)   [A-2]

2. (c)   [A-1]

Interest = principal × rate ×   time
$1,200 = $40,000 × 0.09 × 120/360

3. (d)   [A-2] The present value of the note is computed using the following formula:

$$\frac{\text{face value of note}}{(1 + r)^n} = \frac{\$10,000}{(1 + 0.1)^3} = \$7,513$$

The discount to be recorded is the difference between the face value and the present value of the note ($10,000 − 7,513 = $2,487).

4. (b)   [A-2-d]

5. (d)   [A-4]

6. (b)   [A-4-a]

7. (d)   [B-4]

8. (c)   [D]

9. (d)   [D-3]

10. (c)   [C-1-a(1); Chapter 9, F-2-a(1) (a)]

$600/24 months = $25/month
$25/month × 7 months = $175 insurance expense

11. (c)   [B]

12. (b)   [A-3]

13. (c)   [B-5]

14. (b)   [B-1] Since allowance for uncollectible accounts has a $2,000 debit balance, the adjusting journal entry must be made for $102,000 in order to have an ending balance of $100,000 in allowance for uncollectible accounts after adjustment.

15. (a)   [D-3]

16. (c)   [B-3] $2,000,000 \times 0.01 = \$20,000$

17. (a)   [B-2] $588,000 \times 0.035 = \$20,580$

Since $20,580 is the ending credit balance we wish to have in the allowance for uncollectible accounts, the adjusting journal entry would have to be made for $19,580 ($20,580 − $1,000 credit balance already in the account).

18. (d)   [B-6]

19. (c)   [A-4-a] Maturity value is equal to the principal plus the interest on the note.

Principal +   interest   = maturity value
$10,000   + ($10,000 \times 0.10 \times 90/360) = $ $10,250

20. (d)   [A-4-c] The bank discount in this problem is equal to the maturity value $\times$ the bank discount rate $\times$ the length of time the bank will hold the note.

Maturity value $\times$ bank discount rate $\times$ time = bank discount
    $10,250 $\times$ 0.12 $\times 60/360 =$ $205

Maturity value − bank discount = proceeds
    $10,250   −   205   = $10,045

21. (b)   [A-4-d]

22. (c)   [A-4-f] Frank Co. must pay the bank the maturity value of the note plus the protest fee. Frank Co. would then record an account receivable from Alex Co. for the amount paid to the bank.

CHAPTER 15

Debt Equities or Liabilities

OVERVIEW

This chapter is intended to introduce the candidate to the accounting procedures used in recording and reporting liabilities. Many liabilities, such as accounts payable and accrued liabilities, have been discussed in earlier chapters. The accounting for notes payable and bonds payable is very similar to the accounting for notes and bonds receivable. The candidate may find it useful to review Chapter 11.

The candidate should know the accounting procedures used for interest-bearing and noninterest-bearing notes payable, the calculation of simple and compound interest, the definitions of term and installment notes payable, the treatment of accounts payable, the recording of accrued liabilities, and the accounting for long-term liabilities, including notes, mortgages, and bonds.

KEY TERMS

Bearer bonds	Mortgage
Bond sinking fund	Mortgage bond
Callable bonds	Registered bond
Compound interest	Serial bonds
Convertible bond	Simple interest
Debenture	Term bonds
Installment note payable	Term notes payable

A. Short-Term Obligations

Short-term obligations are current liabilities that will require payment within the next operating cycle. The following are the basic types of short-term obligations:

1. *Notes Payable*: Notes payable are written documents promising to pay an amount to a creditor on a specific date. Short-term notes payable can be interest bearing or noninterest bearing. Notes payable could be given in exchange for goods or services, for purchase of real estate or equipment, or to a bank in exchange for cash.

a. *Interest-bearing notes payable*: Interest-bearing notes payable require the payment of principal and interest at their maturity date. Interest-bearing notes payable should be recorded at their face value. If the accounting period ends before the note matures, an adjusting entry should be made to record any accrued interest on the note.

EXAMPLE: This example shows the accounting entries for an interest-bearing note payable. Assume that on May 1 Johnson Company issued a $5,000 six-month 12 percent note payable to Jones Company in exchange for merchandise. Johnson Company uses a periodic inventory system. The entry to record the issuance of the note would be:

	dr	cr
May 1 Purchases	5,000	
Notes payable		5,000

To record issuance of six-month 12% note in exchange for goods.

Assuming that Johnson Company's year end is December 31, the entry to record payment of the note on November 1 would be:

	dr	cr
Nov. 1 Notes payable	5,000	
Interest expense	300	
Cash		5,300

Paid six-month note to Jones Co. with interest ($5,000 × 0.12 × 6/12).

If Johnson Company's year end were August 31, the following adjusting entry would be needed to record the accrued interest expense:

	dr	cr
Aug. 31 Interest expense	200	
Accrued interest payable		200

To record interest accrued from May 1 through August 31 on Jones Co. note payable ($5,000 × 12 × 4/12).

Assuming that Johnson Company's year end was August 31, the entry to record payment of the note on November 1 would be:

	dr	cr
Nov. 1 Notes payable	5,000	
Accrued interest payable	200	
Interest expense	100	
Cash		5,300

Paid six-month note to Jones Co.

(1) *Simple interest*: Simple interest is calculated for a single period of time and is computed only on the amount of the principal of the note. The formula for calculation of simple interest is

$$\text{Interest} = \text{principal} \times \text{rate of interest for one period} \times \text{number of periods or fraction of a period}$$

Note: All examples of the calculation of interest made above are calculations of simple interest.

(2) *Compound or add-on interest*: Compound interest refers to the calculation of interest on the principal and on any interest that is earned but has not yet been paid. Any interest earned during a period earns interest in subsequent periods. Compounding of interest takes place at periodic intervals which may vary in length. For example, many savings accounts compound interest on a daily basis. Interest might also be compounded on a weekly, monthly, quarterly, or yearly basis. The more often that interest is compounded, the greater is the total amount of interest earned. Tables are available to aid in solving compound interest problems. The following example shows the calculation of simple and compound interest.

EXAMPLE: Assume that Sara Stein invested $1,000 at 10 percent interest for five years. The calculation of the total amount that she would earn on the investment, assuming simple interest versus compound interest (compounded yearly), would be:

Year	Interest Computation	Simple Interest	Compound Interest
1	Interest on principal ($1,000 × 0.10)	$100.00	$100.00
2	Interest on principal ($1,000 × 0.10)	100.00	100.00
	Interest on interest ($100 × 0.10)		10.00
3	Interest on principal ($1,000 × 0.10)	100.00	100.00
	Interest on interest ($210 × 0.10)		21.00
4	Interest on principal ($1,000 × 0.10)	100.00	100.00
	Interest on interest ($331 × 0.10)		33.10
5	Interest on principal ($1,000 × 0.10)	100.00	100.00
	Interest on interest ($464.10 × 0.10)		46.41
	Total interest earned	$500.00	$610.51

b. *Noninterest-bearing notes payable*: Noninterest-bearing notes payable do not require the payment of interest. Only the payment of the principal amount is required. Since money has a time value, a portion of the payment of the note at maturity is for implied interest. Although theoretically all noninterest-bearing notes should be reported at their present value, it is acceptable to treat notes issued for a short period of time (less than one year) as noninterest bearing since any interest included in the face value is normally immaterial.

c. *Discounted note payable*: A company may issue its own noninterest-bearing note payable to a bank in exchange for cash. The bank discounts the note and pays the discounted amount to the borrower. The bank calculates the discount as follows:

> Face value of note
> × Discount rate
> × Period of time note will be outstanding
> = Discount

The face value of the note less the discount equals the proceeds the borrower will receive. The discount on the note represents interest expense to the borrower.

EXAMPLE: This example shows the accounting entries for a noninterest-bearing note payable discounted with a bank. Robert Corp. discounted its own 90-day note payable for $5,000 at Security National Bank. The bank discount rate is 10 percent. The proceeds received by Robert Corp. are calculated as follows:

Face value	5,000
Less: Discount	
($5,000 × 0.10 × 90/360)	− 125
Proceeds	4,875

The entry to record the loan would be:

	dr	cr
Cash	4,875	
Discount on notes payable	125	
Notes payable		5,000

To record discounting of 90-day note with Security National Bank at 10%.

The entry to record payment of the note when it matures would be:

	dr	cr
Notes payable	5,000	
Interest expense	125	
Discount on notes payable		125
Cash		5,000

To record payment of loan from Security National Bank.

d. *Term notes payable*: Term notes payable are repaid in a lump sum on a specific date. They have a specified term of life after which the principal, or principal plus interest, must be repaid.

e. *Installment notes payable*: Installment notes payable are repaid through a series of periodic payments. Each payment represents a payment of a portion of the principal plus interest. Purchase of a television set to be paid for in 20 equal monthly installments would represent an installment note payable.

2. *Accounts Payable*: Accounts payable result from the purchase of merchandise or services on open account. Accounts payable are not formal written documents and usually do not require the payment of interest. The accountant must be careful to ensure that all accounts payable are recorded. Cash (or purchase) discounts are often offered for prompt payment of accounts payable. Companies should take advantage of cash discounts whenever possible since a substantial cash savings results from doing so.

3. *Accruals*: Accruals are liabilities recorded through year-end (or monthly) adjusting entries. The recording of accrued liabilities is discussed in Chapter 9, Section F.

EXAMPLES: Accrued interest payable, accrued salaries payable, and accrued payroll taxes payable.

B. Long-Term Obligations	Long-term liabilities will not require repayment within the next operating cycle. Long-term liabilities could include mortgages, long-term notes payable, bonds payable, leases, and pensions.

1. *Notes Payable*: Long-term notes payable might be issued when large items such as machinery, equipment, or real estate are purchased. Long-term notes payable are accounted for in the same way as short-term notes payable. Most long-term notes payable are interest bearing, and any applicable interest should be accrued at the end of each accounting period. If a long-term note payable is noninterest bearing, the interest imputed on the note should be recorded as a discount on notes payable. The discount on the notes payable account is a contra-liability which is shown as a deduction from notes payable on the balance sheet. By using a discount account, the note is valued on the balance sheet at its present value. If the discount were not recorded, the cost of the item obtained in exchange for the note would be overstated. Interest should also be imputed on any long-term notes payable that have unreasonably low rates of interest. The discount on notes payable account is amortized to interest expense over the life of the note.

    The following example is based on the same information as the example in Chapter 14, Section A-2. Accounting for noninterest-bearing notes payable parallels the accounting for noninterest-bearing notes receivable. The candidate should review both examples together in order to ensure a complete understanding of the concept.

    EXAMPLE: Zebo Company issued a $10,000 two-year noninterest-bearing note payable to Moomey Company on January 1, 19XA. The note was given in exchange for merchandise. The interest rate normally charged in this type of transaction is 10 percent. The computation of interest to be imputed is

    $$\frac{\$10,000}{1.21} = \$8,264 \text{ (See Chapter 14, Section A-2, for the formula.)}$$

    The discount (interest) on the note would be

    $$\$10,000 - 8,264 = \underline{\underline{\$1,736}}$$

    The journal entry to record the issuance of the note would be:

	dr	cr
Jan. 1 Purchases	8,264	
Discount on notes payable	1,736	
Notes payable		10,000

    Issued a two-year noninterest-bearing note to Moomey Co. Interest was imputed at 10%.

    The journal entry to accrue the first year's interest would be:

	dr	cr
Dec. 31 Interest expense	826	
Discount on notes payable		826

    To record interest accrued on the Moomey Co. note payable (carrying value × interest rate × time, or $8,264 × 0.10 × 1 year).

    The journal entry to record the payment of the note on December 31, 19XB, would be:

		dr	cr
Dec. 31	Notes payable	10,000	
	Interest expense	910	
	Discount on notes payable		910
	Cash		10,000

To record payment of the Moomey Co. note and to write off the balance in the discount account.

2. *Mortgages*: Mortgages are legal agreements that protect the lender by giving him or her the right to be paid from the sale of specific assets that belong to the borrower.

   a. *Installment payments*: Mortgages usually require equal monthly installment payments. These payments include a portion for payment of interest and a portion for payment of principal on the loan.

   b. *Security*: Mortgages are usually secured by the asset (often real estate) which has been purchased with the mortgage.

Mortgages and installment notes are accounted for in the same way. The current portion of any mortgage (that portion which is to be paid within the next operating cycle) should be classified as a current asset.

EXAMPLE: This example illustrates typical accounting entries used for mortgages or installment notes. Assume that Lloyd Corp. purchases real estate for $100,000 on January 1. The firm pays $25,000 cash and obtains a 4-year 12 percent mortgage for $75,000. Lloyd Corp. makes the following entry to record the purchase of the real estate:

	dr	cr
Land	20,000	
Building	80,000	
Cash		25,000
Mortgage payable		75,000

Purchased real estate using cash and a 4-year 12% mortgage.

The monthly mortgage payments are $1,975. The following schedule shows the calculation of the portion of each payment which relates to interest and to principal for three months:

Payment Date	Monthly Payment	Interest of 12% on Principal Balance	Principal Reduction	Unpaid Principal Balance
1/1				$75,000.00
2/1	$1,975.00	$750.00[a]	$1,225.00	73,775.00
3/1	1,975.00	737.75[b]	1,237.25	72,537.75
4/1	1,975.00	725.38[c]	1,249.62	71,288.13

[a]$(75,000.00 \times 0.12 \times 1/12)$.
[b]$(73,775.00 \times 0.12 \times 1/12)$.
[c]$(72,537.75 \times 0.12 \times 1/12)$.

The entries to record the payments in February and March would be:

		dr	cr
Feb. 1	Interest expense	750.00	
	Mortgage payable	1,225.00	
	Cash		1,975.00
	Paid monthly mortgage payment.		
Mar. 1	Interest expense	737.75	
	Mortgage payable	1,237.25	
	Cash		1,975.00
	Paid monthly mortgage payment.		

3. *Bonds Payable*: When an accounting entity wishes to raise a large sum of money, long-term bonds payable might be issued. Bonds are usually sold to numerous investors. Bonds normally have a face value of $1,000 each and pay interest semiannually on the face value of the bond. Bonds are usually issued by large corporations or governmental entities.

   a. *Types of bonds payable*: There are many different types of bonds payable. The basic characteristics of some of these types are shown here.

      (1) *Debentures*: Debentures are unsecured bonds payable. Debentures are usually issued by large, financially sound companies.

      (2) *Mortgage bonds*: Mortgage bonds are secured by specific assets.

      (3) *Term bonds*: Term bonds have a single fixed date of maturity.

      (4) *Serial bonds*: Serial bonds have varying maturity dates but are issued at the same time. Issuing serial bonds avoids the cash flow drain that might occur when term bonds mature.

      (5) *Callable bonds*: Callable bonds may be redeemed by the issuer prior to their maturity date through payment of a stipulated call price. Callable bonds allow the company to take advantage of interest rate changes over time.

      (6) *Convertible bonds*: Convertible bonds have a special provision that allows the bond holder to convert the bonds into common stock of the issuing company. Convertible bonds are often issued as inducements to the lender.

      (7) *Registered bonds*: Registered bonds have the name of the owner registered with the issuing company. The issuing company mails the interest checks to the registered owner.

      (8) *Coupon bonds or bearer bonds*: Bearer bonds are not registered to a specific person. The owner of a bearer bond is assumed to be the person who has possession of the bond. Bearer bonds have coupons attached to them which, when an interest payment is due, the owner sends to the issuing company or to a bank acting as trustee. The issuer then pays the bond interest when the coupon is received.

   b. *Sale of bonds*: Bonds are traded regularly on securities exchanges. Bonds may be held to maturity, or they may be sold on the market prior to maturity.

c. *Interest accrued on bonds sold*: When bonds are sold between interest dates, the purchaser must pay the seller for any interest that has accrued on the bonds. When the next interest payment date arrives, the issuer then pays the holder interest for the full six-month period.

EXAMPLE: Assume that Weller Corp. sells $1,000,000 of 10-year 12 percent bonds payable on March 1, 19XA. Interest is paid on the bonds on January 1 and July 1. The bonds are sold at face value. The entry to record the sale is:

	dr	cr
Mar. 1 Cash	1,020,000	
Bonds payable		1,000,000
Bond interest payable		20,000

To record issuance of $1,000,000 of 10-year 12% bonds at face value plus two months' accrued interest ($1,000,000 \times 0.12 \times 2/12$).

The entry to record the semiannual interest payment on July 1 is:

	dr	cr
July 1 Interest expense	40,000	
Bond interest payable	20,000	
Cash		60,000

Paid semiannual interest on 12% bonds ($1,000,000 \times 0.12 \times 2/12$).

d. *Recording of bonds payable*: Bonds payable are always recorded in the accounts at face value. However, bonds may be sold at an amount different from their face value. For example, assume that the market rate of interest for bonds of the same grade as those sold by Weller Corp. was 15 percent. When Weller Corp. attempted to sell their 12 percent bonds on the market, investors would be unwilling to pay a full $1,000 for the bonds. This is because the bonds pay interest at an amount lower than the market rate of interest. The purchaser would be willing to pay only enough for the bond so that the effective rate of interest on the bond would be equal to market rate of interest. Usually, the coupon rate (also called contract or stated rate) is fairly close to the market rate at the time of initial issue.

(1) Bond prices are quoted as a percentage of the bond's stated face value.

EXAMPLES:

A $1,000 stated value bond quoted at 98 is selling at 98 percent of face value, or $980 ($1,000 \times 0.98$).

A bond quoted at 104 is selling at 104 percent of face value, or $1,040 ($1,000 \times 1.04$).

(2) When the market rate of interest is higher than the stated rate of interest paid by the bond, the bond will sell at a discount.

EXAMPLE: Onsi Corp. issued $1,000,000 of 20-year 8 percent bonds on July 1, 19XA. The market rate of interest for bonds of the same grade was higher than 8 percent so the bonds sold at 97 ($970 for each $1,000 bond). The bonds were sold on an interest payment date. The entry to record issuance of the bonds would be:

	dr	cr
July 1 Cash	970,000	
Discount on bonds payable	30,000	
Bonds payable		1,000,000
Issued 1,000 8% bonds at 97.		

Note that bonds payable are always recorded at face value, as compared to bonds receivable which are recorded at cost. Discount on bonds payable is a contra-liability account and is shown as a deduction from bonds payable on the balance sheet.

(3) When the market rate of interest is lower than the stated rate of interest paid by the bond, the bond will sell at a premium.

EXAMPLE: Zeta Corp. issued $1,000,000 of 10-year 15 percent bonds on January 1, 1982. The market rate of interest for bonds of the same grade was lower than 15 percent, so the bonds sold at 105 ($1,050 for each $1,000 bond). The bonds were sold on an interest payment date. The entry to record issuance of the bonds would be:

	dr	cr
Jan. 1 Cash	1,050,000	
Premium on bonds payable		50,000
Bonds payable		1,000,000
Issued 1,000 15% bonds at 105.		

Bond premium is an adjunct account. An adjunct account is related to another account and has a balance that is on the same side of an account as the account to which it is related. Premium on bonds payable is added to bonds payable on the balance sheet to report book value of the bonds.

(4) Bond premium or discount should be amortized to interest expense over the life of the bond. There are two methods of bond premium or discount amortization: the straight-line method and the effective-interest method. The purpose of the amortization of bond premium or discount is to reflect the effective rate of interest paid by the issuer on the bonds. The effective-interest method is a more accurate method of adjusting the interest paid to the effective rate.

e. *Bond redemption*: When bonds payable mature, the issuer pays the bond holders the face value of the bonds. At maturity, all of the bond premium or discount has been amortized and the carrying value of the bonds is equal to the face value.

EXAMPLE: Assume that Zeta Corp. redeemed the $1,000,000 of bonds on their maturity date, January 1, 19XA. The entry to record the redemption would be:

	dr	cr
Jan. 1 Bonds payable	1,000,000	
Cash		1,000,000
Retired 15% bonds at maturity.		

(1) *Sinking fund*: Some bonds provide for the establishment of a sinking fund to accumulate sufficient funds to retire the bonds when they mature. The bond issuer makes periodic cash payments into the sinking fund, and the money is invested to earn a return. The sinking fund should cover the cost of retiring the bonds when they mature. Sinking funds are reported as a long-term investment on the balance sheet.

(2) *Redemption prior to maturity date*: Bonds may be redeemed prior to their maturity date, either through payment of the call price or by purchasing the bonds on the market. A gain or loss might be reported on the early redemption of bonds payable. Gains or losses from bond retirements should be reported as extraordinary items.

Review Questions

DIRECTIONS: Select the best answer from the four alternatives. Write the letter of your answer in the blank to the left of the number. Assume 360 days per year in all interest calculations.

_____ 1. Interest-bearing notes

    a. require payment of principal and interest at maturity.
    b. are reported at face value on the balance sheet.
    c. necessitate the recording of any accrued interest at year end.
    d. All of the statements above are true.

_____ 2. Which of the following statements is true?

    a. Simple interest is calculated based only on the principal amount of the note.
    b. If two securities with a two-year life are identical in all ways except that one earns simple interest and the other earns compound interest, with monthly compounding, the security earning simple interest will earn the larger amount of interest.
    c. The more often interest is compounded, the less the total amount of interest that is earned.
    d. Interest must be imputed on short-term noninterest-bearing notes.

_____ 3. The method of calculating interest in which interest is earned on both principal and previously accumulated interest is called

    a. imputed interest.
    b. accrued interest.
    c. simple interest.
    d. compound interest.

_____ 4. A $20,000, two-year, noninterest-bearing note payable is issued. What is the amount of the discount on notes payable that should be recorded if the interest rate for comparable transactions is 5 percent? (Round your answer to the nearest dollar.)

    a. $10,141
    b. $1,859
    c. $9,524
    d. $2,000

_____ **5.** Discount on notes payable is

      a. an owners' equity account.
      b. a liability account.
      c. a contra-liability account.
      d. a contra-asset account.

_____ **6.** Jones Co. discounts their own $10,000 note payable (noninterest-bearing) at the Second Security Bank. The bank discount rate is 9 percent. The note is due in 180 days. The proceeds received by Jones Co. are

      a. $9,000.
      b. $9,100.
      c. $9,550.
      d. $10,000.

_____ **7.** A legal agreement that gives the lender the right to be paid from the sale of specific assets that belong to the borrower is a/an

      a. installment note.
      b. bond.
      c. debenture.
      d. mortgage.

_____ **8.** Bonds payable

      a. may be traded on securities exchanges.
      b. may be sold for more or less than their face value depending on the relationship between the current market rate of interest and the contract rate of interest printed on the bond.
      c. normally pay interest semiannually.
      d. are characterized by all of the statements above.

_____ **9.** A fund provided to accumulate a sufficient amount to repay bonds when they mature is usually called a/an

      a. bond sinking fund.
      b. bond redemption fund.
      c. bond call fund.
      d. investment fund.

_____ **10.** Zeb Co. issued $100,000 of 10 percent (contract rate) bonds on May 1, 19XA. The market rate of interest for similar bonds on May 1, 19XA, was 8 percent. The bonds were sold

      a. at a discount.
      b. at face value.

    c. at a premium.

    d. at an amount that cannot be determined from the information given.

_____ **11.** When bonds sell for less than face value, the difference between the selling price of the bonds and face value is called

    a. adjunct on bonds payable.

    b. premium on bonds payable.

    c. discount on bonds payable.

    d. contra bonds payable.

_____ **12.** Bond premium is

    a. a liability account.

    b. a contra account.

    c. deducted from bonds payable on the balance sheet.

    d. added to bonds payable on the balance sheet.

_____ **13.** A bond that is quoted at 103 would sell for

    a. $1,003.

    b. $1,030.

    c. $1,300.

    d. $1,033.

_____ **14.** The entry to record payment of a $10,000 90-day 9 percent note payable would include

    a. a credit to notes payable for $10,000.

    b. a debit to notes payable for $10,225.

    c. a credit to cash for $10,225.

    d. a debit to interest expense for $900.

_____ **15.** Installment notes payable are repaid through

    a. periodic payments on principal only.

    b. periodic payments on interest only.

    c. periodic payments which include both principal and interest.

    d. a lump-sum payment of principal and interest due.

Use this information in answering Questions 16 and 17. Assume 360 days per year in all interest calculations.

Jack Nimble invested $5,000 at 10 percent for three years.

_____

16. The total interest for the three-year period, assuming simple interest, is

   a. $500.
   b. $5,500.
   c. $1,500.
   d. $6,500.

_____

17. The total interest for the three-year period, assuming compound interest, is

   a. $1,050.
   b. $1,655.
   c. $1,600.
   d. $6,665.

Use this information in answering Questions 18 to 20. Assume 360 days per year in all interest calculations.

Jill Sykes Company made the following journal entry to record a two-year, non-interest-bearing note payable:

	dr	cr
Equipment	24,793	
Discount on notes payable	5,207	
Notes payable		30,000

The equipment was purchased on October 1, 19XA, and the interest rate was assumed to be 10 percent. Jill Sykes Company's year end is December 31.

_____

18. The amount of interest expense to be recorded on December 31, 19XA, would be (rounded to the nearest dollar)

   a. $620.
   b. $2,479.
   c. $651.
   d. $521.

_____

19. The entry made by Jill Sykes Company to record the accrued interest would include

   a. a debit to interest expense and a credit to interest payable.
   b. a debit to interest receivable and a credit to interest income.

c. a debit to discount on notes payable and a credit to interest income.

d. a debit to interest expense and a credit to discount on notes payable.

_____

20. The carrying value of the note on Jill Sykes Company's December 31, 19XA, balance sheet would be

a. $24,793.

b. $30,000.

c. $25,413.

d. $29,479.

Solutions

Answer	Refer to:

1. (d)   [A-1-a]

2. (a)   [A-1-a(1)]

3. (d)   [A-1-a(2)]

4. (b)   [B-1]

$$\frac{\$20,000}{(1 + 0.05)^2} = \frac{\$20,000}{1.1025} = \$18,141 \text{ (present value of note)}$$

Face value of note − present value of note = discount
$20,000   − $18,141   = $1,859

5. (c)   [B-1]

6. (c)   [A-1-c]

Discount = $10,000 × 0.09 × 180/360 = $450

Proceeds = face value − discount
$9,550   = $10,000   − $450

7. (d)   [B-2]

8. (d)   [B-3]

9. (a)   [B-3-e(1)]

10. (c)   [B-3-d(3)]

11. (c)   [B-3-d(2)]

12. (d)   [B-3-d(3)]

13. (b)   [B-3-d(1)]

$1,000 × 1.03 = $1,030

14. (c)   [A-1-a]

Interest expense = $10,000 × 0.09 × 90/360 = $225

The journal entry to record payment of the note would be:

	dr	cr
Notes payable	10,000	
Interest expense	225	
Cash		10,225

15. (c)   [A-1-e]

16. (c)   [A-1-a(1)]
$$\$5,000 \times 0.10 \times 3 \text{ years} = \$1,500$$

17. (b)   [A-1-a(2)]

Year 1	$5,000	$\times 0.10 =$	$ 500
Year 2	($5,000 + 500)	$\times 0.10 =$	550
Year 3	($5,000 + 500 + 550) $\times 0.10 =$		605
Total interest			$1,655

18. (a)   [B-1] Interest expense would be computed as follows:
carrying value $\times$ interest rate $\times$ time = interest
$$\$24,793^a \quad \times \quad 0.10 \quad \times 3/12 = \quad \$620$$

19. (d)   [B-1]

20. (c)   [B-1]

Notes payable	$30,000
− Discount on notes payable	− 4,587[b]
Carrying value of the note	$25,413

[a]Carrying value is equal to the face value of the note less the balance in the discount on notes payable account ($30,000 − $5,207 = $24,793).
[b]Discount on notes payable = $5,207 − $620 = $4,587.

CHAPTER 16

Owners' Equity

OVERVIEW

This chapter covers accounting and reporting for owners' equity. The three forms of business entities were introduced in Chapter 6 and are elaborated on further in this chapter. In Chapter 8 we introduced the recording of owners' equity on the balance sheet. The candidate might wish to first review the owners' equity section of Chapter 8, where we emphasize accounting for the owners' equity of sole proprietorships, partnerships, and corporations. Accounting for the owners' equity of a corporation is more complex than accounting for the owners' equity of a sole proprietorship or a partnership, so the majority of the material in this chapter relates to corporations.

The candidate should understand the three basic types of business entities and their advantages and disadvantages. The candidate should understand the recording of transactions affecting owners' equity in a sole proprietorship and a partnership. The candidate should also understand the following topics pertaining to corporations: the rights of and accounting for common and preferred stock, accounting for treasury stock, calculation of book value of stock, securities markets, and accounting for unappropriated and appropriated retained earnings.

KEY TERMS

Appropriated retained earnings
Authorized shares of capital stock
Book value
Callable preferred stock
Convertible preferred stock
Cumulative preferred stock
Dividends in arrears
Issued shares
Limited liability

Organized stock exchanges
Outstanding shares
Over-the-counter market
Participative preferred stock
Par value
Private placement
Treasury stock
Unappropriated retained earnings
Unlimited liability

A. Sole Proprietorships and Parterships

As discussed in Chapter 6, sole proprietorships are businesses owned by one individual. Partnerships are businesses with two or more co-owners who share profits and losses. These forms of business carry with them certain advantages and disadvantages.

1. *Advantages of Sole Proprietorships and Partnerships:* The following advantages are common to both sole proprietorships and partnerships:

   a. *Formation*: Formation is relatively easy. No legal formalities are required to create the business.

   b. *Regulation*: There is less regulation of the business during its existence than that involved in a corporation.

   c. *Tax advantage*: There exists a possible tax advantage. There is no double taxation of the business firm since no tax is assessed at the business level. All taxable income is passed through to the owners. Losses, too, may be passed through. However, the tax laws are extremely complicated, so it is best to seek expert advice relating to tax matters before deciding which form of business organization to use.

2. *Disadvantages of Sole Proprietorships and Partnerships*: Both these forms of business enterprises do not create new legal entities, as happens when a corporation is formed. There are several disadvantages that are common to both sole proprietorships and partnerships.

   a. *Limited life*: Because the form of business is not a legal entity, the business terminates on the death or withdrawal of an owner.

   b. *Unlimited liability*: The sole owner in a sole proprietorship and each general partner in a partnership are liable for the debts of the business, not only from business assets but also from personal assets.

   c. *Limited capital-raising ability*: As compared to a corporation, both sole proprietorships and partnerships have far less ability to generate capital from contributors.

3. *Accounting for Owners' Equity*: In sole proprietorships and partnerships, accounting for owners' equity may be handled in the following ways:

   a. *Sole proprietorships*: The accounting for a sole proprietorship is relatively simple (see Chapter 8). Owners' equity consists of one capital account which records all increases and decreases in owners' equity.

   b. *Partnerships*: The accounting for a partnership was discussed in Chapter 8. In a partnership, capital accounts for each individual partner record the increases and decreases in the owner's equity for individual partners. Since there is more than one capital account in a partnership, one of the major differences between accounting for a sole proprietorship and a partnership is in the division of profit or loss.

      (1) If no agreement is apparent among partners as to the sharing of profits, the division will be made equally, even if time or capital contributions devoted to the business are not equal. Losses will also be shared equally. However, if any agreement has been reached, either oral or written, that agreement will hold for both profits and losses in the same manner unless otherwise specified.

(2)   The division of profits and losses can take many forms, depending on the agreement of the partners. Division may be according to a fixed ratio (e.g., 3:2:4) or a ratio reflecting capital contributed. Salaries may be allowed as a distribution of profit as well as interest on the capital balances.

Note: If salaries and/or interest are allowed as part of the distribution of income, they are not recorded as salary expense or interest expense.

EXAMPLE: Assume a partnership of P and Q which has a net income for the period of $25,000. The written agreement between P and Q specifies that each partner is to be allowed a salary of $7,000 and interest on invested capital of 10 percent. P has invested $40,000 capital and Q $30,000. The division of profit is to be equal after salaries and interest are accounted for. Division of profits is as follows:

Net income				$25,000
Salaries:	P	$7,000		
	Q	7,000	$14,000	
Interest:	P	$4,000		
	Q	3,000	7,000	(21,000)
Remaining profit to be divided:				$ 4,000
		To P		$ 2,000
		To Q		$ 2,000

Each partner will then receive:

	P	Q
Salaries	$ 7,000	$ 7,000
Interest	4,000	3,000
Remainder	2,000	2,000
Totals	$13,000	$12,000

The $25,000 net income has been divided according to the partners' agreement.

The journal entry to record the distribution of income would be:

	dr	cr
Income summary	25,000	
P, capital		13,000
Q, capital		12,000

To record distribution of net income for the period.

B.   Corporations

As discussed in Chapter 6, corporations are entities created by state or federal law which are separate and distinct from ownership interests. A corporation can hold and dispose of property, can contract in its own name, can sue and be sued. This type of business entity carries with it certain advantages and disadvantages.

1.   *Advantages of the Corporate Form of Ownership*: Corporations have a number of advantages, including limited liability for the shareholders, continuity of existence, capital-raising capacity, and quality of management.

a. *Limited liability*: The shareholder, or owner, in a corporation risks only the amount of his/her investment. Such a shareholder's personal assets are protected from corporate creditors by the limited liability feature.

b. *Continuity of life*: Since the corporation is a creature of law, its existence does not depend on continuous ownership by one or a group of individuals. This feature leads to free transferability of ownership interests. Shares in a corporation may be bought and sold freely without the issuing corporation's interference and without affecting the operations of the corporation.

c. *Capital-raising capacity*: The corporation is efficient as a mechanism for pooling the investments of many individuals. Not only can it raise large amounts of capital, but it can also use several means of raising capital. For example, bonds and several types of capital stock may be issued.

d. *Quality of management*: Owners need not devote time and energy to managing the entity. Instead, they can employ professional executives to accept the responsibility of management.

2. *Disadvantages of the Corporate Form*: Double taxation and regulation costs are two of the primary disadvantages of the corporate form of business enterprise.

a. *Double taxation*: Since the corporation is considered a legal entity, it is taxed on its earnings. The distribution of these earnings to the owners in the form of cash dividends is considered to be personal income to the shareholders and is again taxed. (See comments about taxation with respect to the sole proprietor.)

b. *Regulation costs*: A corporation is regulated by federal and state governments, securities exchanges, and other bodies. The costs of this regulation may be high compared to other types of business entities.

C. Accounting for Stockholders' Equity in a Corporation

The ownership of a corporation consists of individuals who hold the shares of capital stock originally issued by the corporation in exchange for contributions of cash, property, or services. The stockholders' equity section of the balance sheet will display this contributed capital. Contributions are not the only source of capital for a corporation. If the business is successful and has income, management may want to retain some of these earnings in the corporation. The stockholders' equity section of the balance sheet allows for the recording of the retention of earnings.

1. *Contributed Capital*: A corporation has flexibility in the amounts and types of capital stock that it offers in exchange for capital. The amount of capital stock that can be offered to individuals is determined by the corporate charter filed with the state of incorporation. This is known as the *authorized amount* and cannot be exceeded. The amount of stock that has actually been issued to investors is known as the *issued amount*. The amount that is in the hands of stockholders is the *outstanding amount*. These three amounts may be identical; however, they need not be the same. (Some authorized shares may not have been issued to investors, and some shares that were issued to investors may have been repurchased by the company and are no longer considered outstanding. When a corporation holds treasury stock, the treasury shares are still classified as issued; but they are no longer considered outstanding since they are not in the hands of shareholders.) Flexibility in

the types of capital stock offered to investors exists. There are two major types of capital stock: common stock and preferred stock.

a. *Common stock*: Common stock is the basic unit of ownership in a corporation. If a corporation has only one class of capital stock, it will be common stock. Common stock carries with it four basic rights which are inherent in its ownership unless specified otherwise by the corporation on issue or waived by the stockholder after issuance. These rights are:

(1) *The right to have a voice in management*: Stockholders elect the board of directors, which is responsible for the overall management of the firm. Stockholders are also able to vote on matters such as the issuance of long-term debt or the amendment of the state charter.

(2) *The right to share in profits on distribution*: Each shareholder is entitled to obtain a proportionate share of the earnings of the corporation in the form of dividends based on the number of shares owned. This right does not begin until and unless dividends are declared by the board of directors.

(3) *The right to maintain percentage ownership in the corporation*: Each shareholder may have the right to purchase additional shares of stock in new issues at market value in order to maintain his or her percentage of ownership in the firm. This is often called the *preemptive right*.

(4) *The right to share in assets on liquidation*: Common stockholders have a residual claim: in the event of liquidation, common stockholders cannot receive any distributions unless creditors and preferred stockholders, if any, have received their claims. Once these claims have been paid, common shareholders are entitled to the remaining or residual assets in relation to proportional ownership in the firm.

b. *Basic accounting for common stock:*

(1) *Issuance of common stock*: At authorization in the corporate charter, common stock may be given a par value. *Par value* is a fixed amount printed on the face of the stock certificate. In many states, par value represents the minimum legal capital of the corporation. This means that an individual who buys stock from a corporation must give the corporation at least par value for the stock or be liable for the difference. Most states prohibit the issuance of stock at less than par value. Although par value may bear some relationship to the original price, it is often set arbitrarily and should not be confused with market value in any way. On the issuance of par value common stock, the asset cash is increased with a debit for the total amount received by the corporation. The common stock account is increased or credited for par value. The remainder, if any, is a credit and is placed in the paid-in capital in excess of par account.

EXAMPLE: Zeta Company issues 100 shares of its $10 par value stock for $28 per share. The journal entry to record this transaction is as follows:

	dr	cr
Cash	2,800	
Common stock		1,000
Paid-in capital in excess of par		1,800

Issued 100 shares of common stock @ $28 per share ($10 par × 100 shares par value; $2,800 − $1,000 = $1,800 paid-in capital in excess of par).

(a) The issuance of common stock for assets other than cash is recorded in the same manner, with the asset account increased (debited) for market value of the asset and common stock and paid-in capital increased (credited) exactly as in the Zeta Company example.

(b) At one time it was required that all stocks have a par value. Since par value might mislead investors as to the "true value" of a share of stock and sale of stock at less than par value results in a contingent liability, the issuance of stock that does not have a par value (no-par stock) was allowed. The main advantage of no-par stock is that it may be issued at any price. When no-par stock is issued, the asset cash is debited for the amount received, and the common stock account is credited for the total amount received.

Note here that these entries are only for the original issuance of stock by the corporation. Subsequent trading of the stock by investing individuals does not necessitate any entries on the part of the corporation due to the transferability characteristic of corporate stock.

(2) *Dividend payments on common stock*:

(a) *Cash dividends*: Cash dividends on common stock are not an expense of the corporation but are rather a distribution of earnings to the owners. Dividend declarations are at the discretion of the board of directors. Once declared, the cash dividend amount becomes a liability of the corporation until paid.

On declaration, the debit is to dividends declared (or retained earnings). The credit increases the liability account, dividends payable. The date of payment occurs a few weeks later. At this date the liability is removed with a debit, and cash is decreased with a credit. A cash dividend, then, reduces both assets and stockholders' equity since funds are severed from the business. Dividends declared is a temporary account that is closed to retained earnings.

The entry to record declaration of a $1,000 cash dividend is:

	dr	cr
Dividends declared	1,000	
Dividends payable		1,000

The entry to record payment of the $1,000 cash dividend previously declared is:

	dr	cr
Dividends payable	1,000	
Cash		1,000

(b) *Stock dividends*: A stock dividend of common stock is a distribution of additional shares of common stock to existing common stockholders based on the quantity of shares currently held. A stock dividend is a distribution of earnings just as is a cash dividend. The difference lies in the payment: stock rather than cash.

On declaration, the stock dividends declared (or retained earnings) account is debited, and a stockholders' equity account, stock dividends to be distributed, is credited. There is no liability since there is no obligation to pay cash or any other asset. On payment, stock dividends to be distributed is cleared with a debit and common stock is credited. Note that the net effect of this event merely reduces one stockholders' equity account (retained earnings) and increases another (common stock). The total stockholders' equity remains unchanged as well as each stockholder's relative ownership percentage. Stock dividends declared is a temporary account that is closed to retained earnings.

The entry to record declaration of a $1,000 stock dividend is:

	dr	cr
Stock dividend declared	1,000	
Stock dividends to be distributed		1,000

The entry to record the distribution of the $1,000 stock dividend declared above is:

	dr	cr
Stock dividends to be distributed	1,000	
Common stock		1,000

c. *Preferred stock*: Preferred stock is a form of contributed capital with features that distinguish it from common stock. Generally, preferred stock will have a preference over common stock with respect to one or more of the rights of common stock (such as dividend payments or receipt of assets if the corporation liquidates) with a sacrifice of another of the rights (voting power or participation in the distribution of earnings past some specified date). The basic accounting for preferred stock involves its issuance, dividend payments, and termination of the preferred status.

(1) *Issuance of preferred stock*: The issuance of preferred stock is similar to the issuance of common stock, except that the par value, if any, is entered into a preferred stock account.

EXAMPLE: If 10 shares of Beta Company's preferred stock (par value $100) are issued for $105 each, the entry would be:

	dr	cr
Cash	1,050	
Preferred stock		1,000
Paid-in capital in excess of par/preferred stock		50
Issued 10 shares of preferred stock for $105 ($100 par × 10 shares par value;		
$1,050 − $1,000 = $50 paid-in capital in excess of par).		

(2) *Dividend payments on preferred stock*: Dividend payments on preferred stock are in cash and are stated as a percentage of par value.

EXAMPLE: If par is $100 on a share of preferred stock and the dividend rate is 9 percent, the dividend payment would be

$$9\% \times \$100 \text{ par} = 0.09 \times 100 = \$9 \text{ per share}$$

This stock may also be referred to as $9 preferred.

(a) *Payment of dividends*: Dividends are payable only at the discretion of the board of directors. Once dividends are declared, preferred dividends normally take precedence over dividends on common stock.

EXAMPLE: The Miller Corporation has 100 shares of $9 preferred stock and 1,000 shares of common stock, and the board of directors declares a $2,000 dividend. The distribution will be as follows:

Preferred stock		$ 900
($9 × 100 shares)		
Common stock		1,100
($2,000 − 900 = $1,100)		
Per share:		
Preferred stock	$9.00	
Common stock	$1.10	
($1,100/1,000 shares)		

(b) *Cumulative dividends and participation*: Two features with respect to dividends make preferred stock a more attractive investment. These two features are cumulative dividends and participation.

One reason for investment in preferred stock is the expectation of a regular stream of dividends of a fixed amount. Without a cumulative dividends feature, any dividends not declared in a period will be lost forever. Therefore, most preferred stock is issued with a *cumulative dividends* feature which signifies that any dividends not paid in any one period to the preferred stockholders (called *dividends in arrears*) must be made up before any current dividends to preferred or common stock can be distributed. These dividends in arrears are not a liability since no liability exists until declaration. Dividends in arrears are not recorded in the accounting records.

Normally, preferred stock has no right to share in earnings above the stated rate, even if the corporation has high earnings. One desirable feature of preferred stock is *participation*. Participation means that preferred shareholders may receive not only their stated dividend but may also share in earnings of the corporation when they are high. Participating preferred stock will never receive less than the stated dividend when dividends are declared. Many preferred stock issues contain the cumulative feature, with relatively few participating.

(3) *Termination of the preferred status*: Some preferred stocks carry features which make them terminable at the option of either the issuing corporation or the stockholder.

    (a) *Callable preferred stock*: If a preferred stock is callable, the issuing corporation may call, or redeem, the stock at a date after issue for a stipulated price, usually slightly higher than the issue price. Callable preferred stock allows the issuing corporation to raise capital without the loss of control by the existing shareholders. The corporation has the prerogative of redeeming the stock should the funds prove unnecessary in the future.

    (b) *Convertible preferred stock*: If a preferred stock is convertible, the stockholder can exchange the preferred stock at his or her option for a predetermined number of shares of common stock. Convertible preferred stock allows the shareholder to participate in periods of high growth by conversion to higher common stock dividends and market value. In this way the former preferred shareholder now has an equity interest in higher earnings, which usually translate to higher market value of the stock.

d. *Treasury stock*: The shares of its own capital stock reacquired by a corporation are referred to as *treasury stock*. Treasury stock is reacquired for various purposes (for example, to be used in an employee bonus plan). Treasury stock can be reissued at any time or held in the treasury indefinitely. While in the treasury, the stock carries none of the rights of the other shares in its class (such as cash dividends or voting). On the acquisition of shares for the treasury, the stockholders' equity contra-account, treasury stock, is debited to increase the account, and the cash account is credited for the cost of the treasury stock.

EXAMPLE: The reacquisition of 10 shares of $100 par common stock originally issued at $115 per share for $1,300 ($130 per share) would be recorded as:

	dr	cr
Treasury stock	1,300	
Cash		1,300
To record reacquisition of 10 shares.		

Even though it has a debit balance, the treasury stock account does not represent an asset. It is deducted from total stockholders' equity on the balance sheet at its reacquisition cost, since the company, in effect, has become smaller.

e. *Book value*: Book value per share of common stock is a numerical measure of the net assets of a corporation as reflected in a single share of common stock. Book value is not market value but rather is computed by referring to the accounting records. Assume stockholders' equity as presented below:

Common stock (100,000 shares)	$ 200,000
Preferred stock (2,000 shares)	200,000
Paid-in capital in excess of par	500,000
Retained earnings	900,000
Total stockholders' equity	$1,800,000

Since the common shares have a residual claim, all of the net assets belong to the common stockholders except that which belongs to the preferred shareholders. In this example, book value per common share would be:

Total stockholders' equity	$1,800,000
Less: Par value of preferred stock	
($100 × 2,000 shares)	− 200,000
Equity allocated to common stock	$1,600,000
Divided by: Number of common shares outstanding	100,000
Book value per share of common stock	$16

The number of common shares which is divided into the equity allocated to common stock represents the shares outstanding, which indicates that any unissued or treasury shares would not be included in the computation.

    f. *Securities markets*:

        (1) *Original issues markets*: The issuing corporation offers its securities in exchange for capital. A new issue of securities may be offered to the public through an investment banker (or underwriter) who is a specialist in marketing securities to investors. Original issues of securities may also be sold through private placement. *Private placement* is the sale of an entire issue of securities by the issuing corporation directly to one or a few large institutional investors. The offering is not open to the public.

        (2) *Secondary markets*: Securities are exchanged among the general public in the secondary markets. Organized stock exchanges are markets for securities where buy and sell orders are matched at public auction. Organized exchanges may be national (New York Stock Exchange and American Stock Exchange) or may be regional or local. The over-the-counter market consists of all markets for securities except organized exchanges. In the over-the-counter market, securities dealers maintain inventories of over-the-counter securities and sell these to the public at bid-and-ask prices.

2. *Retained Earnings*: Retained earnings is the portion of stockholders' equity that arises from the retention of earnings in the corporation. The retained earnings account is a historical record of all net income (or loss) from the time of incorporation to the present date less any distributions of earnings to stockholders in the form of cash or stock dividends.

    a. *Increases in retained earnings*: The retained earnings account has a normal credit balance, but may have a debit balance should accumulated losses be large. In this case, it is presented on the balance sheet as a deficit or negative balance. The retained earnings account is increased with a credit entry.

Increases result from net income in any period. Increases will also result from releases from the appropriations account.

b. *Decreases in retained earnings*: The retained earnings account is decreased with a debit entry. Decreases will result from a net loss in any period or a transfer to an appropriations account. Decreases will also result from the declaration of cash or stock dividends.

c. *Appropriated retained earnings*: The division of the retained earnings account into two or more separate accounts is achieved by the appropriation of retained earnings. The purpose of this segregation is to inform the financial statement reader that a portion of retained earnings is not available for the payment of dividends. Since the declaration of dividends is at the discretion of the board of directors in all cases, appropriations are not a mandatory accounting procedure. Alternatively, this information may be given in a footnote, which is the most prevalent practice.

Should an appropriation of retained earnings be desired, the entry will be a debit to reduce unappropriated retained earnings and a credit to establish one or more appropriations accounts:

	dr	*cr*
Unappropriated retained earnings	xx	
Retained earnings appropriated		xx

The total amount of retained earnings remains the same. This appropriation may be voluntary, as in the case of plant expansion, or it may result from contractual or legal obligations such as long-term loan covenants restricting the payment of cash dividends. Note that the appropriation of retained earnings does not provide cash or other assets. It is not a source of funds. Conversely, a lack of an appropriations account does not ensure that cash will be available for the declaration of cash dividends. An appropriation of retained earnings is a convention of accounting designed to provide information only. The retained earnings account has its own financial statement presentation (refer to Chapter 8).

Figure 16–1 shows an example of a complete owners' equity section shown in financial statement format, illustrating all the points discussed in this chapter.

Figure 16–1   Owners' Equity Section/Financial Statement

Stockholders' equity		
Cumulative 10% preferred stock, $100 par, 9,000 shares authorized and issued	900,000	
Common stock, $1 par, authorized 1,000,000 shares, issued 500,000 shares of which 2,000 shares are held in the treasury	500,000	
Paid-in capital in excess of par value	3,100,000	
Total contributed capital		4,500,000
Retained earnings		
Appropriated for contingencies	800,000	
Unappropriated retained earnings	2,524,000	3,324,000
Total paid-in capital and retained earnings		7,824,000
Less: Treasury stock 2,000 shares (at cost)		20,000
Total stockholders' equity		7,804,000

Review Questions

DIRECTIONS: Select the best answer from the four alternatives. Write the letter of your answer in the blank to the left of the number.

_____ 1. An arbitrary value placed on a share of stock at the time a corporation seeks authorization is called

    a. preferred value.
    b. statutory value.
    c. market value.
    d. par value.

_____ 2. Which of the following statements is false?

    a. Each partner in a general partnership is personally liable for all of the partnership's business debts.
    b. A corporation must apply for and receive a charter before it comes into existence.
    c. Formation of a partnership requires the approval of the state.
    d. Corporate stockholders normally have limited liability for debts of the corporation.

_____ 3. In a corporation

    a. dividends in arrears are a liability on the balance sheet.
    b. par value establishes the amount a share of stock will sell for.
    c. declaration of dividends reduces retained earnings.
    d. common stock dividends normally take precedence over dividends on preferred stock.

_____ 4. Which of the following is not normally a right of common stockholders?

    a. The right to share in assets upon liquidation
    b. The right to maintain their percentage of ownership in the corporation
    c. The right to share in profits on distribution
    d. The right to vote on _all_ decisions affecting the company

_____ 5. Treasury stock

    a. is an asset account.
    b. should be shown as a reduction from stockholders' equity on the balance sheet.

c. has the right to receive cash dividends on declaration.
d. cannot be reissued by the company.

_____

6. Retained earnings

a. is a record of cash available for projects which results from earnings kept in the business.
b. is increased when additional investments are made by owners.
c. is increased by net income and decreased by net losses.
d. All of the statements above are true.

_____

7. Joe and Alex own a partnership. They have not signed a partnership agreement as to the division of profits resulting from the business. Which of the following statements is true?

a. Since Joe contributed twice as much capital as Alex, the ratio for sharing profits is 2:1.
b. If their agreement is oral, it is invalid.
c. If there is no oral agreement between the partners regarding the division of profits, both profits and losses will be split equally.
d. In partnership agreements, profits and losses must be divided in the same manner.

_____

8. Preferred stock

a. is a class of stock given priority status over common stock with respect to one or more of the rights of common stock, such as dividend payments or receipt of assets on liquidation.
b. always carries a feature which signifies that any dividends not paid to the preferred stockholders in any one period must be made up before any current dividends to preferred or common stock can be distributed.
c. normally has the right to vote.
d. All of the statements above are true.

_____

9. The right of common stockholders to maintain their proportionate interest in a corporation is called

a. the preemptive right.
b. the proportional right.
c. a proxy.
d. the participative right.

10. On June 30, 19XA, XYZ Corporation declared a dividend of $1.00 per share to the common stockholders of record July 10, 19XA, to be paid July 20, 19XA. XYZ Corporation has 5,000 authorized shares and 3,000 outstanding shares. The journal entry to be made on June 30 would be:

	dr	cr
a. Dividends declared	5,000	
Common dividends payable		5,000
b. Dividends declared	3,000	
Common dividends payable		3,000
c. Retained earnings	3,000	
Dividends declared		3,000
d. No journal entry would be made on June 30.		

11. Using the information from question 10, the journal entry to be made on July 20 would be:

	dr	cr
a. Dividends declared	3,000	
Cash		3,000
b. Common dividends payable	5,000	
Cash		5,000
c. Common dividends payable	3,000	
Cash		3,000
d. No journal entry would be made on July 20.		

12. Zeno Corporation issued 10,000 shares of $1.00 par value common stock for $10 per share. The journal entry to record this transaction would include

a. a credit to common stock for $100,000.
b. a debit to cash for $90,000.
c. a credit to common stock for $10,000.
d. a debit to cash for $10,000.

13. Original issues of stock may be sold

a. by private placement to large institutional investors.
b. on the American Stock Exchange.
c. over the counter.
d. through all of the means noted above.

14. The paid-in capital in excess of par account

a. is shown as part of the contributed capital section of stockholders' equity on the income statement.
b. is credited for the excess of market price over par value on the original issuance of stock.

c. is used only when stock is sold for cash.
d. is described by all of the above.

15. Failure to record the declaration and distribution of a stock dividend (dividend issued in stock) would

a. cause assets to be overstated.
b. cause total stockholders' equity to be overstated.
c. cause total stockholders' equity to be understated.
d. have no effect on total stockholders' equity.

16. An appropriation of retained earnings

a. reduces the total retained earnings of the company.
b. is used to inform the financial statement readers that a portion of retained earnings is not available for the payment of dividends.
c. is a mandatory procedure when all of the retained earnings of the company are not available for dividend payment.
d. is characterized by all of the above.

Use this information in answering Questions 17 to 19.

Bob and Sally own a partnership. The written agreement between Bob and Sally specifies that each partner is to be allowed a salary of $10,000 and interest on invested capital of 12 percent. Sally has invested $60,000 in the partnership, and Bob has invested $20,000. The division of profit after salaries and interest have been accounted for is to be made equally.

17. Assuming that the partnership has net income of $40,000 for the period, the amount allocated to Bob would be

a. $20,000.
b. $22,400.
c. $17,600.
d. none of the above.

18. Assuming that the partnership has net income of $20,000 for the period, the amount allocated to Sally would be

a. $12,400.
b. $7,600.
c. $22,000.
d. ($4,800).

19. Assuming that the partnership has net income of $20,000, the journal entry to record the distribution of earnings would include

a. a debit to each partner's capital account and a credit to income summary.
b. a debit to income summary and a credit to each partner's capital account.

c. a debit to salaries expense, a debit to interest expense, a debit to income summary, and a credit to each partner's capital account.

d. a debit to cash and a credit to each partner's capital account.

20. The stockholders' equity of Martin Corporation is as follows:

Preferred stock, $100 par value	
100 shares outstanding	$100,000
Common stock, $10 par value	
10,000 shares outstanding	100,000
Paid-in capital in excess of par—	
common	100,000
Retained earnings	500,000
	$800,000
Less treasury stock (2,000 shares)	− 150,000
Total stockholders' equity	$650,000

What is the book value per common share?

a. $25.00
b. $87.50
c. $75.00
d. $68.75

Use this information in answering Questions 21 and 22.

Morgan Corporation has 100 shares of $100 par 10 percent cumulative preferred stock outstanding. Two years' dividends are in arrears on the preferred stock. (No dividends were paid in 19XA and 19XB.) There are 10,000 shares of common stock outstanding. Morgan Corporation declares a $10,000 cash dividend at the end of 19XC.

21. The total amount of the $10,000 dividend that will be paid to the preferred shareholders is

a. $3,000.
b. $1,000.
c. $2,000.
d. $100.

22. The amount that common stockholders will receive per share is

a. $1.00.
b. $0.70.
c. $0.80.
d. $0.99.

Solutions

Answer	Refer to:
1. (d)	[C-1-b(1)]
2. (c)	[A-1-a]
3. (c)	[C-1-b(2)]
4. (d)	[C-1-a]
5. (b)	[C-1-d]
6. (c)	[C-2]
7. (c)	[A-3-b]
8. (a)	[C-1-c]
9. (a)	[C-1-a(3)]
10. (b)	[C-1-b(2) (a)] Dividends are paid to outstanding shares (3,000 shares × $1.00 per share).
11. (c)	[C-1-b(2) (a)]

12. (c) [C-1-b(1)] The journal entry to record this transaction would be:

Cash	100,000[a]	
Common stock (at par)		10,000[b]
Paid-in capital in excess of par		90,000[c]

13. (a) [C-1-f(1)]

14. (b) [C-1-b(1)]

15. (d) [C-1-b(2) (b)] A stock dividend results in a transfer from retained earnings to contributed capital. If this entry were omitted, total stockholders' equity would be correct, but the components of stockholders' equity would be misstated.

[a]10,000 shares × $10.00 per share = $100,000.
[b]10,000 shares × $1.00 per share = $10,000.
[c]Cash paid − par value = $100,000 − $10,000 = $90,000.

16. (b)   [C-2-c]

17. (c)   [A-3-b] The allocation of income would be:

	Sally	Bob	Total
Income to be split			$40,000
Salary	$10,000	$10,000	(20,000)
Interest	7,200	2,400	(9,600)
Balance to be			$10,400
split equally	5,200	5,200	(10,400)
	$22,400	$17,600	0

18. (a)   [A-3-b] The allocation of income would be:

	Sally	Bob	Total
Income to be split			$20,000
Salary	$10,000	$10,000	(20,000)
Interest	7,200	2,400	(9,600)
Balance to be			$ 9,600
split equally	(4,800)	(4,800)	(9,600)
	$12,400	$ 7,600	0

19. (b)   [A-3-b]

20. (d)   [C-1-e]

Total stockholders' equity $650,000
Less: Par value of preferred stock   (100,000)
Equity available to common shares $550,000

$$\frac{\text{Equity available to common shares}}{\text{Common shares outstanding}} = \frac{\$550,000}{8,000^d} = \$68.75$$

21. (a)   [C-1-c(2) (b)]

Dividends in arrears 19XA $1,000
    (100 × $100 × 0.10)
Dividends in arrears 19XB   1,000
Current dividend   19XC   1,000
    Total preferred dividend $3,000

22. (b)   [C-1-b(2) (a)]
$7,000^e /10,000 shares = $0.70/share

CHANGE 17

CHAPTER 17

Income Statement Accounts

OVERVIEW

This chapter covers accounting for revenues and expenses. (The general accounting for revenue and expense accounts is covered in Chapter 7.) The candidate should review this material if necessary. In this chapter we emphasize accounting for payroll, payroll-related expenses, and accounting for individual federal income taxes. In studying the material related to payroll and income taxes, the candidate should focus review on definitions and methods of recording rather than tax rates or amounts of exclusions, since these amounts are subject to frequent change by the federal government.

The candidate should understand the recording of revenues and expenses in general; the specific treatment of payroll, payroll taxes, and payroll fringe benefits; and the treatment of individual federal income taxes.

KEY TERMS

Capital assets	FICA tax
Capital gain	Long-term capital gain or loss
Capital loss	Short-term capital gain or loss

A. Revenues

Revenues are earnings resulting from the receipt of cash or other assets (or the reduction of a liability) in exchange for goods sold by an entity or services performed by an entity. (A complete discussion of revenues is presented in Chapter 7.)

B. Expenses

Expenses are the cost of goods and services consumed (used up) by an entity as a result of earning revenue. (A complete discussion of expenses is presented in Chapter 7.)

1. *Operating Expenses*: Operating expenses are those expenses related to the normal operations of a business. They include selling expenses and general or administrative expenses.

317

EXAMPLES OF OPERATING EXPENSES: Salaries, payroll taxes, sales commissions, advertising, state and local taxes, telephone, legal fees, insurance, depreciation, and bad debt expense.

a. *Payroll accounting*: Accounting for payroll expenses includes more than just recording the cash paid out for salaries. Companies must also account for health insurance (if provided), employees' income tax which is withheld, social security (FICA) taxes, union dues (if applicable), pension plans, savings bond purchases, and employer payroll taxes.

   (1) *Income tax withheld*: Employers are required to withhold a portion of their employees' gross wages for payment of federal income taxes. They are also required to keep records of the tax withheld. These taxes must be remitted to the federal government periodically. State and local income taxes might also be required to be withheld from the employees' pay. The amount withheld for federal income tax purposes is based on withholding tax tables provided by the government. These tables are based on the amount of the employees' earnings, the frequency of pay periods, and the number of exemptions to which each employee is entitled.

   (2) *FICA tax*: Federal Insurance Contributions Act (social security) tax must also be withheld from each employee's pay. Employers withhold a specific percentage of each employee's earnings until a maximum limit is reached. The employer must also pay a tax at the same rate as the employee. The rate used to calculate FICA tax and the base salary (maximum amount that will be taxed) have changed frequently in recent years. The rate in effect in 1990 was 7.65 percent on the first $51,300 of gross income. For simplicity, it is assumed in this module that the rate is 7 percent on the first $50,000 of income.

   EXAMPLE: Assume that Chase Co. has two employees, Harlan Howe and George Peters. Harlan Howe earned $2,000 for the month of May. Harlan's gross pay for the year as of May 1 was $10,000. George Peters earned $12,000 for the month of May. George's gross pay for the year as of May 1 was $47,000. Chase Co. would withhold $140 of Harlan's earnings for payment of FICA taxes ($2,000 × 0.07 = $140). Chase Co. would withhold $210 of George's earnings for payment of FICA taxes ($3,000 × 0.07 = $210). Only $3,000 of George's May earnings are subject to FICA tax since George reached the $50,000 limit in May. Chase Co. will have to match the amount paid by the employees, so they must remit a total of $700 to the federal government for FICA taxes related to payroll in May.

   (3) *Voluntary deductions from employees' pay*: The employee might also have other amounts withheld from pay, such as insurance premiums, pension plan payments, and purchase of savings bonds. The employer must keep records of all voluntary deductions.

   Note: Amounts withheld from employees' pay are part of salary expense to the company. The amount withheld represents a liability for the company since employees' earnings are held until payment is remitted to the appropriate party.

(4) *Employer payroll expenses*:

(a) *FICA tax*: The employer's portion of the FICA tax is an employer payroll expense.

(b) *Federal unemployment insurance tax*: Employers must pay an amount for Federal Unemployment Insurance Tax. This tax is levied only on the employer, and no portion is deducted from the employee's pay. Like FICA taxes, the rates used to calculate federal unemployment tax change periodically. The rate in effect in 1990 was 6.2 percent on the first $7,000 paid to an employee. The employer is allowed to take a maximum credit of 5.4 percent for contributions to state unemployment programs. For most companies, the net federal tax is 0.8 percent on the first $7,000.

(c) *State unemployment tax*: The states administer distribution of unemployment insurance payments and also collect a state unemployment tax. Most states only tax the employer for unemployment tax, but a few states also tax the employee. Many states use 5.4 percent on the first $7,000 as the basic rate for unemployment taxes. Most states assign a merit rating based on the employment history of the company. A company that has a favorable merit rating will normally have its state unemployment tax rate reduced.

(d) *Employee fringe benefits*: The employer might also provide fringe benefits such as paid vacations, health insurance (the employer might pay all or a portion of the premiums), retirement plans, and paid holidays. These fringe benefits are a substantial amount for most companies.

EXAMPLE: This example illustrates the recording of payroll and related expenses for one payroll period. Nelson Company's employees earned gross pay of $10,000 for the week ending August 31, 19XA. The net cash paid out to employees was $7,000. The following amounts were withheld from the employees' gross pay:

Federal income tax	$2,000
State income tax	200
FICA tax	700
Health insurance premiums	100

The employer payroll taxes were $700 for FICA, $60 for federal unemployment tax, and $180 for state unemployment tax. The employer expenses for fringe benefits were $750 for the retirement plan and $200 for health insurance. The entries to record the payroll and related expenditures were:

	dr	cr
Aug. 31 Salary expense	10,000	
Federal income tax withholding payable		2,000
State income tax withholding payable		200
FICA tax withholding payable		700
Insurance withholding payable		100
Salaries payable		7,000

To record salaries for the week of August 31.

	dr	cr
Aug. 31 Salaries payable	7,000	
Cash		7,000
To record payment of August 31 salaries.		
Aug. 31 Payroll taxes expense	940	
FICA tax payable		700
State unemployment tax payable		60
Federal unemployment tax payable		180
To record employer payroll taxes for salaries for the week of August 31.		
Aug. 31 Payroll benefits expense	950	
Retirement plan payable		750
Health insurance payable		200
To record expenses for benefits associated with August 31 payroll.		

(5) *Accrual of payroll-related taxes and expenses*: When payroll is accrued at the end of the accounting period, all of the payroll-related taxes and expenses should also be accrued. This results in proper matching of revenues and expenses. Payroll taxes are not a legal liability until the salaries are paid. Therefore, some businesses do not accrue payroll taxes.

(6) *Payroll liabilities*: Liabilities related to payroll are recorded as current liabilities.

(7) *Filing of quarterly reports*: A business must file quarterly reports with the government showing the amounts withheld from employees' earnings for federal income taxes and FICA taxes. Payroll taxes must be accounted for on a calendar-year basis in reporting to the government. Amounts withheld from employees must be deposited periodically. The frequency of deposit depends on the amount of taxes withheld. If the total amount is very small, it may be remitted with the quarterly tax returns. If the amounts withheld are significant, they must be deposited with a Federal Reserve Bank or a designated commercial bank on a frequent basis.

2. *Federal Individual Income Taxes*: Individuals must pay federal income tax on the amount of taxable income they earn. Taxable income is calculated as follows:

> Income
> Less: Adjustments to income
> Adjusted gross income (AGI)
> Less: Personal and dependency exemptions
>   Itemized deductions or standard deductions (whichever is greater)
> = Taxable income

a. *Income*: Some of the common items included in income are: wages, salaries, tips, taxable interest income, dividend income, taxable refunds of state and local income tax, alimony received, business income, capital gains, rents, bonuses, and royalties. Some of the common items excluded from gross income include: accident insurance proceeds, child support payments, cost-of-living allowances (for military), damages for personal injury or sickness, gifts, disability benefits, life insurance paid on death, a limited amount of social security benefits, certain scholarship grants, and inheritances.

b. *Gains and losses from property transactions*: When property is disposed of, a gain or loss may result. Gains are generally recognizable for income tax purposes. Losses from the disposition of property held for personal use (not for investment or used in a trade or business) are not recognizable for tax purposes. To determine the appropriate tax treatment of a recognizable gain or loss, the amount of the gain or loss must be classified as *ordinary* or *capital*. Usually, ordinary gains and losses result from the disposition of assets not classified as capital items.

c. *Capital gains and losses*: Capital gains and losses result from the disposition of capital assets. The U.S. Internal Revenue Code defines capital assets as any property a taxpayer holds that is not listed in Section 1221. Section 1221 property includes inventory, accounts receivable, and depreciable property or real estate used in a business.

EXAMPLE: Individual capital assets include property held for personal use, such as a house or a car, and assets held for investment purposes, such as securities.

Capital gains must be classified as short term or long term in nature to determine the appropriate tax treatment.

(1) *Short-term capital gains or losses*: Short-term capital gains or losses result from dispositions of capital assets held for one year or less. Short-term gains and losses must initially be offset to determine net short-term capital gain or loss.

(2) *Long-term capital gains or losses*: Long-term capital gains or losses result from dispositions of capital assets held for more than one year. Long-term capital losses are used to offset long-term capital gains.

(3) *Net short-term capital gains or losses*: Next, any net short-term capital losses are offset against any net long-term capital gains. If the taxpayer has net long-term capital losses and net short-term capital gains, they are also offset.

(4) *Taxing of net capital gains*: Net capital gains (short-term or long-term) are currently taxed as ordinary income. Prior to 1988, net long-term capital gains were afforded special beneficial tax treatment.

(5) *Deduction of net capital losses*: Net capital losses are deductible (as a deduction from adjusted gross income) to a maximum of $3,000 per year. Any unused amount of net capital loss may be carried forward indefinitely.

d. *Deductions (business/personal)*: Deductions allowed to individual taxpayers include deductions from gross income to arrive at adjusted gross income and deductions from adjusted gross income:

(1) *Adjusted gross income*: Some of the deductions from gross income to arrive at adjusted gross income are:

(a) Ordinary and necessary expenses incurred in a trade or business

(b) Employee business expenses that are reimbursed by the employer

    (c)   Penalties on early withdrawal of savings

    (d)   Alimony paid

    (e)   Capital loss deduction

    (f)   Some IRA payments

    (g)   Certain retirement plan contributions

(2) *Itemized deductions*: Certain personal expenses are allowed as itemized deductions from adjusted gross income (AGI). Some of the items that may be included as itemized deductions are:

    (a)   Medical expenses that exceed 7.5 percent of adjusted gross income (AGI)

    (b)   Real estate taxes

    (c)   Personal property taxes

    (d)   Interest on a home mortgage

    (e)   Charitable contributions

    (f)   Casualty and theft losses that exceed 10 percent of AGI

    (g)   Moving expenses

    (h)   Job expenses and other miscellaneous deductions (only the total amount that exceeds 2 percent of AGI is deductible):

- Union dues
- Professional dues and subscriptions
- Job education
- Job travel (with limitations)
- Tax return preparation fees
- Investment counsel fees
- Safety deposit box fees

Note: Items that are allowed as a deduction from gross income to arrive at adjusted gross income provide a greater potential benefit for the taxpayer than itemized deductions from AGI. This is because the taxpayer will always benefit from the deduction for AGI. Itemized deductions will benefit the taxpayer only if the total amount of itemized deductions exceeds the amount of the standard deduction allowed for the taxpayer. The amount of the standard deduction is specified by Congress and depends on the filing status of the taxpayer.

Review Questions

DIRECTIONS: Select the best answer from the four alternatives. Write the letter of your answer in the blank to the left of the number.

_____ 1. Which of the following is legally required to be withheld from employees' pay?

   a. Federal unemployment taxes
   b. FICA taxes
   c. Insurance premiums
   d. IRA deductions

_____ 2. Which of the following items would be recorded in the payroll taxes expense account?

   a. Federal income tax withheld
   b. Company pension plan contributions
   c. Federal Unemployment Tax Act payments
   d. State income tax withheld

_____ 3. Which of the following items deducted from employees' pay *must* be matched by an equal contribution by the employer?

   a. Insurance premiums
   b. Company pension plan contributions
   c. Federal income tax withheld
   d. FICA tax

_____ 4. Items withheld from employees' pay should be classified by the employer as

   a. current liabilities.
   b. long-term liabilities.
   c. expenses.
   d. current assets.

_____ 5. When a company records payroll, salaries or wages expense should be

   a. debited for the amount of net pay.
   b. debited for the amount of gross pay.
   c. credited for the amount of net pay.
   d. credited for the amount of gross pay.

_____ **6.** Which of the following statements about payroll is false?

a. Employers are allowed to take a credit on their federal unemployment taxes for contributions made to their state unemployment programs.
b. FICA tax is subject to a maximum earnings limit. (Taxes are no longer paid once the employee has reached that maximum limit.)
c. Employees may choose to have amounts voluntarily withheld from their pay.
d. State unemployment taxes are normally levied only on the employee.

_____ **7.** Short-term capital gains

a. could result from sales of any asset held for one year or less.
b. could result from the sale of capital assets held for two years or less.
c. could result from the disposition of a capital asset held for one year or less.
d. may be carried forward indefinitely.

_____ **8.** In the United States, long-term capital gains

a. are currently given preferential tax treatment.
b. may be carried forward indefinitely.
c. could result from the sale of Section 1221 property.
d. could result from the sale of investments held by an individual for more than one year.

_____ **9.** Which of the following items would not be included in gross income for individual income tax purposes?

a. Wages
b. Tips
c. Life insurance proceeds paid on death of insured
d. Alimony received

_____ **10.** Which of the following statements about capital gains and losses is false?

a. Net capital losses are deductible to a maximum of $3,000 per year.
b. Net capital gains are currently taxed as ordinary income.
c. Since capital gains are no longer afforded preferential tax treatment, there is no need to net capital gains and losses.
d. The sale of inventory would not result in a capital gain or loss.

_____ **11.** The sale of a personal automobile at a loss

a. could be used to offset any capital gains earned by the owner during the year.
b. would not be recognizable for tax purposes.

c. would be deductible as an ordinary expense item.

d. would be deductible only if the loss was long term in nature.

12. Operating expenses normally include all of the following except

a. sales commissions.

b. payroll taxes.

c. advertising.

d. interest.

Use this information in answering Questions 13 and 14.

Young Company has an employee named Charles Wiley. During the past week Charles earned gross pay of $1,500. Charles' federal income tax withholding based on the federal tax tables is $200 and his state income tax withholding is $20. Charles has requested that a $10 insurance premium and $2 in union dues be withheld from his check each week. Assume that the FICA rate is 7 percent on the first $50,000, the federal unemployment tax rate is 0.8 percent on the first $7,000, and the state unemployment tax rate is 2 percent on the first $7,000. Charles' gross pay to date for this year is $6,000.

13. Charles Wiley's take home pay (net pay) would be

a. $1,268.

b. $1,500.

c. $1,175.

d. $1,163.

14. Young Company's total payroll tax expense related to Charles' earnings for the week would be

a. $133.

b. $105.

c. $147.

d. $353.

Solutions

Answer	Refer to:
1. (b)	[B-1-a(2)]
2. (c)	[B-1-a(4)]
3. (d)	[B-1-a(2)]
4. (a)	[B-1-a(6)]
5. (b)	[B-1-a(4) (d)]
6. (d)	[B-1-a(4) (c)]
7. (c)	[B-2-c(1)]
8. (d)	[B-2-c(2)]
9. (c)	[B-2-a]
10. (c)	[B-2-c(4)]
11. (b)	[B-2-b]
12. (d)	[Chapter 8, B-5-a(2)]

13. (d) [B-1-a]

Gross pay		$1,500
Less:		
Federal income tax withheld	$200	
State income tax withheld	20	
Insurance withheld	10	
Union dues withheld	2	
FICA withheld ($1,500 × 0.07)	105	337
Net pay or take-home pay		$1,163

14. (a) [B-1-a(4)]

FICA ($1,500 × 0.07)	$ 105
Federal unemployment tax ($1,000 × 0.008)	8
State unemployment tax ($1,000 × 0.02)	20
Total payroll tax expense	$ 133

CHAPTER 18

OVERVIEW

Users of financial statements have developed techniques to evaluate the financial data contained in published statements. To a skilled reader, the statements themselves show a wealth of information. A balance sheet can give a good indication of the amount and composition of a firm's assets and liabilities. The income statement displays the results of operations. Finally, the statement of cash flows indicates from where a firm is obtaining cash and how it is being used. When prepared on a consistent basis, comparative statements allow trend analysis, that is, how a firm is progressing through time. Ratio analysis is another widely used technique for evaluating a firm's activities.

The balance sheet, income statement, and statement of retained earnings were discussed in Chapter 8. The candidate should review those particular topics at this time.

KEY TERMS

Cash flow statement
Comparative financial statements
Financing activities
Investing activities
Operating activities

Ratio
Source of working capital
Use of working capital
Working capital

A. Statement of Changes in Financial Position

The balance sheet provides a picture of the status of the firm at a particular time. Comparative balance sheets give an indication of change over time in the composition of the firm's assets and liabilities. Prior to 1988, the statement of changes in financial position was a required financial statement that incorporated input from comparative balance sheets and the income statement to show formally the changes in the balance sheet. This was often done by showing the sources and uses of working capital for the firm.

In November 1987, the Financial Accounting Standards Board (FASB) issued Statement of Financial Accounting Standards No. 75, "Statement of Cash Flows," which requires the presentation of a statement of cash flows in place of the statement of changes in financial position.

Note: The material covering the statement of changes in financial position was left in this chapter because the CPS Study Outline still includes this topic. Concepts used in developing a statement of changes in financial position on a working capital basis should also aid the candidate in understanding and interpreting financial statements.

1. *Working Capital*: Working capital is defined as current assets minus current liabilities. Working capital is employed as a basis for preparing the statement of changes in financial position. The statement shows the sources and uses of working capital during a period.

   a. *Source of working capital*:

      (1) *Resources provided by operations*: If a firm is operating profitably, working capital will increase. The actual net income figure as reported in the income statement must be adjusted for items which are included in the calculation of net income that do not affect working capital.

         (a) *Additions to net income*: Certain expenses must be added back to net income in arriving at resources provided by operations. For example, the entry to record depreciation expense would be:

	dr	cr
Depreciation expense	xx	
Accumulated depreciation		xx

         The depreciation expense account is closed to the income statement, and the accumulated depreciation account remains on the balance sheet as a contra-asset until the depreciable asset is disposed of. No working capital account is affected, yet net income is reduced by the appropriate amount. Therefore, to determine resources (working capital) provided by operations, the amount of depreciation expense must be added back to net income. Other income statement items that must be added back include amortization of goodwill, amortization of bond discount, and losses on disposal of assets.

         (b) *Subtractions from net income*: Similarly, certain items are added to net income, yet provide no working capital. These items must be subtracted from net income to arrive at income provided by operations. Examples include: amortization of bond premium and gains on disposal of assets.

         EXAMPLE OF WORKING CAPITAL:

         Resources provided by operations

Net income		xx
Add: Expenses not affecting working capital		
Depreciation	xx	
Amortization of bond discount	xx	
Loss on sale of assets	xx	

Less: Items not affecting working capital
Amortization of bond premium	(xx)	
Gain on sale of assets	(xx)	xx
Working capital provided by operations		xxx

(2) *Sale of noncurrent assets*: When noncurrent assets are sold for cash, working capital is increased. The amount provided to resources of the firm is irrespective of any gain or loss on the disposition. For example, if land with a book value of $10,000 is sold for $12,000, the entry is:

	dr	cr
Cash	12,000	
Land		10,000
Gain		2,000

In the statement of changes in financial position, the $12,000 is recorded as a source of working capital.

(3) *Borrowing through the use of long-term debt*: When a firm issues long-term debt for cash, working capital is increased. If bonds are sold at a discount or premium, it is the amount of cash received, not the face value of the bonds, which is shown as a source of funds.

(4) *Sale of capital stock*: When a firm sells additional shares of capital stock, working capital is increased.

b. *Uses of working capital*:

(1) *Net loss*: An adjusted net loss decreases a firm's working capital. A failure to operate profitably is thus a use of working capital.

(2) *Purchase of noncurrent assets*: When noncurrent assets are purchased, working capital is decreased. Each acquisition or class of acquisitions is usually shown separately. Note that purchase of inventory is not a use of working capital since inventory is a current asset.

(3) *Declaration of cash dividends*: When cash dividends are declared, working capital decreases. The declaration of a cash dividend creates a current liability, dividends payable. The payment of a cash dividend that has already been declared does not affect working capital.

(4) *Repayment of long-term debt*: Payment of long-term debt that is outstanding reduces the amount of working capital available.

(5) *Repurchase of common stock*: The repurchase of outstanding common stock reduces the amount of working capital available.

c. *All-financial-resources concept*: Some transactions that do not affect working capital are also shown on the statement of changes in financial position. If common stock is exchanged for a noncurrent asset, there is no change in working capital. To better present the sources and uses of resources, such transactions are treated as if two transactions had occurred. The common stock is shown as a source of working capital, and the acquisition is shown as a use of working capital. This procedure was referred to as the all-financial-resources concept, and its use was required by generally accepted accounting principles prior to the issuance of FASB Statement 75.

d. *Reading the statement of changes in financial position*: To the trained reader, the statement of changes in financial position provides a wealth of information. Management's performance can be evaluated in terms of how resources were obtained and utilized. A set of comparative balance sheets will show only the net change in the accounts whereas the statement of changes in financial position will show each change in the accounts. For example, if land with a historical cost of $10,000 is sold for book value and land costing $12,000 is bought, comparative balance sheets will show a net change of $2,000 while the statement of changes in financial position will show a source of working capital of $10,000 and a use of $12,000. The additional information is intended to help users of financial statements make a more effective evaluation for their purposes.

Figure 18–1 shows an example of the statement of changes in financial position.

B. Statement of Cash Flows

The statement of cash flows explains the differences between the beginning and ending balances of cash (including cash equivalents). Cash equivalents are generally short-term temporary investments that are readily convertible to a known amount of cash *and* sufficiently close to their maturity date so that their market value is relatively insensitive to changes in interest rates. Generally, only investments purchased within three months of their maturity dates meet these two criteria. Short-term investments in Treasury bills, investments in money market funds, and some investments in commercial paper would normally qualify as cash equivalents. The statement of cash flows presents information about cash flows from operating, investing, and financing activities.

1. *Operating Activities*: Operating activities generally include transactions that relate to the calculation of net income. These items are usually related to the production and sale of goods and services.

Figure 18–1   Statement of Changes in Financial Position, Lee Company

Sources of working capital		
Resources provided by operations		
Net income	50,000	
Add: Expenses not requiring use of working capital		
Depreciation	20,000	
Loss on sale of assets	5,000	
Total working capital provided by operations		75,000
Sale of bonds		50,000
Sale of long-term assets		10,000
Sale of capital stock		50,000
Total sources of working capital		185,000
Uses of working capital		
Purchase of equipment		60,000
Retirement of bonds payable		70,000
Declaration of cash dividends		30,000
Total uses of working capital		160,000
Increase in working capital		25,000

       a. *Operating cash inflows*: Typical operating cash inflows include:

          (1) Cash sales to customers

          (2) Cash collections from credit sales

          (3) Cash dividends received from stock investments

          (4) Interest payments received

          (5) Refunds from suppliers

       b. *Operating cash outflows*: Typical operating cash outflows include:

          (1) Payments for salaries and wages

          (2) Payments made for goods and services used by the company

          (3) Interest payments

          (4) Payments to the government for taxes

          (5) Payments for other normal business expenses

    2. *Investing Activities*: Investing activities include transactions that involve the investment of a company's cash.

       a. *Investing cash inflows*: Typical investing cash inflows include:

          (1) Cash received from sale of investments (stocks or bonds of other firms)

          (2) Cash received from the sale of property, plant, and equipment

          (3) Cash received from repayment of loans made by the company to other entities

          (4) Cash received from the sale (discounting) of loans made by the company to other entities

       b. *Investing cash outflows*: Typical investing cash outflows include:

          (1) Payments made to buy property, plant, and equipment

          (2) Payments made in purchasing stocks of other entities as an investment

          (3) Payments made to purchase debt securities of other entities as an investment (excluding cash equivalents)

          (4) Payments made in making loans to other entities

3. *Financing Activities*: Financing activities include transactions with the company's owners and long-term creditors.

   a. *Financing cash inflows*: Typical financing cash inflows include:

      (1) Cash received from sale of stock

      (2) Cash received from the issuance of bonds or nonoperating notes payable

   b. *Financing cash outflows*: Typical financing cash outflows include:

      (1) Payment of dividends to owners

      (2) Payments of the principal amount on nonoperating loans or bonds payable

      (3) Payments made to acquire treasury stock

4. *Noncash Investing and Financing Activities*: Some important investing and financing transactions do not involve cash. For example, a company might purchase equipment and issue a long-term note payable to the seller. This transaction does not involve an inflow or an outflow of cash, but both financing and investing activities are involved. Since the statement of cash flows would omit significant financing and investing activities if noncash financing and investing transactions were excluded, the FASB requires that noncash investing and financing transactions be disclosed in a separate schedule on the statement of cash flows. Examples of noncash investing and financing activities that must be disclosed are:

   • Conversion of bonds payable to stock

   • Conversion of preferred stock to common stock

   • Exchange of one noncash asset for another noncash asset

   • Purchase of long-term assets through the issuance of a note payable to the seller

   • Purchase of a building by securing a mortgage loan

   • Purchase of noncash assets in exchange for stock

   • Leasing of assets in a transaction that involves a lease classified as a capital lease

5. *Presentation of a Statement of Cash Flows*: An example of a statement of cash flows is presented in Figure 18–2a. The cash flows from operating activities may be presented in either a direct or an indirect fashion.

   a. *Direct method*: The direct method involves the calculation and presentation of individual operating cash inflows and outflows (examples are cash received from customers and cash paid to suppliers). Figure 18–2a shows a statement of cash flows using the direct method. The FASB recommends that the direct method be used in presenting the statement of cash flows. When the direct method is used, a reconciliation of net income to net cash provided (or used) by operating activities must be presented. This reconciliation shows the same information as the indirect method in the same format.

Figure 18–2a Schmaus Company Statement of Cash Flows

Schmaus Company
Statement of Cash Flows
For the Year Ended December 31, 19XA

Cash flows from operating activities			
Cash received from customers	$220,000		
Dividends received	9,000		
Cash inflows from operating activities		$229,000	
Less cash paid for:			
Payments for merchandise	$ 98,000		
Payments for salaries and wages	64,000		
Payments for taxes	9,250		
Payment of interest	2,300		
Cash disbursed for operating activities		173,550	
Net cash provided by operating activities			$55,450
Cash flows from investing activities			
Proceeds from sale of equipment	$ 20,000		
Proceeds from sale of investments	40,000		
Purchase of building	(55,000)		
Purchase of land	(40,000)		
Net cash used by investing activities			(35,000)
Cash flows from financing activities			
Proceeds from bond issue	$ 50,000		
Payment of long-term note	(30,000)		
Payment of dividends	(6,000)		
Net cash provided by financing activities			14,000
Net increase (decrease) in cash			$34,450
Cash balance, January 1, 19XA			40,250
Cash balance, December 31, 19XA			$74,700
Schedule of noncash investing/financing activities			
Purchase of equipment through the			
issuance of a long-term note payable		$100,000	

b. *Indirect method*: Although the direct method is preferred by the FASB, the presentation of a statement of cash flows using the indirect method is allowed. Because the indirect method is required to be shown as a reconciliation when the direct method is used, most companies use the indirect method. When the indirect method is used, net income must be adjusted for items included in net income that do not affect cash.

EXAMPLES: Depreciation expense, amortization expense, losses on the sale of long-term assets, and changes in current asset and current liability accounts.

The procedures for adjusting net income to cash flow are beyond the scope of this chapter.

Figure 18–2b   Partial Statement of Cash Flows

Schmaus Company
Partial Statement of Cash Flows
For the Year Ended December 31, 19XA
(Indirect Method)

Cash flows from operating activities

Net income		$50,750
Adjustments to reconcile net income to net cash flow from operating activities		
Depreciation expense	$5,000	
Gain on sale of equipment	(4,000)	
Loss on sale of investments	3,300	
Decrease in accounts receivable	6,000	
Increase in merchandise inventory	(4,500)	
Increase in accounts payable	1,500	
Decrease in salaries payable	(2,600)	
Total adjustments		4,700
Net cash provided by operating activities		$55,450

Figure 18–2b shows an example of the cash flows from the operating activities section presented on an indirect basis. The remainder of the statement of cash flows on an indirect basis would be the same as shown in Figure 18–2a.

C.   Comparative Statements

Firms often present financial data for several years in annual statements to allow comparison of current performance to previous performance. To allow such comparison, it is important that the statements be prepared on a consistent basis. Any consistency exceptions are prominently noted in the auditor's report and the financial statements themselves. A common practice is to show percent increases or decreases in selected items. Financial analysts often get a better idea of the progress of a firm by such reports.

D.   Ratio Analysis

Ratio analysis essentially studies the relationships between various amounts on financial statements. A ratio for a given firm can be compared to others in the same industry. Such ratios are printed regularly by publishing services. Ratios from the current year are often compared to the same ratio in preceding years to provide information about changes within the company.

1. *Liquidity Ratios*: Liquidity ratios are concerned with a firm's ability to meet current obligations. For purposes of short-term financing, these ratios are very important. Creditors are often interested in liquidity ratios.

    a. *Current ratio*: The current ratio is expressed as

    $$\frac{\text{current assets}}{\text{current liabilities}}$$

    b. *Acid-test ratio or quick ratio*: Since inventories and prepaid expenses may be difficult to liquidate quickly, the acid-test ratio is often computed as a supplement to the current ratio. The acid-test ratio compares only the highly liquid assets of cash, marketable securities, and receivables with current liabilities:

$$\frac{\text{cash + marketable securities + receivables}}{\text{current liabilities}}$$

c.   *Receivables turnover*: This ratio shows how often, or how quickly, a firm's receivables are collected. Too large a ratio may indicate too lenient a credit policy. This is important, as receivables are often interest-free. A firm may be giving credit to customers at no charge for extended periods while paying interest on its own short-term debt to finance the receivables. The ratio is

$$\frac{\text{credit sales}}{\text{average receivables}}$$

If credit sales are not available, net sales may be used. Average receivables is a better number to use than year-end receivables, as the average allows for the effects of seasonal business.

d.   *Inventory turnover*: Inventory turnover is identical in concept to the receivables turnover. A low ratio may indicate overstocking of inventory or the presence of obsolete inventory, usually financed with short-term debt. The inventory turnover ratio is

$$\frac{\text{cost of goods sold}}{\text{average inventory}}$$

Note that cost of goods sold, rather than sales, is comparable to inventory cost.

2.   *Debt Ratios*: Debt ratios are more concerned with a firm's policy on long-term debt. The capital structure of a corporation is composed of both debt and owners' equity. A firm that is financed primarily by debt must be able to service that debt in a timely manner to maintain its credit standing.

a.   *Debt-to-equity ratio*: The debt-to-equity ratio measures the balance between the portion of assets provided by stockholders and the portion provided by creditors:

$$\frac{\text{total liabilities}}{\text{total stockholders' equity}}$$

This ratio often is expressed as long-term debt over equity.

b.   *Debt-to-total-assets ratio*: The debt-to-total-assets ratio is similar to the debt-to-equity ratio. This ratio shows the percentage of assets financed by debt:

$$\frac{\text{total liabilities}}{\text{total assets}}$$

c.   *Times-interest-earned ratio*: This ratio relates to a firm's ability to service debt from earnings. Obviously, a firm that is barely able to generate sufficient earnings to make interest payments is a suspect investment. The ratio may be calculated in different ways. In general, a good representation of the ratio is

$$\frac{\text{earnings before interest expense and income taxes}}{\text{interest expense}}$$

A weakness of the ratio is that principal must also be repaid, as well as the fact that payments are made from cash rather than earnings. Nevertheless, if there aren't sufficient earnings, there will not be enough cash generation in the long run.

3. *Profitability Ratios*: Profitability ratios are designed to measure a firm's efficiency in generating profits in relation to sales and in relation to investment. Investors are generally interested in profitability ratios.

   a. *Earnings per share*: This is one of the most common ratios. This ratio relates to shares of common stock only. If preferred stock exists, the earnings must be adjusted for the dividends. The ratio is

   $$\frac{\text{net income less preferred stock dividend}}{\text{average shares of common stock outstanding}}$$

   Treasury stock is not included in the denominator. Average shares of common stock are calculated using a weighted average. For example, if 750 shares of common stock are outstanding on January 1, 19XA, and 500 shares are issued on June 30, 19XA, average shares at the end of the year can be calculated as:

   $$
   \begin{array}{lr}
   750 \times 12 \text{ months} = & 9,000 \\
   500 \times 6 \text{ months} = & \underline{3,000} \\
   \text{Total shares} & 12,000
   \end{array}
   $$

   $$\frac{12,000}{12 \text{ months}} = 1,000 \text{ average shares outstanding}$$

   Such computations as primary earnings per share and fully diluted earnings per share are also calculated for firms with complex capital structures.

   b. *Dividend yield*: Yield is an investor's tool for comparing the cash return by means of dividends in relation to the market value of the stock. The ratio is

   $$\frac{\text{dividend per share}}{\text{market value per share}}$$

   c. *Price–earnings ratio*: An investor might use the price–earnings ratio to determine whether the price of the stock is suitable for his/her purposes, considering the earnings of the stock. The price–earnings ratio compares the market price of the stock with the earnings per share of the stock:

   $$\frac{\text{market price per share}}{\text{earnings per share}}$$

   d. *Gross profit margin*: The gross profit margin is an indicator of a firm's efficiency at producing goods and pricing them for sale. The ratio is calculated as

   $$\frac{\text{sales} - \text{cost of goods sold}}{\text{sales}}$$

A net profit margin may also be calculated by

$$\frac{\text{net income}}{\text{sales}}$$

Two firms may produce the same product and sell it at the same price, yet have different profit margins.

e. *Return on investment*: There are many different ways to calculate return on investment. The easiest method is simply

$$\frac{\text{net income}}{\text{tangible assets}}$$

Intangible assets are usually subtracted from total assets in arriving at this figure. For purposes of evaluating management performance, the DuPont method is often employed as follows:

$$\frac{\text{sales}}{\text{tangible assets}} \times \frac{\text{net income}}{\text{sales}}$$

f. *Book value*: Book value per share is a marginally useful number that is computed in this way:

$$\frac{\text{owners' equity} - \text{par value of preferred stock}}{\text{number of shares common stock outstanding}}$$

The reason book value per share is not particularly useful is the reliance on historical cost in preparation of financial statements.

The ratios discussed in this chapter represent many of the most common ratios used in analyzing financial statements. Numerous other ratios might be used as well.

Figure 18–3c shows the calculation of the ratios presented in this chapter. The calculations are based on the financial statements for the XYZ Company shown in Figures 18–3a and 18–3b. (see accompanying sheets)

Figure 18–3a Consolidated Balance Sheet

XYZ Company
Consolidated Balance Sheet
December 31, 19XB

Assets	19XB	19XA	Liabilities and Stockholders' Equity	19XB	19XA
Current assets			Current liabilities		
Cash	20,000	15,000	Accounts payable	125,000	100,000
Marketable securities	100,000	80,000	Notes payable	220,000	200,000
Accounts receivable	300,000	280,000	Accrued liabilities	100,000	80,000
Inventories	280,000	260,000	Total current liabilities	445,000	380,000
Total current assets	700,000	635,000	Long-term debts		
Investments	250,000	200,000	Bonds payable	700,000	700,000
Fixed assets			Notes payable	25,000	50,000
Plant and equipment	2,150,000	1,800,000	Total long-term debts	725,000	750,000
Less: Accumulated depreciation	(800,000)	(600,000)	Total liabilities	1,170,000	1,130,000
Total fixed assets	1,350,000	1,200,000	Stockholders' equity		
Total assets	2,300,000	2,035,000	Common stock	150,000	150,000
			Additional paid-in capital	600,000	600,000
			Retained earnings	380,000	155,000
			Total stockholders' equity	1,130,000	905,000
			Total liabilities and stockholders equity	2,300,000	2,035,000

Figure 18–3b   Statement of Income

XYZ Company
Statement of Income
For the Year Ended December 31, 19XB

	19XB	19XA
Revenues		
Net sales	1,500,000	1,300,000
Interest income	5,000	10,000
Other income	20,000	35,000
Total revenue	1,525,000	1,345,000
Expenses		
Cost of goods sold	750,000	670,000
Depreciation expense	200,000	160,000
Selling and administrative expenses	145,000	115,000
Interest expense	72,500	75,000
Total expenses	1,167,500	1,020,000
Net income before income taxes	357,500	325,000
Less: Income tax expense	82,500	75,000
Net income after taxes	275,000	250,000
Earnings per share	$5.50	$5.00

Additional information:
   50,000 shares of common stock were outstanding during 19XA and 19XB.
   Cash dividends were $50,000 or $1.00 per share.
   All sales were made on credit.
   Market price of XYZ's stock at the end of 19XB was $50 per share.

Figure 18–3c   Summary of Financial Ratios

Ratio	Calculation	Example
1. Liquidity ratios		
a. Current ratio	$\dfrac{\text{Current assets}}{\text{Current liabilities}}$	$\dfrac{700{,}000}{445{,}000} = 1.57$ times or 1.57 to 1
b. Acid-test ratio	$\dfrac{\text{Cash} + \text{Marketable securities} + \text{Receivables}}{\text{Current liabilities}}$	$\dfrac{\begin{array}{r}20{,}000\\+100{,}000\\+300{,}000\end{array}}{445{,}000} = .94$ times or .94 to 1
c. Receivables turnover	$\dfrac{\text{Credit sales}}{\text{Average receivables}}$	$\dfrac{1{,}500{,}000}{290{,}000} = 5.17$ times
d. Inventory turnover	$\dfrac{\text{Cost of goods sold}}{\text{Average inventory}}$	$\dfrac{750{,}000}{270{,}000} = 2.78$ times
2. Debt ratios		
a. Debt-to-equity ratio	$\dfrac{\text{Total liabilities}}{\text{Total stockholders' equity}}$	$\dfrac{1{,}615{,}000}{1{,}130{,}000} = 1.43$ or 143%
b. Debt-to-total assets ratio	$\dfrac{\text{Total liabilities}}{\text{Total assets}}$	$\dfrac{1{,}615{,}000}{2{,}300{,}000} = 70.22\%$
c. Times-interest-earned ratio	$\dfrac{\text{Earnings before interest expense and income taxes}}{\text{Interest expense}}$	$\dfrac{430{,}000^{a}}{72{,}500} = 5.93$ times
3. Profitability ratios		
a. Earnings per share	$\dfrac{\text{Net income} - \text{preferred stock dividend}}{\text{Average shares of common stock outstanding}}$	$\dfrac{275{,}000}{50{,}000} = \$5.50$
b. Dividend yield	$\dfrac{\text{Dividend per share}}{\text{Market value per share}}$	$\dfrac{\$1.00}{\$50.00} = 2\%$
c. Price–earnings ratio	$\dfrac{\text{Market price per share}}{\text{Earnings per share}}$	$\dfrac{\$50.00}{\$5.50} = \$9.09$
d. Gross profit margin	$\dfrac{\text{Sales - cost of goods sold}}{\text{Sales}}$	$\dfrac{\begin{array}{r}1{,}500{,}000\\-750{,}000\end{array}}{1{,}500{,}000} = 50\%$
e. Return on investment	$\dfrac{\text{Net income}}{\text{Tangible assets}}$	$\dfrac{275{,}000}{2{,}300{,}000} = 11.96\%$
f. Book value	$\dfrac{\text{Owners' equity less par value of preferred stock}}{\text{Number of shares of common stock outstanding}}$	$\dfrac{1{,}310{,}000}{50{,}000} = \$22.60$

[a]Net income before income taxes plus interest expense = 357,500 + 72,500 = 430,000.

Review Questions

DIRECTIONS: Select the best answer from the four alternatives. Write the letter of your answer in the blank to the left of the number.

_____ 1. The financial statement that shows the differences between the beginning and ending balances of cash, including cash equivalents, is called the

   a. statement of changes in financial position working capital basis.
   b. statement of cash flows.
   c. income statement.
   d. balance sheet.

_____ 2. Comparative financial statements

   a. need not be prepared on a consistent basis.
   b. are not useful in determining trends affecting a business.
   c. allow financial statement users to make comparisons between current performance and past performance.
   d. are characterized by all of the above.

_____ 3. Which of the following transactions will result in a reduction of Y Company's current 2:1 ratio?

   a. Borrowing money from the bank in exchange for a note payable due in five months
   b. Selling a fixed asset for a loss
   c. Collection of an account receivable
   d. Sale of common stock

_____ 4. Which of the following ratios would normally be used to analyze a firm's ability to pay its short-term obligations?

   a. Price–earnings ratio
   b. Return on investment
   c. Earnings per share
   d. Acid-test ratio

_____ 5. If a building were acquired by signing a mortgage note payable, the transaction would be reported on the statement of cash flows in the

   a. operating activities section.
   b. investing activities section.

c. schedule of noncash investing/financing activities.

d. financing activities section.

_____ 6. Which of the following methods does the FASB recommend be used in preparing a statement of cash flows?

a. The indirect method

b. The direct method

c. The working-capital method

d. The accrual method

_____ 7. Current assets minus current liabilities is called

a. working capital.

b. the current ratio.

c. the acid-test ratio.

d. changes in financial position.

_____ 8. Which of the following is a source of working capital?

a. Purchase of equipment

b. Declaration of cash dividends on capital stock

c. Repurchase of common stock

d. Sale of equipment used in the business

_____ 9. Which of the following items would not be included in the schedule of noncash investing/financing activities?

a. Purchase of merchandise on account

b. Conversion of bonds to common stock

c. Exchange of common stock for land

d. Conversion of preferred stock to common stock

_____ 10. The term used to describe the ratio between cost of goods sold and merchandise inventory is

a. accounts receivable turnover.

b. debt-to-equity ratio.

c. return on investment.

d. merchandise inventory turnover.

_____ 11. Which of the following is considered to be a liquidity ratio?

a. Times-interest-earned ratio

b. Earnings per share

c. Current ratio
d. Dividend yield

Use this information in answering Questions 12 to 14.

The following financial information for the years 19XA and 19XB is available for the ABC Company:

	19XA	19XB
Current assets		
Cash	20,000	30,000
Accounts receivable	90,000	85,000
Inventory	90,000	98,000
Prepaid expenses	5,000	6,000
Total current assets	205,000	219,000
Current liabilities		
Accounts payable	10,000	12,000
Notes payable	40,000	30,000
Accrued liabilities	12,000	11,000
Total current liabilities	62,000	53,000

_____ 12. What is the current ratio for 19XB? (Round your answer to two decimal places.)

  a. 4.13
  b. 3.31
  c. 0.26
  d. 2.00

_____ 13. If credit sales are equal to $890,000, what is receivables turnover for 19XB? (Round your answer to two decimal places.)

  a. 10.47
  b. 9.89
  c. 10.17
  d. 12.45

_____ 14. What is the acid-test ratio for 19XA? (Round your answer to two decimal places.)

  a. 3.23
  b. 1.85
  c. 1.77
  d. 2.20

_____ **15.** Cargo Company had net income of $20,000, which was 10 percent of net sales. Cost of goods sold was 60 percent of sales. The dollar amount of gross profit (or gross margin) for the company was

    a. $200,000.
    b. $120,000.
    c. $60,000.
    d. $80,000.

Solutions

Answer	Refer to:
1. (b)	[B]
2. (c)	[C]
3. (a)	[D-1-a]
4. (d)	[D-1-b]
5. (c)	[B-4]
6. (b)	[B-5-a]
7. (a)	[A-1]
8. (d)	[A-1-a(2)]
9. (a)	[B-4]
10. (d)	[D-1-d]
11. (c)	[D-1]

12. (a) [D-1-a]

$$\frac{\text{current assets}}{\text{current liabilities}}$$

$$\frac{\$219,000}{\$53,000} = 4.13$$

13. (c) [D-1-c]

$$\frac{\text{credit sales}}{\text{average receivables}}$$

$$\frac{\$890,000}{\$87,500^a} = 10.17$$

14. (c) [D-1-b]

$$\frac{\text{cash + marketable securities + accounts receivable}}{\text{current liabilities}}$$

$$\frac{\$20,000 + 0 + \$90,000}{\$62,000} = 1.77$$

a($90,000 + $85,000)/2 = $87,500.

347

15. (d)   [D-3-d] The solution is calculated as follows:

Sales	$200,000[b]	100%
− Cost of goods sold	− 120,000	60%
Gross profit	$ 80,000	40%

[b]Net income = 0.10 × sales
$20,000 = 0.10 × sales
$200,000 = sales

CHAPTER 19

Managerial Accounting

OVERVIEW

Managerial accounting is concerned with aiding managers in planning and controlling the operations of a business. The candidate should be familiar with basic techniques used in managerial accounting.

   The candidate needs to understand the difference between fixed and variable costs and the effects of different costs on the decision-making process (cost–volume profit analysis). The candidate needs to understand the differences between accounting for a merchandising firm and accounting for a manufacturing firm.

   Another topic that the candidate needs to understand is the budgeting process. The candidate may already be familiar with budgeting from the standpoint of preparing a personal budget. Budgeting for a business firm is more complex, but the same basic task is being performed. A plan (budget) is prepared and used to aid in making decisions during the period. At the end of the period, actual results should be compared to the plan to see how well the business met its objectives.

KEY TERMS

Breakeven point	Manufacturing overhead
Budget	Mixed cost
Contribution margin	Predetermined overhead rate
Cost behavior	Process costing
Direct labor	Proforma financial statement
Direct materials	Relevant range
Fixed costs	Standard cost
Forecasting	Variable cost
Job order costing	Variance

A. Cost Analysis

Costs are analyzed in various ways in managerial accounting. One of the most important ways in which costs are classified in managerial accounting is by cost behavior. Cost behavior refers to changes in a cost when changes in the output of goods or services occur.

1. *Determining Unit Costs*: The per unit cost of an item is calculated as follows:

$$\frac{\text{total cost of the item}}{\text{total number of units of output}}$$

EXAMPLE: Assume Quik-Copy, Inc. produced 10,000 copies during the month of June. The total cost of copying fluid for the month was $1,000. The per unit cost of copying fluid would be $0.10 ($1,000/10,000).

2. *Variable and Fixed Costs*:

   a. *Variable costs*: Variable costs vary in total directly with the level of output. As production increases, the total amount of a variable cost will increase proportionately while the per unit cost will remain the same. Raw materials are an example of a variable cost.

   EXAMPLE: Assume that Quik-Copy, Inc. pays $0.01 for each sheet of paper it uses in making copies. If 10 copies are made, the total cost is 10 × $0.01 = $0.10. If 10,000 copies are made, the total cost is 10,000 × $0.01 = $100. The per unit cost remains at $0.01 regardless of the level of activity.

   b. *Fixed costs*: Fixed costs remain constant in total despite changes in the volume of output. The per unit amount of a fixed cost varies as the level of activity changes. For example, if Quik-Copy, Inc. rents a building for $500 per month, the $500 rental expense will be incurred whether Quik-Copy produces 0 copies, 100 copies, or 10,000 copies. Depreciation, insurance, and advertising are other examples of fixed costs.

   EXAMPLE: Assume Quik-Copy, Inc. has $200 per month in insurance expense, which is a fixed cost. If Quik-Copy produced 10 copies in a month, the total cost of insurance expense would be $200 and the per unit cost would be $20 ($200/10 copies). If Quik-Copy produced 10,000 copies in a month, the total cost of insurance would be $200 and the per unit cost would be $0.02 ($200/10,000).

   c. *Mixed or semivariable costs*: Mixed costs vary with level of activity but by less than a proportionate amount. A common example of a mixed cost is electricity. The cost of electricity is not constant or fixed, yet it does not vary directly with production. The cost of electricity could be separated into fixed and variable portions. This might be done by various methods, such as regression analysis, simultaneous equations, or the high–low method.

   EXAMPLE: Assume that Quik-Copy, Inc. is able to separate the mixed cost of maintenance into the following components: $100 per month plus $0.001 per copy. If Quik-Copy produced 10,000 copies, the cost of maintenance would be $110 [$100 + (10,000 × $0.001)]. If Quik-Copy produced 100,000 copies, the cost of maintenance would be $200 [$100 + (100,000 × $0.001)].

   d. *Relevant range*: Fixed and variable costs retain their characteristics within a certain relevant range. Outside the relevant range, the assumptions made about cost behavior are not valid.

3. *Cost–Volume Profit Analysis*: Cost–volume profit analysis, also called breakeven analysis, is a powerful management tool used for budgeting, forecasting, pricing, and decision making.

a. *Contribution margin*: In managerial accounting, the income statement is often classified in the following manner:

Sales
− Variable costs
Contribution margin
− Fixed costs
Net income

b. *Breakeven analysis*: The central concept of breakeven analysis rests on the equation

sales = fixed costs + variable costs + profit

The breakeven point is the point where total revenues are equal to total expenses and net income is equal to zero. Thus the breakeven point is where

sales revenue = variable expenses + fixed expenses

This equation may be rewritten as

$$SP(SQ) = VC(SQ) + \text{fixed expenses}$$

where SP is selling price, VC is variable cost per unit, and SQ is sales quantity.

EXAMPLE: Quik-Copy wants to know its breakeven point in number of copies if it sells copies for $0.05 each. Costs are as follows:

Fixed costs
Rent $500
Electricity   150
Depreciation   100
    Total fixed costs $750

Variable costs
Materials $0.01/copy
Labor   0.01/copy
    Total variable cost
        per copy $0.02/copy

The breakeven point is then calculated:

sales   = variable expenses + fixed expenses
($0.05)(SQ) =   ($0.02)(SQ)   + $750

Simplifying the equation, we get

$$($0.03)(SQ) = $750$$
$$SQ = 25{,}000$$

The breakeven number of copies is 25,000. The breakeven amount in sales dollars is equal to

$$25{,}000 \text{ copies} \times \$0.05/\text{copy} = \$1{,}250$$

c. *Contribution margin approach to breakeven analysis*: The contribution margin ratio is equal to

$$\frac{\text{sales (in dollars)} - \text{variable expenses (in dollars)}}{\text{sales (in dollars)}}$$

The breakeven point (BEP) in sales dollars is equal to

$$\text{breakeven point (BEP)} = \frac{\text{fixed expenses}}{\text{contribution margin ratio}}$$

EXAMPLE: The Quik-Copy breakeven problem could be solved using the contribution margin approach as follows:

$$\text{contribution margin ratio} = \frac{0.05 - 0.02}{0.05} = 0.60$$

$$\text{breakeven point (BEP)} = \frac{\$750}{0.60} = \$1,250$$

d. *Cost–volume profit analysis for planning*: If a company wishes to use cost–volume profit analysis for planning purposes, various quantities may be inserted into the cost–volume profit equation.

EXAMPLE: To determine profit when 60,000 units are sold, multiply the unit prices by 60,000.

sales = variable expenses + fixed expenses + profit

60,000($0.05) = 60,000($0.02) + $750 + profit

$1,050 = profit

By changing the variables for sales price, fixed expenses, and variable expenses, the effects of such changes on profitability can be forecast.

e. *Graphical analysis*: The cost–volume–profit relationships may be shown in a graphical manner as shown in Figure 19–1. Fixed costs are shown as a straight horizontal line. Since the costs do not change with an increase in volume, the slope of this line is zero. The total cost line is equal to fixed costs at zero volume and increases with volume with a slope equal to variable costs per unit. The revenue line is equal to zero at zero volume and increases with volume with a slope equal to sales price. The breakeven point is where total costs intersect total revenue. Note that volume refers to sales quantity, not to quantity produced.

Using data for Quik-Copy, Inc., the graph shown in Figure 19–1 can be prepared. The fixed cost line is drawn at $750. Since total costs are fixed costs at zero volume, only one other point must be calculated to draw the total cost line. At 40,000 copies, total costs are $750 + 40,000(0.02) = $1,550. Total revenue is zero at zero volume, so one other point is needed to draw a revenue line. At 40,000 copies, revenue is equal to 40,000(0.05) = $2,000. The intersection of the total revenue and total expense lines is the breakeven point. The

Figure 19–1 Breakeven Point

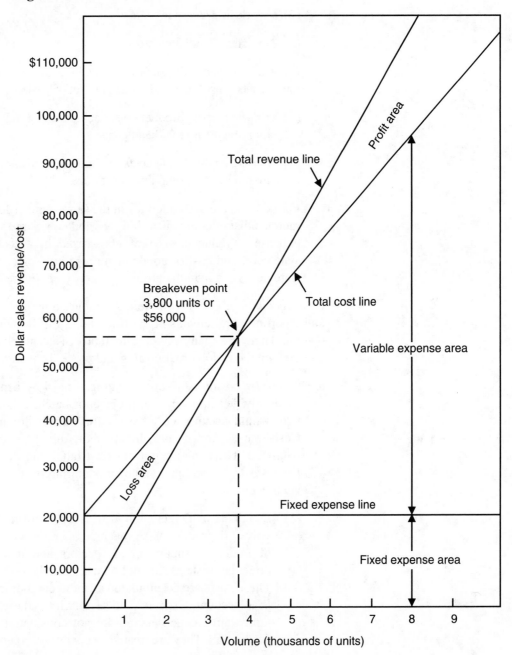

distance between the lines at any given volume is the amount of profit or loss associated with sales at the volume given, assuming that all other relationships remain the same.

4. *Reporting for a Manufacturing Concern*:

   a. *Balance sheet*: The balance sheet of a manufacturing company is the same as that of a merchandising company except that three inventory accounts are shown. A manufacturing company maintains the following three inventory accounts:

       (1)   Raw materials inventory

       (2)   Work-in-process inventory

       (3)   Finished goods inventory

b. *Income statement*: To prepare an income statement for a manufacturing company, costs must be classified as product or period costs.

       (1)   *Product costs*: Product costs include direct materials, direct labor, and all manufacturing overhead costs.

       (2)   *Period costs*: Period costs include those costs which are not related to the manufacturing of a unit of product.

Period costs are accounted for in the same manner for both manufacturing and merchandising companies. Most period costs are treated as part of operating expenses. Product costs are summarized in a cost of goods manufactured statement, and cost of goods manufactured replaces purchases in the income statement for a manufacturing company (see Figure 19–2).

5. *Cost Accounting*: Costs for a unit of product must be determined to satisfy legal and reporting requirements of the firm and to fulfill management's need for information. There are many possible methods of accumulating costs. The two most common methods, job order costing and process costing, are discussed below.

a. *Job order costing*: Job order costing is used by firms with production that is easily divided into separate projects or batches. For example, a construction firm would accumulate all costs for each building on a separate job card. Costs are separated into direct labor, direct materials, and manufacturing overhead. The combination of direct labor and direct materials is known as *prime costs*. Direct labor and manufacturing overhead together are called *conversion costs*.

       (1)   *Direct labor*: Direct labor is all labor performed by personnel directly involved in production. A machine operator's wage is direct labor. Salaries of production supervisors, inspectors, and maintenance personnel are not direct labor. These are not related directly to the production of a product. These costs are accumulated as indirect labor in the manufacturing overhead account. Officers' and secretaries' salaries are considered to be administrative expenses and are not considered to be part of the cost of production. They are treated as operating expenses.

       (2)   *Direct materials*: Direct materials are raw materials that are readily identified with an individual product. In the production of furniture, wood and cloth would be direct materials. Other items, such as the glue and nails, which are either difficult to measure or of such small value that accurate measurement is not worthwhile, are classified as *indirect materials*. Indirect materials are part of the manufacturing overhead account.

       (3)   *Manufacturing overhead*: Manufacturing overhead contains all other costs of production. The unique aspect of manufacturing overhead is that while direct labor and direct materials are variable costs, manufacturing overhead is composed of both fixed and variable costs. Fixed costs could

Figure 19–2   Partial Income Statement with Statement
of Cost of Goods Manufactured

Jones Manufacturing Co.
Partial Income Statement
For the Period Ending December 31, 19XA

Sales		200,000
Cost of goods sold		
Beginning finished goods inventory	10,000	
Cost of goods manufactured[a]	120,000	
Goods available for sale	130,000	
Less: Ending finished goods inventory	20,000	
Cost of goods sold		110,000
Gross profit		90,000

[a]From statement below.

Jones Manufacturing Co.
Statement of Cost of Goods Manufactured
For the Period Ending December 31, 19XA

Beginning work-in-process inventory			30,000
Direct materials		50,000	
Direct labor		50,000	
Manufacturing overhead			
Indirect materials	2,000		
Indirect labor	10,000		
Depreciation—factory	20,000		
Utilities—factory	5,000		
Maintenance	5,000		
Insurance	5,000	47,000	
Total manufacturing costs			147,000
Total cost of work-in-process during the period			177,000
Less: Ending work-in-process inventory			57,000
Cost of goods manufactured			120,000

include salaries, rent, and depreciation, while variable costs could include electricity, indirect materials, or any other expense that varies with volume. Manufacturing overhead is a control account in which numerous expenses are accumulated.

(4)   *Cost flows in job order costing*: In job order costing, each project has a job card on which costs are accumulated. The job cards are subsidiary records of the costs which are recorded in the work-in-process inventory account. The flow of costs in job order costing is as follows:

(a)   When raw materials are purchased, the raw materials inventory account is debited and accounts payable is credited.

Raw Materials Inventory

(a) 15,000 |

Accounts Payable

| 15,000 (a)

(b)   When materials are requisitioned by the production department, the raw materials inventory account is credited for the total amount requisitioned. The work-in-process inventory account is debited for the portion of the materials requisitioned which are direct materials (DM), and the manufacturing overhead account is debited for the indirect materials (IM) portion.

Raw Materials Inventory

(a) 15,000	10,000 (b)

Work-in-Process Inventory

DM (b) 9,500	

Manufacturing Overhead

IM (b) 500	

The amount of direct materials used on each job is also recorded on the individual job cost sheets.

(c)   When employees perform work on the product, the wages payable account is credited for the total labor cost related to the product. The work-in-process inventory account is debited for the direct labor cost (DL), and the manufacturing overhead account is debited for the indirect labor cost (IL).

Wages Payable

	12,000 (c)

Work-in-Process Inventory

DM (b) 9,500	
DL (c) 10,000	

Manufacturing Overhead

IM (b) 500	
IL (c) 2,000	

The amount of direct labor incurred on each individual job is also recorded on the individual job cost sheets.

(d)   As items of manufacturing overhead other than indirect materials and indirect labor are incurred, the manufacturing overhead account is debited and the related payable account (or cash) is credited.

Manufacturing Overhead

IM (b) 500	
IL (c) 2,000	
Electricity (d) 1,000	
Rent (d) 5,000	

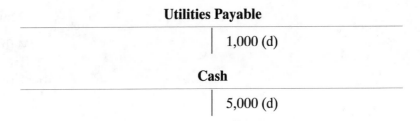

Utilities Payable

| | 1,000 (d) |

Cash

| | 5,000 (d) |

(e)   Manufacturing overhead is applied to individual jobs based on a predetermined overhead rate. The predetermined overhead rate is used to allocate manufacturing overhead costs to the jobs included in the work-in-process inventory and to the jobs completed during the period. A predetermined overhead rate is used to avoid charging individual jobs with different overhead amounts due to seasonal variations in production volume.

To calculate the predetermined overhead rate, total overhead costs are estimated for the period and the total overhead application base for the period is estimated. The overhead application base chosen should be common to all jobs worked on during the period, and it should reflect each job's utilization of the manufacturing overhead incurred. Direct labor hours, direct labor cost, and machine hours are examples of commonly used overhead application bases. The formula for calculating the predetermined overhead rate is

$$\text{predetermined overhead rate} = \frac{\text{estimated total manufacturing overhead costs}}{\text{estimated total units in the application base}}$$

EXAMPLE: Assume that total manufacturing overhead costs were estimated to be $9,000 for the period and that overhead is to be applied on the basis of direct labor hours. Assume that the total direct labor hours for the period are estimated to be 6,000 hours. The predetermined overhead rate would be $9,000/6,000 hours, which is $1.50 per direct labor hour. Assume that 5,800 direct labor hours were worked during the period and all jobs worked on are still in work-in-process inventory, that is, no jobs have been completed and transferred to finished goods inventory during the period. The company would apply $8,700 (5,800 direct labor hours worked $\times$ $1.50 per direct labor hour) of manufacturing overhead to the work-in-process inventory account. The entry to record the application of manufacturing overhead would be a debit to work-in-process inventory and a credit to manufacturing overhead.

Work-in-Process Inventory

DM (b) 9,500	
DL (c) 10,.000	
ManOH (e) 8,700	

Manufacturing Overhead

IM (b) 500	8,700 (e) Mfg.
IL (c) 2,000	overhead
Electricity (d) 1,000	applied
Rent (d) 5,000	
	200 Overapplied
	mfg. overhead

Based on the predetermined overhead rate, $8,700 of manufacturing overhead was applied to work-in-process inventory, but only $8,500 of actual manufacturing overhead was incurred during the period. Since more overhead was applied than was incurred, there is a $200 credit balance in the manufacturing overhead account which is called overapplied manufacturing overhead. *If more manufacturing overhead was incurred than was applied during a period, the manufacturing overhead account would have a debit balance, which would be called* underapplied manufacturing overhead.

Overapplied or underapplied manufacturing overhead is normally closed to cost of goods sold at the end of the period. Overhead applied to individual jobs is recorded on the individual job cost sheet. If 200 direct labor hours have been worked on job C, $300 of manufacturing overhead would be applied to job C (200 direct labor hours × $1.50 per direct labor hour).

(f)   As individual jobs are completed, the costs of producing the units within the job are transferred from the work-in-process inventory account to the finished goods inventory account. Assume that job C has been completed using $400 of direct materials, $450 of direct labor, and $300 of manufacturing overhead. The total cost of the job is $1,150, which would be transferred to finished goods by debiting the finished goods inventory for $1,150 and crediting the work-in-process inventory for $1,150. If 50 widgets were produced in job C, the per unit cost of an individual widget would be $23 per unit ($1,150/50 units).

(g)   The cost of any units sold during the period is transferred from the finished goods inventory to cost of goods sold. If 20 widgets from job C were sold, cost of goods sold would be debited for $460 (20 units × $23 per unit) and finished goods inventory would be credited for $460.

b.   *Process costing*: Process costing is a method of product costing used to cost products in companies that employ a continuous manufacturing process to produce a homogeneous product. The same accounts are utilized as in job order costing: direct labor, direct materials, and manufacturing overhead. When work is in process at the end of a period, costs may be allocated to the ending inventory on a weighted average or FIFO basis. The inventory pricing is based on equivalent units of production. The actual technique is complicated and can be found in any cost accounting textbook.

B.	**Budgets**	A *budget* is a detailed plan that shows proposed acquisitions of financial resources and uses of financial resources during a period of time. Budgets are a powerful planning and control tool of management. Their uses are many, including cash management, inventory planning, production scheduling, profit planning, and performance evaluation. The budgeting process is sequential, beginning with the sales budget; there is great interdependence between budgets. Normally, a firm will make only the quantity of goods that it intends to sell and will purchase only the required raw materials for the quantity that it intends to make. This is the key to the planning function of budgeting. After the fact, budgets may also be used to compare actual results with planned objectives and evaluate the firm's and management's performance.

1. *Types of Budgets*:

   a. *Sales budget*: The sales budget is the foundation for all other budgets. Various scientific and not-so-scientific methods of preparing a sales budget exist. This is essentially a marketing function and is passed on to management and accounting when completed. The sales budget must include the *quantity* and *timing of sales*. More sophisticated budgets also include the place where a sale is to occur.

      EXAMPLE:

	Jan.	Feb.	Mar.	Apr.
Sales (in thousands)	20	24	32	50
Sales price	0.05	0.05	0.05	0.05
Total sales	$1,000	$1,200	$1,600	$2,500

      Another schedule related to the sales budget is the cash collection schedule. If sales are made on an account, there may be a time lag between delivery of the product and collection of cash. Usually, depending on a firm's credit policy, a certain amount will prove to be uncollectible. These data are critical for cash planning.

      EXAMPLE: Assuming that 25 percent of sales are made on account and are collected in the next month, a cash collection schedule would show:

	Jan.	Feb.	Mar.	Apr.
Current sales	750	900	1,200	1,875
(75% of current sales)				
Collections on account				
(25% of previous month's sales)	0	250	300	400
Total sales and collections	$750	$1,150	$1,500	$2,275

   b. *Production budget*: The production budget is prepared next. The production budget shows the quantity and timing of units required to be produced during the period to meet sales and inventory requirements. Usually, there is a time lag between production and sales. Orders might be produced in advance, and some standard items might be kept in stock. If 20 percent of orders can be produced in advance, the production budget would appear as follows:

EXAMPLE:

	Jan.	Feb.	Mar.	Apr.	
Current req.	20,000	24,000	32,000	50,000	Current sales
End inventory	4,800	6,400	10,000	?	29% of next month's sales
Totals	24,800	30,400	42,000		Total production needs
Less beg. inv.	0	4,800	6,400		Amount already produced
To be produced	24,800	25,600	35,600		

c. *Raw materials budget*: The timing and quantity of materials purchases can now be planned in the raw materials budget. This is important, as many materials must be ordered in advance. A shortage of raw materials will cause delays in production and sales losses in the short run and potential long-term customer dissatisfaction. The process is identical to the production budget in terms of planning ending inventory and purchases to accommodate the firm's needs.

d. *Labor budget*: The labor budget shows the quantity of labor expected to be needed during the period. The labor budget is identical to the production and materials budgets above except that labor cannot be stored in inventory. Management can plan to have sufficiently trained labor available and plan the necessary cash needed to pay them in a timely fashion. Management might plan to start with two employees and add one employee in March. If each employee earns $600 per month, the labor budget is:

	Jan.	Feb.	Mar.	Apr.
Salary	600	600	600	600
Number of employees	2	2	3	3
	1,200	1,200	1,200	1,200

Another aspect, which is omitted for simplicity, is the timing and amount of withholding payments and employment taxes usually paid no later than the following month. Large firms often must make deposits every few days.

e. *Manufacturing overhead budget*: Overhead includes both fixed and variable components. A budget is prepared for each aspect. The fixed portion is constant for any volume by definition, whereas the variable portion is largely dependent on the production schedule. Some of the costs are discretionary as to timing and even as to incurrence. Machine maintenance costs may be higher in slack periods and lower in peak periods, due to management policy.

f. *Selling expense budget*: Like manufacturing overhead, selling expenses are composed of fixed and variable elements. The fixed elements remain constant, although some may be discretionary, such as advertising. The variable elements will vary with sales volume, not production volume as manufacturing overhead does.

g. *Administrative expense budget*: Like the manufacturing overhead and selling expense budgets, the administrative expense budget has fixed and variable components. Administrative expenses are dependent on management policy for amount and timing of expenditures.

h. *Cash budget*: The cash budget is very important to the success of a firm. The timing and quantity of cash inflows and outflows need to be estimated to the best of management's ability to provide sufficient funds to continue operations. With many firms, the seasonal nature of sales will result in a cash surplus in some months and a cash deficiency in other months. In times of surplus, excess funds are invested in such a manner as to maximize returns while maintaining liquidity.

i. *Master budget*: After all of the individual sales, production, and expense budgets are prepared, they are combined into a master budget that is approved by the board of directors and becomes the plan or objective for the period. Master budgets are usually prepared on a quarterly or annual basis. The master budget serves as the financial and operating plan for the period.

j. *Capital budget*: A capital budget is a long-range budget that includes plans for addition of new product lines or purchase of any new plant or equipment items. A capital budget might cover a period as long as five to 10 years.

2. *Factors Considered in Budget Preparation*:

a. *Participative budgeting*: Budgets are used as a motivational tool to help managers understand and meet the company's goals and objectives. When the individuals responsible for implementing the budget provide input into the budgeting process, it is called *participative budgeting*. When individuals help to draft a plan or budget, it is assumed that they will want to try to meet the budget goals. Participative budgeting is used to aid in getting employees to accept the budget as their goal and improve motivation within the company.

b. *Zero-base budgeting*: Zero-base budgeting is a method of budgeting where managers are required to start at zero budget levels each year. They must justify all costs as if they were first-time costs. Frequently, traditional budgets are prepared by starting with last year's budget and adding to it or subtracting from it. With zero-base budgeting every expenditure is reviewed, not just taken for granted.

c. *Continuous budgeting*: When continuous budgeting is followed, the budget is continually updated and reviewed each month. At any time, a continuous budget covers a 12-month period since it is updated every month.

d. *Using budgets as control tools*: To use budgeting effectively, a company must use budgets not only as planning tools but also as control tools. Control involves the methods through which management assures that the company is operating in such a way as to attain the goals set out in the plan. One part of the control process is budget variation and analysis.

3. *Budget Variation and Analysis*: After a period for which a budget had been prepared has ended, the performance of the firm and responsible personnel can be evaluated by comparing budgeted items to actual results. Any difference between the two is known as a *variance*. A favorable variance occurs when an actual expense is less than a budgeted expense or an actual revenue is greater than a budgeted revenue. An unfavorable variance occurs when an actual expense is greater than a budgeted expense or an actual revenue is less than a budgeted revenue.

Actual expense > budgeted expense
Actual revenue < budgeted revenue } Unfavorable variance

Actual expense < budgeted expense
Actual revenue > budgeted revenue } Favorable variance

If actual results are compared to budgeted items for only one level of activity, the budget is known as a *static* budget. A better means of evaluating performance is by means of a *flexible* budget. Flexible budgets have varying amounts budgeted for different levels of activity. Variable costs are budgeted at an appropriate amount for the attained output. Static or fixed budgets are a good planning tool but are less meaningful for control or evaluation purposes.

EXAMPLE: Assume that the following information is budgeted for ABC Company:

Fixed costs	$750
Variable manufacturing costs	0.02/unit
Variable selling costs	0.01/unit
Sales price	0.05/unit

Assume a static budget for 60,000 units was prepared and compared to the actual results.

	Static Budget	Actual Results
Sales	60,000 × 0.05 = 3,000	65,000 × 0.05 = 3,250
Variable mfg. cost	60,000 × 0.02 = 1,200	65,000 × 0.025 = 1,625
Variable selling cost	60,000 × 0.01 = 600	65,000 × 0.009 = 585
Fixed costs	= 750	= 750
Profit	750	290

Analysis of the static budget as compared to the actual results gives the following variances.

Sales variance	$250	Favorable	(3,000–3,250)
Variable mfg. variance	(425)	Unfavorable	(1,200–1,625)
Variable selling variance	15	Favorable	(600– 585)
Total variance	(160)		

a. *Static budget*: When a static budget is compared to actual results line by line, the variances computed may have little meaning. This is because efficiency, level of sales quantity, and changes in prices are lumped into one amount. For example, we would expect that the actual variable manufacturing cost for ABC Company would be greater than the budgeted cost per the static budget because ABC Company produced more units than they anticipated. The variance does not provide information about whether the 65,000 units were produced efficiently. Variances that provide information about cost efficiency are based on a flexible budget related to the actual level of activity. Two variances are often calculated using the master or static budget: the sales price variance and the sales volume variance.

(1) *Sales price variance*: The sales price variance is computed by multiplying the difference between budgeted selling price and actual selling price per unit by the number of units sold.

(2) *Sales volume variance*: The sales volume variance is determined by multiplying the difference between actual sales and budgeted sales (in units) by the budgeted contribution margin per unit. The sales volume variance is considered to be a measure of the effectiveness of management for a given period.

EXAMPLE: Using the static budget and actual results from the previous ABC Company example, the sales price and sales volume variance would be calculated as follows:

Sales price variance = actual units sold (ASP − BSP)

where BSP is the budgeted selling price per unit and ASP is the actual selling price per unit.

Sales price variance = 65,000(0.05 − 0.05) = 0

This variance is zero since budgeted selling price and actual selling price were equal.

Sales volume variance = budgeted CM (ASU − BSU)

where CM is the contribution margin, ASU is the actual number of units sold, and BSU is the budgeted number of units expected to be sold.

Sales volume variance = 0.02(65,000 − 60,000) = 100   Favorable

The budgeted contribution margin is (0.05 − 0.03) = 0.02.

b. *Flexible budget*: A flexible budget is a budget that is prepared for different levels of activity. After actual production for the period is known, a flexible budget can be prepared that shows budgeted production costs for the actual level of activity.

EXAMPLE: Now assume that a flexible budget for three different levels of activity was prepared as follows:

	Level of Activity		
	50,000 Units	*60,000 Units*	*70,000 Units*
Sales	$2,500	$3,000	$3,500
Variable mfg. costs	1,000	1,200	1,400
Variable selling costs	500	600	700
Fixed costs	750	750	750
Profit	$ 250	$ 450	$ 650

This is very similar to cost–volume–profit analysis in providing expectations of revenues and expenditures at varying levels of activity. Actual results are now compared to budgeted allowances for the actual activity level.

	Flexible Budget	Actual Results
Sales	65,000 × 0.05 = 3,250	65,000 × 0.05 = 3,250
Variable mfg. cost	65,000 × 0.02 = 1,300	65,000 × 0.025 = 1,625
Variable selling cost	65,000 × 0.01 = 650	65,000 × 0.009 = 585
Fixed costs	= 750	= 750
Profit	550	290

Analysis of results:

Sales variance	$ 0	
Variable mfg. variance	(325)	Unfavorable
Variable selling variance	65	Favorable
Total variance	(260)	Unfavorable

The flexible budget variances may be split into price and efficiency variances. (See Section C-2 of this chapter.)

C. Standard Costing and Variance Analysis

A standard cost is a predetermined estimate of the cost per unit for materials, labor, and manufacturing overhead. A *standard cost* is the cost that should be incurred to produce a product or perform an operation efficiently. When a standard costing system is used, managers compare actual results with the predetermined standard goal to determine whether performance was satisfactory.

1. *Management by Exception*: A standard costing system allows managers to direct their attention to those areas that require corrective action. This is called *management by exception*. When a standard costing system is used, managers do not spend time reviewing areas that do not differ significantly from standard cost.

2. *Variance*: The difference between standard cost and actual cost is called the *variance*. A *favorable variance* occurs when actual cost is less than standard cost. An *unfavorable variance* occurs when actual cost is more than standard cost. The following example shows the calculation of the most common standard costing variances.

EXAMPLE: Assume that Hamsmith Co. has established the following cost standards for its product Snac:

Material (1 pound per unit @ $5 per pound)	$ 5.00
Direct labor (1 hour per unit @ $10 per hour)	10.00
Overhead ($5 per standard direct labor hour)	5.00
Total standard cost of one Snac	$20.00

Direct material variances:

Hamsmith Co. produced 1,000 units of Snac. They used 1,100 pounds of raw materials which cost $4.95 per pound to produce the 1,000 Snacs.

Actual cost (1,100 lb @ $4.95)	$5,445
− Standard cost (1,000 lb @ $5.00)	5,000
Total direct material variance (unfavorable)	−$ 445

The total direct material variance (flexible budget variance) may be divided into price and efficiency components as follows:

Price variance:

Actual units used × actual price:	
1,100 lb × $4.95	$5,445
− Actual units used × standard price:	
1,100 lb × $5.00	5,500
Direct material price variance (favorable)	+$ 55

Efficiency variance (also called quantity variance):

Actual units × standard price:	
1,100 lb × $5.00	$5,500
− Standard units allowed × standard price:	
1,000 lb × $5.00	5,000
Direct material efficiency variance (unfavorable)	−$ 500

Direct material price variance	+$ 55 (favorable)
+ Direct material efficiency variance	− 500 (unfavorable)
Total direct material variance	−$445 (unfavorable)

Direct labor variances:

Hamsmith Co. used 1,110 hours costing $10.10 per hour to produce the 1,000 units of Snac.

Actual labor cost:	
1,110 hours × $10.10	$11,211
− Standard labor cost:	
1,000 hours × $10.00	10,000
Total direct labor variance (unfavorable)	−$ 1,211

The total direct labor variance (flexible budget variance) may be divided into price and efficiency components as follows:

Direct labor price variance:

Actual hours used × actual price:	
1,110 × $10.10 =	$11,211
− Actual hours used × standard price:	
1,110 × $10.00 =	11,100
Direct labor price variance (unfavorable)	−$ 111

Direct labor efficiency variance:

Actual hours used × standard price:	
1,110 × $10.00	$11,100
− Standard hours allowed × standard price:	
1,000 × $10.00	10,000
Direct labor efficiency variance (unfavorable)	$ 1,100

Direct labor price variance (unfavorable)	−$ 111
± Direct labor efficiency variance (unfavorable)	−1,100
Total direct labor variance (unfavorable)	−$1,211

Overhead variances may be computed in several ways. When standard costs are used, overhead is applied to production on the basis of a predetermined standard overhead rate. The calculation of overhead variances is beyond the scope of this chapter. The candidate should refer to an elementary managerial accounting textbook for further discussion of this topic.

D. Forecasting

Forecasting is the prediction of a value of a variable in the future. This prediction may be based on past values of the variable, values of related variables, or expert judgment. Forecasts are needed in business to plan for the future development of the company.

1. *Types of Forecasts*: Forecasts may be short term, medium term, or long term in nature. Short-term forecasts cover a period of only a few months. Medium-term forecasts cover the period from about three months to two years in the future. Long-term forecasts cover periods beyond two years into the future. Forecasts that cover a shorter time frame are generally more accurate than long-term forecasts.

    a. *Sales forecast*: A sales forecast is generally the first step in preparing a budget. After sales are forecast, production needs can be estimated based on the forecasted level of sales.

    b. *Capital expenditures forecast*: A company also needs to forecast what its capital expenditure requirements will be in the future. Advance planning is necessary to ensure that sufficient funds are available to purchase additional capital equipment.

    c. *Product demand forecast*: Forecasts of demand for a company's products are useful in preparing sales forecasts and in determining where new products should be introduced and old product lines dropped.

    d. *Other forecasts*: The different types of items that might be forecast are endless. Any item of information that would aid management in meeting goals and objectives of the company might be forecast.

2. *Factors Considered in Preparation of Forecasts*: A number of different methods can be used to prepare a forecast.

    a. *Forecasting methods*: These methods may be quantitative or qualitative in nature.

        (1) Quantitative forecasts are based on past data. It is assumed that the trends observed in the past will continue in the future. Time-series models base the forecast on past values of the variable. Regression models assume that the variable to be forecast exhibits a cause-and-effect relationship with another variable or variables.

        (2) Qualitative forecasts are not based on past data but on intuitive thinking, judgment, and expert knowledge.

        The type of method that should be used depends on the individual situation. In making forecasts pertaining to new products, there may be no relevant past data. Many firms use a combination of methods to forecast.

    b. *Accuracy of forecast*: A forecast is usually inaccurate. It might be useful to provide more than one value for a forecasted item. For example, pessimistic, most likely, and optimistic values of the forecast might be provided or a range might be provided (that is, $10,000 ± 15 percent).

    c. *Monitoring actual performance*: After a forecast is prepared, actual performance of the variable should be monitored to determine the accuracy of the forecast and to aid in preparing future forecasts.

3. *Proforma Statements*: Proforma statements are forecasted financial statements. After the budgeting process is complete, a forecasted balance sheet and income statement can be prepared. These are called proforma financial statements and are used for planning and evaluation purposes.

Review Questions

DIRECTIONS: Select the best answer from the four alternatives. Write the letter of your answer in the blank to the left of the number.

_____

1. A variable cost

   a. will not be affected by changes in activity from period to period.
   b. will remain constant in total as the level of activity changes.
   c. increases or decreases proportionately (in total) with changes in the level of activity.
   d. will increase on a per unit basis as the level of activity increases.

_____

2. Which of the following costs is variable?

   a. Straight-line depreciation on machinery
   b. Direct labor
   c. The salary of the controller
   d. Rent on the sales building

_____

3. As the number of units produced by a manufacturing company decreases,

   a. the variable cost per unit increases.
   b. fixed costs per unit remain the same.
   c. fixed costs in total remain the same.
   d. the variable cost in total increases.

_____

4. Which of the following costs is fixed?

   a. Direct materials
   b. Property taxes on the factory land and building
   c. Wages of maintenance employees
   d. Freight-out on goods sold

_____

5. When a company's actual sales for a period are equal to its breakeven sales,

   a. total contribution margin for the company will be equal to total fixed expenses for the period.
   b. total revenues will be equal to total expenses.
   c. net income for the period will be zero.
   d. all of the above conditions will occur.

6. Janet Company produces a game that sells for $20 per game. Variable costs are $12 per game, and fixed costs total $172,000 annually. The breakeven point in units is (rounded to the nearest unit)

a. 19,111 units.
b. 10,118 units.
c. 21,500 units.
d. 24,000 units.

7. Karl Company produces dolls. Each doll sells for $15 per unit and has a contribution margin ratio of 60 percent. Total annual fixed expenses are $240,000. If Karl Company wishes to earn $30,000 of net income, how many dolls must be sold?

a. 28,667 dolls
b. 30,000 dolls
c. 18,000 dolls
d. 45,000 dolls

8. In a job order cost system, the entry to record the requisition of direct materials for use in production would include

a. a debit to the direct materials account.
b. a credit to the manufacturing overhead account.
c. a debit to the work-in-process inventory account.
d. a credit to accounts payable.

9. In a job order cost system, the entry to record the wages paid to factory maintenance workers would include

a. a debit to the work-in-process inventory account.
b. a credit to the manufacturing overhead account.
c. a debit to the direct labor account.
d. a debit to the manufacturing overhead account.

10. In a job order cost system, the entry to record the application of overhead to a job would include

a. a debit to the manufacturing overhead account.
b. a debit to the work-in-process inventory account.
c. a credit to the work-in-process inventory account.
d. a credit to the cost of goods sold account.

11. Assume XYZ Company applies overhead to production on the basis of a predetermined overhead rate. A debit balance in the manufacturing overhead account at the end of the period means

  a. the overhead cost that was actually incurred was greater than the amount applied to production.
  b. the overhead cost that was actually incurred was less than the amount applied to production.
  c. the amount of manufacturing overhead incurred was equal to the manufacturing overhead applied during the period.
  d. more hours were actually worked during the period than were predicted in calculating the predetermined overhead rate.

12. Which of the following companies would be most likely to use process costing?

  a. A custom home builder
  b. A manufacturer of specialized machine tools
  c. A contractor building bridges
  d. A company that manufactures tint base for paint

13. Electricity is a mixed cost for ABC Company. ABC Company estimates that the fixed portion of the monthly electrical cost is $500 and the variable portion is $0.10 per machine hour. If ABC Company used 10,000 machine hours in April, their estimate of total electrical cost for the month would be

  a. $600.
  b. $1,500.
  c. $1,000.
  d. $500.

14. The fixed cost per unit for rent is $0.50 at a production level of 100,000 units. If 125,000 units are produced, the total fixed cost for rent would be

  a. $65,500.
  b. $100,000.
  c. $50,000.
  d. $125,000.

15. Kilo Company applies overhead to units of product based on machine hours. At the beginning of the period Kilo Company estimated that total manufacturing overhead would be $500,000 and that the number of machine hours used during the period would be 200,000. Kilo Company actually used 210,000 machine hours during the period. The total amount of overhead applied for this period was

  a. $500,000.
  b. $84,000.

c. $210,000.
d. $525,000.

16. Budgets can be used for

   a. production scheduling.
   b. cash management.
   c. inventory planning.
   d. all of the above.

17. When the individuals responsible for implementing the budget are involved in preparing the budget, it is called

   a. participative budgeting.
   b. collective budgeting.
   c. zero-base budgeting.
   d. employee budgeting.

18. The budget that is used to plan for long-range purchases of new plant and equipment is called the

   a. cash budget.
   b. continuous budget.
   c. capital budget.
   d. production budget.

19. Farley Enterprises has budgeted sales in units of:

   May   5,000 units
   June   6,000 units
   July   4,000 units

   Farley Enterprises desires to have an ending inventory equal to 25 percent of next month's sales needs. The beginning inventory on May 1 was 1,250 units. The total units to be produced in May are

   a. 5,000.
   b. 5,250.
   c. 5,500.
   d. 4,750.

20. An unfavorable variance results when

   a. actual revenue is greater than budgeted revenue.
   b. actual expense is less than budgeted expense.

c. actual revenue is greater than actual expense.
d. actual expense is greater than budgeted expense.

_____ 21. A method of budgeting where managers are expected to justify all costs as if they were first-time expenditures is called

a. capital budgeting.
b. participative budgeting.
c. continuous budgeting.
d. zero-base budgeting.

_____ 22. A predetermined estimate of the cost per unit for materials, labor, or manufacturing overhead is called

a. a standard cost.
b. management by exception.
c. a unit cost.
d. a variance cost.

_____ 23. Which of the following statements about forecasts is false?

a. A forecast is a prediction of the future.
b. Forecasts can be based on past data.
c. Forecasts are based only on quantitative information.
d. Pessimistic, most likely, and optimistic estimates can be prepared for a given forecast.

_____ 24. Forecasted financial statements are called

a. estimated financial statements.
b. proforma financial statements.
c. futuristic financial statements.
d. flexible financial statements.

Use the following financial information pertaining to the sales activities of the 4R Corporation for the year 19XA in answering Questions 25 to 27.

Selling price per unit	$ 20
Variable production cost per unit	12
Fixed production cost	3,000
Selling commission per unit	2
Fixed selling expenses	2,400
Number of units sold in 19XA	6,000

25. The total contribution margin generated in 19XA was (rounded to the nearest dollar)

   a. $36,000.
   b. $48,000.
   c. $45,000.
   d. $30,600.

26. The breakeven point in dollars is (rounded to the nearest dollar)

   a. $89,400.
   b. $13,500.
   c. $18,000.
   d. $75,000.

27. Assuming that the cost information does not change, how many units would the company have to sell in 19XB to earn a $50,000 profit (rounded to the nearest unit)?

   a. 10,000
   b. 3,400
   c. 1,870
   d. 9,233

Use this information in answering Questions 28 and 29.

Jones Company budgeted to sell 10,000 units at $10 per unit. Variable manufacturing costs at $5 per unit were included in the budget. Jones Company actually sold 9,000 units at a price of $11.00 per unit. Their actual variable manufacturing costs were $5.50 per unit. (F, favorable; U, unfavorable)

28. The sales price variance would be

   a. $9,000 F.
   b. $9,000 U.
   c. $10,000 F.
   d. $10,000 U.

29. The sales volume variance would be

   a. $5,000 U.
   b. $5,500 F.
   c. $10,000 U.
   d. $500 U.

Use this information in answering Questions 30 to 34.

The standard costs for a unit of finished product are as follows:

	Standard Quantity	Standard Price
Direct materials	10 feet	$ 2.00 per foot
Direct labor	2 hours	$15.00 per hour

The company actually produced 10,000 units. The actual quantity used was 105,000 feet; the actual cost of materials was $199,500. The company actually used 18,000 direct labor hours at a cost of $279,000.

30. The direct material price variance would be

a. $500 F.
b. $10,000 F.
c. $10,500 F.
d. none of the above.

31. The direct material quantity variance would be

a. $10,000 U.
b. $950 U.
c. $10,000 F.
d. none of the above.

32. The flexible budget variance for direct materials would be

a. $500 F.
b. $500 U.
c. $10,000 F.
d. none of the above.

33. The direct labor rate (price) variance would be

a. $21,000 F.
b. $9,000 U.
c. $10,000 U.
d. none of the above.

34. The direct labor efficiency variance would be

a. $30,000 F.
b. $30,000 U.
c. $21,000 F.
d. $27,000 F.

Solutions

Answer	Refer to:

1. (c)   [A-2-a]

2. (b)   [A-2-a]

3. (c)   [A-2-b]

4. (b)   [A-2-b]

5. (d)   [A-3-b]

6. (c)   [A-3-b]

$$\frac{\text{fixed expenses}}{\text{contribution margin/unit}} = \text{breakeven point in units}$$

$$\frac{\$172,000}{\$20 - 12} = 21,500 \text{ units}$$

7. (b)   [A-3] The formula to solve this question is

$$\frac{\text{fixed expenses} + \text{desired net income}}{\text{contribution margin per unit}} = \text{breakeven point in units}$$

$$\frac{\$240,000 + \$30,000}{\$9 \text{ per unit}} = 30,000 \text{ dolls}$$

If the selling price per unit is $15 and the contribution margin ratio is 60 percent, the per unit contribution margin is $9.

Selling price	$15	100%
− Variable cost	− 6	40%
Contribution margin	$ 9	60%

8. (c)   [A-5-a(4) (b)]

9. (d)   [A-5-a(4) (c)]

10. (b)   [A-5-a(4) (e)]

11. (a)   [A-5-a(4) (e)]

12. (d)   [A-5-b]

13. (b)   [A-2-c]

Total cost = variable cost + fixed cost
$1,500   = $0.10(10,000) + $500

14. (c)   [A-2-b]
$100,000 \times \$0.50 = \$50,000$
Since fixed cost remains constant in total regardless of the level of activity (within the relevant range), the total fixed cost would be the same whether 100,000 units or 125,000 units were produced.

15. (d)   [A-5-a(4) (e)]

$$\text{predetermined overhead rate} = \frac{\text{estimated total overhead}}{\text{estimated quantity of the application base}}$$

$$\$2.50 \text{ per machine hour} = \frac{\$500,000}{200,000 \text{ hours}}$$

$\$525,000 = 210,000$ machine hours $\times \$2.50$/machine hour

16. (d)   [B]

17. (a)   [B-2-a]

18. (c)   [B-1-j]

19. (b)   [B-1-b]

Sales	5,000	
+ Desired ending inventory	1,500	$(6,000 \times 0.25)$
	6,500	
– Beginning inventory already available	–1,250	
Units to be produced	5,250	

20. (d)   [B-3]

21. (d)   [B-2-b]

22. (a)   [C]

23. (c)   [D-2]

24. (b)   [D-3]

25. (a)   [A-3-a]
sales – variable expenses = contribution margin

Sales ($20.00 \times 6,000$)		$120,000
– Variable expenses:		
Variable production $12.00 \times 6,000$	$72,000	
Variable selling $2.00 \times 6,000$	12,000	84,000
Contribution margin		$ 36,000

26. (c)   [A-3-c]
$$\frac{\text{fixed expenses}}{\text{contribution margin ratio}} = \text{breakeven point in dollars}$$

$$\frac{\$5,400}{0.30} = \$18,000$$

Contribution margin ratio = $36,000/$120,000 = 0.30

27. (d)   [A-3-d]
$$\frac{\text{fixed expenses + desired net income}}{\text{contribution margin per unit}} = \text{BEP in units}$$

$$\frac{\$5,400 + \$50,000}{\$6/\text{unit}} = 9,233$$

Contribution margin per unit = $20 – 14 = $6

28. (a)   [B-3-a(1)]
Sales price variance = actual units sold (ASP–BSP) where ASP = actual selling price and BSP = budgeted selling price.

$9,000 = 9,000 units sold (11.00 – 10.00)

The variance is favorable because the actual selling price was greater than the budgeted selling price. When actual revenue > budgeted revenue, the variance is favorable.

29. (a)   [B-3-a(2)]
Sales volume variance = budgeted CM (ASU – BSU) where CM = contribution margin, ASU = actual sales in units, and BSU = budgeted sales in units.

–$5,000 = $5.00(9,000 – 10,000)

Budgeted contribution margin = $10.00 – 5.00 = $5.00

This variance is unfavorable because actual cost exceeded budgeted cost.

30. (c)   [C-2] The direct material price variance is equal to

AQ(AP) – AQ(SP)
where AQ = actual quantity of units used, AP = actual price of units purchased, and SP = standard price per unit of material.

The actual price of the units was $1.90 ($199,500/ 105,000).

105,000($1.90) – 105,000($2.00) = $10,500

This variance is favorable because the actual price paid was less than the standard price allowed.

Note: It is also possible to base the material price variance on units purchased rather than units used.

31. (a)   [C-2] The direct material quantity variance is equal to AQ(SP) – SQ(SP) where AQ = actual quantity of units used, SP = standard price per unit of material, and SQ = standard units allowed.

Standard units allowed is equal to units produced times the standard quantity of material allowed per finished unit.

SQ = 10,000 units × 10 feet = 100,000 feet
DM quantity variance = 105,000($2.00) – 100,000($2.00)
DM quantity variance = $10,000

This variance is unfavorable because the actual quantity of feet used was greater than the standard quantity of feet allowed.

32. (a)   [C-2] The flexible budget variance is the difference between the actual cost for materials and the standard cost allowed for materials. It is also equal to the sum of the DM price variance and the DM quantity variance.

Actual cost	$199,500
– Standard cost allowed	– 200,000
Flexible budget variance	$ 500

Standard cost allowed is equal to the standard quantity allowed times the standard price (100,000 × $2.00).

This variance is favorable because actual cost was less than standard cost.

33. (b)   [C-2] The direct labor rate (price) variance is equal to AH(AP) – AH(SP) where AH = actual hours used, AP = actual price paid per hour, and SP = standard price allowed per hour.

18,000 hours($15.50) – 18,000 hours($15.00) = $9,000

Actual price paid is equal to $270,000/18,000 hours = $15.50/hour.

This variance is unfavorable because the actual rate paid was greater than the standard rate allowed.

34. (a)   [C-2] The direct labor efficiency variance is equal to AH(SP) – SH(SP) where AH = actual hours used, SP = standard price allowed per hour, and SH = standard hours allowed.

Standard hours allowed is equal to the number of units produced times the standard number of hours allowed per finished unit.

SH = 10,000 units × 2 hours/unit = 20,000 hours
DL efficiency variance = 18,000($15.00) – 20,000($15.00)
DL efficiency variance = $30,000

This variance is favorable because the actual number of hours used was less than the standard number of hours allowed.

CHAPTER 20

Introduction to Business Law

OVERVIEW

Law provides a consistent means of defining rights and resolving disputes. Since the business community desires an atmosphere of stability, business law in particular must be sound and predictable. To gain an adequate understanding of law, one should be familiar with the sources of law, including their hierarchy. Basic legal terminology needs to be mastered and an awareness developed of the major areas of law.

This chapter serves as a basic introduction to law. In the chapters that follow we explore specific areas of law in greater detail.

KEY TERMS

Civil law	Procedural law
Common law	Promulgate
Constitutional law	Regulation
Criminal law	Stare decisis
Executive order	Statutory law
Felony	Strict liability
Misdemeanor	Substantive law
Precedent	Tort law

A.   Origin of Law

The origin of our legal system is the English common law. With the signing of the Magna Charta in 1215, King John formally recognized certain rights of landowners and provided a means of adjudicating those rights. Over time, a court system evolved and judicial opinions were recorded. These opinions became precedent for future cases involving similar facts. The vast body of case law that has developed is known as *common law.*

1. *Common Law*: Common law is case law. Our common law actually includes the case law and custom of England prior to the American Revolution insofar as it has not been expressly superseded or overruled by cases or laws of the United States. Our common law also includes all published opinions of courts in the United States. Needless to say, the common law is an immense body of case law that is the subject of much legal research by attorneys and legal scholars.

   a. *Basis for common law*: Common law is based on the concept of precedent. A goal of the common law is consistency. Once a legal principle is established, it should be followed. Thus, once a case is decided, it becomes a precedent to be considered by future courts in adjudicating similar issues.

   b. *The doctrine of stare decisis*: The doctrine that precedent should be followed is known as *stare decisis* (the decision stands). In applying stare decisis, a court would follow precedent and decide the same legal issue consistent with the earlier court's ruling.

2. *Constitutional Law*: Constitutional law is derived from the United States Constitution. The Constitution and the accompanying Bill of Rights are the highest law of the land. The Constitution prevails over any other law.

   a. *Supreme Court opinions*: The Constitution has been interpreted in numerous cases decided by the Supreme Court. These Supreme Court opinions are part of what is commonly known as constitutional law.

   b. *Final authority*: The Supreme Court of the United States is the final authority on what the Constitution means.

3. *Statutory Law*: Statutory law is enacted by legislative bodies.

   a. *Congressional acts*: The Congress of the United States enacts federal statutes that apply throughout the United States.

   b. *State legislative statutes*: The legislature of each state enacts statutes that apply within the boundaries of that state.

   c. *Federal law*: Federal law governs over any inconsistent state law.

   d. *An unconstitutional statute*: A statute, state or federal, may be declared unconstitutional by the Supreme Court.

4. *Regulations*: Regulations are promulgated by administrative agencies (see Chapter 25).

   a. *Regulatory agencies*: Congress has created regulatory agencies and has granted rule-making authority to some of them.

      (1) Agency employees are capable of acquiring a high level of expertise in a given field.

      (2) Agencies can only promulgate regulations within the scope of the authority granted by Congress.

      (3) Specific procedures exist for rule making by agencies (see Chapter 25).

   b. *Prevailing statute*: A statute prevails over a conflicting regulation.

5.   *Executive Orders:* Executive orders are laws issued by the President of the United States.

    a.   *Authority:* The President's authority to issue executive orders is limited. Such authority must be traceable to an act of Congress or to the Constitution.

    b.   *Prevailing statute:* A federal statute prevails over a conflicting executive order.

B.   Classifications of Law

Although there are many subdivisions of law, in this chapter we address only several broad classifications.

1.   *Civil Law:* Civil law pertains to private, as opposed to public, rights.

EXAMPLES OF CIVIL LAW: Contract law (Chapter 21) and property law (Chapters 27 and 28).

2.   *Tort Law:* Tort law is a broad area of civil law. Tort law is the law of civil wrongs, which include intentional wrongs and negligence.

    a.   *Negligence:* Negligence is the breach of a duty of care owed to another person.

    EXAMPLE: One who drives an automobile owes a duty of care to other motorists and to pedestrians. A breach of that duty of care may consist of driving too fast and not maintaining a proper lookout.

    If such negligent conduct results in injury, the injured party may sue and recover for his/her losses.

    b.   *Strict liability:* Strict liability provides a basis for an injured party to sue for and recover damages without having to prove negligence.

        (1)   *Dangerous activities:* Strict liability is limited to highly dangerous activities.

        EXAMPLE: Al decides to use dynamite to clear his property of old tree stumps. Blasting dynamite is a highly dangerous activity. Al is legally responsible for any damage caused by the blasting even if he employs all reasonable precautions.

        (2)   *No real defense:* When strict liability exists, there is no real defense. The trial would focus on the extent of damage to be compensated.

3.   *Criminal Law:* Criminal law defines offenses against the government and provides penal sanctions for such violations.

    a.   *Criminal suit:* A criminal case is brought in the name of and on behalf of the state or federal government against the alleged violator.

    b.   *Protection of individual rights:* Because the liberty of one charged with a crime is at stake, the individual's rights are carefully protected. A person charged with a crime has a right to remain silent and, if jail is a possibility, a right to free legal representation if he or she cannot afford to hire a lawyer.

    c.   *Presumption of innocence:* The prosecution is required to prove guilt beyond a reasonable doubt before there can be a conviction. The person charged with a crime is presumed innocent until proven guilty.

    d.   *Felony*: A felony is a crime punishable by one year or more in prison.

    e.   *Misdemeanor*: A misdemeanor is a crime punishable by up to one year of incarceration.

    f.   *Tort or crime*: The same act may be both a tort and a crime.

4. *Procedural Law*: Procedural law consists of rules governing the enforcement of laws and rights. Lawsuits are governed by these procedural rules.

EXAMPLE: A statute may set forth the exact method of jury selection to be used in that state. This is a procedural law.

5. *Substantive Law*: Substantive law defines rights and duties.

EXAMPLE: A statute may bestow a right to sue for damages in certain types of cases where no such right is specifically guaranteed by the Constitution and where no such right is recognized as common law. Such a statute is substantive law.

Thus, while substantive law defines rights, procedural law provides the means or rules whereby these rights are enforceable.

CHAPTER 21

Contracts

OVERVIEW

Modern business transactions involve numerous agreements: employment agreements; agreements to buy or sell goods; agreements to buy, sell, or lease land; and agreements to lend or borrow money, to name just a few. Not all agreements, however, are legally enforceable. The legal principles used to determine which agreements are enforceable are embodied in the law of contracts. In this chapter we present a look at the major principles of contract law.

Although knowledge of the terms and principles presented in this chapter is essential to an understanding of contract law, mere knowledge is not enough for success on the examination. The candidate must be able to apply the principles of contract law to fact situations and determine whether a contract exists. In some cases it will also be necessary to determine what type of contract is involved and what remedies are available in the event the contract is breached.

KEY TERMS

Acceptance	Express contract
Assignee	Formal contract
Assignment	Goods
Assignor	Gratuitous assignment
Bilateral contract	Illusory promise
Breach of contract	Implied contract
Common law	Merchant
Consideration	Novation
Contract	Offer
Contractual capacity	Offeree
Delegation	Offeror
Disaffirmance	Quasi-contract
Duress	Ratification

Restitution   Uniform Commercial Code (UCC)
Revocation   Unilateral contract
Simple contract   Void contract
Statute   Voidable contract

A. Common Law   **1.** *Common Law*: The origin of contract law is the common law. Common law con-
versus Sales Law   tract law resulted from case precedents. Although the common law evolved in
                                each state, there are basic principles that are generally accepted in all states which
                                will be presented in this chapter.

                       2. *Establishment of the Universal Commercial Code (UCC)*: To promote greater uni-
                                formity in interstate commercial transactions, the Uniform Commercial Code
                                (UCC) was developed as a model law for state consideration and enactment.
                                Today, the UCC has been adopted by every state. The UCC applies to a wide
                                range of business applications, such as the sale of goods (contracts for the sale of
                                goods), commercial paper (discussed in Chapter 22), and security interests in per-
                                sonal property.

                       3. *Application of Article 2*: Article 2 of the UCC, Sales, applies to the sale of goods.
                                Where applicable, Article 2 supersedes the common law. Although this chapter
                                will focus on the common law, the following sales terms and concepts should be
                                noted.

                       a. *Goods*: Goods are tangible personal property.

                                EXAMPLES:

                                A football, car, loaf of bread, this book, and similar items are all goods.

                                The sale of land and the providing of a service are not *goods.*

                       b. *Merchant*: A merchant is a person who regularly deals in the kind of goods in-
                                volved.

                                *EXAMPLE: A hardware store owner is a merchant for goods regularly sold at
                                his store. However, he is not a merchant for the sale of a used refrigerator at a
                                garage sale at his house.*

                                Some Article 2 rules apply only to a merchant [such as the firm offer, dis-
                                cussed in Section C-2-b(2)] or to merchants [the battle of forms, discussed in
                                Section C-3-b(2)].

                       c. *Good faith*: The UCC requires good faith of all parties involved in the sale of
                                goods. Good faith is defined as honesty in fact.

                       d. *Focus on performance*: Article 2 has greater emphasis than the common law
                                on rules and expectations of performance of a contract, including possible
                                warranties.

                                Unless stated otherwise, the law presented in this chapter is common law contract
                                law. However, many of the Article 2 provisions are similar or identical to the com-
                                mon law, especially with regard to the elements of a contract (discussed in
                                Sections B-1 to B-5).

| **B. Elements of a Contract** | For an agreement to be a legally enforceable contract, five elements must be present. First, the agreement must be legal as to both subject matter and purpose. Second, there must be mutuality of agreement. Third, there must be legal consideration. Fourth, the parties to the agreement must have contractual capacity. Fifth, the agreement must conform to any specific, additional requirements imposed by statute. |

1. *Legality*: Courts will not enforce illegal agreements. If the law were otherwise, the courts would actually be facilitating the breaking of the law. Consider the absurdity of a court enforcing the following agreement:

   EXAMPLE: Al agrees to pay Bob $50 in return for Bob's promise to break Chad's arm. Al cannot enforce this agreement by obtaining a court order directing Bob to perform as promised. Similarly, if he had actually broken Chad's arm, Bob could not obtain a judgment against Al for the promised $50.

   a. *Subject matter*: Agreements may be found to be illegal for various reasons. The subject matter may be illegal.

      EXAMPLE: Alice agrees to sell a gram of cocaine to Barb for $200.

   b. *Purpose*: The purpose of the agreement may be illegal.

      EXAMPLE: Sam promises to pay Wally $100 in return for Wally's promise to testify falsely at Sam's criminal trial that Sam was visiting Wally in another city at the time the crime was committed. The purpose of this agreement is for Wally to commit perjury to assist Sam in defending himself against the charge.

   c. *Violation of statute*: The agreement may violate a statute.

      EXAMPLES:

      Sally and Pam bet $100 on the outcome of a football game. Gambling is outlawed by a state statute. (Some states permit certain types of regulated gambling.)

      Peter agrees to loan Paul $300 in return for Paul's promise to repay the $300 with 50 percent interest at the end of one year. Most states have usury statutes regulating the maximum amount of interest that may be charged. An agreement that requires the payment of interest in excess of the statutory maximum is illegal. (Such excess interest is called usury *and is said to be usurious.)*

      Don hires Ed to remove a tumor surgically from Don's arm. Ed is not licensed to practice medicine. Each state has laws requiring that persons practicing trades or professions such as medicine, law, dentistry, architecture, building, and plumbing be licensed by the state. An agreement that requires an unlicensed party to perform such work is illegal.

   d. *Public policy*: The agreement may be against public policy.

      EXAMPLE: The Acme Catering Company, which provides food for wedding receptions and banquets, requires its customers to sign an agreement that relieves Acme of any liability resulting from its negligence in preparing or serving food. Such an exculpatory clause is illegal because it violates public policy. The public has an interest in ensuring that the food served at such functions is safe to eat. Removing liability from the preparer and server of the food takes away a major incentive for the exercise of due care and is likely to leave the injured parties without an effective legal remedy.

e. *Partial legality*: Some agreements are only partially illegal. If the legal portion of a partially illegal agreement can be severed from the illegal part, the court will probably enforce the legal portion.

EXAMPLE: The Atlas Pharmaceutical Company agrees to sell 300 units of drug A (illegal) for $600 and 300 units of drug B (legal) for $300 to Hamilton Drug Stores, Inc. The court will probably enforce the part of the agreement pertaining to the legal drug B. Because that part carried a separate price term, the contract is severable.

2. *Mutuality of Agreement*: For there to be a contract, the words or conduct of the parties must indicate that there is an agreement between them.

a. *Intent of parties*: The law does not ordinarily delve into the minds of the parties to find what they actually were thinking; instead, it judges their intent from their words and conduct.

EXAMPLE: Kevin offers to sell a new Garth Brooks compact disk to Angie for $5. Angie agrees. Kevin then refuses to go through with their deal because he had meant his offer to be a joke. If a reasonable third party would have thought the "offer" to have been an actual offer, Kevin would be bound regardless of his subjective (persona) intent.

b. *Mutual assent*: In some situations, even though it *appears* that there is mutual assent, underlying facts make it clear that the agreement of a party was not voluntary.

(1) *Duress*: The expression of assent may be the result of duress. Duress is present when a party uses an improper threat to obtain another party's assent.

EXAMPLE: Ed threatens to break Jim's arm unless Jim signs a contract. As a result of the threat, Jim signs the contract. If Ed sues Jim to enforce the contract, duress provides a valid defense for Jim.

(2) *Undue influence*: The expression of assent may be the result of undue influence. Undue influence is present when a party takes unfair advantage of the high level of trust and confidence another person has placed in him/her in order to obtain that person's expression of assent. For undue influence to apply, the relationship between the parties must be a close one built on trust.

EXAMPLE: Joan is an 86-year-old invalid who relies on her sister Jane to care for her and handle her financial affairs. Jane tells Joan to invest all of her savings in stock of the Green Company. Trusting Jane, Joan agrees to make the investment. Joan does not know that Jane and her husband operate the Green Company, which is deeply in debt. Joan's assent was obtained through undue influence. Joan, therefore, has a valid defense if Jane attempts to enforce the agreement.

(3) *Fraud*: The expression of assent may be the result of fraud.

(a) Fraud requires that there be a false representation.

(b)   The false statement must be one of fact, not of opinion.

(c)   The falsely stated fact must be likely to influence the decision of the person to whom it is made. (In other words, the falsely stated fact must be material to the agreement.)

(d)   The false statement must be made by one who has knowledge of its falsity and intent to deceive.

(e)   The false statement must be justifiably relied on by the party to whom it was made.

EXAMPLES:

George offers to sell his airplane to Mel. George says to Mel, "I think you will really enjoy owning this plane." In fact, George does not believe Mel will enjoy owning the plane. There is no fraud because George's statement was one of opinion, not of fact.

George offers to sell his airplane to Mel. George tells Mel that the plane has never been in a crash. In fact, the plane was damaged in a crash. George had the plane repaired. There is no apparent evidence of the earlier damage. If Mel agrees to buy the plane based on George's statement, fraud has occurred and Mel can succeed in having the agreement set aside and may collect any damage from George.

(4)   *Misrepresentation*: The expression of assent may be the result of *innocent misrepresentation*.

(a)   The elements of innocent misrepresentation are the same as those of fraud, with one exception. There is no requirement that the party making the statement know of its falsity.

EXAMPLE: George offers to sell his airplane to Mel. George tells Mel that the plane has never been in a crash. Unknown to George, the plane was in a crash before he purchased it. George has made an innocent misrepresentation.

(b)   The victim of innocent misrepresentation may succeed in having the agreement set aside but cannot collect punitive damages from the party making the representation.

(5)   *Mutual mistake*: The expression of assent may be the result of a mutual mistake.

(a)   If both parties agreed to enter into an agreement based on a fundamental mistake as to the subject of the agreement, the contract may be set aside.

EXAMPLE: Angie agrees to sell her motorcycle to Sara. Unknown to either party, the motorcycle was totally destroyed by fire the day before their agreement. Their mistake was a mutual one that went to the very subject matter of the agreement.

(b)   If the mistake is not mutual, it does not affect the expression of assent.

EXAMPLE: Angie agrees to sell her motorcycle to Sara for $600. Angie mistakenly believes that the motorcycle has a market value of $600. In fact, it has a market value of $800. Angie's mistake does not affect the agreement. It is not mutual. Moreover, it does not involve the fundamental nature of the subject matter but relates only to its value.

3. *Consideration*: For there to be a contract, there must be a bargained-for exchange of something of value. The legal term for this requirement is *consideration*.

    a. *Exchange of value*: Consideration may consist of a party giving up a legal right in return for something else of value.

    EXAMPLES:

    Sue agrees to refrain from smoking any cigarettes for six months in return for Gail's promise to pay Sue $100 at the end of that time. Sue has given up her right to smoke, and Gail has promised to give up $100. Consideration is present.

    Adam has sued Ryan for striking him in the face and breaking his nose. Adam agrees to dismiss the suit in return for Ryan's promise to pay for his medical expenses. Adam has given up his legal right to pursue the case. Consideration is present.

    b. *Bargained-for exchange*: Without a bargained-for exchange, there can be no consideration.

    EXAMPLE: Feeling guilty for having injured Adam, Ryan promises to pay for Adam's medical expenses. Adam, in a gesture of forgiveness, promises to dismiss the suit he had filed against Ryan. There is no consideration. The promises were not exchanged. Each was made without a return promise.

    c. *Exchange of equal value not required*: The bargained-for exchange need not involve things of equal value in order to constitute consideration.

    EXAMPLE: Paul agrees to pay Dan $50 for a fishing pole that Dan had recently purchased for $3. The courts are not concerned with the adequacy of what a party gets under the terms of the agreement. The courts are only concerned that there be an exchange of something of some value.

    d. *Promise to pay for services already rendered*: A promise to pay for work already performed does not involve consideration.

    EXAMPLE: Upon returning from vacation and finding that his neighbor has trimmed his hedges, Frank promises to pay his neighbor $20. There is no consideration. At the time of Frank's promise, the work had already been completed. Frank's promise is unenforceable.

    e. *Preexisting legal duty*: A promise to pay someone to do what that person is already legally bound to do does not involve consideration.

    EXAMPLES:

    Dick promises to pay John $35 in return for John's promise not to break any of Dick's windows during the month of May. Breaking Dick's windows is a violation of the law. John is obligated to obey the law. Therefore, Dick's *promise is not legally enforceable. He has merely promised to pay John to obey the law—something John is already obligated to do.*

Wilson contracted to paint James' house for $400. Wilson stopped painting when he was only half finished. He refused to continue unless James promised to pay him an additional $100. James made the promise. Wilson then finished painting the house. James is not legally obligated to pay the additional $100. His promise to pay it was not part of a bargained-for exchange of something of value because Wilson did nothing more than promise to do what he was already legally obligated to do. Wilson gave up nothing in return for the additional promise.

f.   *Illusory promise*: An illusory promise does not provide a basis for consideration. An illusory promise is one that does not impose an enforceable obligation on the promisor.

EXAMPLE: In return for receiving a 10 percent discount, Joe of Joe's Ice Cream Parlour promises to purchase all of the ice cream he wants from Jake's Wholesale Company. Joe may avoid any further obligation by stating he does not want any more ice cream from Jake's. The result would be the same if Joe had used the word "desire" instead of "want."

g.   *Promise to buy one's needs*: A promise to buy all of one's *needs* or *requirements* can serve as a basis for consideration. Courts regard such a promise as being enforceable. A good faith requirement is imposed on the promisor. Needs or requirements can be determined with reasonable definiteness. The same is true of a promise to sell all of one's output to a particular customer.

4.   *Capacity of Parties*: Both parties to a contract must have *contractual capacity* if the agreement is to be fully enforceable.

a.   *Age of majority*: In order to have contractual capacity, a party must have attained the age of majority. Anyone who has not attained that age is a minor. The age of majority at common law was 21 years of age. Today in nearly all states the age of majority is 18 years of age.

(1)   *Minor's right to void contract*: A minor who enters into a contract has the right to avoid (to make void) the contract if he/she elects to do so. When this happens, the minor is said to have *disaffirmed* the contract.

(2)   *Minor's right to enforce contract*: A minor who has entered into a contract with an adult has the right to enforce the contract against the adult.

EXAMPLE: Dennis, who is 16 years old, contracts with Curt, who is an adult. Under the terms of the contract, Dennis is to pay Curt $20 per month for 14 months in return for Curt's jukebox. Dennis may elect to disaffirm the contract. In doing so, he must return the jukebox. Instead, Dennis might elect to treat the contract as a binding one. If Curt failed to deliver the jukebox, for instance, Dennis could enforce the agreement. Only the minor has the option of disaffirming the contract.

(3)   *Return of contract items*: Upon disaffirming a contract, a minor must return to the adult anything the minor received under the contract. If the minor no longer has what was received, however, most courts will nevertheless allow the minor to disaffirm.

(4) *Reasonable time for disaffirmance*: A minor may disaffirm anytime during minority and within a reasonable time after reaching majority.

(5) *Contract for necessary items*: Upon disaffirming a contract for necessary items such as food, clothing, or emergency medical care, the minor must pay the reasonable value of the necessities.

(6) *Ratification of contract by minor*: One who entered a contract while a minor may *ratify* the contract upon reaching majority. Once the contract is ratified, it may no longer be disaffirmed.

   (a) *Words or actions*: Ratification may result from words or actions of the minor that indicate an intent to recognize the contract as an enforceable obligation.

   (b) *Majority*: Ratification can occur after the age of majority has been attained.

     EXAMPLE: While 17 years old, Shirley entered into a contract to purchase a camera. Under the terms of the contract, she was to pay $15 per month for three years. Shirley made six monthly payments after her eighteenth birthday. Shirley will be deemed to have ratified the contract. Shirley can no longer disaffirm.

b. *Contractual capacity*: A party who has attained the age of majority is presumed to have contractual capacity. Not all adults, however, have contractual capacity. There are two types of situations in which an adult will be found to lack capacity.

(1) *Mental deficiency*: A person who is unable to understand the nature of the contract because of mental deficiency lacks contractual capacity.

   (a) The mental deficiency must have existed at the time the contract was formed.

   (b) The mental deficiency must be more severe than a mere lacking of normal intelligence. It must deprive the person of the ability to understand the subject matter of the agreement and its consequences.

   (c) The lack of capacity need not be permanent.

(2) *Intoxication*: A person who is so intoxicated by alcohol or drugs that he/she is incapable of understanding the nature of the contract lacks contractual capacity.

c. *Disaffirmance of contract*: Adults who lack capacity because of mental deficiency or intoxication may disaffirm a contract if they are able to substantially restore the other party to the precontractual position. The contract is said to be voidable.

d. *Ratification of contract*: One who entered a contract while suffering from incapacity because of mental deficiency or intoxication may ratify the contract after capacity is regained.

5. *Form Required by Law*: Specific statutes require that certain types of agreements be in writing or meet other special requirements as to form. The statute of frauds is discussed in Section F. Other statutes vary from state to state and have narrow application in their coverage. Negotiable instruments are discussed in Chapter 22.

C. Formation

An agreement is usually formed with an offer and an acceptance.

1. *Offer*: An offer is a communication of an intent to be bound to the terms of a specific proposed contract. The communication invites acceptance on the part of the intended recipient. There are three basic requirements for a valid offer:

    a. *Intent*: An offer must express an intent to enter into a contract.

    EXAMPLE: Tom, whose new car has stalled at a busy intersection, says to Bill, "I will sell you this heap of junk for $10." There is no offer because Tom's words are uttered in anger and do not actually express an intent on his part to enter into such a contract.

    b. *Definite terms*: An offer must be sufficiently definite in its terms.

    EXAMPLE: If Tina says to Wilma, "I offer to sell you my typewriter," there is no valid offer. The communication lacks definiteness.

    c. *Communication of offer*: An offer must be communicated to the intended party.

    EXAMPLES:

    Tina writes a note, "Dear Wilma: I offer to sell you my only typewriter for $25." There can be no offer unless the note is communicated to Wilma.

    Ordinarily, a catalog entry, newspaper advertisement, or magazine advertisement is regarded merely as an invitation for offers and is not itself regarded as an offer.

2. *Termination*: A valid offer may be terminated in the following ways:

    a. *Lapse of time*: If the expiration date contained in the offer has passed, the offer is terminated. If there is no express expiration date, the offer expires after the passage of a reasonable time.

    b. *Revocation*: As a general rule, the offeror may revoke the offer anytime prior to acceptance. There are three main exceptions to this rule:

        (1) *Option to purchase*: If the offeror has granted an option to purchase, the offer cannot be revoked for the period stated in the option. An option is a promise not to revoke an offer in return for something of value. Consideration must be present for there to be an option.

        (2) *Firm offer*: Under the UCC, if a merchant promises, in a signed writing, to hold open an offer to buy or sell goods for any period less than three months, the offer cannot be revoked during the stated time period. If the stated time period exceeds three months, the offer nevertheless becomes revocable after three months. This exception is known as the merchant's *firm offer*. It does not require consideration. Because this exception is statutory, each element must exist or the exception does not apply.

        (3) *Reasonable time*: If the offeror should have known that the offeree would change his/her position in reliance on the offer for a unilateral

contract, the offeror will not be allowed to revoke until the offeree has had a reasonable time to complete the performance.

EXAMPLE: Peggy says to Pat, "I will pay you $5,000 if you run all the way across the state." In reliance on the promise, Pat began to run across the state. After nearly 24 hours, Peggy announces that she is revoking the offer. Peggy must allow Pat a reasonable time to complete performance. Peggy should have known that Pat would rely on the offer. It would be unfair to allow her to revoke before Pat has an opportunity to complete his performance.

    c. *Rejection of offer*: When the offeree rejects the offer, the offer is terminated. A mere inquiry on the part of the offeree does not amount to a rejection.

EXAMPLE: Mike says to Peter, "I offer to sell you my bicycle for $20." Peter responds, "$20 seems rather high. Would you consider $15?" Peter has not rejected the offer.

        (1) *Rejection*: The offeree rejects an offer when he/she expresses an unwillingness to accept the offered terms.

EXAMPLE: Mike says to Peter, "I offer to sell you my bicycle for $20." Peter responds, "No, I really don't want to buy it for that price." Peter has rejected the offer.

        (2) *Counteroffer*: A counteroffer by the offeree operates as a rejection. The counteroffer stops the original offer and starts a new offer.

EXAMPLE: Mike says to Peter, "I offer to sell you my bicycle for $20." Peter responds, "I offer you $15 for your bicycle." Peter has rejected the original offer, causing it to terminate. He has also made an offer of his own, known as a counteroffer.

    d. *Death or insanity*: The death or insanity of either party terminates automatically the offer (unless there is a valid option in effect).

    e. *Destruction of subject matter*: If the subject matter of the offer is destroyed, the offer is terminated automatically.

    f. *Illegality of the offer*: If an offer that is legal when made later becomes illegal because of a change in the law, the offer is terminated.

EXAMPLE: The Metropolis Mineral Company offers to sell four grams of cryptonite to Luthor for $20,000. Before Luthor accepts, however, the legislature enacts a law outlawing the sale of cryptonite. The offer is terminated at the time the law becomes effective.

  3. *Acceptance*: A clear expression by the offeree to the offeror of an agreement to the terms of the offer constitutes an acceptance.

    a. *Clarity of acceptance*: An acceptance must be positive and clear.

    b. *Acceptance of terms of offer*: An acceptance cannot vary the terms of the offer in any way. Common law requires that the acceptance "mirror" the terms of the offer.

(1) *Counteroffer*: An attempted acceptance that varies from the terms of the offer will probably be interpreted as a counteroffer, which terminates the original offer.

(2) *Battle of forms*: The Uniform Commercial Code (UCC) greatly relaxes the mirror-image requirement of the common law where the sale of goods is involved. Under its battle of forms section, the UCC provides that when the sale of goods is involved, the acceptance need not mirror the terms of the offer as long as the intent to accept the terms offered is clearly expressed. This means that the offeree can add terms, modify terms, or ask that terms be deleted as long as the acceptance is not made *conditional* on the requested changes becoming part of the contract.

EXAMPLE: ABC Company offers to sell XYZ Company 100 Pluto Computers for $150,000 to be shipped via Speedway Express. XYZ responds, "Accept your offer. Ship via Olympic Express." There is a contract for the computers because the acceptance is not conditional. XYZ Company's modification would not likely be considered material so it becomes a part of the accepted contract.

c. *Communication of acceptance*: If an acceptance is sent through an authorized means of communication, it is effective upon being sent. If it is sent through an unauthorized means of communication, it is not effective until it is received.

(1) *Authorized means of communication*: Any means of communication specifically approved by the offeror is authorized. Unless the offeror indicates otherwise, any reasonable means of communication that is at least as reliable and as prompt as that used by the offeror is an authorized means. Thus, the offeree should use the same or better means of communication than the offeror used.

EXAMPLES:

Pam writes to Diane, "I offer to sell you my typewriter for $30." The offer is mailed on May 1. On May 3 Diane receives the offer and writes, "I accept." The acceptance is mailed on May 3. On May 4 Pam mails a note to Diane in which she says, "I revoke my offer." On May 5 Pam receives Diane's acceptance. On May 6 Diane receives Pam's attempted revocation. There is a contract. The acceptance, having been sent through an authorized means of communication, is effective upon being sent (May 3). The revocation cannot be effective until it is received. Because it was received after the acceptance had become effective, it is of no consequence.

Pam writes to Diane, "I offer to sell you my typewriter for $30. Your acceptance must be by phone on or before May 5." Diane writes, "I accept." Diane mails the acceptance on May 4. Pam receives the acceptance on May 6. There is no contract. The acceptance was not effective upon being sent because the mail was not an authorized means of acceptance according to the terms of the offer.

(2) *Receipt of first communication*: If the offeree first responds by sending a rejection and follows by sending an acceptance, the acceptance is not ef-

fective upon being sent. The first communication received by the offeror is effective.

EXAMPLE: Pam writes to Diane on May 1, "I offer to sell you my type-writer for $30." On May 3 Diane receives the offer and writes, "I will not pay $30. I offer you $20." On May 4 Diane writes, "I accept your offer of May 1." On May 5 Pam receives Diane's rejection. On May 6 Pam receives Diane's acceptance. There is no contract. The rejection was effective upon receipt. It terminated the offer.

    d. *Silence as acceptance*: Ordinarily, silence will not constitute an acceptance.

EXAMPLE: Al receives a letter from Ray offering to mow his yard this season. The letter ended with the following: "If I do not hear from you in five days, I will presume you accept." Al cannot be forced to respond to avoid such an offer. Therefore, silence would not be an acceptance.

D. Types of Contracts

The basic types of contracts are quasi-contracts, unilateral contracts, bilateral contracts, express contracts, implied contracts, formal contracts, and simple contracts.

    1. *Quasi-contract*: The so-called quasi-contract is not a contract in the true sense because there is no mutual assent. The law imposes an obligation under some circumstances where there is no agreement between the parties to prevent an injustice from occurring. Frequently, a quasi-contract is found to exist to prevent unjust enrichment of a party.

EXAMPLE: Neal owed $100 to Mike for the repayment of a loan from Mike. Without knowing that Mike had moved, Neal went to Mike's former apartment. Finding no one home, Neal placed the $100 in a plain folder and left it inside the door. Ozzi, the new occupant of the apartment, returned home later and found the money. Upon discovering what happened, Neal demands that Ozzi return the money. The law imposes a duty on Ozzi to return the money to Neal. Ozzi would be unjustly enriched if he were allowed to keep the money.

    2. *Unilateral Contract*: A unilateral contract is one in which the offer is accepted by performance of the requested act. In a unilateral contract the offer invites acceptance only by performance of the requested act, not by a return promise.

EXAMPLE: Tim's dog, Lassie, has disappeared. Tim offers to pay $100 to anyone who returns Lassie to him. Jeff learns of the offer and promises Tim that he will find the dog and return it. There is no contract. The offer can only be accepted by actual performance. If Jeff returns Lassie to Tim, there is a unilateral contract.

    3. *Bilateral Contract*: A bilateral contract involves an exchange of promises. The offer is accepted by a return promise from the offeree. Unless the offer provides that acceptance is to be by actual performance, a promise to perform will usually suffice as an acceptance.

EXAMPLE: Jean says to Debbie: "I offer you $10 to shovel my sidewalk. Will you agree to do it?" Debbie says, "Yes, I accept." A bilateral contract has been formed. Jean invited acceptance by return promise.

If it is not clear whether an offer is for a unilateral or bilateral contract, the courts will find that a bilateral contract was intended.

4. *Implied Contract*: An implied contract is one in which the parties' agreement is expressed by their conduct instead of by their words.

EXAMPLE: Harold drove his car to a self-service gas station. Without saying a word, he filled his tank with gasoline. The station attendant watched as Harold pumped the gasoline. By their conduct, the parties formed an implied contract for the sale of the gasoline. By his actions, Harold promised to pay the listed price of the gasoline he pumped into his tank.

E. Statute of Limitations

The law of each state establishes a time period within which suits for breach of contract must be brought. If the suit is not brought within the relevant time period following the breach, the right to sue for a remedy is lost. A typical statute of limitations requires that a suit based on an oral contract must be brought within five years of the breach and that a suit based on breach of a written contract must be brought within 10 years of the breach.

F. Statute of Frauds

The law that requires certain types of contracts to be in writing is generally known as the *statute of frauds*. When the statute of frauds applies, the contract cannot be enforced in court unless it is in writing and signed by the party being sued.

1. *Sale of Land*: Contracts for the sale of land are covered by the statute of frauds.

2. *Sale of Goods*: A contract for the sale of goods for $500 or more requires a writing.

3. *Promise in Consideration of Marriage*: A promise to give goods or money in return for a promise to marry must be in writing to be enforceable.

EXAMPLE: Jones says to Anderson, "If you marry me, I will give you $10,000." Jones' promise is not enforceable unless it is in writing and signed by Jones.

4. *Promise to Perform for Another Party*: A promise to be responsible for the obligation of another party must be in a signed writing to be enforceable. (This promise is called a *surety promise*.)

EXAMPLE: Sam accompanies Wilbur to the bank and tells the banker, "Give Wilbur the loan he wants. If he fails to pay, I will pay." Sam's promise is not enforceable unless it is in writing and signed by him.

5. *Contracts That Cannot Be Performed within One Year*: Contracts that cannot be performed within one year are covered by the statute of frauds.

   a. *Time for contract performance*: The time runs from the time the contract is entered into, not from the time actual performance is to take place.

   EXAMPLE: On May 1, Tina hires Melba to work in Tina's store for six months beginning on January 2. The contract must be in writing because it cannot be performed within one year from the date it was made.

   b. *Contract performance within one year*: If the contract could possibly be performed within one year, it is not covered by the statute of frauds.

   EXAMPLE: David hired Phil to write a dictionary. Even though it is most unlikely that the dictionary can be completed within the year, it is possible. The contract, therefore, is not covered by the statute of frauds. Here the law considers possibilities, not probabilities.

6. *Promise of Responsibility for Obligation of Estate*: A promise from one who is the court-appointed manager of the estate of a deceased person to be personally responsible for an obligation of the estate must be in writing and signed.

EXAMPLE: James died while owing money to Bob. James's son, James Jr., was appointed by the court to manage his deceased father's estate. The estate does not have enough money to pay the debt owed to Bob. James Jr. promised to pay the debt himself. His promise is not enforceable unless it is in writing and signed by him.

G. Assignment of Rights and Delegation of Duties

Sometimes a person who was not a party to the formation of the original contract acquires rights or undertakes responsibilities provided for in the contract.

1. *Assignment*: An assignment is a transfer of a contract right to one who is not a party to the contract. One who makes assignment is known as an *assignor*. One to whom an assignment is made is known as an *assignee*.

    a. *Assignable contract rights*: Most contract rights are assignable. The law provides, however, that certain rights are nonassignable. The contract may state that it is nonassignable. The prohibition on assignment of certain types of rights is for the protection of the nonassigning party to the contract.

        (1) An assignment that materially increases the burden or risk of the nonassigning party is prohibited.

        EXAMPLE: The Acme Pest Control Company contracted with Tim to spray Tim's house each time a roach was discovered. Tim is not permitted by law to assign his rights under the contract to Joe, who owns a hardware store. Such an assignment changes the risk of Acme.

        (2) Rights that are highly personal in nature cannot be assigned.

        EXAMPLES:

        Dr. Jones contracted to perform cosmetic surgery on Myron's face for $2,000. Myron cannot assign his rights under such a contract.

        Hank, a lawyer, contracted to make a will for Wilma. Wilma cannot assign her rights to another person.

        (3) An assignment that is specifically outlawed by a statute cannot legally be made. For instance, some statutes prohibit wage assignments.

        (4) A mere statement in a contract that there can be no assignment does not necessarily mean that no assignment can be made. The assignor would be in breach of the contract and, therefore, liable for any damages caused to the nonassigning party, but an assignment could still be made.

    b. *Gratuitous assignment*: The law does not require that there be consideration in order for an assignment to be valid. An assignment made without consideration is known as a *gratuitous assignment*.

> *EXAMPLE: Jake owes $100 to Sandra. Sandra assigns her right to receive the money to Carla. Even though there was no bargained-for exchange between Sandra and Carla, the assignment is nevertheless valid.*

   c. *Enforcement of assigned rights*: The assignee can enforce the assigned rights against the nonassigning party.

> *EXAMPLE: Al contracted to purchase a boat from Bob for $300. Bob delivered the boat to Al. Under the contract Al was obligated to pay the purchase price within six months. Bob assigned his right to receive the $300 to Carl. If Al fails to pay within the six-month period, Carl can sue Al to enforce his right to receive the money.*

      (1) *Full performance of contractual duties*: If the nonassigning party has already rendered full performance of the contractual duties to the assignor, the assignee cannot require a second performance of them.

      (2) *Notification to nonassigning party*: If, however, the nonassigning party has been notified of the assignment and still renders performance to the assignor, he/she may be required to perform again for the assignee.

> *EXAMPLE: Wanda owes $50 to Gloria. Gloria assigns her right to receive the money to Sally. Before being notified of the assignment, Wanda pays the $50 to Gloria. Wanda has a good defense against a suit brought by Sally. If Wanda had paid the money to Gloria after receiving notice of the assignment, Wanda would not have a valid defense to a suit brought by Sally.*

      (3) *Assignment of contract rights only*: The assignor cannot assign greater rights than he has under the contract. The assignee merely stands in the shoes of the assignor.

2. *Delegation*: A delegation is a transfer of one's contractual obligation to another person. It may involve all of one's obligations under a contract or only part of them.

   a. *Nondelegation of duties*: Some duties may not be delegated.

      (1) *Duties requiring skill or judgment*: Duties that involve the exercise of skill or judgment cannot be delegated.

      EXAMPLES:

> *Wayne hired Omar to paint a portrait of Wayne. Omar cannot delegate his duty to paint the portrait because it involves a special skill.*

> *Curt hired Daryl to mow Curt's lawn. Daryl can delegate his duty because it does not require special skill or judgment. However, Daryl is still responsible for the yard being mowed.*

      (2) *Delegation prohibited by contract*: If delegation is prohibited in the contract, a party cannot delegate duties.

   b. *Novation*: The delegating party remains responsible for performance of the contractual duties unless there is a novation. If the nondelegating party expressly agrees to release the delegating party from further responsibility and accepts the delegating party's promise to perform, a novation has occurred.

EXAMPLES:

The Gold Star Disposal Company contracted with Dan to pick up and remove garbage from Dan's farmhouse twice per week. Gold Star delegated this duty to the Victory Disposal Company. Victory failed to pick up Dan's garbage. Dan can successfully sue Gold Star because the delegation did not relieve Gold Star of its contractual obligations.

Assume in the above situation described that Dan had expressly agreed to release Gold Star from its obligations in return for Victory's promise to perform the same duties. Dan could then successfully sue only Victory.

H. Breach of Contracts— Remedies

When a party fails to perform its contractual obligations, the issue of what constitutes an appropriate remedy becomes relevant. A party breaches a contract when, without justification, it fails to perform its obligations under the terms of the agreement. The nonbreaching party is entitled to a remedy as compensation for the loss suffered as a result of the breach. The most commonly sought remedies are money damages, specific performance, and restitution.

1. *Money Damages*: The nonbreaching party may sue to recover the amount of money required to put the property in as good a position as it would have been in had there been no breach (that is, had the contract been performed as promised).

   EXAMPLE: Howard contracted to paint Don's car for $300. Howard failed to paint the car. Don hired someone else to paint the car for $450. Assuming that $450 was a reasonable price negotiated in good faith, Don is entitled to recover $150 from Howard.

   a. *Nominal damages*: If a party cannot prove that a loss was suffered as a result of the breach, only nominal damages are awarded. Nominal damages are a small amount, often one dollar, which the court grants to recognize that a breach of contract did in fact occur, but that no real loss was proven.

      EXAMPLE: If in the situation described above, Don hired someone else to paint his car for $300, he could recover from Howard only the value of the time and effort he expended to find someone else to paint the car.

   b. *Liquidated damages*: At the time they enter into the contract, the parties may agree on the money damages to be paid in the event of a breach. These predetermined damages are known as *liquidated damages*. The courts will enforce a liquidated-damages clause only if the stated damages bear a close relationship to those which could be reasonably expected to occur in the event of a breach. If the liquidated-damages clause amounts to a penalty for the breaching party further than an attempt to compensate the nonbreaching party reasonably, it will not be enforced.

2. *Specific Performance*: The nonbreaching party may sue for a court order requiring the breaching party to perform its contractual duties. In order to obtain specific performance, the nonbreaching party must convince the court that no amount of money damages will put it in the position it would have been in had there been no breach.

EXAMPLES:

Cindy contracted to sell her home to Paula. Cindy breached the contract. If Paula sues for specific performance to require Cindy to complete the sale, Paula will succeed. The law recognizes that no two pieces of land are the same and, therefore, money damages would be inadequate.

George contracted to sell 20 pounds of salt to Myron for $20. If George breaches the contract, Myron will not succeed in obtaining specific performance because money damages would be adequate.

3. *Restitution*: The nonbreaching party may sue to require the breaching party to return what it received under the contract.

EXAMPLES:

Linda contracted to sell her antique bicycle to Floyd for $800. Under the terms of the agreement, Floyd took possession of the bicycle and was to pay the purchase price in four installments. Floyd breached the contract by failing to make the payments. Linda may sue for restitution and recover the bicycle from Floyd.

Ann contracted to purchase a gold ring from Bernice. In compliance with the terms of the contract, Ann paid $400 for the ring. Bernice breached the contract by failing to deliver the ring. Ann may sue for restitution and recover the $400 she paid to Bernice.

Review Questions

DIRECTIONS: Select the best answer from the four alternatives. Write the letter of your answer in the blank to the left of the number.

_____ 1. George is employed by the City of Greenville as a street commissioner. In the course of his work for the city, George uses a concrete mixing machine owned by the city. Bob, a citizen of a nearby town, offered to rent the machine from George for one day at a cost of $150. When George rejected the offer because he feared losing his job for leasing city property to an unauthorized person in violation of a city ordinance, Bob offered to pay a rental of $250. George accepted the offer. Bob returned the machine after using it, but he refused to pay the $250 to George. If George sues Bob to enforce the contract,

   a. George will succeed in collecting the $250.
   b. George will succeed in collecting only a reasonable amount.
   c. George will succeed in collecting the fair rental value of the equipment.
   d. George will not succeed in collecting anything from Bob.

_____ 2. For months Matt has attempted to purchase an antique car owned by Paul. Matt's latest offer of $5,000 was rejected by Paul. The next day Matt observed Paul leaving a theater which was showing an X-rated movie. Matt took a picture of Paul and threatened to circulate the picture at Paul's workplace if Paul did not contract to sell the car to Matt. Fearing that he would lose his job if the picture was circulated, Paul signed a contract to sell the car to Matt for $5,500. When Paul refused to deliver the car, Matt sued him for breach of contract.

   a. Matt will win because the agreement is in writing and signed by Paul.
   b. Paul will win because his agreement was obtained by fraud.
   c. Paul will win because his signature was obtained by duress.
   d. Paul will win because his signature was obtained by undue influence.

_____ 3. Jane offered to sell her television set to Becky for $200. Jane told Becky that the set was two years old and that a new picture tube had just been installed. Relying on these statements, Becky agreed to purchase the set. Two days later Becky learned that the set had its original picture tube. Becky sues Jane, seeking the return of the sale price.

   a. Becky will succeed in having the sale set aside. She must return the set, and Jane must return the $200.
   b. Becky will not succeed in recovering the money because the agreement involved a mutual mistake.

c. Becky will not succeed in recovering the money because of the legal principle of "buyer beware."

d. Becky could succeed in recovering the money only if she is a minor.

_____

4. Mona, who is a nurse, offered her friend Rona $100 if Rona would lose 25 pounds. Mona showed Rona a study which indicated that weight loss would improve her health. Rona accepted Mona's offer. She lost 25 pounds. Mona, however, refused to pay Rona the $100. Mona claims that the weight loss was good for Rona but that she received no benefit from it. Rona sues Mona to collect the $100.

a. Mona will win the suit because there was no consideration.

b. Mona will win the suit because the agreement violates public policy.

c. Mona will win the suit because there was no bargained-for exchange of something of value.

d. Rona will win.

_____

5. Judy's mother was hospitalized from May 1 to June 1 while Judy was in Europe on business. Upon her return to town, Judy visited the hospital. She told the head of the hospital's billing department that she was so thankful her mother had been properly cared for over that month that she would pay the bill if her mother failed to pay. Later, however, Judy refused to pay the bill. The hospital brings suit against Judy based on her promise to pay.

a. The hospital will win because there was no consideration.

b. The hospital will win because Judy promised to answer for the debt of another person.

c. Judy will win because undue influence is present.

d. Judy will win because there was no consideration.

_____

6. Bill hired Jim to panel Bill's basement. The written contract provided that Jim would remove the wallpaper and install a specified kind of paneling for $1,700, including labor. After Jim had removed the wallpaper and paneled half of the basement, he refused to complete the job unless Bill promised to pay him an additional $100. Jim realized the job was taking longer than expected. Bill promised to pay the additional $100. Upon completion of the work, however, Bill refused to pay the extra $100. Jim sues Bill to collect the $100.

a. Bill will win because there was no consideration.

b. Bill will win because the agreement to pay the $100 was illegal.

c. Jim will win because there was a mutual mistake as to how long the job would take.

d. Jim will win because Bill is guilty of fraud in promising to pay the $100, which he never intended to pay.

7. The accountancy firm of Wilson, Jones, and Smith contracted to purchase all pencils that the firm needed for the coming year from the Sharp Pencil Company at a price of 7 cents per pencil. One month into the year covered by the contract the firm began purchasing pencils from another company at 5 cents per pencil. Sharp sues the firm for breach of contract.

a. Sharp will lose because the firm's promise was illusory.
b. Sharp will lose because there was no consideration.
c. Sharp will win because the firm's promise is enforceable.
d. Sharp will win because the firm is guilty of fraudulent misrepresentation.

8. Mike, who is 15 years old, contracted to buy a set of golf clubs for $85 from Sam, who is 45 years of age.

a. The contract is void.
b. The contract is voidable by Mike.
c. The contract is voidable by Sam.
d. The contract is voidable by either Sam or Mike.

9. Rick, who is 15 years of age, ran away from home. He checked into a hotel one evening when the temperature dropped to 10°F. The next day Rick notified the hotel clerk that he was a minor and claimed that he owed the hotel nothing because he was disaffirming the contract. The hotel clerk argued that Rick was legally obligated to pay the $92 per night fee which the hotel charges all its guests. Who is correct?

a. Rick is correct. The law allows him to disaffirm.
b. The hotel clerk is correct. Because lodging was a necessary item to Rick, he is obligated to pay the contract price.
c. The hotel clerk is correct. Rick's minority is irrelevant.
d. Neither party is correct.

10. Mary, a 17-year-old high school student, contracted to purchase stereo equipment from National Sales. Under the terms of the contract, Mary was to pay $10 per month for 45 months. After reaching 18, the age of majority in her state, Mary continued making the monthly payments for another five months. Mary then notified National that she was disaffirming the contract. National argued that Mary cannot disaffirm.

a. National is correct because a minor can disaffirm only during minority.
b. National is correct because Mary ratified the contract upon making the first payment after her sixteenth birthday.
c. National is correct because the stereo equipment is a necessity.
d. National is correct because Mary has ratified the contract.

11. Jack wrote a note to Todd that read, "Todd, I offer to sell you my calculator for $10. (Signed) Jack." Jack placed the note on a table in his own home. Later that evening Todd made an unannounced visit to Jack's house. While Jack was in the kitchen getting refreshments, Todd found the note and read it. When Jack reentered the room, Todd laid out a $10 bill and said, "I accept." Is there a contract?

    a. No, because there was no valid offer.
    b. No, because there was no valid acceptance.
    c. No, because there was no consideration.
    d. Yes, there is a contract.

12. Alice, a college professor, offered to sell her desk to Brenda for $350. Alice promised to hold the offer open for one week. The next day, however, Alice sold the desk to Rupert for $420. When Alice told Brenda of the sale later that same day, Brenda took $350 to Alice and said, "I accept your offer." Brenda claims that she has contracted to purchase the desk. Alice claims the offer to Brenda has been revoked. Who is correct?

    a. Brenda is correct. Alice was legally obligated to hold the offer open for a week as promised.
    b. Alice is correct. The offer was revoked when Alice told Brenda of the sale.
    c. Alice is correct. The offer was revoked when Alice refused to take Brenda's $350.
    d. Brenda is correct. Alice's offer was a firm offer that cannot be revoked for three months.

13. Sally, a book company sales agent, wrote to Tom, a book store purchasing agent, "I offer to sell you 300 volumes of *How to Become a Millionaire* for $900. This offer will remain open for two months. (Signed) Sally." A week later, however, before Tom had responded to the offer, Sally phoned Tom and told him that she revoked the offer. Tom argues that Sally cannot revoke for the two-month period. Sally claims that she can revoke any time prior to acceptance. Who is correct?

    a. Sally is correct.
    b. Tom is correct because there was a valid option.
    c. Tom is correct because there was a merchant's firm offer.
    d. Neither party is correct. Sally can revoke after the passage of a reasonable time.

14. Alex said to Barry, "I offer to sell you this briefcase for $30." Barry responded, "I offer you $25 for it." Alex said, "No, that is not enough." Barry then said, "O.K., I accept your offer." Is there a contract at this point?

    a. Yes, there is a contract.
    b. No, because there is no consideration.
    c. No, because the offer was not in writing.
    d. No, because the offer had terminated before Barry's attempted acceptance.

15. Frank wrote to Jenny, "I offer to sell you my lawn mower for $50." Jenny wrote back, "I accept. Include a gallon of gasoline." Is there a contract?

    a. No, because the attempted acceptance does not match the terms of the offer.
    b. No, because the parties are not merchants.
    c. Yes, because the acceptance was mailed.
    d. Yes, because the acceptance was not conditional.

16. On May 1 Sandy wrote to Burt, "I offer to sell you my banjo for $50." On May 3 Burt received Sandy's offer and wrote back, "I accept your offer." On May 4 Sally sold the banjo to Ed. She phoned Burt on May 4 and told him the offer was revoked. On May 5 Sandy received Burt's letter of acceptance. Is there a contract between Sandy and Burt?

    a. No, because the offer was revoked before the acceptance was received.
    b. No, because performance became impossible when Sandy sold the banjo to Ed on May 4.
    c. Yes, because the acceptance became effective on May 3.
    d. Yes, because the offer was made prior to May 3.

17. On June 1 Al wrote to Bob, "I offer to sell you my window fan for $25." On June 3 Bob received Al's offer and wrote to Al, "No, thank you. Your price is higher than I can pay." On June 4 Bob changed his mind and wrote to Al, "I accept your offer." On June 5 Al received Bob's letter of rejection. On June 6 Al received Bob's letter of acceptance. Is there a contract between Al and Bob?

    a. Yes, because the acceptance was effective upon being mailed.
    b. Yes, because the offer had not been terminated on June 6 when the acceptance was received.
    c. No, because the rejection was effective when mailed on June 3.
    d. No, because the rejection was effective on June 5 before the acceptance was received.

18. Mike lost his watch. He placed an ad in the local newspaper which read, "I offer $20 to anyone who returns my watch to me." It included a description of the watch and his address. Ken read the ad and later found the watch. He returned it to Mike and collected the reward. What kind of contract existed between Mike and Ken?

    a. Unilateral contract
    b. Bilateral contract
    c. Quasi-contract
    d. Implied contract

19. Curt agreed to purchase a small strip of land from Dick for $499. The agreement was not put in writing. Curt later denied that he had made such an agreement. Dick sues Curt to enforce the agreement.

   a. Dick will win. The contract need not be in writing because less than $500 is involved.
   b. Dick will win. The statute of frauds does not apply to sales of land.
   c. Curt will win because there was no consideration.
   d. Curt will win because the agreement was not in writing and signed by him.

20. Clyde owned and operated a restaurant. He contracted to purchase 400 dozen plates from Susan. Susan failed to deliver the plates. Clyde sues Susan. Clyde seeks specific performance. Will the court order specific performance?

   a. Yes.
   b. Yes, but only if Clyde proves that Susan breached the contract.
   c. No, because specific performance cannot be awarded in a breach of contract suit.
   d. Yes, but only if money damages are inadequate.

Use this information in answering Questions 21 to 23.

Ted and Mary were robbed of all their cash and belongings while vacationing in a large city. Since they had left home without traveler's checks or credit cards, they contacted Jane, a friend who lived in the city. On her way to work Jane accompanied Ted to a camera shop and told the proprietor, "Let him pick out any camera under $300, and I will pay for it on the way back home this afternoon." She then took Mary to a clothing store and told the clerk, "Mary will select the clothes she wants up to $400. If she doesn't pay, I will." The next day she accompanied Mary to a furniture store, where Mary ordered an $800 couch to be delivered in 30 days. Jane told the salesperson, "I will pay for it."

21. Assume that the camera shop sues Jane to recover the $250 sale price of the camera Ted selected and took home.

   a. The camera shop will win because Jane's promise was a direct promise to pay for goods under $500.
   b. The camera shop will win because the goods are valued at under $1,000.
   c. Jane will win because her promise was to pay for the debt of another.
   d. Jane will win because the camera's value is more than $200.

22. Assume that the clothing store sues Jane to collect the $350 sale price of the clothing Mary selected and took home. The correctly reasoned answer is

   a. the clothing store will win because Jane's promise was a direct promise to pay for goods under $500.
   b. the clothing store will win because the goods are valued at under $500.

c. Jane will win because her promise was to pay for the debt of another and was not in writing.

d. Jane will win because the promise to pay for the debt of another is never enforceable.

23. Assume that the furniture store sues Jane for the price of the couch. The correctly reasoned result is

a. the furniture store will win because Jane's promise is a direct promise to pay.

b. the furniture store will win because the price of the couch is under $1,000.

c. Jane will win because her promise is indirect.

d. Jane will win because her promise to pay for goods over $500 is not in writing.

Use this information in answering Questions 24 and 25.

Sandra owned an antique coffee grinder that Tony, Randall, and Kathy each wanted to buy. On June 1 Sandra mailed to each of the interested parties an offer to sell the item for $300. On June 3 each of the interested parties received the offer. On June 3 Tony mailed a note which read, "$300 is too high. I offer $250." This was received by Sandra on June 4. On June 3 Randall mailed the following response, "Would you consider $250?" Also, on June 3 Kathy wrote, "I do not have $300 to spend. Sell it to someone else." On June 4 Sandra received Randall's note but did not receive Kathy's because it had been mailed to an incorrect address.

Also, on June 4 Tony, Randall, and Kathy, acting independently of one another, each mailed the following communication: "I accept your offer of June 1. Enclosed is my money order for $300." On June 5 Sandra received Kathy's first response. On June 6 she received all of the responses mailed on June 4.

24. With whom does Sandra have a contract?

a. Tony

b. Randall

c. Kathy

d. Randall and Kathy

25. If Sandra had hand delivered the following note to each of the other parties on June 3, "My offer of June 1 is hereby revoked," the delivery of the note would

a. revoke the offer.

b. have no effect.

c. revoke the offer only if delivered before the other party's receipt of the offer.

d. revoke the offer only as to Tony and Kathy.

Use this information in answering Questions 26 and 27.

On May 1 Joan loaned $200 to Todd. The loan was payable with 5 percent interest on January 30. On July 1 Joan assigned her right to receive the money to Ann. Todd was not notified. On January 30 Todd paid the required amount to Joan. On February 1, Ann demands that Todd pay her.

_____

26. The correct outcome is

    a. Todd must pay Ann.
    b. Ann may collect from Todd and then from Joan.
    c. Ann may recover the money from Joan.
    d. Ann is not entitled to any recovery.

_____

27. If Todd had been notified of the assignment on January 29

    a. it would make no difference.
    b. Todd could be required to pay Ann even after he paid Joan.
    c. Todd cannot be required to pay twice.
    d. Ann is not entitled to any recovery.

Solutions

Answer	Refer to:
1. (d)	[B-1-c] The agreement is illegal. A city ordinance prohibits the leasing of city property to unauthorized persons. Because the agreement is illegal, it is not an enforceable contract. George, therefore, will lose his suit.
2. (c)	[B-2-b(1)] Matt's threat to circulate the picture caused Paul to lose free will. His apparent agreement to the terms of the sale was obtained by duress. Paul feared the loss of his job if the picture was released. Matt's conduct did not amount to undue influence because there was no close relationship between the parties. There was no fraud because Matt did not make a false representation to Paul.
3. (a)	[B-2-b(3), (4)] Becky will succeed in having the agreement set aside. Jane's statement that the set had a new picture tube was a false statement of fact. It was reasonably relied upon by Becky. If Jane knew that her statement was false, it amounts to fraud. If Jane reasonably believed that her statement was true, it amounts to an innocent misrepresentation. In either event, Becky is entitled to have the agreement set aside. She will be required to return the television set and will be entitled to the return of the money.
4. (d)	[B-3-a] Rona will win because all the elements required for a valid contract are present. Rona surrendered her right to maintain her weight. She performed the act requested by Mona. Whether Mona received anything of value is unimportant. The fact that Rona benefited from the weight loss is unimportant.
5. (d)	[B-3-d] Judy will win because there was no consideration. The care that the hospital rendered to her mother had already been performed. There was, therefore, no bargained-for exchange, Moreover, Judy merely told the hospital employee that she would pay the bill if her mother failed to pay. Since this is a promise to answer for the debt of another person, the law requires that it be in writing. There was no evidence to support a claim of undue influence.
6. (a)	[B-3-e] There was no consideration to support Bill's promise. Jim was doing nothing in return for the extra $100. He was merely doing what he had already contracted to do. He was legally obligated to perform his contractual duties.
7. (c)	[B-3-g] A promise to buy all of the goods that a party needs or requires is enforceable. The Uniform Commercial Code imposes a standard of good faith, thus making the quantity involved in such a promise reasonably

certain. Had the promise been to buy all the pencils the firm wanted or desired, it would have been illusory and, therefore, unenforceable. As stated, the promise provides a basis for consideration.

8. (b) [B-4-a(1), (4)] A contract entered into by a minor is voidable at the option of the minor. The minor may elect to enforce the contract against the adult. Mike may avoid the contract by disaffirming it during his minority or within a reasonable time after reaching his majority.

9. (d) [B-4-a(1), (5)] Rick is allowed to disaffirm, but since lodging was a necessity to him, he must pay the reasonable value of the lodging. The reasonable value may differ from the $92 that the hotel charges its customers.

10. (d) [B-4-a(6) (a), (b)] By making five monthly payments after reaching majority and remaining in possession of the stereo equipment, Mary has ratified the contract. It is also true that more than a reasonable time has passed since she reached her majority. Mary, therefore, cannot now disaffirm.

11. (a) [C-1-c] The offer was not communicated to Todd with Jack's intent. Since Jack had not sent the note, there is a chance he would reconsider it and not communicate it to Todd. When Todd found and read the note in Jack's house, he learned of the note's contents without Jack intending for him to learn of it at that time. The law requires that an offer be communicated with the intent of the offeror.

12. (b) [C-2-b] As a general rule, the offeror may revoke the offer at any time prior to acceptance. Alice told Brenda of the sale to Rupert before Brenda tendered the money and indicated her intent to accept.

13. (c) [C-2-b(2)] All of the elements of a merchant's firm offer are present. Sally is a merchant (she sells books on a regular basis). Her offer is in writing. It is an offer to sell goods. It is signed by her, and it contains a promise that the offer will be held open for a period of time. The offer is not revocable for two months.

14. (d) [C-2-c(2)] Barry made a counteroffer that terminated Alex's original offer. Answer (c) is incorrect because there is no requirement that such agreements be in writing. Answer (b) is incorrect because were it not for the termination, consideration would be present.

15. (d) [C-3-b(2)] Since this is a contract for the sale of goods, the Uniform Commercial Code applies. As long as the offeree expresses an intent to accept the offer and does not make acceptance conditional on new or different terms, acceptance is effective. In this case, the acceptance is not conditioned upon the additional term.

16. (c) [C-3-c(1)] The mail was an authorized means of communication since it was used by the offeror and there was nothing in the offer to indicate that the mail would be unacceptable. The acceptance, therefore, was effective upon being sent. Since the offer was accepted on May 3, the attempted revocation on May 4 was of no legal effect.

17. (d) [C-3-c(2)] Because the offeree's first response was the sending of a rejection, the acceptance was not effective upon being sent. In such a case, whichever communication arrives first is the one that is effective. Since the rejection was received before the acceptance was received, the rejection governs and there is no contract.

18. (a) [D-2] The only way that Mike's offer could be accepted was by performance. It was, therefore, a unilateral offer. When Ken performed the requested act, he accepted the offer.

19. (d) [F-1] A contract for the sale of land must be in writing and signed by the party being sued. The $500 requirement applies only when goods are involved.

20. (d) [H-2] Specific performance is available only in cases where money damages are inadequate. In this case Clyde could only get specific performance if he could prove that the plates he contracted for were so unique that he could not purchase similar plates with any sum of money. It is extremely doubtful that Clyde can prove that. He will be limited to receiving money damages in his suit.

21. (a) [F-2] Jane's promise was a direct promise to pay for the camera. The promise was not conditional. Since the goods are valued under $500, there is no requirement for the promise to be in writing.

22. (c) [F-4] Jane's promise was to pay for the debt of Mary. It was not a direct promise to pay. Rather, the promise was conditional on Mary's failure to pay. Since the promise was to pay for Mary's debt, the law requires that it be in writing.

23. (d) [F-2] Although Jane's promise was a direct promise to pay, the law required that it be in writing because the value of the goods exceeds $500.

24. (b) [C-3] Randall's first communication was a mere inquiry, which did not constitute a rejection of the offer. His second communication was a valid acceptance. Kathy and Tony had rejected Sandra's offer in their first communications, which Sandra received before she received their attempted acceptances.

25. (a) [C-2] Generally, an offer may be revoked by the offeror any time prior to its acceptance. Sandra's actual delivery of the revocation before any of the offerees had accepted was a valid revocation.

26. (c)   [G-1-c] Todd was not notified of the assignment before he performed his obligation fully. He cannot, therefore, be required to perform twice.

27. (b)   [G-1-c(2)] Once he is notified of the assignment, Todd must honor it or risk being required to pay twice.

CHAPTER 22

Negotiable Instruments

OVERVIEW

In the modern business world the use of checks, drafts, and promissory notes is taken for granted. Yet if such instruments were not available, business transactions would, by necessity, be based on the actual transfer of cash. If cash were required, the risk and inconvenience of transporting the money would retard the conduct of business. Moreover, credit would become more difficult to arrange, and efforts to finance transactions would be hampered.

It is the use of negotiable instruments as substitutes for money that makes today's streamlined transactions possible. In this chapter we present the fundamentals of the law of negotiable instruments. The candidate should become familiar with the concept of negotiability and the elements it requires, the types of negotiable instruments, the requirements for a valid transfer of such instruments, and the defenses that the law recognizes against the holder of such instruments.

KEY TERMS

Bearer
Cashier's check
Draft
Drawee
Drawer
Holder
Holder in due course
Indorsee
Indorsement without recourse

Indorser
Maker
Negotiable instrument
Negotiation
Payee
Promissory note
Restrictive indorsement
Special indorsement

A. The Significance of Negotiability

Negotiability is a valued characteristic because it is possible for the recipient of a negotiable instrument to be free of many of the defenses that the promisor could assert against the original owner of the document.

1. *Legal Requirements*: The law establishes certain requirements for negotiability (see Section B). These are contained in the Uniform Commercial Code (UCC).

2. *Effect of Negotiability*: A document containing a promise that can be transferred to another party in a manner that entitles the recipient to enforce the promise without being subject to all the defenses that could be asserted against the original owner is said to be negotiable. To appreciate fully the effect of the transfer of a negotiable instrument, it should be compared to the ordinary assignment of contract rights.

   a. *Assignable contract rights*: Most contract rights are assignable (see Chapter 21). However, the assignee is subject to the same defenses to which the assignor is subject. The assignee merely stands in the shoes of the assignor.

      EXAMPLE: Al contracted to deliver a certain rare coin to Bob in return for Bob's promise to install new carpeting in Al's living room. Bob assigned his rights in the contract to Cal. When Cal sued Al to collect the coin, Al defended on the grounds that Bob had failed to install new carpeting. Al is permitted to assert this defense against Cal. Bob's contract right was assignable, but the contract was not negotiable within the meaning of the law. Thus Cal was subject to all defenses that Al could assert against Bob.

   b. *Assignable rights free of defenses*: A document that meets all the legal requirements for negotiability is worth more to other parties because, unlike an ordinary contract, its recipient, if he or she qualifies as a holder in due course [see Section B-6-c(6)], may take rights free of most defenses. It therefore involves less risk.

      EXAMPLE: Al signed a properly drawn check in the amount of $200 and delivered it to Bob in return for Bob's promise to carpet Al's living room. Bob endorsed the check and delivered it to Cal, to whom he owed $200. Cal cashed the check. Even if Bob did not carpet Al's room as he promised, Cal, assuming he took the check without any knowledge of Bob's failure to perform, is free of Al's claims.

B. Elements of a Negotiable Instrument

The Uniform Commercial Code (UCC) establishes the legal requirements for a negotiable instrument. If all of these requirements are not met, a document may be a contract capable of being assigned, but it is not a negotiable instrument. The difference between a mere contract and a negotiable instrument is important to those to whom the document is transferred (see Section A-2).

1. *Writing*: A negotiable instrument must be in writing. The requirement serves two main functions:

   a. *Fraud*: It minimizes the risk of fraud.

   b. *Transfer*: It allows for ease and certainty in transferring the promise to other parties.

   The UCC does not require that the writing be on paper. The writing requirement will be satisfied if the material on which the writing is done is in "tangible form." The material should, of course, be of the type that is likely to last for a considerable time.

EXAMPLE: Unhappy with his hotel room on his vacation to Hawaii, Lance paid his bill with a check he carved on a coconut. The instrument meets the writing requirement of the UCC.

2. *Signature*: To qualify as a negotiable instrument, a writing must be signed in accordance with the UCC.

   a. *Maker's signature*: If the instrument is a note, it must be signed by its maker.

   b. *Drawer's signature*: If the instrument is a check or a draft, it must be signed by the drawer.

   c. *Type of signature required*: A traditional signature is not required. Any mark made or adopted by a party with the intention of authenticating the writing will suffice as a signature.

      (1) An *X* or other mark will serve as a signature if it was the intent of the person making the mark to authenticate the document.

      (2) A rubber stamp that imprints a party's name may be used by the party or the party's authorized agent as the party's signature.

      (3) The signature may appear any place on the document.

3. *Unconditional Promise*: A negotiable instrument must contain an unconditional promise or order to pay.

   a. *Promise to pay*: A writing that merely recognizes a debt does not satisfy the requirement of a promise to pay.

      EXAMPLE: Don agreed to purchase Tina's lawn mower for $40. Upon receiving the lawn mower, Don wrote on a piece of paper, "Tina, I owe you $40. (Signed) Don." The promise requirement is not satisfied.

   b. *Order to pay*: A check that bears the name of a bank and words such as "Pay to the order of . . . " satisfies the order requirement.

      (1) The order to pay is clear and certain.

         (a) Words such as "please pay" are sufficiently clear and definite.

         (b) Words such as "I hope you will pay" or "I wish you would pay" are *not* sufficiently clear and definite.

      (2) The bank's name on the check identifies the party that must pay pursuant to the order and thus satisfies the legal requirement that the order to pay be directed to a specific, identifiable party.

   c. *Unconditional promise*: The promise must not be conditional.

      (1) If the promise states that it is subject to another agreement, the promise is conditional and does not meet the requirements for a negotiable instrument.

      (2) If the promise to pay states that payment can *only* be made from a particular source or fund, the promise does not meet the requirement for a negotiable instrument.

EXAMPLE: Willis signed a document that read, "I promise to pay to the bearer of this note $5,000 on May 1, 1995. Payment is to be made only from my travel account."

    (a)   Because it is possible that a specified fund will not be in existence when payment becomes due, the promise is conditional.

    (b)   If the word *only* were omitted, the preceding promise would satisfy the promise requirement for a negotiable instrument.

d. *Reference to agreement*: A mere reference to an agreement does not render a promise to pay conditional.

    (1)   The instrument may contain a statement of the parties' agreement.

    EXAMPLE: George writes, "I promise to pay Jane $100 on May 1 in payment of the desk she will deliver to me on that date. (Signed) George." George's promise is not conditional. He merely stated the terms of the agreement.

    (2)   The instrument may contain a reference to a separate agreement as long as the promise to pay is not made conditional on the other agreement.

    EXAMPLE: Susan writes, "I promise to pay Jack $35. Jack agrees to return the books he borrowed from me last semester. (Signed) Susan." Susan's promise merely refers to another agreement. Because the promise to pay is not subject to Jack's agreement to return the books, it is not a conditional promise.

4. *Specific Sum of Money*: The promise to pay must be expressed in terms of a specific sum of money.

    a. *Stated or ascertainable sum*: The sum must either be stated on the face of the instrument or be ascertainable without the necessity of referring to another source.

    EXAMPLE: A promise to pay "$100 with 9 percent interest upon demand" expresses a specific sum because the interest can be calculated without reference to any other source of information.

    b. *Promise to pay money*: The promise to pay must not include a promise to pay in something other than money.

    EXAMPLE: A promise to pay $300 and deliver a new light fixture will not suffice for a negotiable instrument because the promise includes a commitment to pay in something other than money.

    c. *Promise to pay in foreign currency*: The promise may be expressed in terms of a foreign nation's money. The UCC recognizes as money "a medium of exchange authorized or adopted by a domestic or foreign government as part of its currency."

    EXAMPLE: Boris writes, "I promise to pay 10,000 rubles on June 1." Rubles are recognized as money in Russia, so Boris's promise states a specific sum of money.

5. *Payable at Specific Time or Upon Demand*: To meet the requirements of a negotiable instrument, the promise must make the payment due at a specific time or upon demand.

    a. *Statement of due date*: To be considered payable at a specific time, the document must either state a certain date or express the due date in terms that allow the time to be ascertained with certainty.

    EXAMPLES:

    Bill promises to pay "$500 sixty days after the birth of Lou's next child." The due date cannot be ascertained because the birth date of the child is uncertain.

    Sally promises to pay "$200 on or before July 1, 1995." The due date is sufficiently definite. Although Sally may elect to pay before the stated date, the payment is due on July 1, 1995.

    b. *Payment upon demand*: Promises to pay *upon demand, at sight,* or *upon presentment* satisfy the requirement.

6. *Payable to Order or Bearer*: To be negotiable, an instrument must make it clear that the promisor intended for the instrument to be transferable by the promisee to another party.

    a. *Acceptable word usage*: Words such as *pay to the order of Gregg Wilson* or *payable to the bearer* satisfy this requirement.

    b. *Transfer of instrument*: If the instrument is simply made payable to a named party, it may still be transferred, but the rights of the transferee will be limited. The transferee will not be considered a holder [see Sections B-6-c(5) and (6) below].

    c. *Parties to negotiable instruments*: The parties involved in the making and transferring of negotiable instruments are known in the law by various names. Familiarity with the basic terminology employed by the UCC is helpful in understanding negotiable instruments.

        (1) *Drawer*: A drawer is one who issues a check or other draft.

        (2) *Drawee*: A drawee is a party who is ordered by the drawer to pay a certain sum of money to a party known as a *payee*.

        EXAMPLE: Alice writes a check in the amount of $10 payable to Barb. Alice is the drawer; Barb is the payee. Alice's bank is the drawee.

        (3) *Maker*: A maker is one who signs a promissory note promising to pay a certain sum of money to another party.

        (4) *Indorser and indorsee*: An indorser is a payee who transfers the instrument by signing it and delivering it to one known as an indorsee. (An indorsee can become an indorser.)

        EXAMPLE: Barb is named as the payee on a check. She signs the check and delivers it to Cathy. Barb is the indorser. Cathy is the indorsee.

        (5) *Holder*: A holder is one who possesses an instrument that is issued or indorsed to that person or is payable to the bearer.

(6) *Holder in due course*: A holder in due course is one who gives value for an instrument and takes it in good faith without knowledge of any defect. A holder in due course is free of many defenses to which an ordinary assignee is subject (see Section E).

C. Types of Negotiable Instruments

The UCC recognizes two types of instruments: drafts and promissory notes.

1. *Drafts*: A draft is an instrument that contains an unconditional order by the drawer, directing the drawee to pay money to a payee (see Section B-6-c).

    EXAMPLE: A check.

2. *Promissory Notes*: A promissory note is an instrument that contains a promise by the maker to pay a certain sum of money to another party at a specific time or on demand.

D. Transfer of Negotiable Instruments

A negotiable instrument may be transferred by assignment or by negotiation.

1. *Assignment*: An assignment is a transfer of contract rights. Assignments are governed by contract law (see Chapter 21, Section G). Because the assignee stands in the shoes of the assignor, the assignee is subject to the same defenses as those to which the assignor is subject. Thus one of the main advantages of a negotiable instrument is lost when it is merely assigned.

2. *Negotiation*: Negotiation is the transfer of an instrument in such form that the transferee becomes a holder [see Section B-6-c(5)]. Negotiation may occur in two ways.

    a. *Negotiation by delivery*: If the negotiable instrument is payable to the bearer, it is negotiated by delivery.

        EXAMPLE: Dick signed a check reading, "Pay to the order of cash, $100." He delivered the check to Mary. The act of delivery constituted negotiation. Mary became the holder.

    b. *Negotiation by indorsement and delivery*: If the negotiable instrument is payable to the order of a party, the instrument is negotiated when the named party indorses it and delivers it to a holder.

        EXAMPLE: Dick signed a check reading, "Pay to the order of Mary Johnson, $100." Mary took the check to the bank, indorsed it by signing her name on the back, and received the $100. The bank became the holder.

        (1) *Blank indorsement*: A blank indorsement is one that does not specify an indorsee. An instrument that is payable to the order of a payee becomes payable to the bearer once the payee indorses it in blank.

             EXAMPLE: Mary signed a check that read, "Pay to the order of Debbie Black, $20." Debbie indorsed the check in blank by signing the back of it. The check became payable to the bearer when she indorsed it in blank.

        (2) *Special indorsement*: A special indorsement is one that names the party to whom the indorser makes the instrument payable.

EXAMPLE: Ellen signed a check that read, "Pay to the order of Peter Jones, $40." Peter specially indorsed the check by writing on the back, "Pay to the order of Glen Hall. (Signed) Peter Jones."

A party who receives a negotiable instrument indorsed in blank may make it a specially indorsed instrument by writing over the signature of the blank indorser.

EXAMPLE: Ed Green received a check that had been made payable to Joe Lane. Joe Lane had indorsed the check in blank by signing his name on the back. Ed may write over Joe's signature, "Pay to Ed Green." Ed has made the check into one that is specially indorsed.

    (3) *Indorsement without recourse*: An indorsement without recourse is one in which the indorser disclaims liability in the event that the maker or drawer fails to pay.

EXAMPLE: Tim manages several apartments for Mike. A tenant gave Tim a check for rent. The check was made payable to the order of Tim. Instead of merely indorsing the check, Tim writes "without recourse" above his signature. This ensures that Tim will not be held liable in the event that the check is not paid.

    (4) *Restrictive indorsement*: A restrictive indorsement is one that requires the indorsee to follow certain instructions.

EXAMPLE: Ann signed a check payable to the order of Brenda. Brenda indorsed the check on the back by writing, "Pay to Clara, provided that she graduates from college by May 30, 1995." Brenda signed beneath the statement. Clara or any subsequent holder cannot collect payment until the condition is met. (Brenda could not put such a condition in a check on which she is the drawer without making the check nonnegotiable, but she is permitted to indorse a check conditionally.)

E. Defenses

There are two main categories of defenses: personal defenses and real defenses. Real defenses are specified by the UCC. Any defense not so specified is a personal defense.

  1. *Real Defenses*: Real defenses are valid against all holders, including holders in due course. Real defenses are sometimes referred to as universal defenses.

    a. *Forgery*:

      (1) One whose signature is forged on a negotiable instrument may use forgery as a defense even against a holder in due course.

      (2) If an agent has signed a negotiable instrument on behalf of a principal, the principal may assert the signer's lack of *any* authority as a defense even against a holder in due course.

    b. *Fraud in the execution (real fraud)*: [See Chapter 21, Section B-2-b(3).]

EXAMPLE: Burt, a movie star, is asked by a fan to autograph a picture. Later the fan lifts the picture off the promissory note that it was covering. Burt's signature appears on the note. Since Burt was deceived as to what he was signing, he has a valid defense even against a holder in due course.

c. *Material alteration*: A material alteration of the instrument is a real defense. A material alteration is one that changes the amount, the interest, the date, the signature, or the parties. If an alteration is material, it is a defense against any ordinary holder. A holder in due course may enforce the instrument as originally drawn or written.

EXAMPLE: Roy raises an $80 check to $800. Mary, a holder in due course, acquires the check. The drawer has a real defense to the raised amount, but Mary can enforce the check to the original amount, $80.

d. A *discharge in bankruptcy*: Federal bankruptcy prevails over the interest of a holder in due course. If the debt is discharged in bankruptcy court, the holder has no right to payment.

e. *Illegality that renders an instrument void*: If the instrument is merely voidable, it provides only a personal defense (see Section E-1-c).

f. *Mental incompetence*: A person who has actually been found by a court to be mentally incompetent cannot issue a negotiable instrument that is enforceable against him or her. Such a person has a real defense. If at the time the instrument is signed the person has not yet been adjudged by a court to be mentally incompetent, the instrument is merely voidable and provides only a personal defense.

g. *Threat*: If a signature was obtained by the threat of force or immediate violence, the instrument is void. This type of extreme duress provides a real defense.

h. *Minority*: Minority is a real defense to the same extent that it is a defense to the enforcement of a simple contract.

2. *Personal Defenses*: Personal defenses are valid only against an ordinary holder. Personal defenses will not allow a party to avoid paying a holder in due course [see Section B-6-c(6)]. Personal defenses include the following:

a. *Breach of contract*: Negotiable instruments are usually issued as a result of a contract between two parties. If a third party gives value for that negotiable instrument and takes it without any knowledge of the breach, the third party is free from the defense of breach of contract.

EXAMPLE: Leon contracted to purchase four copy machines from True-Copy, Inc. Under the agreement Leon gave True-Copy a promissory note for $4,000 payable in two months. True-Copy sold the note to XYZ, Inc. for $3,600. When the note became due, XYZ presented it for payment. Leon claimed that because he only received three machines, he was not obligated for the full amount of the note. XYZ is free of Leon's personal defense because XYZ qualifies as a holder in due course provided that it had no knowledge of any breach at the time it acquired the note for value.

b. *Fraud in the inducement (personal fraud)*: A party who issues a negotiable instrument based on a fraudulent representation [see Chapter 21, Section B-2-b(3) (a)] cannot use fraud as a defense against a holder in due course.

EXAMPLE: Based on Lloyd's representation that a certain rock had been brought from the moon to earth by astronauts, Jake agreed to purchase the *rock for $5,000. Jake issued a promissory note to Lloyd in that amount. Later Jake learned that Lloyd had misrepresented the rock's origin and that in fact Lloyd had found the rock in his yard. Although Jake would have a valid defense against Lloyd or an ordinary holder, if Lloyd has transferred the note to a holder in due course, Jake must pay the note. (Jake could still sue Lloyd for breach of contract.)*

c. *Duress and undue influence*: These are considered personal defenses as long as the abuse involved did not become so outrageous that the issuer of the instrument lost his or her will as a result of threats of physical harm.

EXAMPLE: Mike threatens to organize all of the local hardware-store owners and obtain their promise never to buy from ABC Manufacturing, Inc., unless ABC issues a note to him for $10,000 for his services as a consultant. When ABC issues the note to Mike, he quickly sells it to Irv for $9,450. Irv had no knowledge of any threat. ABC cannot assert the defense of duress against Irv, who is a holder in due course.

d. *Mental incapacity*: This is not a valid defense against a holder in due course unless the incapacity is so extreme that the instrument is void rather than merely voidable.

e. *Payment of the instrument*: Upon paying the amount of the negotiable instrument, the maker should obtain the return of the instrument or at least have it marked *canceled*. If such a precaution is not taken, the instrument may come into the possession of a holder in due course against whom payment would not be a valid defense.

f. *Writing without authority*: The defense that someone acted without authority and completed an incomplete instrument is a personal defense.

EXAMPLE: Lucy asked Georgia to go to the grocery store for her and purchase the items on a grocery list. Lucy gave Georgia a check that she had signed. The check was left blank as to the payee and the amount. Georgia wrote her name in as the payee and wrote in $200 as the amount. Georgia then indorsed the check and delivered it to a holder in due course. The unauthorized completion would constitute a valid defense against Georgia or an ordinary holder but not against a holder in due course.

Review Questions

DIRECTIONS: Select the best answer from the four alternatives. Write the letter of your answer in the blank to the left of the number.

_____

1. Wes contracted to deliver his motorcycle to Ed in return for Ed's promise to paint Wes's house. Ed assigned his rights in the contract to Ted. When Ted sued Wes to obtain the motorcycle, Wes defended on the grounds that Ed had not painted the house. Is Wes permitted to assert the defense against Ted?

   a. Yes, because Ted is subject to the same defenses to which Ed would be subject.
   b. Only if Ted knew that Ed had not completed painting the house at the time Ted took the assignment.
   c. No, because the contract was a negotiable instrument.
   d. None of the above.

_____

2. Mel owed a disputed debt to the Acme Farm Implement Company. Angry and frustrated at his inability to resolve the dispute, Mel carved a check on a pumpkin and delivered it to Acme. Does the pumpkin qualify as a negotiable instrument?

   a. No, the UCC requires the writing to be on paper.
   b. No, pumpkins are among the items specifically excluded by the UCC as media for negotiable instruments.
   c. Yes, if all the elements of negotiability are met.
   d. Yes, because pumpkins are goods under the UCC.

_____

3. Alex wrote on a slip of paper, "Barb, I owe you $55. (Signed) Alex." Is this a negotiable instrument?

   a. Yes, because all requirements of the UCC are met.
   b. No, because the signature was not notarized.
   c. No, because the promise was conditional.
   d. No, because the writing does not contain a promise to pay.

_____

4. Jack wrote, "I promise to pay Wayne $150 if Wayne delivers his 13-inch color television set to my home by May 1. (Signed) Jack." Is this writing a negotiable instrument?

   a. Yes, because all requirements of the UCC are met.
   b. No, because the sum of money is not certain.
   c. No, because the promise to pay is conditional.
   d. No, because it is not payable to the bearer.

423

5. Luke wrote a check payable to the order of Sandra. The check is drawn on the First National Bank. Which of the following is true?

a. Luke is the drawer, Sandra the drawee, and the bank the payee.
b. Luke is the drawer, Sandra the payee, and the bank the drawee.
c. Luke is the maker, Sandra the holder, and the bank the indorsee.
d. Luke is the maker, Sandra the indorsee, and the bank the drawee.

6. William contracted to purchase a new oven for his restaurant from the Universal Supply Company. Under the terms of the agreement, William gave Universal a promissory note for $6,000 payable in three months. Universal negotiated the note to Max in return for $5,200. When the note became due, Max presented it for payment. William claimed that the oven Universal had delivered did not comply with the contract. Is Max subject to William's defense?

a. No.
b. No, provided that Max had no knowledge of any breach of the contract at the time he purchased the note.
c. Yes, because breach of contract is a real defense.
d. Yes, because a promissory note is not a negotiable instrument.

7. Which of the following is a real defense?

a. Fraud in the inducement
b. Payment on the instrument
c. Forgery
d. Breach of contract

8. An important difference between a real defense and a personal defense is that

a. a personal defense can be asserted against a holder in due course, but a real defense cannot.
b. a real defense can be asserted against a holder in due course, but a personal defense cannot.
c. a personal defense requires two witnesses, but a real defense requires only one.
d. none of the above.

9. Susan signed a check made payable to the order of Pamela. Pamela indorsed the check by writing on the back of it, "Pay to Louise provided that she registers to vote by October 1, 1995." Pamela signed her name below the statement. Pamela has made a/an

a. restrictive indorsement.
b. indorsement without recourse.
c. assignment.
d. forgery.

10. Which of the following would not constitute a material alteration of a negotiable instrument?

    a. A change in the amount of money listed
    b. A change in the stated rate of interest
    c. A change in the date
    d. A change in the stated address of the maker for the purpose of correcting it

11. Hugh is a holder in due course of a note made by Chet. When Hugh demanded payment on the note, Chet claimed that he had already paid the full amount to Greg, the previous holder. Which of the following statements is true?

    a. Chet may assert the defense against Hugh because payment is a real defense.
    b. Chet will succeed with the defense if he can prove that he actually paid the full amount to Greg.
    c. Both (a) and (b) are true.
    d. Hugh is not subject to the defense of payment.

12. Assume that in the preceding situation Hugh sued Chet on the note. Before the case came to trial, however, Chet obtained a discharge of the debt in federal bankruptcy court. Which of the following statements is true regarding Hugh's right to collect on the note?

    a. Hugh can collect only if he proves that he obtained the note prior to Chet's filing for bankruptcy.
    b. Hugh can recover only if he proves that he obtained the note prior to the date on which Chet obtained the discharge in bankruptcy.
    c. Hugh can recover regardless of the timing of the bankruptcy.
    d. None of the above.

13. A material alteration of a negotiable instrument provides a defense against

    a. any holder (ordinary holders and holders in due course).
    b. only ordinary holders.
    c. ordinary holders and holders in due course if the alteration is apparent.
    d. none of the above.

14. Lenny, a delivery person for a flower shop, delivered flowers to Jim. Lenny showed Jim a receipt and asked him to sign on a certain line. While Jim went to get a pen, Lenny substituted a promissory note for the receipt. Thinking he was signing the same document he had just examined, Jim signed the note. Lenny negotiated the note to Howard, a holder in due course. When Howard demanded payment, Jim asserted the defense of fraud. May Jim's defense be used against a holder in due course?

    a. No, because fraud is a personal defense.
    b. Yes, because Lenny's conduct amounts to fraud in the execution.

c. No, because Lenny's conduct amounts to fraud in the inducement.
d. Yes, because Lenny's conduct amounts to duress.

Use this information in answering Questions 15 and 16.

William had several fake diamonds that he attempted to sell as real diamonds. On May 1 he sold one of these to Rita in return for a promissory note in the amount of $200. Also on May 1 he sold one to Mark in return for a promissory note in the amount of $250. On May 2 William transferred Rita's note to Wanda in return for $175. Wanda had no knowledge of any misrepresentation. On May 8 William transferred Mark's note to Barry in return for $20. Barry knew at the time of this transfer that Mark planned to sue William for misrepresentation concerning the "diamond" sale.

15. When Rita's note became due, Wanda sued Rita to collect the $200. Which is the correct result?

a. Rita can use the defense of misrepresentation against Wanda.
b. Rita will win because a promissory note is nontransferable.
c. Wanda will win if she can prove that the misrepresentation was fraud in the execution.
d. Wanda will win because she is a holder in due course.

16. When Mark's note became due, Barry sued to collect the $250. Which is the correct result?

a. Mark can use the defense of misrepresentation against Barry.
b. Barry can collect $20 from Mark, but not the full amount of the note.
c. Barry will win because he is a holder in due course.
d. Barry will win because misrepresentation is no defense in a suit based on a promissory note.

Use this information in answering Questions 17 and 18.

Adam is a holder in due course of a promissory note purportedly signed by Bruce. When Adam sued to collect on the note, Bruce claimed that the signature was forged.

17. Which of the following is a correct statement?

a. Bruce can assert the defense of forgery against Adam.
b. Bruce cannot assert the defense of forgery against Adam.

    c. As a holder in due course, Adam can collect on the note only from the party who negotiated the note to him.

    d. As a holder in due course, Adam cannot collect on the promissory note.

18. Assume that Bruce, instead of claiming forgery, claims that the note was altered after he signed it. Which of the following is correct?

    a. Any alteration will be a defense against Adam.

    b. Any material alteration will be a defense against Adam.

    c. Any apparent alteration will be a defense against Adam.

    d. Only apparent and material alterations will be a defense against Adam.

Use this information in answering Questions 19 and 20.

Helen signed a draft that read, "Pay to the order of Wayne, $100." She delivered the draft to Wayne.

19. To negotiate the draft, Wayne must

    a. indorse it.

    b. deliver it.

    c. indorse and deliver it.

    d. Wayne cannot indorse the draft since it is payable to him.

20. Assume that Helen signed a draft which read, "Pay to bearer, $100." She delivered it to Wayne. To negotiate the draft, Wayne must

    a. indorse it.

    b. deliver it.

    c. indorse and deliver it.

    d. Wayne cannot negotiate the draft because it is payable to the bearer.

Solutions

Answer	Refer to:
1. (a)	[D-1] Ted is merely an assignee. As such he stands in the shoes of Ed, the assignor. Since Ed would be subject to Wes's defense, Ted is also subject to that defense. The contract did not qualify as a negotiable instrument. Among other things, the contract did not contain an unconditional promise to pay a certain sum of money.
2. (c)	[B-1] The Uniform Commercial Code requires only that the writing be in tangible form. Since a carving on a pumpkin is tangible, this requirement is met.
3. (d)	[B-3-a] Alex's writing merely acknowledges a debt. It does not contain an express promise to pay the money. There is no requirement that the signature be notarized.
4. (c)	[B-3-c(1)] Jack's promise is conditioned on Wayne's delivery of the television set. The writing does not, therefore, qualify as a negotiable instrument.
5. (b)	[B-6-c] As the issuer of the check, Luke is the drawer. As the party that is ordered to pay the money, the bank is the drawee. Sandra, the party to whom the check is payable, is the payee.
6. (b)	[E-1-a] If Max had no knowledge of the alleged breach, he qualifies as a holder in due course and therefore takes free of William's defense.
7. (c)	[E-2-a] Forgery is a real defense. All of the others listed are personal defenses, which cannot be asserted successfully against a holder in due course.
8. (b)	[E-1] Only real defenses can be asserted successfully against a holder in due course.
9. (a)	[D-2-b(4)] Pamela has made a restrictive indorsement. Louise, the indorsee, must perform the stated act in order to collect payment on the check. If Pamela had been the drawer of the check, she could not include such a condition without making the check nonnegotiable. As the payee, however, Pamela may make such an indorsement.
10. (d)	(E-2) Answers (a), (b), and (c) relate to important aspects of the instrument that affect the amount due or the date the money is payable. A correction of the address of the maker, however, does not change the nature of the obligation.

11. (d) [E-1-f] Payment is a personal defense. Because Hugh is a holder in due course, he is not subject to such a defense. Chet should have insisted that Greg return the note to him when he paid Greg. At least Chet should have had the note marked canceled.

12. (d) [E-1-d] A discharge in bankruptcy is a real defense. It therefore applies even against a holder in due course.

13. (c) [E-1-c] A material alteration provides a valid defense against all ordinary holders. In addition, it provides a defense against a holder in due course if the alteration is an obvious one.

14. (b) [E-1-b] Since Lenny actually deceived Jim into signing something other than what he thought he was signing, fraud in the execution occurred. Unlike fraud in the inducement, fraud in the execution is a real defense. It is therefore valid even against a holder in due course.

15. (d) [E-2-b] Since Wanda gave value for the instrument and took it in good faith without knowledge of any defenses, she is a holder in due course who takes free of the personal defense of fraud in the inducement.

16. (a) [E-2-b] Since Barry did not take the instrument in good faith without knowledge of the defense, he is not a holder in due course. He is therefore subject to the defense of fraud in the inducement.

17. (a) [E-1-a] Forgery is a real defense that may be asserted even against a holder in due course.

18. (d) [E-1-c] Since Adam is a holder in due course, he takes free from even a claim of material alteration unless the alteration is an apparent one.

19. (c) [D-2-b] Because this instrument is payable to Wayne, he must both indorse and deliver it in order to negotiate the instrument.

20. (b) [D-2-a] Since this negotiable instrument is payable to the bearer, it is negotiated by mere delivery.

CHAPTER 23

Agency

OVERVIEW

Agents make it possible for a party to expand its business dealings. Corporations could not act without agents, and partnerships would be greatly impaired by such a limitation. Without agents, an individual party could transact business only in person. Yet with the advantages of agency come complications. What is the relationship between the principal and agent? What is the nature of the relationship between the agent and third parties with whom the agent deals on behalf of the principal? Moreover, when does an agency relationship exist, and how is it terminated? The answers to these questions are to be found in the law of agency. In this chapter we present the major rules of agency law.

In studying agency, the candidate should become aware of the different types of authority that an agent may possess. The candidate should know the types of agency relationships and the legal consequences of each. The details of agency law are better understood when viewed in the context of the agency relationship itself and the purposes it is designed to achieve. Accordingly, this chapter begins with a look at the creation of the agency relationship.

KEY TERMS

Agency
Agent
Apparent authority
Authority
Conflict of interest
Disclosed principal
Emergency authority
Employee
Express authority
Fraud

General agent
Implied authority
Independent contractor
Negligent conduct
Partially disclosed principal
Power of attorney
Principal
Special agent
Third party
Undisclosed principal

A. Creation
An agency relationship exists when it is agreed among parties that one will act for and on behalf of the other. The party acting on behalf of the other is known as the *agent*. The one on whose behalf the agent is acting is known as the *principal*.

1. *Consideration Not Required*: Consideration is not required for the creation of an agency.

   EXAMPLE: Frank says to Bruno, "Do me a favor and take my wagon to town and sell it for the highest price that you can negotiate." Bruno agrees. There is a valid agency relationship. No consideration is required.

2. *No General Requirement for Writing*: Only certain agency agreements must be in writing.

   a. *Agency agreements not in writing*: Unless the contract the agent is authorized to enter on behalf of the principal is legally required to be in writing or a specific state statute requires that the agency agreement be in writing, the agency agreement need not be in writing.

      EXAMPLE: Patricia hires Alice to work as Patricia's agent for purposes of selling suntan oil at the local beach. The agreement is subject to the general rule that agency agreements need not be in writing.

   b. *Agency agreements that must be in writing*: If the contract which an agent is authorized to enter on behalf of the principal is legally required to be in writing, then the agency agreement itself must be in writing.

      (1) *General statutes*: The statute of frauds and the Uniform Commercial Code dictate which contracts must be in writing (see Chapter 21).

         EXAMPLES:

         Al agrees to act as Paul's agent for the purpose of selling Paul's house. The agreement must be in writing. Because a contract for the sale of land must be in writing, an agreement authorizing an agency to buy or sell land must also be in writing.

         Paul authorizes Al to sell Paul's car for $1,000. The agency agreement must be in writing. A contract for the sale of goods for $500 or more must be in writing. Therefore, an agreement authorizing an agent to sell such goods must be in writing.

         Paul authorizes Al to hire a sales representative for Al's company to serve for a three-year period. The agency agreement between Paul and Al must be in writing because the contract that Al is authorized to enter on behalf of Paul cannot be completed within one year and therefore must be in writing.

      (2) *Special statutes*: Other specific state statutes may require that certain kinds of agency agreements be in writing. For example, the law in most states requires that powers of attorney, whereby one party is formally authorized to represent another in certain matters, be in writing.

3. *Capacity of Principal*: A principal can only accomplish through an agency those things that the principal personally has capacity to do. A corporation or a partnership may serve as a principal. It is the capacity of the principal, not that of the

agent, that affects the contracts entered by the agent on behalf of the principal. (For a review of capacity, see Chapter 21).

EXAMPLE: John, who is 16 years old, hired Bob, a 25-year-old, to act as John's agent for the purpose of purchasing an antique vase. Because John, the principal, is a minor, the contract Bob enters on John's behalf can be disaffirmed by John (see Chapter 21).

4. *Capacity of Agent*: Any party capable of understanding the nature of the task to be performed may serve as an agent. A corporation or a partnership may serve as an agent. Even though the agent may lack contractual capacity because of minority or mental incapacity, the agent can nevertheless enter into a binding contract on behalf of the principal.

EXAMPLE: Bonnie, an adult, hires Angie, a minor, to serve as Bonnie's agent for the purpose of purchasing certain stereo equipment. The contract that Angie enters on Bonnie's behalf is not voidable. It is Bonnie's capacity as the principal that is relevant (see Section A-3).

B. Types of Agencies

There are three basic types of agencies. Under some circumstances, the type of agency affects the rights and liabilities of the parties. It is therefore important to be able to recognize the various types.

1. *Disclosed Principal*: If the identity of the principal is known to the third party with whom the agent deals, the agency is one with a *disclosed principal*.

EXAMPLE: Ann acts as Peter's agent in dealing with Thomas. Thomas knows Peter's identity and knows that Ann is acting as Peter's agent. Peter is a disclosed principal.

2. *Partially Disclosed Principal*: If only the existence of the principal is known to the third party with whom the agent deals, the agency is one with a *partially disclosed principal*. The third party knows there is a principal but does not know who it is.

EXAMPLE: Ann acts as Peter's agent in dealing with Thomas. Thomas knows that Ann is acting on behalf of a principal but does not know who the principal is. Peter is a partially disclosed principal.

3. *Undisclosed Principal*: If the third party is unaware that the agent is representing anyone, the agency is one with an undisclosed principal.

EXAMPLE: Ann acts as Peter's agent in dealing with Thomas. Thomas thinks that Ann is acting on Ann's own behalf. Peter is an undisclosed principal.

C. Types of Employment

The law recognizes various types of employment: general agent, special agent, independent contractor, and employee.

1. *General Agent*: A general agent is authorized to represent the principal in a number of transactions over a period of time.

EXAMPLE: The Brown Company, a shoe manufacturer, hires Tony to serve as its agent for the purpose of selling shoes to retail stores in a three-state area for a period of one year. Tony is a general agent.

2. *Special Agent*: A special agent is authorized to perform a single task or to achieve a single goal.

EXAMPLE: Esther hires Sarah to serve as Esther's agent for the purpose of selling Esther's boat. Sarah is a special agent.

3. *Independent Contractor*: An individual who is retained by the principal to achieve desired results and who has substantial freedom in the manner used to accomplish these goals is an *independent contractor*. The principal does not have the right to control the physical conduct of the independent contractor.

EXAMPLE: George hires Brenda, a lawyer, to represent him in a lawsuit that is going to trial. Because the lawyer is expected to use her own skills and judgment in trying a case, Brenda is an independent contractor.

4. *Employee*: An employed person without legal authority to bind the employer is simply called an *employee*.

EXAMPLES: Bookkeeper, salesclerk, receptionist, or secretary.

D. Types of Authority

An agent may possess four types of authority: express authority, implied authority, emergency authority, and apparent authority.

1. *Express Authority*: A principal's written or oral instructions to an agent constitute express authority.

2. *Implied Authority*: An agent may have implied authority to do those things that are reasonably necessary to exercise the express authority of an agent and to achieve the objectives of the agency. Although authority to do such things is not expressly stated, the agent reasonably believes that the principal intended the agent to have such authority.

EXAMPLE: The Chemex Company hires Jack as its agent for purposes of selling the company's new industrial-strength cleaning fluid. Jack's contract states that he has authority to sell the product to factories in a three-state area at a stated price. To accomplish the objective of the agency, Jack mails letters to hundreds of factories in the stated area, phones the factories, and makes trips to visit interested factories to demonstrate the product. Jack makes a number of sales at the established price. Jack has express authority to make the sales. He has implied authority to mail letters, phone potential customers, and make personal visits for the purpose of promoting sales.

3. *Emergency Authority*: A type of implied authority, emergency authority, exists during a sudden, unexpected happening or unforeseen combination of circumstances that requires immediate action. Emergency authority permits an agent to take reasonably necessary steps to carry out tasks that are within the scope of the agent's actual authority.

EXAMPLE: Vince was employed as a sales agent for ACE Copy Machines, Inc. He was scheduled to make a critical sales presentation to WorldWide Communicators, Inc. at 8:00 A.M. World Wide was an extremely important potential client. Vince injured his back while getting out of bed on the morning of the presentation. Because of the injury, he was unable to lift the copy machine that was an essential part of the sales presentation. Vince hired Arnold, the only available person, to carry the machine for him to WorldWide's office. Vince had emergency authority to obtain assistance.

4. *Apparent Authority*: Apparent authority stems from the circumstances that the principal allows to exist. If, based on these circumstances, a third party who deals with the agent reasonably believes that the agent has certain authority, the law permits the third party to rely on that reasonable belief. In other words, the law allows the third party to rely on the appearance of things, even though there may not be express or implied authority on the part of the agent. The authority that derives not from the words or intentions of the principal, but from the circumstances the principal allows to exist, is known as apparent authority.

EXAMPLE: Mike owns a furniture store. He hires Joe to work as a janitor. One day Mike has to make a short trip to the local bank to make a deposit. Instead of closing the store, Mike simply asks Joe to watch the store and tell any customers who enter that Mike will return within a half hour. Freda enters the store for the first time. She sees Joe standing behind the cash register. Assuming that Joe is a salesclerk, she asks him how much a certain chair costs. Joe responds by stating that the chair is on sale for $100. In fact, the chair is priced at $300. Freda purchases the chair and takes it home. Upon discovering what happened, Mike seeks to recover the chair or the $200 difference between the actual price and what Freda paid. Mike will not succeed. Joe had apparent authority. Mike knowingly allowed the circumstances to exist under which Freda could reasonably believe that Joe had authority to sell the chair.

E. Obligations of Agent to Principal

The agent owes the highest duty of loyalty to the principal.

1. *Duty to Act within Authority*: The agent has a duty to act within his or her actual authority, that is, not to exceed power to the detriment of the principal.

   EXAMPLE: Sharon leaves her bicycle with Lisa. Sharon tells Lisa, "Rent my bicycle if you can to someone for $3 per day, but do not sell it." Lisa sells the bicycle to Clyde. Lisa has breached her duty to Sharon by not acting within her actual authority. Lisa is liable to Sharon for the value of the bicycle.

2. *Duty to Perform*: The agent has a duty to personally perform the duties undertaken in the agency agreement. The law permits the agent to delegate his or her duties only in certain limited circumstances.

   a. *Delegation of performance*: If the task is extremely simple, requiring no skill or expertise, it may be delegated.

   b. *Customary delegation*: If it is customary for such tasks to be delegated, the agent may delegate unless the agent has specifically agreed to perform personally.

3. *Duty to Exercise Care and Skill*: The agent has a duty to exercise reasonable care and skill in performing services for the principal. The agent is liable for any damages that failure to exercise reasonable care and skill causes the principal to suffer.

   EXAMPLE: Tom hires Warren to serve as his agent for the purpose of purchasing milking cows to be used on Tom's dairy farm. Warren is an experienced purchaser of milking cows. Warren nevertheless fails to inspect a dozen cows that he pur-

chases on Tom's behalf. The cows are obviously diseased and unfit for use as milking cows. Warren has breached his duty of exercising reasonable care and skill in serving as Tom's agent. Warren is liable to Tom for the damage his breach of duty caused.

4. *Duty to Account to Principal*: The agent has a duty to account to the principal for all money or other property that the agent has handled on behalf of the principal.

5. *Duty Not to Commingle Property*: The agent has a duty not to commingle personal funds or other property with that of the principal.

    EXAMPLE: Bill serves as Walter's agent for purposes of renting apartments owned by Walter. Bill receives security deposits from tenants and places the money in his personal bank account along with his personal funds. Bill has breached his duty to Walter because Bill did not keep his principal's funds separate from his own.

6. *Duty to Inform Principal*: The agent has a duty to inform the principal of relevant information that comes to the attention of the agent.

    EXAMPLE: Wendy is employed as a sales agent by Modern Fashions, Inc., a corporation that manufactures and sells clothing. She discovers that Mirror Image, Inc., a competitor of Modern Fashions, has manufactured a line of clothing practically identical to Modern Fashions' latest line. Wendy is obligated to pass this information on to her employer.

7. *Duty to Avoid Conflicts of Interest*: The agent has a duty to avoid conflicts of interest.

    a. *Competition with principal*: The agent must not compete against the principal or work for a competitor of the principal.

    b. *Conflict of interest*: If a conflict of interest does develop, the agent must promptly inform the principal of the conflict. Only if the principal, with full knowledge of the conflict, consents to the agent's continued service can the agent maintain this position.

        EXAMPLE: Bob works as a purchasing agent for Ajax Used Auto Parts, Inc., a corporation that buys used auto parts. Bob takes a part-time job as a purchasing agent for Baxter, Inc., a competitor of Ajax. Bob has breached his duty to Ajax because he has undertaken a job that conflicts with his duty of loyalty to Ajax. Only if Bob fully discloses the conflict to Ajax and obtains Ajax's approval can he continue to work for Baxter.

    c. *Seizing principal's opportunity*: The agent must not seize the principal's opportunity.

        EXAMPLE: Alice serves as a sales representative for Lowell Industries, a rapidly growing company that is looking for an attractive site for a new corporate headquarters. In the course of her work for Lowell Industries, Alice has a conversation with Rick, who informs her of the availability of an ideal site for such a building. Alice acts to buy the land for herself. She has breached the duty of loyalty to her principal by taking advantage of the principal's opportunity.

d.   *Divulging confidential information of principal*: The agent must not divulge confidential information of the principal.

> *EXAMPLE: Jane is employed as a paralegal by Shirley, who is a lawyer. Jane releases information from a confidential file to Mary, who is suing one of Shirley's clients. Jane divulged the information in the hope of obtaining a higher-paying job with Mary. Jane has breached her duty of loyalty to Shirley.*

8.   *Duty to Make No Secret Profit*: The agent has a duty not to make a secret profit. Any money or other property obtained by the agent must be reported to the principal.

> *EXAMPLE: Andrew serves as a purchasing agent for Rainbow Industries, Inc., a company that purchases 20 new cars each year for use by company executives. Andrew received a secret payment of $10,000 in return for purchasing 20 cars from Smiley Motors, a local car dealer, on behalf of the company. Andrew has breached his duty of loyalty to Rainbow by receiving this secret profit.*

F.   Obligations of Agent to Third Party

The obligation of an agent to a third party often depends on the type of agency involved (see Sections B-1, B-2, and B-3).

1.   *Contract on Behalf of Disclosed Principal*: An agent who enters a contract on behalf of a disclosed principal incurs no liability on the contract.

> *EXAMPLE: Alan, acting within his actual authority, enters a contract with Tom, who knows that Alan is acting merely as Paul's agent. Alan is not personally liable on the contract. If Paul breaches the contract, Tom can recover damages from Paul only.*

2.   *Contract on Behalf of Partially Disclosed Principal*: An agent who enters a contract on behalf of a partially disclosed principal can be held liable to the third party.

> *EXAMPLE: Amy, acting within her actual authority, enters a contract with Theresa, who knows that Amy is acting as an agent but does not know the identity of Amy's principal, Phyllis. If the contract is breached, Theresa can recover damages from Amy. Because Theresa did not know of Phyllis's identity, she relied on Amy's background and reputation in contracting with Amy. Thus, Theresa is allowed to hold Amy responsible in the event the contract is breached.*

Note: If the third party determines the identity of the principal, that party may enforce or pursue either the principal or the agent.

3.   *Contract on Behalf of Undisclosed Principal*: An agent who enters a contract on behalf of an undisclosed principal can be held liable to the third party.

If the third party suffers a loss as a result of the agent's fraud, deceit, or negligent conduct, the agent is liable and the third party may recover such loss.

> *EXAMPLE: Alex, acting within his actual authority, enters a contract with Terry, who does not know that Alex is acting as an agent for Paulette. Terry reasonably believes that Alex is acting on Alex's own behalf. If the contract is breached, Terry can recover damages from Alex. Because Terry reasonably believed that Alex was acting for himself, Terry relied on Alex's background and reputation in contracting with Alex. Terry is, therefore, allowed to hold Alex responsible in the event the contract is breached.*

G. Obligations of Principal to Agent

The principal's duties to the agent may be divided into four categories: duty to compensate, duty to honor contract terms, duty to reimburse expenses, and duty to indemnify.

1. *Duty to Compensate*: Unless it is agreed that the agent will serve without being compensated for services (a gratuitous agent), the principal is obligated to pay the agent for the services rendered.

2. *Duty to Honor Contract Terms*: In addition to the duty to compensate the agent in the absence of a contrary agreement, a principal who has contracted with an agent must abide by the terms of the contract.

   EXAMPLE: Arnold agreed to serve as Paul's agent for the purpose of selling Paul's race horse, Molasses. When Arnold attempted to show the horse to a prospective buyer, Paul would not give Arnold the keys to the stable. When Arnold attempted to make other arrangements to show the horse, Paul refused. Paul has breached his implied promise not to interfere unreasonably with Arnold's efforts to sell the horse.

3. *Duty to Reimburse Expenses*: The principal is obligated to reimburse the agent for authorized expenditures the agent has made.

   EXAMPLE: Pam hires Ann to serve as her agent in managing Pam's clothing store. To prevent the electricity from being turned off while Pam was vacationing in Europe, Ann paid the store's electricity bill. Pam is obligated to reimburse Ann for the payment.

4. *Duty to Indemnify*: The principal is obligated to indemnify the agent for losses suffered by the agent in the course of the agent's duties.

   EXAMPLE: Peter hires Andy to serve as his agent for the purpose of purchasing a yacht from Tom. Peter directs Andy to make no mention of the agency relationship and to act as if Andy is purchasing the boat for himself. Andy follows these instructions and enters into a contract with Tom for the purchase of the yacht on the terms that Peter had indicated he would find acceptable. Peter forwards the down payment to Andy. After Peter takes possession of the boat, however, he fails to make any further payments. Tom sues Andy and wins a judgment, which Andy pays. Andy is entitled to reimbursement from Peter.

H. Obligations of Principal to Third Parties

The principal's liability to third parties may result from contracts entered into by an agent on the principal's behalf or from injuries caused by the agent's conduct within the scope of the agent's employment.

1. *Principal's Duty to Perform Contract*: The principal has a duty to perform on contracts entered into on the principal's behalf by an agent who acted with authority.

   a. *Authorized acts of agent*: The principal is bound by the authorized acts of his or her agent whether the principal is disclosed, partially disclosed, or undisclosed (see Section B in this chapter).

   (1) Even though the third party did not know the identity of a partially disclosed principal, the party may nevertheless hold the principal liable on contracts entered on behalf of the principal by an authorized agent.

(2)   Even though the third party did not know of the existence of a principal at the time of entering into the contract, the party may, upon learning of the principal, hold the principal liable.

EXAMPLE: Alex acted as Patrick's agent in dealing with Terrence. Terrence thought that Alex was acting on Alex's own behalf. Terrence entered into a contract with Alex. Later, upon learning that Alex was acting on behalf of Patrick, Terrence elects to hold Patrick responsible for performing the contract. Patrick is responsible to Terrence.

b.   *Ratification of agent's acts*: If the agent acted without authority, the principal may still be bound if he or she ratifies the acts of the agent.

(1)   Ratification occurs when the principal adopts the unauthorized acts of the agent.

(2)   Ratification need not be stated in words. If the principal accepts the benefits of the agent's unauthorized acts with the intent of ratifying those acts, the principal has ratified.

(3)   The principal can ratify only if he or she has knowledge of all relevant facts.

EXAMPLE: While serving as Patrick's agent, Alex acted beyond his authority and entered into a contract with Terrence. Upon learning of the unauthorized act and the resulting contract, Patrick accepted the benefits of the contract with the intent of being bound by its terms. Patrick has ratified Alex's unauthorized act.

2.   *Principal's Liability for Injuries to Third Parties*: The principal is liable to third parties for injuries caused by negligent or intentional acts of an employee acting within the scope of employment. This legal doctrine is known as *respondent superior*.

a.   *Injuries by independent contractor*: A principal is not ordinarily liable for injuries caused by an independent contractor (see Section C-3).

b.   *Interests served by employees*: In determining whether an employee is acting within the scope of the employee's authority, courts consider the interest the employee was serving at the time the employee caused the injury.

EXAMPLES:

Ralph employs Jim to travel from store to store in Central City to solicit sales for Ralph's awning business. While driving between stores, Jim negligently injures Mike. Ralph is liable to Mike.

Assume that at the time he negligently injured Mike, Jim had decided to take the rest of the day off and was 20 miles outside Central City on his way to a lake. Ralph, Jim's employer, is not liable to Mike. Jim was serving only his own purpose. He had abandoned his duties to Ralph and was outside the scope of his employment.

I. Obligations of Third Parties to Principals and Agents

Third parties are bound to perform on contracts they enter into with agents.

1. *Contract with Agent for Disclosed Principal*: A third party who contracts with an agent who is acting on behalf of a disclosed principal owes a duty to the principal to perform contractual obligations.

2. *Contract with Agent for Partially Disclosed Principal*: A third party who contracts with an agent acting on behalf of a partially disclosed principal owes a duty to the principal and to the agent to perform contractual obligations.

   EXAMPLE: Tess contracts with Annette, who is acting for Pam, a partially disclosed principal. If Tess fails to perform under the contract, either Annette or Pam may sue Tess for breach of contract.

3. *Contract with Agent for Undisclosed Principal*: A third party who contracts with an agent who is acting on behalf of an undisclosed principal owes a duty of performance to the agent and, in most cases, to the principal.

   a. *Duty of performance to agent*: The third party owes a duty of performance to the agent because he or she contracted with the agent, thinking that the agent was acting on the agent's behalf.

   b. *Duty of performance to undisclosed principal*: The third party owes a duty of performance to the undisclosed principal unless one of the following situations exists:

      (1) If the contract requires the agent to perform contractual duties personally, the undisclosed principal cannot hold the third party liable for breach of contract.

      (2) If the agent lies to the third party by denying that he or she is acting as an agent, the undisclosed principal cannot hold the third party liable for breach of contract.

      (3) If the agent or undisclosed principal knows, or should know, that the third party would not agree to do business with the principal, the undisclosed principal cannot hold the third party liable for breach of contract.

4. *Third-Party Performance on Contract*: Under no circumstances can the third party be required to perform contractual duties twice. Even where both the agent and the principal can hold the third party responsible for performance, once performance is rendered or once damages are paid, the third party is relieved of further obligation.

J. Termination of Agency Relationship

An agency may be terminated in the following ways:

1. *Mutual Agreement*: The principal and agent can terminate the agency by mutual agreement.

2. *Agency Agreement*: The agency agreement itself may provide for termination of the agency.

   a. *Accomplishment of agency purpose*: If the purpose of the agency, as specified in the agreement, is accomplished, the agency terminates.

   b. *Expiration of time*: The agreement may specify that the agency is to last only for a specified time. The agency terminates when that time expires.

3. *Notification of Intent to Terminate Agency*: Either the principal or the agent may terminate the agency by notifying the other party of his or her intent to terminate.

   a. *Limited right to terminate*: While either party has the *power* to terminate the agency, the right to terminate may be limited by the agency agreement.

   b. *Liability for damages*: If a party exercises his or her power to terminate without having the right to terminate, he or she is liable to the other party for any damages the termination caused.

   EXAMPLE: Patricia and Anthony agree that their agency relationship will last for one year. After only two months, Patricia acts to terminate the agency. Patricia is liable for any damages the termination has caused Anthony to suffer.

4. *Death*: The death of either the principal or agent terminates the agency.

5. *Insanity*: The insanity of either the principal or agent terminates the agency.

6. *Impossibility of Performance*: When the objective of the agency becomes impossible to accomplish, the agency is terminated.

   EXAMPLE: Rick agrees to serve as Bob's agent for the purpose of selling Bob's motorcycle. When the motorcycle is destroyed by fire, the agency is terminated.

7. *Illegality of Agency Agreement*: When the agency agreement becomes illegal because of a change in the law, the agency is terminated.

   EXAMPLE: Sam hires Bill to serve as his agent for the purpose of purchasing a certain type of hunting rifle. After Sam and Bill enter into an agency relationship, the legislature of their state enacts a law making the purchase of such a gun illegal. The agency is terminated when the law becomes effective.

8. *Change in Circumstances*: The agency terminates when the agent should know from the change in circumstances that the principal no longer desires the agent to perform under the agency agreement.

   EXAMPLE: Dick agrees to serve as Hal's agent for the purpose of purchasing auto parts for Hal's 1932 Ford automobile. When Dick learns that Hal has sold the car, the agency terminates. Dick should know that Hal no longer desires him to acquire parts for the vehicle.

K. Notification of Termination of Agency Relationship

When the agency is terminated, the principal should notify all parties who had knowledge of the agency. Such notice will eliminate apparent authority. In the absence of such notice, the principal may be bound by an agent acting with apparent authority.

1. *Oral or Written Notice*: Parties who previously dealt with the agent must be notified orally or in writing.

2. *Notice Published in Newspaper*: Other parties can be notified by a notice published in a newspaper of general circulation in the area where the agent was operating.

3. *No Formal Notification Needed*: If the agency was terminated by death, illegality, or insanity, it may not be necessary for the principal to notify others of the termination.

Review Questions

DIRECTIONS: Select the best answer from the four alternatives. Write the letter of your answer in the blank to the left of the number.

1. Wally agrees to offer Ernie's snowblower for sale for $150 at Wally's garage sale. Their agreement is oral. Wally is not entitled to any compensation under the terms of the agreement. Is there an agency relationship between Wally and Ernie?

   a. No, because the agreement is not in writing.
   b. No, because there was no consideration.
   c. Both (a) and (b) are correct.
   d. Yes, there is an agency relationship.

2. Connie, a 16-year-old, hired Ann, a 22-year-old, to act as Connie's agent for the purpose of purchasing some fishing equipment. Ann contracted to purchase the designated equipment as Connie's agent. Connie, however, wishes to disaffirm the purchase contract. May Connie legally disaffirm the purchase contract?

   a. Yes, because she is a minor.
   b. No, because the capacity of the agent governs.
   c. No, because she did not disaffirm the agency agreement before the purchase contract was entered into by the agent.
   d. Connie can only disaffirm if the sale price of the equipment exceeded $500.

3. Al acts as Paul's agent in dealing with Tom. Tom knows that Al is acting on behalf of a principal, but Tom does not know who the principal is. Paul is

   a. a disclosed principal.
   b. a partially disclosed principal.
   c. an undisclosed principal.
   d. an illegal principal.

4. St. Peter's Church hired Mike to paint a detailed religious scene on the ceiling of its new church. Mike was authorized to select the colors and materials to be used. He was recognized as an expert in his field. Mike became very busy and delegated his duties to Angelo, a young unknown and inexperienced artist. The church claims that Mike is not legally permitted to delegate his duties. Is the church correct?

   a. No, because the law permits an agent to delegate duties in all cases.
   b. No, because Mike didn't know he would become very busy.

c. Yes, because Mike's duties required special skill and expertise.
d. Yes, because an agent may never delegate duties.

_____ 5. Jennifer is employed as a purchasing agent by Alpha, Inc., a company that purchases many chemicals. Jennifer owns a significant amount of stock in the Beta Chemical Company. Jennifer contracted on behalf of Alpha to purchase chemicals from Beta. Has Jennifer breached the duty she owes to Alpha?

a. Yes, unless Jennifer notified Alpha of her conflict of interest and received Alpha's authorization to contract with Beta despite her conflict of interest.
b. No, there is no evidence that the purchase from Beta was a poor deal.
c. Yes, there is no way that an agent can contract with another party on behalf of the principal when a conflict of interest exists.
d. No, the mere fact that Jennifer had an interest in Beta is irrelevant.

_____ 6. Which of the following kinds of authority must an agent have to bind the principal to a contract?

a. Express authority
b. Implied authority
c. Apparent authority
d. Any one of the above

_____ 7. An agent who enters into an authorized contract on behalf of the principal is *not* liable on the contract in which of the following circumstances?

a. If the agent acted for a disclosed principal.
b. If the agent acted for a partially disclosed principal.
c. If the agent acted for an undisclosed principal.
d. None of the above.

_____ 8. Paula hired Alice as her agent for the purpose of selling Paula's ring. The ring has an imitation diamond. Alice falsely represented to Tanya that the diamond was genuine. Based on that representation, Tanya paid $3,000 for the ring. May Tanya recover the money from Alice?

a. Yes, an agent is liable for losses caused by the agent's fraud or deceit.
b. Yes, an agent is always liable under contracts entered into on behalf of the principal.
c. No, an agent cannot be held liable under a contract entered into on behalf of a principal.
d. No, only the principal, Paula, is liable.

9. Which of the following is an obligation of the principal?

   a. Duty to reimburse the agent for any expenditures
   b. Duty to indemnify the agent for losses suffered by the agent as a result of the principal's failure to honor an authorized contract which the agent entered on the principal's behalf
   c. Duty to indemnify the agent for losses suffered as a result of the agent's negligent conduct.
   d. Duty to reimburse the agent for authorized expenditures even if the agent acts in a deceitful manner.

10. A principal has a duty to perform on contracts entered into on the principal's behalf by an agent who acted without authority if

   a. the agent is indemnified.
   b. the contract is ratified.
   c. the contract is fair.
   d. none of the above.

11. Andy is employed as a salesperson in Paula's hardware store. Andy negligently dropped a heavy box on the toe of Sam, a customer. Against whom may Sam recover for his injury?

   a. Paula, the principal.
   b. Andy, the agent.
   c. Sam may recover against Paula or Andy.
   d. Sam cannot recover against Andy or Paula.

12. A third party who contracts with an agent owes a duty of performance to the principal

   a. if the principal is disclosed.
   b. if the principal is partially disclosed.
   c. in most cases in which the principal is undisclosed.
   d. All of the above.

13. Pete and Dick entered into an agency agreement that, by its terms, was to run for two years. Pete was to serve as Dick's agent. Pete notified Dick that he was terminating the agency after only two weeks had passed. Dick claims that Pete cannot terminate the agency. Which of the following is true?

   a. Pete has the power to terminate, but not the right.
   b. Pete has the right to terminate, but not the power.

c. Pete cannot terminate the agency.

d. Pete has both the power and the right to terminate the agency.

14. Kate was employed as Wanda's agent for the purpose of selling encyclopedias. Claude had previously dealt with Kate while she was acting as Wanda's agent. Wanda fired Kate. After being fired, Kate, representing herself as Wanda's agent, contracted to sell encyclopedias to Claude. Claude paid Kate $100 as a down payment. Kate then left town. Can Claude enforce the contract against Wanda?

a. No, because the agency had been terminated.

b. No, because Claude was not entitled to actual notice of the termination.

c. Yes, because Kate had apparent authority.

d. Yes, because Kate need not have authority in order to bind Wanda.

Use this information in answering Questions 15 and 16.

Susan, president of a small advertising firm, obtained approval from the board of directors to purchase all new office furniture and to sell the used furniture. She placed an ad in the local paper announcing that used furniture would be sold on a particular Saturday. On the designated day Susan left Gil in charge of the sale. She told him, however, not to sell any lamps because the board had decided to keep all lamps and light fixtures.

Gil sold all of the furniture, including seven lamps, to parties who responded to the ad. He placed the money obtained from the sale in his personal bank account without writing down the exact amount of the sale proceeds. He cannot remember how much of the deposit was from sale proceeds and how much was from his winnings at the race track that afternoon.

15. Upon learning of these events, Susan's firm seeks to recover the lamps from the purchaser who has now been identified as Sandy. Which of the following statements is true?

a. The firm will recover the lamps from Sandy because Gil had no actual authority to sell them.

b. The firm will recover the lamps from Sandy because Gil had been specifically instructed by his principal not to sell them.

c. Sandy will be permitted to keep the lamps because Gil possessed emergency authority to sell them.

d. Sandy will be permitted to keep the lamps because Gil had apparent authority to sell them.

16. Which of the following duties of an agent did Gil *not* violate?

a. Duty to use care and skill

b. Duty not to commingle

c. Duty not to use agency-related information for personal gain
d. Duty to account to principal

Use this information in answering Questions 17 and 18.

George started a pharmaceutical firm to market a new drug known as Tridol. He hired Al, Barb, and Connie as sales agents. Each signed an agency agreement for one year. Each was given a certain sales territory. One month later Al notified George that he was terminating his agency relationship. The next month Barb died after using Tridol. The next month the federal Food and Drug Administration declared the sale of Tridol illegal.

17. Which statement concerning Al's agency relationship is correct?

a. The agency terminated upon Al's notification of George.
b. The agency terminated when the sale of Tridol was made illegal.
c. The agency will terminate at the end of the one-year period.
d. The agency will remain in effect until it is mutually terminated.

18. Which of the following statements is correct?

a. The agency relationship of both Barb and Connie terminated upon Al's notification of George.
b. The agency relationship of both Barb and Connie terminated upon the death of Barb.
c. The agency relationship of both Barb and Connie terminated when the sale of Tridol was made illegal.
d. Barb's agency relationship terminated upon her death, but Connie's did not terminate until the sale of Tridol was made illegal.

Use this information in answering Questions 19 to 21.

Warner is employed by Mediocre Foods as a sales and delivery person. He drives a company truck along a specified route and fills orders from his truck. While unloading some frozen meat, Warner bumped Ann, causing her to fall and injure her arm. While driving to the next store on the route, Warner bumped into the back of a garbage truck and injured Bill, who was loading garbage into the truck. Warner decided to take the remainder of the day off and visit his grandmother at a nursing home. After driving 10 miles off his route, Warner crashed into a vehicle stopped at a red light, causing injury to Cal, its driver.

19. Which of the following statements is true?

a. Mediocre Foods is liable to Ann, Bill, and Cal.
b. Warner is liable to Ann, Bill, and Cal.

c. Mediocre Foods is liable only to Ann.
d. Warner is liable only to Cal.

_____

20. Mediocre Foods notified Warner of his termination. Nevertheless, he later went to Able's Foods, a customer he had sold to for seven years and took advance payment for a large order. Able's Foods now seeks to collect from Mediocre Foods because the delivery of its order was never made. Which of the following statements is accurate?

   a. Able has no right to recover because Warner's agency had already been terminated.
   b. Able can recover unless Mediocre published a notice of termination in a newspaper of general circulation in the area where Able does business.
   c. Able can recover if it was notified both orally and in writing of the termination.
   d. Able can recover unless it was notified either orally or in writing of the termination.

_____

21. Two weeks after being terminated, Warner introduced himself at Bentley's Grocery as an agent for Mediocre Foods. Warner had never been to Bentley's before. He took advance payment for a large order. Which of the following statements is true concerning Bentley's right to recover its payment from Mediocre?

   a. Bentley's cannot recover because the agency had already been terminated.
   b. Bentley's cannot recover because it was not notified orally or in writing of the termination.
   c. Bentley's can probably recover unless notice of Warner's termination was published in a newspaper of general circulation in the area where Bentley was operating.
   d. Bentley's cannot recover because no notice to third parties is required when an agent is fired.

Solutions

Answer	Refer to:

1. (d)   [A-1, A-2-b] There is an agency relationship between the parties. As a general rule, agency agreements need not be in writing. Only if the contract that the agent is authorized to enter on behalf of the principal is legally required to be in writing must the agency agreement be in writing. In this case Wally is authorized to enter into a contract to sell a snowblower (goods) for Ernie for $150. Because this is under $500, the contract would not have to be in writing.

2. (a)   [A-3] It is the capacity of the principal that is important in determining whether a contract entered into by an authorized agent can be disaffirmed. Because Connie, the principal, is a minor, she is permitted to disaffirm. It is not necessary that the minor principal have disaffirmed the agency agreement before disaffirming the contract entered into by the agent.

3. (b)   [B-2] The third party (Tom) knows of the existence of the principal but does not know the principal's identity, so Paul is therefore a partially disclosed principal. If Tom had known of Paul's identity, Paul would be a disclosed principal. If Tom had reasonably believed that Al was acting on his own behalf without any principal being involved, Paul would be an undisclosed principal.

4. (c)   [E-2-a] An agent may delegate duties only in certain limited circumstances. In this case Mike's duties require special skill and therefore cannot be delegated. The mere fact that Mike became very busy does not allow him to delegate his duties.

5. (a)   [E-7-b] An agent has a duty to avoid conflicts of interest. Jennifer owned stock in Beta, and a conflict of interest therefore existed. Jennifer was obligated to notify Alpha of the conflict. Unless Alpha, with full knowledge of the conflict, approved of the transaction with Beta, Jennifer would be in breach of her duty of loyalty.

6. (d)   [D-1, D-2, D-4] An agent who possesses express, implied, or apparent authority can bind the principal to a contract.

7. (a)   [F-1] An agent who enters into a contract on behalf of an undisclosed or partially disclosed principal is liable on the contract. Only the agent who acts for the disclosed principal can avoid liability on the contracts entered into on behalf of the principal.

8. (a)   [F] An agent is liable for losses caused by the agent's fraud or deceit.

9. (b)   [F] The principal is obligated to indemnify the agent for losses suffered by the agent in the course of carrying out his/her duties as an agent.

10. (b)   [H-1-b] A principal may ratify an unauthorized contract and thereby become bound by its terms. Ratification requires that the principal have knowledge of all relevant facts and that the principal accept the benefits of the contract with the intent of being bound by its terms. Without ratification, a principal is not bound by an unauthorized contract.

11. (c)   [F, H-2-b] Because Andy was negligent, he is liable for the injury he caused. Because the negligent act occurred in the course of the agent's employment, the principal is also liable. Andy was an employee, not an independent contractor.

12. (d)   [I-1, I-2, I-3] The principal can enforce the contract against the third party if the principal was disclosed or partially disclosed. In addition, an undisclosed principal can enforce the contract in most cases. Only if the contract required the agent to perform personally, or if the agent denied to the third party that he or she was acting as an agent, or if the agent should have known that the third party would not agree with the principal, can the third party refuse to perform the contract for the principal.

13. (a)   [J-3-a] Either the principal or the agent has the power to terminate the agency at any time. In this case the parties have limited their right to terminate. Pete had no right to terminate for two years. Pete therefore can terminate the agency, but he is liable for any damages that his termination causes because he exercised his power to terminate without possessing the right to terminate.

14. (c)   [K-1] Because Claude had previously dealt with Kate acting as Wanda's agent, he was entitled to actual notice. No notice of termination was given. Kate had apparent authority to bind her principal. Kate, of course, is liable to Wanda for her wrongdoing.

15. (d)   [D-4] By leaving Gil in charge of the sale after advertising it as a furniture sale, the firm allowed circumstances to exist that would lead a reasonable person to conclude that Gil had authority to sell the lamps. Sandy was allowed to rely on the appearance of things, even though Gil lacked actual authority to sell the lamps.

16. (c)   [E] Gil breached each of the listed duties except using agency-related information for personal gain.

17. (a)   [J-3] Although Al lacked the right to terminate the agency after one month, he had the power to do so.

18. (d)   [J] Both death and illegality cause termination of an agency. Barb's agency was terminated when she died. Connie's remained, but was terminated by the FDA's action when the sale of Tridol became illegal.

19. (b)   [F] An agent is always liable for his own negligence, whether or not the principal can also be held liable. Mediocre Foods can also be held liable for injuries to Ann and Bill that occurred in the scope of Warner's employment.

20. (d)   [K-1] Since Able had previously dealt with Warner in his capacity as an agent of Mediocre Foods, Able was entitled to either oral or written notification of the termination.

21. (c)   [K-2] Since Bentley's had not dealt with Warner before, it was entitled only to notice by publication. Had the agency been terminated by death, illegality, or insanity, no notice would have been required.

CHAPTER 24

Basic Business Entity Law

OVERVIEW

In this chapter we provide a very basic review of the laws governing the formation, creation, and termination of sole entrepreneurships, partnerships, and corporations. A candidate should be able to visualize the life cycle of a business entity: the manner of formation, business operation, and the termination.

The agency-law concepts learned earlier may be applied to the study of business entities. For example, a partner, when acting on behalf of the partnership, always acts as an agent, not a principal. Therefore, a partner will have the authority to act that a general agent would normally possess (actual plus implied authority). In contrast, a shareholder of a corporation has no agency authority to bind the corporation. Shareholders are considered investors with very limited decision-making input. Directors determine policy, and officers, who are the agents of the corporation, implement policy and handle day-to-day transactions.

The candidate should attempt to understand the basic similarities and distinctions between partnerships and corporations.

KEY TERMS

Articles of incorporation
Bylaws
Common stock
Estoppel
Joint and several liability
Joint liability

Limited partner
Partnership
Preferred stock
Promoter
Sole entrepreneurship

A. Sole Entrepreneurship

A sole entrepreneurship, sometimes called a sole proprietorship, is a business owned and operated by one person.

1. *Formation of Sole Entrepreneurship*:

   a. *Single owner*: This type of business has only one owner and is *not* incorporated (not a corporation).

   b. *Variable size*: Although there is a single owner, there can be any number of employees. A business may be large or small and still be in the form of a sole entrepreneurship.

   c. *Unlimited liability*: As the only owner, a sole proprietor can potentially be liable for all the debts of the business (plus the owner's personal debts).

2. *Creation of Sole Entrepreneurship*: A sole entrepreneurship is created subject to state law. Generally, no detailed procedures are required for the creation of a sole entrepreneurship. Generally, the true owner's name must be registered in the local courthouse, along with the trade and/or business name if the name of the business is not to be the owner's name.

   EXAMPLE: If John Doe begins a business called Lucky Pizza, he would have to register the business name (Lucky Pizza) along with his name as the sole owner. This is a sole entrepreneurship.

3. *Operation*:

   a. *Government regulation*: The sole entrepreneurship is generally subject to governmental regulations, just as any partnership or corporation might be. Small businesses (regardless of the business form), however, are often exempt from laws and/or regulations for reasons such as these:

      (1) The business has little impact, if any, upon interstate commerce.

      (2) The size of the business is small (few employees or small gross sales).

          EXAMPLE: Title VII of the Civil Rights Act of 1964, the basic law concerning employment discrimination, applies only to businesses having 15 or more employees.

   b. *Income tax applicable*: The sole entrepreneurship, as an entity, pays no income tax. (Profits or losses are reflected on the owner's personal income tax return.)

   c. *Employee benefits provided*: Workers' compensation, unemployment compensation, and FICA payments are all required of the sole entrepreneurship just as they are required of a partnership or a corporation.

   d. *Agency*: The laws of agency apply to the sole entrepreneurship.

      (1) The owner is the principal.

      (2) Any agents have whatever express authority is given by the principal plus that authority resulting from their agency position and/or standard trade practices.

   e. *Termination*: No formal procedure exists for the sole owner to terminate the business. As long as no fraud results as to creditors, the owner may simply cease doing business.

B. Partnership	A partnership is a business entity owned and operated by two or more persons (called partners). The formal definition of a partnership is an association of two or more persons to carry on as co-owners of a business for profit.

1. *Formation of Partnerships*: Partnerships are governed by state laws (statutes). Many states have adopted the Uniform Partnership Act (UPA), a model act, as the state's partnership law. The purpose of the UPA is to achieve uniformity among states concerning partnership laws.

2. *Creation of Partnerships*: Partnerships may be created by an express partnership agreement, by determination of the courts, and by estoppel.

   a. *Express partnership agreement*: A written partnership agreement (articles of partnership) is always advisable to assure clarity and understanding of the intent of the partners. However, an oral partnership agreement is legally enforceable, as long as a writing is not required under the statute of frauds.

      EXAMPLE: Andrew, Betty, and Charles form the ABC Partnership, which is to exist for 10 years. The agreement must be in writing because it will not be completed within one year.

   b. *Determination of the courts*: Sometimes it is not clear whether or not a partnership exists. In these cases a court may be called upon to examine the overall facts and determine whether or not a partnership exists. No one test need be met, but courts place the most emphasis upon whether the parties agree to share profits and losses.

      EXAMPLE: Al and Bob jointly open a record shop. They agree to share profits. A court would probably find a partnership.

   c. *Partnership by estoppel*: Partnership by estoppel is based on the same theory as agency by estoppel. *Estoppel* means that a party to a lawsuit will be precluded (stopped) from raising a defense. In partnership law, the fact that no partnership actually exists among persons who are involved will not be allowed as a defense by these persons. A court finds "partnership by estoppel" to avoid inequity to an innocent third party.

      EXAMPLES:

      Andrew, Betty, and Charles represent to a bank that they are partners in a restaurant to facilitate the lending of monies to Andrew, the actual owner. Andrew, Betty, and Charles will be considered a partnership as to the bank.

      Assume that Alice and Bob are not actual partners. In front of Alice, Bob tells Phyllis that Alice and Bob are partners. Alice would be liable as if she were, in fact, a partner for Phyllis's loan to the supposed partnership of Alice and Bob.

3. *Types of Partnerships*: Partnerships may be general or limited, depending on the nature of the partnership formed.

   a. *General partnership*: This type of partnership is sometimes called an ordinary or regular partnership.

   b. *Limited partnership* (created specially by state statute): This type of partnership has been established in many states to allow persons to invest in the partnership business without fear of personal loss beyond the original investment.

In this type of partnership, there must be at least one general (regular) partner and one limited partner. The general partner is similar to the partner in a general partnership.

(1) Without specific state law authorizing a limited partnership, there cannot be one. A limited partnership agreement must be filed with the state (usually not required for a general partnership).

(2) A limited partner is treated as the equivalent of a shareholder in a corporation.

    (a) A limited partner's potential liability for the partnership debt is limited to the limited partner's capital contribution.

    (b) A limited partner may not participate in the active, day-to-day management of the partnership.

    EXAMPLE: Ben is a limited partner in the ABC Partnership. Ben may not be actively involved in partnership business decisions.

    (c) A limited partner shares in profits according to the partnership agreement.

    (d) A limited partner may not lend his or her name to the partnership name.

    (e) A limited partner has no inherent agency authority to bind the limited partnership.

    EXAMPLE: Using the same example, Ben has no authority to bind the partnership to any contracts with third parties.

    (f) A limited partner who acts as a general partner loses statutory protection and will be liable as any other general partner.

4. *Partnership Operations*: Five basic rules exist under the UPA in regard to the operation of a partnership.

    a. *Agency*: Every partner is an agent of the partnership.

    EXAMPLE: Michael is a partner of XYZ Partnership. Therefore, he is an agent of the partnership. When Michael acts on behalf of the partnership, he is acting as an agent, not as a principal.

    b. *Profit/loss sharing*: Partners share profits and losses equally (unless otherwise stated in their partnership agreement).

    EXAMPLE: The partnership agreement of Golden Company is silent as to the sharing of profits among the five partners. Accordingly, each partner will receive 20 percent of the profits even if one partner had put up 50 percent of the capital.

    c. *Partners' liability*: Every partner is potentially personally liable for all the debts of the partnership.

    EXAMPLE: Partner X and the XYZ Partnership become bankrupt. Partners Y and Z may be held individually liable for all the remaining debts of the partnership (but not for partner X's personal debts).

    d. *Admission of new partners*: Unanimous consent is required to admit a new partner (unless a partnership agreement exists to the contrary).

    e. *Management of partnership*: The partners have equal management rights (unless there is a partnership agreement to the contrary). In essence, each partner has one vote in partnership matters.

5. *Relationship of Partners to Third Persons*:

    a. *Authority to bind partnership*: A partner's authority to bind the partnership to third persons is determined by the following:

        (1) The laws of agency apply when a partner acts on behalf of the partnership.

        (2) A partner acts as an agent, not as a principal, when acting for or on behalf of a partnership.

        (3) A partner can bind the partnership as the result of using express, implied, or apparent authority, the usual types of agency authority (see Chapter 23).

        EXAMPLE: Partner A visits a building for sale and signs a contract for the partnership to buy it. Unless the partnership deals in buildings in its ordinary course of business or unless specific partnership authority exists, the partnership will not be bound up to the seller.

    b. *Contract liability—joint liability*: Partners have joint liability for the contract obligations of the partnership. In essence, this means that if a suit is brought against the partnership, all partners must be sued individually for partnership contract obligations.

    EXAMPLE: ABC Partnership owes Patrick $5,000. Patrick must include A, B, and C if he includes any partner in conjunction with the suit against the partnership.

    c. *Tort liability*: Partners have joint and several liability for tort actions of partners and/or employees occurring within the scope of employment. *Joint and several* means that the party bringing suit may sue the partnership and any combination of the partners.

    EXAMPLE: Ellen brings a tort action against the ABC Partnership. Ellen may sue the partnership and any combination of the partners individually, such as ABC Partnership plus B.

    An individual partner is always liable for personal tortious actions even if acting for the partnership.

6. *Partnership Dissolution*: A partnership dissolution occurs when there is a change of partners. In essence, this means that the old partnership terminates and a new one is begun (if the partnership continues after a partner's departure).

EXAMPLE: Partner A of the ABC Partnership retires, but B and C wish to continue. The partnership of ABC will terminate, and the partnership of BC will exist thereafter.

C. Corporation   A corporation is considered distinct from the individuals who own it (the shareholders). A corporation is a legal entity, which means that it can be sued or sue directly. A corporation must be formed according to procedures established by state law and must pay annual income taxes, whereas a partnership does not.

    1. *Organization of a Corporation*:

        a. *Ownership and management of a corporation*: The owners of a corporation are the shareholders, while the directors are involved in establishing corporate policy and the officers of the corporation are involved in the management functions. Figure 24–1 shows how a corporation may be organized.

            (1) *Shareholders:* Although shareholders are owners, they are neither managers nor agents. Shareholders are considered to be investors, with a corporate voice only in extraordinary policy matters. Only a majority shareholder may owe fiduciary duties to the corporation and to the minority shareholders.

                EXAMPLE: Mary owns 50 shares of General Motors stock. Mary may also buy Ford shares. If Mary should invent a new type of battery, she would have no duty to provide it to General Motors (assuming that Mary is not otherwise affiliated with General Motors).

            (2) *Directors*: The shareholders have the power to elect and remove the directors of the corporation. Directors have the responsibility to establish corporate policies. They are neither managers nor agents, but they do

Figure 24–1 Corporation Organization

owe fiduciary duties to the corporation. Directors need not be shareholders or officers. The board of directors of the corporation is empowered to elect the officers of the corporation or, if necessary, to remove them from office.

EXAMPLE: A director of Ace Corporation discovers an excellent building lot location for Ace's expansion. The director has no inherent authority, as a director, to be able to obligate the corporation for the purchase of the lot. The director also cannot purchase the lot for personal gain and thereafter sell it to the corporation.

    (3) *Officers*: Officers implement policy, manage, and serve as agents for the corporation. Officers owe fiduciary duties to the corporation.

EXAMPLE: Ace Corporation's board of directors votes to acquire a building for Ace's expansion. Corporate officers would be told to carry out the board's directive.

  b. *Advantages of corporate form*: The primary advantages of the corporate form of business organization include the capital investment potential, limited liability for investors, perpetuity, and corporate control, among others.

    (1) *Capital investment*: The corporation is designed to raise substantial capital from a large number of investors.

    (2) *Limited liability for investors*: There is limited liability for investors, which means that shareholders' personal liability for corporation losses is limited to the original purchase price paid for the stock (the original investment).

    (3) *Perpetuity*: Perpetual business existence is possible.

    (4) *Corporate control*: It is possible for effective control of the corporation to be vested in those with a minority of the investment (by using such techniques as nonvoting and/or preferred stock).

    (5) *Employee benefits*: An investor-employee may be entitled to normal employee benefits (such as workers' compensation).

    (6) *Ability to resell*: Corporate stock is generally easier for the shareholder to sell than would be a partnership interest.

  c. *Disadvantages of corporate form*: Some of the primary disadvantages of the corporate form of business organization include the higher cost of formation, corporate income taxes required, licensing, and government regulation affecting corporations.

    (1) *High cost of formation*: The cost of formation and maintenance could be particularly significant for a small corporation because of

        (a) *License fees*

        (b) *Franchise taxes*

        (c) *Attorney fees*: An attorney must be utilized in any corporate litigation.

     (d) *State corporate rules and regulations*: Numerous rules and regulations may not practically apply to a small corporation but must still be complied with.

   (2) *Operation*: Greater procedural rules of operation exist as to who can do what in regard to ownership (shareholders) versus management (board of directors setting policy, officers implementing policy).

   (3) *Income taxes*: The corporation pays income taxes on income earned, and shareholders later pay income taxes on dividends received (double taxation).

   (4) *Government regulation*: A corporation is often subject to more overall regulation than are other types of business entities.

2. *Formation of a Corporation*: Corporations are formed under state laws, not federal. The sale of stocks and bonds (both securities) may be controlled by the Securities and Exchange Commission (federal) or state laws.

  a. *The role of the promoter*: A promoter is the person who organizes and forms a new corporation.

   (1) A promoter assembles the necessary assets and financing for the new corporation.

   (2) A promoter seeks stock purchasers, known as subscribers to the corporate stock.

   (3) A promoter is not an agent of the corporation to be formed since no principal is yet existing.

   (4) A promoter owes fiduciary duties to fellow promoters and/or subscribers. This means that the promoter must act in good faith and without known personal gain. A promoter must disclose any situation of private gain even though the corporation may also receive a benefit.

   EXAMPLE: A promoter must disclose his or her interest in a parcel of land being considered for the site of the new business.

   (5) A promoter is allowed to make a profit if full disclosure is made and there is subsequent acceptance by the new corporation.

   EXAMPLE: Promoter C sells an owned building to the newly formed XYZ Corporation. C is allowed to keep his profit if a full disclosure was made and appropriate approval was received.

  b. *Articles of incorporation*: A new corporation is formed by the filing of articles of incorporation with a state and receiving back a corporate charter. In effect, the articles of incorporation are the corporation's constitution and, as such, contain

   (1) Name of corporation being formed

   (2) Address of corporation

   (3) Duration of time the corporation is to exist

   (4) Purpose (often stated in very broad terms, such as "any legal purpose")

       (5)   The names of the incorporators of the new corporation

       (6)   Number and types of shares

       (7)   The name of the statutory agent (a person appointed by the incorporators who is available to receive complaints and summonses if the corporation is involved in litigation)

          EXAMPLE: Cajun Corporation's articles of incorporation authorize 1,000 shares of voting common stock and 500 shares of nonvoting preferred stock.

  c. *First shareholders' meeting of new corporation*: The agenda of the first shareholders' meeting will include the issuance of stock to the subscribers and the election of the board of directors.

  d. *First meeting of board of directors*: Items of business for the initial board of directors meeting should include

       (1)   Establishment of bylaws (the internal governing rules of the corporation)

       (2)   Election of officers

       (3)   General acceptance or rejection of preincorporation contracts of the promoters

          (a)   The corporation is not liable on such contracts unless the directors have approved adoption (implied or express) of such contracts.

          (b)   The promoter continues personal liability even though a contract has been adopted unless it was a conditional contract (no liability to promoter if corporation is not formed or does not adopt) or a novation occurs (third party agrees to release the promoter from liability and looks only to the corporation for performance).

3. *Corporate Finances—Stock*:

  a. *Common stock*: Common stock represents ownership in a corporation. Each share of stock may earn a dividend only after all corporate obligations, including those to owners of preferred stock, are satisfied.

       (1)   *Dividends*: Common shareholders have no priority as to dividends paid.

       (2)   *Voting*: Generally, there is one vote per share of common stock owned.

  b. *Preferred stock*: Preferred stock also represents ownership in a corporation that entitles the shareholder to certain advantages not available to owners of common stock. The owner of preferred stock is usually entitled to receive a dividend before it is granted to owners of common stock.

DIRECTIONS: Select the best answer from the four alternatives. Write the letter of your answer in the blank to the left of the number.

_____ 1. A partnership is being sued by Jackson for injuries suffered in an auto accident. The evidence shows that Burns, an employee of the partnership, was negligent in causing the accident. In a court action

    a. Jackson would win against Burns only if Burns was not acting within the scope of employment.
    b. the partners would be jointly liable.
    c. the partnership would be liable if Burns was acting within the scope of employment.
    d. the partnership would win versus Jackson because Burns is not a partner.

_____ 2. The following are part of the five basic rules in regard to the operation of a partnership *except*

    a. Every partner is an agent of the partnership.
    b. Admission of a new partner must be by majority vote.
    c. Partners share profits and losses equally.
    d. Partners have equal management rights.

_____ 3. R, S, and T form a new partnership. R contributes $50,000; S contributes $25,000; and T contributes expertise but no money. The partnership agreement is silent as to the sharing of profits. The partnership makes $30,000 profit in its first year, which it now wishes to pay partners.

    a. Partner T should receive nothing.
    b. Partner R should receive $10,000.
    c. Partner R should receive $20,000.
    d. Partner S should receive $15,000.

_____ 4. Alex is a promoter for a new corporation to be formed, the Denver Corporation. Which of the following statements is true?

    a. Alex is an agent for the Denver Corporation.
    b. The Denver Corporation will be liable for Alex's contracts made prior to incorporation.
    c. Alex owes fiduciary duties to the new corporation.
    d. Alex is considered a corporate officer.

5. A shareholder

    a. has limited liability.
    b. has implied authority to bind the corporation.
    c. has a role similar to that of partners in a partnership.
    d. None of the above.

6. Articles of incorporation must include which of the following?

    a. Name of new corporation
    b. Purpose of corporation
    c. Names of the incorporators
    d. All of the above

7. The advantages of the corporate mode of doing business include all of the following *except*

    a. operation of business.
    b. limited liability for shareholders.
    c. perpetual existence.
    d. ability to raise capital more effectively from investors.

Use this information in answering Questions 8 to 10.

John Austin is contemplating opening an athletic store, Heflin Aerobics Sports, focusing primarily on running, swimming, and biking. Austin already owns the property that will be used for the store. Austin will initially begin business without any other persons joining him as co-owners. From a previous business experience, Austin knows that he wants somehow to retain control if and when he does accept co-owners. He presently expects future co-owners also to be managers of new store locations.

8. The easiest form of business for Austin to choose to begin business would be the

    a. sole entrepreneurship.
    b. general partnership.
    c. limited partnership.
    d. corporation.

9. The form of business most compatible with Austin's goals and most appropriate for new co-owners would be

    a. sole entrepreneurship.
    b. partnership.

    c. limited partnership.

    d. corporation.

_____

10. Assume that Austin has formed a corporation. Austin would be considered an agent of the corporation if acting as

    a. the promoter.

    b. a shareholder.

    c. a director.

    d. an officer.

Solutions

Answer	*Refer to:*

1. (c)   [B-5-c] The employee's negligence will cause the partnership to be liable if the employee was acting within the scope of employment.

2. (b)   [B-4-d] The admittance of a new partner must generally be by unanimous vote.

3. (b)   [B-4-b] Where a partnership agreement is silent as to the manner of sharing profits and losses, the Uniform Partnership Act calls for an equal sharing. T shares in profits and losses regardless of capital contribution.

4. (c)   [C-2-a] A promoter is someone involved in the creation of a new corporation. A promoter owes both prospective shareholders and the formed corporation fiduciary duties: full disclosure, fair dealing, and full accountability.

5. (a)   [C-1-a(1)] Unlike a partner in a partnership, a shareholder of a corporation is treated as an investor and is liable only to the extent of capital contributions. A shareholder is not an agent of the corporation and has no authority to bind the corporation.

6. (d)   [C-2-b] All items listed must ordinarily be part of the articles of incorporation.

7. (a)   [C-1-c(2)] The corporate mode of operations is more involved than that of a sole proprietorship or partnership.

8. (a)   [A-2] A sole entrepreneurship is the easiest form of business to begin.

9. (d)   [C] A corporation would be best for purposes of control and the ability of co-owners to be actively involved in the day-to-day business operations.

10. (d)   [Figure 24–1] Officers are the only agents of a corporation.

CHAPTER 25

Regulation of Business and Employment

OVERVIEW

In this chapter we focus on government regulation of business and employment. The overall role of administrative agencies and antitrust laws is described and presented in detail. The candidate should review the following key points:

- The role and basic operations of an administrative agency

- The basic scope of antitrust laws (enforced by both the Department of Justice and the Federal Trade Commission)

  The regulation of employment focuses on three separate parts:

- Laws of the workplace

- Laws governing employment discrimination

- Laws pertaining to labor–management relations

Laws of the workplace include such legislation as social security, minimum wage, overtime, unemployment compensation, workers' compensation, and occupational safety and health legislation. The candidate should be able to distinguish these different laws and set forth the applicable requirements of each.

Laws governing employment discrimination deal with all aspects of employment discrimination: race, color, sex, religion, and national origin (included in Title VII) as well as discrimination in regard to age or handicaps. The candidate should be familiar with the various types of discrimination, bona fide occupational qualifications, and the role of the Equal Employment Opportunity Commission in monitoring employment practices.

Labor–management relations law deals with legislation covering the private-sector workforce. The candidate should understand what the National Labor Relations Act is, the role of the National Labor Relations Board, the role of an arbitrator, how a union may be recognized, and what is meant by unfair labor practices. This subject matter area is quite broad and detailed. Included here is a basic overview of labor laws as they are most likely to be covered on the CPS Examination.

KEY TERMS

Administrative agency
Administrative law judge
Age Discrimination in Employment Act (ADEA)
Americans with Disabilities Act
Bona fide occupational qualification (BFOQ)
Divestiture
Employee Retirement Income Security Act (ERISA)
Employment discrimination
Equal Employment Opportunity Commission (EEOC)
Equal Pay for Equal Work Act
Executive branch
Fair Labor Standards Act
Federal Insurance Contribution Act (FICA)

General counsel
Landrum–Griffin Act
National Labor Relations Act (NLRA)
National Labor Relations Board (NLRB)
Occupational Safety and Health Act (OSHA)
Price discrimination
Price fixing
Rehabilitation Act of 1973
Right-to-work law
Taft–Hartley Act
Title VII—Civil Rights Act of 1964
Treble damages
Unemployment insurance
Unfair labor practices
Wagner Act
Workers' compensation

A. Administrative Agencies

An administrative agency is a subdivision of the government with expertise and jurisdiction to regulate a specialized area of government operation.

1. *Relationship to Other Branches of Government*: Administrative agencies are often considered the fourth branch of government because of their significant impact on everyday life. In fact, administrative agencies fall under the jurisdiction of the executive branch (the president). Figure 25–1 illustrates the branches of government and their interrelationship with administrative agencies.

2. *Administrative Agency Functions*: Administrative agencies have been established for many specialized areas of government and/or governmental regulation. All existing agencies encompass basic similarities in the types of functions performed. Administrative agencies generally encompass similar executive, legislative, and judicial functions performed by the three branches of government.

   EXAMPLE: The administrative agency may issue regulations interpreting statutes, enforce existing statutes and regulations under the agency's jurisdiction, and/or determine liability for failure to comply with statutes/regulations.

3. *Administrative Agency Configuration*:

   a. *Establishment of commission or board*: As a general rule, administrative agencies are headed by a commission or board.

Figure 25–1 Relationship of Administrative Agencies to Legislative and Judicial Branches

(1) The commission or board is composed of an odd number of members, usually from five to seven.

(2) Members are appointed by the President and approved by Congress. The majority of board members are usually of the same party in control of the presidency.

(3) Members serve set terms of office, often four years, and members can be removed by the President only for wrongdoing.

b. *General counsel*: Agencies usually have a general counsel, appointed by the President, charged with deciding which cases should be brought by the agency.

c. *Regional agency offices*: Administrative agencies often have regional offices at different locations around the country. A regional office administers agency matters for a given geographical area.

EXAMPLE: Alice claims that she has been discriminated against in promotion by her employer because of her sex. Her complaint would be processed and prosecuted by a regional office of the Equal Employment Opportunity Commission (EEOC) in Chicago if she is working in the Chicago area.

d. *Administrative law judge*: Administrative law judges (ALJs) within each agency hear administrative cases brought by the agency.

(1) An administrative law judge hears witnesses and receives evidence in a similar manner as a court. The ALJ, however, is not a judge in the judicial branch.

(2) An ALJ's decision is reviewable by the full board or commission of the agency.

e. *Court review and/or enforcement*: Decisions of ALJs can be appealed to the full board or commission of an administrative agency, as discussed. An appeal is thereafter possible from the board or commission to a court of appeals. The court will not hear any witnesses or admit new evidence.

B. Antitrust Laws

1. *Applicable Statutes*: Three major acts make up the federal antitrust laws:

   a. *Sherman Act*: Antitrust legislation enacted in 1890 (see Section B-5).

   b. *Clayton Act*: Antitrust legislation enacted in 1914 (see Section B-6).

   c. *Robinson–Patman Act*: Antitrust legislation enacted in 1936, actually an amendment to the Clayton Act (see Section B-7).

2. *Major Objectives of Antitrust Laws*: The major objectives of antitrust legislation include

   a. *A competitive society*: The preservation, protection, and promotion of a competitive society.

   b. *Economic opportunity*: Many smaller, independent businesses are favored over fewer, larger businesses in an industry.

   c. *Protection of the public*: The public is to be protected against monopolistic control of the economies (protected against monopolies).

3. *Types of Offenses*: Antitrust violations are one of two types of offenses: rule of reason violations or per se violations.

   a. *Rule of reason violations*: In these types of alleged violations the defendant(s) can attempt to show that the alleged improper conduct is not an unreasonable restraint of trade.

      EXAMPLE: Favoring one buyer over another because of savings resulting from a quantity order would not be price discrimination.

   b. *Per se violations*: In these types of violations, once improper conduct is shown, there can be no defense raised and recognized by the defendant.

      EXAMPLE: Price fixing between two major competitors would be a per se violation.

4. *Possible Sanctions (Punishments) and/or Remedies*: Possible sanctions and/or remedies for antitrust violations are as follows:

   a. *Civil*: Civil remedies can be sought by the federal government (FTC or Department of Justice), competitors, victims, or state governments. Remedies include

      (1) *Injunction*: A court ordering a person or company not to do something.

      (2) *Treble damages*: Actual damages incurred, times 3.

         EXAMPLE: If actual damages were $5 million, the winning plaintiff would receive $15 million.

      (3) *Divestiture*: A court order that a corporation divest (sell) some of its particular operations and/or assets.

         EXAMPLE: Ford Motor Company was required to divest itself of Autolite, a manufacturer of automobile lights.

   b. *Criminal*: Criminal prosecution can be brought only by the federal government (Department of Justice) and only for alleged violations of the Sherman or Robinson–Patman acts. Possible sanctions include

    (1) Treble damages

    (2) Fine(s)

    (3) Prison sentence(s)

5. *Violations under the Sherman Act*: Violations under the Sherman Act can involve the sale of either goods or services. Violations include

  a. *Price fixing (per se violation)*: Price fixing occurs when two or more competitors agree on the price at which to sell goods or services.

    EXAMPLE: It would be price fixing for two competing airlines to agree to a price for the Dallas-to-Chicago air route. (It is not a violation for one to match the other without an agreement.)

  b. *Horizontal territorial allocation (per se offense)*: This would take place when two or more competitors agree to divide sales territories.

    EXAMPLE: It would be a per se violation for one soft drink company to agree to only sell east and another to only sell west of the Mississippi River.

  c. *Vertical territorial allocation (rule of reason offense)*: An agreement among companies to provide goods or services needed for the operation of a particular business can be a violation if the business owner attempts to create a monopoly or monopolize any market. Franchises are not considered a violation but are seen as reasonable even though this form of business organization involves all functions, goods, or services needed for the operation of the business. A franchise is purchased from a parent organization that has already established policies and procedures. In other words, controls are already in place for the franchisee to follow.

    EXAMPLE: It is not a violation for McDonald's to create different sales territories for McDonald's Restaurants in St. Louis. It would be a per se violation if McDonald's divided St. Louis with Burger King (an example of a horizontal territorial allocation).

  d. *Monopoly (rule of reason offense)*: An illegal monopoly is one that has the *power* and the *intent* to control prices and/or exclude competition.

    EXAMPLE: Regional telephone companies were divested from AT&T because of the telephone company's monopoly power in the telephone market.

6. *Clayton Act Violations (not applicable to sales of services)*: The Clayton Act has some overlap with the Sherman Act. Common violations include

  a. *Tying contracts (rule of reason offense)*: A tying contract occurs where the seller uses control of one market item to require buyers of that item to buy another item which the seller does not control.

    EXAMPLE: Years ago IBM was found to have improperly tied the lease of IBM punchcard machines to the usage of IBM punchcards. But for this tying arrangement the lessee would have been able to acquire proper punchcards easily from a number of sources.

b. *Reciprocal dealing contracts (per se offense)*: It is a violation for a stronger contracting party to require a weaker party to sell to it or buy from it as a condition of the stronger party buying or selling.

EXAMPLE: It would be a violation for General Motors to require a supplier of steering wheels to buy only GM vehicles as a condition of doing business with GM. (As a practical matter, the supplier would probably buy GM vehicles if GM were a significant customer.)

c. *Improper mergers (rule of reason offense)*: A merger of two or more companies into one company is illegal where the reasonable probability or effect would be to substantially lessen competition or tend to create a monopoly.

EXAMPLE: Mobil Oil was not permitted to merge with Marathon, another oil company (which was subsequently acquired by U. S. Steel).

7. *Robinson–Patman Act (price discrimination/rule of reason defense)*: The Robinson–Patman Act applies only to price discrimination—charging a buyer a different price for the same merchandise of identical grade or quality than the price charged another buyer for the same goods.

EXAMPLE: ABC Company sells the same ladder for $20 to Joe's Hardware, a little hardware store, and $18 to K-Mart, a large retail corporation. This would be an offense unless covered by a recognized defense (most probably a permissible discount because of proven savings by volume of sales).

a. *Overview of the act*: The primary features of this legislation include the following elements:

(1) Permits criminal prosecution

(2) Is not applicable to the sale of services

(3) Does not apply to sales by retailers to consumers

b. *Violation (rule of reason offense)*: It is a violation knowingly to give or receive a price discrimination.

c. *Defenses*: Appropriate defenses include the following:

(1) Meeting the price of competitor

   EXAMPLE: American Airlines matches a fare rate charged by Delta between Dallas and Chicago.

(2) Functional or quantity discount

   EXAMPLE: Ladders to be sold in K-mart stores are delivered to a central K-mart location. From that location K-mart trucks distribute the ladders to retail stores.

(3) Change in market conditions

   EXAMPLE: Santa Claus outfits are more valuable before Christmas than afterward.

(4) Change in marketability of item involved

   EXAMPLE: Fruit about to rot is worth less than fresh, ripe fruit.

C. Federal Laws Regulating the Workplace

Federal laws regulating the workplace include laws regulating minimum wage and overtime pay (Fair Labor Standards Act), unemployment compensation, social security, and occupational safety and health (Occupational Safety and Health Act).

1. *Fair Labor Standards Act*: This act, also known as the Wage and Hour Law, established the requirements for an employer to pay employees a minimum wage and "time and a half" for overtime worked over 40 hours per week. To limit child abuse, the act provides rules limiting the use of children in employment. In addition, the act was amended in 1963 to require equal pay for men and women who are performing equal work (the Equal Pay Act; see Section E-2).

   a. *Employees covered by the act*: Employees involved in interstate commerce or producing goods for interstate commerce are covered by the act. As a practical matter, very few private employers are able to escape application of the act on this basis. Those who might will generally be covered by a similar type of state law. The act applies to both union and nonunion employees.

   b. *Minimum wage*: Each year Congress reviews and sets the minimum wage employers are required to pay to employees. In figuring the minimum wage, an employer may include the reasonable value of room and board (if furnished), tips, commissions, and bonuses. In addition, an employee may be paid according to piece rate (payment for units handled or worked) as long as the probable earnings equate to the minimum wage.

   c. *Overtime pay*: An employee who works over 40 hours in a week's time is due time and a half by the employer. This means that if an employee makes $5 an hour, he or she will be due $7.50 per hour for each hour worked beyond 40 in a week. It is important to note that this law does not require time-and-a-half pay for hours worked in excess of eight hours per day.

   EXAMPLE: Sara works 12 hours on Monday, Tuesday, and Wednesday and four hours on Thursday. Sara would not be entitled to any overtime pay under the act. (Sara's company may pay overtime over eight hours worked, but this is not required by the act.)

   d. *Exemptions to minimum wage and overtime payment requirements*: Employees in the following categories are not covered by the minimum wage and overtime pay provisions of the act:

      (1) Fishing industry

      (2) Seasonal employees

      (3) Executive, professional, managerial, and supervisory personnel

      (4) Outside salespersons

      (5) Partial exemptions for learners, apprentices, students, and handicapped persons

   e. *Child-labor laws*: To reduce the likelihood of abuse of children at work, the act generally prohibits the employment of children under the age of 16. Two exceptions apply:

(1) *Age exceptions*: Children who are age 14 or 15 may do light work, such as clerical or sales work, as long as limited hours exist that do not conflict with school hours.

(2) *Work exceptions*: Newspaper delivery, child actors, children who work-for their parents, and agricultural work are work exceptions according to the act.

f. *Equal Pay for Equal Work Act*: This act is an amendment to the Fair Labor Standards Act and requires equal pay for women who are performing work substantially equal to that performed by men. A detailed explanation of the Equal Pay Act is included in Section E-2.

g. *Enforcement/remedies*:

(1) *Civil actions*: Among the available civil remedies are back pay, fines, and injunction. In addition, the government may seize goods moving in interstate commerce that were made in violation of child labor laws.

(2) *Criminal actions*: Fines and/or imprisonment may occur in exceptional cases.

2. *Unemployment Insurance (Part of the Social Security Act)*: Unemployment insurance, as its name implies, is for workers who, without fault, become unemployed. The federal unemployment insurance coverage was implemented to spur the creation of such benefit programs by states at the state level. All states today have unemployment insurance programs. Employers are permitted to take as a credit a percentage of the state unemployment tax permitted.

a. *Calculation of amount owed*: An employer's tax is dependent on unemployment claims made against it. A good claims record will result in lower employer-required payments. In addition, the employer is permitted to offset a percentage of the state payment, as discussed in the preceding paragraph.

EXAMPLE: Fast-food businesses often have a very high turnover rate, which results in a higher unemployment rate than that in more stable employment businesses.

b. *Special exemptions*: Family employees working in the family business and agricultural employees for small farm operations are not covered by the law.

c. *Requirements to receive unemployment benefits*: An employee who loses his/her job is entitled to compensation only if he or she has worked a minimum number of weeks and is ready, able, and willing to take equivalent new employment. It is not necessary that the terminated employee be in financial need of the benefits.

EXAMPLE: Scott, a bartender, is laid off by a bar because of slow business. Scott is eligible for unemployment benefits even if he is independently wealthy as long as he has earlier worked a minimum number of weeks.

d. *Disqualification*: In most states, an employee who was discharged for good cause, quit voluntarily (unless to take a better job), or refuses to accept equivalent work will be ineligible for benefits. In other states, the applicant may be penalized before receiving benefits if termination has been based on one of these reasons.

EXAMPLE: If in the example above, Scott refuses to take a bartender position in a similar type of bar in a similar area, he will lose his unemployment benefits.

3.   *Social Security (FICA)*: The social security system has undergone great scrutiny and has had many changes made by Congress because of the concern over its financial stability. The following are the basic aspects of the system:

   a.   *Benefits covered*: The benefits covered by the social security system include

      (1)   Medicare

      (2)   Retirement

      (3)   Disability

      (4)   Death benefits to surviving family members

   b.   *Employees covered*: This area of the law has undergone great change. Formerly, government employees were exempt from social security taxes (except the military), but this has now been changed as to new employees in state or federal government.

      (1)   If covered, an employee does not have a choice to opt out of the social security system.

      (2)   Self-employed persons are not exempt from coverage.

   c.   *Computation of withholding rates*: Congress has the authority to set the rates and earning limits for the collection of the social security payments due. The following contributions are required:

      (1)   *Employee*: An employee has his or her FICA contribution deducted at the time of payment by the employer. If the employer should fail to deduct the employee's contribution, the government will assess the employer for the amount.

      (2)   *Employer*: The employer is required to pay an additional amount for each employee.

      (3)   *Self-employed individual*: The rate for self-employed individuals is approximately double that of the individual employee rate.

4.   *Employee Retirement Income Security Act (ERISA)*: ERISA was passed in 1974 in an attempt to better regulate private pension plans. ERISA does not require an employer to establish a pension plan or set any minimum level of benefits if a pension plan is established.

   a.   *Purposes of the act*: The primary purposes of ERISA include the following:

      (1)   To ensure that an employer's pension plan, if one exists, does not favor management and is sufficiently broad-based in employee coverage.

      (2)   To ensure that an employee will have his or her interest *vest* without the passage of an unreasonable amount of time. (*Vest* means that the employee has the legal right to receive those payments that have been contributed into the pension on his or her behalf by the employer.)

      (3)   To establish financial control rules relating to pension trust funds.

(4) To provide pension termination insurance via the Pension Benefit Guaranty Corporation (PBGC).

   b. *Pension Benefit Guaranty Corporation (PBGC)*: This federal corporation provides protection to pensions in a fashion similar to the Federal Deposit Insurance Corporation's protection of bank savings accounts. If a covered pension plan should have insufficient assets to make the required payments to beneficiaries, the PBGC would cover the deficient amounts.

5. *Occupational Safety and Health Act*: This act is administered by the Occupational Safety and Health Administration (OSHA) under the Secretary of Labor. Established in 1970, OSHA received much media attention for its workplace rules, which were often contradictory, unclear, and unnecessary. Today OSHA has attempted to reduce its exhaustive set of miscellaneous rules and concentrates instead on major problem areas.

   a. *Purposes of the act*: There are two major purposes of this legislation:

   (1) To ensure safe workplaces for employees

   (2) To establish safety and health standards for the workplace

   b. *Workplace inspections*:

   (1) By law, OSHA investigators must not inform an employer of a pending investigation. The purpose of this rule is to reduce the likelihood that the employer will cover up problems that would otherwise have been detected and ordered remedied.

   (2) OSHA investigations may be prompted by employee complaints or by the initiation of OSHA alone. An employee cannot be subjected to retaliation by the employer.

   (3) An employer has the right to insist that an OSHA investigator secure a search warrant before being granted access to the plant. As a practical matter, a search warrant is very easily obtained by the investigator.

   (4) If OSHA violations are found during the inspection, the employer is given a *citation* (notice of violation). A citation recites the alleged violations and what OSHA is demanding the employer do to rectify the situation. An employer may appeal.

   c. *Potential penalties*:

   (1) *Civil actions*: Fines (where greater than 10 violations are found) and temporary injunctions are possible. A *temporary injunction* is issued where such danger exists that could cause great bodily harm or the possibility of death.

   (2) *Criminal actions*.

   d. *New directions for OSHA*: Because of the tremendous amount of criticism of OSHA operations and rules, OSHA has undergone a major reorganization.

   (1) *Fewer inspections*: OSHA now permits small businesses or businesses with few problems in the past to conduct their own investigations. Results of these investigations are sent to OSHA, which always reserves

the right to make an actual investigation. Inspections in the more danger-ous industries have continued.

(2) *Greater focus on health standards*: OSHA initially stressed safety stan-dards almost exclusively.

D. State Legislation— Workers' Compensation

1. *Purpose of Legislation*: The purpose of workers' compensation is to provide cov-erage to employees who are incapacitated because of accidental injury, disease, or death incurred while on the job.

2. *Employer Requirements*: The state fund method requires that payments be based on claims experience and the number of employees. All states have state fund plans, but employers may be able to self-insure.

3. *Employee Eligibility for Benefits*: An employee becomes eligible for benefits if ac-cidental injury, disease, or death was incurred while on the job.

   a. *Liberal interpretation*: Courts liberally construe "while on the job" so as to give employee compensation.

   EXAMPLE: An employee kicked the plant cafeteria vending machine after it took his money without returning the desired soda. The employee recovered workers' compensation for a broken foot that resulted from the kick.

   b. *Recovery of workers' compensation*: The employee recovers even though the injury occurred because he or she negligently failed to follow directions.

E. Employment Discrimination

Laws governing employment discrimination deal with all aspects of employment dis-crimination: race, color, sex, religion, and national origin (included in Title VII of the Civil Rights Act of 1964), as well as age or handicaps. Employment discrimination legislation and executive orders have been created to augment the Constitution. As such, they provide the means and/or procedures for effective redress of employment discrimination problems.

Employment discrimination laws generally prohibit discrimination in hiring, compensation, employment terms and conditions, promotion, retention, and discharge. In essence, no discrimination is to be tolerated in any aspect of employment.

1. *Title VII*: Title VII of the Civil Rights Act of 1964 brought fundamental changes to employment. The act created the Equal Employment Opportunity Commission (EEOC) to promulgate and enforce employment discrimination regulations for employers with 15 or more employees.

   a. *Coverage of act*: Title VII prohibits discrimination in any form of employ-ment based on

      (1) Race

      (2) Color

      (3) Religion

      (4) Sex

      (5) National origin

b. *Scope of coverage*: An employer may not discriminate in hiring, retaining, promoting, or laying off persons.

    (1) In assessing the employer's conduct, a court can consider the disparate (unequal) impact on the workforce of the employer's employment practices.

    (2) A court will look with great scrutiny on any employment requirements that have the effect of eliminating a protected minority group, such as an applicant's arrest record, education (unless relevant to the position), marital status, and religion.

    (3) Applicants are not to be refused summarily simply because of preconceived notions. Applicants should be considered individually and tested against relevant work expectations.

    EXAMPLE: Utility companies formerly often denied employment opportunities to women on work crews because the work was dangerous and/or involved hard work or lifting.

    (4) Employers must attempt to make reasonable accommodations for persons claiming religious discrimination.

    EXAMPLE: It is generally considered reasonable to expect an employer to accommodate a full-time employee's day of worship.

    (5) Sexual harassment, a form of sex discrimination, is recognized in two situations:

        (a) The traditional approach is where some personnel action is made dependent on sexual favors.

        EXAMPLE: Debra was asked by her manager to spend a weekend with her manager to get to "know her better" and to "discuss a possible promotion."

        (b) The more recent type of recognized sexual harassment deals with the workplace environment. A hostile working environment may result in a sexual harassment action.

        EXAMPLE: A workplace where frequent sexual-innuendo jokes are permitted and/or tolerated may result in a hostile working environment. It should be noted that this may occur even though the person subjected directly to such behavior does not object but others working in the area do object.

c. *Bona fide occupational qualifications (BFOQs)*: In very limited situations involving reasonable business necessity, an employer may legally discriminate based on sex, national origin, or religion.

    (1) This limited defense is called the bona fide occupational qualification defense.

    EXAMPLES:

    A Catholic church could limit employees to Catholics.

    A theater could require that Cleopatra be a woman.

The owner of a French restaurant could insist on French natives to be employed as waiters and waitresses; however, he or she could not then reject a black French native.

(2) The BFOQ defense is *not* available for discrimination involving race or color.

d. *Enforcement/procedure for relief from discrimination*: The overall enforcement of Title VII is through the Equal Employment Opportunity Commission (EEOC).

(1) *Filing of complaints*:

(a) Complainants must first file their complaints with a state equivalent of the EEOC, if it exists.

(b) If a complaint is filed with a state or local agency, the EEOC cannot act until that agency has had 60 days to resolve the matter.

(2) *Role of the EEOC*: The EEOC may be involved in any of the following activities designed to assist with a solution:

(a) Investigation of the complaint

(b) An attempt to reach an administrative solution with the employer

(c) Filing of suit against the employer on behalf of the claimant(s)

(d) Dismissal of the complaint

(3) *Private action*: If the complainant fails to achieve the desired relief after the preceding steps are taken, a private lawsuit may be brought against the employer by the employee(s).

e. *Burden of proof*:

(1) *Prima facie case of discrimination*: Plaintiff, whether complaining employee(s) or EEOC on behalf of complaining employee(s), must establish a prima facie case of discrimination.

EXAMPLES:

Charles, a black laborer, applied for a job with ACE Corporation. Although qualified, Charles was not hired and the job remained open.

Karen was qualified to receive a promotion with ACE Corporation. Ken was promoted instead, even though he had less experience and poorer qualifications.

(2) *Employer accountability*: The employer has the burden to account for the apparent discrimination.

f. *Potential remedies*:

(1) Injunction prohibiting illegal action

(2) Damages (back pay)

(3) Reinstatement if fired or forced out improperly

          (4)   Promotion to position denied improperly

          (5)   Other remedies suitable to redress the employer's wrongdoing

2. *Equal Pay for Equal Work Act*: This act, a part of the Fair Labor Standards Act, requires equal pay for equal work regardless of sex. The term *equal work* means that two or more employees are doing substantially equal work under similar working conditions.

    EXAMPLE: A man is paid 25 cents more per hour than the women on an assembly line because he is required to empty a 50-gallon drum twice a day. A court would probably find that this is not enough difference to justify the greater pay. (Perhaps the drum could be emptied more often, smaller drums could be utilized, or a mechanical device such as a two-wheeled cart could be used.)

    a. *Permitted pay differences*: A difference in pay between sexes is permissible if due to piecework rates of production (quantity of production), seniority on the job, or merit. There might still be a violation of Title VII, however, because of the discriminatory effects of the seniority system.

    b. *Remedy for violation*: If an equal-pay violation is found, the wages of the employees discriminated against will be raised to the wages of the favored sex. (The reverse *never* occurs: the higher-wage earners are never reduced to the wage rates of the discriminated-against workers.)

3. *Age Discrimination in Employment Act (ADEA)*: Even though the Age Discrimination in Employment Act (ADEA) was not a part of Title VII, the Equal Employment Opportunity Commission is the enforcing agency. The ADEA applies to employees over the age of 40 and employers with 19 or more employees. (*Note*: The original law applied to employees between the ages of 40 and 70 years of age.)

    a. *Effect*: There is no mandatory retirement or discrimination in regard to hiring, promotion, and retention because of age if not at least 40 years old.

    b. *Exceptions*:

        (1) Exceptions include certain occupations, such as airline pilots, police, and firemen, where innocent third parties rely on critical physical skills.

        (2) A bona fide executive and/or high policymaker of a private company can be forced into early retirement if he or she will be receiving a pension of $27,000 or more per year.

    c. *Potential damages*:

        (1) Reinstatement in position

        (2) Back pay

        (3) Attorney fees

4. *Rehabilitation Act of 1973*: This legislation requires employers who participate in government contracts to make reasonable accommodation to employ and promote qualified handicapped individuals. The Equal Employment Opportunity Commission (EEOC) has the power of enforcement for this legislation, even though this act is not a part of Title VII. The act seeks to have employers meet the individual needs of handicapped persons.

   a. *Coverage*:

      (1) Federal government employees are covered under this act.

      (2) Employers with federal government contracts of $2,500 or more per year are also included within this act.

      (3) Extended coverage occurs as a general contractor with a government contract is required to make its subcontractors agree to follow the act.

   b. *Requirements for covered employer*: Employers who participate in government contracts of $2,500 or more per year are required to take affirmative action in employing qualified handicapped individuals.

      (1) *Affirmative action*: Employers must take affirmative action to hire, promote, and retain handicapped employees.

      (2) *Employment*: The legislation applies to all levels of employment.

      (3) *Accessibility to work*: Working conditions and accessibility for handicapped individuals must be remedied as necessary to accommodate the handicapped person. Such remedies must not pose an undue hardship for the employer.

   c. *Qualifications for employment*: For employee coverage, the handicapped individual must be able to show that he or she is otherwise qualified for the job.

      (1) The individual must be able to perform the job or perform with reasonable accommodations.

      (2) Alcoholics and drug abusers are specifically not covered under the act. Persons with symptomatic HIV infection (AIDS) now are covered by regulation.

   d. *Damages*: The government may require the following damages as settlement:

      (1) *Severance*: The government may sever the contract with the employer.

      (2) *Hiring or reinstatement*: The government may require hiring or reinstatement of minority workers.

      (3) *Payment of back wages*: The government may require back wages to be paid.

5. *The Americans with Disabilities Act (ADA)*: The Civil Rights Act of 1964 was extended in 1992 to cover the physically and mentally disabled, including AIDS patients, cancer patients, and treated, recovering substance abusers. Individuals with emotional disorders, however, are excluded. Businesses must make reasonable accommodations to workers and job applicants with disabilities unless the required changes present an undue hardship for the business. The act is considered the most comprehensive civil rights legislation in 30 years.

   a. *General areas of the act*: The provisions of the act range from public services and building codes to employment practices concerning physically and mentally disabled persons.

(1) *Public services*: One of the major provisions of the act mandates that disabled persons not be excluded from participating in any municipal activities. Disabled persons cannot be denied services provided routinely for other citizens. Building codes will need to be modified to include accommodation for disabled persons.

EXAMPLE: Public transportation must be available and accessible for those citizens with a disability.

(2) *Employment*: Employers cannot discriminate against an applicant on the basis of the disability if the person can perform the basic responsibilities of the job. Employers must make reasonable accommodation to assist the disabled employee.

EXAMPLES:

Job duties may need to be restructured so that the employee can perform these duties. Such restructuring must not cause the employer an undue hardship, however.

Office equipment may need to be modified for the disabled person.

b. *Passage of the act*: The legislation was passed in July 1990, with provisions taking effect July 26, 1991, except for the employment sections. Those sections took effect July 26, 1992, for employers with 25 or more workers.

The President's Committee for Employment of People with Disabilities states that two-thirds of the nation's disabled adults are unemployed, and the majority receive public assistance. Therefore, the ADA is seen as a national response to the specific needs of an important group of citizens.

F. Labor–Management Relations (Private Employers)

Labor–management relations law deals with legislation covering the private-sector workforce. The National Labor Relations Act (NLRA) covers labor–management relations of private employers. This act consists of the Wagner Act (1935), the Taft–Hartley Act (1947), and the Landrum–Griffin Act (1959).

1. *The National Labor Relations Act (NLRA)*:

    a. *Administration of the act*: The NLRA is enforced by the National Labor Relations Board (NLRB).

        (1) The board is composed of five members.

        (2) A general counsel oversees operation of the NLRB and all investigations.

        (3) Regional offices exist to handle NLRA matters.

    b. *Coverage of the act*: Any employer engaged in private business affecting commerce is potentially covered. A business "affects commerce" if it is involved in interstate selling and/or purchasing.

    c. *Purposes of the NLRA*:

        (1) Protect employees in forming, joining, and being members of a union, or the alternative, their refraining from being so involved.

(2) Ensure fair union election.

(3) Enforce collective bargaining obligations.

(4) Oversee unfair labor practices of management or the union.

2. *The Wagner Act (1935)*: The Wagner Act established union election procedures and the requirement that employers must bargain in good faith with the winning union. The National Labor Relations Board (NLRB) was established. The act identified unfair labor practices of employers and the right of employees to assist, form, and join a union.

3. *Taft–Hartley Act (1947)*: The Taft–Hartley Act identified union unfair labor practices. The act also created the Federal Mediation and Conciliation Service.

   a. *Free speech*: The act established the right of the employer to engage in free speech as long as "no threat of reprisal or force or promise of benefit" is made.

   EXAMPLE: It is all right for an employer to tell employees that he or she hopes the employees will vote against a union. It is wrong to threaten retaliation.

   b. *Union shop*: The employee also has the right to refrain from union involvement except to the extent of required membership by union shop. A *union shop* is where the collective bargaining agreement requires employees to join the recognized union as a condition of employment.

   EXAMPLE: Most union shop agreements require a new employee to join the union within 30 days of work.

   c. *Right-to-work law*: The act established the right of states to outlaw union shops in their states (known as the right-to-work law).

   EXAMPLE: In a right-to-work state, an employee could choose not to join the UAW, for example, even though it represents the plant employees at a General Motors plant.

   Workers choosing not to belong to the union are still covered by the union collective bargaining agreement and must be represented by the union if proper grievance is filed.

4. *Landrum–Griffin Act (1959)*: The Landrum–Griffin Act essentially deals with the internal operation and management of unions and establishes specific union member rights, such as

   a. *Election of union officers*: Union members have the right to vote.

   b. *Conduct of meetings*: Union members have the right to attend and vote.

   c. *Management of union funds*.

5. *Means and Effect of Union Recognition*:

   a. *Voluntary recognition of union*: Voluntary recognition of a union by the employer may occur where the union represents a majority of employees in the particular bargaining unit.

   (1) The bargaining unit is the particular grouping of employees.

        (2)   The bargaining-unit employees must have sufficient common interests.

   b. *Involuntary recognition of union*: Involuntary recognition of a union occurs in situations where

        (1)   A union wins a union election.

        (2)   An employer engaged in such grievous unfair labor practices that a fair election was and/or is impossible.

           EXAMPLE: Mass firing of a group of employees because of union favoritism prior to an election.

   c. *Union recognition*: The effect of union recognition is that the union represents all employees within the bargaining unit.

6. *The Election Process*:

   a. *Order for election*: A union receiving authorization cards from 30 percent or more employees within a proposed bargaining unit will cause the NLRB to order an election.

   b. *Union election*: The NLRB investigates the proposed bargaining unit and, if appropriate, orders and conducts a union election at the employer's plant.

       EXAMPLE: The NLRB generally holds that a single store within a chain is still an appropriate bargaining unit.

   c. *Majority vote*: The union must secure the vote of a majority of the employees of the proposed bargaining unit *who vote*.

       EXAMPLE: Union A wins if it secures 150 votes to 145 no-union votes even though 20 employees abstain from voting.

   d. *Union campaign*: During the union campaign period, an employer may not

        (1)   Spy on employees

        (2)   Take polls of employees

        (3)   Offer new benefits or change existing working conditions

        (4)   Fire any employee because of union sympathy

        (5)   Restrict or forbid solicitation or distribution of information during working hours, if similar activity allowed previously for nonunion purposes such as the United Way

   e. *Refusal of employer to recognize union*: An employer may refuse to recognize a union voluntarily and require the union to seek an election even though the union can show a majority interest via authorization cards.

   f. *New election ordered*: If either management or the union engages in activities that cause the other party to lose unfairly, a new election may be ordered.

       EXAMPLE: An employer illegally polls employees regarding their views of the union.

7. *Unfair Labor Practices by Employer*:

   a. *Interference with employee's rights*: The employer may not interfere with the employee's rights to form, join, or belong to a union.

   b. *Domination of union*: The employer may not dominate the union.

      EXAMPLE: An employer may not establish a union for its employees.

   c. *Discrimination*: The employer may not discriminate in the hiring or firing of an employee because of union activity and/or affiliation.

   d. *Refusal to bargain in good faith*: The employer may be unwilling to bargain in good faith.

8. *Unfair Labor Practices by Union*:

   a. *Refusal to bargain in good faith*: Union representatives refuse to bargain in good faith.

   b. *Striking*: Where a no-strike clause exists, the union will exhibit an unfair labor practice by striking.

   c. *Picketing*: Certain types of picketing may be seen as unfair practice.

9. *The Role of the Arbitrator*:

   a. *Settlement of disputes*: It is quite common for collective bargaining agreements to include a clause requiring disputes to be settled by an arbitrator.

   b. *Arbitration clause*: Where an arbitration clause exists and applies, a union may not strike where the matter is resolved by the arbitrator.

   c. *Unfair practices*: It is possible for an arbitrator to decide a matter that is also an unfair labor practice.

   d. *Ruling*: An arbitrator's ruling has the same force of law as does a court decision or NLRB decision.

10. *Potential NLRB Remedies*: The NLRB may utilize any of the following remedies:

    a. *Injunction*: The NLRB may issue an injunction.

    b. *New election*: The NLRB may order a new election.

    c. *Union recognition*: The NLRB may require an employer to recognize a union.

    d. *Good-faith bargaining*: The NLRB may order bargaining in good faith.

    If the offending party refuses to comply, the enforcement will be ordered via the federal courts of appeal.

G. Emerging Employment Issues

During the late 1980s and early 1990s a number of new employment issues began to emerge. These issues are being addressed by both statute and court cases.

1. *Decline of the Employment At-Will Doctrine*: In common law an employer had the power to fire any worker not subject to an employment contract for any reason (or no reason). Employees without a contract subject to such removal were known as employees at-will.

EXAMPLES:

John is hired as an assembler at ABC Manufacturing Company. John is not covered by a collective bargaining agreement and not hired for a set period of time. John could be freely terminated at any time under the common law.

Referring to the example above, John is covered by a collective bargaining agreement. Now John can probably not be discharged unless just cause exists.

a. *Limitation of employer powers*:

(1) Employment discrimination laws have greatly reduced the ability of employers to discharge employees for impermissible discriminatory reasons.

EXAMPLE: It would be a violation of Title VII for an employer to fire a person because of race or sex.

(2) Court cases and, in some states, state statutes have begun to limit employer termination rights as to other discharges that are contrary to public policy or employee handbooks.

EXAMPLES:

An employee is given a subpoena for jury duty. The employer tells the employee that he or she will be fired if the employee reports for jury duty. The employee reports to court for jury duty. The employee is subsequently fired. The court may reinstate and/or award damages.

The employee handbook states that an employee is probationary for the first six months of service and then becomes permanent. Permanent may be interpreted as meaning that the employee cannot be removed without cause.

b. *Emphasis on proper employment practices*: The employment at-will doctrine is slowly eroding, primarily by state court decision precedents. The emerging abolition of the doctrine, however, has caused employers to put greater emphasis on proper employment practices policies.

2. *Employee Privacy Issues*: A number of new employee privacy issues arose during the 1980s. These include the following:

a. *Lie detector tests*: The Employee Polygraph Protection Act of 1988 forbids the usage of polygraph (lie detector) tests in most situations of employment, including hiring.

b. *Drug testing*:

(1) Employer drug testing of employees has increased dramatically as a result of a number of reasons, including the Drug-Free Workplace Act of 1988, which requires employers with federal government contracts to maintain a drug-free workplace.

(2) Permissible ways and situations in which to test employees are still not clearly defined.

EXAMPLE: A court is more likely to approve random drug testing for employees of an electrical utility company working at a nuclear plant than accounting personnel at the home office.

c.   *Privilege against defamation*: Many terminated employees have begun to win lawsuits against former employers who, after termination, make untrue statements about their employment, integrity, or person. As a result, many employers are limiting their exposure to lawsuits by what they will say about a former employee, good or bad.

d.   *Intrusions into personal privacy*: Employers are prohibited from unreasonable intrusions into the personal privacy of employees.

EXAMPLE: A retail chain store manager was found to have violated an employee's right of personal privacy when he severed the employee's personal lock on a store locker while looking for possible stolen store inventory. (Because the employee was allowed to apply her own lock, there was a higher expectation of privacy.)

Review Questions

DIRECTIONS: Select the best answer from the four alternatives. Write the letter of your answer in the blank to the left of the number.

_____ 1. Administrative agencies are

  a. part of the legislative branch.
  b. part of the judicial branch.
  c. part of the executive branch.
  d. in fact a fourth branch of government.

_____ 2. Witnesses will be heard and evidence admitted in an administrative agency matter at which stage?

  a. Before the administrative law judge.
  b. Before the agency board itself.
  c. Before the federal court of appeals.
  d. Witnesses are never heard in an administrative agency matter.

_____ 3. A criminal violation for monopoly activity is possible under the

  a. Sherman Act.
  b. Clayton Act.
  c. Robinson–Patman Act.
  d. FTC Act.

_____ 4. Arrow Corporation and Phoenix, Inc. have been charged with price fixing. Which of the following statements is correct?

  a. Price fixing is a Robinson–Patman Act violation.
  b. Arrow and Phoenix should prevail if the alleged price fixing actually resulted in lower consumer prices.
  c. Price fixing is a per se rule violation.
  d. Price fixing cannot result in a criminal trial.

_____ 5. A situation where a seller will sell you product A only if you also agree to buy product B, a product readily available elsewhere, is called

  a. a tying contract.
  b. a vertical territorial allocation.
  c. a horizontal territorial allocation.
  d. price discrimination.

6. Martin, Inc. has been charged with price discrimination to buyers Smith and Pace. Which defense below would *not* be recognized?

a. Martin is a retailer.
b. Martin's price to Pace was because the particular product was damaged by water from a flood.
c. Pace's price reduction was because of a functional discount.
d. Smith was selling Martin's product at a discount causing Pace to lose sales.

7. Which antitrust act applies to both the sale of goods and the sale of services?

a. Clayton Act
b. Robinson–Patman Act
c. Securities Act of 1933
d. Sherman Act

8. Skyler Corporation has been charged with sex discrimination. Which defense could be recognized?

a. Lifting of heavier weights is involved in the designated men's positions.
b. Men and women are paid the same piecemeal rate.
c. The employees are represented by a union.
d. Women are excluded because the work involved is extremely dangerous.

9. John was injured while working for Acme Manufacturing because he failed to use a machine's safety mechanism. John's claim for workers' compensation will be

a. denied if John was negligent.
b. denied if John was grossly negligent.
c. reduced by the amount of damages attributable to John's own fault.
d. paid in full.

10. Under the Fair Labor Standards Act, the following is required:

a. double time on Sundays or holidays if hours worked for week exceed 40.
b. minimum wage.
c. pay for hours worked in excess of eight hours for any day must be time and a half.
d. children under the age of 16 can work only for their parent(s).

11. Which of the following statements about social security is correct?

a. A self-employed individual is exempt from social security coverage.
b. An employer must make contributions for each employee.

c. Social security coverage is optional.

d. An employer may decide whether to make contributions for each employee.

_____

12. Calvin was laid off by Atlas Corporation. Calvin might be denied unemployment compensation

a. if he had not worked enough weeks prior to being laid off.

b. if he is wealthy and does not need it.

c. if the employer was forced to lay off Calvin because of the economy.

d. if he is an hourly employee.

_____

13. ABC Corporation would have to recognize union A if

a. union A had recognition cards from 60 percent of the ABC employees.

b. in an election 100 workers voted for the union, 95 voted for no union, and 7 abstained from voting.

c. an employer strongly urged employees to vote against the union.

d. union A represented ABC's major competitor.

_____

14. The federal agency that directly oversees private employer–union relationships is

a. the Equal Employment Opportunity Commission.

b. the National Labor Relations Board.

c. the Occupational Safety and Health Act.

d. the Department of Labor.

_____

15. Union A is trying to organize the employees of Huskie Corporation. In a speech to the Huskie employees, the corporation president may

a. state the corporation wishes no union.

b. tell employees that the usual Christmas bonus will be suspended pending the election.

c. poll the employees as to their preference.

d. threaten retaliation if the union should win.

_____

16. The first comprehensive labor act was

a. the Equal Pay Act.

b. the Landrum–Griffin Act.

c. the Taft–Hartley Act.

d. the Wagner Act.

_____ **17.** Which of the following is totally a matter of state law?

a. Workplace safety rules
b. Unemployment compensation
c. Workers' compensation
d. Child-labor laws

_____ **18.** Which statement concerning the employment at-will doctrine is incorrect?

a. The doctrine is being challenged in many courts today.
b. The doctrine is not applicable to persons subject to a collective bargaining agreement.
c. The doctrine prohibits removal of an employee except for cause.
d. The doctrine has especially been challenged in regard to public policy matters.

Use this information in answering Questions 19 to 21.

Revel, Inc. employs 20 persons in the production of sport watches. The plant is unionized.

_____ **19.** Revel has had some serious employee theft problems that they wish to deter. Revel seeks your counsel. Which of the following ideas would probably be legal?

a. Begin random testing for drugs.
b. Use random lie detector tests.
c. Fire all of the union employees and hire a new workforce.
d. Search outer garments of workers as they exit the plant.

_____ **20.** Revel changed the working schedules of five employees from eight hours a day/five days a week to 10 hours a day/four days a week. These workers

a. may be eligible for workers' compensation.
b. would be eligible for time-and-a-half pay for hours worked above eight hours each day.
c. would deserve a pay adjustment under the Equal Pay Act.
d. would have no claim under the Fair Labor Standards Act.

_____ **21.** Revel has a right-to-work workforce. One employee, not a member of the union, was discharged for a third violation of drinking on the job. The discharge was consistent with Revel policies and past actions. Which of the following statements is correct?

a. The employee has no right to union assistance.
b. If the employee is a minority covered by Title VII, the employer will probably lose.
c. The employee will probably be eligible for unemployment compensation.
d. The discharge would probably not violate the NLRA.

Solutions

Answer	Refer to:

1. (c) [A-1] Administrative agencies are often considered the fourth branch of government but actually are part of the executive branch.

2. (a) [A-3-d] Administrative law judges act as the equivalent to trial judges in hearing administrative cases.

3. (a) [B-4-b, 5-d] Monopoly is a violation under the Sherman Act. Criminal prosecution is possible under the Sherman Act.

4. (c) [B-5-a] Price fixing is a per se violation under the Sherman Act. It does not matter whether the agreed on price is a fair price.

5. (a) [B-6-a] The described actions would result in a tying contract.

6. (d) [B-7-c] The fact that Smith is selling the product at a discount is not an acceptable reason for Martin to sell the same product at a lesser price to Pace.

7. (d) [B-5] The Sherman Act is the only antitrust act that applies to both the sale of goods and the sale of services. (The Clayton and Robinson–Patman Acts apply only to the sale of goods.)

8. (b) [E-2-a] A bona fide piecemeal plan is a legal defense under the Equal Pay Act even if it generally results in higher net pay for men.

9. (d) [D-3-b] An employee recovers under *workers' compensation* for all injuries suffered during work except intentional injuries. The employee either recovers the full permissible amount or none.

10. (b) [C-1-b, C-1-d] The Fair Labor Standards Act provides for a minimum wage to be paid employees except for some specific exemptions.

11. (b) [C-3-c] The amount deducted for FICA for an employee must be supplemented by an additional amount contributed by the employer.

12. (a) [C-2-c] To recover unemployment compensation, an employee must show substantial past employment and involuntary severance.

13. (b) [F-5-b] An employer must recognize a union when the union gets the majority of votes in a union-choice election.

14. (b)   [F-1] The National Labor Relations Board is the agency with the responsibility of overseeing private employer–union relationships.

15. (a)   [F-3-a] Answer (a) is correct as long as no threats or inducement accompany the free speech.

16. (d)   [F-2] The Wagner Act (1935) created the National Labor Relations Board.

17. (c)   [D] Workers' compensation is the correct answer. All other choices are matters of both state and federal concern and involvement.

18. (c)   [G-1-a] The employment at-will doctrine permitted just the reverse: termination without any cause (or even bad cause).

19. (d)   [G-2-d] Given the problems of theft in the plant, the search of outer garments would probably not be considered to be an unreasonable intrusion into the personal privacy of the workers.

20. (d)   [C-1-c] As long as the employees are not working more than 40 hours a week, they have no right to overtime.

21. (d)   [F-7] A discharge of an employee for cause would not result in a violation of the NLRA.

CHAPTER 26

Regulatory Law

In this chapter we focus on government regulation of business by regulatory agencies. The overall role of government regulatory agencies, with a review of several federal regulatory agencies, is described and presented in detail. The candidate should review the overall objectives of the following federal government commissions or agencies:

- Interstate Commerce Commission (ICC)

- Federal Energy Regulatory Commission (FERC)

- Federal Communications Commission (FCC)

- Environmental Protection Agency (EPA)

- Consumer Product Safety Commission (CPSC)

- Federal Trade Commission (FTC)

- Food and Drug Administration (FDA)

- Securities Exchange Commission (SEC)

In addition, the candidate should understand the purposes and functions of state public utility commissions.

Bait and switch	Interstate commerce	Security
Broker	Intrastate commerce	16b Insider
Cease and desist order	Issuer	Tariff
Consent decree	Prospectus	10b-5 Insider
Federal Trade Commission (FTC)	Proxy	Tender offer
	Registration statement	Underwriter

A. Government Regulatory Agencies

Within the executive branch of government exist a number of government regulatory agencies established for specific purposes through legislative acts. Some of these regulatory agencies are supervised directly by the President of the United States; others report directly to cabinet departments of the executive branch. The regulatory agencies highlighted in this section represent some of the more influential agencies in power at this time.

1. *Interstate Commerce Commission (ICC)*: The Interstate Commerce Commission (ICC) was established in 1887 and is one of the oldest of the federal administrative bodies. The ICC is presently subject to much deregulation by Congress. The requirement for ICC jurisdiction is that the carrier be engaged in interstate commerce. This is met by crossing state lines. ICC powers include investigation of interstate commerce and the establishment of rules and regulations governing interstate commerce.

   a. *Interstate commerce*: ICC investigations relate to interstate carriers and freight forwarders.

      EXAMPLE: The ICC will investigate allegations of prejudicial rate fixing between transit users.

   b. *Rules and regulations*: Establishment of rules and regulations concerning interstate shipments, keeping of accounts, and responsibilities to users are primary powers of the ICC.

      EXAMPLE: Railroads engaged in interstate commerce are required to maintain accounting books in a prescribed, uniform manner.

      EXAMPLE OF NEW ICC REFORM: Trucking companies have recently been exempted from such accounting rules.

   c. *Other responsibilities*: The ICC is responsible for the establishment and review of

      (1) Certificates of public convenience (the ICC award of a right to do business over a given route)

      (2) Rates, fares, and charges to be legally allowed

      (3) The number of carriers to be permitted per given route

      (4) Approval before a merger may occur between two or more interstate railroads or between two or more interstate motor carriers

      (5) Approval of any sale or purchase of an ICC-granted route from one business to another

2. *Federal Energy Regulatory Commission (FERC)*: The Federal Energy Regulatory Commission is an independent regulatory agency, established within the Department of Energy.

   a. *Responsibilities*: The FERC is empowered with many of the responsibilities of the former Federal Power Commission. Primarily, its charge includes the following priorities:

      (1) *Monitoring electrical rates*: The FERC establishes and monitors rates charged for electricity.

(2) *Monitoring rates for pipeline transportation*: The FERC establishes and monitors rates charged for the transportation of oil and gas by pipeline.

b. *General organization*: The FERC was established within the Department of Energy as part of the Department of Energy Organization Act enacted by Congress on August 2, 1977. The head of the FERC is responsible only to the President of the United States. The Economic Regulatory Administration (ERA), a division within the Department of Energy, is responsible for administering many of the directives handed down by the FERC. The ERA also has the power to order that electrical utility companies convert their operations to use coal instead of scarcer oil and natural gas resources.

EXAMPLE: In 1978, one of the ERA's first activities was to hold hearings to set rates for oil transported through the Trans-Alaska Pipeline.

3. *Federal Communications Commission (FCC)*: In essence, the Federal Communications Commission regulates all interstate communication except the awarding of cable television franchises, which local government units generally award. The FCC has the preemption power to decide franchise cable license awards but has chosen not to exercise this power.

a. *Areas of communication under FCC jurisdiction*: Specific communication areas directly under the jurisdiction of the FCC include

(1) Telephone (interstate operations)

(2) Radio (licensing and operations)

(3) Television (licensing and operations)

(4) Cable television (operations only)

(5) Communication satellites

(6) Telex

(7) Mobile telephone service

b. *Functions of the FCC*: The FCC's primary functions at the present time are quite broad and include the following specific operations:

(1) Establishing rules and regulations governing those matters over which the FCC has jurisdiction.

EXAMPLE: The prime-time-access rule, also known as the family viewing hour, reserves one evening hour per day to local television stations to program non-network shows.

(2) Granting and renewing licenses to operate (awarding of certificates of public necessity).

EXAMPLE: The FCC grants licenses to television and radio stations.

(3) Investigating potential violations of FCC regulations and rules.

EXAMPLE: The FCC investigates charges of outrageous conduct by radio station disc jockeys. Fines or even revocation of licenses may result.

    c. *Limitations of FCC powers*:

        (1) *Regulation of radio/television programming*: The FCC regulates radio and television to determine what constitutes the public interest. The FCC may prevent the airing of certain programs or commercials on television (example: cigarette advertisements), require equal time for political candidates, and impose fairness standards. The FCC may not specifically detail what overall scheduling and programming radio and television stations will follow.

        (2) *Effect on network policies*: The FCC seldom becomes concerned with individual stations until it is time for license renewal (every five years for television stations and every seven years for radio stations). Accordingly, the FCC's policies appear to affect network policies more directly than they affect individual stations.

    d. *Trends of the FCC*:

        (1) The FCC is in the process of lessening or removing regulations in many areas.

            EXAMPLE: The FCC has greatly relaxed the licensing requirements for pay TV (where a television station transmits a scrambled signal that can only be unscrambled with a decoder machine).

        (2) Radio and television station license renewals are likely to remain under close FCC scrutiny.

        (3) As new communications technology surfaces, it is probable that the FCC jurisdiction will be expanded to apply.

            EXAMPLE: The FCC jurisdiction was broadened to include communication satellites and mobile telephone services as these technologies evolved.

        (4) The FCC favors a maximum diffusion of control of radio and television stations. Local control and ownership will generally prevail over non-local control in the granting of station licenses.

    e. *FCC jurisdiction*:

        (1) The FCC has primary jurisdiction to resolve disputes concerning interstate communications matters.

            EXAMPLE: An allegation of improper conduct by a radio station would be tried before an administrative law judge for the FCC and not a court.

        (2) Federal courts may be utilized only on appeal of FCC rulings.

4. *Environmental Protection Agency (EPA)*: The Environmental Protection Agency was established in 1970 to consolidate the federal government's efforts in protecting the environment.

    a. *Functions of the EPA*:

        (1) *Regulation of external pollutants*: The EPA regulates industry as to external pollutants.

        (a) Pollutant discharges of factories, such as smokestack pollution at a steel plant.

        (b) Pollutant discharges of consumer goods, such as auto emission standards.

    (2) *Types of external pollutants*: The EPA's regulation of external pollutants by industry includes the following types of pollution:

        (a) Air

        (b) Water

        (c) Pesticides

        (d) Solid waste (land pollution)

        (e) Noise

        (f) Radiation

b. *Civil or criminal sanctions*: The EPA monitors pollution discharges. If discharges exceed the discharge standards, the violator is subject to civil or criminal sanctions.

    (1) *Civil sanctions*: Fines, injunctions, and/or seizure.

    (2) *Criminal sanctions*: Fines and/or imprisonment.

c. *Environmental impact studies*: Federal agencies are required to perform environmental impact studies before federal dollars are spent on programs that will affect the environment.

5. *Consumer Product Safety Commission (CPSC)*: Consumer product safety protection legislation is monitored by the Consumer Product Safety Commission (CPSC).

a. *Consumer Product Safety Act*: The overall purpose of the act is to protect the public from dangerous products and to provide for the evaluation of product safety hazards.

b. *Major functions of the CPSC*:

    (1) Establishes *consumer* product safety standards.

    (2) Analyzes product injury data (investigation).

    (3) Enforces consumer product safety standards:

        (a) Quality of the product

        (b) Design of the product

        (c) Labeling of the product (warnings)

        (d) Performance of the product

        (e) Manufacturing of the product

    (4) Establishes industry standards:

        (a) Notice of proposed standards must be given to the public.

(b) Public hearings are held by the CPSC. The CPSC must evaluate the cost of a proposed product safety standard in relation to the expected consumer benefit.

EXAMPLE: The CPSC wishes to require a reduction of potentially dangerous microwave oven leakages. The CPSC would have to calculate the probable costs to the microwave manufacturing industry and contrast this with the protected consumer benefit. In short, the CPSC would have to conduct a cost–benefit analysis.

c. *Product injury analysis function—investigation*: The Injury Information Clearinghouse of the CPSC serves three primary purposes:

(1) *Data collection*: Data on injuries, illness, or death caused by various consumer products is collected.

(2) *Cooperation from manufacturer*: Manufacturer cooperation is sought in voluntarily correcting, removing, and/or stopping the manufacture of a defective consumer product.

(3) *Public warnings*: Consumer warnings are issued to the public about dangerous products.

d. *Enforcement of Consumer Product Safety Act*:

(1) *Hearings*: Administrative hearings are similar to those described concerning the FTC.

(2) *Remedies*: Possible remedies include requiring the manufacturer to

(a) Provide notice and/or warning of a defective consumer product to consumers

(b) Repair or replace a defective product or provide a refund to consumers

(c) Recall a product for repair or replacement

6. *The Federal Trade Commission (FTC)*: The Federal Trade Commission is a federal administrative agency whose primary responsibility is to keep business competition fair, free, and open. In essence, the FTC is a "watchdog" over business conduct and activity.

a. *Areas of commerce*: The areas of commerce regulated by the FTC include

(1) Advertising

(2) Antitrust laws (Clayton Act and Robinson–Patman Act)

(3) Consumer credit

(4) Product safety

(5) Unfair methods of competition

b. *Functions of the FTC*:

(1) *Regulation*: The FTC makes rules (regulations) which implement and/or interpret laws of Congress. Regulations have the force of law.

(2) *Advice to businesses*: The FTC gives advice and provides guidelines to businesses and/or industries.

(3) *Investigation of business practices*: The FTC investigates activities and practices that may be in violation of FTC regulations or statutes.

(4) *Hearings*: The FTC conducts adjudicative hearings to determine whether violations actually exist. Hearings may result from FTC-initiated investigations or from actions begun by third parties such as consumers or competitors.

c. *The FTC's role in regulation of advertising*:

(1) *Substantiation of product claims*: All product claims must be capable of being substantiated as true and not unfair or deceptive.

EXAMPLES:

A product endorsement by a famous person is illegal if the product is not actually used by that person.

A claim of consumer preference must be through a fair and actual objective determination.

Competitor price comparisons must not be deceptive or misleading. (Comparing a "stripped" car price vs. a competitor's make "fully loaded" would be misleading.)

Advertising special and/or sale prices which, in fact, are not special or sale prices are deceptive.

Advertising a product just to lure customers in to get them to buy a different or more expensive product (bait and switch) is deceptive. (A store advertises a low price on a basic white washing machine, but has in stock or sells only more expensive machines.)

Usage of simulation vs. actual showing of the product, without adequate disclosure, is unfair and deceptive.

(2) *Issuance of industry-wide rules*: The FTC may issue industry-wide rules regulating commercial advertising. (This power has been a very controversial matter before Congress.)

(3) *Issuance of cease and desist orders*: The FTC can issue cease and desist orders preventing and/or forbidding deceptive and/or unfair advertising.

EXAMPLE: The FTC could order an advertisement discontinued where a professional ball player claims that he always eats a certain cereal, whereas, in fact, he does not.

d. *Regulation of credit*: The FTC has the responsibility for the protection of consumer credit transactions, including the borrowing of money, the reporting of credit history, billing and collection practices. This is done as a result of four major federal legislative acts.

(1) *Truth in Lending Act (TILA)*: The purpose of this act is to provide consumers with information about the costs of borrowing money prior to the actual commitment to borrow money for a consumer purpose. With this

knowledge, consumers are better able to shop around for the best credit opportunity.

    (a) *Consumer purpose*: The borrowing of money must be for a consumer purpose (defined to be for personal, family, or household purposes only).

        EXAMPLE: Carol wishes to borrow $2,500 to purchase a computer for home usage. This would be a loan subject to the TILA. However, the purchase of the same computer for her floral shop would not be.

    (b) *Limitations of the act*: TILA does not regulate the amount lenders may charge for credit.

  (2) *Equal Credit Opportunity Act (ECOA)*: The purpose of this act is to make credit available to all worthy applicants without regard for race, marital status, religion, or sex (among detailed factors). A consumer denied credit has the right to be told the specific reason(s) for being denied.

      EXAMPLE: Susan is denied credit from General Motors Acceptance Corporation for the purchase of a new Camaro. Susan has a right to be told why.

  (3) *Fair Credit Reporting Act*: The purpose of this act is to regulate consumer credit agencies in regard to consumer credit histories and the release of consumer credit information.

      EXAMPLE: In learning why she was turned down for her loan, in the previous example, Susan discovers that her credit record contains a false report of failure to pay a loan. Susan has a right to have the record corrected.

  (4) *Fair Debt Collection Practices Act*: The purpose of this act is to prevent abusive practices in the collection of consumer data.

      EXAMPLE: A bill collector is prohibited from representing himself as an attorney if he is not. Continuous calls at all hours of the day are prohibited.

  e. *Regulation of antitrust activity*: (See Section B of Chapter 25 for an explanation of antitrust laws.)

7. *Food and Drug Administration (FDA)*: The objective of the Federal Food, Drug, and Cosmetic Act is to exclude impure, defective, or misbranded food, drugs, and/or cosmetic products from interstate commerce. The act is enforced by the Food and Drug Administration (FDA). (Generally, states also enact and enforce health standard laws.)

  a. *Enforcement powers of the FDA*:

    (1) The seizure of defective products

    (2) Securing injunctions against the creation, handling, and/or storage of defective products

        (3) Bringing civil actions for money damages and/or fines

        (4) Bringing criminal actions against violators

  b. *Product evaluation by the FDA*:

        (1) Tests and certifies new drugs

        (2) Tests products overall to discover impure, defective, or mishandled food, drug, and/or cosmetic products

        (3) Investigates manufacturing, processing, and handling procedures relating to health standards

           EXAMPLE: The FDA may inspect food warehouses to ensure that foods handled therein are not subject to rodents, cockroaches, or other pests.

8. *Securities and Exchange Commission (SEC)*: To protect the investing public, the Securities and Exchange Commission (SEC) was established to ensure disclosure of relevant, accurate, and truthful information by sellers of new securities. In addition, the SEC has the authority to establish rules needed to ensure the integrity of the securities market and protect the investing public from fraud and/or manipulation in the sale or purchase of securities. The three major legislative acts involving the SEC are the Securities Act of 1933 (the Truth in Securities Law), the Securities Exchange Act of 1934, and the Foreign Corrupt Practices Act of 1977.

  a. *The Securities Act of 1933*: This act, also known as the Truth in Securities Law, regulates the issuance (sale) of new securities to investors.

        (1) *Securities*: Essentially, a security is an investment. For the investment to be called a security, the investor

           (a) Must not be actively engaged in the management of the business

           (b) Must be expecting investment returns (profits) primarily from the efforts of others

              EXAMPLE: The buyer of an IBM bond does not expect nor receive the right to be actively involved in the management of IBM.

        Unless an exemption applies, a seller of new securities must receive SEC approval before offering new securities to the public.

        EXAMPLES OF SECURITIES:

        Stock of a corporation

        Bonds (where some of the seller's assets are put up as security to ensure payment of the debt)

        Debentures (where no specific seller's assets are put up to secure repayment of the debt)

        Limited partnership interest

        Real estate investment trust interest (REIT)

        In some cases, a franchise business (where the franchisee's actions are so completely controlled by the franchisor)

(2) *Procedure for SEC approval of new security sales*: The procedure for obtaining SEC approval of the sale of new securities includes the following:

   (a) The seller must file a *registration statement* with the SEC. The registration statement provides basic information as to the seller's operations, the proposed use of the monies to be received, and the manner of distributing the new securities. It must include financial statements, certified by a CPA as to accuracy and truthfulness.

   (b) The SEC reviews the registration statement. Only 20 days are allowed to review it unless additional information is needed.

   (c) The SEC evaluates the registration statement only to determine if sufficient information exists so as to enable the prospective investor to decide to buy or not to buy.

   EXAMPLE: New Fangle Corporation wishes to sell stock to raise money to produce silver widgets. If the SEC approves the registration statement, it does not mean that the SEC believes it to be a good idea or a good investment. SEC approval simply means enough information is available for the investor to make a purchase decision.

   During the SEC review process, the seller may not make any offers or accept any sales.

   (d) If the SEC approves the sale offering, the seller sells to the public through use of a prospectus. A prospectus provides basic information to prospective purchasers. In essence, a prospectus is a summarized registration statement and constitutes the official offering of a security for sale to the public. Announcement of offerings generally appear in "tombstone ads."

   EXAMPLE: Look at the Wall Street Journal, *near the market reports, for examples of "tombstone ads."*

   (e) The potential sellers of new securities who are required to file with the SEC include

   • *An issuer*: Normally, the entity (business) selling the security.

   • *An underwriter*: The distributor of an issuer's securities.

   • *A broker*: An individual who acts in the role of an underwriter.

(3) *Exempted securities*: The seller of exempted securities need not file with the SEC regardless of the amount of money involved. Some types of exempted securities include

   (a) Securities being sold by any governmental body or agency

   (b) Commercial paper (checks, notes) which is payable within nine months

   (c) Securities of charitable nonprofit organizations: for example, private schools, churches, Girl Scouts

(d) Small public offerings (SEC Regulation A):

- The offering must not be greater than $5 million issuance.

- An offering circular must be provided prospective purchasers (similar in nature to a prospectus but in more condensed fashion).

- There may be any number of offerees or purchasers.

(e) Regulation D, Rule 505:

- There are $5 million of issuances per 12-month period.

- The offering is limited to 35 unaccredited purchasers (institutional or sophisticated investors).

- Less detailed information than the prospectus or offering circular must be provided prospective buyers.

(f) Exchanges between the issuer and its existing security holders:

- It is presumed that existing security holders are already knowledgeable.

- The rule covers stock splits, reorganizations.

(g) Intrastate offerings (seldom utilized):

- Securities are offered and sold exclusively to residents of issuer's state of incorporation.

- Good faith on behalf of issuer is no defense where there is an out-of-state offeree or purchaser.

(4) *Potential liability under the 1933 Act*: Antifraud provisions apply to any seller(s) of securities using telephone or mail (interstate communications) to defraud prospective or actual purchasers.

(a) Civil or criminal violations are possible.

(b) Who may sue?

- Any party who can show actual knowledge of a false statement or a misleading omission in the registration statement and/or prospectus.

- It is sufficient that the plaintiff simply purchased the security. There is no need to prove direct reliance.

(c) Who may be sued?

- The issuer.

- Any person who signed the registration statement.

- All directors named in the registration statement.

- Any expert providing attributed statements in the registration statement. Such experts are likely to be CPAs, attorneys, engineers, or other professionals.

      (d)   Burden of proof is on the defendant(s) after plaintiff shows actual knowledge of false statement or misleading omission and damages.

      (e)   Due diligence is the major available defense:

- A reasonable investigation was undertaken before signing the registration statement.

- In good faith, the registration statement was believed to be true.

b. *The Securities Exchange Act of 1934*: This act created the Securities and Exchange Commission (SEC). Primary purposes of the act include the following:

(1) *Proxies*: The act applies to proxies (granting of authority to another to vote one's shares) and tender offers (offers to purchase the shares of a corporation).

(2) *Required reporting*: Regular reports are required from companies that have total assets in excess of $5 million and 500 or more shareholders.

(3) *Rule 16b*: Rule 16b prohibits short-swing profits of *insiders* (officers, directors, and principal shareholders representing 10 percent or more of the ownership; trader on security exchange).

      (a)   Insiders may not sell, then buy—or buy, then sell—within a six-month period.

          EXAMPLE: John, a 16b insider, purchased 50 shares of Ace stock on January 9. John may not sell any Ace stock for six months thereafter, or he will lose his profits.

      (b)   Insider gains belong to the corporation.

      (c)   Losses averted belong to the corporation if the insider should thereafter repurchase corporate stock.

(4) *Rule 10b-5*: Rule 10b-5 prohibits insider usage of knowledge.

      (a)   An insider is defined as anyone with proprietary (inside) knowledge, whether involved with the corporation or not. Insider information is information not generally available to the public in the purchase or sale of securities.

          EXAMPLES:

          Corporation clerical workers typing information

          "Tippees"—people given tips

          Anyone who knows and uses inside information

      (b)   An insider must allow inside news to be publicly released and disseminated before acting personally in buying or selling.

      (c)   A violation of 10b-5 results in loss of the profits to any party injured by the sale to the insider.

      (d)   The plaintiff must prove that the defendant

- Had actual knowledge of the falsity
- Used reckless disregard of the truth in making a false statement
- Intentionally made a material omission or false statement

(e) The question posed by 10b-5 is whether a prudent investor would be expected to respond to such information if already inclined to buy or sell the security.

(f) Plaintiff need not prove actual reliance.

EXAMPLE: Tom buys 100 shares of ABC stock from Ken without telling Ken that ABC Corporation will announce a major oil field discovery in three days. If the stock should thereafter go up, the profits would rightfully belong to Ken.

c. *The Foreign Corrupt Practice Act of 1977*: An amendment to the 1934 act, this law prohibits all U.S. corporations (their officers, agents, or employees) from bribing foreign governmental or political officials.

(1) The act imposes internal control requirements for corporate financial statements so as to allow the SEC to better detect possible bribing violations.

(2) Criminal fine and/or imprisonment is possible for violators of this law.

B. State Public Utility Commissions

State public utility commissions have jurisdiction over intrastate rates, routes, and services for gas, electricity, water, common carriers, and telephone communications. The state commissions have no authority as to interstate utility rates, routes, and/or concerns. A state must be careful not to burden interstate commerce unduly with its state laws.

EXAMPLE: Louisiana was not permitted to tax the passage of offshore oil extracted beyond its state coastline authority.

1. *Purposes of State Utility Regulation*:

a. *Licensing of utility services*: State public utility commissions provide certificates of necessity.

b. *Utility services*: Commissions prescribe mode and manner of utility service to the public.

c. *Rates, services, and operations*: Commissions also establish rates, variety of services, and means of operations for utilities as well as later review.

EXAMPLE: An electrical utility company must secure state approval for any rate increase.

d. *Issuance of certificates of necessity*: A certificate of necessity is a right to do business and to compete. It may be an exclusive or a nonexclusive right.

(1) Exclusive franchise right.

EXAMPLE: Awarding intrastate electrical franchise for a given part of the state to an electrical company.

       (2)   Nonexclusive franchise right.

           EXAMPLE: Establishing two independent carrier routes between two in-state cities.

2. *State Delegation of Utility Regulation*:

  a. States may delegate regulatory powers to local government units (cities, counties).

  b. Some regulatory areas are fully delegated to local government units such as the awarding of cable television franchises.

3. *Tariffs*: Tariffs are descriptions of available services, equipment, rates, rules, and regulations between the user and the utility company.

  a. *Tariff approval*: Tariffs must be approved by the appropriate utility commission and publicly filed.

  b. *The effect of tariffs*: Tariffs have the effect of law.

  c. *A tariff rate-change procedure*:

       (1)   Request for new tariff rate is filed with the appropriate utility commission.

       (2)   Public notice of hearing is made.

       (3)   Memorandum and evidence of need are submitted by the utility company.

       (4)   Commission conducts a public hearing to establish the need for a rate hike. The following factors are generally considered:

           (a)   Operating expenses

           (b)   Past earnings or losses

           (c)   Apparent need

           (d)   Potential effect on the user

       (5)   After the finding of fact is concluded by the commission, the tariff request may be denied, partially approved, or fully approved.

Review Questions

DIRECTIONS: Select the best answer from the four alternatives. Write the letter of your answer in the blank to the left of the number.

_____ 1. The FTC has authority to act in each of these areas except

    a. product safety.
    b. consumer credit.
    c. food impurities.
    d. antitrust actions.

_____ 2. The following remedies for unsafe products may be sought by the Consumer Product Safety Commission except for

    a. warnings on products and/or packages.
    b. treble damages.
    c. requiring manufacturers to replace products.
    d. requiring manufacturers to provide a refund.

_____ 3. Which of the following agencies deals with the regulation of the sale and exchange of stock?

    a. Federal Trade Commission
    b. Interstate Commerce Commission
    c. Securities and Exchange Commission
    d. Federal Communications Commission

_____ 4. The Securities Act of 1933 accomplished which of the following?

    a. Creation of the Securities and Exchange Commission
    b. Regulation of issuance of new securities
    c. Established rules as to insiders
    d. Established the Foreign Corrupt Practices Act

_____ 5. The following are all securities under the Securities Act of 1933 except

    a. corporate stock.
    b. bonds.
    c. limited partnership interest.
    d. checks.

      6. A prospectus approved by the SEC assures a prospective investor that

          a. the sale will be free of any fraud.
          b. the offered security is at least not a bad investment risk.
          c. the SEC has reviewed the prospectus for adequacy of investor information.
          d. the SEC will stand behind any losses suffered.

      7. The FCC has jurisdiction to do all of the following things except

          a. require the showing of specific programs.
          b. require one hour of prime-time television access for local television stations.
          c. require an opportunity for opponents of a major issue to rebut on a television show.
          d. require equal time for all qualified candidates for a public office.

      8. The granting of a specific route by the ICC is called a

          a. certificate of public necessity.
          b. certificate of public convenience.
          c. forwarder's certificate.
          d. controlled airspace.

      9. A state public utility commission would potentially have jurisdiction over

          a. licensing of television stations in the state.
          b. the interstate telephone rates for its residents.
          c. the rates for electricity sold to its residents.
          d. federal clean water laws.

     10. The FTC's regulation of consumer credit is intended to accomplish all of the following *except*

          a. regulate the amount lenders can charge consumers for borrowing money.
          b. prevent discrimination in lending because of sex.
          c. allow consumer challenge to errant credit report information.
          d. make creditors specify to consumers the reason credit was denied.

     11. The agency most likely to have authority over a defective toy telephone for children would be

          a. the Securities and Exchange Commission.
          b. the Consumer Products Safety Commission.
          c. the Federal Communications Commission.
          d. the Federal Trade Commission.

Use this information in answering Questions 12 and 13.

Star Corporation is an independent oil refining company. Star needed money for expansion of refining capacity, so it filed a registration statement and a prospectus with the SEC to sell $10 million worth of stock. Star failed to disclose an ongoing major investigation by the EPA concerning air pollutant emissions at their major refinery. Oswald Oil, another independent oil refining company, is seeking to acquire Star Corporation.

12. Concerning the registration statement and prospectus:

   a. the registration statement provides information as to the seller's operations.
   b. the SEC reviews the registration statement to approve it as to its soundness of investment.
   c. the SEC may accept offers but not sales during the SEC review process.
   d. the registration statement is what is actually given investors.

13. The EPA could seek all of the remedies listed below against Star Corporation except

   a. criminal fines.
   b. an injunction to stop the emissions.
   c. imprisonment of responsible corporate officers.
   d. treble damages.

Solutions

Answer	Refer to:

1. (c)   [A-6-a] The FTC has broad authority but not over food impurities.

2. (b)   [A-5-d] Treble damages are not available for violations of the Consumer Product Safety Act.

3. (c)   [A-8] The SEC is the federal administrative agency responsible for overseeing the issuance of new securities.

4. (b)   [A-8-a] The regulation of the issuance of new securities came into the law with the Securities Act of 1933.

5. (d)   [A-8-a(1)] Checks are not an example of securities; they are not considered an investment.

6. (c)   [A-8-a(2) (d)] The SEC reviews the registration statement and prospectus to determine the adequacy of investor information so that an investor can reasonably decide whether to invest.

7. (a)   [A-3-c(1)] The FCC cannot require the showing of specific programs.

8. (b)   [A-1-c(1)] The ICC regularly issues certificates of public convenience, the right to do business over a given route.

9. (c)   [B] State utility commissions are involved primarily with setting rates and awarding service areas for in-state service of customers.

10. (a)   [A-6-d] The FTC's regulation of credit does not apply to the interest rates that lenders can charge consumers. Such laws, known as usury laws, are a matter of state law.

11. (b)   [A-5-a] The Consumer Product Safety Commission (CPSC) has jurisdiction over child toy safety.

12. (a)   [A-8-a(2) (a)] A registration statement provides background information about the issuer, including information about the issuer's operations.

13. (d)   [A-4-b] Treble damages are not available for a breach of environmental laws.

CHAPTER 27

Personal and Intellectual Property

Anything that is capable of being owned is property. Ownership includes the right to possess, control use, or transfer. Land, including attached buildings, fixtures, and crops, is called *real property* and is dealt with in Chapter 28. Property other than real property is known as *personal property*. If the property has physical existence, it is considered *tangible*. If not, it is *intangible* property (shares of stock, checks, or other such representation of value). Finally, property is either *public* (owned by the government) or *private*.

Copyright, patent, and trademark interests are also considered property. These legal interests are commonly referred to as *intellectual property*. To encourage creative thinking and innovative advances in technology, federal law affords the author or inventor certain protection for his/her work. For instance, one who writes a poem, book, or computer program may apply for copyright protection. One who invents a new tool or a unique design for a ballpoint pen may apply for a patent. A business may wish to obtain trademark protection for the distinctive marking it places on its products. Copyrights and patents give the protected parties the exclusive right to market and profit from their works. Anyone who violates the copyright or patent will be held liable for damages. In this chapter we review the law of personal property, including copyrights, patents, and trademarks.

KEY TERMS

Chattel mortgage	Literary works
Copyright	Patent
Fair use	Patent and Trademark Office
Fixtures	Personal property
Infringement	Real property

517

A. Classification of Property

Land, including attached buildings, fixtures, and crops, is called *real property*. Property other than real property is known as *personal property*. Personal property that is attached to real property and becomes a part of it is known as a *fixture*.

EXAMPLE: Paneling constitutes personal property when brought to a construction site. When installed in offices in a building, paneling becomes a fixture.

1. *Types of Personal Property*:

    a. *Tangible*: Personal property having a physical existence—capable of physical possession—is known as tangible personal property.

    EXAMPLES: A book, an automobile, a stereo set.

    b. *Intangible*: Personal property not existing in physical form—incapable of physical possession—is known as intangible personal property.

    EXAMPLES:

    Stock certificates only represent the ownership of stocks in a corporation. Corporate ownership is determined solely by the corporation's shareholder records.

    Patents, copyrights, and accounts receivable.

2. *Acquisition of Ownership*: Individuals acquire ownership of personal property through purchase, gift, finding abandoned or lost property, and by will or descent.

    a. *Acquisition by purchase*:

    EXAMPLE: Ed buys a can of paint at the local Sears store.

    b. *Acquisition by gift*:

    (1) *Parties*:

        (a) *Donor*: Person making the gift.

        (b) *Donee*: Person receiving the gift.

    (2) *Required elements of gift*:

        (a) Present donor intent to make a gift to the donee

        (b) Delivery of property and/or title thereto

        (c) Acceptance of the gift by the donee

    (3) *Types of gifts*:

        (a) *Intervivos gift*: A gift made during the donor's lifetime.

        (b) *Testamentary gift*: Personal property may be transferred through a will that becomes effective upon the death of its maker.

        (c) *Causa mortis*: This type of gift requires a fear of imminent death in the donor. If the donor survives or dies of another cause, the gift is considered legally canceled.

            EXAMPLE: Al was told by his doctor that he has terminal, inoperable cancer and is not expected to live more than 60 days. Al decides to give his antique desk to Sue and arranges to have it moved to her home. Through a medical miracle, Al survives and is completely cured. The gift is canceled.

   c. *Acquisition by finding property*:

     (1) *Abandoned property*: If property is abandoned, the finder receives full ownership rights. Property is considered abandoned when it is obvious that the previous owner intended to relinquish ownership rights. The manner, place, and time of the previous owner's parting with the property are relevant in determining whether abandonment has occurred.

     EXAMPLE: Adam finds some Indian arrowheads while tilling his garden.

     (2) *Lost or mislaid property*: If property is lost, the finder has rights superior to everyone but the rightful owner. If property is mislaid, the owner of the premises upon which it is found has rights superior to all but the rightful owner.

     EXAMPLE: Lassie, a dog, wanders onto Hector's property. Hector would not get good title to the lost dog because title is still held by Lassie's owners.

     (3) *Other types of ownership claims*: It is often difficult to ascertain whether property is lost, mislaid, or abandoned. Much case law exists regarding determination of conflicting ownership claims to such property.

   d. *Acquisition by descent*: Personal property can be acquired by relatives of a deceased person who dies without a will by descent. Each state has its own law establishing the order of descent. This is known as the *law of intestacy*.

3. *Chattel Mortgages on Personal Property*: A chattel mortgage represents the giving of security interest in personal property, similar to that of giving a mortgage on real property. Today, UCC Article IX is in effect and governs the issuance of chattel mortgages, except in Louisiana.

B. Copyrights

A *copyright* is legal protection available to the author of a literary work. A copyright gives the author the exclusive right to use the work subject to certain legally recognized exceptions.

1. *Protection of Rights in Literary Works*: Copyright protection is available to the author of a literary work. A literary work may take various forms, such as

- Books, magazines, journals, and newspapers
- Plays, lectures, and musical compositions
- Artworks, photographs, and graphic designs
- Motion pictures and recordings
- Computer programs and data bases
- Audiovisual displays
- Any other verbal or numerical symbols

2. *Protection Is Not Automatic*: The author of a literary work must take certain precautions to qualify for copyright protection.

   a. *Release of work*: The author must not allow the work to be released to the public unless it bears an indication of the author's intent to copyright the work.

      (1) *Intent*: The intent may consist of the word *copyright*, the year the work is released, and the name of the author.

      (2) *Copyright symbol*: The copyright symbol © should be used on all works the author intends to copyright because it is recognized in many countries besides the United States.

   b. *Registration of copyright*: To enforce his or her rights fully in court, the author must register the copyright with the Copyright Office in the Library of Congress in Washington, D.C. This requires filing an application form, which is accepted by the Register of Copyrights.

3. *Duration of Copyright Protection*:

   a. *Author known*: Copyright protection lasts for the lifetime of the author plus 50 years.

   b. *Author unknown*: If the author is unknown or if the work is done under the name of a fictitious person, the duration of copyright protection is 75 years from the date the work was first released to the public (or 100 years from the date the work was created if its creation preceded its release by more than 28 years).

   c. *Work created prior to January 1978*: If the work was created before January 1, 1978, its copyright protection is for only 28 years. (An additional 47 years of protection may be applied for upon the expiration of the first 25 years.)

4. *Nature of Copyright Protection*: The author of a copyrighted work has the right to the exclusive use of the work subject to certain legal exceptions.

   a. *Permission to use copyrighted work*: The holder of a copyright may grant permission to another party to use the copyrighted work. The permission might be obtained in return for the payment of a fee, or it might be granted without payment.

   b. *Fair uses of copyrighted work*: The law recognizes certain fair uses as exceptions to the copyright holder's exclusive right to the copyrighted work.

      (1) Copying a copyrighted work for purposes of studying it or using it in the course of one's research is permissible.

      (2) Using copyrighted material for limited purposes in a classroom for instructing students is permissible if the work is relatively short, and it would be impractical to obtain the consent of the copyright holder. If the material is a major part of the class material or if it is used from year to year, the author's consent may be required.

      (3) Other fair uses are permitted if they do not affect the potential market for the work or otherwise decrease the value of the work. If there is a ques-

tion as to whether a particular use is permitted under copyright laws, a legal expert should be consulted.

5. *Enforcement of Copyrights*: A party who has violated copyright law may be prosecuted for a criminal offense or sued by the copyright holder for damages.

   a. *Criminal violation*: In a criminal case, the intentional violator may be fined or imprisoned.

   b. *Civil violation*: In a civil suit for damages, the violator will be ordered to pay damages to the copyright holder.

   c. *Court orders*:

      (1) A court may enter an order directing a party to stop a practice that constitutes a copyright violation. If the party defies the order, he or she will be subject to contempt of court proceedings.

      (2) A court may order a party to turn over or destroy all illegal copies of copyrighted material.

   d. *Prosecution*: A violator may be prosecuted in a criminal case and sued for damages in another suit for the same violation.

C. Patents

A *patent* is legal protection available to the inventor of a machine, process, product, chemical, a new variety of nonpollinating plant life, or other new useful invention. A patent gives the inventor the right to prevent others from using the patented invention in the United States and its territories and possessions.

1. *Protection of Rights of Inventors*: One who invents or discovers a new process or machine may qualify for patent protection.

   EXAMPLES:

   Patent protection is also available for an inventor who manufactures a new product.

   One who discovers a new chemical, a new chemical compound, or a plant may apply for patent protection.

   One who invents or discovers useful improvements in existing machines, processes, products, chemicals, or plants may also apply for patent protection.

2. *New and Useful Requirement*: An invention must be new and useful to qualify for a patent.

   a. *Known or used*: If the invention has been known or used by others or if it is merely an obvious extension of an existing invention, it does not qualify for a patent.

   b. *Nonperformance*: If the invention does not perform the intended purpose or is otherwise not useful, it does not qualify for a patent.

3. *Obtaining a Patent*: To obtain a patent, the inventor must apply to the Patent and Trademark Office in Washington, D.C. The law does not require that the inventor be represented by a lawyer, but it is highly advisable that the inventor obtain expert assistance.

4. *Duration of Patent Protection*: Patent protection lasts for 17 years from the date the patent is granted.

5. *Nature of Patent Protection*: A patent gives the inventor the right to prevent others from making, using, or selling the invention in the United States and its territories and possessions.

    a. *No right to make*: A patent does not give the inventor the right to make, use, or sell the invention. The invention must comply with all relevant state and federal laws.

        EXAMPLE: Floyd invented a new kind of lawn mower and obtained a patent for it. The mower, however, does not comply with the standards of the Environmental Protection Agency. Floyd cannot legally market the mower unless he complies with all relevant laws. Mere possession of a patent does not give him the right to market the product. It only gives him the right to prevent others from using his invention.

    b. *Outside the United States*: It may be possible to obtain a patent protection in other countries. The United States has entered into a treaty with many other nations for the purpose of making international patent protection easier to obtain. Expert assistance should be obtained to expand patent protection beyond the United States and its territories and possessions.

    c. *Licensing*: The patent holder may grant a license permitting another party to use the invention.

6. *Enforcement of Patent Rights*: A patent holder may sue one who infringes upon the patent.

    a. *Stop practice*: The court may enter an order directing a party to stop a practice that constitutes patent infringement. If the party defies the order, it will be subject to contempt of court proceedings.

    b. *Pay damages*: The court may order the infringing party to pay damages to the patent holder.

    c. *Challenge validity*: In a patent-infringement suit, the party being sued may challenge the validity of the patent.

    d. *Countersuit*: One who is threatened with a patent-infringement suit may sue the patent holder to obtain a court ruling on the issue.

    e. *Government use*: The government may use patented inventions without permission from the patent holder. The patent holder is entitled to receive fair compensation, however, for the use of the invention.

D. Trademarks

A *trademark* is a distinctive marking, motto, or device that is placed on products to identify their source.

1. *Qualification as a Trademark*: To qualify as a trademark, the marking, motto, or device must be distinctive and must not be merely descriptive of the product or its use.

    EXAMPLE: The maker of a new soft drink places the words A Refreshing Drink *on its beverage containers. This phrase does not qualify as a trademark because it is descriptive of the product. It would be unfair to prevent competitors from describing their beverages as refreshing drinks. If the phrase was accompanied by a distinctive design, it could, with the design, qualify as a trademark.*

2. *Registration Not Required*: A trademark need not be registered with the government to be protected from infringement. Registration does add to the protection of a trademark, however, by providing proof of the date of the trademark's use.

   EXAMPLE: Two businesses use the same symbol on their products. Each claims the symbol as a trademark. One of the businesses had registered its trademark with the government in 1961. The other never registered the symbol as a trademark and cannot prove that it used the symbol on products prior to that time.

3. *Infringement*: The holder of a trademark is entitled to sue anyone who infringes upon it and to recover lost profits and a court order prohibiting further unauthorized use of the trademark.

Review Questions

DIRECTIONS: Select the best answer from the four alternatives. Write the letter of your answer in the blank to the left of the number.

_____ 1. A stock certificate is personal property. Which factor listed below is a property aspect of the stock certificate?

    a. A stock certificate is considered tangible property.
    b. A stock certificate is considered intangible property.
    c. A stock certificate could be a fixture.
    d. A stock certificate is not considered property.

_____ 2. To make a valid intervivos gift, all of the following must be present except

    a. donative intent by the donor.
    b. delivery to the donee.
    c. fear of imminent death.
    d. acceptance by the donee.

_____ 3. Copyright protection may be obtained for an original work in each of the following categories except

    a. books, magazines, journals, and newspapers.
    b. computer programs.
    c. photographs.
    d. Original works in each of the categories above may be copyrighted.

_____ 4. Copyright protection lasts for

    a. 17 years.
    b. 50 years.
    c. life of the author plus 50 years.
    d. forever.

_____ 5. Tom invented a new engine for automobiles that makes it possible to get 73 miles per gallon. Tom was granted a patent by the Patent and Trademark Office in Washington, D.C. When Tom attempted to sell cars with his new engine in them, however, he was informed by the Environmental Protection Agency that the engine did not conform to the applicable standards. Tom claims that the patent permits him to sell the engines. Is Tom correct?

    a. Yes, because patent law prevails over other applicable regulations.
    b. Yes, because patent law prevails over administrative agency regulations, but not over other federal legislation.

c. No, because patent laws merely give the inventor the right to prevent others from using the invention.

d. No, because he should have obtained copyright protection.

6. Patent protection lasts for

a. 17 years.
b. 50 years.
c. the inventor's life plus 50 years.
d. the inventor's life plus 17 years.

7. Sally obtained a patent on a new ballpoint pen she invented. She discovered Hal making and selling similar pens without permission. Sally sued Hal. Which of the following is true?

a. In the suit Hal may challenge the validity of Sally's patent.
b. The court may order Hal to stop making and selling the pens if he is found to be violating Sally's patent rights.
c. The court may order Hal to pay damages to Sally if he is found to be violating Sally's patent rights.
d. All of the above.

8. At a picnic table along the side of the highway, Elmer found a map that had directions and phone numbers written upon it. Hugo claims that the map is his and can prove that he owned it on an earlier date. Elmer's interest in the map will prevail over Hugo's if it is determined that

a. Hugo had lost the map.
b. Hugo had abandoned the map.
c. Hugo had mislaid the map.
d. Hugo had made the map.

9. Ann and her niece Susan were passengers on an airplane. The pilot announced that the plane had run out of gas and that an emergency landing would be attempted. Ann began crying and removed her diamond ring and gave it to Susan saying, "Here, this is for you. I'm going to be dead in a few minutes." The plane made a miracle landing, and Ann suffered only a sprained ankle. Susan refuses to return the ring. Which of the following statements is true?

a. Susan is entitled to keep the ring because the gift was completed.
b. Susan is entitled to keep the ring because the ring was mislaid property.
c. Ann is entitled to the return of the ring because it was a gift in contemplation of death.
d. Ann is entitled to the return of the ring because it was a fixture.

Use this information in answering Questions 10 to 12.

Bates invented a low-calorie chocolate candy formula. He called it Light Chocolate. He also wrote a book describing his seven-year ordeal in developing and perfecting the formula.

10. If Bates wants to apply for legal protection of his new formula, he should apply for

    a. copyright protection.
    b. patent protection.
    c. trademark protection.
    d. civil rights protection.

11. If Bates wishes to obtain maximum legal protection for the term *Light Chocolate* that will appear on his product, he should apply for

    a. copyright protection.
    b. trademark protection.
    c. patent protection.
    d. civil rights protection.

12. If Bates wishes to obtain maximum legal protection for his book, he should apply for

    a. copyright protection.
    b. trademark protection.
    c. patent protection.
    d. civil rights protection.

Solutions

Answer	*Refer to:*

1. (b)   [A-1-b] A stock certificate is intangible property—not having physical existence and incapable of physical possession.

2. (c)   [A-2-b(3)] A fear of imminent death is only required for a gift causa mortis.

3. (d)   [B-1] The items listed in answers (a), (b), and (c) are considered literary works subject to the copyright laws.

4. (c)   [B-3] Copyright protection lasts for the life of the author plus 50 years.

5. (c)   [C-1, C-5] The inventor must still comply with all other applicable laws and regulations. Patent protection only allows the inventor to prevent others from using the invention.

6. (a)   [C-4] Patent protection lasts for 17 years.

7. (d)   [C-6] Answers (a), (b), and (c) are correct statements regarding patent-infringement suits.

8. (b)   [A-2-c] The finder of abandoned property prevails over the previous owner. The finder of lost or mislaid property takes subject to the previous owner's interest.

9. (c)   [A-2-c] A gift made in contemplation of death is canceled if the donor does not die as he or she anticipated. Since Ann survived, the gift is canceled and she is entitled to the return of the ring.

10. (b)   [C-1] Patent protection includes protection to the inventor of a process, product, or chemical.

11. (b)   [D-1] Trademark protection is available for distinctive markings or slogans attached to products to identify their source.

12. (a)   [B-1] Copyright protection is available for literary works.

CHAPTER 28

Real Property

OVERVIEW

Anything that is owned or can be owned is property. Ownership means the right to possess, control use, and/or transfer. Land, including attached buildings, fixtures, and crops, is called *real property*. Property owned other than real property is known as *personal property*. If the property has physical existence, such as a computer, it is considered *tangible*. If not, it is *intangible* property (shares of stock, checks, or other such representation of value). Finally, property is either *public* (owned by the government) or *private* (owned by individuals).

The most effective approach to studying property is to understand the distinction between the various concepts, to be able to define specific terms, and know how they relate to each other, for example, selling mortgaged property subject to the mortgage versus a sale with the assumption of a mortgage. Practical applications will help the candidate visualize the various concepts as they are presented in this chapter. For example, a husband and wife may buy a house in joint tenancy, receive a warranty deed, assume a loan, be subject to a utility company easement for electrical lines, and have the title checked to make sure no unknown liens exist. In this example, real property is both private and tangible.

Besides real and personal property, the candidate must master the distinctions between different types of deeds to real property (warranty, quitclaim), forms of ownership (estate in severalty, tenancy in common, joint tenancy, tenancy by the entirety), methods of selling mortgaged property (subject to the mortgage or assumption of the mortgage), and various methods of acquiring and/or possessing property (deed, adverse possession, gifts).

Landlord-tenancy law requires the candidate to focus on the classifications of tenancies, rights, duties, and remedies. Fitness for use, habitability, and termination methods and reasons should be understood.

KEY TERMS   Adverse possession   Personal property
                    Easement   Quitclaim deed
                    Fixtures   Real estate mortgage
                    Foreclosure   Real property
                    Grantee   Redemption
                    Grantor   Second mortgage
                    Joint tenancy   Security interest
                    Mortgage   Tenancy in common
                    Mortgagee   Warranty deed
                    Mortgagor
                    Novation

A. Classification of Property

Property means ownership: the right to possess, use, and/or transfer real and personal property. Land, including attached buildings, fixtures, and crops, is called *real property*. Property owned that is other than real property is known as *personal property*.

1. *Real Property*: Land and any improvements on or connected with the land is *real property*. Trees and crops are considered real property until severed.

    EXAMPLES: Land, buildings, airspace above the land, minerals, and trees.

    a. *Ownership*: An owner of real property owns not only the surface but that above and below the surface. Below-surface ownership rights in minerals (oil, gas, coal, water) may be sold or leased separately from the surface real estate.

        EXAMPLE: Mary sells a firm, Black Acre, to John but retains oil and gas interests. Mary could later sell, lease, or use this retained interest.

    b. *Use of airspace*: Airspace is limited to the amount that the owner may reasonably use. Government restrictions often exist that restrict the permitted height of buildings and towers.

        EXAMPLE: Building heights are restricted close to airports so as not to interfere with airplane takeoffs and landings.

    c. *Legal interest of others*: Real property is often subject to legal interests of others, for example, utility lines, easements (right of passageway), and tenants.

        EXAMPLE: If Karen signs a one-year lease on March 1, she will have a right to remain in her apartment for one year even if the building is sold the very next day.

2. *Personal Property*: All other property that is not real property is called *personal property*. (See Chapter 27 for complete explanation of personal property.) *Fixtures* are items of personal property that have been attached to real property so as to become a part thereof.

    EXAMPLE: Bookshelves or paneling attached permanently to walls in an office.

B. Acquisition of Real Property

Real property may be acquired through purchase, gift or adverse possession, condemnation, lease, or forfeiture.

1. *Purchase*: This is the most common manner in which real property is transferred.

    a. *Writing required*: A writing (written contract) is required under the statute of frauds for the sale of land (and affixed buildings and fixtures thereon). The written contract sets forth the terms and conditions of sale, such as when the closing will be, the purchase price, and the actual items to pass with the property. It must be signed by the seller.

    EXAMPLE: Sharon agrees orally to purchase Ted's house. The contract is unenforceable because no writing (written contract) exists.

    b. *Conveyance of deed*: A deed is delivered by the seller to the buyer evidencing the sale of the property. The deed represents title to the property.

    c. *Recording of deed*: The buyer records the deed in the county courthouse so as to provide public record of ownership. The failure to record the deed would allow the seller to resell the property to another buyer if the third-party purchaser bought in good faith, for value, and without notice of prior sale.

2. *Gift*: The voluntary giving of the property to another without charge is called a *gift*. For a gift to be considered a *valid* gift, the following elements must be present:

    a. *Intent to make a gift by donor (giver)*: The donor intends to make an unconditional present gift.

    EXAMPLE: Roger tells Eugene that he is to have Roger's farm when Roger dies. This is not a present intent.

    b. *Delivery of a deed to donee (recipient)*: Delivery of a deed may be directly to the donee or to someone who accepts the gift on behalf of the donee (constructive delivery).

    c. *Acceptance of the gift by donee*: Acceptance is generally presumed where not otherwise indicated.

3. *Adverse Possession*: The taking of property from another without consent or payment may legally be accomplished by adverse possession. Acquisition by adverse possession must be

    a. *Notorious*: The adverse possessor is actually using the property.

    b. *Open*: The adverse possession is obvious in actual usage. If the usage is not sufficiently visible, adverse possession is not possible.

    EXAMPLE: James erects a garage that extends four feet onto his neighbor's property. If no consent and/or objection occurs, the land belongs to James after the number of years set by statute.

    c. *Adverse*: The possession is without permission. In essence, the taker by adverse possession is a squatter who is trespassing. Therefore, no adverse possession may occur where the person is present with consent.

    EXAMPLE: Alvin was a tenant for 23 years in a house owned by John. Alvin has no right to the house.

    d. *Hostile*: The adverse possessor is a trespasser, using the property without permission of the owner.

> **e.** *Under a claim of right*: The adverse possessor must actually claim ownership over a period of time. The statutory requirement of years of adverse possession before the property may legally be taken varies by state from 5 to 20 years. The "tacking" of years toward meeting this statutory requirement is possible.
>
> *EXAMPLE: James (see example in Section B-3-b) lived at his property for 11 years and then sold it to Elizabeth. If the adverse possession period is 20 years total, Elizabeth would have to possess the property only 9 more years.*

C. Types of Deeds

Deeds represent the giving of written title from the seller to the buyer. Specific types of deeds include quitclaim deeds, warranty deeds, and special warranty deeds.

1. *Quitclaim Deed*: The grantor (seller) conveys all he or she owns, if anything, in the property.

EXAMPLE: Kathi could give Sandy a quitclaim deed to the White House. Sandy would get no legal interest, however, because Kathi does not have any legal interest to give.

   a. *No warranties made*: If the grantor owns nothing, the grantee (buyer) receives nothing. If the grantor owns a house and conveys by quitclaim deed, the grantee receives good and rightful title.

   b. *Representation of ownership*: The grantor could be independently liable from the deed for misrepresentation or fraud in the inducement concerning false representations of ownership, if any exist.

EXAMPLE: Brenda has no real-property warranty obligations to Evan if she gives Evan a quitclaim deed to a farm that she claims to own but actually does not own and wants to convey to him legally. Brenda may, however, yet face tort liability for fraud.

2. *Warranty Deed*: In essence, a warranty deed represents a warranty by the grantor (the property seller) that the property is transferred free from all unknown defects or claims.

   a. *Warranties by grantor*: In the warranty deed, the grantor warrants that

   (1) He or she owns the property being transferred.

   (2) He or she has the right to convey the property.

   (3) The property is free from undisclosed encumbrances such as easements or mortgages.

   (4) Grantee's legal right to possession will not be disturbed.

   (5) The title to the property is good.

   EXAMPLE: Carl acquires Black Acre, a farm, from Robert by warranty deed. If Robert did not actually own Black Acre, then Carl would have a right of recovery against Robert.

   b. *Purchaser's knowledge of legal interests*: A purchaser of property is charged with knowledge, whether actually known or not, of any legal interest properly recorded against the property in the county courthouse, any defect in title evident from an inspection of the property being sold, or the zoning.

EXAMPLES:

An electric power line runs across the back lot line of Al's property. If the power line is evident, the buyer would be charged with knowledge. Thus, a buyer should carefully inspect the property.

If the electric power line (above) was a buried cable, the purchaser of the property would be charged with knowledge of it if the easement (right of passage) was recorded in the county courthouse. Thus, a buyer should carefully inspect the legal title at the county courthouse.

3. *Special Warranty Deeds*: These instruments are also known as bargain and sale deeds. All warranties of the general warranty deed described above are covered. The warranties, however, apply only to the time during which the grantor actually owned the property.

). Types of Ownership

Real property is either owned by a sole owner (only one person or entity owns the property) or by multiple owners (more than one person or entity owns the property). When there are multiple owners of the property, ownership may be characterized by joint tenancy, tenancy by the entirety, tenancy in common, or community property.

1. *Joint Tenancy*: Joint tenancy exists when there is simultaneous (concurrent) ownership of property by two or more owners with a right of survivorship. The owners must acquire their interest at exactly the same time and must be clearly designated in the deed as joint tenants.

   a. *Equal undivided interests*: Each joint tenant owns an equal undivided interest with equal rights of possession.

      EXAMPLE: If there are two joint tenants for a particular piece of real property, each owns one half, regardless of which joint tenant, if either, paid greater monies toward the purchase. If there are three joint tenants, each would own one third.

   b. *Conveyance of interest*: A joint tenant may convey his or her interest to another. The transferee becomes a tenant in common (see Section D-2) with the remaining joint tenant(s).

      EXAMPLE: A, B, and C own a farm in joint tenancy. A sells his undivided one-third interest to X. X is a tenant in common as to B and C but as to the remaining two-thirds interest B and C remain joint tenants.

   c. *Survivorship*: The surviving joint tenant(s) automatically receives the interest of a joint tenant who dies. A will has no effect.

      EXAMPLE: Kyle and Peter own a farm in joint tenancy. Kyle's will says that Kyle's son is to receive Kyle's share of the farm when Kyle dies. Peter would prevail.

   d. *Statement of joint tenancy*: When receiving real property in joint tenancy, the joint tenants must be sure that this is clearly stated. If they do not, the ownership of the property will be presumed to be tenancy in common.

2. *Tenancy in Common*: Concurrent ownership exists by two or more owners with no right of survivorship. Surviving co-owners do not receive the property.

    a. *Undivided interest*: The owners have an undivided interest (like joint tenancy).

    b. *Equality of interest*: Ownership need not be equal (unlike joint tenancy).

    EXAMPLE: A may own two-thirds while B owns one-third of a farm.

    c. *Survivorship*: When a tenant in common dies, his or her share passes by will or by descent to heirs. There is no legal right by the surviving co-owner to the property unless will or descent would so direct.

When ownership interest is not clear, it is presumed to be a tenancy in common. This is the most common means of ownership where no family connection exists.

3. *Tenancy by the Entirety*: A joint-ownership interest exists between husband and wife. This type of ownership is *not* recognized in all states.

    a. *Conveyance of interest*: Tenancy by the entirety is essentially like a joint tenancy, except that a spouse may not sell his or her share without the consent of the other.

    b. *Survivorship*: The surviving spouse receives the property as in joint tenancy.

    c. *Termination*: Tenancy by the entirety is terminated by a divorce.

4. *Community Property*: Property that is owned by husband and wife is called *community property*. Community property is recognized in only eight states.

    a. *Survivorship*: Owners have the right of survivorship (as in joint tenancy).

    b. *Ownership*: Property acquired during marriage automatically becomes community property (one-half belonging to each spouse).

E. Mortgages

In general, a mortgage represents a nonpossessory interest (lien) in real property that is given to secure a debt. People often confuse mortgages so as to believe that lenders are giving home mortgages. In fact, lenders are lending money that is secured by the house, the mortgaged property. Thus, the borrower is the *mortgagor* because he or she is giving a mortgage (interest in the property to secure a loan) to the lender, the *mortgagee*. A mortgage must be in writing because an interest in land is being conveyed. If the mortgagor defaults on the mortgage, not making required payments, a mortgagee may foreclose on the mortgage (deprive the mortgagor the right to redeem the property).

Property that is already subject to a mortgage may be mortgaged again if a lender is willing to take a second mortgage for security. The second mortgage is, of course, junior to the original mortgage. Only if the first mortgage is fully satisfied can the holder of the second mortgage recover anything.

F. Easements

In general, an easement is a nonpossessory interest in the land of another either to use (affirmative easement) or prevent usage (negative easement) in a particular manner.

Figure 28–1   Illustration of Easement

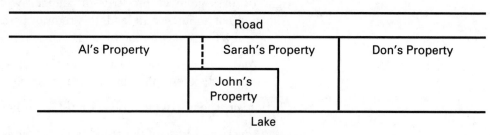

EXAMPLES:

As shown in Figure 28–1, John has a right to cross Sarah's land to reach his cabin on a lake. This right is called an affirmative easement.

John has the right to receive sunlight crossing Sarah's property. This is a negative easement, referring to the prevention of land usage by the grantor in a way detrimental to the grantee. Sarah would not be allowed to build a tall structure that would block the sunlight crossing John's property.

1. *Characteristics of an Easement*:

   a. *Nonpossessory*: The easement only provides access across another individual's property.

      EXAMPLE: In the example illustrated in Figure 28–1, John may use his access right across Sarah's property but could not erect a garage, plant a garden, or substantially alter the passageway as to usage or size.

   b. *Maintenance*: The easement must be maintained by the individual who has the right to use the property.

      EXAMPLE: John must maintain the easement.

   c. *Interference*: The property owner may not interfere with the use of the easement.

      EXAMPLE: Sarah may not interfere with John's use of the easement passageway.

2. *The Nature of Easements*: The creation of an easement interest may occur in one of three ways:

   a. *Express grant or resolution*: This easement must be in writing.

   b. *By necessity*: This is possible only where an owner of land divides the land into two or more parcels without providing a means of access. (A buyer is not to be left landlocked by the seller.)

      EXAMPLE: If Sarah had sold John his property without mention of any right of passageway across her property, he would still have a legal right because of a necessity (see Figure 28–1).

    c. *By prescription*: By continuous adverse passage, the adverse passer secures a right of passage over property of another without consent or payment. Although not an interest in land, this right of passage is achieved in a similar manner as adverse possession of land. The adverse passage must be

        (1) *Notorious*: The adverse passer must be actually using the property, and it is publicly known that the adverse passer is doing so.

        (2) *Open*: The use of the property must be sufficiently visible.

        (3) *Adverse*: The use of the property is without permission of the owner.

        (4) *Hostile*: The adverse passer is a trespasser, using the property without the permission of the owner.

        EXAMPLE: Henry gives Patti permission to go across his property on her horse. Patti can get no adverse passage right (prescriptive easement) as her passage is with Henry's consent.

        The required number of years necessary to secure a prescriptive easement may be gained by "tacking," as in adverse possession cases. The adverse passer gets the right of passageway, a nonpossessory interest versus actual possession rights that the adverse possessor gets.

        EXAMPLE: If Bill builds his garage five feet over onto Harry's property without permission and the required years go by without action by Harry, Bill is actually considered to own the five feet. Thereafter, Bill can do anything with it that one normally can do with land. A prescriptive easement would have given Bill a right of passageway forever over Harry's land but not legal title to the land or usage other than passage alone.

    3. *Termination of an Easement*:

        a. *Lapse*: The termination of time permitted to the passer has occurred.

        b. *Abandonment*: Nonusage of the easement has occurred. Generally, abandonment requires an affirmative act besides nonusage.

        c. *Merger*: Dominant and servient parcels of land have been united.

        EXAMPLE: Sarah purchases John's property.

        d. *Misuse of easement*: The easement is being used for an improper purpose.

G. The Landlord–Tenant Relationship

Property owners may lease or rent property to others. A contract known as a lease outlines the conditions of such a relationship. Most states have specific statutes regulating the landlord–tenant relationship. Below appear the general common law rules that have been changed in many places by statutes.

    1. *The Nature of the Lease*: A lease is both a contract and a conveyance of *real property*. The *lessee* (the renter) secures possession rights for a given period of time from the *lessor* (the landlord). A lease is not required to be in writing if it will be completed within one year's time. The lease is not terminated by the death of either the lessor or lessee. A purchaser of a building takes subject to any existing leases.

2. *Types of Leasehold Estates*:

    a. *Estate for years*: Tenancy is for a fixed time only, but not necessarily for only one year.

    EXAMPLE: A lease of a warehouse for 60 days is an estate for years as a lease for a set period of time.

    b. *Periodic tenancies*: Tenancy for a specified period of time, which will continue for similar periods of time until terminated, is known as periodic tenancy. Timely notice must be provided to terminate such leases.

    EXAMPLE: A month-to-month lease.

    c. *Tenancy at sufferance*: This type of tenancy occurs when a tenant holds over (stays) beyond the lease termination date or date otherwise agreed as to the termination date.

3. *Rights of Landlord*:

    a. *Rent*: The landlord receives the rent.

    b. *Lease term*: If tenant stays beyond the lease, the landlord may

        (1) Evict the tenant

        (2) Treat the tenant as a holdover with period-to-period lease

    c. *Abandonment of lease*: If the tenant wrongfully abandons the lease, the landlord may

        (1) Do nothing and sue for rent as it comes due, or

        (2) Rent the property and hold the tenant liable for any deficiencies in rent money

        Note: In some states, a landlord must show evidence of having tried to rent the lease premises (known as mitigation of damages).

4. *Duties of Landlord to Tenant*:

    a. *Implied warranty of habitability*: Warranty to the tenant that the premises are fit for human occupancy (generally applies only to residential leases).

    EXAMPLE: The warranty is breached where landlord rents apartment without heat in the winter.

    b. *Providing safe common areas*: The landlord must provide safe areas such as stairways and hallways.

    c. *Warranty of quiet enjoyment*: The warranty of quiet enjoyment is a warranty to the tenant that the landlord has the legal right to lease out the premises and that the tenant will not be removed without just cause during the term of the lease.

    d. *Termination of lease by tenant*: A breach of the landlord's duties does not legally permit the tenant to terminate the lease. Many courts, however, are finding *constructive eviction* where an apartment becomes uninhabitable. In essence, this means the tenant may move out without further legal duties to the landlord.

5. *Tenant's Transfer of Interest*:

    a. *Assignment*: The transfer of a tenant's entire interest in a lease is an assignment.

        (1) *Novation*: The original tenant, the assignor, is still liable unless there is a novation from the landlord. *Novation* is the release of a party to a contract in exchange for another being liable.

        (2) *Tenant liability*: The new tenant, the assignee, becomes personally liable to the landlord.

    b. *Sublease*: The transfer of less than the tenant's entire interest to the sublettor is known as a sublease.

        (1) *Tenant liability*: As in assignment, the assignor (the original tenant) is still liable on the lease.

        (2) *Binding terms*: The assignee is not personally liable to the landlord for a sublease. The terms and conditions of the lease are still binding on the assignee, however.

A landlord may prohibit either subleasing or assignment, or both, if so stipulated in the lease. If just subleasing is prohibited, however, the tenant may still assign the lease, and vice versa.

EXAMPLE: Ginger's lease prohibits her from assigning the lease to her apartment. She is not prohibited from subleasing, however.

Review Questions

1. Howard signs a 10-year lease for a building with Anderson. Howard agrees in the lease not to assign it. The lease could be terminated if

   a. Howard dies.
   b. Anderson sells the building to Quincy.
   c. Howard sublets the building to Morkle.
   d. Howard assigns the lease without permission.

2. Fernando has a year's lease with Maria, the landlord. Connie has agreed to take over Fernando's lease, and Maria has agreed to release Fernando from his lease obligations.

   a. Fernando received a novation.
   b. Fernando would not have been liable any longer to Maria regardless of her release.
   c. Connie would not have been personally liable on the lease if Fernando had not been released.
   d. This is an example of a sublet.

3. Curt just purchased a cabin on a lake from Milton. Although there was a passageway to the highway via Milton's property, Milton had traveled the old hunter's path across Jason's property. Jason has now erected a barrier across this passageway.

   a. Since Curt would not have used the hunter's path for sufficient time, no prescriptive easement could exist.
   b. If Curt's own passageway got washed out, he could use Jason's path because of necessity.
   c. Milton could have gained a prescriptive easement only if he was an adverse passer.
   d. A prescriptive easement would have to be in writing to be effective.

4. John mortgaged his farm to Delta Bank. Delta Bank recorded the mortgage. When John defaulted, it was learned by Delta Bank that John had earlier given a mortgage to Alex.

   a. If Alex failed to record, Delta Bank would prevail over Alex.
   b. If Alex failed to record, John would prevail over Alex.

c. If both Alex and Delta Bank file properly, they will share foreclosure proceeds, if any, on a pro rata basis.

d. In both cases, John was the mortgagee.

5. The following must be created by a writing, if created by an express grant, *except*

   a. an easement.
   b. a six-month lease.
   c. a mortgage.
   d. a quitclaim deed.

6. A six-month lease is an example of

   a. periodic tenancy.
   b. tenancy at sufferance.
   c. estate for years.
   d. an easement.

7. Gen gave First Federal a mortgage for a $75,000 loan. Gen defaulted on the loan.

   a. First Federal may foreclose on the mortgage.
   b. Because Gen has defaulted, she could not redeem the property.
   c. First Federal was the mortgagor.
   d. Gen's mortgage could have been oral.

8. Which of the following actually represents legal title to property (meaning ownership of the property)?

   a. A contract to sell the property
   b. An easement to cross the property
   c. A deed received at closing
   d. Title insurance

9. Assuming that you have the choice about which deed you will receive from a seller, your best choice would be a/an

   a. quitclaim deed.
   b. general warranty deed (sometimes simply called warranty deed).
   c. special warranty deed.
   d. implied warranty deed.

10. All of the terms listed below are elements of adverse possession *except*

    a. notorious.
    b. open.

    c. hostile.
    d. permission.

Use this information in answering Questions 11 to 13.

Cindy and David Brix, newlyweds, are buying their first home together from a person transferred to a new location, Ben Smith. They are unsure of what to expect at their first home closing or the legal significance of several matters that will be involved in the closing. They have sought your assistance.

11. Which item below is unlikely to be involved at the closing?

    a. A lease for the home
    b. A bill of sale for the personal property to be transferred with the home
    c. A note from Cindy and David to a lender
    d. A deed from Ben Smith

12. Cindy and David are to receive a special warranty deed. This means that

    a. defects in title prior to Ben Smith's ownership will not be covered.
    b. it is likely that defects existed prior to Ben Smith's ownership.
    c. their deed will be considered more valuable than both a general warranty deed and a quitclaim deed.
    d. the deed assures the same ownership interest as if a quitclaim deed had been received.

13. Cindy and David will own their home as tenants by the entirety. This type of ownership is

    a. recognized in all states.
    b. another name for community property.
    c. quite similar in operation to joint tenancy.
    d. quite similar in operation to tenancy in common.

Solutions

Answer	Refer to:

1. (d) [G-5] A lease that restricts assignment can be terminated by the landlord if the tenant assigns the lease without the landlord's approval.

2. (a) [G-5-a] Fernando received a novation when Maria agreed to release him and look only to Connie.

3. (c) [F-2-c] To gain a prescriptive easement, one must be an adverse passer, not having consent. There may be "tacking," the adding of the years Milton used the property to Curt's time. To tack, there must not have been any interruption of usage.

4. (a) [B-1-c, E] Delta Bank would win if it otherwise had no knowledge of the prior mortgage. John is still liable to Alex.

5. (b) [G-1] A writing is not required for the lease because it will be completed within one year's time. An express grant easement, mortgage, or quit-claim deed must be in writing.

6. (c) [G-2-a] A lease for a stated duration is an *estate for years* even though it may be less than a year in length.

7. (a) [E] A mortgagee may foreclose on a mortgage in a situation where the mortgagor defaults on the mortgage.

8. (c) [C] A deed represents the seller's passing of ownership to the buyer. The buyer records the deed in the courthouse for the county where the property is located to give official notice to third parties.

9. (b) [C-2] A general warranty deed, often simply called a warranty deed, provides the greatest protection to the buyer and is the most respected by lenders.

10. (d) [B-3-c] No adverse possession may occur where the person is present with consent.

11. (a) [G] A lease will seldom be involved in the sale of a home from a person who has been living in the home.

12. (a) [C-3] The special warranty deed operates exactly like the warranty deed except that it applies only to the time during which the grantor actually owned the property.

13. (c) [D-3-b] Upon the death of Cindy or David, if still married at death, the property will go automatically to the survivor as in joint tenancy.

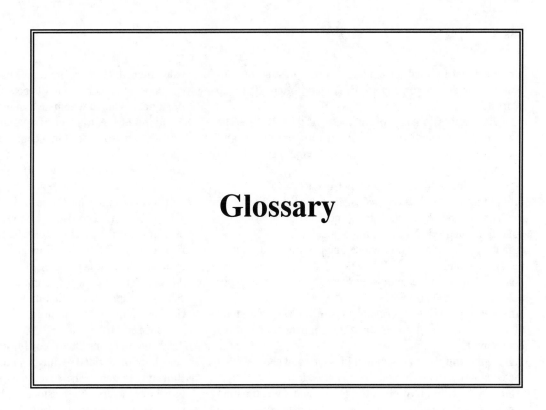

Glossary

Absolute advantage The ability of one country to produce a commodity at a cost lower than that of other countries. (5)*

Accelerated depreciation method A depreciation method that assigns more depreciation expense to the earlier years of an asset's useful life than to its later years of useful life. (13)

Acceptance A clear expression by the offeree of agreement to the terms of the offer. (21)

Account A device used to collect and summarize information. (7)

Account balance The difference between the total debits and total credits recorded in an account. (7)

Accounting The process of recording, measuring, summarizing, analyzing, and interpreting financial information and communicating this information to various users. (6)

Accounting cycle All of the procedures performed during an accounting period, including analyzing and journalizing of transactions, posting, taking a trial balance, preparing a worksheet, preparing financial statements, journalizing and posting adjusting entries, closing the temporary accounts, and taking a post-closing trial balance. (9)

Accounting entity Any business, individual, or not-for-profit organization whose financial affairs can be viewed as being distinct from those of any other entity or unit. (6)

Accounting equation Assets = liabilities + owners' equity or, stated another way, assets − liabilities = owners' equity. (7)

Accounts payable The account used for recording the liabilities a company has incurred for goods or services purchased on open account. (7)

Accounts receivable The account used to record the right a company has to receive payment for sales made on open account. (7)

Accrual The concept that states that revenues should be reported when earned rather than when received and expenses should be reported when incurred rather than when paid. (7)

Ad valorem "According to value"; rates of duty on a percentage of the invoice value, not on weight or quantity. (5)

Adjusting entries A journal entry made at the end of an accounting period to bring an account balance to the correct amount. (9)

Administrative agency A subdivision of the government with expertise and jurisdiction to regulate a specialized area of government operation. (25)

Administrative law judge An official who hears cases within an administrative agency. (25)

Adverse possession The taking of real property belong-

---

*The number in parentheses after each entry indicates the chapter location in the text.

ing to another by notorious, adverse, open, hostile, or continuous possession for a period of years, often 10 to 20 years. (28)

Age Discrimination in Employment Act (ADEA) The law prohibiting employment discrimination on the basis of age for persons over the age of 40 and employers with 19 or more employees. (25)

Age Discrimination in Employment Act of 1967 An act prohibiting discrimination against individuals between the ages of 40 and 70 in the hiring, compensation, working conditions, and privileges of employment. (4)

Agency A relationship in which one party acts for and on behalf of another party. (23)

Agent One who has authority to act for and on behalf of another party (the principal). (23)

Aggregate demand (aggregate expenditures) The total amount consumers, business, and government spend in the economy. (2)

Aggregate supply The amount of goods and services that the economy will produce at various price levels. (2)

Aging of accounts receivable A method of estimating the amount of the allowance for uncollectible accounts and bad debt expense. This method groups the individual accounts according to the length of time they have been outstanding. The amount of uncollectible accounts is then estimated for each group. (14)

Allowance for uncollectible accounts Contra-account to the accounts receivable account used for reporting accounts receivable at the amount that is expected to be received. (8)

Americans with Disabilities Act (ADA) The extension of the Civil Rights Act of 1964, that first became effective in 1992, to provide public services, building codes, and employment accommodations for physically and mentally disabled individuals. (4, 25)

Amortization The systematic writing off as an expense of the balance in an account over a period of time. Amortization is usually associated with intangible asset accounts. (14)

Antitrust laws A set of laws designed to control monopolistic practices and monopoly power. (4)

Apparent authority Authority that a third party reasonably believes an agent possesses based upon circumstances which the principal has allowed to exist, even though the agent in fact does not have the express or implied authority. (23)

Appropriated retained earnings Retained earnings that have been segregated into a separate account to inform the financial statement reader that a portion of retained earnings is not available for the payment of dividends. (16)

Articles of incorporation The legal framework in which a corporation operates. It is filed with the state at the time of incorporation. (24)

Assets Economic resources from which an entity can expect to receive benefits now or in the future, a thing of value owned. (1) Economic resources from which an entity can expect to receive benefits now or in the future. (7)

Assignee One to whom an assignment is made. (21)

Assignment A transfer of a contractual right to one who is not a party to the original contract. (21)

Assignor One who makes an assignment. (21)

Audit (independent external) An examination of the financial statements of an entity by an independent accountant to determine the fairness of the financial statements. The accounting records are referred to in assessing the fairness of the financial statements. (6)

Authority The power granted to an agent by a principal to enter into contracts. (23)

Authorized shares of capital stock The number of shares of capital stock that may legally be sold. The authorized amount of capital stock is determined by the corporate charter. (16)

Average propensity to consume (APC) The level of consumption divided by the level of income. (2)

Bait and switch The advertising ploy whereby the advertiser lures buyers into the store on the pretense of wishing to sell one item, whereas his or her objective is to have the consumer purchase another, often more costly, product. (26)

Balance of payments A summary record of all economic transactions of a nation with the rest of the world in a specific period of time. (5)

Balance sheet A financial statement that shows the financial position of an entity as of a specific time. Although *balance sheet* is the common term for this financial statement, the formal title is the *statement of financial position*. (8)

Bank reconciliation A report that explains the difference between the balance per the bank statement and the balance per the general ledger cash account. (10)

Bearer bond Bonds that are not registered in the name of the owner are assumed to be owned by the individual who possesses the bond (also known as coupon bonds). (15)

Bearer One who is in possession of a negotiable instrument. (22)

Bilateral contract A contract in which the parties make a bargained-for exchange of promises. (21)

Bona fide occupational qualification (BFOQ). In limited situations, an employer is permitted to discriminate on the basis of sex, religion, or national origin if any of these characteristics are required as occupational qualifications. (25)

Bond A debt security issued in stated dollar denominations with a stated interest rate and maturity date. The most commonly stated dollar value is $1,000. (11)

Bond discount The difference between the face value of a bond and the amount it sells for when the bond sells for less than its face value. (11)

Bond premium The difference between the face value of a bond and the amount it sells for when the bond sells for more than its face value. (11)

Bond sinking fund An investment fund established to ensure that sufficient funds are available to retire the bonds at maturity. (15)

Bonds payable Long-term liabilities consisting of securities normally issued in stated denominations with a stated interest rate and maturity date. There are numerous types of bonds. (8)

Bookkeeping The record-keeping phase of accounting. (6)

Book value or carrying value The carrying value of an asset on the books, that is the original cost less any accumulated depreciation related to that asset. (8) Book value per share of common stock is a numerical measure of the net assets of a corporation as reflected in a single share of common stock. (16)

Breach of contract A failure by a party to a contract to perform the duties imposed by the terms of the agreement. (21)

Breakeven point The point where a company has zero profit or loss (total revenue for the company is equal to total costs). (19)

Broker An individual who acts in the role of an underwriter. (26)

Budget A detailed plan that shows acquisitions and uses of financial resources for a period of time. (19)

Built-in stabilizers Automatic forces that operate to restrain fluctuations in gross national product (GNP). (2)

Bylaws Regulations of the corporation that govern internal management and day-to-day operational structure. (24)

Callable bonds Bonds with a provision stating that the issuer may redeem the bonds prior to maturity by payment of a stipulated call price. (15)

Callable preferred stock Callable preferred stock may be redeemed by the issuing corporation at a stipulated call price. (16)

Capital Goods that are produced by humans, then used in the production of something else; capital should not be confused with monetary capital (money value of capital goods). (1)

Capital assets Any property a taxpayer holds that is not listed in Section 1221 of the U.S. Internal Revenue Code. Section 1221 property includes inventory, accounts receivable, and depreciable property or real estate used in a business. Examples of capital assets are investments in stocks, bonds, or real estate that are not used in a trade or business. (17)

Capital consumption allowance An estimated amount of depreciation of the nation's capital within a time period. (2)

Capital gain A gain resulting from the disposition of a capital asset. (17)

Capital loss A loss resulting from the disposition of a capital asset. (17)

Capital stock Ownership of a corporation is evidenced by shares of capital stock. Capital stock is also the title of the account used to record the total investment in shares of stock of a corporation. (7)

Cash Coins, paper money, checks, money orders, and money on deposit in banks. (10)

Cash disbursements journal A special journal used to record all disbursements of cash. (10)

Cash discount A reduction in the total amount due on an invoice offered if the invoice is paid within a designated period of time. (10)

Cash flow statement A cash flow statement accounts for the increase or decrease in a company's cash during a period by showing where the company got cash and the uses it made of cash. (18)

Cash receipts journal A special journal used to record receipts of cash. (10)

Cashier's check A check drawn by a bank on itself. (22)

Casualty insurance Insurance coverage that is primarily for the liability of a party that results from negligent acts or omissions resulting in bodily injury and/or property damage to another party. (14)

Cease and desist order An administrative agency's demand that the defendant stop a certain action and not resume it (similar to a court's injunction). (26)

Certified check A check that is guaranteed by the depositor's bank. (10)

Ceteris paribus A Latin phrase meaning that all other things remaining equal. (2)

Chattel mortgage The legal document used when the collateral securing a loan is personal property, such as in the purchase of a car financed through a lender. (27)

Check register The form of the cash disbursements journal used in conjunction with a voucher system. (10)

Civil law Law pertaining to private as opposed to public rights. (20)

Civil Rights Act of 1964. This act created the Federal Fair Employment Practice Law covering all industries involved in interstate commerce. The fair employment practice law bars discrimination by employers, unions, employment agencies, and others, based on race, color, sex, religion, or national origin. (4)

Classical school of economics Pioneered by Adam Smith, David Ricardo, and Thomas Malthus, the classical school of economic thought advocates concepts such as economic freedom of choice and private property and the general principle that individuals in a society are more prosperous without government intervention into the economy. (2)

Closing entry A journal entry made at the end of an accounting period, which transfers the balance of a temporary account to the owners' equity or retained earnings account. (9)

Co-insurance A provision in some insurance contracts that requires the insured party to insure property for at least a specified minimum percentage of its fair market value, or to share the loss proportionately with the insurance company. (14)

Command economy   A type of economic system in that the basic decisions of what, how, and for whom to produce are answered by an individual or small group of individuals. (1)

Common law   A vast body of law, consisting of decided case law, which includes the case law and custom of England prior to the American Revolution to the extent that it has not been expressly superseded or overruled by cases or laws of the United States. Common law includes all published opinions of courts in the United States. (20) A vast body of recorded cases that have been decided by courts (past decision). (21)

Common market (European Economic Community)   An economic, social, and political organization of some of the european countries [Germany, France, England, Italy, the Netherlands, Belgium, Luxembourg, and (as new members) Greece and Spain]. (5)

Common stock   A classification of capital stock that has no preferences relative to the corporation's other classes of stock. Common stockholders have the right to all residual assets left after the claims of creditors and preferred stockholders have been met. (8) Stock that represents ownership in a corporation. Each share of stock may earn a dividend only after all corporate obligations, including those to owners of preferred stock, are satisfied. (24)

Comparative advantage   A principle that explains why one country would specialize in producing certain goods and importing others rather than producing all goods domestically. (5)

Comparative financial statements   Financial statements that show financial data for a series of years in adjacent columns. (18)

Complementary goods   Goods that are used in connection with other goods (tennis balls and tennis rackets). (1)

Compound interest   When a security earns compound interest, it earns interest on the principal of the security and on any interest that has been earned but not yet paid. (15)

Compound tariff   A tariff based both on ad valorem and physical units; increases the price of the foreign good in the country imposing the tariff. (5)

Conflict of interest   A conflict between personal interest and the official responsibilities of a person in a position of trust, such as an agent. (23)

Consent decree   An agreement whereby the defendant admits no guilt but agrees to pay damages, cease an action, and/or other remedial action. (26)

Conservatism   The principle which requires that the accounting method which is least likely to overstate income and financial position be used. (6)

Consideration   The bargained-for exchange of something

of value; an essential element of an enforceable contract. (21)

Consistency   The principle that requires that once an accounting or reporting method is selected, it should be used from one period to another. (6)

Consolidated statements   The combination of two or more accounting entities into one entity for financial reporting purposes. This is done when one entity possesses a controlling interest over the other entity or entities. (11)

Constitutional law   Law derived from the United States Constitution and the Bill of Rights. (20)

Consumerism   A movement whose principal view is that corporations consider the interests of consumers and general public interests, as well as those of stockholders. (4)

Consumer price index (CPI)   An index created to measure changes in the cost of living of households throughout the years by comparing the cost to purchase a "typical market basket" of commodities by households. (2)

Consumption   The act of consuming goods and services. (1) Using goods and services to satisfy wants and needs. (2)

Contingent liability   A potential liability that could become an actual liability only if certain events occur. (14)

Contra-asset account   An account that is related to a specific asset account and has a credit balance. Contra-assets are reported as deductions from the related asset on the balance sheet. Allowance for uncollectible accounts and accumulated depreciation are examples of contra-asset accounts. (8)

Contract   A legally enforceable agreement. (21)

Contractual capacity   The ability to understand the subject matter and consequences of an agreement; only adults may possess this kind of capacity. (21)

Contribution margin   Contribution margin is equal to sales minus variable expenses. (19)

Control account   An account with a balance representing the total of all the account balances of a related subsidiary ledger. (10)

Convertible bond   A bond with a provision allowing the holder to convert the bond into common stock of the issuing company. (15)

Convertible preferred stock   Convertible preferred stock may be exchanged by the stockholder for a predetermined number of shares of common stock. (16)

Copyright   Legal protection available to the author of a literary work. A copyright gives the author the exclusive right to use the work subject to certain legally recognized exceptions. (27)

Corporation   A business entity that is created by state or federal law and has a separate legal existence from that of its owners. (6)

Cost behavior   Cost behavior refers to changes in a cost when changes in the level of activity occur. (19)

Cost–benefit analysis   A method of evaluating the implications of alternative courses of action in terms of their costs and benefits. (4)

Cost of goods sold The cost of merchandise sold to customers, that is shown as a deduction from sales on the income statement to arrive at gross margin (gross profit). (8)

Cost-push inflation Price increases caused by increased costs of resources used in production. (2)

Credit An entry recorded on the right-hand side of an account. (7)

Criminal law Law that defines offenses against the government (representing all of society) and provides penal sanctions. (20)

Cumulative preferred stock Cumulative preferred stock is cumulative with respect to dividends. This means that any dividends not paid in one period must be made up before any current dividends may be paid to common shareholders. (16)

Currency Coins and printed paper used as money (medium of exchange), stamped by a government to certify their value. (3)

Current assets Those assets that are expected to be used in operations of the business within the operating cycle of the business or one year, whichever is longer. (8)

Current liabilities Obligations of a business that are to be repaid during the next operating cycle or one year, whichever is longer. (8)

Cyclical unemployment A type of unemployment caused by declines in the business cycle. (2)

Debenture An unsecured bond backed only by the general credit of the company. (15)

Debit An entry recorded on the left-hand side of an account. (7)

Delegation A transfer of one's contractual duties to another party. (21)

Demand The quantity of goods or services that individuals will buy at various prices within a given time period. (1)

Demand-pull inflation (inflationary gap) increase in the price level caused by increased demand for goods and services when the level of employment is near full employment. (2)

Depletion The amount a natural resource is reduced due to usage (i.e., cutting timber, mining ore, or pumping oil). (13)

Deposits in transit Bank deposits that have been recorded on the books of a company but have not yet been received and recorded by the bank. (10)

Depreciation A systematic and rational allocation of the cost of an asset over its useful life. (8)

Direct labor All labor performed by employees directly involved in production. (19)

Direct materials Raw materials that become a part of the company's end product and can be traced easily to that end product. (19)

Direct write-off method A method of recording bad debt expense that does not use an allowance for uncollectible accounts or attempt to match bad debt expense with related revenue. When the direct write-off method is used, worthless accounts are written off as a debit to bad debt expense and a credit to accounts receivable. This method does not conform to GAAP. (14)

Disaffirmance An expression by a person lacking contractual capacity of an intent not to be bound by the terms of an agreement. (21)

Disclosed principal A principal whose identity is known to the third party with whom the principal's agent deals. (23)

Discounting of a note receivable When a note receivable is discounted, it is sold to a bank for cash. The seller remains contingently liable for payment of the note if the maker defaults. (14)

Discount rate An interest rate at which member banks can borrow from the Federal Reserve System. (3)

Discrimination Equals being treated unequally or unequals being treated equally. (4)

Disposable personal income (DPI). The amount of income available to households for spending and saving (personal income minus taxes). (2)

Divestiture A court order that a corporation divest (sell) some of its particular operations and/or assets. (25)

Dividend A distribution of assets by a corporation to its owners. (7)

Dividends in arrears Dividends earned on cumulative preferred stock that have not yet been declared. (16)

Double-declining-balance depreciation (DDB) An accelerated depreciation method that uses a depreciation rate that is twice the straight-line rate. (13)

Double-entry accounting In double-entry accounting, an equal dollar amount of debits and credits must be recorded in the accounts whenever an accounting transaction is recorded. This is also called the duality principle. (7)

Draft A negotiable instrument that contains an unconditional order directing another to pay a certain sum of money. (22)

Drawee A party who is ordered by the terms of a draft to pay a certain sum of money. (22)

Drawer One who issues a check or other draft. (22)

Duress The use of a wrongful threat that causes a person to enter into an agreement which the person would otherwise have rejected. (21)

Earnings per share The amount of net income earned per share of common stock during an accounting period. (8)

Easement The right of a nonowner to use a piece of land in a specific way (affirmative) or to prevent the owner from using his or her own land in a specific way (negative). (28)

Economic efficiency   The production of goods and services at the least possible cost. (1)

Economic equity   The more equal the distribution of income is in the minds of most people, the more equitable the distribution is. (1)

Economic freedom   The ability of individuals to purchase goods and services that they need or want and to sell their resources, including labor, to whom they please. (1)

Economic growth   An increase in per capita real gross national product in a given period of time. (2)

Economic security   The reduction of risk to the individual incurring costs associated with unpredictable and/or unusual events. (1)

Economics of pollution   A study of pollution to evaluate and compare its costs and benefits to individuals, firms, and institutions in society. (4)

Economic stability   Low levels of price changes and low levels of unemployment within society. (1)

Elasticity   A measure of the responsiveness of individuals to the change of the price of a good or service. (1)

Embargo   The prohibition of shipping to or receiving products from a country. (5)

Emergency authority   A type of implied authority that exists during a sudden, unexpected happening or unforeseen combination of circumstances that requires immediate action. (23)

Employee   An employed person without legal authority to bind the employer; an agent may be, but need not be, an employee. (23)

Employee Retirement Income Security Act (ERISA)   A federal pension law; an employer is not required to have a pension plan for employees, but ERISA applies if the employer does have a pension plan for employees. (25)

Employment discrimination   Workplace decisions based upon race, color, sex, religion, national origin, age, or handicaps that affect employed individuals adversely. (25)

Entrepreneur   One who owns and assumes the risk of running a business for the purpose of making a profit. (1)

Entrepreneurial ability   The unique talents some individuals have for combining resources to produce goods or services more efficiently than other individuals. (1)

Environmental Protection Agency (EPA)   A federal agency, founded in 1970, to develop and enforce standards for clean air and water and establish standards to control pollution of any sort. (4)

Equal Employment Opportunity Act of 1972   A series of amendments to the Civil Rights Act of 1964; the most significant amendment created the equal employment opportunity commission (EEOC). (4)

Equal Employment Opportunity Commission (EEOC)   The administrative agency that oversees the enforcement of Title VII of the Civil Rights Act and other employment discrimination laws. (4, 25)

Equal Pay for Equal Work Act   An amendment to the Fair Labor Standards Act that requires equal pay for women who are performing work substantially equal to that of men; also known as the equal pay act. (25)

Equilibrium price   The price at which the quantity demanded and the quantity supplied are equal. (1)

Equity method   A method used to account for investments in common stock where the investor has significant control over the operations of the investee. (11)

Estimation   Much of what is included in financial reports is the result of an estimate. (6)

Estoppel   A party to a lawsuit will be precluded (stopped) from raising a defense. (24)

Excess reserves   The amount of reserves that are held by a commercial bank in excess of the legally required reserves. (3)

Excise tax   A tax on the purchase of specific domestically produced commodities. (5)

Executive branch   The President or governor and the administrative agencies thereunder (the bureaucracy). (25)

Executive order   A law issued by the President of the United States. (20)

Expenses   The costs of goods and services consumed (used up) by an entity in order to earn revenues. (7)

Explicit costs   Costs incurred by business for which direct monetary payment is made. (1)

Express authority   Authority granted by the principal in words, whether they be written or oral. (23)

Express contract   A contract in which the agreement is put into words, either written or oral. (21)

External financial reports   The standard financial reports issued by entities primarily for the use of decision makers other than the management of the entity (the balance sheet, the income statement, and the statement of cash flows). (6)

External users   Users of accounting information who are not part of the management of the company (examples: bankers, creditors, investors). (6)

Extraordinary repairs   Repairs that either prolong the useful life of the asset or change the quality of service provided by the asset. (13)

Factors of production   Land, labor, capital, entrepreneurial ability; the resources used to produce other goods and services. (1) Land (land and raw materials), labor, capital, and entrepreneurial ability. (2)

Fair Labor Standards Act   Legislation known as the Wage and Hour Law which established the requirements for an employer to pay employees a minimum wage and "time and a half" for overtime worked over 40 hours per week; provided for limited use of children in employment. (25)

Fair use   Legally recognized exceptions to copyright protection that allow those other than the author to use the copyrighted work for certain limited purposes. (27)

Federal Aviation Administration (FAA)   An agency

chartered to provide for the regulation and promotion of civil aviation in such a manner as to best foster its development and safety and to provide for the safe and efficient use of the air space by both civil and military aircraft. (4)

Federal Deposit Insurance Corporation (FDIC) A government insurance institution that guarantees the payment of the amount deposited in banks (up to $100,000) to the depositor in case of the bank's failure. (3)

Federal Food and Drug Administration (FDA) An agency established in 1930 by federal legislation. The FDA develops standards and conducts research with respect to reliability and safety of drugs, evaluates new drug reaction programs, establishes a nationwide network of poison control, and advises the justice department on the results of its research. (4)

Federal Housing Administration (FHA) The government agency that carries out the provisions of the National Housing Act of 1934. The FHA promotes the ownership of homes and the renovation or remodeling of residences through government-guaranteed loans to homeowners. (3)

Federal Insurance Contribution Act (FICA). The federal legislation that created the social security system. (25)

Federal Power Commission (FPC) A government agency established in 1930 to regulate interstate operation of private utilities in matters of their issuance of securities, rates, and location of sites. (4)

Federal Reserve note A paper bill issued by a Federal Reserve bank. (3)

Federal Reserve System (FED) The network of 12 federal reserve banks in the United States responsible for the regulation of most nationally chartered financial institutions and the regulation of the country's money supply. (3)

Federal Trade Commission (FTC) A national agency created in 1914 whose main tasks are to promote free and fair competition by prevention of price-fixing agreements, boycotts, and unlawful price discrimination. (4, 26)

Federal reserve note A paper bill issued by a federal reserve bank. (3)

Felony A crime punishable by one year or more of incarceration. (20)

FICA tax The Federal Insurance Contributions Act (FICA) tax; commonly called social security tax. (17)

Fidelity bond Insurance that guarantees that the insurance company will pay for losses of money or property that result from the dishonest acts of bonded employees. (14)

FIFO The *first- in first-out* method of valuing inventory, which assumes that the earliest units purchased are sold first and that ending inventory is made up of the latest purchases. (12)

Financing activities Transactions with the company's owners and long-term creditors. (18)

Fiscal policy The use of government spending and taxing policies to alter general employment and national income levels. (2)

Fixed assets Long-lived assets used in the operation of the business. (8)

Fixed costs Costs that remain constant in total despite changes in the volume of output of a company. (19)

Fixtures Personal property so attached to real property as to become a part thereof, for example, paneling in a home; hot water heater. (27, 28)

Forecasting The prediction of a value of a variable in the future. (19)

Foreclosure The act of the mortgagee (lender) in forcing the sale of property secured to a loan as a result of default by the mortgagor (borrower/owner of property). (28)

Foreign exchange rate A rate at which the currency of one country can be exchanged for the currency of another country. (5)

Formal contract A contract that complies with a specific form required by law for contracts of that particular type. (21)

Fraud A misstatement or misrepresentation of a material fact made with knowledge of its falsity. (23)

Frictional unemployment People in the labor force who are unemployed as a result of changing jobs, entering the labor force, or being laid off seasonally. (2)

Full disclosure The accounting principle that requires all information that may be relevant to decision makers to be included in the financial statements. (6)

Gains Revenues generated from an activity that is not part of the normal operations of the business. (8)

General agent An agent who is authorized to represent a principal in a number of transactions over a period of time. (23)

General counsel The person within an administrative agency who oversees agency enforcement prosecution. (25)

Generally accepted accounting principles (GAAP) The standards governing the recording and reporting of information published in external financial statements. (6)

Geographic specialization A situation whereby natural resources, geographic location, climate, or market conditions of a certain region of a country might create certain advantages to producing a certain good or goods. (5)

GNP implicit price deflator index An index computed once a year using the prices of all goods and services produced in the United States to present the most accurate measure of price increases. (2)

Going concern The assumption that an entity will exist for an indefinite period of time. (6)

Goods Tangible personal property. (21)

Grantee One to whom property is conveyed. (28)

Grantor One who conveys property. (28)

Gratuitous assignment An assignment made without consideration. (21)

Gresham's law When two kinds of money of equal commodity value but of unequal use value are in circulation, the one of lesser use value tends to drive the one of better use value out of circulation. (3)

Gross margin (or Gross profit) The amount that remains after deducting the cost of goods sold from net sales. (8)

Gross National Product (GNP) Total market value of all final goods and services produced in the economy over some period of time (usually one year). (2)

Gross profit method A method of inventory estimation based on the use of the past gross profit percentage experienced by the company. (12)

Historical cost The concept that assets should be recorded at their original purchase cost. (6)

Holder One who possesses an instrument that is issued or indorsed to him or her or is payable to the bearer. (22)

Holder in due course A holder who has given value for an instrument and has taken it in good faith without knowledge of any defect. (22)

Illusory promise A promise that does not impose a legally enforceable obligation upon the promisor. (21)

Imperfect competition The production environment in which one of the four conditions for perfect competition is not met; imperfect competition typically results in higher prices and less production than under perfect competition. (1)

Implicit costs The value of resources used by businesses for which direct payment is not made because resources are owned by entrepreneurs. (1)

Implied authority Authority to do those things that are reasonably necessary to the exercise of express authority and to the achievement of the objectives of the agency. (23)

Implied contract A contract in which the parties' agreement is expressed by their conduct rather than by their words. (21)

Import quota A maximum limit imposed on imports to protect an industry and its workers. (5)

Import tariff A set of taxes imposed on the importation of foreign goods on behalf of national interest. (5)

Income statement A financial statement that summarizes the operations of a business showing revenues, expenses, gains, and losses over an accounting period. (8)

Independent contractor One who is retained to achieve a desired result and who is given substantial freedom in deciding the manner to be used to accomplish the objective. An agent may be, but need not be, an independent contractor. (23)

Indorsee One who receives an indorsed instrument. (*Note:* the word *endorse* is commonly used in business. The word *indorse* is used in the UCC.) (22)

Indorsement without recourse An indorsement in which the indorser disclaims liability in the event that the maker or drawer fails to pay. (22)

Indorser A payee who transfers an instrument by signing it and delivering it to an indorsee. (22)

Inelastic demand A change in price results in a small change in quantity bought. (1)

Inelastic supply A large change in price results in a small change in quantity supplied. (1)

Inflation A rise in the general price level of all goods. (2)

Infringement Illegal use of patented or copyrighted work. (27)

Installment note payable A note payable that is due in equal periodic payments. (15)

Intangible assets Long-lived assets that do not have any tangible existence. Examples are patents, copyrights, goodwill, and trademarks. (8)

Interest-bearing note receivable A note receivable that requires payment of the principal of the note plus a stated amount of interest on the maturity date. (14)

Internal controls The methods and procedures adopted by a business to control its operations and protect its assets from waste, fraud, and theft. (10)

Internal financial reports Reports issued for use by managers of an entity that are usually more detailed than external reports. These reports are also called managerial accounting reports. (6)

Internal users The managers of an entity who use accounting information. (6)

International finance The movement of monies from one country to another. (5)

Interstate commerce Sales, purchases, or transit (commerce) among states. (26)

Intrastate commerce Sales, purchases, or transit (commerce) within a state. (26)

Inventory An asset account that is comprised of goods or merchandise held for future sale. (7)

Investing activities Transactions that involve the investment of a company's cash. (18)

Investment Expenditure on capital goods that are, in turn, used by business firms to produce goods and services. (2) Long-term asset held by the company for investment purposes rather than for use in the operations of the business. (8, 11) An asset held for investment purposes rather than for use in the operation of the business.

Issued shares Shares that have been issued to shareholders at any time. (16)

Issuer A seller of new securities. (26)

Job order costing The form of product costing used most often by firms that produce a number of products; these products can easily be divided into separate projects or batches. (19)

Joint and several liability In partnership law, a party suing the partnership on a tort claim may include any number of partners in the suit; responsibility either as a group or individually. (24)

Joint liability In partnership law, a party suing the partnership on a contract claim must sue all partners individually if any partner(s) is (are) included in the suit; responsibility as a group. (24)

Joint tenancy Co-ownership of property whereby a deceased party's interest goes to the surviving party(ies). (28)

Journal An accounting record where business transactions are recorded in chronological order; also known as the book of original entry. (7)

Keynesian economics A school of economic thought advanced by the British economist, John Maynard Keynes; Keynesian theory states that a condition of economic equilibrium could exist without full employment of the factors of production and that a major cause for economic crises is a failure of the system to maintain the proper relationship between investment and savings, therefore resulting in the need for government spending. (2)

Labor One of the four factors of production. The term *labor* encompasses both the quantity and quality of people available in the labor force. (1)

Laissez faire Economic organization that emphasizes the free operation of market forces. (1) A principle of economic conduct that advocates "let things proceed without interference." The principle further asserts that an individual is more productive when he or she is allowed to follow his or her own self-interest without external restrictions. (4)

Land One of the four factors of production. To an economist, land includes all natural resources that come directly from the land (iron ore, coal, etc.). (1)

Landrum–Griffin Act Federal legislation that established rights of individuals with union and union internal affairs. (25)

Law of demand The law that states that there is an inverse relationship between price of a good or service and quantity demanded. (1)

Law of supply The law that states that there is a direct relationship between the price of a good or service and the quantity supplied. (1)

Ledger A collection of all the accounts of a business. Information contained in the journals is posted to the ledger. (7)

Liability An obligation or debt of an entity owed to another party. (7)

Life and health insurance Business life and health coverage provides funds for normal maintenance of a business in the event of a loss of a key person. (14)

LIFO The *last-in first-out* method of valuing inventory, that assumes that the latest units purchased are sold first and that ending inventory is made up of the earliest units purchased. (12)

Limited liability Shareholders of a corporation are liable for the debts of the corporation only to the amount of their investment in the corporation. (16)

Limited partner The partner is treated as an investor only and may not engage in active day-to-day management of the business or lend his or her name to the partnership name. A limited partner is potentially liable on partnership debts only to the extent of capital contribution. (24)

Liquidity The more easily an asset can be converted to cash, the higher is its liquidity. (8)

Literary works Works such as books, magazines, newspapers, plays, musical compositions, artwork, photographs, motion pictures, recordings, computer programs, data bases, and other verbal or numerical symbols that can be copyrighted by the author. (27)

Long-term capital gain or loss A gain or loss resulting from the disposition of a capital asset held for more than one year. (17)

Long-term liabilities Obligations of an entity that will not come due during the next year or operating cycle. (8)

Losses Expenses or decreases in owners' equity that do not result from normal operations of the business. (8)

Lower of cost or market The rule which requires that certain assets (such as inventory and temporary investments) be recorded at market value if their market value is below their cost. (12)

Maker One who signs a promissory note. (22)

Manufacturing overhead Overhead that includes all costs of production except direct materials and direct labor. (19)

Margin requirements The fraction of a stock price that must be paid in cash when stock is purchased; the remainder can be a loan. (3)

Marginal propensity to consume (MPC) Change in the consumption generated by the change in income. (2)

Marginal tax rate The proportion of a unit of income paid into taxes. In the case of federal income tax, there is an increasing marginal tax rate. The proportion of income paid into taxes increases as income increases. (2)

Market An environment in which exchange of goods and services takes place. (1)

Matching The principle that states that expenses incurred in earning revenues should be matched with those revenues in order to determine net income. (7)

Materiality The accounting principle that states that insignificant items need not be accounted for in the same manner as more relevant or significant items. (6)

Maturity date of a note The date on which a note and any interest are due and payable. (14)

Merchant A person who regularly deals in the kinds of goods involved. (21)

Misdemeanor A crime punishable by up to one year of incarceration. (20)

Mixed cost A cost that is composed of both variable and fixed elements. (19)

Mixed economy A combination of laissez-faire and command economic force; the United States is an example of a mixed economy. (1)

Modified accelerated cost recovery system (MACRS) An accelerated method of depreciation required for income tax purposes. (13)

Monetary policy Activity of the Federal Reserve System designed to alter the money supply. (2) A policy enacted to influence the course of the national economy by the Federal Reserve System through the use of monetary tools such as reserve requirements and open market operations to control the money supply. (3)

Money Anything used as a medium of exchange, a store of value, and a unit of account (a standard to evaluate all assets and liabilities. (3)

Money measurement A common unit of measure (money) used to record all information in the accounting records. (6)

Moral suasion An attempt by the Federal Reserve System to influence member banks to adopt what the FED regards as more socially beneficial policy. (3)

Mortgage A long-term obligation that is normally secured by real estate and is normally repaid in installments. (8) A legal agreement that gives the lender the right to be paid from the sale of specific assets that belong to the borrower if the borrower does not repay the loan. (15) The legal document used when collateral securing a loan is real or personal property. (28)

Mortgage bond A bond secured by specific assets of the issuing company. (15)

Mortgagee The lender; party to whom the mortgage is given. (28)

Mortgagor The borrower; party putting up property to secure a loan. (28)

National income Total value of all incomes generated by all legal productive agents, individuals, and businesses in the nation's economy over a specific time period. (2)

Nationalism Under any economic circumstances, it is a way of acting to maximize the national interest and patriotism. (5)

National Labor Relations Act (NLRA) The federal act that deals with private employer-union relations. (25)

National Labor Relations Board (NLRB) The administrative agency established by the National Labor Relations Act that oversees and monitors union-management relations in the private sector. (25)

Near money Financial assets that can easily be converted into money. (2)

Negligent conduct Careless behavior that results in injury to another person or organization. (23)

Negotiable instrument A written document containing a signed, unconditional promise or order to pay a certain sum of money at a specified time or upon demand to the order of a named party or to the bearer. (22)

Negotiation The transfer of an instrument in such form that the transferee becomes a holder. (22)

Net income Revenues − expenses = net income (or net loss if revenues < expenses). (7)

Net national product (NNP) Gross national product less depreciation. (2)

Non-interest-bearing note receivable A note in that no provision is included for the payment of interest; only the payment of principal is required. (14)

Notes payable Obligations of an entity consisting of signed documents that promise to pay specific amounts of money plus interest on specific future dates. (8)

Notes receivable Signed documents given to an entity by a customer promising to pay a specific amount of money plus interest on a specific future date. (8)

Novation An agreement by a party to a contract to release the other party from its contractual obligation and to accept another party's promise to perform those duties. (21) The release of a party to a contract in consideration of the assumed liability of another, that is, the substitution of a new contract for an old contract. (28)

NOW account A transaction account on that negotiable orders of withdrawal can be written. (3)

NSF check A check that has been written on a bank account in that there are insufficient funds deposited to cover the amount of the check; commonly called a "bad check." (10)

Objectivity The accounting principle that requires that financial information be factual, verifiable, and unbiased. (6)

Occupational Safety and Health Act (OSHA) Federal law that provides for the establishment of health and safety standards for the workplace. (25)

Offer A communication of an intent to be bound to the terms of a specific proposed contract. The communication invites acceptance on the part of the intended recipient. (21)

Offeree One to whom an offer is made. (21)

Offeror One who makes an offer. (21)

Open market operations The buying and selling of domestic government securities by the Federal Reserve System. (3)

Operating activities Transactions that relate to the calculation of net income. These items are usually related to the production and sale of goods and services. (18)

Operating cycle The period of time it takes for a firm to buy merchandise, sell the merchandise, collect the accounts receivable resulting from the sale of the merchandise, and pay the accounts payable of the firm. (8)

Opportunity cost What must be given up to do something; the value of the next best alternative. (1)

Organized stock exchanges Established markets for securities where buy and sell orders are matched at public auction. Examples of organized stock exchanges are the

New York Stock Exchange and the American Stock Exchange. (16)

Other assets The balance sheet classification used for assets that do not fit under the normal balance sheet classifications of current assets, investments, fixed assets, or intangible assets. (8)

Other liabilities The balance sheet classification used for liabilities that do not fit under the normal balance sheet classifications of current liabilities or long-term liabilities. (8)

Output per capita A nation's total output divided by its population. (2)

Outstanding checks Checks issued by a company that have not yet been presented to the bank for payment. (10)

Outstanding shares The shares that are currently in the hands of stockholders. (16)

Over-the-counter market All markets for securities except organized stock exchanges. (16)

Owners' equity The resources invested in the business by owners plus profits from successful operations that have been retained in the business. Owners' equity may also be called capital, net worth, or proprietorship. (7)

Parent company A company that owns the majority of the voting stock of another company. (11)

Partially disclosed principal A principal whose existence is known but whose identity is unknown to the third party with whom the principal's agent deals. (23)

Participative preferred stock Shares of preferred stock that enable the stockholders to receive not only their stated dividend but also to share in dividend distributions of earnings of the corporation. (16)

Partnership An association of two or more persons to carry on a business for profit as co-owners. (6, 24)

Par value An arbitrary value placed on a share of stock at the time the corporation seeks authorization of the stock. (16)

Patent Legal protection available to the inventor of a machine, process, product, chemical, a new variety of nonpollinating plant life, or other new useful invention. A patent gives the inventor the right to prevent others from using the patented invention in the United States and its territories and possessions. (27)

Patent and Trademark Office Federal agency in U.S. Department of Commerce that administers patent law. (27)

Payee The party to whom a check or draft is made payable. (22)

Perfect competition An environment in which business firms produce under circumstances where no one producer can have an effect on the market price, there is freedom of entry and exit, homogeneous goods are produced, and complete information is available to all producers and consumers. Perfect competition guarantees economic efficiency in production at a given level of technology. (1)

Periodic inventory system A system of accounting for inventory that requires the use of a physical count of inventory at the end of the accounting period in order to determine ending inventory and to calculate cost of goods sold. (12)

Periodicity The concept in accounting that requires that the life of a business be broken down into specific time periods for periodic reporting purposes. The normal accounting period is one year. (6)

Permanent accounts Asset, liability, and owners' equity accounts (balance sheet accounts). These may also be called real accounts. (7)

Perpetual inventory system A system of accounting for inventory that maintains a continuous record of all inventory transactions. (12)

Personal income (PI) Total income received by households from all sources. (2)

Personal property Property owned other than real property. (27, 28)

Petty cash fund A fund established to pay for small expenditures that would be inconvenient to pay by check. (10)

Pollution Use of the environment (air, land, and water) by producers and consumers as a dumping ground for waste. (4)

Posting The process of transferring the information contained in the journal to the ledger accounts. (7)

Power of attorney A document that formally authorizes one person to act on behalf of another person as to matters stated in the document. (23)

Precedent A previously decided case. (20)

Predetermined overhead rate The rate that is determined in advance and used to allocate manufacturing overhead costs to the jobs in work in process inventory and to the jobs completed during the period. The predetermined overhead rate is calculated by dividing estimated total manufacturing overhead costs by estimated total units in the application base. (19)

Preferred stock A form of capital stock of a corporation that entitles its owners to certain preferences, such as receipt of a guaranteed amount of annual dividends before common shareholders may receive dividends. (8) Stock that represents ownership in a corporation entitling the stockholder to certain advantages not available to owners of common stock. (24)

Prepaid expenses Expenses that consist of the cost of goods or services bought for use in the business that are not used up at the end of the accounting period. (8)

Price ceiling A legal maximum price that can be charged for a product. (4)

Price discrimination A seller's sale of identical goods at different prices to different buyers without legal justification. (Robinson–Patman Act) (25)

Price fixing The agreement by one party with one or

more others as to the setting of a price of a good or type of good. (Sherman Act) (25)

Primary deposit   Money placed in a transaction account by an account owner. (3)

Prime interest rate   The interest rate charged to large corporations with large equity for loans. (2)

Principal   One who acts through an agent. (23)

Private goods   Goods and services that can only be used if purchased. (1)

Private placement   The sale of an entire issue of securities by the issuing corporation directly to one or a few large institutional investors. (16)

Private property   Individual ownership of property and other resources. (1)

Procedural law   Law that specifies rules governing how rights are to be enforced. (20)

Process costing   The method of product costing most often used by firms that produce a homogeneous product using a continuous manufacturing process. (19)

Producer price index (PPI)   An index that attempts to measure average changes in the producer's cost of items throughout the years. A representative sampling of goods is used. (2)

Production possibility curve (PPC)   Identification of the various combinations of goods and services that can be produced at a given time with a given level of technology and full, efficient use of resources. (1) All the alternative combinations of commodities that can be produced with fixed amounts of product inputs and fixed technology. (2)

Productivity   The amount of output produced per unit of input. (4)

Profit   The revenue received minus the cost of production (both explicit and implicit). (1)

Proforma financial statement   A forecasted (or budgeted) financial statement. (19)

Promissory note   A negotiable instrument that contains a promise by the maker to pay a certain sum of money to another party at a specified time or on demand. (22)

Promoter   The person(s) who organizes (creates) a new corporation and solicits stock subscriptions. (24)

Promulgate   A term describing the act of an administrative agency in creating a regulation. (20)

Property insurance   Insurance protection of the property (assets) of the company from damage or destruction by fire, smoke, vandalism, and so on. (14)

Prospectus   A summarized version of the registration statement provided investors before purchase of securities. (26)

Protective tariff   A tariff placed on imported goods to protect the sale of domestically produced goods. (5)

Proxy   Granting of authority to another to vote one's shares. (26)

Public goods   Goods anyone can consume without dimin-

ishing the amount available for others to consume; goods provided or controlled by government. (1)

Purchases journal   A special journal used to record purchases of inventory on account. The purchases journal may also include purchases of supplies on credit. (10)

Quasi-contract   A legally enforceable obligation that does not stem from the agreement between the parties, but rather from the court's interest in preventing an injustice. (21)

Quitclaim deed   Grantor (the party conveying the property) transfers entire interest, if any, without any warranty of title. (28)

Ratification   An expression of an intent to be bound by the terms of an agreement that was entered into at a time when the party was lacking in contractual capacity. Ratification can occur only after capacity is attained. (21)

Ratio   The relationship of one amount to another. (18)

Real estate mortgage   The giving of a certain type of security interest in land owned or being purchased by the mortgagor. (28)

Real income (purchasing power)   The measurement of a household's income in terms of the amount of goods and services that can be purchased. (2)

Real property   Land and permanent attachments thereto such as crops, buildings, and fixtures. (27, 28)

Redemption   The mortgagor's statutory right to pay overdue payments and penalties and be restored to predefault status. (28)

Registered bond   A bond that has the holder's name registered with the issuing company. (15)

Registration statement   A statement filed by the issuer with the Securities and Exchange Commission to gain approval of the sale of new securities. (26)

Regulation   A law promulgated by an administrative agency. (20)

Rehabilitation Act of 1973   Legislation that required employers who participate in government contracts to make reasonable accommodation to employ and promote qualified handicapped individuals. (25)

Relevant range   The range over which assumptions made about the nature of cost behavior (i.e., fixed or variable) are valid. (19)

Required reserves   A requirement that a bank hold a dollar amount of designated assets as a percentage of certain liabilities. (3)

Reserve ratio   The percentage of deposits required by law to be held in reserve. (3)

Restitution   A remedy for a breach of contract that involves the return of things received under the contract in an effort to put the parties in the position they were in before the contract. (21)

Restrictive indorsement   An indorsement that requires the indorsee to accept the instrument subject to certain specified conditions. (22)

Retained earnings The portion of the stockholders' equity consisting of earnings of the corporation that have been retained in the corporation rather than paid out as dividends. (7)

Revenue Earnings resulting from the receipt of cash or other assets in exchange for goods sold by the entity or services performed by the entity. (7)

Revenue realization The principle that states that revenue is usually recognized only after an exchange has taken place or a service has been performed. (7)

Revenue tariff A tariff with the major purpose of producing revenue. (5)

Revocation The withdrawal of an offer by the offeror. (21)

Right-to-work law One of the provisions of the National Labor Relations Act that permits states to decide whether union shops may exist and whether an employee can be forced to join a union as a condition of continued employment. (25)

Sales journal A special journal used to record sales of merchandise on account. (10)

Salvage value The residual value an asset is expected to have when its useful life is over. (13)

Scarcity A condition where individuals desire more goods or services than are available at zero price. (1)

Secondary deposit Money placed in a transaction account by a paper transaction within the financial institution. (3)

Second mortgage Any mortgage secured after the original (or first) mortgage. (28)

Security The evidence of ownership in a business enterprise such as a stock certificate. (26)

Security interest The giving of a legal interest (lien) in one's property to another to secure a loan. (28)

Serial bonds Bonds issued at the same time but coming due at various maturity dates. Issuing serial bonds alleviates some of the cash flow drain that occurs when bonds mature. (15)

Shortage Excess quantity demanded at a given market price. (1)

Short-term capital gain or loss A gain or loss resulting from the sale of a capital asset held for one year or less. (17)

Simple contract A contract that does not come within the narrow category of formal contracts. (21)

Simple interest Interest that is computed only on the principal of the loan for a single period of time. (15)

16b Insider Officer, director, or shareholder of 10 percent ownership shares. (26)

Small Business Administration (SBA) A federal agency established in 1953 to advise and assist the nation's small businesses; the SBA provides loans, loan guarantees, and other financial assistance and offers loans to victims of natural disasters. The SBA also conducts research on conditions affecting small businesses. (3)

Sole entrepreneurship A business owned and operated by only one person. (24)

Source document The document that is normally prepared when an accounting transaction occurs. Source documents serve as the source of information for making journal entries. (7)

Source of working capital Any transaction that results in an increase in working capital. (18)

Special agent An agent who is authorized by a principal to perform a single task or to achieve a narrow goal on behalf of the principal. (23)

Special indorsement An indorsement that names the party to whom the indorser makes the instrument payable. (22)

Special journal A journal used to record routine transactions that occur frequently. The use of special journals simplifies the posting procedure. (10)

Specific tariff A per unit tariff tax on an imported commodity. (5)

Standard cost The cost that should be incurred when producing a product or performing an operation efficiently. (19)

Stare decisis The doctrine that precedent should be followed. (20)

Statement of cash flows The financial statement that shows the operating, investing, and financing cash flows of a company. (8)

Statement of changes in capital The financial statement that explains the changes in the capital (owners' equity) account for the period. (8)

Statement of retained earnings The financial statement that shows the changes in retained earnings from one period to the next. (8)

Statute A law passed by a legislative body. (21)

Statutory law Law enacted by legislative bodies. (20)

Stock dividend A dividend distributed in the form of additional shares of stock. (11)

Stockholders' equity The term used for the owners' equity in a corporation. (7)

Straight-line depreciation A depreciation method that assigns an equal amount of depreciation expense to each period of the asset's useful life. (13)

Strict liability A legal doctrine that requires one engaged in a highly dangerous activity to compensate those injured as a result of the activity even in the absence of any negligence. One who sells a product in a defective, unreasonably dangerous condition is liable for physical harm caused to the consumer or user of the product if the seller is in the business of selling such a product and the product is expected to and does reach the consumer or user without substantial change in the condition in which it is sold. (20)

Structural unemployment A type of unemployment that occurs when there is a change in the structure of the economy (i.e., a change in technology requring a different mix of skills) to which the labor force cannot readily adapt. (2)

Subsidiary account An individual detailed account of the amount due from a customer owed to a supplier or other detailed information such as specific items of inventory on hand. (10)

Subsidiary company A company that is controlled by a parent company. (11)

Substantive law Law that defines rights and duties. (20)

Substitute goods Goods that can be substituted for other goods. (1)

Sum-of-the-years' digits depreciation (SYD). An accelerated depreciation method that uses a decreasing fraction as the depreciation rate which is used to allocate the cost less salvage value of an asset over its useful life. (13)

Supply The quantity that will be made available for sale by producers within a given period of time at various price levels. (1)

Supply of money Total amount of money in the economy. (3)

Supply-side economics A contemporary school of thought advocating the idea that policies undertaken to alter aggregate supply are more influential in the economy than policies influencing demand. (2)

Surety bond A contract under which one party agrees to make good the debt or default of another party. (14)

Surplus The business state that exists when the quantity supplied is greater than the quantity demanded at a given market price. (1)

T-account A representation of an account that is used for instructional or problem-solving purposes. (7)

Taft–Hartley Act Federal legislation that established free-speech rights for employees and identified union unfair labor practices. (25)

Tariff A fee placed on imported goods before they can be sold. (5) Description of available services, equipment, rates, rules, and regulations between the user and the utility company. (26)

Tariff quota Placement of a low tariff, or no tariff, upon goods imported into the country up to a certain amount. (5)

Technological unemployment Unemployment as a result of changes in technology. (2)

Temporary accounts Revenue, expense, and drawing accounts; temporary accounts are closed to owners' equity at the end of an accounting period. (7)

Temporary investments Investments in marketable securities that are expected to be held for a short period of time; may also be referred to as marketable securities. (8)

Tenancy in common Co-ownership of property whereby a deceased party's interest passes according to the will and/or inheritance laws. (28)

10b-5 Insider Anyone using proprietary (inside, nonpublic) information to make an investment decision. (26)

Tender offer Offer to purchase the shares of a corporation. (26)

Term bonds Bonds that have a single fixed maturity date. (15)

Term notes payable A note payable repaid in one lump sum on a specific maturity date. (15)

Third party One who deals with an agent who is representing a principal. (23)

Title VII—Civil Rights Act of 1964 The law that prohibits employment discrimination on the basis of race, color, religion, sex, or national origin. (25)

Tort law The law of civil wrongs, including intentional acts, negligence, and strict liability. (20)

Trade discount A reduction from the list price of goods that is offered by manufacturers or wholesalers to their dealers; a method of determining the sales price. (10)

Transaction account An account in a financial institution on which one can write checks, negotiable orders of withdrawal, or share drafts. (3)

Transfer payments Income payments that are not related to the productive activity of individuals (social security payments, unemployment benefits). (2)

Treasury stock The shares of a corporation's own capital stock reacquired by the corporation. (16)

Treble damages Triple the amount of actual damages given in some lawsuits to strongly discourage certain kinds of wrongful actions. A statute must authorize treble damages; most antitrust statutes do just that. (25)

Trial balance A listing of all the account balances in the general ledger that is used to verify that the total dollar amount of debits is equal to the total dollar amount of credits. (9)

Unappropriated retained earnings The portion of the retained earnings of a corporation that have not been appropriated for a specific purpose. (16)

Underwriter The distributor of an issuer's securities. (26)

Undisclosed principal A principal whose existence is unknown to the third party with whom the principal's agent deals. (23)

Unemployment insurance Payments made to employees because of involuntary severance from work; to qualify, the employee must have worked a minimum number of weeks and be ready, able, and willing to take equivalent new employment. (25)

Unfair labor practices Management and union practices that are deemed to be unfair and illegal as set forth in the National Labor Relations Act. (25)

Uniform Commercial Code (UCC) A body of law that governs many commercial transactions; it has been adopted in every state. (Louisiana has adopted major parts of the UCC, but not all of it.) (21)

Unilateral contract A contract in which the offer is accepted by performance of the requested act. Only one promise is involved. (21)

Units-of-production method A depreciation method that computes depreciation expense based on the total estimated productive output of the asset. (13)

Unlimited liability The liability of sole proprietors and partners for business debts not only from business assets but also from personal assets. (16)

Use of working capital Any transaction that results in a decrease in working capital. (18)

Usury laws Laws that limit the maximum interest rate that can be charged. (3)

Utility The satisfaction derived from consumption of goods and services. (1)

Variable cost A cost that varies in total in direct proportion to changes in the level of activity. (19)

Variance The difference between the amount budgeted for an item and the amount that actually results for that item at the end of the period. (19)

Vocational Rehabilitation Act of 1973 An act that specifically eliminated job-related discrimination against handicapped individuals. (4)

Voidable contract A contract that may be set aside at the option of one of the parties. (21)

Void contract An attempt at forming a contract that failed due to the absence of an essential element. (21)

Voucher A business paper used in summarizing a transaction and approving it for recording and payment. (10)

Voucher system A system of internal control over cash disbursements that requires that a voucher be prepared and verified before any payments may be made. (10)

Wagner Act The first comprehensive labor act to regulate private employment; this act provides protection for employees to engage in concerted union activity. (6, 25)

Wants Individual desires that can be satisfied by consuming goods and services. (1)

Warranty deed In essence, a warranty by the grantor that the property is transferred free from all unknown defects or claims. (28)

Weighted-average method The method that uses a weighted-average unit cost to value ending inventory and cost of goods sold. (12)

Workers' compensation Laws passed in most states to pay money to employees who are injured on the job, even though the employee failed to follow directions and/or was negligent as long as there was no intentional infliction of injury. (25)

Working capital Current assets minus current liabilities. (18)

Worksheet An accounting tool used to make the end-of-period accounting procedures easier. (9)

Premiere CPS ®
Video Review

Make the Grade...
Whether you are preparing for the Certified Professional Secretary® examination, earning points towards CPS® recertification, or building your skills as an office professional, this video review course is designed for you.

☎ Overview of our Course
Our Premiere CPS® Video Review includes all three parts of the CPS® Exam on 1/2" VHS tapes.

☎ The Video Advantage
Video presentation provides a "mental picture" to help candidates remember key topics at test time.

☎ Be in a Class by Yourself
Our Home Study Plan is designed for the individual whose professional and personal schedules will not permit enrolling in a review course.

☎ Highly Rated Instructors
Our instructors are experts in their field.

☎ Materials
Our course uses the Regents/Prentice Hall Modules for the CPS® examination, the recognized leader in CPS® exam preparation.

☎ Affordable
This hard-hitting video review course can be purchased in parts or as a complete set.

1) Phone
Call us at:
1-800-239-8833 (US & Canada)
615-526-8833

2) Fax
Complete the information request form at right and fax it to us at:
615-528-5888

3) Mail
Complete the information request form at right and mail it to:
The Resource Network
P.O. Box 3561
Cookeville, TN 38502

☐ Yes, rush me information about the Premiere CPS® Video

I will take the CPS exam on _____ / _____
                              month   year

Company _____

Name _____

Address _____

City _____ State _____ Zip _____

Attention: _____

Day Phone # (____) _____

NOTE: The CPS® is a registered trademark of Professional Secretaries International. This video course is not approved or sponsored by PSI®, the owner and administrator of the CPS® examination.